Slave Culture

Slave Culture

A Documentary Collection of the Slave Narratives from the Federal Writers' Project

Volume 3

SPENCER CREW, LONNIE BUNCH,
AND CLEMENT PRICE, EDITORS

GREENWOOD

AN IMPRINT OF ABC-CLIO, LLC
Santa Barbara, California • Denver, Colorado • Oxford, England

Library of Congress Cataloging-in-Publication Data

Slave culture : a documentary collection of the slave narratives from the Federal Writers' Project / Spencer Crew, Lonnie Bunch, and Clement Price, editors.
    volumes cm
    ISBN 978-1-4408-0086-3 (hardback) — ISBN 978-1-4408-0087-0 (ebook)
1. Slave narratives—United States. 2. Slavery—United States—History—Sources.
3. African Americans—History—Sources. 4. African Americans—Interviews.
I. Crew, Spencer R., 1949–, editor of compilation. II. Bunch, Lonnie G., editor of compilation. III. Price, Clement Alexander, 1945–, editor of compilation. IV. Federal Writers' Project.
    E444.S55 2014
    306.3'620973—dc23   2013042627

ISBN: 978-1-4408-0086-3
EISBN: 978-1-4408-0087-0

18 17 16 15 14   1 2 3 4 5

This book is also available on the World Wide Web as an eBook.
Visit www.abc-clio.com for details.

Greenwood
An Imprint of ABC-CLIO, LLC

ABC-CLIO, LLC
130 Cremona Drive, P.O. Box 1911
Santa Barbara, California 93116-1911

This book is printed on acid-free paper ∞

Manufactured in the United States of America

Contents

Preface

The slave narratives created by the Federal Writers' Project (FWP) of the U.S. Works Progress Administration happened almost by accident. The original assignment to the FWP in 1936 was to capture and preserve the life stories of older residents of the country. It was discovered in this process that the testimonies offered by a number of the African Americans interviewed were from persons who had been enslaved. They were among the last survivors of that institution and had valuable perspectives to share about the impact slavery had upon their lives. They talked about slavery from the point of view of the enslaved, which offered a unique view into how it functioned and how it affected their lives. Their testimonies were both touching and frightening. The narratives collected from 17 states, mainly in the South, were quickly recognized as a valuable resource for understanding slavery from the perspective of the enslaved.

Upon completion of the project, the final collection of more than 2,300 individual interviews was sent to the U.S. Library of Congress, where the interviews were organized by state. While it was good to have the material in one location it presented two challenges. First, its location at the Library of Congress limited access to the material as one had to travel to Washington, D.C., to use it. Second, the state-by-state organization made identifying common themes within the narratives a painstaking process, as one had to go through the individual testimonies to reveal commonalties in their testimonies.

Although the Library of Congress's slave narrative collection is now online, it is searchable only by name of the person interviewed, by state, or by keyword. Moreover, many narratives did not reach the Washington office of the WPA or the Library of Congress. They had been residing in other state collections. (There were various reasons for this, possibly including deliberate suppression.) In 1973, George P. Rawick, with Ken Lawrence and Jan Hillegas, began their search for any remaining narratives. What they found was compiled in 22 volumes, published by Greenwood Press in 1978 and 1979, called *The American Slave: A Composite Autobiography*. This massive scholarly undertaking, which included both the narratives from the Library of Congress collection and additionally discovered narratives, yielded 4,000 documents, nearly 2,000 more than the number in the Library of Congress collection.

SCOPE

The intent of *Slave Culture: A Documentary Collection of the Slave Narratives from the Federal Writers' Project* is to ameliorate some of these impediments in the use of the slave narratives for researchers and educators. The editors of these volumes have reviewed the narratives and selected approximately 4,500 excerpts from slave narratives for this book. These excerpts are arranged by topic in seven chapters, providing a very different point of entry into the holdings. The book draws from both the Library of Congress's materials and from the additional narratives George Rawick discovered from other archives.

To craft this topical framework, the original interviews were systematically reviewed and pertinent portions of the testimonies extracted for their emphasis on specific issues. The goal was to identify those ideas that reoccurred most often in the discussions with the enslaved and to highlight those concepts from the interviews. What most often dominated these conversations were discussions focused on family, running away, childhood, work, punishment, culture, gender, and emancipation. Consequently, these topics are the organizational foundation for this exploration of the slave narratives. Each chapter is devoted to a major topic and subdivided into three to six subtopics, each of which features introductory context and numerous excerpts from the narratives of the formerly enslaved. Within subtopics, narratives are arranged alphabetically by the names of the formerly enslaved.

Chapters 1–7 offer introductory background, context, and explanation for the narrative excerpts that illustrate the following topics:

- Chapter 1 reveals a community culture of the enslaved, including religion (both approved and hidden worship), recreations and celebrations, weddings, funerals, and music and other forms of cultural expression.
- Chapter 2 has recollections of childhood by the enslaved, from their work in the fields and homes of slave masters to their games.
- Chapter 3 features excerpts from narratives about the enslaved family and its powerful challenges from the institution of slavery.
- Chapter 4 describes the particular issues and perils that constantly faced enslaved women.
- Chapter 5 informs readers about work for the enslaved, from backbreaking field and domestic work to skilled craft and labor and being hired out to other plantations or homes.
- Chapter 6 provides the difficult narratives about the severe and often sadistic punishment and threats that most enslaved people experienced or were threatened by.
- Chapter 7 tells the stories of those who attempted escape, those who succeeded in escaping, and what happened to enslaved people upon emancipation.

In the seven chapters, it is not surprising that family, work, abuse, and running away were topics that represented a reoccurring theme in the conversations of the enslaved. These concepts were important factors that were central to their existence, gave meaning to their lives, or offered emotional or physical ways to escape from their enslaved circumstances. Work dominated everything else in the existence of the enslaved. It was the most important contribution they made to the slaveholders who controlled their lives. The tasks they performed varied from geographic location to geographic location, but work defined their condition. Physical abuse was linked to work as a means of extracting as much productivity as possible from the enslaved. It was extraordinary if at some point an enslaved person didn't experience physical abuse, witness the abuse of someone close to him or her, or suffer through separation from a loved one as a result of a sale. When a person decided to take the risk of running away these experiences were often the catalysts. The penalties for running were severe enough that making that choice was not done casually but was driven by extraordinary motivations.

Ties to family were a counterbalance to running away. Most enslaved people were part of a nuclear or extended family unit. These connections provided emotional support in the midst of slavery and were a fondly recalled oasis within the institution. Children looked to family to protect them from the worst aspects of enslavement or to provide guidance on how to navigate its vicissitudes. The warmth of a parent's arms or a parent's words of encouragement were important balms for an unhappy child. Words of guidance from a parent were especially important for enslaved females. They faced exploitation not only of their labor but also of their bodies by white men. Parents sought to protect their daughters when they could and to help them when their resistance to unwanted advances proved futile. A tragic fact of life for many enslaved children was that they were deliberately separated from their parents so that the slaveholders could sell parents and child separately to make more money, making the life of an enslaved child even more lonely, difficult, perhaps hopeless, and dangerous.

The enslaved savored unscheduled time that allowed them time away from the work routine. Special occasions like Christmas, the Fourth of July, and weddings were particularly significant in that regard. They offered a respite from the normal work routine and were occasions to rest and enjoy leisure periods with family and friends. The enslaved looked to leverage these moments in ways that were advantageous to them. Weddings, for example, were a time to celebrate a commitment to family and marriage in spite of the limited control the enslaved had over their futures. Religious services served parallel purposes and allowed the enslaved to ignore Bible lessons of fidelity preached by slaveholders. Instead, they used their private religious gatherings to pray for freedom and a better life.

When reorganized into these categories that were frequently the focus of the slave narratives, the testimonies of the enslaved take on an added dimension. No longer are they solely individual reflections on a life of enslavement, but rather they offer a macro view of crosscutting issues of significance to many of these individuals. The hopes, dreams, and disappointments of the enslaved as a group emerge and give the reader an opportunity to better understand what aspects of enslavement reverberated most forcefully for them as well as why they were important. Under these circumstances the enslaved can be seen as a community that shared certain feelings and concerns. It gives their voices a focus and a clearer delineation of the realities of slavery for them as a group. It also reveals more readily discernible patterns that can be explored more easily. The ultimate goal in this book is to allow the voices of these formerly enslaved persons to provide even deeper insights into the reality of their lives under the institution of slavery. They have much to offer and we have much to learn from them.

OTHER FEATURES

Slave Culture: A Documentary Collection of the Slave Narratives from the Federal Writers' Project also includes features that provide more history and context to the slave narratives and to the study of enslaved African Americans in the United States.

Critical Thinking about the Slave Narratives

The introduction, "The History of the Slave Narratives," tells how the slave narratives came to be in the 1930s, under the Federal Writers' Project, a program of President Franklin D. Roosevelt's Works Progress Administration. It is particularly useful for understanding the slave narratives, as it cautions readers to consider the conditions of the interviews conducted, which resulted in the narratives. Especially when conducted by white interviewers in the South in the 1930s, whether intentionally or unintentionally, the process sometimes resulted in the elderly African Americans painting more rosy pictures than was the truth of their lives as people who were enslaved and of their treatment by slaveholders.

Chronology

The "Chronology of Slavery in the United States" gives readers a timeline, from the arrival in 1619 in Virginia of the first Africans captured in a British slave ship, up to 21st-century publications based on slave narratives.

The Long Road to the Cabin Door: Historians on American Slavery

"The Long Road to the Cabin Door: Historians on American Slavery" is an appendix that covers the study of the history, or historiography, of U.S. slavery, beginning in the 19th century and continuing to contemporary times. The essay traces works by black and white historians, starting with the agonizing truth of slavery offered by the African American George Washington Williams in 1884 and moving to the racist attitudes of some Southern white historians of the first half of the 20th century who, although acknowledging slavery as morally indefensible, still praised the institution for bringing Christianity and civilizing to an "inferior race." The appendix concludes with a discussion of historians, both black and white, who were influenced in their writing about slavery by black protest against long-standing injustices in the nation's public and private spheres.

The book ends with recommended resources for the study of slavery in the United States, including books, online resources, and videos and films. Finally, a comprehensive index provides access to the three volumes.

Note: The excerpts from the slave narratives included in this work sometimes use dialect and phonetic spellings to capture the person's speech; in other cases, the words of the formerly enslaved are reported in standard English. It was the decision of the original interviewer in the 1930s, or perhaps an editor, whether dialect or standard English was used. The excerpts from the narratives are copied as they were transcribed and typed, in most cases in 1937 and 1938. No attempt has been made to correct possible mistakes, with this exception: Quotation marks were sometimes added to make it more clear who was speaking, the formerly enslaved man or woman or the interviewer who was narrating the history told by the formerly enslaved person.

It should also be understood that people used language that can be offensive or disturbing, but it is a reflection of the attitudes, lack of access to education, and language used at that time and place.

ACKNOWLEDGMENTS

The editors of these volumes are grateful for the help of several people who assisted us in the creation of this volume. They helped make the task much easier and more enjoyable. In particular we are thankful to Sabrina Berns, Alexandra Bradwhaw, Lisa Struckmeyer, Laura Troiano, and Debora Scriber-Miller for their contributions. They brought different perspectives to the work, which helped us think about the words in the individual testimonies in new ways.

Each of us is further indebted to our partners in life who understand us well enough to know when to encourage us or prod us at different stages of the effort. They are the ones that make the task worthwhile. Sandra Prioleau Crew, Maria Marble-Bunch, and Mary Sue Sweeney Price are remarkable women to whom each of us owes more than we can ever put into words. Hopefully, a heartfelt thanks will in a small way begin to convey our admiration for each of them.

All slave narrative excerpts used in this book were originally published in either the Library of Congress's collection, which is now available online: *Born in Slavery: Slave Narratives from the Federal Writers' Project, 1936–1938.* 2001. http://memory.loc.gov/ammem/snhtml/snhome.html, or they came from additional narratives published in the collections edited by George P. Rawick, with Jan Hillegas and Ken Lawrence, *The American Slave: A Composite Autobiography: Supplement, Series 1,* 12 volumes, Greenwood, 1977; and Rawick's subsequent collection, *The American Slave: A Composite Autobiography,* Supplement, Series 2. 10 Volumes, Greenwood, 1979.

Introduction: The History of the Slave Narratives

The slave narrative project, created by the Works Progress Administration (WPA) during the presidency of Franklin Delano Roosevelt, represents a valuable compendium of information about the institution of slavery. The project contains the recollections of elderly African Americans living in the 1930s who grew up during the era of slavery in the United States. In their testimonies these men and woman describe the difficulties of life under slavery and the steps they took to create safe places where they could preserve their humanity and nurture their relationships with family and friends. Their words are both powerful and poignant, making their existence under slavery a very tangible and personal experience for readers of their words. They offer a view of the institution of slavery from the inside out. Their testimonies provide a sense of the day-to-day challenges faced by enslaved people. Their experiences at times are very hard to read. Brutality and mistreatment are routine occurrences in their lives. Learning how to protect themselves and their families from the worst aspects of the institution is important to their survival. Theirs is a very different view of slavery than the perspective offered by slaveholders of the period. It was not the benign institution many apologists for slavery have described. Although sentimental bonds did occur between the enslaved and their enslavers, most often slavery was harsh as well as physically and emotionally exhausting. The people whose reminiscences were captured were among the lucky ones who survived enslavement and lived long enough to share their stories with the interviewers who recorded their experiences. Both moments of joy and moments of immense sorrow characterize their accounts.

It is interesting that the stories of these formerly enslaved persons might have been lost had not the nation suffered economic duress. The stock market crash of 1929 was a catastrophe for the country. People lost their jobs, homes, and at times their hope for the future. The economic depression that followed led to the election of Franklin Delano Roosevelt as president and his subsequent endeavors to identify actions that might slow or end the economic downturn. Among the many ideas he implemented was the creation of programs to provide employment for some of the thousands of people out of work. The WPA. established in 1935, was created specifically to give jobs to the unemployed to toil on public work projects, such as constructing bridges, dams, roads, or buildings. One of the offshoots of the WPA was the Federal Writers' Project, also created in 1935. Its agenda was to provide work for historians, teachers, writers, and other white-collar workers on projects that leveraged their skills and education. The project's initial goal was to produce a series of guide books, called *The American Guide,* for different sections of the country. These guides were to highlight cultural, economic, historic, and scenic resources in each of those regions. As part of this project the workers identified and interviewed residents living in their areas. Through their testimonies the state projects hoped to learn more about their individual lives and about the history of the regions in which they lived.

As the work of the Federal Writers' Project moved forward its scope broadened. An interest developed in capturing the life histories of older Americans from many different backgrounds. The end goal was to produce an anthology creating a permanent record of their remembrances. It was an ambitious effort that resulted in one of the largest first-person narratives projects in the history of the country (Banks 1981, xiii). Initially, there was no specific interest in collecting slave narratives. Coincidentally, as subjects were identified for interviewing, among them were African Americans who had been enslaved as youths. Many of the early interviews of these persons were arranged by African American employees of the Writers' Project in several southern states. African Americans working in the Writers' Project in Florida were particularly active in this effort in the early years. The director of the Florida group, Carita Doggett Corse, was a historian who had conducted interviews of formerly enslaved persons in her previous work and had found the interviews to be invaluable historical sources. She encouraged the African American workers in Florida, who included Zora Neale Hurston, to make sure the formerly enslaved were among their interviewees. By 1936, the group had collected numerous interviews. which they hoped would be part of the guide for Florida (McDonogh 1993).

No special attention at the national level was given to interviewing the formerly enslaved until John Lomax became involved in the project in 1937. Lomax was the first folklore editor of the Writers' Project. He was a highly respected anthropologist whose work emphasized the importance of preserving southern and rural historical and anthropological materials. In his own work he actively and meticulously collected folklore as well as the life histories of his subjects. Earlier in his career he traveled to Texas prison farms recording the work songs of African American prisoners like Huddie Ledbetter (Lead Belly) and James "Iron Head" Baker (Lomax 1947). His work in Texas heightened his interest in African American culture and made him particularly sensitive to the value of interviews of older African Americans. As a consequence he recognized the significance of interviewing the formerly enslaved and encouraged participants in the Writers' Project to capture the life histories of these people. Because many of the workers in the Writers' Project did not have backgrounds in oral interviewing, Lomax composed a questionnaire fieldworkers could use in their interviews. He also provided instructions on how to conduct the interviews. His goal was to make the interviews as accurate and authentic as possible.

Lomax's interest and encouragement of the state units resulted in an extensive program of slave narrative collection. Projects were launched in all of the southern states and many of the border states. Narratives were also collected in a few northern states, including New York and Rhode Island. The most productive effort

The Facts Slave Narratives Collected after the Civil War

In 1929, scholars at African American colleges, John B. Cade at Southern University (Baton Rouge, Louisiana) and Charles S. Johnson at Fisk University (Nashville, Tennessee) first collected memories of formerly enslaved people, resulting in 82 narratives.

Lawrence D. Reddick of Kentucky State College in Frankfort produced 250 interviews in 1934.

John A. Lomax, the first folklore editor of the Federal Writers' Project, became involved in the slave narrative project in 1937; he directed it and devised a questionnaire for interviewers. A prominent anthropologist, he was also a musicologist and folklorist, who helped to preserve through recordings and writings some of the music of African Americans, including blues, spirituals and hymns, field hollers, and work songs, as well as other types from other groups around the country.

The slave narrative project of the Federal Writers' Project yielded 2,300 narratives and additional documents that were collected into 17 bound volumes, called "A Folk History of Slavery," and given to the U.S. Library of Congress in Washington, D.C., in 1941.

Of these narratives, Arkansas provided the most, nearly 700 interviews. In contrast, only 26 interviews were collected from Mississippi, a major slave state.

Florida had the most African American interviewers, employing 10. North Carolina, South Carolina, and Alabama only employed one African American interviewer among them.

States where the Federal Writers' Project narratives were collected and are represented in the Library of Congress collection: Alabama, Arkansas, Florida, Georgia, Indiana, Kansas, Kentucky, Maryland, Mississippi, Missouri, North Carolina, Ohio, Oklahoma, South Carolina, Tennessee, Texas, and Virginia.

In the 1970s, scholar George P. Rawick, believing there had to be more interviews, went on to find nearly 2,000 additional narratives from archives all around the country.

In addition to more narratives found from Mississippi and in the other states originally included in the Library of Congress collection, Rawick and his researchers located additional interviews in archives in Arizona, Colorado, the District of Columbia, Minnesota, Nebraska, New York, Oregon, Rhode Island, and Washington State.

---

operated in Arkansas, where nearly 700 interviews were collected. The result of this overall effort was the creation of the slave narrative collection, which consisted of more than 2,300 interviews from a broad variety of individuals and geographic locales. The interviews were conducted primarily between 1937 and 1938. They slowed and finally came to an end in 1938 as WPA resources were shifted to other projects and then funding for the entire program was eliminated at the federal level in 1939.

Although the project became the largest effort to collect slave narratives in the nation, it was not the first. Earlier efforts were performed by scholars at African American educational institutions. In 1929, projects were launched at Southern

University and Fisk University. These efforts focused on gathering the recollections of African Americans in nearby communities who had been enslaved. John B. Cade at Southern University and Charles S. Johnson at Fisk University led these efforts. While teaching at Southern, Cade had his students, most of whom were teachers, interview local residents who had lived during the slavery era. Their efforts garnered 82 narratives that talked about "food, clothing, housing facilities, working conditions, amusements, religious practices, educational opportunities, family life, punishment and any other information obtainable" (Cade 1935, 295). The interviews provided fascinating views into the lives of enslaved people, which Cade later analyzed in his article "Out of the Mouths of Ex-Slaves" in the *Journal of Negro History*. Similar field trips took place at Fisk University, which also recognized the value of the information that these older residents possessed and the desire to capture it before it was too late. Lawrence D. Reddick of Kentucky State College launched an analogous project in 1934 that produced 250 interviews. He operated this project with federal funding after he suggested that the Federal Emergency Relief Administration support interviewing former slaves as a way to provide employment to out-of-work African American college graduates. The effort eventually ended because of organizational and funding problems.

If John Lomax was not aware of the efforts at these African American institutions when he became editor of the Writers' Project, one of the men working with him certainly was. Sterling Brown, an English professor at Howard University, became a member of the team, serving as "Editor on Negro Affairs" with the specific task of including more African Americans in the project. He had taught for a year at Fisk at the time of the Cade research and with his interest in folk culture must have been aware of Cade's work. Lomax and Brown, after reading the results of the work going on in Florida, put in place plans to launch similar programs in other states. Lomax directed that 17 states, most of them in the South, include a specific focus on slave testimonies as a part of their work. As these programs moved forward Brown pushed for the inclusion of more African Americans to serve as interviewers in these state projects. The employment of African Americans had become more of an issue for the Roosevelt administration when African Americans like Mary McLeod Bethune and Robert Weaver were appointed to influential positions in government departments. As part of what has been called Roosevelt's "Black Cabinet," they lobbied for greater inclusion of African Americans in the programs initiated by the Roosevelt administration, especially the WPA and the Federal Writers' Project.

The inclusion of African Americans in state projects as a result of pressure from Washington was uneven. Bowing to local customs when southern states sought to hire African Americans, Writers' Project offices established separate units, which increased the cost of their operation. The added expense, in conjunction with southern reluctance to work with African Americans, meant that only a few southern states included African American workers. Active units operated in Virginia, Louisiana, Arkansas, and Florida, but they focused primarily on capturing information only from African Americans. The Louisiana unit operated out of Dillard University, and in Virginia the Negro Studies project was sponsored by Hampton Institute.

INTERVIEWING FORMERLY ENSLAVED PEOPLE

Consequently, in most southern states interviews of formerly enslaved persons were conducted by whites. North Carolina, South Carolina, and Alabama only employed one African American interviewer among them. Florida was better: at its highest levels it employed 10 African Americans in its unit (Mormino 1988, 405). Arkansas, which conducted the largest number of interviews of any state, had just two African American interviewers in its 20-person unit gathering testimonies of formerly enslaved persons. Arkansas, like other state units, was guided by the instructions Lomax sent to them from Washington. Among other points, he directed that the interviewers use a 20-multiple-part questionnaire to guide them. In conducting an interview, Lomax specifically preferred that "The details of the interview should be reported as accurately as possible in the language of the original statements. It should be remembered that the Federal Writers' Project is not interested in taking sides on any question. The worker should not censor any materials collected regardless of its nature" (Spurgeon 2011). Lomax's hope was that this guidance might create more consistent and better-quality interrogations from a workforce with limited experience in conducting oral interviews.

But with an interviewing group that was primarily white interviewing an African American clientele there were many issues to be overcome to acquire the best possible testimonies. Southern customs that buttressed a segregated society and insisted that African Americans behave in proscribed ways were critical obstacles hovering over these interviews. African Americans who did not follow those customs could easily find themselves in difficult if not life-threatening circumstances. Violence toward African Americans living in the South was not uncommon. Thirty-four lynchings of African Americans were recorded between 1935 and 1937 when many of these interviews were taking place ("Lynching in America" n.d.). These realities meant that African Americans needed to carefully control as much as they could their interactions with whites. They could never be sure what reactions they might provoke from a white person by what they said or did. A misstep might prove fatal.

An interview conducted in Mississippi offered an insight into the worries of the formerly enslaved when they were approached. When 90-year-old Liza McGhee was interviewed in Marshall County, Mississippi, a WPA worker found her "hesitant about talking freely as she feared the white people were planning to enslave her again. 'I remember some things about old slave days,' she said, 'but I don't want to say nothing that will get me in bondage again. I am too old now to be a slave. I couldn't stand it.'" McGhee was not the only one to have these concerns and to carefully choose her words. Martin Johnson told another interviewer. "Lots of old slaves closes the door before they tell the truth about their days of slavery. When the door is open, they tell how kind their masters was and how rosy it all was" (McMillen 2005).

The reality of the racial environment in the South consequently had to hover like an ominous cloud over interracial interviews in those regions. Even if the white interviewer did not recognize its presence, the African American being interviewed

Critical Points to Consider about the Slave Narratives

In the 1930s, a time of active lynchings and harsh segregation in the South, many formerly enslaved people, now elderly, were wary of what might happen if they told the truth about their experiences in slavery, especially if the person interviewing them was white.

In the late 1930s, many people were still suffering the effects of the Depression, such as poor living conditions and not enough to eat. Formerly enslaved people may have been especially impoverished, because Jim Crow laws meant they lacked opportunities, and to some, life on the plantation may have seemed almost preferable.

By 1937 and 1938, the people interviewed would have been in their seventies and up to 100 years old and more, which many said they were. Some did not know how old they were. The youngest people interviewed, although born into enslavement, would have been very young at the time, and they would describe what their parents and grandparents and others had experienced.

One theme of southern white historians from the 1920s until perhaps the 1960s argued that slavery helped to "tame" Africans and make them good Christians, but it is clear from reading many narratives that some slaveholders did just the opposite, forbidding and punishing worship, including Christian worship, as well as any kind of education.

Many former slaves, not afraid to tell the details of slavery, were blunt and still anguished about how they and fellow African Americans were treated. In an interview in 1937 in Livingston, Alabama, after describing some terrible punishments he had witnessed, 91-year-old George Young had a question for his interviewer: "Miss whar was de Lord in dem days? Whut was he doin'?"

felt it and the consequences if he or she were to say something considered objectionable, even if it was the truth. The key to a successful interview, as noted by the director of the Arkansas project, was "establishing friendly relations, and drawing them out over a period of time" (Spurgeon 2011). This task was much more difficult when the interviewer was white and the subject African American. The interviewer could have the best possible intentions and have as the only goal to capture the true experiences of the interviewee during the era of slavery. But given life for African Americans in the South, the interviewee could never be truly sure of the goals of the interview.

Candidness was even harder to capture when the interviewer was a white southerner who brought along predetermined ideas and terminology and these views were overtly or inadvertently transmitted to the person being interviewed. In Georgia, many white interviewers described their subjects as "old darky" and "typical old Negro mammy," which, if nothing else, offered a clue to the kind of behavior and possibly the kind of answers they expected (Trap 2011). It was not unusual for editors at the state level to have to edit out inappropriate remarks or comments made by unskilled or biased interviewers. As a result the propensity to provide answers they thought white interviewers expected must have been had a strong influence on these older, probably economically distressed, African Americans. There was much to be gained from giving acceptable answers rather than ones that were critical of slaveholders who were possibly the ancestors of the persons giving the interviews. One had to have a great deal of courage, confidence in the interviewer, or determination to share one's true feelings about the time of enslavement. How much these factors influenced the content of the testimonies is impossible to determine but has to be considered.

Gaining the confidence of a formerly enslaved person was likely easier for an African American interviewer than their white counterparts. For example, in Arkansas the best interviews were conducted by Samuel Taylor, an African American who was described as one of the preeminent interviewers in the entire nationwide program. Also, in a careful analysis of the slave narratives, 72 percent of the formerly enslaved persons interviewed rated the food they received while enslaved as very good when interviewed by whites. When the subject was interviewed by African Americans only 46 percent responded in a positive manner. Similar patterns appeared when they were asked about their former slaveholders. According to author Paul Escott, 74 percent spoke positively about their slaveholder when questioned by a white interviewer but only 61 percent answered similarly when talking to an African American interviewer (Escott 1979). In his work based on the Arkansas slave narratives, George Lankford reinforced this disparity when he noted that important issues to consider when reading the interviews were the racial identity of the interviewer and the racial climate of the era (Spurgeon 2011).

Another issue that also had to be taken into account was the age of the interviewees and the quality of their memories. Those with firsthand memories of enslavement were usually born no later than 1860, which meant they were at least five years old when the war ended in 1865. By 1936, when the Florida unit began interviewing formerly enslaved people who were children during enslavement, their subjects were 76 years old. If they were born earlier they would have been in their eighties, nineties, or older at the time of the interview. It has been estimated that the average age of the persons interviewed was 85 (McMillen 2005). Events connected to their enslavement would have occurred at least 70 years earlier. That gap was a long expanse of time from which to recall detailed information. Certainly very noteworthy moments representing joyous or traumatic events would have been easier to recollect. Less significant events likely were harder to remember. If they were suffering any physical infirmities at the time of the interview, it may have made the interview process even more challenging. Modern research has found that as we age our brains lose cells and our ability to learn new ideas and to remember things from the distant past diminishes. This problem can be further heightened by immobility or physical illness. We also know that memories are not fixed commodities locked away in secure places in our brains. They are evolving, impressionable commodities that are affected by conversations with others or by the perceived expectations of the people with whom we are interacting.

Leading Questions from Some Interviewers

Excerpts from interviews of a formerly enslaved woman, Susan Hamlin, who thought she was 104 years old, in Charleston, South Carolina, between 1937 and 1938, show some of the problems with some narratives. Although most interviewers were well trained and tried not to insert themselves into the interviews with formerly enslaved people, some did ask leading questions. Whether intentional or not, Hamlin's interviewer implies that slavery might not have been so bad. And many elderly formerly enslaved people, either trying to be agreeable to the interviewer, or concerned about telling the truth, may have answered in kind. The interviewer's questions and remarks are shown *in italics*.

"Mrs. Hamlin begins by discussing how she was hired out by her master, as a caregiver to children in another family:

"I got seven dollars a month for looking after children, not taking them out, you understand, just minding them. I did not got the money, Mausa got it." *"Don't you think that was fair?" I asked. "If you were fed and clothed by him, shouldn't he be paid for your work?"* "Course it been fair," *she answered,* "I belong to him and he got to get something to take care of me…"

"Were most of the masters kind?" I asked. "Well you know," she answered, "times den was just like dey is now, some was kind and some was mean; heaps of wickedness went on just de same as now. All my people was good people. I see some wickedness and I hear 'bout all kinds of t'ings but you don't know whether it was lie or not. Mr. Fuller been a Christian man."

"Do you think it would have been better if the Negroes had never left Africa?" was the next question I asked. "No Ma'am, (emphatically) dem heathen didn't have no religion. I tell you how I t'ink it is. The Lord made t'ree nations, the white, the red and the black, and put dem in different places on de earth where dey was to stay. . . ."

These realities about aging and memory make the interview process an even more delicate task. It also places even greater emphasis on the sensitivity and skill of the interviewer. If the interviewer approaches the conversation with predetermined expectations about what he or she will learn it can affect the responses received from an elderly person. If the interviewer believes slavery was a benevolent institution and the enslaved were treated kindly, it increases the possibility that he or she will receive responses that reinforce that concept. If the interviewer uses condescending terms to address the interviewee it also will likely shape the nature of the answers received. These factors further emphasize the critical importance of a good rapport between the participants in the interview to obtain the best possible responses. For white interviewers, even those with the best of intentions, this was a hard condition to achieve and must be part of the equation when evaluating the content of the interviews. Some white interviewers successfully built good rapport and generated valuable interviews. Stetson Kennedy, a white Floridian who later wrote an exposé of the Ku Klux Klan, believed there were people he worked with in Florida who had the skills and sensitivity to develop a strong rapport with the people they interviewed despite their different backgrounds (Crew and Goodman 2002).

But possible issues with the interviews were not solely connected to the skill of the interviewers. The information they received was not normally captured on a recorder. Most of the testimonies were secured in handwritten field notes of the interviewer. As interviewers asked questions they wrote quick notes that they filled in after the conversation was completed. In the best instances they tried to be as faithful as possible to the responses of their subject interviewers, but the reality was that their recollections of the conversations were an important part of the transcripts they produced, and it was only as accurate as their notes or memory allowed.

Complicating the production of the transcripts was the challenge of capturing the language and dialects used by their subjects. Guidelines from John Lomax cautioned interviewers that "The details of the interview should be reported as accurately as possible in the language of the original statements" (Lomax 1937). This guideline meant that whatever imperfections in language used by the respondents should be a part of the written record of the conversation. As a result, as much as possible, the transcribed field notes were expected to capture the verbal cadence of the interviewee, whose spoken language was not always easy to follow let alone duplicate in writing.

Most interviewers tried to visit their subject more than once to get as much information as possible. Sometimes photographs were taken and included for the record. The transcripts from the field were then passed along to supervisors who edited them with the goal of producing a more readable and useable record of the interviews. Each interview file included the name of the interviewer, the name of the person interviewed, the time and place of the interview, the race of the interviewer, and photographs when available. The task of the supervisor/editor was to keep the final transcript as close to the original interview as possible, but this was not necessarily a straightforward task. Editors had to decipher the writing of the field interviewers, who had varying levels of skill. At times they also had to edit out judgmental comments or incorrect information included by the interviewer. They sometimes needed to edit out what they considered wholly false information or allegations from the subject or the interviewer. How closely the final testimony paralleled what the interviewer turned in to the supervisor could vary widely from state to state and depended on the perspective of the supervisor in charge of the project. The interview of Angie Garrett of Alabama (see pp. xxiv–xxvii) is an illustration of editing done by the person reviewing narratives in that state.

The overall impact of the many factors that influenced the interviews certainly made the individual state slave narrative collections less than perfect. But despite these problems, the information gathered was a unique and very personal look into the lives of the last surviving generation of African American enslaved persons. What made the interviews special was that they reflected the idiosyncratic views and experiences of each person questioned. The testimonies spoke to what each interviewee remembered and what he or she went through while under the yoke of slavery. Each individual testimony might not be entirely accurate or might have been affected by the person who conducted the interview, or the questions that were asked or not asked. But as a collection of narratives they illustrate experiences and challenges that were common to the general experiences of the enslaved and to the personal impact the institution had on each individual. Their words offered new considerations on what it meant to be enslaved.

Alabama   10224   Ruby Pickens Tartt,   133
        -Photo-   Livingston, Alabama.

MULES BE EATIN' AND
NIGGERS BE EATIN'.

She sat in the door of her ~~small cabin, a short distance from~~ shanty and

Livingston, Alabama in philsophical reflection. Time has not softened

her memories. ~~As she told these facts an occasional expression of~~

~~bitterness passed over her face.~~

"I'se Angie Garrett," she said. ~~"I was about sixteen years, at beginning uv~~

de Wa'. ~~I was born~~ in De Kalb, Mississippi. My mother was Betty Scott,

an' I didn't know my father's name. I had four brothers, Ember, Johnny,

Jimmie, and Henry; and three sisters, Delphie, Lizzie Sue, and Frankie,

and my grandmother was Sukie Scott. She lived five miles from Gainesville

across Noxubee Creek ~~(in full, Oka-Noxubee)~~ an' I lived wid her. Never

axed 'bout my grand daddy, 'caze wa'n't no tellin'. My mammy lived right

here in Gainesville an' belonged to Mr. Sam Harwood.

"I b'longed to de Moorings and Cap'en Mooring run on a boat to Mo-

bile from Aberdeen, Mississippi, ~~'twus~~ on de 'Bigbee river, and 'twus call-

ed deCremonia. I was de house gal, and nuss, and I slep' on a pallet in

old Miss's room. I had a plenty to eat long as us was on dat boat, and

nt sho' was good. But when us was in De Kalb, vittles was giv' out at

de smoke house, a slice o' meat and piece of bread and peas, and 'twus

sarnt out ter de fiel'. Mules be eatin' and niggers be eatin'.

"I nussed de Moorings little boy Johnny. De little gal had died. Mr.

Scott in De Kalb had 'bout fifty slaves and a big plantation and a over-

seer name' Barnes. He was a haughty man, and niggers was skeered to

death 'caze he would come in a-cussin'.

"Us would git up 'fo' daylight. 'Twus dark ~~when~~ tr go out, dark ~~when~~ ter

come in. Us make a little fire in de fiel' some mawnin's, hit beeze so

cold; den us let hit go out 'fo' de overseer come. Ef he seed you he'd

make yer lay down flat on yo' belly, foots tied out and han's tied out
and whoop yer, ~~mid slapper~~ leather strap wid a handle, a sho-nuff slapper. ~~But I was laid~~
'cross a cheer. I been whooped 'tel I tell lies on myself to make 'em
quit. Say dey whoop 'till I'd tell de troof, so I had ter lie 'bout myse'f keep 'em from killin' me. Dis here race is mo' lac' like de chillun er ob
Isreal, 'cept dey didn't have ter to shoot no gun ter set um dem free.

~~"I was sole ter Mr. Johnny Mooring, 'caze de property was in debt.
And den fuss I b'longed ter Mrs. Scott at De Kalb, and her sole me, an' I
sno' was glad. I walked here to Gainesville frum De Kalb, Mississippi.
Us wa'n't 'lowed to learn nothin'~~ Sometimes us sing and have a little
prayer meetin', but 'twus mighty easy and quiet like. Gran'ma Sukey use'
to sing "Travel on, travel on, Soon be Over."

"Ef any us died in dem days, buried us quick as dey could and got
out of dere and got to work. At night dey blow'd de horn for 'em to
bring in de cotton w'ut de women spinned. Dey made all de clof. Us worked nights too, but us rested Sundays. Us didn't git no presents at Christmas. Sometimes us had a corn shuckin', and no celebration for no marriage.
Dat was called "jumpin' de broom," jes' taken up wid 'em. Dey all want
you to have plenty of chillun, though.

"Us wo' asfedity 'roun' us neck keep off de small pox and measles.
Us didn't have much medicine and some of um was always full of bad com-
plaints lac' Carrie, my neighbor, whut you axed about. I bees a-hurtin',
but I can't never git in edgeways for her. Always got a lot excuses; doan
never 'spects to die 'thout folks knows whut ails her. But she brought
me some black-eyed peas today, and I lac's um 'caze dey biles sof', and
I say 'ef de devil brought hit, God sarnt hit.' Sometimes I bees hongry,
an' I say, 'Whut is I'm gwinter eat?', and along come somebody wid sumpin'.

"Wish you could of heered dat calliope on de Cremonia. Dey dance
some time 'mos' all night, but dey didn't act lac' dey do now. 'Twus

nice behaviour. Look lac' ev'ything goin' back ter heathenisam, and hits
on de way now. But de good Lord he'ps me. He hol's my han'. I ain't
got nothin' 'gin nobody. I doan see no need of fussin' and fightin' an'
a-drinkin' whiskey. Us livin' in a new worl' and I go on makin' de bes'
I kin of hit. Some I lac, some I doan'.

"I got one daughter, Fannie Watson, a good washer and ironer right
here in Gainesville, and I got a son,too, say he ain't gonna marry 'tel
he kin treat de 'oman good as she kin treat herse'f. I makes him wait
on me, and he gits mighty raw sometimes, but I tells him I'm jes' much
older den he is now as I was when he was bawn. Den he gives me a old
dirty dime, but now wid dese here tokens, you gotter pay some of hit fer
spendin'. Dey tells me hit's de Governor, and I say 'let him carry 'em;
he kin tote 'em, I ain't able.' Well, once ain't always, and twice ain't
ferever.

"No'm, I doan never go ter church no mo'. De preacher's here is
goin' bline about money. Dey ain't interested in dey soul. Some folks
b'longs ter de church an' ain't been changed. De church ain't all of
hit. I 'members day uv 'mancipation. Yankees tole us we was free, and
dey call us up frum de fiel' to sign up an' see ef us wanted to stay on
wid 'em. I stayed dat year wid de Moorings, den I bargain for lan', but
couldn't never pay fer hit. Turned loose 'thout nothin'.

"But dey was a coal black free born nigger name George Wright,
had a floatin' mill right here on de 'Bigbee River, stayed at de p'int
of de woods jes' 'bove de spring branch, and hit did a good service.
But he got in debt and he sole his five boys. Dey was his own chillun,
and he could sell 'em under de law. De names was Eber, Eli, Ezekiel,
Enoch, and Ezra, an' he sole 'em ter de highes' bidder right yonder
front of de Pos' Uffice for cash. And Jack Tom was another free nigger

Alabama   - 4 -   136

here and he bought some of 'em, and dey others de white folks bought, and
I never heerd no complaint and I seed 'em long as dey lived. Dey was
a heap of things went on. Some I lac's to remember, some I doan. But
I'd rather be free now. I never seed Mr. Lincoln, but when dey tole
me 'bout him, I thought he was partly God.

     "But Mr. John Rogers right here,(he's dead an' gone now), he was
whut he was and wasn't 'ceitful. Go to him ef you got into anything,
and he more'n apt to tell you whut to do. He was wile when he was
young, but he settle down and was de bes' white man to de niggers I ever
know'd. He'd he'p me right now ef he was livin' and seen me wearin'
dis here rag nasty, he sho' would.

Washington Copy,
6/15/37.
L. H.

Angie Garrett. (Library of Congress)

Lomax and Brown recognized the significance of the narratives, as did many of the state programs that captured the testimonies. To them the testimonies represented an invaluable resource on the African American experience. Unfortunately, others in the federal government did not share this opinion about the slave narratives or the Federal Writers' Project. Congress cut funds for the WPA, which affected the Federal Writers' Project. Consequently, interviewing of formerly enslaved persons slowed dramatically as the Writers' Project reordered its priorities and shifted funds to other activities. This decision was influenced by concerns about what was seen as the repetitious nature of the interviews, the ultimate disposition of the interviews already compiled, and the belief that all of the formerly enslaved persons had been identified and interviewed. For all practical purposes the program ceased operating in 1939.

With the conclusion of the slave narrative project the disposition of the collection became the responsibility of the Library of Congress and its Writers Unit. Under the guidance of the noted folklorist Benjamin A. Botkin, the materials from the state projects were forwarded to the Library of Congress for processing. The collection included more than 2,300 interviews and nearly a thousand related documents ranging from advertisements for runaways to bills of sale for slaves. Botkin, who believed strongly in the need to give voice to the voiceless in order to create greater empathy between different communities, carefully oversaw the organization and preservation of the narratives (Hirsch 1987; Yetman 2001). The accounts were assembled into bond volumes titled "A Folk History of Slavery in the United States" and placed in the holdings of the Library in 1941. Botkin, like Lomax and others, saw the narratives as a valuable resource.

Benjamin Botkin in fact made use of portions of the slave narratives in his 1945 publication *Lay My Burden Down.* His was the second publication to make use of the narratives. The first was *The Negro in Virginia,* which looked at slavery in that state and was produced by the Virginia Writers' Project. In his book Botkin used the words of the respondents to generate insights into African American life and culture during the era of slavery. Among the concepts he discussed were general remembrances of slavery, the use of mother wit, work regimens, and the Civil War. One reviewer found the testimonies engaging and thought their stories describing enslavement "come closer to reality than do the history books" (Powdermaker 1946).

Although Botkin's book introduced the slave narratives to a wider audience, it did not generate a surge of additional volumes based on the collection. In part this was due to their limited accessibility at the Library of Congress. The collection did not circulate outside of the rare books section of the library, which limited access to researchers willing and patient enough to spend long hours going through the individual interviews. This was a formidable prospect that likely discouraged their exploration.

CONTROVERSY OVER USE OF THE NARRATIVES

For many years after the slave narratives were deposited in the Library of Congress scholars tended to marginalize them. In part this was based on concerns regarding the frailties of memory and skepticism about oral histories from the historical profession. From the last quarter of the 19th century historians had sought to professionalize the field as a way of solidifying their stature as scholars. To this end increased emphasis was placed on objective history and history as a social science. The goal was to make use of solid primary sources that were considered reliable and to ensure that writers presented the facts as accurately as possible. The closer the information used was connected to the time and location of the matter under study the greater its value. As a result, material acquired from respected and timely sources was given high value while information from less reliable, less timely sources was devalued. This scientific approach emerged from the work of Leopold von Ranke in Germany (1795–1886), who strongly endorsed reliance on the narratives of eyewitnesses and "immediate documents."

Under these guidelines oral histories gained from interviews conducted years after the historical moment were suspect. Many scholars believed issues of the reliability of memory over time hurt the usefulness of these testimonies. They worried about their accuracy and the possibilities that the interviewee would selectively recall some events and exclude others based on personal whims. Moreover, if the interviewee was not a respected member of the community the accuracy of the testimony was even more suspect. Interviews of uneducated, poor, or less revered persons at the bottom of society certainly were suspect. It was believed they did not have the facility to provide a thoughtful, objective view of events. The best oral sources, if they were to be used, came from the more thoughtful and influential members of society who brought perspective to their commentary.

Also impeding the mining of the slave narratives was the predominant assessment of the institution of slavery prevalent among scholars at the time. In the years subsequent to the Civil War historians sympathetic to a southern view of slavery dominated the scholarship concerning slavery in the United States. Underlying this perspective were idiosyncratic views about race that held sway. These views embraced racial inferiority with regard to people of color and the resulting responsibility of the "white man's burden." This burden decreed that the white race had to control and watch over races perceived to be inferior. With regard to slavery it was a means of rationalizing the institution, declaring it a necessary and useful operation functioning largely to the benefit of the people it enslaved.

The leading voice in this school of thought was the historian Ulrich Bonnell Phillips. One of the earliest and foremost southern scholars, Phillips established himself as an expert on plantation life. He based his work on detailed research of plantation records, letters, southern newspapers, and other southern primary data. In his main works on the subject, *American Negro Slavery* (1918) and *Life and Labor in the Old South* (1929), Phillips put forth his analysis of the institution. Essentially he offered the view that slavery was a necessary institution for controlling the enslaved, who were innately inferior (Smith 2003). He further argued that slavery was more benign than oppressive. Phillips's perspective on the useful and civilizing attributes of slavery was echoed by other influential historians and appeared in history textbooks used in high schools and colleges.

Although dissent from the Phillips school existed, it did not begin to have real energy until the advent of the civil rights movement, which built momentum after World War II. As African Americans took issue with long-held traditions regarding segregation and race, particularly in the South, more historians began to offer alternative analyses of slavery. John Hope Franklin, in his landmark 1947 publication *From Slavery to Freedom,* looked at the enslaved and slavery in a more sympathetic and humane fashion. He did not view the enslaved as inferior or infantile but as victims of an oppressive system designed to overcome any resistance they might consider. His work reflected the perspective of African American scholars and others who disagreed with Phillips's perspective.

As other works reexamined slavery and its operation, new interpretations emerged that were more in accordance with the views of Franklin than those of Phillips. These works looked with new eyes at the sources used by Phillips and consulted additional sources that offered points of view besides those of southern slaveholders and apologists. These historians who were interested in social history sought to better understand the experiences and views of people in society not as often researched. Their interest in history from the bottom up rather than the top down caused them to depend more heavily on nontraditional sources to reveal the history of this often overlooked group. Among the sources used with regard to slavery were the slave narratives. For social historians these testimonies became a valuable vehicle for viewing the day-to-day vicissitudes of slavery through the eyes of the enslaved. Their words often conflicted with the picture of a kindly institution as described by Phillips. These were not people content with their status or who thought they benefited from being enslaved.

GROWING RESPECT FOR ORAL HISTORIES

Growing respect for oral history as a research source also encouraged increased recognition of the slave narratives. In 1949, historian Allan Nevins established the Columbia Oral History Research Office at Columbia University, which boosted the creditability of oral history. Nevins was a well-respected scholar whose embrace of oral history helped raise its standing. Although the Columbia program focused on interviewing those "who have contributed significantly to society or who were close affiliates of world leaders," the quality of its work helped increase acceptance of the use of oral history as a research source. In the 1960s, the founding of oral history organizations in the United States and Great Britain further solidified the value of oral histories. These groups brought together leaders in the field to establish standards for conducting oral history interviews and proving the legitimacy of their work.

The changing environment regarding African American history and oral history offered fertile ground for renewed interest in the slave narratives. Botkin's book *Lay My Burden Down* made use of only a small portion of the slave narratives. In 1970, Norman R. Yetman's book *Voices from Slavery and Life under the "Peculiar Institution": Selections from the Slave Narrative Collection* made more extensive use of the narratives. It contained 100 complete interviews with the goal of revealing the rich information within them. Slave auctions and other painful aspects of enslavement were highlighted along with survival strategies of the enslaved. Although Yetman's book used less than 5 percent of the slave narrative collection, it offered a powerful glimpse of their richness and usefulness for scholars interested in slavery.

Yetman's work was an important step forward in better publicizing the slave narratives. However, it did not solve the problem of the difficult accessibility to them at the Library of Congress, where they remained in the Rare Book reading room. The solution to this dilemma came when Greenwood Press sponsored the publication of the entire slave narrative collection. *The American Slave: A Composite Autobiography* was edited by George P. Rawick in 1972. Looking at the Library of Congress collection, Rawick saw a problem.

> As I reread the material from the Rare Book Room of the Library of Congress collection several times, I was most struck by the fact that for many states we had only a small number of narratives. Most particularly, I noted that there were only 174 pages of narratives for Mississippi, a total of twenty-six interviews. This total, I felt, could hardly represent more than a mere sample of the narratives that should have been recorded in such an important slave state. I surmised either that the project

had been deliberately curtailed by those who did not want such material in existence or that the bulk of the collection had never been sent to the national offices of the Federal Writers' Project in Washington, as they should have been, and might still be somewhere in Mississippi. Both guesses turned out to be correct. (Rawick 1978, x–xi)

In his work of more than 4,000 documents, Rawick also included WPA slave narratives from archives scattered across the country that had not been given to the Library of Congress. This included material from Florida, Arkansas, and other states. For the first time all of the interviews were readily available to researchers to use in their exploration of slavery. It gave the voices and experiences of the formerly enslaved a larger stage on which they could be explored and presented an alternative view of enslavement to the one proffered in plantation documents.

The availability of the narratives was an important component in the upsurge of studies of American slavery in the last three decades of the 20th century. They allowed scholars to look more closely at the dynamics of enslavement and the strategies the enslaved used to navigate it. They have also encouraged an important shift in the historiography of the life of the enslaved. They have allowed a richer, more complex view of enslaved life to emerge. More than the childlike, content, or sometimes surly persons represented by slavery apologists, the individuals who emerge from the slave narratives are real people seeking ways to cope with an untenable existence. They laugh, they cry, they work, and they are emotionally tied to family and friends. They are like other actors in history who are seeking ways to survive and perhaps thrive despite the circumstances in which they find themselves.

The strength of the Rawick publication was that it included as many of the narratives as were available at the time. This compilation made it a valuable source to explore for insights into the experiences of the enslaved. Its strength, however, was also its greatest challenge for researchers seeking to explore specific aspects of enslaved life in depth. There was not an easy way to explore a specific thread of inquiry that might interest researchers. Each narrative was unique unto itself and represented the specific experiences of one person's life. Although interviewers had a set of questions they used to guide their inquiries, the topics covered in response were wide ranging. The interviewees might choose to talk about a particularly important event in their lives, their relationship with the family who enslaved them, or any other issue they wished to explore. This made for very rich content and coverage of topics interviewers would not have covered otherwise, but it also made the consistency of the topics covered less straightforward. A researcher seeking to explore a specific aspect of enslaved life had to read or scan numerous individual testimonies to develop a pattern of how that issue affected enslaved life in general.

An important step in helping to solve this dilemma was the Library of Congress's decision to digitize the narratives in their collection and put them online (Library of Congress 2001). While it did not solve all of the challenges of using the interviews, partly because it includes only the collection of 2,300 documents made in 1941, the Library of Congress's choice was a significant one. The electronic version added an important new dimension to navigating the narratives. Interested researchers did not have to travel to the library to use them. With the online database they could access more of the narratives through their computers, which made them a more complete and readily available resource. Also, searching for particular themes or ideas was no longer a sequential process of reading through each interview to see if it addressed the topics of interest to researchers. The online electronic database allowed for much quicker perusal of the material to identify information of relevance. This new format consequently made the slave narratives a more usable and even more applicable resource.

The online slave narrative database also allowed the voices of the enslaved to have a larger stage from which to be heard. More researchers could read what they had to say and more closely examine their experiences as enslaved people. This had an impact on the way scholars of slavery thought about and interpreted the institution of slavery and those forced to live within its confines. It allowed the true complexity of the relationships between slaveholders and the enslaved to surface. Both the enslaved and their enslavers had a variety of reactions to enslavement and a variety of ways in which they interacted with one another. Both terrible acts and empathetic actions characterized their interactions. The power of the slave narratives was that it made this interaction a two-way conversation. To truly understand the inner workings of slavery it is critical that the views of the persons who were enslaved are heard. The slave narratives provide that voice, and the fact that they are more readily available has allowed the enslaved to speak authoritatively about their views of that institution. And it has allowed researchers to think more creatively about the myriad aspects of the operation of slavery as an institution dependent on the forced labor of people of African descent.

References

Banks, Ann, ed. 1981. *First Person America.* New York: Norton.

Cade, John C. 1935. "Out of the Mouths of Ex-Slaves." *The Journal of Negro History* 20 (3): 294–337.

Crew, Spencer, and Cynthia Goodman. 2002. *Unchained Memories: Readings from the Slave Narratives.* Boston: Bulfinch Press.

Escott, Paul D. 1979. *Slavery Remembered: A Record of Twentieth-Century Slave Narratives.* Chapel Hill: University of North Carolina Press.

Hirsch, Jerrold. 1987. "Folklore in the Making: B. A. Botkin." *The Journal of American Folklore* 100 (395): 3–38.

Lomax, John. 1937. "Supplementary Instructions #9-E To The American Guide Manual Folklore Stories from Ex-Slaves." April 22. In Selected Records Bearing on the History of the Slave Narratives, Library of Congress. http://www.gutenberg.org/files/13847/13847-h/13847-h.htm.

Lomax, John A. 1947. *Adventures of a Ballad Hunter.* New York: Macmillan Co.

"Lynching in America: Statistics, Information, Images." n.d. University of Missouri at Kansas City. http://law2.umkc.edu/faculty/projects/ftrials/shipp/lynchstats.html.

McDonogh, Gary W., ed. 1993. *The Florida Negro: A Federal Writers' Project Legacy.* Jackson: University of Mississippi Press. (A previously unpublished product of the Florida Writers' Project, which relied extensively on interviews with African Americans.)

McMillen, Neil R. 2005. "WPA Slave Narratives." *Mississippi History Now,* The Online Publication of the Mississippi Historical Society. http://mshistorynow.mdah.state.ms.us/articles/64/wpa-slave-narratives

Mormino, Gary. 1988. "Florida Slave Narratives." *The Florida Historical Quarterly* 66 (4): 399–41905.

Powdermaker, Hortense. 1946. "A Review of *Lay My Burden Down: A Folk History of Slavery.* B. A. Botkin (Editor)." *American Anthropologist* 48 (4): 631–632.

Rawick, George P., general ed.; Jan Hillegas, Ken Lawrence, eds. 1977. *The American Slave: A Composite Autobiography: Supplement, Series 1,* 12 vols. Santa Barbara, CA: Greenwood Publishing Co.

Rawick, George P., general ed. 1979. *The American Slave: A Composite Autobiography.* Supplement, Series 2. 10 vols. Santa Barbara, CA: Greenwood Publishing Co.

Rawick, George P. 1978. *The American Slave: A Composite Autobiography Supplement,* Series 1, *Contributions in Afro-American and African Studies,* No.35. Santa Barbara, CA: Greenwood Publishing Co.

Smith, John David. 2003. "Ulrich Bonnell Phillips (1877–1934)." *The New Georgia Encyclopedia, History and Archaeology.* Available at http://www.georgiaencyclopedia.org/nge/Article.jsp?id=h-856.

Spurgeon, John. 2011. "WPA Slave Narratives." *The Encyclopedia of Arkansas History and Culture.* Available at http://www.encyclopediaofarkansas.net/encyclopedia/entry-detail.aspx?entryID=4041.

Trap, Diane. 2011. "Slave Narratives." *The New Georgia Encyclopedia.* http://www.georgiaencyclopedia.org/nge/Article.jsp?path=/Literature/Nonfiction/Works-1&id=h-3007.

U.S. Library of Congress. 2001. Born in Slavery: Slave Narratives from the Federal Writers' Project, 1936–1938. http://memory.loc.gov/ammem/snhtml/snhome.html.

Yetman, Norman. 2001. "An Introduction to the WPA Slave Narratives," Born in Slavery: Slave Narratives from the Federal Writers Project, 1936–1938. Available at http://memory.loc.gov/ammem/snhtml/snhome.html .

Chronology of Slavery in the United States

1619	Twenty Africans arrive in Virginia at Point Comfort on the James River on the English ship *White Lion*. They are sold in exchange for food, and some are taken to Jamestown where they are sold again.
1634	Maryland begins to import enslaved Africans.
1636	Slave trade begins in colonial North America with the voyage of the American slave ship *Desire*, which was built and launched in Massachusetts.
1640	A court case in Virginia sentences three runaway servants differently. The two white servants have additional years added to their servitude while the black runaway, John Punch, is given a sentence of life servitude for his transgression. This is the first documentations of someone being made a slave for life.
1641	The colony of Massachusetts is the first British North American colony to make slavery legal.
1644	In New Netherlands, 11 Africans petition for their freedom. They are given their freedom when it is determined that they had completed their time in servitude.
1646	The Massachusetts Bay Colony has two Africans returned to the Guinea coast of Africa. The court made this ruling to indicate their opposition to man-stealing, which they describe as "heinous."
1652	The Dutch allow New Netherlands to import slaves.
1662	The House of Burgess in Virginia passes legislation providing that a child retains the legal status of the mother. The laws mean all children born of an enslaved mother are enslaved despite the status of their father.
1676	Bacon's Rebellion of black slaves and black and white indentured servants takes place in Virginia. Because of its moderate success, the white elite fear that poor whites will join blacks in other uprisings. This, in turn, leads to the concept of enslavement only of blacks and the idea of hereditary slaves, where slaves cannot gain freedom and can only be born into slavery.

1682	Virginia declares that all black servants are enslaved for life.
1688	Quakers in Pennsylvania endorse an antislavery resolution.
1691	The first law against miscegenation is passed in Virginia. It is primarily directed toward marriages of whites with Africans or Native Americans. The first comprehensive slave laws are passed in South Carolina.
1692	Enslaved women are among those accused of being witches in Salem, Massachusetts.
1694	The cultivation of rice in the Carolinas results in the rapid increased importation of enslaved people.
1696	New England merchants join the slave trade when the Royal African Trade Company has its monopoly removed.
1700	Slavery is legalized in Pennsylvania.
1705	Virginia strengthens its slave codes by more clearly defining the status of the enslaved as Christians and as property. The new laws dramatically reduce any rights the enslaved had as people.
1708	People of African descent become the majority in South Carolina. A slave revolt in Newton, Long Island results in the death of several whites. Three enslaved people (one Indian) are hanged and an African woman burned alive.
1711	Armed raids by fugitive slaves cause great concern in South Carolina.
1712	Violent outbreaks, described as a slave revolt, take place in New York. The alleged uprising results in the death of nine whites and the execution of 18 enslaved persons. South Carolina implements a slave code that becomes the model used by other English colonies.
1715	Maryland declares that all enslaved persons entering the province and their descendants are enslaved for life.
1716	Several ships containing enslaved people arrive in French-controlled Louisiana for the first time.
1720	A large-scale slave revolt takes place in Charleston, South Carolina. Several enslaved people are executed and others banished for their participation.
1722	A plot to kill whites near Rappahannock River in Virginia is discovered. The enslaved plotters escape.
1723	Virginia takes away the rights of free African Americans to vote or participate in the legal system as jurors, testifiers, or witnesses. It also makes manumission illegal.

1724	French-owned Louisiana enacts slave codes.
1731	In a change of policy the Spanish decide they will not return enslaved persons who escape from South Carolina to Florida.
1735	A revolt on the slave ship *Dolphin* results in the death of everyone in an explosion.
1738	In a change of policy the trustees of Georgia decide to allow the importation of slaves from Africa. Spain offers land and freedom to runaways who reach Florida.
1739	An uprising of enslaved people in Stono, South Carolina, results in an attack on an armory and the death of white residents. Before they can reach Florida the rebels are defeated by the militia.
1740	A law entitled the "Negro Act" is passed in South Carolina. It places extensive restrictions on the ability to travel, to gather together, to earn money, and other rights for the enslaved.
1741	Fires that break out in New York are blamed on a conspiracy of enslaved people and poor whites. The so-called revolt results in the hanging of more than 30 people.
1758	Quakers in Pennsylvania decide to stop their members from taking part in the slave trade or owning an enslaved person.
1769	The Virginia House of Burgess rejects Thomas Jefferson's bill decreeing the emancipation of the enslaved.
1770	The fugitive slave Crispus Attucks, a fugitive from slavery, is one of the first to be shot and killed by the British at the Boston Massacre.
1772	The first slave autobiography is written by James Albert Gronniosaw. A court decision issued by Chief Justice Lord Mansfield in England abolishes slavery there but not in English colonies.
1773	Enslaved persons in Massachusetts petition for their freedom but fail.
1774	The Continental Congress pledges to end the slave trade.
1775	Enslaved men serve as substitutes in the Continental Army for their slaveholders. Others are given their freedom when they enlist in the Continental Army. In Philadelphia the first colonial abolition society is established. Black Minutemen fight at the battles of Lexington and Concord, Massachusetts. George Washington decides not to allow free people of color to join the Continental Army. Later in the year he changes his mind. Lord John Dunmore, the British governor of Virginia, issues a proclamation offering freedom to any enslaved person fighting on the side of the British.

1776	Members of the Continental Congress sign the Declaration of Independence.
1777	Vermont is the first colony to abolish slavery.
1779	Rhode Island forbids the removal of enslaved people from the state.
1780	Pennsylvania passes laws supporting gradual emancipation.
1781	Enslaved persons in Williamsburg, Virginia, rebel and set fire to buildings. In Massachusetts Mum Bett wins her freedom in the case *Brom and Bett v. Ashley*.
1783	A freedom clause in the Massachusetts constitution is interpreted as an abolishment of slavery. Massachusetts enfranchises all men regardless of race.
1784	Methodist Episcopal churches issue a mandate to members condemning slavery. Thomas Jefferson's proposal in the U.S. Congress to prevent the expansion of slavery westward fails.
1785	The Rhode Island Society for Abolishing the Slave-Trade is founded.
1787	The Northwest Ordinance stops the spread of slavery into the Northwest Territory. The first African American fraternal organization, the African Mason Lodge, is founded by Prince Hall in Boston.
1788	The U.S. Constitution is passed and includes a clause that counts enslaved persons as three-fifths of a person for tax and representation purposes. The first African Baptist Church is established in Savannah, Georgia, and led by Andrew Bryan, an enslaved man.
1789	*The Interesting Narrative of the Life of Olaudah Equiano, or Gustavus Vassa, the African, written by Himself* is published.
1790	Congress decides to let individual states make decisions about the continued existence of slavery within their borders. The Quakers present petition to Congress requesting the abolition of slavery. Congress takes the position that the Constitution prevents them from acting on the request.
1791	The Virginia Antislavery Society is formed. A revolt by enslaved Haitians is led by Toussaint L'Ouverture.
1793	Eli Whitney patents the cotton gin. It eventually increases cotton production, which results in increasing values for the enslaved labor needed to grow cotton for sale. The passage of the first Fugitive Slave Law permits slaveholders to cross state lines to recover fugitives. Aiding a runaway becomes an offense subject to arrest.

1794	Congress bans the slave trade. The American Convention of Abolition Societies meeting is held in Philadelphia, Pennsylvania. France abolishes slavery.
1795	A plotted slave revolt is discovered north of New Orleans, Louisiana. The participants are executed.
1797	Four enslaved men from North Carolina petition Congress to overturn a state law that requires the return of "illegally freed slaves" to their enslavers. Congress does not act on their request.
1799	An unsuccessful rebellion of enslaved Virginians takes place in Southampton.
1800	Gabriel Prosser, an enslaved man, organizes approximately 1,100 slaves near Richmond, Virginia, to revolt against their enslavers. His plans are betrayed and Prosser is executed.
1803	President Thomas Jefferson purchases the Louisiana Territory from the French. France under Napoleon decides to reestablish the code noir and slavery.
1808	Congress passes a law banning the importation of slaves with the goal of ending the external slave trade.
1811	Charles Deslandes leads more than 300 enslaved persons in a revolt near New Orleans. They attack several plantations before they are overwhelmed by state and federal troops mustered against them.
1816	George Boxley, a white military officer, unsuccessfully plans to free the enslaved in Spotsylvania, Virginia. He escapes, and six enslaved people are hanged.
1817	The American Colonization Society is established to relocate free African Americans in Africa. African American leaders in Philadelphia meet and formally oppose the work of the American Colonization Society. They view its work as an effort to exile free African Americans to Africa. Approximately 200 enslaved people attack whites with sticks in St. Mary's County, Maryland. Police eventually break up the altercation.
1817–19	Fugitive slaves in Florida and Native Americans join together to fight against the United States in the First Seminole War.
1819	Congress passes legislation declaring slave trading by any U.S. citizen to be a capital offense. Canada refuses to allow the U.S. government to hunt runaway slaves within its borders.
1820	The Missouri Compromise is passed. It does not allow slavery beyond the southern border of Missouri. Maine enters the Union as a free state and Missouri as a slave state. Congress passes legislation that classifies trading in foreign slaves an act of piracy.

1821   In the *Hall v. Mullin* case, the Maryland Supreme Court rules that an enslaved person cannot legally own property.

1822   The American Colonization Society establishes Liberia as a colony for African Americans leaving America. Denmark Vesey, a free African American, is tried for organizing a massive slave uprising in South Carolina. Vesey and 40 other people are executed.

1823   The U.S. Circuit Court in Washington, D.C., rules that if an enslaved person is moved into a free state, he or she becomes free. It also rules that inhumane treatment of the enslaved is indictable under common law.

1831   A literate enslaved preacher, Nat Turner, organizes an uprising in Southampton, Virginia. At least 57 whites are killed. Turner is captured and hanged in Jerusalem, Virginia. *The Liberator,* an abolitionist newspaper is created by William Lloyd Garrison in Boston. Maria W. Stewart, of Boston, Massachusetts, is the first free African American woman to give a public lecture against slavery.

1832   The New England Anti-Slavery Society is founded. African American women in Salem, Massachusetts, organize the first Female Anti-Slavery Society. Their efforts are later duplicated by women in other northern cities.

1834   The American Anti-Slavery Society is formed in Philadelphia.

1834/1835   New York City and Philadelphia suffer riots against African Americans and antislavery advocates.

1836   Texas wins independence from Mexico and legalizes slavery. Free blacks and mulattos are forbidden from entering the state. The U.S. House of Representatives adopts a gag rule that automatically tables abolitionist materials sent to it. The rule is not rescinded until 1844.

1837   The first National Anti-Slavery Society Convention meets in New York City. The first Convention of the Anti-Slavery Society of American Women takes place in New York. Both black and white women attend.

1838   Pro-slavery mobs attack the second Anti-Slavery Convention of American Women, which is meeting in Philadelphia. Frederick Douglass escapes from slavery in Maryland.

1839   Fifty-three Africans aboard the Spanish slave ship *Amistad* take over the ship and kill the captain and several crew members. The ship eventually lands off the coast of Long Island, NY. They are freed after a trial and allowed to return to their homes in Africa in 1841. The Liberty Party, the first antislavery political party, is created in Warsaw, New York.

1840   The World Anti-Slavery Convention is held in London, England.

1842   The *Prigg v. Commonwealth of Pennsylvania* Supreme Court Case upholds the Fugitive Slave Law of 1793 and rules that individual states may not hinder efforts to return fugitives. George Latimer is captured in Boston and attempts to return him to enslavement are met with strong abolitionist opposition, which eventually results in the purchase of his freedom.

1843   At the National Convention of Colored Men in Buffalo, New York, Henry Highland Garnett delivers a fiery speech in which he counsels the enslaved to use violence to take their liberty.

1844   More than 70 enslaved people in Maryland arm themselves and begin marching to Pennsylvania to freedom. They are attacked; many are captured but several manage to escape.

1846   In Congress David Wilmot offers a resolution banning slavery in territory acquired from Mexico. It is the subject of acrimonious debate but is eventually defeated.

1848   The Free Soil Party, a combination of antislavery political groups, is formed. Its key goal is to prevent the extension of slavery into land given to the United States as a result of the Mexican War. Seneca Falls, New York, hosts the first Women's Rights Convention. The group is strongly opposed to slavery.

1850   The passage of the Compromise of 1850 includes a stronger fugitive slave law that benefits slaveholders. It allows California to enter the Union as a free state, bans the slave trade in Washington, D.C., and allows the residents of New Mexico and Utah to decide if they will allow slavery.

1851   Thomas Sims is arrested in Boston at the request of a Georgia slaveholder who claims Sims belongs to him. After his trial Sims is returned to Georgia. This is the first major test of the strength of federal support of the 1850 Fugitive Slave Law.

1852   Harriet Beecher Stowe's novel *Uncle Tom's Cabin* is published.

1854   Anthony Burns, who escaped enslavement in Virginia, is arrested in Boston. He is tried and found guilty under the 1850 Fugitive Slave Law. The federal government deploys marines and artillery to ensure his return to enslavement and emphasize its support of the return of fugitive slaves. The territories of Kansas and Nebraska are created by the Kansas-Nebraska Act. The residents of these territories through popular vote are to decide if they will allow slavery within their borders. The act overturns the antislavery clause in the Missouri Compromise.

1856   The Republican Party is established. It emerges from the Free Soil Party. Fighting breaks out between pro-slavery and Free Soil groups in what is referred to as Bleeding Kansas. In Pottawatomie, Kansas, John Brown and his followers kill five pro-slavery men. This is followed by more violence from both sides.

1857   In the *Dred Scott v. Sanford* case the U.S. Supreme Court, under Chief Justice Roger B. Taney, denies citizenship to all African Americans, enslaved or free, and denies Congress the right to prohibit slavery in the territories.

1859   The *Clothilde*, the last slave ship to bring slaves into the United States, lands in Mobile Bay, Alabama. John Brown leads an unsuccessful raid on Harpers Ferry, Virginia. He heads up an interracial group hoping to start a slave rebellion as an attack on the institution of slavery.

1860   Abraham Lincoln is elected president of the United States. A conspiracy planned by enslaved workers to capture arms and escape by ship is uncovered in Plymouth, North Carolina.

1861   Eleven southern states, led by South Carolina, secede from the Union. They form the Union of Confederate States and elect Jefferson Davis president. Congress abolishes slavery in Washington, D.C., and the territories. Lincoln encourages the border states to adopt gradual, compensated emancipation. The Second Confiscation Act provides freedom for enslaved people in the possession of supporters of the Confederacy. The Militia Act gives enemy-owned slaves freedom in return for their service to the Union Army. The First South Carolina Volunteers is created and manned primarily by formerly enslaved men. West Virginia is admitted to the Union as a free state, and Utah abolishes slavery within its borders.

1863   On January 1, Lincoln issues the Emancipation Proclamation, which gives freedom to enslaved people in areas in rebellion against the United States. The 54th Massachusetts Colored Infantry is organized. It is the first black regiment from the northern states. African American soldiers, including formerly enslaved men, are recruited and trained across the North. Maryland abolishes slavery.

1864   President Lincoln and Congress repeal the Fugitive Slave Laws. Slavery is ended in Louisiana, Arkansas, and Missouri. African American troops are massacred at Fort Pillow, Tennessee, after surrendering and laying down their arms. Three enslaved men judged disloyal to the Confederacy are hanged in Brooks County, Georgia.

1865   The Thirteenth Amendment to the Constitution abolishes slavery. The Confederacy passes a Negro Soldier Bill that allows enslaved men to enlist in the Confederate army. General Robert E. Lee, commander of the Confederate Army, surrenders to General Ulysses S. Grant at the Appomattox Court House in Virginia ending the Civil War. Lincoln is assassinated at Ford's Theater. Congress establishes the Bureau of Refugees, Freedmen and Abandoned Lands (The Freedmen's Bureau). Its assignment is to aid the formerly enslaved as they adjust to freedom. On June 19, the arrival of Union troops at Galveston ends slavery in Texas. The first meeting of the National Equal Rights League takes place in Cleveland, Ohio. The attendees urge African Americans to buy property, get an education, and live in a manner that demands respect and acceptance by others. The Ku Klux Klan is organized in Pulaski, Tennessee, by Nathan B. Forrest, a former Confederate general under Robert E. Lee.

1866   Congress passes the Fourteenth Amendment guaranteeing citizenship to the former slaves and threatening states with a loss of representation if they deny freedmen the vote. Race riots engulf Memphis, Tennessee, and New Orleans, Louisiana. Nearly 15,000 people gather in Washington, D.C., to celebrate emancipation. Southern states create black codes to nullify the impact of the Thirteenth Amendment.

1867   Congress passes Reconstruction acts that are passed to create political and social reform in the South. Military districts are created in the former states of the Confederacy (except Tennessee) to protect African American political rights and to ensure the ratification of the Fourteenth Amendment to the Constitution. African Americans receive the right to vote in the District of Columbia.

1868   South Carolina elects the first and last state legislature with an African American majority. The Opelousas Massacre in Louisiana results in the death of 200 to 300 African Americans.

1870   Congress passes the Fifteenth Amendment guaranteeing freedmen the right to vote.

1871   The passage of the Ku Klux Klan Act allows the federal government to use military force and punishment in places where civil rights laws are being denied. The Second Enforcement Act is passed to support the Thirteenth and Fourteenth Amendments to the Constitution and the rights of African Americans.

1872   The Freedmen's Bureau closes.

1873   In Colfax, Louisiana, more than 60 African Americans are killed in a confrontation between predominantly African American state militia and whites who oppose African American participation in government.

1874   Democrats control both houses of Congress. Whites gain control of the South Carolina legislature.

1875   Congress passes a Civil Rights Act providing African Americans equal access to public accommodations. More than 20 African Americans are killed in the Clinton Massacre in Mississippi.

1877   As a result of the Compromise of 1877, Republican Rutherford B. Hayes is elected president and federal troops are withdrawn from the South, marking the end of Reconstruction.

1878   Formerly enslaved men and women in large numbers begin relocating to Kansas, Colorado, and Oklahoma in search of better opportunity and greater freedom. These people, called Exodusters, hope to find improved opportunity and freedom outside the South.

1881   Tennessee segregates the railroads in the state, creating one of the first Jim Crow laws in the nation. Other states soon follow their example.

1929   Interviews of formerly enslaved persons are conducted by John B. Cade of Southern University and Charles S. Johnson at Fisk University.

1934   Lawrence D. Reddick of Kentucky State College launches a project interviewing 250 formerly enslaved persons.

1935   John B. Cade publishes "Out of the Mouths of Ex-Slaves" in the *Journal of Negro History.*

1936–1938   The Slave Narrative Project is conducted by the Federal Writers' Project under the auspices of the U.S. government's Works Progress Administration; the narrative project is directed by John Lomax.

1941   Benjamin A. Botkin, who becomes folklore editor of the Federal Writers' Project after John Lomax, oversees the preparation of the 2,300 slave narratives and additional documents into 17 bound volumes called "A Folk History of Slavery," which is given to the U.S. Library of Congress in Washington, D.C. Anyone wishing to read the narratives must go to the Library of Congress.

1945   *Lay My Burden Down,* published by the University of Chicago Press, publicizes the existence of the slave narratives. Compiled and edited by Benjamin Botkin, it includes excerpts from the FWP narratives and 20 complete narratives.

1970   *Voices from Slavery,* compiled and edited by Norman R. Yetman, is published by Holt, Rinehart, and Winston; it includes 100 complete Federal Writers' Project interviews (narratives), making the work more accessible to the public.

1972   The entire series of the slave narratives in the Library of Congress collection is published in an 18-volume set by Greenwood Press in

The American Slave: A Composite Autobiography, edited by George P. Rawick.

1973   George Rawick, with Ken Lawrence and Jan Hillegas, begins searching for additional narratives not included in the Library of Congress collection. Some are from the original Federal Writers' Project slave interview project and some are from other oral history projects.

1979   Rawick publishes nearly 2,000 additional slave narratives, compiled in two sets, totaling 22 volumes, called *The American Slave: A Composite Autobiography, Supplement, Series 1,* and *Supplement, Series 2,* published by Greenwood Press, in 1978 and 1979.

2001   *Born in Slavery: Slave Narratives from the Federal Writers' Project, 1936–1938,* resulting from digitizing all 2,300 of the slave narratives collected by the Library of Congress, along with 500 photographs, is provided online at the Library of Congress website (http://memory.loc.gov/ammem/snhtml/snhome.html).

2002   Dover Publications publishes *When I Was a Slave: Memoirs from the Slave Narrative Collection,* introduced and edited by Norman R. Yetman. It is a collection of selected unedited narratives from the Library of Congress Slave Narrative Collection, some of which were also included in the 1970 *Voices from Slavery.*

Please note: When reading the narratives, it is important to remember their context. Although the language used in the interviews can be offensive or disturbing, it is a reflection of the attitudes of the time and place.

5

Work and Slavery

The economic success of the South revolved around slavery and agriculture. In the years before the American Revolution slavery grew in importance, particularly in southern colonies where they sought to create a stable labor force to support the production of indigo, tobacco, and rice. Over time, Africans enslaved for life became the preferred labor sources over white indentured servants or Indians. Their agricultural skills, the color of their skin, and their lack of familiarity with the environment made them the best choice as workers in the eyes of southern landowners. Consequently, the enslaved population in the South grew steadily as the nation moved toward independence.

After the Revolutionary War the advent of the Industrial Revolution and the invention of the cotton gin gave added impetus to the southern economy. Southerners moved westward from Virginia, the Carolinas, and Georgia into Alabama, Mississippi, Louisiana, Tennessee, and Texas. There they opened up new acreage on which to grow mainly cotton. As cotton increased in importance as a cash crop so did the need for additional labor to prepare the land and cultivate the crop for market. Consequently, the demand for slaves grew rapidly in conjunction with the expanding demand for cotton in the mills of England and New England. In this process enslaved people were the unpaid labor force that supplied the brawn needed for these agricultural activities. Their involvement reduced production costs and increased the profits of southern landowners. Therefore, the slaveholder's goal was to extract as much labor from the enslaved as they could. Otherwise, the system could not work as effectively.

The institution of slavery was absolutely critical to the successful and profitable operation of the southern economy. This was particularly the case for large plantation owners, who needed large numbers of enslaved people to cultivate multiple acres of crops. Though this group represented only a small percentage of southerners, they were among the most economically influential landowners in the South and the nation. Though less than one percent of slaveholders had 50 or more enslaved people in their operations, an estimated 25 percent of enslaved people lived on such plantations, and more than 50 percent lived on places with 20 or more enslaved people.

FIELD WORKERS

Most of the enslaved worked on the land or in outdoors pursuits. They toiled long days under close scrutiny and were expected to meet a proscribed production

THE FIRST COTTON-GIN.—DRAWN BY WILLIAM L. SHEPPARD.

The enslaved using a cotton gin. (Library of Congress)

level. Falling short of expectations resulted in punishment. Although the enslaved sought to avoid mistreatment, they also sought ways to ease their work burden without detection whenever they could. They did not relish the labor they exerted, which only benefited the slaveholder and not themselves. There was a constant tension between the work expected and the effort they desired to expend.

On the larger-scale operations the work schedule was the most rigid and fixed. With larger groups of workers, it was critical to ensure that they functioned at a fast pace and produced a successful crop. Workers were closely watched and expected to meet the expectations of the slaveholder, overseer, or slave driver. To meet these goals the enslaved had to put in as many as 10 or more hours of work each day. The day began early and ended late, and there was little let up in the course of the day. "We would always be in the field by the time it was light enough to work and stayed until dark run us in," said David Byrd of Texas. Similarly, in Georgia, Alice Green's overseer had her, "in de field by sunup and he wuked 'em 'til sundown." As Henry Cheatum of Alabama put it, " de mos' us did wuz wurk from 'can 'til can't.'"

In this routine enslaved workers were up as early as four in the morning. Wake-up time was announced in a variety of ways. On some plantations the slaveholder or his proxy would come to the quarters and announce loudly that is was time to wake and head to the fields. Other places announced the beginning of the work day through blowing a horn or conch shell or ringing a bell. On the Mississippi plantation on which Orris Harris lived, he recalled that the overseer "made de slaves git up ebery mornin' by ringin' dat big bell. Dat bell wus hangin' on a scafful in de side yard, an' he rung it 'fore day to git de han' off ter wurk and he rung it ergain ter call dem ter dinner." In Texas, where Jeff Calhoun worked in the fields, "'De horn wuz blowed at four in de mornin yer had to git up to feed and do your chores, eat you'se breakfast and be in the fild and ready to work."

Calhoun was fortunate in that he and his fellow workers were allowed to prepare and eat breakfast before they headed to the field. This was not the case in every situation. Work came before eating where Phillis Fox of Mississippi lived: "I 'member de field hands went to de field before day. Lots O' times dey would have to leave before dey had et breakfast an' us lads would have to carry de breakfast to de field to em."

What the enslaved got to sustain them varied greatly from place to place. Ash cakes made of cornmeal baked in the ashes of the fireplace were often one component of breakfast. They might be supplemented by a variety of foods, including fried meat, pickled pork, bread, molasses, coffee, sassafras tea, or sometimes milk. What the enslaved field hands ate was not often of great concern to the slaveholder, however. Getting food in their stomachs was the primary goal. As Herb Griffin of Georgia noted, "Whether this amount of food was sufficient for a morning's meal didn't matter to their master. They simply had to make it last them until dinner."

The fields were not always the first stop in the workday for the enslaved. Often there were chores to complete before they headed out. There were animals to feed, cows to milk, and wood to cut before the workday began. All of this had to be accomplished before they tended the crops. In Texas, John Bates described the following routine: "De young marster usually comes out early in de mornin bout foah clock and hollers and dat means fer us ter git up, we would gits up and while de women foks was gitten breakfast, de men foks would do de milkin and feeding and den eats breakfast, and be in de field fore sun up and works til sun down."

When the workers reached the field the expectations were demanding. A prescribed level of production was expected of each laborer. On cotton, sugar, and tobacco operations, the gang system of work was usually employed, and for most of the year the workers operated in specific units. As John Moore of Texas explained, "Dey have Niggers in de fields in different squads, a hoe squad and a plow squad, and de overseer was pretty rapid. Iffen dey don' do de work dey buck dem down and whip dem."

At harvest time the routine changed, and each enslaved worker was expected to pick a certain amount of cotton or cut a certain amount of sugar cane. Austin Grant's Texas farm had the following system: "They would give us 200 or 300 pounds of cotton to bring in and you would git it, and if you didn' git it, you better, or you would git it tomorrow, or your back would git it. Or you'd git it from someone else, maybe steal it from their sacks."

On rice plantations the work pattern differed. There the land was subdivided into plots in which the rice was planted. Workers were then given a task to complete each day. It might vary from weeding an entire plot to lowering or raising the water level for the plants. Ben Horry noted how challenging task work was in

The most common task of enslaved men and women was working in the fields growing cotton, rice, or sugar cane. It was hard backbreaking work. (MPI/Getty images)

South Carolina: "How much been task? A quarter (acre) if you mashing ground. Ten compass digging ground. Cutting rice one half acre a day (awful job)."

But no matter which crop was cultivated the workers were expected to meet the slaveholder or overseer's production expectations. If a worker fell short, or even if the overseer thought a worker was not performing up to expectations, punishment was swift and often very severe. According to Sol Walton of Texas, "The hands worked from sun to sun, and if the overseer seed 'em slackin' up he cussed 'em and sometimes whacked 'em with a bullwhip. I seed 'em whipped till their shirt stuck to their back. … Heaps of 'em was whipped jus' 'cause they could be whipped. The severity of the punishments suffered by the enslaved varied from place to place, but the threat of violence was almost universal and was used because slaveholders recognized that slavery demanded work from people who provided it grudgingly. The oppressiveness of the work, discouraging work environment, and lack of return for their efforts provided little incentive for the enslaved to work with enthusiasm.

Working conditions were difficult, and in addition to the draining sunup to sundown workday, the oppressive heat of the sun took its toll on field hands. Shade was not always provided or available, and although younger children might bring water to the workers, it was not always enough. According to Charlie Webb of Texas, "Sometimes dey would work 'em hard. Sometimes dey fall dead in d' fiel' dey was so hot. I seen 'em fall dead with sunstroke. But dey said it wouldn' spell much if dey did." The enslaved were expected to work regardless of the weather, and cold weather, rain, or other elements were not an excuse. Andrew Boone's slaveholder in North Carolina was particularly unconcerned about the impact of the elements: "We wurked from sun to sun. If we had a fire in cold weather where we wus wurkin' marster or de overseer would come an' put it out."

Seeking a Break from the Work Routine

Unsurprisingly, with this relentless work regime enslaved workers turned to a variety of devices to gain some relief from the work at hand. They might grab a quick nap or just stop working when the opportunity presented itself, as was the case with the mother of Lizzie Dillard of Mississippi: "One day, my mother felt unusually tired so slipped out to the bushes to rest a bit, while there she fell asleep, her hoe was taken to the house and for this she was given one of her first whippings."

Sometimes they pretended they were sick to avoid work. As Chana Littlejohn of North Carolina observed, "Some of de women played off sick an' went home an' washed an' ironed an' got by wid it." On occasion, larger groups were able to gain some rest by establishing systems to fool those in authority. Richard Carruthers was an accomplice in such a scheme: "I kep' a eye on the niggers down in the cotton patch. Sometime they lazy 'round and if I see the overseer comin' from the big house I sings a song to warn 'em, so they not git whupped, and it go like this: 'Hold up, hold up, American Spirit! Hold up, hold up, H-O-O-O-O-O-O-O!'"

The other method of getting respite from the work routine was to run away. This option was chosen fairly regularly on many plantations. An enslaved worker might grow tired of the work or punishments and decide to slip away to nearby woods, hills, or swamps. Usually they would stay away for several days or weeks and then, because of hunger, loneliness, and/or cold, would return. Abe Kelley remembered this happening in Mississippi: "Some of the niggers would run away off in the woods. Old Master had a woman, Nancy, that stayed in the woods three years." However unlike feigning sickness or sneaking a nap, which might escape detection and reprisal, running away nearly always resulted in punishment. Often it was done in a very public way to discourage others from considering the same choice. The threat of punishment had the desired effect on Emma Taylor of Texas, who "never did run when I was fixin to git a whippin. I seen some of dem run, and den they tied dem up wid chains to a post, and dey got lots worse whippins dan iffin day had jist been still."

Like Emma most enslaved people decided it was wiser to endure the hardships of the work regime rather than to resist in ways that brought retribution. Instead, they pushed through the numbing routine of working in the fields from "sun to sun," which left them weary at the end of each day. Hannah Scott of Texas said, "Bout 9 o'clock dey hollers 'cotton up,' and dat's de quitting signal. We goes to de quarters, and sometimes jes' drop on de bunk and go to sleep without nothing to eat."

What added to the length of the day, however, was that when the work was finished in the fields their tasks were not always completed. The same animals they tended in the morning needed attention in the evening. And for women there were meals to prepare and often weaving or sewing to do for the slaveholder before the workday was completed. Jeff Calhoun of Texas noted that "After you'se was through in the field you'se had to shuck co'n er haul in fodder and de women would spin er weave, de men would also pack out cotton and gin it at night in the fall."

Child Workers

Children were not exempt from work. Even before they reached their teen years children were enlisted to perform tasks that supported the work of older workers. One role was to serve as nursemaids for younger siblings while their parents went off to work. If an older adult was not available to perform this task, it often fell on the older children. This responsibility was given to Silva Witherspoon of Alabama who "stayed in de quarters an' nussed my mammy's chilluns, while she worked in de fiel's. She would tie de smalles' baby on my back so's I could play widout no inconvenience."

Preteens also tackled tasks that directly supported older enslaved field workers. They hauled water, cleared stones, fed livestock, and did other odd jobs. George Caulton of Georgia said their "master owned over a hundred grown slaves and the children were 'thick as blackbirds.' Some worked in the master's house, some did the washing, others drove the horses, and others did the same kind of work for the overseer. The majority of them helped in the tobacco fields."

As they reached their teen years enslaved children took on more responsible tasks in the field. In North Carolina, China Littlejohn's "Marster would not let us work until we were thirteen years old. Den he put us to plowin' in soft lan', an' de men in rough lan'." And the young workers were expected to quickly learn how to work efficiently:

> I 'member I helt a hoe handle mighty onsteady when they put a old women to larn me and some other chillun to scrape the fields. That old woman would be in a frantic. She'd show me and then turn 'bout to show some other li'l nigger, and I'd have the young corn cut clean as the grass. She say, 'For the love of Gawd, you better larn it right, or Solomon will beat the breath out you body.' Old man Solomon was the nigger driver. (Mary Reynolds, Texas)

Youth was not an excuse for underperforming. Once they were sent to work in the fields they were no longer children but field hands expected to pull their weight or suffer the consequences.

NARRATIVES

Charlie Aarons, Alabama

"I was a man able to do a man's work so I 'spects I was eighteen or twenty years old."

"Mr. Jason Harris had about sixty slaves, and a large plantation of a hundred acres, the men and women worked in the fields from six to six, except on Saturday, when they had half day holiday to clean up generally."

Frank Adams, Texas

"In slav'ry days, I hoed in de cotton fiel', didn' earn no money befo' freedom come. Us use' to hab plenty to eat, sich as co'n bread, sweet 'taters, 'possum baked wid 'taters, an' I like eb'ryt'ing we hab to eat."

"Our marster hab a big log house an' a hunnerd acres in his plantation. It was two miles soufwes' er Jasper. We all go up by ourse'fs in de mawnin', iffen we didn' dey blowed de ho'n to call us. We wuk all day an' went fishin' on hol'days."

Louisa Adams, North Carolina

"They sent many of the chillun to work at the salt mines, where we went to git salt. My brother Soloman wuz sent to the salt mines. Luke looked atter the sheep. He knocked down china berries for 'em. (Dad and mammie had their own gardens and hogs.)"

"My missus wuz kind to me, but Mars. Tom wuz the bugger. It wuz a mighty bit plantation. I don't know how many slaves wuz on it, there were a lot of dem do'. Dere were overseers two of 'em. One wuz named Bob Covington and the other Charles Covington. They were colored men. I rode with them. I rode wid 'em in the carriage sometimes. De carriage had seats dat folded up. Bob wuz overseer in de field, and Charles wuz carriage driver.

Louisa Adams. (Library of Congress)

All de plantation wuz fenced in, dat is all de fields, wid rails; de rails wuz ten feet long. We drawed water wid a sweep and pail. De well wuz in the yard. De mules for the slaves wuz in town, dere were none on the plantation. Dey had 'em in town; dey waked us time de chicken crowed, and we went to work just as soon as we could see how to make a lick wid a hoe."

"We hab our tasks lay out Satiday mawnin' an' if we finish' by noon, we could go fishin'."

Rachel Adams, Georgia

"Dere was hunderds of acres in dat dere plantation. Marse Lewis had a heap of slaves. De overseer, he had a bugle what he blowed to wake up de slaves. He blowed it long fore day so dat dey could eat breakfast and be out dere in de fields waitin' for de sun to rise so dey could see how to wuk, and dey stayed out dar and wulked 'til black dark. When a rainy spell come and de grass got to growin' fast, dey wukked dem slaves at night, even when de moon warn't shinin'. On dem dark nights one set of slaves helt lanterns for de others to see how to chop de weeds out of de cotton and corn. Wuk was sho' tight dem days. Evvy slave had a task to do atter dey got back to dem cabins at night. Dey each one had to spin deir stint some as de 'omans, evvy night."

"Young and old washed deir clothes Sadday nights. Dey hardly knowed that Sunday was. Dey didn't have but one day in de Christmas, and de only diff'unce dey seed dat day was dat dey give 'em some biscuits on Christmas day. New Year's Day was rail-splittin' day. Dey was told how many rails was to be cut, and dem Niggers better split dat many or somebody was gwine to git beat up."

S. B. Adams, Texas

"We worked on a farm, raised cattle an' mos' ebery thing needed 'bout de place. De goods fer our close was made at home. De ole spinnin' wheel an' loom was used to make de goods for clothin' an' de close was made by de women with dere fingers, mos'ly at night by candle light, some made clothes by a brush fire light."

Victoria Adams, North Carolina

"My massa's name was Samuel Black and missus was named Martha. She used to be Martha Kirkland befo' she married. There was five chillun in de family; they was: Alice, Manning, Sally, Kirkland, and de baby, Eugene. De white folks live in a great big house up on a hill; it was right pretty, too."

"You wants to know how large de plantation was I lived on? Well, I don't know 'zackly but it was mighty large. There was forty of us slaves in all and it took all of us to keep de plantation goin'. De most of de niggers work in de field. They went rk 'til two. All of them work on 'til it git almost dark. No ma'am, they ain't do much work at night after they gits home."

"Massa Samuel ain't had no overseer, he look after his own plantation. My old granddaddy help him a whole heap though. He was a good nigger and massa trust him."

"After de crops was all gathered, de slaves still had plenty of work to do. I stayed in de house wid de white folks. De most I had to do was to keep de house clean up and nurse de chillun. I had a heap of pretty clothes to wear, 'cause my missus give me de old clothes and shoes dat Missy Sally throw 'way."

Will Adams, Texas

"My Pa was 'leader' on the farm, there warn't no overseer or Driver. When Pa whipped you, you needn't go to the old man. He would say, 'Go on your way, Nigger, Freeman didn't whip you for nothing.' Master Dave believed what Pa said, he knowed it was that way. During slavery a Jew peddler come to our house. He was a treacherous man. After supper he went to the lot to see about his pony. Pa had fed him fifteen ears of co'n, but the Jew wanted him to have a half bushel. He come to the house and said to Master, 'That Nigger ain't fed my pony.' Master got mad and say to him, 'Be on your way if you is going to 'cuse my darkies of lying. Freeman told me he give your horse fifteen ears of co'n and no Jew ain't going to say he didn't.' Then the Jew wanted to pay Master a dime for the feed."

"The hands worked from sun to sun. They didn't do like they do now, they worked. If they needed a whipping, Pa put it on them. There was one man who done all the feeding. Pa come along behind him and if he didn't do it up brown, you would hear him hollering down to the lot. Master give his hands little crops and let them work them on Saturday. Then he bought the crops and the darkies went to Jefferson and bought clothes and such like. Big boats would drive up there. They fired wood. Lots of them saved their money and bought their freedom 'fore the war was over. They couldn't go 'bout as they pleased though, but had to have a dictator."

John Aldrich, Texas

"My daddy was a plow hand. Mother, she work in de field with a hoe. Marster used to work 'em from 'kin to can't.' If he ax you if you could you better not say 'yes.' If you say 'yes' he say, 'come here. I git you warm.' Den he beat you. He git your back hot for you. He work de niggers right along. It take a very severe rain to bring you out de field."

Barney Alford, Mississippi

"My pappy wus named Jourdan, en he wurk in de field, en druv the team uf oxen ter Covin'ton, Louisiana, wid a big waggin loaded wid cotton, all dat four yoke uf oxen culd pull atter time. He wus allus gone er week en when he cum back de waggin wus filled wid flour, en salt, en sugar, en one time he brung a barrell of mackeral, en I stole sum uf dat en wus whipped er gin."

Rev. W. B. Allen, Alabama

"My Master was a very kind man in many respects, but did not allow his slaves—male or female—to idle. All worked in the fields from the crack of day until dark, weather permitting."

"When I was a little fellow, the first bell was rung on the plantation at three o'clock in the mornin' during summer time. That was a signal for the slaves to rise, get their breakfasts and be ready to go to the fields when the second bell rang—at four o'clock. Of course, I was so young then that I didn't have to get up with the first bell, but I usually waked up and can remember that my old black mother always sang as she prepared breakfast in the big, open fireplace (we had no stove)."

Andy Anderson, Texas

"Let me tell yous how we cut an' thresh de wheat. Thar am no binders, or threshin' machines, so weuns cut de wheat by han', usin' a cradle. To thresh de grain, it am hung over a rail wid de heads down, an' de heads am beat wid a stick. Dat knocks de kernels out an' dey falls on a canvass dat am spread to catch dem. Now, to clean de wheat, weuns have to wait fo' a day w'en de wind am blowin' jus' right. W'en dat day comes, weuns pick de wheat up wid pails, raise it up an' pour it out an' de wind blows de chaff an' sich away."

Wash Armstrong, Texas

"Marse kep' fo' [four] fam'ly of slaves, dey was 'bout fo'ty or fifty head. Dey wuk from sun-up to sun-down."

Sarah Ashley, Texas

"I was wukin' in d' fiel' den. I uster wuk fo' a ol' lady, 73 year ol'. Dey uster nab niggers t' wait on d' ol' people w'en dey git disable'. I uster hafter wait on her all t'roo d' night. She was real sickly fo' t'ree year. D' ol' lady was like a mudder t' me. Dat was ol' Mistus Betsy. Den dey was Mandy Davis 'n' Mose Davis, d' marster 'n' mistus. On d' day dey bury po' Miz Betsy, atter d' fun'ral Mister Mose he come t' me 'n' say, 'Pack up all yo' clo's, you comin' home t' wuk in d' fiel'.' I wuk in d' cotton fiel'. I sho' did hate it w'en dat ol' lady die."

"I uster hafter pick cotton. Sometime' I pick t'ree hunnerd poun' 'r' cotton 'n' tote it a mile t' d' cotton house. Some pick t'ree hunnerd t' eight hunnerd poun's 'r' cotton 'n' hafter tote d' bag fo' a whole mile' t' d' gin. Iffen dey didn' do dey wuk dey git whip 'til dey hab blister on 'em. Den iffen dey didn' do it a man on a hoss went down d' rows 'n' whip wid a paddle mek wid holes in it 'n' bus' d' blisters. I neber git whip cause I alays git my t'ree hunnerd poun'. Us hab t' go in d' fiel' so early, dey blow d' ho'n [horn] so early sometime dey don' hab time to' cook fo' [before] daylight. Us hafter tek us wittles [victuals] t' d' fiel' in a bucket iffen we didn' hab time t' cook 'em."

Lizzie Atkins, Texas

"Maser did'nt have but about 25 acres in his farm. Only had one more slave sides mother, father and me. Old negro that he inherited from his wife's father he woke us up every morning about 5 o'clock except when he would get in a real tight, then he would wake us up early so'es we could tend the stock. And yes he worked us until slam dark, he would whip us if we got smart, sassy or did'nt work, cause he would hardly ever be there himself. We would have to do what his son Maser John told us, if we played off on him we sure got a good whipping when he came home. Yes he has whipped me several times and sent me to bed without anything to eat."

George Austin, Texas

"Tudder thing I well 'members am de six hoss powah cotton gin. De six hoss team walks 'round an' 'round an' a beam am 'tached to dem. Dis beam goes into de middle an' am fixed to a big wheel dat have a 20 foot gin pole dat goes straight up. At de top am a 'rangement wid cogs and so on dat compresses de cotton an' makes bales out of it. De reason I 'members it so powe'ful am dat Ise catches three finger in de cogs on de second story of de buildin'. W'en de fingers am stuck Ise lets out a yell dat stops de team dead still. Den de mens have to back de 'chine up so's dey can git me out an' let me go. Dat's one time I don't git no beatin' an' don't need one. Ise gits lots of beatin's f'om mammy but none f'om de Marster. Reason fo' dat am dat de Marster am powe'ful hard to rile. Him jus' sells off de trubblesome niggers. Fo' to git some 'venge on a nigger him sells de nigger to de mens dat him knows wont spare de leather."

Smith Austin, Texas

"I don't just remember when I was born but my white folks' books say it was in 1847 on the Austin plantation in Tennessee. The place was called Ripley, and it was the county seat in Lorderdale County. Mr. Jim Austin owned us and John Fields was the overseer. Shore was a hard man. All the negroes had to work awful hard. Us went to work in the field when it was too dark to see whar we was gwine. Boss John blowed a horn an' us jus' broke for de field at de toot of dat horn, jerkin' on clothes as us stumbled along. Hardly light nuff to see noddin'. If Boss John got to de field head of us us shore caught a hard whippin'. Dey brought breakfus to us in de field and dinner. Had bread an' sirup an' bacon fer breakfus and diff'rn things for dinner. Corn bread not wheat bread."

Celestia Avery, Georgia

One woman was required to do the work around the house there was also one slave man required to work around the house doing odd jobs. Other than these two every one else was required to do the heavy work in the fields. Work began at "sun up" and lasted until "sun down." In the middle of the day the big bell was rung to summon the workers from the field, for their mid-day lunch. After work hours slaves were then free to dow work around their own cabins, such as sewing, cooking (etc.).

Susan Backstrom, Mississippi

Susan, was first sold at Baltimore, Md. before 1860 to a speculator, who brought her in a drove of other slaves to Mobile, Ala. and resold them to Mr. John Garner, who lived at Mobile, but owned a plantation at Enterprise, Miss. These plantations were run by an overseer. There were two, a man and a woman, the man looked after the plow hands and the woman looked after the hoe hands. Besides having an overseer they had a colored man "slave driver" who did the whipping and flogging when a negro became unruly, all the negroes had to mind. They were given an allowance and when their supply was gone they had to do without, they got hungry sometimes.

Georgia Baker, Georgia

"Ma was cook up at de big house and she died when I was jus' a little gal. Pa was a field hand, and he belonged to Marse Britt Tilly."

"Dere was four of us chillun: me, and Mary, and Frances, and Mack," she counted on the fingers of one hand. "Marse Alec let Marse Jim Johnson have Mack for his bodyguard. Frances, she wuked in de field, and Mary was de baby—she was too little to wuk. Me, I was 14 years old when de war was over. I swept yards, toted water to de field, and played 'round de house and yard wid de rest of de chillun."

"Marse Lordnorth never had no certain early time for his slaves to git up nor no special late time for 'em to quit wuk. De hours dey wuked wes 'cordin' to how much wuk was ahead to be done. Folks in Crawfordville called us 'Stephens' Free Niggers.'"

Henry Baker, Texas

"De slaves wokked from de time dey could see till dey couldn't see. De overse'er rang a bell 'bout four o'clock in de mornin' an' de slaves would git up an' eat an' go to de fiel'. Once in a while whin dey waz up on der wokke dey would git Sat'day 'fternoon off."

Tom Baker, Alabama

"I was a water boy for fifty fiel' han's dat worked in de sun all day long, an' I hadda carry many a bucket from de spring. It was along the one fiel' ober from where most of dem was workin'. De spring run down between some willow trees an' it was powerful cool down dere in de shade. I use' to lie on de moss an' let my bare belly git cool an' put my face in de outlet of de spring an' let de water trickle over my haid. Jus' about de time I gits a little rest one of dem niggers would call: 'Water Boy! Bring dat bucket!' Den I grab up de bucket an' run back out in de hot sun."

Mrs. John Barclay, Texas

"There was 1800 acres in Marster Slade's plantation, we got up at 5:00 o'clock in de mornin' and de field workers would quit after sun-down. We didn' have no jails for slaves. We went to church with de white folks and there was a place in de back of de church for us to sit."

John Barker, Texas

"Plantations! I should say! Cotton and co'n. I have seen de time de rows would be fudder dan Mrs. Bitters' house, yonder (about 250 yards). Dey kep' 'em workin' all de time. I guess dey was about fo'ty or fifty acres in dem plantations. Dey worked, worked, an' wasn't allowed to go to church dem days;

John Barker. (Library of Congress)

not allowed to have no exercise a-tall. Dances nothin'! What did we know about dances in dem times? Dey had no time to go out an' make no money wid nobody. Dey had to be right at dat place where dey had 'em. Some of de people whar I tote water down in de field fo' 'em, dey would give me a nickel, or piece o' money 'bout as big as a dime piece. I would buy candy and stuff like dat till it give out."

Amelia Barnett, Texas

"Durin' de cotton pickin' time a big bell was rung to git us up about four o'clock in de mawnin'. We had to go to de field and pick when it was still dark. Dere was times durin' scrap-pickin' when it was so cold dat we had to make a big fire in de field and wahm our hands."

Darcus Barnett, Texas

"My grandpappy calls dem all out fore sunrise every morning and quit 'bout half-hour by sun every evenin'."

"All of us peoples workin' for Jedge Younger just does up de work after we come in from de fields. He had lots of stock ter feed, but it didn't take long—der was seberal ter do it. Everybody knows it had ter be done and he done it. Dey never did work on Satidy evening and Satidy night, dey just sets 'round and talks. We allus had a big time on Christmas, New Year's and de Foath of July, but we didn't have any other holidays."

Alice Battle, Georgia

Alice's father worked in the fields. There was no regular working hours, for he worked from "sun up to sun down." Her mother was the cook for the "big house." The mistress had a number of servants helping with the house work, the washing and ironing, the weaving and sewing. Alice's oldest sister was one of the maids. There were about fifty slaves on the plantation, and those who did not help at the house did field work. The first work that Alice remembers was "nursin' the chillun" though it was a pleasure for her as she enjoyed pulling the little wagon around and playing the games that they did.

Alice's mother wove the cloth for the clothes, which her mistress superintended the making of. Some of the other slave women did the sewing. Dresses were made very full, buttoned down the front, and with belts sewed in at the waist line.

Harrison Beckett, Texas

"It come to pass dat my mudder work in de field. Sometimes she come in nine or ten 'clock at night outer de field. She be all wore out an' it be so dark she too tired to cook lots of times, but she hafter git some food so we could eat it. Every one had a tin pan. We all git 'round de table and she put it in de pans an' we eat. Us all 'round de table like dat was like a feast. Lots of times though she so tired she go right to bed soon's she git through cooking 'thout eatin' nuthin' herself, an' she go right to sleep."

"De young marster usually comes out early in de mornin bout foah clock and hollers and dat means fer us ter git up, we would gits up and while de women foks was gitten breakfast, de men foks would do de milkin and feeding and den eats breakfast, and be in de field fore sun up and works til sun down. Dis man was a good man ter work, I never did hears him threatin ter whip one of us."

"After we worked all day in de fiels we had ter comes in and do up all de chores such as cuttin wood, toten it in, carry water, milk from eight ter twelve head of cows, feed bout fifty hogs, feeds de mules and hosses, chickens, separate de calves and cows, maybe doctor some stock fer screw worms and jest anything that happens ter need ter be done, and de same thing fore we goes ter work in the morning. We worked every day in de fiels if it warnt rainin and if we was in de grass, but if we wasnt in de grass, we was alowed ter knock off Satdy evenin and fore Uncle Ben got his Bible took way from him we would go ter preachin on Satdy nights if there was any, but after dat, we jest sets round and talks and de same things on Sundays."

"When cotton pickin comes in de fall of the year, de chilluns and grown folks both picks cotton in big baskets and marster Harry Hogan hauled it over ter Mr. Logan Stroud ter gets it ginned as he didn't have no gin."

John C. Bectom, North Carolina

"My father and mother told me stories of how they were treated at different places. When my grandmother was with the Murpheys they would make her get up, and begin burning logs in new grounds before daybreak. They also made her plow, the same as any of the men on the plantation. They plowed till dusk-dark before they left the fields to come to the house."

Virginia Bell, Texas

"Massa Lewis had four or five families of us slaves, but we used to have some fun after work and us young folks would skip rope and play ring games. Durin' week days the field hands would work till the sun was jus' goin' down and then the overseer would holler 'all right' and that was the signal to quit. All hands knocked off Sat'day noon."

"When the War done come 'long it sho' changed things, and we heerd this and that, but we didn' know much what it was about. Then one day Massa Lewis had all the wagons loaded with food and chairs and beds and other things from the house and our quarters, and I heerd him say we was movin' to Polk County, way over in Texas. I know it took us a long time to git there, and when we did I never see so much woods. It sho' was diff'rent from the plantation."

"I had to work in the fields, same as the res', and we stayed there three years and made three crops of cotton, but not so much as on our old place, 'cause there wasn't so much clearin'.'"

Cyrus Bellus, Arkansas

"My father and mother were both field hands. They didn't weave or spin. My grandmother on my mother's side did that. They were supposed to pick—the man, four hundred pounds of cotton, and the woman three hundred. And that was gittin' some cotton. If they didn't come up to the task, they was took out and give a whipping."

Sarah Benjamin, Texas

"I dunno how many acres and how many slaves on dis plantation, dey was all waked up fore daylight and to breakfast, dey works from day light til dark, sometimes specially in cotton pickin dem chillens wouldnt se dem parents til sadty, dey go ter fields so early and gits in so late de chillens warnt awake ter see dem."

"When de slaves would come in from de fields dey would eat and go to bed onless it was moon shine nights if it was dey would work in their tobacco patch, de marster would give each man a terbaccer patch if he made more den he could use he could sell de rest and de money was his'n. I specks my daddy had mo money and had mo ter eat during slavery dan since."

"De corn shuckin started when it started rainin and de harder it rained de harder and longer dem niggahs shucked co'n. Dey all picked cotton in big baskets, and dey could pick some cotton too, dem niggahs would begin singin and pickin cotton. And de women had ter run de gin in de day time, and men at night. Dey fed de gin from baskets, my mammy fed de gin from baskets all day wid a high fever and died dat night. She wouldnt tell de marster for she knew he would make her take medicin and she sho didnt like ter take dat quinine. Der wasnt no marryin or deaths either in marsters family. His wife died fore I can remember and he never married any more. And my mothers death is de only one mong de slaves."

"De women had to run de gin in de daytime and de man at night. Dey fed de old gin from baskets and my mammy fed from dose baskets all day with de high fever and died dat night. She wouldn't tell de marster she sick, for fear she have to take de quinine."

Hariette Benton, Alabama

"I wuz neber large 'nuff during dem days to work. But my maw, why she an' de res' o' dem po' slaves on dat plantation she did work. Mos' o' de women plowed in de cotton field or dey picked cotton. Jes' a few worked in de big house. De chillun whut wuz ol' enough fanned flies off de table and dey helped carry de food in de big house from de kitchen. You know dat de kitchen wuz way out from de big house, don't you? In rainy weather? Why dey done jes' lak dey always done. Dey had a kind o' cover to put over de trays an' dey jes' come on in de house. Cose, de slaves, dey always got drenched to de bone."

Nathan Best, Mississippi

"We raised corn, cotton, peas an' everyting—my ole marster run 16 plows every day, he had 25 or 30 head of horses an' mules. He had a 'ticlar saddle horse an' a 'ticlar buggy horse, dey didn' do nothin' but ca'hy him aroun'.'"

"My mother worked on de farm, an' my father stayed in de woods an' run turpentine. My marster run a big farm, an' worked turpentine, too."

"Dey put me at service when I was eight years ole. Dey put me to foller'n de stock. Dey run out in de big woods, an' dey had to foller dem to keep 'em from breakin' into folkses fiel's."

Ellen Betts, Texas

"Marse sho' good to dem gals and bucks what cuttin' de cane. When dey git done makin' sugar, he give a drink call 'Peach 'n Honey' to de women folk and whiskey and brandy to de men. And of all de dancin' and caperin' you ever seen! My pa was fiddler and we'd cut de pigeon wing and cut de buck and every other kind of dance. Sometime pa git tired and say he ain't gwineter play no more and us gals git busy and pop him corn and make candy, so to 'tice him to play more."

"Marse sho' turn over in he grave did he know 'bout some dat 'lassas. Dem black boys don't care. I seen 'em pull rats out de sugar barrel and dey taste de sugar and say 'Ain't nothin' wrong with dat sugar. It still sweet.' One day a pert one pull a dead scorpion out de syrap kettle and he jes' leugh and say, 'Marse don't want waste none dis syrup,' and he lick de syrup right off dat scorpion's body and legs."

"Lawsy me, I seen thousands and thousands sugar barrels and kettles or syrup in my day. Lawd knows how much cane old Harse have. To dem cuttin' de cane it don't seen so much, but to dem what work hour in, hour out, dem sugar cane fields sho' stretch from one end de earth to de other. Marse ship hogs and hogs of sugar down de bayou. I seen de river boats go down with big signs what say, 'Buy dis here 'lasses' on de side.' And he raise a world or rice and 'taters and corn and peanuts, too."

Arrie Binns, Georgia

Her master died of "the consumption" during the war. She recalls how hard it was after his death. The Syberts had no children and there was none to turn to after his death. Arrie tells of her Master's illness, how she was the housemaid and was called upon to fan him and how she would get so tired and sleepy she would nod a little, the fan dropping from hands into his face. He would take it up and "crack my haid with the handle to wake me up. I wuz allus so sorry when I done that, but I jest had ter nod."

After her master's death Arrie had to go into the field to work. She recalled with a little chuckle, the old cream horse, "Toby" she use to plow. She loved Toby, she said, and they did good work. When not plowing she said she "picked er round in the fields" doing whatever she could. She and the other slaves were not required to do very hard work. Her mother was a field hand, but in the evenings she spun and wove down in their cabin. Aunt Arrie added "an' I did love to hear that old spinnin' wheel. It made a low kind of a whir-ring sound that made me sleepy." She said her mother, with all the other negro women on the place, had "a task of spinnin' a spool at night," and they spun and wove on rainy days too. "Ma made our clothes an' we had pretty dresses too. She dyed some blue and brown striped. We growed she indigo she used fer the blue, right dar on the plantation, and she used bark and leaves to make the tan and brown colors."

Henry Bland, Georgia

He worked with a large number of other slaves (he does not know the exact number) who were divided into two groups, the plow group and the hoe group. His father lappened to be the foreman of the hoe gang. His brothers and sisters also worked here in the fields being required to hoe as well as plow, when picking time came, everyone was required to pick. The usual amount of cotton each person was required to pick was 200 lbs. per day. However, when this amount was not picked by some they were not punished by the overseer, as was the case on neighboring plantations, because Mr. Cox-ton realized that some could do more work than others. Mr. Coxton often told his overser that he had not been hired to whip the slaves, but to teach them how to work.

Rias Body, Alabama

"Spring plowin' an' hoein' times we wukked all day Saddays, but nos'em genully we laid offa wuk at twelve o'clock Sadday. That was dinner time. Sadday nights we played an' danced; sometimes in the cabins an' some-times in the yahds. Effen we diden' have a big stack er fat kin'lin wood lit up to dance by, sometimes the mens an' 'omans would carry torches o' kin'lin' wood whilst they danced, an' it sho' was a sight to see. We danced the 'Turkey Trot,' an' 'Buzzard Lope,' an' how we did love to dance the 'Mary Jane'! We would git in a ring an' when the music started we would begin wukkin' our footses, while we sung, 'You steal mah True Love, an' Ah Steal You'en.'"

"We never did no wuk on Sundays on our plantation."

Manda Boggan, Mississippi

"When I wuz put in de fields, hit wuz wuk from early till late. De fields would be full o' slaves a wukin' hard. Us would look up an see Mars acomin' across de field wid his bible under his arm. He would walk along whar us wuz a wukin' an' read a text, den us would sing an' pray. De song us laked bes' wuz, 'De Day ob Jubilee es come.'" (Here she sings the song.)

James Bolton, Georgia

"The overseer woke us up at sunrise—leas'n they called sunrise! We would finish our vittles and be in the fields ready for wuk befo' we seed any sun! We laid off wuk at sunset and they didn't drive us hard. Leas'wise, they didn' on our plantation. I done heard they was moughty hard on 'em on other plantations. My marster never did 'low his niggers to wuk atter sundown. My employer, I means my marster. didn't have no bell. He had 'em blow bugles to wake up his hands and to call 'em from the fields. Sometimes the overseer blowed it. Mistess done larned the cook to count the clock, but none of the rest of our niggers could count the clock."

Scott Bond, Arkansas

Poultry wire was unknown, the poultry yards were fenced with rails to keep the hogs from devouring the young fowls. Imagine if you can, a rail fence built tight enough to keep the hogs out and little goslings, turkeys and chickens in. It was one of little Scott's principal duties to march around the poultry yard and look after the young fowls. In cold weather the frost would bite his bare feet. In rainy weather he acted as a brooder. Boys in those days wore single garments, a long sack-like slip with holes cut for head and arms. When it rains, goslings will stand with their heads up and drown in a short time if left to themselves. Little Scott would gather little goslings under his slip as the hen hovers her brood and thus protect them from the falling rain. It must have been a ticklish task to have a half hundred little geese under one's single garment scrounging and crowding for warmth.

He regaled me with many other stories of slave life that he had witnessed.

He told me that many a time he would be so tired from his day's work that he would not wake up in the morning until the horn blew for work. He would not have time to cook himself any bread, and that he would run to the meal bowl and put a handful or two of meal in his hat and run with his bridle and catch his mule and while the mule was drinking, he would take water and mix the meal. Then when he got to the field he would go to a burning log-heap, when the overseer was not looking, and rake a place in the ashes and hot embers, put his cake in and cover it. Later, when chance permitted, he would take out his ash cake and eat it as he plowed. Thus he would work until dinner time.

After telling me many other stories of the hardships of the slave, he said that after all, the things that looked hardest to him, were really blessings in disguise. These hardships had developed his self-reliance and resourcefulness, and now that he was a free man and a citizen, he could see a benefit, even in the hardships he had undergone. He said that he knew he was a Christian and that he was respected by all his neighbors, black and white.

Andrew Boone, North Carolina

"We wurked from sun to sun. If we had a fire in cold weather where we wus wurkin' marster or de overseer would come an' put it out. We et frozen meat an' bread many times in cold weather. After de day's wurk in de fields wus over we had a task of pickin' de seed from cotton till we had two ounces of lint or spin two ounces of cotton on a spinnin' wheel. I spun cotton on a spinnin' wheel. Dats de way people got clothes in slavery time."

Alec Bostwick, Georgia

"'Gran'pa Berry wuz too old to wuk in de field so he stayed 'roun' de house an' piddled. He cut up wood, tended to de gyarden an' yard, an' bottomed chairs. Gran'ma Liza done de cookin' an' nussed de white folkses chilluns."

"I wukked in de field 'long side de rest of de Niggers, totin' water an' sich lak, wid de overseer dar all de time wid dat gun."

"'Bout dat overseer he wuz a mean man, if one ever lived. He got de slaves up wid a gun at five o'clock an' wukked 'em 'till way atter sundown, standin' right over 'em wid a gun all de time. If a Nigger lagged or tuk his eyes off his wuk, right den an' dar he would make him strip down his clo'es to his waist, an' he whup him wid a cat-o-nine tails. Evvy lick dey struck him meant he wuz hit nine times, an' it fotch de red evvy time it struck."

"I done tole you 'bout dat overseer; all he done wuz sot 'roun' all day wid a gun an' make de Niggers wuk. But I'se gwine tell you de trufe, he sho' wuz poor white trash wid a house full of snotty-nose chilluns. Old Marster tole him he wuz jus' lak a rabbit, he had so many chillun. I means dis; if dem days comes back I hope de good Lord takes me fus'."

Charley Bowen, Texas

"My owner had a big farm and owned 'bout 200 darkies when freedom come. He lived in a big house up on a hill, and the 'quarters' sot down in the field. The old boss come down and holler 'bout day light for the hands to get going. The children warn't bothered. He kept wood piled up in the winter for to keep a fire for the children. He had no overseer, the boys done the bossing. He had a Nigger foreman of the plow hands and a Nigger foreman of the hoe hands. My father run wagons for him and went to Shreveport and Jefferson with cotton and fetched back loads of rations."

"Sometimes Master give us Saturday off. If we hoe so much during the week, he give us Saturday. At night when the hands come in from the field, they just set round the 'quarters.' Old Master didn't work them, he warn't in that class. We warn't beat and driv' in the rain like most of them. If we didn't obey, we looked for a whipping."

Jennie Bowen, Alabama

"I acted as nuss for massa's three chilluns, an' dey learnt me to read an' write. My pappy was named Burl Fisher an' he come f'um Virginny when Cap'n Fisher brung him. My mammy was named Grace Fisher, in'; she was 'roun' de big house mos' of de time a weavin' an' a cardin' wool for de slaves, who wo' calico spun in de summer an' wool in de winter."

"An ole nigger man rung a bell for us to git up by, an' to call de fiel' han's in de evenin's."

James Boyd, Texas

"I split rails, drove oxen wagons an' odder jobs 'bout de place. I nebber did pick much cotton an' I nebber earnet much money, efen I did, an' was cotched wid eny money it was tooken 'way from me an' sometimes de boss gibe me a whuppen 'case he thought I had more money dan I really had."

James Boyd. (Library of Congress)

"In slavery, on our place, we worked all day Saturday an sometimes on Sunday ef de crops was in a rush. De slave women sewed, washed an ironed fer demselves an dere families on Sundays an at night by a brush fire. On Christmas we allus had a big dinner, both black and white."

"Marster wasn't much on presents an money, but we did have warm clothes an plenty to eat an a dry place to live an dat's more dan lots of de niggers have now."

Jerry Boykins, Texas

" A big ole brass bell rang every mornin' at four o'clock on the plantashun an' when that bell begin its racket, every darky roll out his bed, don't you forget!—and sometimes when we had been makin' a high time 'til late—it seem lak we no more'n git to sleep 'til we mus' git up agin."

Rivana Boynton, Florida

"I had to thin cotton in de fields and mind the flies at the table. I chased then with a fly bush, sometimes a limb from a tree and sometimes wid a fancy bush."

Callie Bracey, Indiana

Mrs. Callie Bracey's mother, Louise Terrell, was bought, when a child, by Andy Ramblet, a farmer, near Jackson, Miss. She had to work very hard in the fields from early morning until as late in the evening, as they could possibly see.

No matter how hard she had worked all day after coming in from the field, she would have to cook for the next day, packing the lunch buckets for the field hands. It made no difference how tired she was, when the horn was blown at 4 a.m., she had to go into the field for another day of hard work.

Monroe Brackins, Texas

"I remember that they tasked the cotton pickers there [in Mississippi]. They had to bring in so many pounds in the evening and if they didn't they got a whipping for it. They told me that I had a sister there, that she had to bring in 900 pounds a day. Well, the cotton was heavier there. She could pick 900 pounds right along. Most any of 'em could do 500 pounds. It was heavier and fluffier. My mother was a good cotton picker. I don't remember how much she picked, but I think they used her principally for work around the house [boss man's]. We left a cotton county, in Mississippi, but nobody knew anything about cotton out here that I know of."

Martha Bradley, Alabama

"Our Marster wuz sho good to all his 'niggers.'" she said. "Us allus had plenty to eat and plenty to wear, but de days now is hard, if white folks gin you a nickel or dime to git you sumpin' t' eat you has to write everything down in a book before you can git it. I allus worked in the field, had to carry big logs, had strops on my arms and them logs was put in de strop and hauled to a pile where they all wuz. One morning hit was rainin' and I didn' wanna go to the field, but de oversee' he come and got me and started whooping me. I jumped on him and bit and kicked him 'til he lemme go. I didn't know no better then. I didn't know he was de one to do dat."

"One day I wuz workin' in de field and de overseer he come 'roun and say sumpin' to me he had no bisness say. I took my hoe and knocked him plum down. I knowed I'se done sumpin' bad so I run to de bushes. Marster Lucas come and got me and started whoopin' me. I say to Marster Lucas whut dat overseer ses to me and Marster Lucas didn' hit me no more. Marse Lucas wuz allus good to us and he wouldn' let nobody run over his niggers."

"In cotton pickin' time us'd stay in de field till way atter dark and us'd pick by candle light and den carry hit and put hit on de scaffold. In de winter time us'd quilt; jes' go from one house to anudder in de quarter. Us'd weave all our ever' day clothes but Marster Lucas'd go to Mobile ever' July and Christmas and git our Sunday clothes, git us dresses aad shoes and we'd sho be proud of 'em."

Martha Bradley. (Library of Congress)

Gus Bradshaw, Texas

"The first work I done was picking cotton. Every fellow was in the fiel' at day light picking cotton, hoeing, or plowing. There was one overseer and two 'Nigger-Drivers.' The overseer whipped them in the fiel' for not doing like he say. I had a Uncle Joe to run off just when the war got gwying [going] good; he never did come back."

Wes Brady, Texas

"Some white folks might want to put me beck in slavery if I tells how we was used in slavery time, but you asks me for the truth. The overseer was straddle his big horse at three o'clock in the morning, rousting the hands off to the fiel'. He got them all lined up and then come back to the house for breakfast. The rows was a mile long and no matter how much grass was in them, if you left one sprig on your row they beat you nearly to death. The hands had to work till after dark. Lots of time they weighed cotton by candle light. They had to be to the house, have supper et and be in bed by ten o'clock. If you move' round at night you was trying to steal something and had to be whipped. All the fiel' hands took dinner with them to the fiel' in buckets. The overseer giv' them fifteen minutes to eat dinner. He didn't tell us when the time to go back to work, but when he started cuffing some of them over the head we knowed it was time to go to work. Every Nigger's bucket was marked. When they was back at work the overseer looked in every bucket to see if a piece of bread or anything was left. Then he go to the house and eat his dinner. When he come back to the fiel' he looked in all the buckets again. If a piece of bread of anything was in the bucket when he left was gone when he come back, he say that meant you was losing time when he warn't there and had to be whipped. I'se seed them drive four stakes in the ground and tie Niggers down and beat them till they was raw."

"The first work I done in slavery was drapping [dropping] co'n. Then I was cow-pen boy and sheep herder. All us house chaps had to shell a half bushel of co'n every night for to feed the sheep. I had a cousin that was as mean as any woman you ever saw. One day she made me churn till I nearly give out. I hear Master say that he needed another hoer in the fiel'. I slipped off from my cousin and got me a broom handle and piece of tin and made me a hoe and went to the fiel'. Master come to the fiel' and say, 'Boy, what you doing here?' I told him and after that he let me work in the fiel till surrender. Many times I has walked through the quarters when I was a little chap crying for my mother."

Clara Brim, Texas

"De ol' master he warn't marry and he eat de same t'ings de slaves eat. He treat' his slaves good. He didn' wuk 'em in de heat of de day. 'Bout 'leben o'clock when de sun git hot he call 'em out of de fiel'. He tell 'em to come out dat hot sun. He give 'em 'til it 'gin to git kinder cool befo' he mek 'em go back in de fiel'. He had li'l boys to bring water to de han's when dey was wukkin' in de fiel'."

"Dey had a woman to do weavin'. Some of de clo's was homemek. Some of de clo'f dey buy from de sto'."

"When de slaves hafter go wuk in de fiel' he give 'em a task. Dat so much wuk, so many rows of cotton to chop or co'n to hoe, and he tell 'em when dey git froo wid dat dey kin do what dey wanter. He do dat on Monday. Some of 'em wuk steady and maybe git froo Thursday night. Den dey kin hire deyself out to somebody else and git pay for what wuk dey do, and mek some money dat way."

Della Briscoe, Georgia

In addition to marketing, Della's father trapped beavers which were plentiful in the swampy part of the plantation bordering the Oconee, selling their pelts to traders in the nearby towns of Augusta and Savannah, where Mr. Ross also marketed his cotton and large quantities of corn. Oxen, instead of mules, were used to make the trips to market and return, each trip consuming six or seven days.

The young children were assigned small tasks, such as piling brush in "new grounds," carrying water to field hands, and driving the calves to pasture.

Ned Broadus, Texas

"We came to Texas by way of Mobile an' New Orleans, 'crost de Mississipp on a flat boat above whar de steam boats loaded. Some places whar we stopt to wuk on our way to Texas, dey wanted to be awful bossy an' mean to us, but Marse Williamson tol' 'em 'No, don't do dat way, dese niggers wuk hard an' behave, yo' let 'em 'lone else I do some dat whippin'.' When we got to de place we goin' in Texas, Marse put us to wuk clearin' land an' fellin' logs fer de houses—big ones for ole Marse an' cabins fer de slaves an' barns fer de stock. We had purty good close an' plenty food. 'Cose, durin' de war, we got less ob some kins 'case dey had to sen' it to de soldiers."

Matilda Brooks, Florida

In seasons other than picking-time for the cotton the children were usually allowed to play in the evenings. When cotton crops were large, however, they spent their evenings picking out seeds from the cotton bolls, in order that their parents might work uninterruptedly in the fields during the day. The cotton, after being picked and separated, would be weighed in balances and packed tightly in "crocus" bags.

Josie Brown, Texas

"My daddy wuk in d' fiel'. He help sow d' rice on d' fiel' 'n' plow it under. W'en dey harves' d' rice dey beat it wid a pestle. Dey raise dey own t'baccy. Dey hab fiel's 'r' it. Dey cut it in piece' 'n' put it in d' crack 'r' d' fence t' press. Den dey dry it on d' barn roof. Dat was smokin' t'baccy. Fo' d' chewin' t'baccy dey soak it in sugar 'r' honey. Us neber see no snuff 'til later. Dey crop t'baccy jus' like green'. Dey raise garden veg'tibbles fo' d' big house. D' marster 'low d' ol'er niggers t' hab a patch 'r' dey own but dey hab t' wuk it at night."

Lizzie Fant Brown, Mississippi

"Ever place had a gin house then. Ours was run with levers and two mules. A child could run it by touching the mules with a long switch onc't in awhile."

"Then we would all jump in the lint room and pack the cotton down tight. Then it was packed in hamper baskets and we toted it to the press."

"The press was made of wood and you could hear the lever just cry. Somebody was always there to sew the cloth at the ends of the cotton bales. They could press four or five bales in a day."

Manus Brown, Mississippi

"My pa an' ma wuz brung from way off some-where. I done can't say if it wuz from North Carolina or Virginia. Dey wuz sole an' traded 'bout lak stock an' at las' landed in de hands o' Marse John Brown. I cant say which one ob 'em he got first. Marse John jes had a small plantation. My pa an' ma an' all us chilluns wuz all de slaves he owned. My pa an' de biggest gals an' boys done all de fiel' wuk, de wuk round de lot, tending to de stock an' a gitting de wood, killing hogs, fixing de fences an' de lak wuz made lak dat too."

Sally Brown, Georgia

"I worked hard always. Honey, you can't 'magine what a hard time I had. I split rails lak a man. How did I do it? I used a huge glut made out'a wood, and a iron wedge drove into the wood with a maul, and this would split the wood."

"I help't spin the cotton into thread fur our clothes. The thread wuz wound on big branches—four branches made four cuts, or one hank. After the thread wuz spun we used a loom to weave the cloth. We had no sewin' machines—had to sew by hand. My mistress had a big silver bird and she would always ketch the cloth in the bird's bill and this would hold it fur her to sew."

George W. Browning, Georgia

Mr. Browning's eyes filled with tears as recollections of his mother came to him. He cried softly for a few minutes and then dried his eyes remarking,

"Whenever I think of my mother plowing in the field I have to cry." He continued with the fact that his father's occupation was that of a fox hunter.

The members of his family are unusually skilled, and fared much better in the time of work than the other slaves on the plantation. There was very little cotton raised, consequently, the work in the winter was much lighter than in the summer. With the spring came the plowing, planting, hoeing and tending of crops. Many vegetables were raised including corn, wheat, etc. Bread for the whole plantation was supplied from the corn and wheat.

Queen Eizabeth Bunts, Georgia

"My father was a field hand and worked from sun up to sun down. My mother was considered a very fine seamstress and sewed for the Norris family. When she wasn't busy sewing she worked as house-woman for Mrs. Norris. My brothers and sisters did field work."

James Burleson, Texas

"De slave wimmen in de slave quarters would go out to de cowpen early in de mawnin', and late at night, and milk all of de cows. Even mammy had to go out at times and help milk dem long-horn cows. A lot of dem cows would jes' run wild in de bushes. We used some of dem big steers fo' plowin' in de fields. I don't think dat no steer ever run away. Den I drove many a yoke of 'em wid a wagon, later in life. Even after slavery, when I was married, I used steers fo' my field work. Sometimes my bosses did have mules dat I could work wid."

Midge Burnett, North Carolina

"I wurked on de farm durin' slavery times, among de cotton, corn, an' sugar cane. De wurk wusn't so hard an' we had plenty of time ter have fun an' ter git inter meanness, dat's why Marse William had ter have so many patterollers on de place."

Wesley Burrell, Texas

"I don' know how many acres in de plantation. We had an overseer so mean de nigger a runned off in de woods; at four o'clock we was waked up. All day we wuked. We was slaves 'cause dey white men stole our parints an' 'cause dey was ignorent. We was punished since we was bringed to America. We have been mixed breeded an' we dosen't seem as African."

Vinnie Busby, Mississippi

"De slaves went to wuk fo' day an' wuked 'till night. Acres an' acres ob land wuz to be plowed an hoed—an in de fall ob de year de fiel's wuz white wid cotton."

Ellen Butler, Texas

"The plantation were a good, big place and they have 'bout 200 head of niggers. When I gets big enough they start me to totin' water to the field. I gits the water out the spring and totes it in gourds. They cut the gourds so that a strip was left round and cross the top and that the handle. They was about a foot 'cross and a foot deep. Us used to have one good gourd us kep' lard in and li'l gourds to drink out of."

Gabe Butler, Mississippi

"I got to be a big boy den dey put me to 'tendin' de sheep; ebery mornin' me an' sum more boys had to drive dem sheep to de pasture an' den go atter dem ebery evenin'; I think dar wus 'bout two hundred uf 'm; when dey wud sheer de sheep, I wud stand 'round an' watch 'em. When we wud take de sheep out we wud sum times see wild turkeys an' deer, but I niver see any uf dem now. Sumtimes dey would go huntin' an' kill de turkey and deer; dat wus good eatin'."

Isaiah Butler, North Carolina

"In slavery time de slaves wuz waked up every morning by de colored over-driver blowin' a horn. Ole man Jake Chisolm wuz his name. Jes' at daybreak, he'd put his horn through a crack in de upper part of de wall to his house an' blow it through dat crack. Den de under-driver would go out an' round 'em up. When dey done all dey day-work, dey come home an' cook dey supper, an' wash up. Den dey blow de horn for 'em to go to bed. Sometime dey have to out de fire an' finish dey supper in de dark. De under-driver, he'd go out den and see who ain't go to bed. He wouldn't say anyt'ing den; but next mornin' he'd report it to de overseer, an' dem as hadn't gone to bed would be whipped. My mother used to tell me dat if any didn't do dey day's work, dey'd be put in de stocks or de bill-bo. You know each wuz given a certain task dat had to be finish dat day. Dat what dey call de day-work. When dey put 'em in de stocks dey tie 'em hand and foot to a stick. Dey could lie down wid dat. I hear of colored folks doin' dat now to dere chillun when dey don't do. Now de bill-bo wuz a stabe [stave)]drove in de ground, an' dey tied dere hands and den dere feet to dat, standin' up."

Marshal Butler, Georgia

"My mammy was maid in de Collar's home and she had many fine dresses— some of them were give to her by her missus. Pappy war a field nigger for ole Ben Butler and I worked in the field when I wuz knee high to a grasshopper. We uns et our breakfast while et war dark and we trooped to the fields at sun-up, carrying our lunch wid us. Nothing fancy but jes' good rib-sticking victuals. We come in from the fields at sun-down and care were a good meal awaiting us in de slave quarters."

"All the niggers worked hard—de cotton pickers had to pick 200 pounds of cotton a day and if a nigger didn't, Marse Frank would take de nigger to the barn and beat him with a switch. He would tell de nigger to hollow loud as he could and de nigger would do so. Then the old Mistress would come in and say! 'What are you doing Frank?' 'Beating a nigger' would be his answer. 'You let him alone, he is my nigger' and both Marse Frank and de whipped nigger would come out of the barn. We all loved Marse and the Mistress. No, we wuz never whipped for stealing—we never stole anything in dose days—much."

Dave Byrd, Texas

"We did farm work of all kinds such, as chop cotton, corn, and plowed. I'se cut lots of rails, cause that was all the kinds of fence we had them days."

"Yes, I drove lots for Maser. He would give me money and I would spend it for candy and tobacco, but if Maser had caught me with tobacco he would have tore me up good and plenty."

"There was about 1000 acres which Maser owned. He worked 60 acres and had 30 slaves. He woke us up every morning about 4:30 on days that we had to work, that was every day 'cept Sunday and Saturday evening. We would always be in the field by the time it was light enough to work and stayed until dark run us in. He always give us one hour in the middle of the day for feed time."

Sarah Byrd, Georgia

The size of the plantation required that the slaves be elassified according to the kind of work each was supposed to do. There ware the "cotton pickers," the "plow hands," the "hoe hands," the "rail splitters," etc "My very fust job," remarked Mrs. Byrd," was that was cotton picking." Mrs Byrd's mother was a full hand.

William Byrd, Texas

"The work I did I split rails, chop cotton, plowed with wooden plow, then I'se drove my master lots because he was trader, dealt in slave trade most of the time. Yessir, he gave me nickel and dime several times and I would buy tobacco and candy when I could git it."

"Master Sam sometimes had hole bunch of slaves, then other times he never had but his regular number, six grown and eleven little slaves. Master, he had great iron piece hanging just out side his door and he hit that every morning at 3:30. The negroes they come tumbling out of there beds. If they didnt master he come round in about thirty minutes with that cat-o-nine tails and begins to let negro have that and when he got through they knew what that bell was the next morning."

Louis Cain, Texas

"We did such work as plow, hoe and split rails. Then Maser he built some rock fences and we would beat up the rock for him. We cut tobacco and tied grass to the butt end and hung it up on a pole so it could dry out, then we would twist this day in and day out making cigars and this oldtime home twisted pipe and cigarette tobacco."

"No, we never did earn any money. Maser use to give us a nickel or dime once and awhile and we bought candy and such things as that."

"No sir, we did not have an overse'er. Maser he done all the work himself with the help of the slaves. He had about 50 acres in his plantation and 12 slaves, besides 3 little negroes. Every work morning he would wake us about 4 o'clock so we could tend to the stock and be in the field by the time we could see how to work. People now don't work like they did in them days. We worked just as long as we could see, then we come in and have 15 or 20 cows to feed and milk that night and 20 to 30 head of work stock to feed. By the time we would get in bed at night it would be about 9 or 10 o'clock. We didn't get very much rest or sleep."

"At night we generally fell in at our quarters as we would be so tired we could hardly move until next morning."

Mariah Calloway, Georgia

"Oh! dey had 'bout a hundred slaves I'm sho', for dere was a heap of 'em. De overseer got 'em up 'bout five o'clock in de mornin' and dat breakfust sho' had better be ready by seben or else somebody gwine to have to pay for it. Dey went to deir cabins 'bout ten at night. Marse was good, but he would whup us if we didn't do right. Miss Marion was allus findin' fault wid some of us."

Walter Calloway, Alabama

"Marse John hab a big plantation an' lots of slaves. Dey treated us purty good, but we hab to wuk hard. Time I was ten years ole I was makin' a reg'lar han' 'hin' de plow."

Simp Campbell, Texas

"Marse's place civered a thousand acres and he had over a hundred slaves, with a overseer, Johnson, and a nigger driver. Us niggers was treated well but the overseer had order to whip us for fightin'. If the nigger driver hit too many licks, the overseer sold him off the place."

"We worked from four till six and done a task after that, and set round and talked till nine and then had to go to bed. On Saturday night you'd hear them fiddles and banjoes playin' and the niggers singin'. All them music gadgets was homemade. The banjoes was made of round pieces of wood, civered with sheepskin and strung with catgut strings."

Polly Turner Cancer, Mississippi

"In July an' August atter de crops wuz laid by de men wud all split rails an' cut de wud, an' de women wud card an' spin de cloth; dey had to reel four cuts ov cloth a day; de grannies wud spin de warp; I'se filled many a shuttle on quills [this information is rather vague as we of this generation do not understand spinning and weaving terms; she also said something about burning out corn cobs for shuttles or something to use.] de reel wud go 'Cr-a-a-ack' ever time a cut wuz finished."

George Caulton, Georgia

George's father cured tobacco and had to stay on the job practically day and night. During the day he would keep a slow fire burning and was able to take naps and rest; but, at night, he had to keep a blazing fire and had no time for sleep at all.

The first work that George ever remembers was cooking food for the cattle. He would gather turnips and other vegetables which he would boil in a huge pot for several hours. When thoroughly cooked he would feed it to a herd of forty head of cattle. George remembered that his master praised him for this work saying, "I got the smartest nigger!"

Ellen Cave, Ohio

While in slavery, Mrs. Cave worked as a maid in the house until she grew older when she was forced to do all kinds of outdoor labor. She remembered sawing logs in the snow all day. In the summer she pitched hay or any other man's work in the field. She was trained to carry three buckets of water at the same time, two in her ahands and one on her head and said she could still do it.

Aunt Cicely Cawthon, Georgia

"The overseer on the plantation had a horn," said Aunt Cicely, "a great big ram's horn. I never did see such a big horn. It was 'bout two feet long. The overseer blowed it about two hours before day. The darkies had to get up and cook their breakfast, and curry their mules and a start for the field. They had better be in that field by sun-up. When the sun went down, they stuck their hoes up in the field and quit. Then they was free for the day."

"Darkies had partic'lar tasks to perform. Now, like if they was gathering up corn, they shucked corn late to get it in the crib to keep it from being rained on. Sometimes, if they didn't get through before dark they held torches to see by."

Abraham Chambers, Alabama

"I was big enough to hoe cotton and de garden. I drive cows and calves in slavery time and fotch water."

Henry Cheatam, Alabama

"In dem days de slaves did all de wurk and carried all de news. De Marsters sent notes from one plantation to anudder, an' when dey wanted de niggers dey would blow de ole horn, an' dey wuld use de horn when dey went 'possum an' coon huntin' at night. Den I 'members at night atter wurkin' in de fiel' us w'uld go to de house an' spin an' sum ob de slaves w'uld weave. I'se spun a many role, an' carded many ob bats uf cotton. I'se also made many a taller candle by tieing strings onto a long stick and dropping dem down into moulds filled wid taller; an' I'se hid a many a nite in de fence corners, when I'd be going sumwhars to git mah maw sum tobaccy. De 'patty rollers' wuld be out'lookin' fo' slaves who didn't hab no pass frum dere o'seer and I'd har dem a cumming and I'd hide 'til dey pass, 'cayse ef dey had katch me I sho' w'uld hab got a sound beatin'."

Mary Childs, Georgia

"I worked under four overseers," Mary continued. "One was named Sanders, one named Saxon, one Rush, and the other I can't 'member. One of them was mean, and he had a big deep voice. When the niggers was at the feed lot, the place where they carried the dinner they brought to the fields, he would hardly give 'em time to eat before he hollered out: 'Git up and go back to work!'"

"When the slaves got hungry before dinner time, they would ask the nursing mothers to bring them back hoe-cake 'corn dodger,' when they went to nurse the babies. Those hot-hoe cakes were eaten in mid-morning, to hold us till dinnertime."

Jeptha Choice, Texas

"I went to the fields when I was about 20 years old, but I didn' have to do much field work, 'cause they was keepin' me good and they didn' want to strain me. In 'puttin' in time' in the spring and 'pickin' time' in the fall, the most slaves went out to the field as soon as it was light, and got in at sundown. During in between times it was easier. The men worked every day except

Saturday afternoon and Sundays. The womenfolks had Saturday off to wash clo'es and do the cleanin'."

"Then in the field was always a big strong nigger to keep peace among the hands. He was called by the other slaves 'nigger traitor' behin' his back, and was sorta like a straw-boss-man. He had to be good with his fists to make the boys who got bad in the field, walk the line. 'Course when Old Massa come to the field, anyone who was actin' up started right in to choppin', and everything would get quiet as could be."

"Come Saturday noon, the field hands all came in and they was no more work till Monday, 'ceptin' the womenfolks washin' clothes. Mos' Saturday afternoons we would go fishin' down in the creek, and it wasn' no job to get a mess of cat fish or perch or silver slides for supper."

Anne Clark, Texas

"You know, the white folks hated to give us up worse thing in the world. I ploughed, hoed, split rails. I done the hardest work ever a man ever did. I was so strong, iffen he needed me I'd pull the men down so the marster could handcuff 'em."

"They'd whop us with a bullwhip. We got up at 3 o'clock, at 4 we done et and hitched up the mules and went to the fiel's. We worked all day pullin' fodder and choppin' cotton. Marster'd say, 'I wan' you to lead dat fiel' today, and if you don' do it I'll put you in de stocks.' Then he'd whop me iffen I didn' know he was talkin' to me."

Charles Coates, Florida

Charles Coates remembers vividly the cruelties practiced on the Hall plantation. His duty was to see that all the slaves reported to work on time. The bell was rung at 5:30 a.m. by one of the slaves. Charles had the ringing of the bell for three years; this was in addition to the carriage driving. He tells with laughter how the slaves would "grab a piece of meat and bread and run to the field" as no time was allowed to sit and eat breakfast. This was a very different way from that of the master he had before, as Mr. L'Angle was much better to his slaves."

Pierce Cody, Georgia

The land was divided into many fields each of which was used to cultivate a particular product. Each field had its special crew and overseer.

Cody's father was one of the feeders who arose at least two hours before sunrise, to feed the stock. A large number of horses and more than two hundred head of cattle had to be fed by sunrise when they were to be turned into the pastures or driven to the field to begin the day's work. After sunrise, his father's duty as foreman for plowers began. Other workers were hoe hands, additional foremen, cooks, weavers, spinners, seamstresses, tailors, shoemakers, etc. As everything used was grown and made on the estate, there was plenty of work for all and in many instances slaves learned trades which they liked and which furnished a livelihood when they were set free.

Betty Cofer, North Carolina

"Colored folks on some of the other plantations wasn't so lucky. Some of 'em had overseers, mean, cruel men. On one plantation the field hands had to hustle to git to the and of the row at eleven o'clock dinner-time 'cause when the cooks brought their dinner they had to stop just where they was and eat, an' the sun was mighty hot out in those fields. They only had ash cakes [corn pone baked in ashes] without salt, and molasses for their dinner, but we had beans an' grits an' salt an' sometimes meat."

Abraham Coker, Texas

"When I got big enough I was a plow-boy. I used a lahge turnin' plow wid iron buttones. I liked to plow, 'cause we had good, big American mules to plow wid, and we didn't have to plow wid oxen."

"Dem niggers would git in de field and pick cotton in big baskets, and dey would put about one hunnert pounds in 'em. Mawster Johnson had his own gin-house right on de place and when we picked a basket ob cotton, we'd take it right to de gin. Dis cotton gin was drove by four big mules, and dey turned de pole aroun' and aroun', wid a little slave boy follerin' 'em, and whoopin' 'em now and den to keep 'em going. Der little boy never did git hurt, 'cause he always stayed fur enough away f'om dem mules. De gin separated de seed f'om de lint, and den de lint was pressed into a square bale, and it weighed f'om four to five hunnert pounds. De cotton seed was placed in a pile as big as a house and in dem days, we had no use fo' de seed. We didn't know whut to do wid it. Sometimes de cows would come over and eat all dat dey wanted. In dem days we fed de cows on cawn, and we didn't know dat de cotton seed was good fo' de milk cows."

Alice Cole, Texas

"Maser, he never had no overseer, said they cost him more than they was worth. He done all that himself. Yes sir, he did have a big plantation something over a 100 acres and near about 40 slaves. Well sir, Maser he woke the slaves every morning about 4:30 o'clock with a large bell that hung just out side his door. Well son, we worked every day just long as we could see how, in other words just as long every day as it was light enough for us to see how to work."

"We just mostly fell in at the door and onto our bed cause we would be almost worked down. Believe me son they sure did work the slaves, they did'nt have very much mercy on the poor old slaves in that way. These days son I'se seen men that drives mules to the plow or wagon and dragging along whip behind them and every time they would slow down or stop, they would shower down on the poor old mules and that reminded me of slavery days, cause every time we slowed down or stopped to get our breath—down on us came that old whip, it did not make any difference how tired or how near give out we would be."

Harrison Cole, Texas

"De field hands lived wid de other folks in de quarters, an' dey wuz up on de hillside whar de flood from Tehuacana did not reach, an' w'en four o'clock in de mornin's cum de bell from de big house rings, an' dis means dat everybody dat is able to work has to get up an' eat his breakfast an' be ready for de nex' bell dat rings at five o'clock to go to de fields w'en dey kin work in dem an' w'en hit too rainy an' cold den dey has other work to do, maybe haulin de wood an' some of de men chops hit an' de wimmen go an work in de house an' help in de kitchen an' some in de sewin' room whar dey still spin an' weave de thread to make de homespun clothes."

"W'en we planted de cotton we would clear up a piece of land an' run a furrow wid de old fashioned bull tongue plow, den we drop de seed in de furrow, throw de dirt on top of hit wid a furrow down de side, an' den leave hit till hit cum's up befo' we work hit, sometimes if we has much rain an' very busy we does not work hit any more, but we makes from half to a bale an' acre on de Tehuacana bottom, de land wuz so rich an' we did not have any insects to bother or Johnson Grass, all dese things like dey has now."

Hattie Cole, Texas

"De wo'k am all 'ranged 'cordin' to rule. Ise use to lak to watch dem in de mo'nin' w'en deys gits ready fo' wo'k. Ise gwine tell yous 'bout it. De bell rings, den yous see de cullud fo'ks pilin' out ob de cabins, an' gwine to de field, de shops, an' tudder places whar deys wo'k. De overseer an' de Marster am talkin' to dis one an' dat one, givin' de ordahs. Some goes to de shoeshop, some to de carpentershop, some to de weavin' room, an' so on. Den thar am big herd ob cows, an' de milkers goes to de milkin'. Yous heah dis one an' dat one shoutin' to somebody 'bout dis an' dat, an' ever'thing am in a hustle. Heah an' thar, yous heah some ob dem singin'. It makes me lonesome w'en Ise think 'bout it."

"Most ob de cullud fo'ks am happy 'cause deys am fed good, an' de Marster am reasonable 'bout de wo'k. He ask de cullud fo'ks to wo'k steady, but don't over rush. If someone feels bad, all deys have to do am tell de Marster, or de overseer, an' dey goes to de cabin an' lays down. W'en someone suffer too much wid some misery, de Marster calls de doctah. If it am small misery, de Marster 'tend to it himse'f. He use herb medicine. If Ise gits sich care now, Ise be glad. Now, m'ybe Ise gits medicine, an' m'ybe no."

Julia Cole, Georgia

"Marse John's son, Marse Willic Grant, blowed de bugle in de mornin's by 4 o'clock to git de slaves up in time to be in de fields by daybreak. When slaves got too old to wuk, dey took keer of de chillun in a house down below de kitchen. Mamma wukked in de field when she was able. Nobody on our place had to wuk in de fields on Sadday evenin's. Dat was de time. de 'omans washed deir clothes and cleaned up."

Thomas Cole, Texas

"Den when a slave gets grown, he is jest lak a mule, dey works for der grub and a few clothes and works jest as hard as a mule. Some of de slaves on de plantation jining ourn, didnt have as easier time as de mules, fer de mules was fed good and de slaves laks ter have starved ter death he jest gives dem nuff ter eat keep dem alive."

"We has ter git up early every day in de year, rain or shine, hot or cold. De slaves was woke up every mornin at four thirty by a slave blowin a horn it was his job ter gits up and blow a bugle and den he would go ter work in de fiels wid de rest of de slaves. Dar was no danger of you not wakin up when de bugle blowed cause he blows it long and loud. He allus gits up of a mornin and gits his bugle down and comes out and climbs up on a platform wintah and summah and blows his bugle. Dis platform was bout eight or ten feet tall. All de slaves gits up at four thirty, breakfast is eat and de men folks goes on ter fiels and as soon as de women finished up de house work and takes care of de babies, dey comes ter work. All de slaves carried der dinnah ter de fiel wid dem and iffen you'se puts it whar de ants or a varmint can git it dat is your hard luck. We all works til noon den we eats our dinnah in de shade and res bout an hour or hour and half iffen it is very hot and iffen it is cold we res bout an hour, den we goes back ter work and stays up wid de lead man all evenin jest lak we did in de mornin, and den between sun down and night we takes out, goes ter de quarters and eats supper and by dat time we is already ter goes ter bed and sleep. You is always tired when you makes a day lak dat on de plantation. You cant git ter go ter a party or dance lak de young folks do now a days and play all night. De young folks now speels all de next day, but we couldnt."

"I played with Massa Cole's chillen all de time, and when I got older he started me workin' by totin' wood and sech odd jobs, and feedin' de hawgs. Us chillen had to pick cotton every fall. De big baskets weigh about seventy-five to a hundred pounds, but us chillen put our pickin's in some growed slave's basket. De growed slaves was jes' like a mule. He work for grub and clothes, and some of dem didn't have as easier a time as a mule, for mules was fed good and slaves was sometimes half starved. But Massa Cole was a smart man and a good man with it. He had 'spect for the slaves' feelin's and didn't treat dem like dumb brutes, and 'lowed dem more privileges dan any other slaveholder round dere. He was one of de best men I ever knows in my whole life and his wife was jes' like him."

Eli Coleman, Texas

"We did all kinds of work such as, chopping cotton, split rails, cut rock and built fences. Also worked in tobacco fields. We would cut that tobacco and hang it in the shed so it could dry. Every stock would have to be hung up just one way and that was by the root or stubble end."

Fannie Coleman, Georgia

"I used to card and spin. Us used to spin and weave our clothes in them days. I worked in de fields too."

Preely Coleman, Texas

"As we grew up an' got big enough to work our first work was to learn to hoe. Massa Tom or Young Master Frank made us use the hoe two years and them to the plow. That was the way they managed things. Chillun made hoe hands for two years, then started to plowing. We had to be up an' ready for the field by daylight. The conk, or mussel shell was blown at eleven-thirty and we had to be back at the field at twelve-thirty. Massa Tom or Young Frank would always holler out of a morning, 'All hands ready for the field.' We always got Saturday afternoon off. The women washed, swept yards, tidied up the house and cooked some. Master wouldn't allow no kind of work to be done on Sunday. If he heard an ax sound he would go out an say, 'Young man haven't you got enough wood up, lay that ax down and go to my wood pile and git enough to do you, then see if you can't get yours up next Saturday.'"

William Coleman, Texas

"Maser woke us up every morning about 4:30 o'clock with a great large bell that hung just outside of his bed. Son I'se dressed several times out behind my quarters cause if we did not get right up when Maser rung that bell, here he come with a rawhide whip and gun buckled on him, and he would whip us all the time we were trying to dress. Maser he would work us from sun to sun or we would be in the field in the morning waiting for daylight to come, then we stayed in the field and worked just as long as we could see how. When we went to the house we had all our night work to do after dark before we got our supper, and went to bed. Well son, I'se seen the slaves whipped for nothing, but then if they did do something to be whipped for they were almost killed before Maser would quit working on them. Yes sir, if one was the least bit stubborn or even acted like he would sass Maser, he was whipped.

I'se seen Maser ride up close to a slave when he was working and whip him good, cause he would be 3 or 4 feet behind the rest of the slaves One time one of the slaves was helping Mistress there in the yard and he passed too close to her as he was hurrying fast as he could, and sort of bumped into her. She never paid him no attention, but Maser saw him and he let him go on ahead and finish what he was doing then he called that poor negro to him and took him out in the pasture, tied his hands together, throwed the other end of the rope over a limb on a tree and pulled that negro's hands up in the air to where that negro had to stand on his tiptoes, and Maser he took all that negro's clothes off and whipped him with that rawhide whip until that negro was plum bloody all over. Then he left that poor negro tied there all the rest of the day and night."

"Well son, I'se done all kinds of work as a kid during slavery such as, cut wood, chop cotton, corn, hoe in the garden. Maser he put us to work just as soon as we could follow or sling a hoe, pick cotton, pulled corn and carry in wood, water and so on for our Mistress or feed, milk the cows and just anything like that for there was some things we could not do, and he would make the older negroes do."

"Well son, I might have earned money as a slave but I did not ever get it, in fact son, I did not know what money was. I often heard the older slaves talk about money and I wondered what they were talking about as I did not know what it was."

"You'se ask me what we done when we went to our quarters at night after our days work was done. Well son I just mostly went to bed cause I was locked in and I'se could not go no where or talk with the rest of the slaves. No sir, Maser did not work us on Saturday evening, he always gives us that day off as it was custom everybody turn their slaves loose from work that evening."

Annie Coley, Mississippi

"We worked in de fiels in de cotton en de corn, from early mawnin' twel sundown. Sat'days, all day, jes' de same. Sundays we could rest. Big Boss giv each cullud man a piece of groun' to mek a crap of cawn en cotton fer hisself. Sundays each niggah worked out his own crap."

"Atter the crap was laid by, we went with Big Boss to his church an set in the back seats. We couldn' none of us read the Bible, so's thet was why Boss made us go to church, so's we could hear it read."

Bill Collins, Texas

"After we got big enough to work in the fields we has to work so hard we never did have any time for playing. When winter time came master bought us all a pair of shoes but we always went barefooted in the summer time. We always wore home spun pants and shirts. They were spun by the older slave women. They did most of this at night. Some of them had to work in the fields all day and spin at night."

"My duties were all kinds of field work. We were awakened by a large plantation bell which rang every morning at four o'clock. The bell called and said, get up I'm coming after you, and said if they did not answer the call the over-seer would whip them."

"The youngest age they worked in the field was twelve. Then they would just give them tasks—mostly carrying water."

"The grown people were in the field early in the morning. It was about six, I reckon. It was early. The master would give them time to eat their breakfast. They had an hour for dinner, and they would stop about dark unless there was something the matter urgent. If it was late in the season and they were afraid the rain or something would catch them, then they would have to work later sometimes. If it were hot in the hot part of summer, they would allow the slaves to stop during the hot part of the day and rest. They worked in the early and late part of the day then."

"In the field, they wore jeans. They made their cloth and their clothes. They would dye the cloth red, blue, or brown. Summer, they wore cotton pants made out of cotton cloth. They called the pants jeans."

"My work was to answer the door bell and wait on my mistress and go round with her wherever she went. I had to sleep in the house with her. Sometimes at night I would have to go down to the quarters for her, and I would run every step of the way."

Martha Colquitt, Georgia

"Ma's house wuz right on de edge of Marse Billie's yard, 'cause she wuz de cook. Grandma lived in de same house wid ma and us chillun, and she worked in de loom house and wove cloth all de time. She wove de checkidy cloth for de slaves clo'es, and she made flannel cloth too, leaseways, it wuz part flannel. She made heaps of kinds of cloth."

"De overseer blowed a horn to wake 'em up just 'fore day, so as everybody could cook, eat, and git out to de fields by sunrise. Dey quit nigh sundown, in time for 'em to feed de stook, do de milkin', tend to bringin' in de wood, and all sorts of other little jobs dat had to be done 'fore it got too dark to see. Dey never wuz no work done at night on our plantation."

Sara Colquitt, Alabama

"Miss Mary was good to us, but us had to work hard and late. I worked in de fields every day from 'fore daylight to almost plumb dark. I usta take my littlest baby wid me. I had two chilluns, and I'd tie hit up to a tree limb to keep off de ants and bugs whilst I hoed and worked de furrow. All us niggers was fed from de big kitchen and wasn't hongry, but sometimes us would steal more food dan was give us anyhow."

"I was one of de spinners, too, and had to do six cuts to de reel at de time and do hit at night plenty times. Us clothes was homespun orsanburgs, what us would dye, sometimes solid and sometimes checked."

· "'Sides working de fields and spinning, sometimes I'd hope wid de cooking up at de Big House when de real cook was sick or us had a passel of company. Us cooked on a great, big fireplace what had arms hanging out over de coals to hang pots on to bile. Den us had three-legged skillets what set right over de coals for frying and sech like. Us cooked sho' 'nuff bread in dem days, ash cakes, de best thing you ever et. Dey ain't nothing like dat dese days."

"He would get us slaves up 'fore day blowing on his big horn and us would work 'twell plumb dark. All de little niggers'd get up, too, and go up to de Big House to be fed from wooden bowls. Den dey'd be called ag'in 'fore us come from de fields and put to bed by dark. I useta stop by de spring house to get de milk, it was good cold too, and tote it up to de Big House for dinner."

Arthur Colson, Georgia

There were about one hundred slaves on the plantation, most of them working in the fields. Of course, there was a cook, washer woman, house maid, and a few others who worked for the master's family. Arthur's grandmother milked, washed clothes and spun. His mother was a plow hand, and his father plowed, hoed and split rails. Carrying water to the field workers was the first work that Authur was required to do. He was never whipped by his master, but his mother and many of the other slaves were. Whipping was the only punishment that a slave knew.

Jake Compton, Texas

"We raised corn, oats, hogs, cattle, sheep, an' goats, an' all de vegetables dat we wanted. With cows an' plenty of milk an' butter we had plenty to eat. We did not raise cotton at first, not until after Freedon, an' when de wimmen bought de calico hit wuz fifty an sixty cents a yard. Dey made de cltoh on de spinnin' wheel an de loom."

Steve Connally, Texas

"No 'm dere warn't no gins like now in slavery time. Us picked de cotton off de seed by han, dat was work fer night times an rainy, cold days when us couldn't do nuffin else. Mos everything us needed was made at home in dose days an dey lasted longer dan now. Ob corse, de white folks had fine boughten close but dey used some home made cloth too."

Mandy McCullough Cosby, Alabama

"My mother was a loomer. She didn't do nothin' but weave. We all hed reg'lar stints of spinnin' to do, when we come from the fiel'. We set down an' eat a good supper, an' ever'night until ten o'clock we spin cuts of cotton, an' reel the thread, an' nex' day, the rolls is carded an' packed in a basket to be wove."

"Spinnin' wheels was in every cabin. Dere was so many of us to be tuk care of, it took lots of spinnin'."

Jane Cotton, Texas

"Son, you ask me what kind of work I did, why I chopped cotton, picked cotton, plowed, and sawed wood son. They used me just about like they did the bunch, cause I was always a big stout healthy woman. No son, I never did earn any money until long time after we was freed. Master he brag on me and give me nickel and dime which I keeps. So's when the war was over I had nearly five dollars in money."

Albert Cox, Mississippi

"I done general wuk round de place an' I wuked in de fiels some, doing sich as hoeing, picking cotton an' de lak. Marse Charlie, he raised a heap o' cotton, corn, some wheat an' tobacco an' all kinds ob small food stuff to feed de slaves on. Deir wuz alwas plenty found ter keep de slaves busy as deir wuz so many to be feed an' kept up wid clo'se an' mos' every thing had to be made by hand at home."

Tony Cox, Mississippi

My fust wuk wuz doin' odd jobs 'round mar's big house, such as totin' in wood, drawing water, keeping' fires, an' runnin' an pedling 'round. Den later I wuz put in de fields, fust pullin' up grass, hoein' an' pickin' cotton. Master wuz good 'nough ter us, but de over-seers wuz what wuz cruel sometimes. Mars didn't mean fer de slaves to be beat lak dey wuz. At times big fields full would be a workin', dey would be a singin', hollerin' an' a prayin'; de overseer would ride up on hes horse an' think 'nough wuk hadn't been done, den he would beat 'em till dey would fall in de fields, an us would haf to tote water to 'em an' bring 'em to."

Sara Crocker, Georgia

Her father worked in the fields for Mr. Hodge, while her mother was the cook for Mr. Fulton's family and also washed their clothes. Her brother and sisters worked in the fields. Sara's first recollection of any work was when she was quite a small girl, and this was field work. There were various kinds of work performed by other slaves on the plantation, such as plowing, chopping, hoeing, weaving cloth, spinning and washing. Most of them did their washing at night.

Ed Crum, Mississippi

"Pappy was a field hand an' mammy was house gal to Mis' Mary Crum. Dey was Mis' Mary an' Marse Jake Crum our owners. Marse Jake was Doc Crumm you know. An' dey was young Mis' Mary, Mis' Betty an' dey boys was Charlie, Vin, an' Billie. Dey libed in a big ole' two story house made out'n logs den sealed ober. I reck'n house had 'bout eight rooms in hit."

"Uncle Sam come roun' an' wak us up 'bout sun up an' we worked in de fields till sun down gen'ally. Now on rainy days mammy an' all de womens would weave an' spin in de loom house makin' clof—lowell you know, fo' us clothes. When we wo' shoes dey was russetts an' one ob de men's on de place made 'em."

Green Cumby, Texas

"Durin' slavery I had purty rough times. My grandfather, Tater Cumby, was cullud overseer for forty slaves and he called us at four in de mornin' and we worked from sun to sun. Most of de time we worked on Sunday, too."

Tempie Cummins, Texas

"Marster had 30 or 40 acres and he raise cotton, and corn and 'tatoes. He used to raise 12 bales cotton a year and then drink it all up. We work from daylight till dark, and after Marster punish them what didn't work hard enough."

Julia Daniels, Texas

"My daddy worked in the fields with Uncle Lot and my brothers, and my Uncle Joe, he's driver. But Briscoe am overseer and he a white man. He can't never whup the growed mens like he wants, 'cause they don't let him unless he ask Old Man Denman. I seed him whup 'em, though. He make 'em take off the shirt and whup with the strap."

Katie Darling, Texas

"When the niggers done anything massa bullwhip them, but didn't skin them up very often. He'd whip the man for half doin' the plowin' or hoein' but if they done it right he'd find something else to whip them for. At night the men had to shuck corn and the women card and spin. Us got two pieces of clothes for winter and two for summer, but us have no shoes. We had to work Saturday all day and if that grass was in the field we didn't git no Sunday, either."

Carey Davenport, Texas

"I was a sheep minder them days. The wolves was bad but they never tackled me, 'cause they'd ruther git the sheep. They like sheep meat better'n man meat. Old Captain wanted me to train he boy to herd sheep and one day young master see a sow with nine pigs and want me to catch them and I wouldn't do it. He tried to beat me up and when we git to the lot we have to go round to the big gate and he had a pine knot, and he catch me in the gate and hit me with that knot. Old Captain sittin' on the gallery and he seed it all. When he heered the story he whipped young master and the old lady, she ain't like it."

Ada Davis, Texas

"I guess dere wuz three hundred acres in de plantation an' 'bout fifty servants. Dere wuz lots ob work, clearin' lan' fer de plantin', an' buildin' fences, barns an' sech; 'sides dat de quarters had to hab chimneys an' fences too. Some de cabins didn't git no floors fer 'bout two years. Jes' as fas' as dey could de men got out clap boards fer de walls ob de big house an' split puncheon slabs fer floors an' palins fer a fence."

Mose Davis, Georgia

Field hands were roused, every morning by the everseer who rang the large bell near the slave quarters. Women young children were permitted to remain at home until 9 o'clock to prepare breakfast. At 9 o'clock these women had to start to the fields where they worked along with the others until sundown. The one break in the day's work was the noon dinner hour. Field hands planted and tended cotton, corn, and the other produce grown on the plantation until harvest time when everybody picked cotton. Slaves usually worked harder during the picking season than at any other time. After harvest, the only remaining work was cleaning out fence corners, splitting rails building fences and numerous other minor tasks. In hot weather, the only work was shelling corn. There was no Sunday work other than caring for the stock.

George Dillard, Alabama

George explained that he was a field hand and had to work hard most of the time.

Sally Dixon, Mississippi

"I has just a misty recollection of my first Mistress, Miss Sally White. I was born on her place near Macon, Georgia. She was a widow lady and lived in a great big beautiful house. My mother, Louise, cooked for her and when I was born, she named me Sally after her. That was many years before the Civil War. Old Miss was old and not very strong. One morning we got the news she done died. I never will forget that funeral, cause I aint never seed one like it. Instead of burying her in the ground like all folks is buried, they buried her in something what looked like a big brick wall. Miss had two sons Mr. Frank and Mr. Crawfort. They was living on their farms near Como, Miss. We, my family, was left to Mr. Crawfort. Old Miss had done put it in her will that he was to have us. He carried us to his place in Mississippi in big covered wagons. Besides my father, Frank, mother, Louise, there was four boys and six girls. The boys was named Larkin, Floyd, Doc, and Ed. The girls was Dosia, Lucy, Tokie, Tooly, Rebecca, and me. I never will forget that trip. There was so many children in the wagons when us comed to the poll gates they would make us all lay real still in the bottom of the wagon so they wouldn't have to pay toll for us all. Mr. Crawfort wasn't married. He lived most of the time with his brother, Frank, and had an overseer to look after his place. He was clearing his place up. It was on the Bogue. We went to work at daylight and worked 'till dark. The nights the big logs was burning some one would have to sit up to watch the fire. We stayed there on that place for seven years when the big overflow came they had to take us all back to the hills. I don't know nothing bout what year it was children wasn't taught about years and months like they is now. That how come I don't know how old I is. Mistress didn't tell my ma what the date was she had put down in the book. I speck if she hader told her, she could have kept all them children's dates in her head. My grandpa, old Uncle Essex White, knowed a lot about figures, but he stayed down in Georgia, and we never seed him again after we left there. The houses we lived in was made of logs and chinked with clay. The chimneys was made of the same clay. They was good and warm. The women on the place wove the cloth our clothes was made of. Every night my ma had to spin six cuts of cotton before she went to bed. Some of the cloth was dyed in colored stripes."

Lucy Donald, Mississippi

"A bgg wuz blowed fer signals. We all knowed whut each blow meant. We knowed by de blows ob de horn when to go to Marse's big kitchen to eat, slave women cooked de food fer everybody. It wuz set on long tables. De horn blowed fer em' to go to wuk an' to come in; an' if a fire broke out, or anything onusual. And we knowed what it meant by signals. De wuk wuz carried on from fo' day 'till after dark. Deir sho wuz a heap o' wuk done in one day."

Douglas Dorsey, Florida

As to plantation life, Dorsey said that the slaves lived in quarters especially built for them on the plantation. They would leave for the fields at "sun up" and remain until "sun-down," stopping only for a meal which they took along with them.

Instead of having an overseer they had what was called a "driver" by the name of January. His duties were to get the slaves together in the morning and see that they went to the fields and assigned them to their tasks. He worked as the other slaves, though, he had more priveliges. He would stop work at any time he pleased and go around to inspect the work of the others, and thus rest himself. Most of the orders from the master were issued to him. The crops consisted of cotton, corn, cane and peas, which was raised in abundance.

When the slaves left the fields, they returned to their cabins and after preparing and eating of their evening meal they gathered around a cabin to sing and moan songs seasoned with African melody. Then to the tune of an old fiddle they danced a dance called the "Green Corn Dance" and "Cut the Pigeon Wing." Sometimes the young men on the plantation would slip away to visit a girl on another plantation. If they were caught by the "Patrols" while on these visits they would be lashed on the bare backs as a penalty for this offense.

Willie Doyld, Arkansas

"My pa was Moster Jin's ox driver. He drove five or six yokes at a time. He walk long side of em, wagons loaded up. He toted a long cowhide whoop. He toted it over his shoulder. When he'd crack it you could hear his whoop half a mile. Knowed he was comin' on up to the house. Them oxen would step long, peartin up when he crack his whoop over em. He'd be haulin' logs, wood, cotton, corn, taters, sorghum cane and stuff. He nearly always walked long side of em; sometimes he'd crawl upon the front wagon an' ride a piece."

Willis Dukes, Florida

He was one of 40 slaves belonging to one John Dukes, who was only in moderate circumstances. His parents were Amos and Mariah Dukes, both born on this plantation, he thinks. As they were a healthy pair they were required to work long hours in the fields, although the master was not actually cruel to them.

George Eason, Georgia

Mr. Eason was about 7 or 8 years of age when he was first sent to work in the field. It was then that his troubles began. He says that he was made to get up each morning at sun-up and that after going to the field he had to toil there all day until the sun went down. He and his fellow slaves had to work in all types of weather, good as well as bad. Although the master or the overseer were not as cruel as some he had heard of they tolerated no looseness of work and in case a person was suspected of loafing the whip was applied freely. Although he was never whipped, he has heard the whip being applied to his mother any number of times. It hurt him, he says, because he had to stand back unable to render any assistance whatever. (This happened before he was sent to the plantation.)

Some nights after he and the other slaves had left the field they were required to do extra work such as ginning cotton and shelling peas and corn, etc. The young women were required to work that in some respects was as hard as that the men did, while the older women usually did lighter work. When the time came to pick the cotton all hands were converted into pickers. Night was the only time that they had to do their washing and to cultivate the small gardens they were allowed to have.

During the months when there was little field work to do they were kept busy repairing fences, etc. on the farm. Every day was considered a working day except Sunday, Thanksgiving and Christmas. They were not allowed to celebrate on these days as were the slaves on other nearby plantations.

Anderson Edwards, Texas

"Mammy was a weaver and made all the clothes and massa give us plenty to eat; fact, he treated us kind-a like he own boys. Course he whipped us when we had to have it, but not like I seed darkies whipped on other place. The other niggers called us Major Gaud's free niggers and we could hear 'em moanin' and cryin' round 'bout, when they was puttin' it on 'em."

"I worked in the field from one year end to t'other and when we come in at dusk we had to eat and be in bed by nine. Massa give us mos' anything he had to eat, 'cept biscuits. That ash cake wasn't sich bad eatin' and it was cooked by puttin' cornmeal batter in shucks and bakin' in the ashes."

Doc Edwards, North Carolina

"We hed big work shops whare we made all de tools, an' even de shovels was made at home. Dey was made out of wood, so was de rakes, pitchforks an' some of de hoes. Our nails was made in de blacksmith shop by han' an' de pisks an' grubbin' hocs, too."

"We had a han' thrashing machine. It was roun' like a stove pipe,—only bigger. We fed de wheat to it an' shook it 'til de wheat was loose from de straw an' when it come out at de other and it fell on a big cloth, bigger den de sheets. We had big curtains all roun' de cloth on de floor, like a tent, so de wheat wouldn' get scattered, Den we took de pitchfork an' lifted de straw up an' down so de wheat would go on de cloth. Den we moved de straw when de wheat was all loose. Den de fanned de wheat wid big pieces of cloth to get de dust an' dirt outen it, so it could be taken to do mill an' groun' when it was wanted."

"When de fall come we had a regular place to do different work. We had han' looms an' wove our cotton an' yarn an' made de cloth what was to make de clothes for us to wear."

Mary Edwards, Texas

"I got give to Massa Felix Vaughn and he brung me to Texas. Dat long 'fore de war fer freedom, but I don't know de year. De most work I done for de

Vaughns was wet nuss de baby son, what name Elijah. His mammy jes' didn't have 'nough milk for him."

"Den I knit de socks and wash de clothes and sometimes I work in de fields. I he'ped make de baskets for de cotton. De man git white-oak weed and we lets it stay in de water for de night and de nex' mornin' and it soft and us split it in strips for makin' of de baskets. Everybody try see who could make de bes' basket."

"Us pick 'bout 100 pound cotton in one basket. I didn't mind pickin' cotton, 'cause I never did have de backache. I pick two and three hunnert pounds a day and one day I picked 400. Sometime de prize give by massa to de slave what pick de most. De prize am a big cake or some clothes. Pickin' cotton not so bad, 'cause us used to it and have de fine time of it. I gits a dress one day and a pair shoes 'nether day for pickin' most. I so fast I take two rows at de time."

"Us have ash-hopper and uses drip-lye for make barrels soap and hominy. De way us test de lye am drop de egg in it and if de egg float de lye ready to put in de grease for makin' de soap. Us threwed greasy bones in de lye and dat make de bes' soap. De lye eat de bones."

Callie Elder, Georgia

"Oh, no Ma'am, I sho' can't tell nothin' t'all 'bout how big dat old plantation was, but it was one whoppin' big place. Dere was too many slaves on dat plantation for me to count. De overseer got 'em up by 4:00 o'clock and de mens had to be in de fields by sunrise. De 'omans went out 'bout 8:00 o'clock. Dey stopped wuk at sundown and by de time dey et and done de chores for de day it was 10:00 o'clock 'fore dey hit de bed. De cabins was built in a circle and de overseer went de rounds evvy night to see if de slaves was in bed."

"Cotton pickin's warn't planned for fun and frolic lak cornshuckin's. If Marse Billy got behind in his crops, he jus' sent us back to de fields at night when de moon was bright and sometimes us picked cotton all night long. Marster give de 'oman what picked de most cotton a day off, and de man what picked de most had de same privilege."

Lawerence Evans, Mississippi

"Ole Marse wuz kind to his slaves but he kept 'em under rule. Deir wuz a time fer everything, de big bell wuz rung fer us to git up in de mornings an' rung fer us to go to de big kitchen to eat an' go to wu'k, an' to come in from de feil's an' on lak dat. An overseer wu'ked us an' he sho' believed in keepin' us busy. Dey raised mostly cotton an' wheat. I wuz to little to wuk fiel's. I can recollect seein' de fiel's white wid cotton an' dem full ob slaves a pickin' hit an' a singin' an' a hollerin'. An' Marse he owned a boling shaft fer de wheat an de wheat growers fer miles an' miles and miles 'round took, deir wheat deir. Dats whar I come in handy wuz toting an' movin' de straw out 'en de way ob de shaft. Everything alwa's went on quiet lak an easy on Marse's plantation. I think it wuz 'cause he had a good agreeable set o' darkies, dey jes naturally neber gib no trouble to amount to anything. Dey didn't hab to be all dat whipping an' carrying on lak I'se heard ob. Us wuz taught ter mind an' ter wuk; us wuz taught good manners an' ter be polite."

Sam and Louisa Everett, Florida

Sam was the son of Peter and Betsy Everett, field hands who spent long back-breaking hours in the cotton fields and came home at nightfall to cultivate their small garden. They lived in constant fear that their master would confiscate most of their vegetables; he so often did.

Martha Everette, Georgia

"My daddy worked in th' field an' so did Maw sometimes."

Lewis Favor, Georgia

These slaves who were field hands were in the field and at work by the time it was light enough to see. They plowed, hoed, and then later in the season gathered the crops. After the harvesting was over the fences were repaired and rails were split. In rainy weather nobody had to work out of doors, instead they shelled the peas and corn and sometimes ginned the cotton. At night the women were required to spin and to weave. In the winter season no work was required at night unless they had not spun as much thread as was required. At such times they had to work at night until the amount set had been reached.

Sarah Felder, Mississippi

"Old Marse wud mek de slaves git ter de fiel' ter wuk an' he wud git on his big fine horse an' ride ober de fiel' wid a big whip hangin' by his side, an' de slaves wud see dat whip an' wurk hard fur dey wus skeer'd uf dat whip."

"We niver hed much time ter rest 'ceptin Sad'ay nights, an' den sum times de older slaves wud git passes an' go sum whar, an' sum times slaves wud cum ter our place but dar wusn't much dancin' only on udder plantashuns. Ebery Sunday we hed ter wrap hair. Old Marse an' Miss Vickey niver 'low'ed us ter rest much."

"Old Marse hed a big gin out behind de barn an' ebery year atter dey wuld gin de cotton dey wud put it on wagons an' send it ter Natchez; De teams wus oxen an' de driver wud start 'bout three days a hed uf old Marster. An den old Marse wud go on his big fine hoss, an' sell dat cotton an' lode de wagon wid ebery thing good ter eat and fine things fur old Mistis, an' it wus all de team culd pull home. Dar wus flour, sugar, coffee, raisins, cheese an' mackerel. Atter while old Marse traded in Magnolia an' it didnt tek dem so long ter go ter town."

John Finnely, Texas

"What we'uns make? 'Low me to 'collect a li'l. Let's see, we'uns make shoes, and leather and clothes and cloth and grinds de meal. And we'uns cures de meat, preserves de fruit and make 'lassas and brown sugar. All de harness for de mules and de hosses is make and de carts for haulin'. Am dat all? Oh, yes, masse make peach brandy and him have he own still."

"Dis nigger never gits whupped 'cept for dis, befo' I's a field hand. Massa use me for huntin' and use me for de gun rest. When him have de long shot I bends over and puts de hands on de knees and massa puts his gun on my back for to git de good aim. What him kills I runs and fetches and carries de game for him. I turns de squirrels for him and dat disaway: de squirrel allus go to udder side from de hunter and I walks 'round de tree and de squirrel see me and go to massa's side de tree and he gits de shot."

"All dat not so bad, but when he shoots de duck in de water and I has to fetch it out, dat give me de worryment. De fust time he tells me to go in de pond I's skeert, powe'ful skeert. I takes off de shirt and pants but there I stands. I steps in de water, den back 'gain, and 'gain. Massa am gittin' mad. He say, 'Swim in dere and git dat duck.' 'Yes, sar, massa,' I says, but I won't go in dat water till massa hit me some licks. I couldn't never git use to bein' de water dog for de ducks."

"De work am 'vided 'twixt de cullud folks and us allus have certain duties to do. I's am de field hand and befo' I's old 'nough for to do dat, dey has me help with de chores and errands."

Laura Ford, Mississippi

"Everything 'bout dis plantation wuz kept gwine by de blow ob de ole cow horn. Dey had a signal fer everything, when to go to Ole Missus's fer meals, to de fiel's an' when to come in an' out lak dat. Dis ole horn wuz over a foot long, it wuz polished up 'till hit wuz plumb shinnin', a cord wuz fastened through a hole at one end an' kept hangin' on de back piazza."

"It wuz wuk, wuk all through de week from day light 'till dark, in de fiels an' 'round de place. On Sundays us wuz good an' ready to res'. De grown up slaves would lie 'round on de cabin gallery flo or on de grass under de trees. De chillun played. When I wuz a little chile we played jumpin' grape vines an' swingin' on grape vine swings an' a makin' doll dresses fer our rag dolls. I wuz put in de fiel's when I wuz ten years ole. We wont taught no book learnin' but how to wuk, to cook, sew, knit an' weave an' de lak ob dat. Den us wuz teached how to be polite an' how to treat white folks."

Sarah Ford, Texas

"Uncle Big Jake sho' work de slaves from early mornin' till night. When you is in de field you better not lag none. When its fallin' weather de hands is put to work fixin' dis and dat. De women what has li'l chillen don't have to work so hard. Dey works 'round de sugar house and come 11 o'clock dey quits, and cares for de babies till 1 o'clock, and den works till 3 o'clock and quits."

Phillis Fox, Mississippi

"Durin' slavery days I worked 'round de house mostly. I'd go to de field some durin' cotton pickin' time. Marsa an' missus treated me very well. Dey gave me plenty to eat an plenty clothes to wear. De workin hands would get new shoes but we wore second hand ones. My sister Lucy was their house girl. I'd go up there an' play with her some. I was allus such a white child when strangers come dey would ask Ole missus if I was her little girl."

"I 'member de field hands went to de field before day. Lots O' times dey would have to leave before dey had et breakfast an' us lads would have to carry de breakfast to de field to em. Lots o' nights dey stayed in de field an picked cotton 'till after dark an weighed it up by candle light."

Ruben Fox, Mississippi

"The place was not very large so Master George looked after it hisself. The big bell was in the yard. He rang it before day every morning for everybody to get up and out. I is knowed them to work as late as ten o'clock at night, when it was the light of the moon, and they was behind with the cotton picking. There warn't no overseers or drivers. Them niggers was just natural good workers, and they didn't need none. Master sure didn't 'low no poor white trash around there. It's them kind of folks what's got things so tore up now. This here young generation is the ones that let them in. The biggest thing the slaves got punished 'bout was fighting amongst their slaves. Boss tried to stop that and sometimes he would have to whip them 'bout it. He didn't always know when they fought so there was mightly little punishment. There was so much to do on that place as we didn't have time to get in much devilment."

"Besides making the crop, we had big herds of sheep and goats to be cared for, cows to be milked, and mules fed. When night came, we was ready to git in our beds and go to sleep. In cold weather we had hog killing. Master's big smoke house was so full of meat you couldn't see the top of it. The only Christmas what we had was the hanging of the stockings by the children. They was filled with candy, cake, and apples. Saturday and Sunday was our rest days."

Anderson Furr, Georgia

"How big was dat plantation? Good Granny; it was so big I never did git all de way over it, and dere must a been 15 or 20 slaves. Old Marster got us up 'bout sunrise and fetched us in at sundown. He was all time knockin' on his Niggers 'bout somepin. He 'lowed dey didn't do dis, or dat, or somepin else right—he allus had to have some 'scuse to knock 'em 'round."

Clayborn Gantling, Florida

"As a child I uster have to tote water to de old people on de farm and tend de cows an' feed de sheep. Now, I can' say right 'zackly how things wuz during slavery 'cause its been a long time ago but we had cotton and corn fields and de hands plowed hard, picked cotton grabbled penders, gathered peas and done all the other hard work to be done on de plantations. I wuz not big 'nuff to do all of dem things but I seed plenty of it done."

Henry Gibbs, Mississippi

"After Mars David bought him he was a Cottrell. My pap was an all round nigger. Plow hand and a cobbler. De man what raised my pap give him to his daughter, when he was sold to the speculator to be brought out to dis country, the daughter come into de kitchen looking so sad."

"Mars Cooper was a horse raiser, and dis young nigger Henry rode his fine horses on de race track. You know dey bet on dem races."

"You know my mammy was a field hand, but when de war come she had to help spin and weave, caise we couldn't get no cloth from Mobile. Mistess, you know befo de war, dey would go to Tibbee swamp and clear up de timbers and make a flat boat and ship cotton to Mobile, Dey would ship de whole crop, and dey would bring back cloth, sugar and coffee and everything dey need, besides what was raised on de place."

Cora Gillam, Arkansas

"Most of the slaves on our place worked in the field—cotton and corn and so on. Had a man for each thing. One would be over the horses, and so on. They raised everything we ate on the farm. Did n't have to buy anything. They would buy their meat, of course. But they did n't have to buy that often, because they raised hogs, and killed and cured their own meat. But in the summer, they would buy fresh meat if they wanted it."

"As I said, there was a man to take care of the horses; a man for the cattle stock—to see that they were in of evenings; one for the hogs. They fed the stock twice—morning and evening. They had hog pens and stables for the cows and horses. Nothing had to stand out in the open, especially in the winter time. We had field hands. All the stock men worked in the field also— so many hours. They had a bell for them to go to work in the morning, a bell for them to get up by, and another one for noon, and another in the evening when they would knock off for dark."

"They had a woman to nurse the children while the mothers were in the field. If the mothers were nursing the baby, they allowed them to come back to the nursery every hour to nurse them. The woman who took care of them was an old woman who was too old to go into the field. She was 'Aunt Kizzie.' I don't know what her real name was. She was a tall brownskin woman. She had children, too, —grand children. But she would treat them all alike. You could n't say she made any difference."

Mattie Gilmore, Texas

"When dey's hoein' cotton or corn, everybody has to keep up with de driver, not hurry so fast, but workin' steady. Some de women what had suckin' babies left dem in de shade while dey worked, and one time a big, bald eagle flew down by one dem babies and picked it up and flew away with it. De mama couldn't git it and we never heared of dat baby 'gain."

Andrew Goodman, Texas

"Marse Bob didn't put his little niggers in the fields till they's big 'nough to work, and the mammies was give time off from the fields to come back to the nursin' home to suck the babies. He didn't never put the niggers out in bad weather. He give us something to do, in out of the weather, like shellin' corn and the women could spin and knit. They made us plenty of good clothes. In summer we wore long shirts, split up the sides, made out of lowerings—that's same as cotton sacks was made out of. In winter we had good jeans and knitted sweaters and knitted socks."

Austin Grant, Texas

"We got up early, you betcha. You would be out there by time you could see and you quit when it was dark. They tasked us. They would give us 200 or 300 pounds of cotton to bring in and you would git it, and if you didn' git it, you better, or you would git it tomorrow, or your back would git it. Or you'd git it from someone else, maybe steal it from their sacks."

"The overseer woke us up. Sometimes he had a kin' of horn to blow, and when you heered that horn, you'd better git up. He would give you a good whippin' iffen he had to come and wake you up. He was the meanest one on the place, worse'n the boss man."

Sarah Gray, Georgia

Sarah's master was Mr. Jim Nesbit, who was the owner of a small plantation in Gwinnett County. The exact number of slaves on the plantation were not known, but there were enough to carry on the work of plowing, hoeing and chopping the cotton and other crops. Women as well as men were expected to turn out the required amount of work, whether it was picking cotton, cutting logs, splitting rails for fences or working in the house.

Alice Green, Georgia

"Mammy said dat atter de slaves had done got through wid deir day's work and finished eatin' supper, dey all had to git busy workin' wid cotton. Some carded bats, some spinned and some weaved cloth. I knows you is done seen dis here checkidy cotton homespun—dat's what dey weaved for our dresses. Dem dresses was made tight and long, and dey made 'em right on de body so as not to waste none of de cloth. All slaves had was homespun clothes and old heavy brogan shoes."

"De overseer, he got de Niggers up 'fore day and dey had done at deir breakfast, 'tended to de stock, and was in de field by sunup and he wuked 'em 'til sundown. De mens didn't do no wuk atter dey got through tendin' to de stock at night, but Mammy and lots of de other 'omans sot up and spun and wove 'til 'leven or twelve o'clock lots of nights."

Isaiah Green, Georgia

The Willis plantation was very large and required many workers. There were 75 plow hands alone, excluding those who were required to do the hoeing. Women as well as men worked in the fields. Isaiah Green declares that his mother could plow as well as any man. He also says that his work was very easy in the spring. He dropped peas into the soft earth between the corn-stalks, and planted them with his heel. Cotton, wheat, corn, and all kinds of vegetables made up the crops. A special group of women did the carding and spinning, and made the cloth on two looms. All garments were made from this homespun cloth. Dyes from roots and berries were used to produce the various colors. Red elm berries and a certain tree bark made one kind of dye.

"All de slaves had to work—my mother was a plow han'. All de aged men an' women had to tend to de hogs an' de cows an' do de weavin' an' de sewin'. Sometimes ol' marster would let us have a frolic an' we could danse all night if we wanted to as long as we wuz ready to go to de fiel' when de overseer blowed de bugle 'fo dey nex' mornin'. De fiel' han's had to git up early enuff to fix dey breakfas' befo' dey went to de fiel'. We chillun took dinner to 'em at twelve o'clock. We used baskets to take de dinner in, an' large pails to take de milk in. Dey had to fix supper for dey selves when dey lef' de fiel' at dark."

Besides acting as midwife, Green's grandmother Betsy Willis, was also a skilled seamstress and able to show the other women different points in the art of sewing.

Jake Green, Alabama

"Cose dey had to begin, an' all us got up 'fo' day. Twan't nothin' strange to be standin' in de fiel' by your plow waitin' for de sun to come up. Ev'body was early risers in dem days. Dey was pretty good to us, but ole Mr. Buck Brasefiel', what had a plantation 'jinin' us'n, was so mean to his'n dat twan't nothin' for 'em to run away. One nigger Rich Parker, runned off one time an' whilst he gone he seed a hoodoo man, so when he got back Mr. Brasefiel' tuck sick an' stayed sick two or three weeks. Some of de darkies tole him, 'Rich been to de hoodoo doctor.' So Mr. Brasefiel' got up outten dat bed an' come a-yellin' in

Jake Green. (Library of Congress)

de fiel', 'You thought you had ole Buck, but by God he rose agin'. Dem niggers was so skeered, dey squatted in de fiel' jes' lack partridges, an' some of
'em whispered, 'I wish to God he had a-died.'"

George Greene, Arkansas

"I learned how to work—work in the field. Wasn't nothing but field work. I
learned how to hoe first. But in Alabama I learned how to plow. I didn't want
to be no hoe man; I wanted to plow. When I went back to Mississippi, they
put me on the plow. I was just eight years old when I learned to plow."

John Gregory, Mississippi

John Gregory of Louisville about 89 years of age (1937) peaceable, industrious,
and reliable, was born in North Carolina and moved from there to Attala
County Mississippi eight miles east of Kosciusko. When about thirty years of
age he moved to Louisville, Winston County. He began working when very
small as water boy for the field hands. Next year he hoed on the same row with
his mother to learn, and the following year was given a row to himself. When
his master was called to fight in the War Between the States John went along
to wait on him, and when his master died John accompanied the body home.

Harriett Gresham, Florida

This was a very large plantation and there was always something for the score of slaves to do. There were the wide acres of cotton that must be planted, hoed and gathered by hand. A special batch of slave women did the spinning and weaving, while those who had been taught to sew, made most of the clothing worn by slaves at that time.

Other products grown here were rice, corn, sugarcane, fruits and vegetables. Much of the food grown on the plantation was reserved to feed the slaves. While they must work hard to complete their tasks in a given time, no one was allowed to go hungry or forced to work if the least ill.

Pauline Grice, Texas

"After breakfas' in de mornin' de niggers am gwine here, dere and everywhere, jus' like de big factory. Every one to he job, some a-whistlin', some a-singin'. Dey sings diff'rent songs and dis am one when deys gwine to work:

Old cotton, old corn, see you every morn,
Old cotton, old corn, see you since I's born.
Old cotton, old corn, hoe you till dawn,
Old cotton, old corn, what for you born?

Abner Griffin, Georgia

"I was born near de Gold Mines, 88 years ago," said Abner, "and I belonged to Felix Griffin. He didn' have no wife, so Miss Fannie took care of his han's." Abner nodded. "Dere was real gold in dem mines, Miss. Far back as 26 years ago I worked in water and mud up to my waist, drilled many a hole and shot it out with dynamite. Worked at mining 14 years, shake it and wash it and it shine dus' as pretty! Flux it and retort it and den dey ship it to North Carolina and make into bars."

Heard Griffin, Georgia

On this plantation was grown corn, cotton, wheat, etc. Long before day light, the master would come to the slave quarters and call each person one by one, "Get up, Get up." Very soon every one was up and fully dressed ready to begin the day's work. First, however, they drank one or two glasses of milk and a piece of corn bread, which was considered breakfast. Whether this amount of food was sufficient for a morning's meal didn't matter to their master. They simply had to make it last them until dinner. Smiling Mr. Griffin remarked, "It wouldn't be long before you would hear the 'geeing and hawing' coming from the fields, the squealing of pigs and the barking of dogs—all sounds mingling together."

Every one had a certain amount of work to complete before the day ended; and each person worked in feverish haste to get it done and avoid the whipping which they knew was in store for them, should they fail. During the day Mr. Griffin's mother worked in the field, hoeing and plowing. At night she, as well as other women, had to spin thread into cloth until bed time. Each woman had to complete four cuts or be punished the next morning. "If it began raining while we worked in the fields, the overseer would tell everyone to put up their horses and to to shelling corn in the cribs," remarked Mr. Griffin.

Minerva Grubbs, Mississippi

"I wuz put in de fields when I wuz big 'nough to hoe. I'se hoed wid de field plumb full ob slaves. Hit wuz wuk but us got some enjiment outen hit too. De slaves would tell tales an' ghos' stories an' all 'bout cungerin' an' hoo-doo-in'. Den dey would git to singin', prayin' an' a shoutin'. When de overseers hear 'em, he alwas' go make 'em be quiet lak. Dat wuz de onliest time de slaves could worship lak dey wanted to, 'caus us didnt hab no church. Us went to de white folks' church, an' sit on back seats, but didn't jine in de worship. You see, de white folks dont git in de spirit, dey don't shout, pray, hum, and sing all through de services lak us do. Dey dont believe in a heap o' things us niggers knows 'bout. Dey tells us dey aint no ghos', but us knows bettern dat."

July Ann Halfen, Mississippi

"My mammy had to spin, card an' weave cloth ebery rainy day. We black folks had to wear lowells an' dat stuff wud neber wear out. I wore shirt tail aprons till afte' de surrender an' neber had any shoes till I wus in my teens."

Molly Harrell, Texas

"Dey use to have de little whip dey use on de women. Course de field hands got it worse, but den, dey was men. Mr. Swansen was good and he was mean. He was nice one day and mean as Hades de next. You never knowed what he gwine to do. But he never punish nobody 'cept dey done somethin'. My father was a field hand, and Mr. Swanson work de fire out dem. Work, work—dat all dey know from time dey git up in de mornin' till dey went to bed at night. But he wasn't hard on dem like some masters was. If dey sick, dey didn't habe to work and he give dem de med'cine hisself. If he cotch dem tryin' play off sick, den he lay into dem, or if he cotch dem leafin'. Course, I don't blame him for dat, 'cause dere ain't anythin' lazier dan a lazy nigger. Will am 'bout de laziest one in de bunch. You ain't never find a lazier nigger dan Will."

Henderson Harris, Georgia

The first work that Henderson remembers doing was "totin peaches to the pigs" and "drapin' peas."

Orris Harris, Mississippi

"My pappy, Warren Bonner, wus Marse Hughey kerrage driver, en w'en he wud start to church wid de Mistress en de giruls, Marse Hughey wud tell him not ter low de horses to run way wid de kerrage en not ter low enything to hap'en to dem. He allus rode horse back."

"He hed no overseer—he seed ter day his slaves wurk. He made de slaves git up ebery mornin' by ringin' dat big bell. Dat bell wus hangin' on a scafful in de side yard, an' he rung it 'fore day to git de han' off ter wurk and he rung it ergain ter call dem ter dinner. When it rained he made de men go in de crib an' shuck corn or go in de barn an' clean up, an' sum time afte' de rain he made dem wurk in de garden."

Virginia Harris, Mississippi

"I didn't work none till after the War. My mother and father both were field hands. They didn't get no money for none of that, but they raised chickens and sold them. What money they made off of that, they was allowed to keep and spend as they pleased. We was fed on pickled pork, corn bread and lasses. In the summer time we got beans, peas, and vegetables out of the big field garden, that was raised for everybody. Every Sunday we got white bread. We sure loved that. If the men could catch possums, coon or fish, we would cook them at night at our own house. We didn't cook our everyday meals at home. That was done in the cook shed. Breakfast and dinner was sent to the fields in wagons. Supper, everybody ate at the cook shed."

"Every morning before day, the plantation bell was rung for to get up. All hands must be in the field when daylight came. They worked till dark. If there was corn to be shucked, or cotton to be put up, off the gin platform, the work went on at night. They didn't punish much on that place. Master didn't allow no beating or knocking. They got whipped if they wouldn't do what they was told to do, or if they runned off. They wasn't put in jail. Didn't have none of them things. Just whipped and let go. Thats all."

G. H. Hawkins, Arkansas

"I've told you the slaves were tasked to the limit. The hours of the slave hands—if it was summer time—he must be in the field when the sun rose. And he must come home and eat his dinner and get back in the field and stay till the sun went down. In the winter time he must be out there by the time it was light enough to see the work and stay out till it was just too dark to see the work with just enough time out to stop and eat his dinner. This was just after slavery that I remember. But the hours were the same then. The average on cotton picking was two hundred pounds a day. Pulling fodder was a hundred bundles. Gathering corn and such as that was all they could do."

Tom Hawkins, Georgia

"Dar was 'bout four or five hunderd acres in our plantation. Miss Annie kept 'bout a hunderd slaves. She was all time sellin' 'em for big prices atter she done trained 'em for to he cooks, housegals, houseboys, carriage drivers, and good wash 'omans. She wukked 75 slaves in her fields. Her Niggers was waked by four o'clock and had to be in de field by sunup. Dey come in 'bout dark. Atter supper, de mens made up shoes, horse collars, and anything else lak dat what was needed; de 'omans spun thread and wove cloth."

"Old Miss give dem dat wanted one a cotton patch and she didn't make her slaves wuk in her fields atter de dinner bell rung on Saddays."

Wash Hayes, Mississippi

"My pappy done fiel' wuk in season but de mos' ob de time he wuz de shoe maker fer all de slaves on Marse's three plantations. Dat kept him busy mos' ob de time. De shoes wuz made from rough cow hide wid brass on put on de toes to keep 'em from wearin' out so soon. When de slaves wuz give a pair ob dem shoes he knowed dey sho' had to las' a long time. Now de clothes dey wore wuz lak de shoes plain an' course. Dey had to wear mos' anything dey could git deir han's on. I'se heard my pa say dat dey had to wash 'en on Saturday nights an' dry 'em by de fire. Dey wore 'bout de same things on Sundays jes' washed up a bit. Deir wasn't no whar to go much back in dem days on Sundays only to Church 'bout one Sunday out ob each month. De slaves mos' an' generally wuz tired out an lay 'round an' rested."

Bill Heard, Georgia

"Folks wuked mighty hard dem days, 'specially durin' plantin' and harvest time, 'til atter de corn was gathered and fotched out of de fields in dem old two-wheel carts dat was used to haul up all de craps."

Emmaline Heard, Georgia

Slaves on the Harper plantation arose when the horn was sounded at four o'clock and hurried to the fields, although they would sometimes have to wait for daylight to dawn to see how to work. The overseer rode over the plantation watching the slaves at work and keeping account of the amount of work performed by each. Any who failed to complete their quota at the close of the day were punished.

Robert Heard, Georgia

"Us went to work 'bout a half hour by sun an' quit at dusty dark. De mens done fiel' wuk en' de wimmins mostly hopped Mistis 'bout de house. Dey washed, milked, made candles, an' worked in de spinnin' room. Us didn't have to buy nothin' caze dey wuz evathing us needed on the plantation."

Benjamin Henderson, Georgia

The Henderson plantation comprised 250 acres and Mr. Henderson owned only five slaves to carry the necessary work. Besides Benjamin's immediate family there was one other man slave, named Aaron. Cotton, cattle, and vegetables were the chief products of the farm. The work was divided as follows: Benjamin's job was to keep the yards clean and bring up the calves at night; his older sister and brother, together with Aaron, did the field work; and his mother worked in the house as general servant.

The master of the Henderson Plantation as well as other plantation owners, allowed their slavas to work individual cotton patches; When the cotton was picked he paid them their price for the amount they had raised. Slaves often earned money, too, by splitting rails at night and selling them to different plantation owners.

Phoebe Henderson, Texas

"After dey brought us to Texas in 1859 I worked in the field many a day, plowin' and hosin', but the children didn't do much work 'cept carry water. When dey git tired, dey'd say dey was sick and the overseer let 'em lie down in de shade.

Phoebe Henderson. (Library of Congress)

He was a good and kindly man and when we do wrong and go tell him he forgave us and he didn't whip the boys 'cause he was afraid they'd run away."

Jefferson Franklin Henry, Georgia

"That old plantation was a large place all right enough; I 'spects thar was 'bout four or five hunderd acres in it. Marse Robert warn't no big slave holder and he didn't have so awful many slaves. His foreman had 'em out in the fields by daylight and wuked 'em 'til dark. The woman had a certain stint of thread to spin and cloth to weave 'fore they could go to bed at night. The menfolks had to shuck corn, mend horse-collars, make baskets, and all sich jobs as that at night, and they had to help the women with the washin' sometimes. Most of that kind of thing was done on days when the weather was too hot for 'em to work in the fields."

Robert Henry, Georgia

"Yes, in spite of the hard work required, life was very pleasant on the plantations. The field hands were at work at sunup and were not allowed to quit until dark."

Tom Holland, Texas

"I chopped cotton and plowed and split rails, then was a horse rider. In them days I could ride the wildest horse what ever made tracks in Texas, but I's never valued very high 'cause I had a glass eye. I don't 'member how I done got it, but there it am. I'd make a dollar or fifty cents to ride wild horses in slavery time and massa let me keep it. I buyed tobacco and candy and if massa cotch me with tobacco I'd git a whippin', but I allus slipped and bought chewin' tobacco."

"Massa Frank had cotton and corn and everything to live on, 'bout three hundred acres, and overseed it himself, and seven growed slaves and five little slaves. He allus waked us real early to be in the field when daylight come and worked us till slap dark, but let us have a hour and a half at noon to eat and rest up. Sometimes when slaves got stubborn he'd whip them and make good Negroes out of them, 'cause he was real good to them."

Bill Homer, Texas

"Some work was hard and some easy, but massa don' 'lieve in overworkin' his slaves. Sat'day afternoon and Sunday, dere was no work. Some whippin' done, but mos' reasonable. If de nigger stubborn, deys whips 'nough for to change his mind. If de nigger runs off, dat calls de good whippin's. If any of de cullud folks has de misery, dey lets him res' in bed and if de misery bad de massa call de doctor."

Laura Hood, Georgia

Laura relates that the darkies worked all the time except Sunday. On Sunday they could do as they pleased so long as they went to church. All the Bank's darkies attended service in the "cooler" [basement] of the First Baptist Church and had a colored preacher.

Rebecca Hooks, Florida

They were treated kindly and cruelly by turns, according to the whims of a master and mistress who were none too stable in their dispositions. There was no "driver" or overseer on this plantation, as "Old Tom was devil enough himself when he wanted to be," observes Rebecca. While she never felt the full force of his cruelties, she often felt sorry for the other slaves who were given a task too heavy to be completed in the given time; this deliberately, so that the master might have some excuse to vent his pentup feelings. Punishment was always in the form of a severe whipping or revocation of a slave's privilege, such as visiting other plantations etc.

The Lowes were not wealthy and it was necessary for them to raise and manufacture as many things on the plantation as possible. Slaves toiled from early morning until night in the corn, cotton, sugar cane and tobacco fields. Others tended the large herds of cattle from which milk, butter, meat and leather was produced. The leather was tanned and made into crude shoes for the slaves for the short winter months. No one wore shoes except during cold weather and on Sundays. Fruit orchards and vegetables were also grown, but not given as much attention as the cotton and corn, as these were the main money crops.

Josephine Howard, Texas

"Marse Tim done git a big farm up by Marshall but only live a year dere and his boys run de place. Dey jes' like dey papa, work us and work us. Lawd have mercy, I hear dat call in de mornin' like it jes' jesterday, 'All right, everybody out, and you better git out iffen you don't want to feel dat bullwhip 'cross you back.'"

Carrie Hudson, Georgia

"Marse Elbert's overseer was a Mr. Alderman. He got de slaves up early in de mornin' and it was black night 'fore he fetched 'em in. Marse Elbert didn't 'low nobody to lay hands on his Niggers but his own self. If any whuppin' had to be done, he done it."

Charles Hudson, Georgia

"My grandma Patsy, Pappy's Ma, knocked 'round lookin' atter de sheep and hogs, close to de house, 'cause she was too old for field wuk. Ma's Mammy was my grandma Rose. Her job was drivin' de oxcart to haul in wood from de new grounds and to take wheat and corn to mill and fetch back good old home-made flour and meal. I never did hear nothin' 'bout my grandpas. Ma done de cookin' for de white folks."

"Evvybody was up early so dat by sunrise dey was out in de fields, jus' a whoopin' and hollsrin'. At sundown dey stopped and come back to de cabins. In wheat harvestin' time dey wukked so hard dey jus' fell out f'um gittin' overhet. Other times dey jus' wukked 'long steady lak."

"When Marse David changed me f'um calf shepherd to cowboy, he sent three or four of us boys to drive de cows to a good place to graze 'cause de male beast was so mean and bad 'bout gittin' atter chillun, he thought if he sont enough of us dere wouldn't be no trouble. Den days, ders warn't no fence law, and calves was jus' turned loose in de pastur to graze. De fust time I went by myself to drive de cows off to graze and come back wid 'em, Aunt Vinnie 'ported a bunch of de cows was missin', 'bout 20 of em, when she dons de milkin' dat night, and I had to go back huntin' den cows. De moon come out, bright and clear, but I couldn't see dem cows nowhar—didn't even hear de bell cow. Atter while I was standin' in de may-berry field a-lookin' crost Dry Fork Crick and dere was dem cows. De bell was pulled so clost on de bell cow's neck whar she was caught in de bushes, dat it couldn't ring. I looked at den cows—den I looked at de crick whar I could see snakes as thick as de fingers on your hand, but I knowed I had to git dem cows back home, so I jus' lit out and loped 'cross dat crick so fast dem snakes never had no chanct to bite me. Dat was de wust racket I ever got in."

Bryant Huff, Georgia

All the slaves worked from sunrise to sunset; the majority did field work. Women, as well as men, shared farm work. Small boys not old enough to be sent to the field, minded horses, drove cows to and from the pasture, and did chores around the "big house." A few woman prepared meals and supervised a group of younger girls who did general work in the big house. Sunday was the only day of rest and usually all the adults attended church.

Easter Huff, Georgia

"Mammy was a plow hand, but us chillun didn't do nothin' much 'cept eat and play and sleep in de grass 'til she got in from de fiel' evvy night."

Frank Hughes, Mississippi

"My mother and her mother worked in de field in de day time, and dere was a task of spinning at night. There were so many hanks of thread to be reeled befo dey went to bed. No, mam dey didn't have Saturdays off. Dey washed at night. She was de mother of nine chillern, I bein the oldest of all. I'm about the onliest one livin.'"

"Dere was an old Mammy too old to work in de field who took care of des chillern while my mammy worked. I members old lady Mandy. She was good to us. All thru de day dem chaps was fed. The house boy would pack us milk to de quarter."

Lizzie Hughes, Texas

"Dr. Newton Fall had a big place at Chireno and a hundred slaves. They lived in li'l houses round the edge of the field. We had everything we needed."

"When master was gone he had a overseer, but tell him not to whip. He didn't 'lieve in rushin' his niggers. All the white folks at Chireno was good to they niggers. On Saturday night master give all the men a jug of syrup and a sack of flour and a ham or middlin' and the smokehouse was allus full of beef and pork. We had a good time on that place and the niggers was happy. I 'member the men go out in the mornin', singin':

I went to the barn with a shinin', bright moon,
I went to the wood a-buntin' a coon.
The coon spied me from a sugar maple tree,
Down went my gun and up the tree went me.
Nigger and coon come tumblin' down,
Give the hide to master to take off to town,
That coon was full of good old fat,
And master brung me a new beaver hat.

"Pert of 'nother song go like this:

Master say; you breath smell of brandy,
Nigger say, no, I's lick 'lasses candy.

"When old master come to the lot and hear the men singin' like that, he say, 'Them boys is lively this mornin'. I's gwine git a big day's plowin' done.' They did, too, 'cause them big Missouri mules sho' tore up that red land. Sometime they sing:

This sin't Christmas mornin', just a long summer day,
Hurry up, yellow boy and don't run 'way,
Grass in the cotton and weeds in the corn,
Get in the field, 'cause it soon be morn.

Matthew Hume, Indiana

His father, Luke Hume, lived in Trimble County Kentucky and was allowed to raise for himself one acre of tobacco, one acre of corn, garden stuff, chickens and have the milk and butter from one cow. He was advised to save his money by the overseer, but always drank it up. On this plantation all the slaves were free from Saturday noon until Monday morning and on Christmas and the Fourth of July. A majority of them would go to Bedford or Milton and drink, gamble and fight. On the neighboring farm the slaves were treated cruelly. Mr. Hume had a brother-in-law, Steve Lewis, sho carried marks on his back. For years sho had a sore that would not heal where his master had struck him with a blacksnake whip.

When Mr. Hume was a small boy he was placed in the fields to hoe, He also wanted a new implement. He was so small he was unable to keep near enough to the men and boys to hear what they were talking about, he remembered bringing up the rear one day, when he saw a large rock he carefully covered it with dirt, then came down hard on it breaking his hoe. He missed a whipping and received a new tool to replace the old one, after this he could keep near enough to hear what the other workers were talking about.

Another of his duties had to go for the cattle, he was to walk around the road about a mile, but was permitted to come back through the fields about a quarter of a mile. One afternoon his mistress told him to bring a load of wood when he came in. In the summer it was the custom to have the children carry the wood from the fields. When he came up he saw his Mistress was angry this peeved him, so that he stalked into the hall and slammed his wood into the box. About this time his Mistress shoved him into a small closet and locked the door. He made such a howl that he brought his mother and father to the rescue and was soon released from his prison.

As soon as the children were old enough they were placed in the fields to prepare the ground for setting tobacco plants. This was a very complicated procedure. The ground was made into hills, each requiring about four feet of soil. The child had to get all the clods broken fine. Then place his foot in the center and leave his track. The plants were to be set out in the center and woe to the youngster who had failed to pulverize his hill. After one plowing the tobacco was hand tended. It was long green and divided into two grades. It was pressed by being placed in large hogsheads and weighted down. One one occasion they were told their tobacco was so eaten up that the worms were sitting on the fence waiting for the leaves to grow but nevertheless in some manner his master hid the defects and received the best price paid in the community.

Emma Hurley, Georgia

The slaves did plenty of hard work done on the plantation. The women labored all day in the fields and then spun at night. Each one was given the task of spinning six broaches a week. On Saturday "a white lady" reeled off the spinning and if one of the women had failed in her task she was severely beaten. The men worked all day and until ten o'clock at night shucking corn or doing other chores by lamp light.

Mose Hursey, Texas

"All week the niggers worked plantin' and hoein' and carin' for the livestock. They raised cotton and corn and veg'tables, and mules and horses and hawgs and sheep."

Charley Hurt, Texas

"Dere am system on dat plantation. Everybody do he own work, sich as field hands, stock hands, de blacksmith and de shoemaker and de weavers and clothes makers. I'm all 'round worker and goes after de mail, jus' runnin' 'round de place."

Carter Ingram, Texas

"Massa Rogers had a 300 acre plantation and 200 in cultivation and he had a overseer and Steve O'Neal was the nigger driver. The horn to git up blowed 'bout four o'clock and if we didn't fell out right now, the overseer was in after us. He tied us up every which way and whip us, and at night he walk the quarters to keep us from runnin' 'round. On Sunday mornin' the overseer come 'round to each nigger cabin with a big sack of shorts and give us 'nough to make bread for one day."

Wash Ingram, Texas

"Master Ingram had a big plantation down near Carthage and lots of niggers. He also buyed land, cleared it and sol' it. I plowed with oxen. We had a overseer and sev'ral taskmasters. Dey whip de niggers for not workin' right, or for runnin' 'way or pilferin' roun' master's house. We woke up at four o'clock and worked from sunup to sundown. Dey give us an hour for dinner. Dem dat work roun' de house et at tables with plates. Dem dat work in de field was drove in from work and fed jus' like hosses at a big, long wooden trough. Dey had to eat with a wooden sppon. De trough and de food was clean and always plenty of it, and we stood up to eat. We want to bed soon after supper durin' de week for dat's 'bout all we feel like doin' after workin' twelve hours. We slep' in wooden beds what had corded rope mattresses."

Squire Irvin, Mississippi

"The only work I was allowed to do was to keep the calves off, while my mother milked. I didn't get no money for doing it. We didn't know nothing about getting no pay for anything."

"At daylight every morning the grown folks was woke up by a horn. They worked until dark. The rule was sun to sun. All the slaves what master had wanted to be men and women. They went right on and did their work as they should. The only punishment what they got was to make them work later till they finished the task if they seed any of them was slacking on the job."

Amanda Jackson, Georgia

"I wuz born in Glasscock county 'bout twelve miles fum Davisboro, Ga. My marster's name wuz Lowry Calboun—he did'nt have no chillun—jes' him an' his wife an' her mother. He wus a rich man ah' he had a big plantation an' 'bout fifty slaves or more—I 'members de big quarters in de back o' his house, where me an' de res' o' de slaves lived, an how we uster git up an' do 'roun'!"

"Besides me I had two sisters an' one brother—Iwuz de younges' child."

"All of de slaves on de lantation worked in de fiel'—even de cook—dat is 'till time fer her to cook de meals. On dis plantation dey raised practically everything—corn, cotton, wheat, an' rye, an' a heap o' live stock. Dey wuz runnin' 'bout twenty-five or thirty plows all de time. Dere wuz one overseer."

"Every mornin' de slaves had to git up an' by de time it wuz light enuff to see dey had to be in de fiel' workin'. When asked how they were awakened Mrs. Jackson replied: 'Dey knowed how to git you up alright—de overseer had a horn dat he blowed an' dem dat did'nt wake up when de horn wuz blowed wuz called by some of de others in de quarters." Continuing, she said, "Dey wuz in de fiel' fore de sun rose an' dere'till after it went down—fum sun to sun."

"De fiel' han's had one hour fer dinner—dem dat had families done dere own cookin' an' dere wuz a special cook fer de single ones. De women whut had families would git up soon in de mornin's 'fore time to go to de fiel' an' put de meat on to boil an' den dey would come in at dinner to come in at dinner time an' put de vegetables in de pot to cook an' when dey come home in de evenin' dey would cook some corn bread in de ashes at de fireplace."

"All dat I could do den wuz sweep de yards, water de cows an' go chickens an' den go to de pasture to git de cows an' de calves—we had two pastures—one fer de calves an' one fer de cows. I had to git de cows so de womens could milk 'em."

"All of de hard work on de plantation wuz done in de summer-time. In rainy weather an' other bad weather all dat dey had to do wuz to shell corn an' to help make cloth. As a rule ol' marster wuz pretty good to his slaves but sometimes some of 'em got whupped kinda bad fer not workin' an' stuff like dat—I seen 'im cut womens on dey shoulders wid a long whip 'till it looked like he wuz gonna cut de skin off'n 'im."

Richard Jackson, Texas

"I 'members mammy allus sayin' the darkies had to pray out in the woods, 'cause they ain't 'lowed to maks no fuss round the house. She say they was fed and clothed well 'nough, but the overseer worked the lights out of the darkies. I wasn't big 'nough to do field work, but 'member goin' to the field to take mammy's pipe to her. They wasn't no matches in them days, and I allus took fire from the house and sot a stump afire in the field, so mammy could light her pipe."

John James, Texas

"After breakfast I'd see a crew go here and a crew go dere. Some of 'em spin and weave and make clothes, and some tann de leather or do de blacksmith

John James. (Library of Congress)

work, and mos' of 'em go out in de field to work. Dey work till dark and den come home and work round de quarters."

Andrew Jackson Jarnagin, Mississippi

"My father was a first-class log hewer and helped hew logs to lay the Mobile and Ohio Railroad. In 1856 the railroad notified the planters to spare what slaves they could, so they could get the railroad to Macon built by the fourth of July. They got it finished and celebrated with a big picnic."

Lewis Jefferson, Mississippi

"Some times when de fiel' wurk wus pushin' he had dem eat in de kitchen an' some times he low'd dem to cook an' eat in deir cabins. My mammy wus named Binky an' my pappy wus named Seab. Dey bofe wurk in de fiel' but my pappy had to wurk at de gin an' den some times he had to drive de wagon to town."

"I had to wait on de table when dey had company an' I heard dem sayin' de big War wus comin' but I didn't kno' whut dat meant."

Thomas Johns, Texas

"We done a good day's work, but didn' have to work after night 'less it was necessary. We was allowed to stop at 12 o'clock and have time for rest 'fore goin' back to work. Other slave owners roun' our place wasn't as good to dere slaves, would work 'em hard and half starve 'em. And some marsters or overseers would whip dere niggers pretty hard, sometimes whip 'em to death. Marster Johns didn' have no overseer. He seed to the work and my father was foreman. For awhile after old Marster died, in 1862 or 1863, I forget which now, we had a overseer, John Sewell. He was mean. He whipped the chillen and my mother told Miss Lucy, old marster's oldest girl."

Benjamin Johnson, Georgia

"De women would be plowin' an' hoein' grain an' de spanish needles an' cockie burrs would be stickin' to dere dresses fum dere knees to dere feet. Further down dere would be a man diggin' a ditch. Every now an' den white folks would walk over to de ditch an' see if it wus de same width all de way."

"We worked in de fiel' every day an' way in de night we shucked an' shelled corn. De cook done all de cookin'. When all of de marster's 75 slaves wus in de fiel' dey had two cooks to feed 'em. At twelve o'clock de cooks would blow a horn at de stump in de yard back o' de cook house. Even de hosses an' de mules knowed dat horn an' dey would'nt go a step further. You had to take de mule out of de harness an' take 'im to de spring am' water 'in an' den take 'im to de house where a colored man up dere named Sam Johnson had all de feed ready fer de hosses. When you git dere all de hosses go to dere own stalls where dere wus ten ears o' corn an' one bundle o' fodder fer each hoss. While dem hosses is eatin' you better be out dare eatin' yo' own. Sarah an' Annie, de cooks had a big wooden tray wid de greens an' de meat all cut up on it an' you pass by wid yo' tin pan an' dey put yo' meat all out up on it along wid de greens an' den you could eat anywhere you wanted to—on de stump or in de big road if you wanted to. Sometimes some of 'ems meat would give out or dere bread would give out an' den day would say: 'I'll give you a piece of my bread for some or yo' meat or I'll give you some of my meat for some of yo' bread.' Some of 'em would have a big ol' ash cake an' some of 'em would have jes' plain corn bread. Dere wus usually a big skillet o' potatoes at de cook house an' when you eat an' drink yo water den you is ready to go back to work. Dey wus goin' to let you lay down in de shade fer 'bout a hour but you would make de time up by workin' till dark. Some of 'em worked so 'till dey back wus gone. Dey could'nt even stand up straight."

Henry Johnson, New York

After he was 21 years old Mr. Johnson was put to work, around the plantation, cutting wheat with a scythe—that is, cutting it from places where the machines (wheat reapers) could not go. He drove horses, hauling wood, chopped down trees and cut them into cord wood, cultivated the garden and did all other types of farm work.

Spence Johnson, Texas

"Us run de hay press to bale cotton on de plantation and took cotton by ox wagons to Shreveport. Seven or eight wagons in a train, with three or four yoke of steers to each wagon. Us made 'lasses and cloth and shoes and lots of things. Old Marse Riley had a nigger who could make shoes and if he had to go to court in Carthage, he'd leave nigger make shoes for him."

Estella Jones, Geogia

"Slaves on our place had a hard time. Dey had to work night and day. Marster had stobs [staves] all over de field to put lights on so dey could see how to work atter dark. De mens, more so dan de womens, had to work every night 'til twelve o'clock. But dey uld feed 'em good. Dey had dey supper sent out in de field to 'em 'bout nine o'clock by a cripple boy who didn't do nothin' but tote water and do things lak dat."

"Whenever anybody wuz late gittin' his cotton picked out, he always give a moonlight cotton pickin' party. Dese parties wuz always give on moonshiny nights and wuz liked by everybody. Atter while dey give everybody somethin' good to eat, and at de end of de party, de pusson who had picked de most cotton got a prize. Sometimes dey had pea shellin's 'stead of corn huskin's, but de parties and frolics wuz all pretty much alike."

"At quiltin' bees, four folks wuz put at every quilt, one at every corner. Dese quilts had been pieced up by old slaves who warn't able to work in de field. Quiltin's always tuk place durin' de winter when dere warn't much to do. A prize wuz always give to de four which finished dere quilt fust. 'Freshments went 'long wid dis too."

Hannah Jones, Alabama

Aunt Hannah Jones lives with her daughter in a small four room house on Tuscaloosa Street, Greensboro. "Lawdy," she said, "It's been so long dat I's mos' forgot 'bout dem slavery days, but I was bawn, in Bunker Hill, Amelia County, Virginny. My pappy was named Simon Johnson an' my mammy was Rhoda Johnson. My Marster was Alfred Wood an' my mistis was Miss Tabby Wood. When Massa died, de 'state was 'vided an' I fell to de son dat was too sick to take care of de place an' de slaves. Soon I was tuk to Richmond an' sold to Jedge Moore of Alabammy for twelve hundred dollars. Dat was de fust time I ever seed a slave sold. I was sixteen years old. When Jedge Moore's plantation was sold de niggers went wid de place an' it was bought by Marse Isaiah an' Marse Bill Smarr. It was called de Gillum Place and dat is east of Prairieville. I was house girl an' hope wid de sewin' an' de spinnin'."

"Our oberseer was Harvey Williamson an' he went 'roun' at nine o'clock to see iffen us niggers was in baid. Sometimes atter he done been 'roun', us'd git up an' have some fun. At de break of day all de slaves would git up an' go to work. Dose goin' way down in de fiel's would have to git up even befo' it was light so's to be dar when de dawn broke to commence de day's work. Den dey would come back at twelve o'clock for dinner an' res' awhile, den go back an' work till sun down."

Lizzie Jones, Texas

"The overseer was named Wade and he woke the han's up at four in the mornin' and kep' them in the field from then till the sun set. Mos' of de women worked in de fields like de men. They'd wash clothes at night and dry them by the fire. The overseer kep' a long coach whip with him and if they didn' work good, he'd thrash them good. Sometime he's pretty hard, on them and strip 'em off and whip 'em till they think he was gonna kill 'em. No nigger ever run off as I 'member."

Abe Kelley, Mississippi

"They raised cotton on the place, then Old Miss had it spun and weaved. She hired a lady to come weave it and she was on the place sometimes two weeks."

"We had to git up at 3 A.M. in the morning, then we carried our breakfast to the field. It was a all right breakfast though—fried meat and bread. When we was working far from the house, we carried our dinner too, but if we was close by, they blowed the horn."

"We didn't raise no chickens. What use did niggers have for chickens? Old Miss raised them; she had about fifteen head o' turkeys and twenty head o' geese."

"Overseers was pretty tight, —so tight that Old Master would tell them to stop, that they was being too tight. Some of the niggers would run away off in the woods. Old Master had a woman, Nancy, that stayed in the woods three years."

Jennie Kendricks, Georgia

In Mr. Moores family were his mother, his wife, and six children (four boys and two girls). This family lived very comfortably in a two storied weatherboard house. With the exception of our grandmother who cooked for the owner's family and slaves, and assisted her mistress with housework all the slaves worked in the fields where they cultivated cotton and the corn, as well as the other produce grown there. Every morning at sunrise they had to get up and go to the fields where they worked until it was too dark to see. At noon each day they were permitted to come to the kitchen, located just a short distance in the rear of the master's house, were they were served dinner. During the course of the day's work the women shared all the men's work except plowing. All of them picked cotton when it was time to gather the crops. Some nights they were required to spin and to help Mrs. Moore, who did all of the weaving. They used to do their own personal work, at night also. Jennie Kendricks says she remembers how her mother and the older girls would go to the spring at night where they washed their clothes and then left them to dry on the surrounding bushes.

Sam Kilgore, Texas

"Do work stock am eighty head of mules and fifty head of hosses and fifteen yoke of oxen. It took plenty feed for all dem and massa have de big field of corn, far as we could see. De plantation am run on system and everything clean and in order, not like lots of plantations with tools scattered 'round and dirt piles here and there. Do chief overseer am white and de second overseers am black. Stien was nigger overseer in de shoemakin' and harness, and Aunty Darkins am overseer of de spinnin' and weavin'."

Emmaline Kilpatrick, Georgia

"Well," she said, "Fore dis hyar railroad wuz made, dey hauled de cotton ter de Pint [She meant Union Point] en sold it dar. De Pint's des' 'bout twelve miles fum hyar. Fo' dey had er railroad thu de Pint, Marse Billie used ter haul his cotton clear down ter Jools ter sell it. My mammy say dat long fo' de War he used ter wait twel all de cotton wuz picked in de fall, en den he would have it all loaded on his waggins. Not long fo' sundown he wud start de waggins off, wid yo' unker Anderson bossin' am, on de all night long ride towards Jools. 'Bout fo' in de mawnin' Marse Billie en yo' grammaw, Miss Margie, 'ud start off in de surrey, driving de bays, en fo' dem waggins git tar Jools Marse Billie done cotch up wid am. He drive er head en lead em on ter de cotton mill in Jools, whar he sell all his cotton. Den him en Miss Margie, dey go tar de mill sto' en buy white sugar en udder things dey doan raise on de plantation, en load 'em on de waggins en start back home."

Robert Kimbrough, Georgia

The old man remembers, and describes interestingly, a type of hand-fed, foot propelled, one-man cotton gin that was more or less common when he was a boy. This gin was pedaled on the same principle as a sewing machine, one man being able to gin about 100 pounds of lint cotton in a day, or a bale in about five days.

Charlie King, Georgia

[Charlie King] said that all the "Niggers" on "ole Master's place had to work, even chillun over 7 or 8 years of age."

The first work that Charlie can remembers during was "toting cawm" for his mother "to drap," and sweeping the yards up at the "big house." He also recalls that many times when he was in the yard at the "big house," "Ole Miss" would call him in and give him a buttered biscuit.

The Negroes on this plantation had to work from sun up till sun down, except Saturday and Sunday; those were free.

The master blew on a big conch shell every morning at 4 o'clock, and when the first long blast was heard the lights "'gin to twinkle in every 'Nigger' cabin." Charlie, chuckling, recalled that "ole Master" blowed that shell so it could-a-been heard for 5 miles. Some of the "Niggers" went to feed the mules and horses, some to milk the cows, some to cook the breakfast in the big house, some to chop the wood, while others were busy cleaning up the "big house."

Nicey Kinney, Georgia

"Marster was too old to go to de war, so he had to stay home and he sho seed dat us done our wuk raisin' somepin t'eat. He had us plant all our cleared ground, and I sho has done some hard wuk down in dem old bottom lands, plowin', hoein', pullin' corn and fodder, and I'se even out cordwood and split rails. Dem was hard times and evvybody had to wuk."

"Did you ever see folks shear sheep, Child? Well, it was a sight in dem days. Marster would tie a sheep on de scaffold, what he had done built for dat job, and den he would have me set on de sheep's head whilst he cut off de wool. He sont it to de factory to have it carded into bats and us chillun spun de thread at home and mammy and Mistess wove it into cloth for our winter clothes. Nobody warn't fixed up better on church days dan Marster's Niggers and he was sho proud of dat."

Larnce Kolt, Texas

"My big brother Eb he tete so many buckets of water te de hands in de field he were all de hair offen de top he head."

Julia Larken, Georgia

"'Fore Grandma Mary got too old to do all de cookin, Mammy wuked in de field. Mammy said she allus woke up early, and she could hear Marster when he started gittin' up. She would hurry and git out 'fore he had time to call 'em. Sometimes she cotch her hoss and rid to the field ahead of de others, 'cause Marster never laked for nobody to be late in de mornin'. One time he got atter one of his young slaves out in de field and told him he was a good mind to have him whupped. Dat night de young Nigger was tellin' a old slave 'bout it, and de old man jus' laughed and said: 'When Marster pesters me dat way I jus' rise up and cuss him out.' Dat young fellow 'cided he would try it out and de next time Marster got atter him dey had a rukus what I ain't never gwine to forgit. Us was all out in de yard et de big house, skeered to git a good breath when us heared Marster tell him to do somepin, 'cause us knowed what he was meanin' to do. He didn't go right ahead and mind Marster lak he had allus been used to doin'. Marster called to him again, and den dat fool Nigger cut loose and he evermore did cuss Marster out. Lordy, Chile, Marster jus' fairly tuk de hide off dat Nigger's back. When he tried to talk to dat old slave 'bout it de old man laughed and said: 'Shucks, I allus waits 'til I gits to de field to cuss Marster so he won't hear me.'"

Cinto Lewis, Texas

"I fast went to do field when I 'bout 15 year old, but they larned us to work when we was chaps, we would he'p our mammas in de rows. My mamma's name Maria Simmons and my papa, Lewis. They rared me up right."

George Lewis, Georgia

In answer to a query concerning the work requirements of the other slaves on this particular plantation Mr. Lewis replied "De sun would never ketch dem at de house. By de time it wus up dey had done got to de fiel'—not jes gwine. I've known men to have to wait till it wus bright enough to see how to plow without 'kivering' the plants up. Dey lef' so early in de morning dat breakfus' had to be sent to dem in de fiel'. De chillun wus de ones who carried de meals dere. Dis wus de first job dat I had. All de pails wus put on a long stick an' somebody hold to each end of de stick. If de fiel' hands wus too far away fum de house at dinner time it wus sent to [illegible text] same as de breakfus'."

All of the slaves on the plantation were awakened each morning by a bugle or a horn which was blown by the overseer. The same overseer gave the signal for dinner hour by blowing on the same horn. All were usually given one hour for dinner. None had to do any work after leaving the field unless it happened to be personal work. No work other than the caring for the stock was required on Sundays.

Abbie Lindsay, Arkansas

"My mother and father worked around the house and yard. Slaves in the field had to pick a certain amount of cotton. The man had to pick from two to three hundred pounds of cotton a day if he wasn't sick, and the woman had to pick about one hundred fifty. Of course some of them could pick more. They worked in a way of speaking from can till can't, from the time they could see until the time they couldn't. They do about the same thing now."

Westly Little, Mississippi

"I wuked 'bout Marse's place in de yard, garden an' lots an' when I wuz ole 'nuf I wuked in de fiel's. I plowed wid de slaves, hoed, an picked cotton. We laked cotton pickin' times. A bunch ob us in a big white fiel' ob cotton whar we could pick an' sing an' joke one another. We knowed plenty to eat wuz waitin' fer us an' a good nights sleep. Give a darkie dat an' he can be as happy as a coon."

Chana Littlejohn, North Carolina

"Marster would not let us work until we were thirteen years old. Den he put us to plowin' in soft lan', an' de men in rough lan'. Some of de women played off sick an' went home an' washed an' ironed an' got by wid it. De oberseer tried to make two of 'em go back to work. Dey flew at him an' whupped him. He told de marster when he come home, marster said, 'Did you 'low dem women to whup you?' 'Yes,' he replied, den marster tole him if women could whup him he didn't want him. But he let him stay on. His name wus Jack Rivers. He wus hired by marster. Marster Rivers did not have any slaves. Dere wus no jail on de plantation, case when er overseer whupped er nigger he did not need any jail."

Jacob Manson, North Carolina

"We wurked all day an some of de night an' a slave who made a week, even atter doin dat, wus lucky if he got off widout gettin' a beatin. We had poor food an' de young slaves wus fed outen troughs. De food wus put in a trough an de little niggers gathered round an' et. Our cabins wus built of poles an had stick an dirt chimleys one door an one little winder at de back end of de cabin. Some of de houses had dirt floors. Our clothin' was poor an homemade."

Jim Martin, Mississippi

"My pappy wus a plow han' and when twant plow time he hoed and sum time wurk at de gin: dat gin wus a big thing: it wus run by horse power, an' when dey put de press on it, yer culd hear it fur more'n a mile. I seed my pappy cum out uf dar ebery day wid his hed civered white wid cotton."

"As us growed up big 'nuf us wuz made to do little odd jobs 'round sich as totin' water and wood, an on to pullin' up de grass an hoein' 'round stumps an in fence corners. I never did git as fer as de hoein' as I wuz to young when wuz freed."

William Mathews, Texas

"De slaves git out in de fields 'fore sun-up and work till black dark. Den dey come home and have to feel dere way in de house, with no light. My mammy and daddy field hands. My grandma was cook, and have to git in de cook pot 'bout four o'clock to git breakfest' by daylight. Dey et by candles or pine torches. One de black boys stand behin' 'em and hold it while dey et."

"De clothes we wore was made out of dyed 'lows.' Dat de stuff dey makes sackin' out of. Summer time us go barefoot but winter time come, dey give you shoes with heels on 'em big an biscuits."

John Matthews, Mississippi

"Dat yard had more cedar trees in it dan eny I kno'd uf. It wus my job to sweep dat yard an' keep it clean an' I kno' no grass wud grow under dem trees. Dar wus a black gal by de name uf Sally who wus to help me sweep dat yard an' we wud quarrell an' sometimes fight 'bout who had de most to do. She sed I played off on her an' made her sweep more den I did, an' I sed she made me do de most uf de work, an' some time old Mistress wud come out dar an' whup us bofe."

"Dey had a big lot full uf cows an' deir wus two wimen who had to milk ebery morn' an' night, an' me an' Sam had to drive dem cows up ebery night an' pen 'em. Didnt have a pasture to keep de cows but let dem run in de woods, but when de crops wus gethered dey wud turn dem cows in de fiel' to eat de scraps an' whut little grass dey cud git."

"Marse Bill had a overseer by de name uf Mr. Filmore an' dat man sho' wus tight on de slaves. He rung dat bell ebery mornin' way 'fore day an' had all de slaves come to de kitchen an' git breakfuss an' he got on his hoss an' driv' dem to de fiel' an' wud sot on dat big bay hoss an' seed to it dat dey wurk'd, an' he neber low'd none uf dem to lag behind."

"I wus jes' learnin' to plow when we wus sot free, an' dat man whupped me two time because I cud not hold de plow straight. I made crooked rows, but I soon learned to do better."

Susan Matthews, Georgia

"My ma, she done the cooking and the washing fer the family and she could work in the fields jes lak a man. She could pick her three hundred pounds of cotton or pull as much fodder as any man. She wuz strong an she had a new baby mos' ev'y year. My marster and Mistis liked for to have a lot of chillen 'cause that helped ter make 'em richer."

Duncan McCastle, Mississippi

"All de time I wuz a slave I wuz to small to wuk in de fields an' I spent de mos' ob my time a playin' 'round de cabin doo'. I wuz dressed in long shirts. I never had on a pair ob pants 'till I wuz 'bout fifteen years ole. I sho had a time tryin' to git use to my fust 'uns. I wuz tickled to death over 'em, but dey wuz so on-comfo'table. I'd wear 'em a little while an' den take 'em off an' git back in my ole shirt. Hit wuz lak breakin' in a ho'se."

"My ma wuz a field wuker an' wuz gone from daylight 'till dark. Us chillun wuz cared fer by de slave cook an' fed at Mars' kitchen. De wukers wuz fed early an' den us went later. We knew when to go by de blow o' de horn."

Alex McCinney, Mississippi

"My mammy was a field hand an' cooked. De cookin' fo de white folks was mostly in Mamma's hands 'cause she wouldn't steal. Some o' de colored women was allus gettin' whippins 'bout stealin'."

Ed McCree, Georgia

"Dere was a thousand or more acres in dat old plantation. It sho' was a big piece of land, and it was plumb full of Niggers—I couldn't say how many, 'cause I done forgot. You could hear dat bugle de overseer blowed to wake up de slaves for miles and miles. He got 'em up long 'fore sunup and wuked 'em in de fields long as dey could see how to wuk. Don't talk 'bout dat overseer whuppin' Niggers. He beat on 'em for most anything. What would dey need no jail for wid dat old overseer a-comin' down on 'em wid dat rawhide bull-whup?"

Lucy McCullough, Georgia

"In all Mr. Hale had eleven children. I had to nurse three of them before I was old enough to go to the field to work."

When asked to tell about the kind of work the slaves had to do Mrs. McDaniel said: "Our felks had to get up at four o'clock every morning and feed the stock first. By the time it was light enough to see they had to be in the fields where they hoed the cotton and the corn as well as the other crops. Between ten and eleven o'clock everybody left the field and went to the house where they worked until it was too dark to see. My first job was to take breakfast to those working in the fields. I used buckets for this. Besides this I had to drive the cows to and from the pasture. The rest of the day was spent in taking care of Mrs. Hale's young children. After a few years of this I was sent to the fields where I planted peas, corn, etc. I also had to pick cotton when that time came, but I never had to hoe and do the heavy work like my mother and sisters did." According to Mrs. McDaniel they were seldom required to work at night after they had left the fields but when such occasions did arise they were usually in the form of spinning thread and weaving cloth. During the winter months this was the only type of work that they did. On days when the weather was too bad for work out of doors they shelled the corn and peas and did other minor types of work not requiring too much exposure. Nobody had to work on Saturday afternoons or on Sundays. It was on Saturdays or at night that the slaves had the chance to do their own work such as the repairing of clothing, etc."

Henry Lewis McGaffey, Mississippi

"Iffen I remember right, old Marse had thirty slaves, an' he made dem wurk in de fiel'—His brudder John, wus de overseer. Dey made corn, an' cotton, an' 'taters, an' 'lasses, an' he bought cotton frum udder people an' put it on boats an' sont it 'way."

"Dem boats wud cum up de Lake loaded wid all kind uf good things an' fine stuff to make clo'se out uf an' always left sum uf it wid my Marse. We chaps uster ter watch dem boats cum an' go an' see de water make big waves as de boats skipped off."

"Old Marse wus hard on his Slaves; he made 'em wurk hard an' I seed him many times tie his slaves and strip dem ter de waist an' beat 'em till de skin wud break. Once I saw him whup my mammy an' de blood run down her bare back, an' den he put salt on it. I cried and he sed 'iffen I didnt shut up he wud beat me,' den I went behind de kitchen ter cry."

William McWhorter, Georgia

"I 'members dat my pa's ma, Grandma Cindy, was a field hand, but by de time I was old 'nough to take things in she was too old for dat sort of wuk and Marster let her do odd jobs 'round de big house. De most I seed her doin' was settin' 'round smokin' her old corncob pipe. I was named for Grandpa Billy, but I never seed him."

"I ain't got no idee how many acres was in dat great big old plantation, but I'se heared 'em say Marse Joe had to keep from 30 to 40 slaves, not countin' chillun, to wuk dat part of it dat was cleared land. Dey told me, atter I was old enough to take it in, dat de overseer sho did drive dem slaves; dey had to be up and in de field 'fore sunup and he wuked 'em 'til slap, black dark. When dey got back to de big house, 'fore dey et supper, de overseer got out his big bull whip and beat de ones dat hadm't done to suit him durin' de day. He made 'em strip off deir clothes down to de waist, and evvywhar dat old bull whip struck it split de skin. Dat was awful, awful! Sometimes slaves dat had been beat and butchered up so bad by dat overseer man would run away, and next day Aunt Suke would be sho to go down to de spring to wash so she could leave some old clothes dar for 'em to git at night. I'se tellin' you, slaves sho did fare common in dem days."

"Dere warn't never no let-up when it come to wuk. When slaves come in from de fields atter sundown and tended de stock and et supper, de mens still had to shuck corn, mend hoss collars, cut wood, and sich lak; de 'omans mended clothes, spun thread, wove cloth, and some of 'em had to go up to de big house and nuss de white folks' babies. One night my ma had been nussin' one of dem white babies, and atter it dozed off to sleep she went to

692   WORK AND SLAVERY

lay it in its little bed. De child's foot cotch itself in Marse Joe's galluses dat he had done hung on de foot of de bed, and when he heared his baby cry Marse Joe woke up and grabbed up a stick of wood and beat ma over de head 'til he 'most kilt her. Ma never did seem right atter dat and when she died she still had a big old knot on her head."

"Dey said on some plantations slaves was let off from wuk when de dinner bell rung on Saddays, but not on our'n; dere warn't never no let-up 'til sundown on Sadday nights atter dey had tended to de stock and et supper."

Susan Merritt, Texas

"The hands was woke with the bit bell and when massa pulls that bell rope the niggers falls out them bunks like rain fallin'. They was in that field 'fore day and stay till dusk dark. They work slap up till Saturday night and then washes their clothes, and sometimes they gits through and has time for the party and plays ring plays. I member part the words to one play and that, 'Rolling river, roll on, the old cow die in cold water … now we's got to drink bad water 'cause old cow die in cold water,' but I can't 'member more'n that. It's too long ago."

"When the hands come in from the field at dusk dark, they has to tote water from the spring and cook and eat and be in bed when that old bell rings at nine o'clock. 'Bout dusk they calls the chillen and gives 'em a piece of cora pone 'bout size my hand and a tin cup milk and puts them to bed, but the growed folks et fat pork and greens and beans and sich like and have plenty milk. Ev'ry Sunday massa give 'em some flour and butter and a chicken. Lots of niggers caught a good cowhiding for slippin' 'round and stealin' a chicken 'fore Sunday."

Ann Miller, Texas

"We comes to Palo Pinto and dat's wild country den. Plenty of Indians, but dey never trouble we'uns. My work, 'twas helpin' wid de chores and pick up de brush whar my pappy was a-clearin' de land. When I gite bigger, I'se plowed, hoed, and done all de goin' to de mill. I'se helps card, spins and cuts de thread. We'uns makes all de cloth for to makes de clothes, but we don' git 'em. In de winter we mos' freeze to death. De weavin' was de night work, after workin' all de day in de fiel'."

Tom Mills, Texas

"They had field work on the place, but a family by the name of Knowles did the farm work. I worked stock nearly all my life. It used to be all the work there was. I think my mother was allowed to make a little money on this cloth business. That is, cloth she made on the outside. And she was the only one of the slaves that could read. I don't know that they cared anything about her readin', but they didn't want her to read it the rest of 'em. I never earned no money; I was too little."

"I remember the cotton they raised on the Patterson place. They picked the seeds out with thier fingers and made cloth out of it. They would take coarse wool—not merino wool, for that was too fine—and use the coarse wool for a filler. That was what they would make me do, pick the seed out of that cotton to keep me out of mischief. I remember that pretty well. Kep' me tied down, and I would beg the old man to let me go, and when he did, if I got into anything, I was back there pickin' seeds pretty quick."

"We would get up about daybreak. They might have got up before I knew anything about it, but sometimes I got up with my mother."

Bob Mobley, Georgia

"He worked in the field," was the answer. "Most of my brothers and sisters worked there too. My mother was the marster's cook. She did all the cookin' for the white fokes an' the niggers, too. Course she had a helper but she had a lots of work to do anyhow. She'd cook for the slaves in great big wash pots."

John Moore, Texas

"Dey have niggers in de fields in different squads, a hoe squad and a plow squad, and de overseer was pretty rapid. Iffen dey don' do de work dey buck dem down and whip dem. Dey tie dey hands and feet togedder and make 'em put de hands 'tween de kneew, and put a long stick 'tween de hands to dey can't pull 'em out, and den dey whip dem in good fashion."

William Moore, Texas

"Marse Tom had five hundred head of sheep, and I spent mos' my time bein' a shepherd boy. I starts out when I'm li'l and larns right fast to keep good 'count of the sheeps."

Mack Mullen, Florida

Plantation Life: The slaves lived in cabins called quarters, which were constructed of lumber and logs. A white man was their overseer, he assigned the slaves their respective tasks. There was also a slave known as a "caller." He came around to the slave cabins every morning at four o'clock and blew a "cow-horn" which was the signal for the slaves to get up and prepare themselves for work in the fields.

All of them on hearing this horn would arise and prepare their meal; by six o'clock they were on their way to the fields. They would work all day, stopping only for a brief period at midday to eat. Mack Mullens says that some of the most beautiful spirituals were sung while they labored.

The women wore towels wrapped around their heads for protection from the sun, and most of them smoked pipes.

The overseer often took Mack with him astride his horse as he made his "rounds" to inspect the work being done. About sundown, the "cow-horn" of the caller was blown and all hands stopped work, and made their way back to their cabins.

Lizzie Norfleet, Mississippi

"The place was so big it took a many a one to work it. I wouldn't have no idea how many acres Master owned. During cotton picking time every body stopped work before dark, so as to get the cotton they had picked to the gin house to be weighed. They carried it to the gin house to be weighed. They carried it in wheel barrows. Every body had to stay till his cotton was weighed to see if they had enough for a day's work. Sometimes the lanterns would have to be lit to see to weigh the last of the cotton."

"When the cotton was ginned, all the seed that was kept for planting was put in the seed house and the rest of them was piled up outside. Whenever my feet got cold I would dig a hole in the seed pile and put my feet in it. They will get just as warm that way as putting them to the fire. Old Sterling Flagg, who helped me drive the mule to run the gin, learned me that."

Richard Orford, Georgia

"All de rest of de slaves wus fiel' hands. Dey spent dere time plowing an' takin' care of de plantation in general. Dere wus some who split rails an' others who took care of de stock an' made de harness—de slaves did everything needed to be done on de plantation. Everybody had to git up 'fore daybreak an' even 'fore it wus light enuff to see dey wus in de fiel' waitin' to see how to run a furrow. 'Long 'bout nine o'clock breakfus' wus sent to de fiel' in a wagon an' all of 'em stopped to eat. At twelve o'clock dey stopped again to eat dinner. After dat dey worked 'till it wus to dark to see. Women in dem days could pick five-hundred pounds of cotton a day wid a child in a sack on dere backs."

"When de weather wus too bad to work in de fiel' de hands cribed an' shucked conn. If dey had any work of dere own to do dey had to do it at night."

Anna Parks, Georgia

"Old Marster had a big fine gyarden. His Negroes wukked it good, and us wuz sho' proud of it. Us lived close in town, and all de Negroes on de place wuz yard and house servants. Us didn't have no gyardens 'round our cabins, kaze all of us et at de big house kitchen. Ole Miss had flowers evvywhar 'round de big house, and she wuz all time givin' us some to plant 'round de cabins."

G. W. Pattillo, Georgia

With a few slaves and a small farm, Master Ingram was very lenient and kind to his slaves and usually worked with them in the fields. "We had no special time to begin or end the work for the day. If he got tired he would say, 'Alright, boys, let's stop and rest,' and sometimes we didn't start working until late in the day."

Lindy Patton, Alabama

"I wukhed in de fiel's an' I worked hard all day long. De white folks useta gimme de clothes of de lil' white chilluns. I was born in Knoxville, Alabama, in Greene County, an' I belonged to Messa Bill Patton."

Ellen Payne, Texas

"I mostly minded the calves and chickens and turkeys. Master Evans had a overseer but he didn't 'low him to cut and slash his niggers and we didn't have no hard taskmaster. They was 'bout thirty slaves on the farm, but I is the only one livin' now. I loved all my white folks and they was sweet to us."

"The hands worked from sun to sun and had a task at night. Some spinned or made baskets or chair bottoms or knit socks. Some the young'uns courted and some jest rambled round most all night. On Saturday was the prayer meetin' in one house and a dance in another. On Sunday some went to church and visitin', but not far, 'cause that was in patterroller times."

Daniel Phillips, Texas

"Marse Dailey raised cotton and co'n on de plantation. On de ranch dey ketches wild horses and I herds dem. When I'm on de ranch I has to drive de wild horses into de pen. De men cotches de wild horses and I has to drive 'em so's dey won't git wild agin."

"Lots of dem wild horses got colts and I has to brand dem. Marse Dailey he helps to cotch de wild horses but I has to drive 'em. In de mornin' I drives dem out and in de evenin' I drives dem back. Dere's sure a lot of dem wild horses."

Lee Pierce, Texas

"Marse Fowler worked 'bout a hundred and fifty acres of land and had sev'ral cullud families. He done overseeing hisself, but had a black man for foreman. I seed plenty niggers whopped for not doin' dey tasks. He'd whop 'em for not pickin' so many hundreds of cotton a day, buckle 'em down hawg fashion and whop 'em with a strap. Us never stopped work no day, lessen Sunday, and not then iffen grass in the field or crops sufferin'."

Dempsey Pitts, Mississippi

"We didn't raise no cotton, in North Carolina. Tobacco was the big money crop. Besides that, we grew indigo, rice, and corn. I didn't work in the field, cause I was raised to be the carriage driver. We didn't get no money, for work we done, but we sure did git plenty something to eat. We didn't have to steal. No sir, you git whipped for that sure. We had plenty hogs, beef, mutton and rabbits. We set out nets, and when the tide come in, caught more fish than we could eat. Didn't have no possum, but that mutton could take its place. We loved that, better than anything. Each person had his own garden and had to work it hisself, like they does now."

Isaac Potter, Mississippi

"One ob my fust duties wuz ter feed de chickens which wuz raised by de hundreds. Dey would send me wid big buckets ob feed to de chickens yard an' I did enji taking long sticks or big rocks an' kill 'em. Dis wuz real fun to me. At fust I wuz afraid to kill many ob 'em, den I got braver and braver and killed more and more."

"My next wuk wuz at de stables, caring fo de horses, dis kept me busy, watering dem, feeding 'em an' keepin' em curred. Mars wanted 'em slick an' shinnin'. I had ter keep de harnesses straight'en."

Betty Powers, Texas

"De field hands works early and late and often all night. Pappy makes de shoes and mammy weaves, and you could hear de bump, bump of dat loom at night, when she done work in de field all day."

Charlie Powers, Mississippi

"My ole Marse raised cotton, corn an' all kinds o' food stuff. He wuz kind to his slaves an' fed an' clo'sed us well. De cabins wuz small wid one room an' a dirt an' straw chimney. De slaves wuked from early till late in de fiel's an' wid de stock an' cattle. Deir wuz big hog killin's, syrup makin' time, deir wuz a heap o' spinnin', quiltin' an' weavin' to be done an' soap an' candles to be made. All de close had to be made by han'. We wore course an' thick clos'e but alwa's went clean. We wuz fed in de kitchen at Ole Marse's in de winner time an' out in de back yard in de summer time."

Jenny Proctor, Texas

"We had some co'n shuckin's sometimes but de white folks gits de fun and de nigger gits de work. We didn' have no kind of cotton pickin's 'cept jes' pick our own cotton. I's can hear dem darkies now, goin' to de cotton patch way 'fore day a singin':

Peggy, does you love me now?
One ole man he sing:
Sat'day night and Sunday too
Young gals on my mind,
Monday mornin' way 'fore day
Ole marster got me gwine.
Chorus:
Peggy, does you love me now?

"Den he whoops a sort of nigger holler, what nobody can do jes' like dem ole time darkies, den on he goes,

Possum up a 'simmon tree,
Rabbit on de ground
Lawd, Lawd, 'possum,
Shake dem 'simmons down.
Peggy, does you love me now?
Holler
Rabbit up a gum stump
'Possum up a holler
Git him out little boy
And I gives you half a dollar.
Peggy, does you love me now?

A. C. Pruitt, Texas

"De field hands stay up in de big barn and shuck corn on rainy days. Dey shuck corn and sing. Us chillen keep de yard clean and tie weeds together to make brooms for de sweepin'. Us sep'rate de seed from de cotton and a old woman do de cardin'. Dey have 'nother old woman what do nothin' on de scene but weave on de loom."

Charlie Pye, Georgia

His mistress was Miss Mary Ealey, who later married a Mr. Watts. Miss Ealey owned a large number of slaves, although she did not own a very large plantation. Quite a few of her slaves were hired out to other owners. The workers on the plantation were divided into two or more groups, each group having a different job to do. For instance, there were the plow hands, hoe hands, log cutters, etc. Mr. Pye's mother was a plow hand and besides this, she often had to cut logs. Mr. Pye was too young to work and spent most of his time playing around the yards.

In every slave home was found a wooden loom which was operated by hands and feet, and from which the cloth for their clothing was made. When the work in the fields was finished women were required to come home and spin one cut (thread) at night. Those who were not successful in completing this work were punished the next morning. Men wore cotton shirts and pants which were dyed different colors with red oak bark, alum and copper. Copper produced an "Indigo blue color." I have often watched dye in the process of being made, remarked Mr. Pye. Mr. Pye's father was a shoemaker and made all shoes needed on the plantation. The hair was removed from the hides by a process known as tanning. Red oak bark was often used for it produced an acid which proved very effective in tanning hides. Slaves were given shoes every three months.

Mary Reynolds, Texas

"The conch shell blowed afore daylight and all hands better git out for roll call or Solomon bust the door down and git them out. It was work hard, git beatin's and half fed. They brung the victuals and water to the fields on a slide pulled by a old mule. Plenty times they was only a half barrel water and it stale and hot, for all us niggers on the hottes' days. Mostly we ate pickled pork and corn bread and peas and beans and 'taters. They never was as much as we needed."

"The times I hated most was pickin' cotton when the frost was on the bolls. My hands git sore and crack open and bleed. We'd have a li'l fire in the fields and iffen the ones with tender hands couldn't stand it no longer, we'd run and warm our hands a li'l bit. When I could steal a 'tater, I used to slip it in the ashes and when I'd run to the fire I'd take it out and eat it on the sly."

Mary Rice, Alabama

Few of the ex-slaves will readily admit that they were mere field hands in the old days. Generally they prefer to leave the impression that they were house servants, or at least stable boys or dairy hands.

But "aunt" Mary Rice, age 92, who lives in Eufaula holds no such view about the superior social position of house servants. She was a "big missy gal" [teen age] during the War, and about her duties on the plantation of Dr. Cullen Battle near Tuskegee, where she was born, she said: "Honey, I lived in de quahter. I was a fiel' nigger, but when I was a lil' gal, I helped around de milk-house, churnin', washing de pails and de lak, and den give all de little niggers milk."

"Yassum, I was jes' as happy bein' a fiel' han' as I would'er been at de Big House; mebbe mo' so. De fiel' han's had a long spell when de crops was laid by in de summer and dat's when Massa Cullen 'lowed us to 'jubilate' [several days of idle celebration]. I was happy all de time in slavery days, but dere ain't much to git happy over now 'cep'n I's livin'—thank de Lawd. Massa Cullen was a rich man, and owned all de worl' from Chestnut Hill to de ribers, and us always had eberything us needed."

Shade Richards, Georgia

Mr. Neal had several plantations in different localities and his family did not live on this one in Pike County but he made regular visits to each one. It had no name, was just called "Neal's Place." It consisted of thirteen hundred acres. There were always two or three hundred slaves on the place, besides the ones he just bought and sold for "tradin'." He didn't like "little nigger men" and when he happened to find one among his slaves he would turn the dogs on him and let them run him down. The boys were not allowed to work in the fields until they were 12 years old, but they had to wait on the hands, such as carrying water, running back to the shop with tools and for tools, driving wagons of corn, wheat etc. to the mill to be ground and any errands they were considered big enough to do. Shade worked in the fields when he became 12 years old.

Dora Roberts, Georgia

"We worked de fields an' kep' up de plantation 'Til freedom, ebry Wednesday de massa come visit us an look ober de plantation ta see dat all is well. He talk ta de obersheer an' find out how good de work is. We lub de massa an' work ha'd fe' him."

Ferebe Rogers, Georgia

"I was a fiel' han' myself. I come up twix' de plow handles. I warn't de fastes' one wid a hoe, but I didn't turn my back on nobody plowin'. No, mam."

Annie Row, Texas

"De marster has two overseers what tends to de work and 'signs each nigger to do de certain work and keep de order. Shoes was made by a shoemaker what am also de tanner. Cloth for de clothes was made by de spinners and weavers and that what they larned me to do. My first work was teasin' de wool. I bets you don't know what teasin' de wool am. It am pickin' de burrs and trash and sich out of de wool for to git it ready for de cardin'."

Martin Ruffin, Texas

"The growed slaves et cornbread and bacon and 'lasses and milk, but all the chillen get was milk and bread and a little 'lasses. Massa have fifteen on twenty women carding and weaving and spinning most all the time. Each nigger had his task and the chillen gathered berries in the woods to make dyes for clothes. Us wore only white lowell clothes, though. They was sho' thick and heavy."

"The overseer was named Charley and there was one driver to see every-one done his task. If he didn't, they fixed him up. Them what fed the stock got up at three and the overseer would tap a bell so many times to make 'em git up. The rest got up at four and worked till good dark. They'd give us a hundred lashes for not doing our task. The overseer put five men on you; one on each hand, one on each foot, and one to hold your head down to the ground. You couldn't do anything but wiggle. The blood would fly 'fore they was through with you."

Julia Rush, Georgia

As a child Mrs. Rush served as playmate to one of the Colonel's daughters and so all that she had to do was to play from morning till night. When she grew older she started working in the kitchen in the master's house. Later she was sent to the fields where she worked side by side with her mother and three sisters from sunup until sundown. Mrs. Rush says that she has plowed so much that she believes she can "outplow" any man.

Instead of the usual white overseer usually found on plantations the Colonel used one of the slaves to act as foreman of the field hands. He was known to the other slaves an the "Nigger Driver" and it was he who awakened all every morning. It was so dark until torch lights had to be used to see by. These women who had babies took them along to the field in a basket which they placed on their heads. All of the hands were given a certain amount of work to perform each day and if the work was not completed a whipping might be forthcoming. Breakfast was sent to the field to the hands and if at dinner time they were not too far away from their cabins they were permitted to go home. At night they prepared their own meals in their individual cabins.

Aaron Russel, Texas

"De bell ring 'fore daylight and de work start. When de cullud folks starts out in de mornin' it like de army. Some goes to de fields, some to de spinain', some to de shoeshop, and so on. De hours am long, but massa am good. No overseer, but de leader for each crew."

Charlie Sandles, Texas

"No I never did earn any money during slavery time. My new Maser would give me a nickel or dime once and awhile, when I could I would spend it for candy or something like that."

"All the slaves he had was my family, which was 8 of us. Maser would wake us every morning about 4 o'clock so we could be up and tend the stock, eat and be in the field when daylight came. Then he worked us just as long as we could see. At night we came in and fed the stock and by the time we went to our quarters it was about 9 or 10 o'clock. Yes Maser would thrash the slaves if they got unruly just like you would a stubborn mule, and he never got mad about either. Thanks to my Lord! he never hit me a lick in his life. I'se seen him whip one of my brothers just exactly like you would one of your own children. He never would bruise them or skin them up. Everyone loved Maser, he hardly ever spoke a harsh word to the slaves and everyone of them would have died for him.

When we went to our quarters we nearly always just fell in the bed. Sometimes if we were not so tired we sat around and talked, but most of the time we went right to bed. Them patterrollers would come there and walk all around in my quarters and I would be plum still until they left because I'se afraid of them, they never did bother me, no sir."

Clarissa Scales, Texas

"My job was tendin' fires and herdin' hawgs. I kep' fire goin' when de washin' bein' done. Dey had plenty wood, but used corn cobs for de fire. Dere a big hill corn cobs near de wash kettle. In de evenin' I had to bring in de hawgs. I had a li'l whoop I druv dem with, a eight-plaited rewhide whoop on de long stick. It a purty sight to see dem hawgs go under de slip-gap, what was a rail took down from de bottom de fence, so de hawgs could run under."

Hannah Scott, Texas

"Marster Bat was mean, too, work de slaves from 'fore daylight to 9 o'clock in de night. At fust, 'fore I's put in de field, I totes water for de hands. I carries de bucket on my head and 'fore long I ain't got no more hair on my head, dan you has in de palm of your hand, no suh!"

"When I gets bigger, de overseer puts me in de field with de rest. Marster Bat grows mostly cotton, and it don't make no diffrunce is you big or little, you better keep up or de drivers burn you up with de whip sure 'nuff. Old Marster Bat never put a lick on me all de years I belong to him, but de drivers sure burnt me plenty times. Sometimes I gets so tired come night dat I has dropped right in de row and gone to sleep. 'Den de drivers come 'long and wham, dey cuts you 'cross de back with de whip and you sure 'nuff wakes up when it lights on you, yes suh.

"'Bout 9 o'clock dey hollers 'cotton up', and dat's de quitting signal. We goes to de quarters, and sometimes jes' drop on de bunk and go to sleep without nothing to eat."

"Yes suh, on old Bat's place dat's all us know is work and more work. 'Bout de onliest time we has off is Sunday, and den we has to do de washing and mending clothes."

"I hears some of de white folks what owned slaves treat 'em good, and give 'em time off and ground what dey can work, but Marster Bat he jes' believe in working his darkies all de time. We had plenty to eat, and plenty warm clothes in de winter time, but we sure has to work. Ain't no foolishness going on 'round his place, no suh, jes' work and more work."

Abram Sells, Texas

"Li'l folks slep' mos's' long as dey want to in day light but de big niggers hab to come outn' dat bed 'bout fo' [four] o'clock w'en de big ho'n blow. De oberseer hab one nigger he wake up early fo' to blow the horn 'n' w'en he blow dis ho'n 'n' mek sich a holler den all de res' 'r' de niggers better git outn' dat bed 'n' 'pear [appear] at de barn, 'bout day light. He might not whip him fo' bein' late de fus' time but dat nigger better not fo'git de secon' time 'n' be late."

George Sells, Texas

"Us nebber have no holiday 'till atter freedom riz up. De slaves wuk from soon's dey kin see in de mawnin' and's long as dey kin see at night, but de white folks tek care of 'em and ain't let 'em suffer. Us white folks help us to l'arn to read and write a li'l, and dat's mol dan mos' of de marsters done."

George Selman, Texas

"The hands were called to dinner by the blowing of the conk. Massa Tom was very good to us. He never had to punish anyone very often. Hit was under Massa Tom's guidance and faithful teachin' that I prossed religion. He was the best man I ever knew. When Saturday noon came we stopped the field work and did our washin', cleaning up and cookin' for Sunday. Massa Tom wouldn't 'low no workin' on Sunday. Aunt Dicey was the cook and Massa Tom and Missa Polly seed to it that Aunt Dicey had plenty vegetables in the house. (We chillun help bring them in from the garden.) The cakes and pies was baked Saturday. Everything fixed so's there'd be no cookin' on Sunday. We went to church once a month, over to the white folks' church. We sat on one side and the white folks on t'other."

"Marster had five families livin' in his yard. Our cabins were made or built in a half circle in the back yard. We chillun jes' played aroun' in the big yard til we got big enough to work. 'Pears like I was Massa Tom's pet. As soon as I was big enough to follow him he allus took me with him to feed the hogs, go to mill or to town. I carried water to the field hands an' thars where I learned to plow. My mother would let me hold the plow handles and walk along with her. Finally she let me go around by myself and I had larn't to plow before Massa Tom know anything about it. He had three farms, some days we worked in the bottom field, some days in the north field and sometimes in the field by the house."

Nancy Settles, Georgia

"Ma, she chop cotton and plow, and I started choppin' cotton when I wuz twelve years old."

Lucindy Hall Shaw, Mississippi

"I had to wurk mity hard; I had to plow in de fiel's in de day an' den at nite when I wuz so tired I cu'dn't hardly stan' I had to spin my cut of cotton befo' I cu'd go to sleep; we had to card, spin, an' reel at nite; I wish I had a dollar fur evry yard ov cloth I has loomed thru dat ole slay."

Will Sheets, Georgia

"Marse Jeff jus' had 'bout four mens and four 'oman slaves and him and young Marse Johnny wukked in de fiel' 'long side of de Niggers. Dey went to de fiel' by daybreak and come in late at night."

"When Marse Jeff got behind wid his crop, he would hire slaves f'um other white folkses, mostly f'um Pa's marster, dat's how Pa come to know my Ma."

"Marse Jeff wukked dem few Niggers so hard dat when dey got to deir cabins at night dey was glad to jus' rest. Dey all knocked off f'um wuk Sadday at 12 o'clock. De 'omans washed, patched, and cleaned up de cabins, and de mens wukked in dey own cotton patches what Marse Jeff give 'em. Some Niggers wouldn't have no cotton patch 'cause dey was too lazy to wuk."

Robert Shepherd, Georgia

"Marse Joe, he had three plantations, but he didn't live on none of 'em. He lived in Lexin'ton. He kept a overseer on each one of his plantations and dey had better be good to his Niggers, or else Marse Joe would sho' git 'em 'way from dar. He never 'lowed 'em to wuk us too hard, and in bad or real cold weather us didn't have to do no outside wuk 'cept evvyday chores what had to be done, come rain or shine, lak milkin', tendin' de stock, fetchin' in wood, and things lak dat. He seed dat us had plenty of good somepin t'eat and all de clothes us needed. Us was lots better off in dem days dan us is now."

Polly Shine, Texas

"Well I has done all kinds of work for a youngster during slavery time. Chopped cotton, hoed corn, milked cows, cooked and washed dishes as Mistress used me lots to help her. I was a young negro and Maser just let me put my time in helping Mistress."

"Maser had about 100 acres in his plantation and about 35 or 40 slaves. He planted it all in cotton, corn and sugar cane. He made syrup out of the sugar cane. Maser woke us every morning about 4 o'clock with a big bell so'es we could get our morning work done, eat and be in the field at daylight or before and be ready to work. Well, no he never had no overseer, he done all that himself and he worked us till plum dark every day, we just quit long enough to eat our dinner at noon then right back to work. That is we worked from sun to sun as we called it then. He would sure tend to the negro if he was lazy, contrary or stubborn. I'se seen him whip some of the slaves terrible but he had some real mean slaves. If he was not with them they were all time into some kind of trouble, if it were not anything but doing something to the rest of the slaves after they would go to their quarters when the days work was done. Otherwise Maser was real good to the slaves, but they must mind him and take off their hats in presence of white people."

"Well when we went to our quarters after the days work was done there on the plantation we usually were so tired that we just fell in at the door right on the ground especially in the summertime, that was where we sleep all that night unless the patterrollers come and made us go to bed right."

Betty Simmons, Texas

"Dey's purty rough on de niggers. Iffen us hab a baby us was on'y 'low to stay in de house for one mont'. Dey hab us card an' spin. Atter de baby one mont' ol' us sont back into de fiel' to de heaby wuk. Dey hab a ho'n up in de house an' dey blow it in de middle of de mawnin' an' atternoon for de mammies to come up an' nuss dey li'l babies."

Emma Simpson, Texas

"Master he would wake us about four o'clock every morning except Sunday morning and we alway had two holiday in the week cause master would never make us work on Saturday. Then we quits work every evenin when dark run us in. Boss, they was never no slaves punished on masters farm."

"They tried to rest when they went to their quarters after the days work was done. We have holiday on Saturday. Master never did work us on Saturday. We have Saturday off all day to wash our clothes, clean out our quarters, then Saturday night we most time have negro dance, banjo pickin, story telling, ring games."

"Sometimes Sunday evenin' we could all set 'round de big fire in de kitchen to de big house. But we couldn't set there 'less we was doin' somethin'. Each 'un had a task to do. Some ob dem was cardin' an' spinnin', and some was pickin' peanuts, an' some was sewing. All de littlest chillun gathered up close to de fire to set potatoes to roast for de breaffast an' watch 'em. If you wouldn't git finished wid what you doin' you was tied on a hoghead barrel or a log an' whipped."

Mr. and Mrs. Alex Smith, Alabama

Unlike the chores of Elizabeth [Mrs. Smith], Mr. Smith had to chop wood, carry water, chop weeds, care for cows, pick bugs from tobacco plants. This little boy had to go barefoot both summer and winter, and remembers the cracking of ice under his bare feet.

Giles Smith, Texas

"Let me s-e-e. I's m'ybe 'membahs de words ob one. Dis am che, an' de way deys do, am dis away, w'en dey raise de axe, or de grubbin' hoe, dey says, 'Hi.' W'en deys swing it down, dey says, 'Ho,' an' w'en de axe hits, deys says, 'Ug,' so de song goes:

Hi, Ho, Ug, Hi, Ho, Ug,
De sharp bit, de strong ahm,
Hi, Ho, Ug, Hi, Ho, Ug,
Dis tree am done 'fo' weuns am wahm

Henry Smith, Texas

"I know dat I done a lot of field work and sich. I done a lot of cotton pickin'. Den at times I had to drive de hosses around and around a hoss-power gin. Den I had to help tromp de cotton down in de baler, and den tie de bale up wid ropes. Dey sure didn't gin cotton in dem days lak dey do now. In dem days it was good work to put out about one bale every hour."

"Dere was times when I had to tote eats out to de field hands. I packed buckets of eats on my head, and took it to de workers. Dey would stop workin', set down in de rows, and staht eatin'."

Jordon Smith, Texas

"Mistress didn't 'low her 'Niggers' to work till they was twenty one. The chil'ren played marbles and run round and kick up their heels till they was grown. She had a overseer and several 'Drivers.' The first work I done was hoeing, and we worked as long as we could see a stalk of cotton or a hill of corn. The hands didn't wo'k on Saturday afternoon. That's when they washed their clothes and went fishing if they wanted to. I'se seed Niggers with munney in slavery time. They stole whiskey or something and slipped off and sold it to get munney. Mistress used to call up the old fo'ks at Christmas and give them a dollar a piece. The rest got a dinner."

Lucinda Smith, Texas

"My mother was a slave on the Jenkins Plantation near Waco, Texas. Her Massa was Lee Jenkins. He was a young man. My mother wo'k hard in the fields. She had to plow and plant crops. My father was killed. The team he was driving ran away; he fell off the wagon and broke his neck. I don't 'member much mo' wh'at my mother told me."

Maria Smith, Georgia

"De suckin' mothers was given light wuk," said Grammaw. "My mother had a track of two acres to tend. I used to tend her suckin' baby and tote it down to de fiel' for her to nuss. Den de baby would go to sleep and we'd lay it down 'twixt de cotton rows and ma would make me holp her. She kep' a long switch and iffen I didn't wuk fast enuf, she switch me. When she got through she could quit. Sometimes she was through by noontime. Den she'd go back to de quarters and iffen it was fruit time, she'd put up some fruit for mistis."

Melvin Smith, Georgia

"Ma an' Pa was field hands an' Ever' mornin' at four clock th' overseer blowed a conchshell an' all us niggers knowed it was time to git up an' go to work. Sometimes he blowed a bugle that'd wake up the nation. Ever'body worked from sunup 'till sundown. If we didn't git up when we was s'posed to we got a beatin'. Marster'd make 'em beat the part that couldn't be bought." Melvin chuckled at his own sly way of saying that the slaves were whipped through their clothes.

Millie Ann Smith, Texas

"We was woke up 'fore day break with a horn and wo'ked till sundown. When we got in from the fiel' there was stock to tend to and chores to do, and cloth to weave 'fore we went to bed. The overseer come 'round at nine o'clock to see if we was in bed then he go back to the house and turn in. When we knowed he was sound sleep we slip out and run 'round and go to the neighbors sometimes. We warn't lowed to go to chu'ch or nowhere without a pass. I think sometime how did we live through it. The Lord took care of us. They locked the young men up in a house there on the place at night and on Sunday to keep them from running 'round. It was a log house and had cracks in it. One time a little nigger boy was sticking his hand through the crack poking fun at the boys on the inside and one of them chopped his fingers off with an ax."

"Marster George had bout fifty er sixty slaves countin chilluns and all and de best I can member, he had bout four er five hundert acres in his plantation. De drivah wakes dem all up at foah clock in de morning, he rings a big bell and you bettah get up too if you aint sick. And dey was in de field fore sun up and works til after sun down, and if you wants a licken jest fool roun likes dey do now, er gets sacy when you is tole ter do a little more."

"Der slaves all worked hard every day in dem days and when dey comes in from work, de chores has ter be done, but if dey was behind wid de work dey would have ter shuck co'n at night, er haul in fodder er hay. Dey never did work on Satity evenins unless dey was behind wid de work, and if dey was behind dey worked night and day ter ketch up. And when Satity night comes dey was all glad ter rest. Sometimes on Sunday we went ter church but not allus."

"When cotton pickin comes along ever body picks cotton, chilluns and all and dey picks in de big baskets. Cotton sacks wasn't heard of den, but dey picks lots of cotton in dem baskets."

Samuel Smith, Texas

"In de winter time we would get up about what would be six in de mornin' now, and some would feed de stock, and some would milk de cows and some would do somethin' else. De same thing in summer, except we would get up about four o'clock 'stead of six, we was all busy, but we didn't have to work so hard."

Tucker Smith, Texas

"Boss I'se could ride the wildest horse that ever had hair on his back, that was most my job riding horses and breaking them so'es they could be gentle. No son I'se never earned money in slavery days but Maser has give me money and I'se buy candy, tobacco and so on like that cause I'se go all over the country on them wild horses learning them to ride."

"Son, I do not know how many acres there was on Maser's ranch but it would take two days to ride clear around his land. We never had very much fences no sir. Well son, Maser he would get us out of bed about 4 o'clock nearly every morning. Yes sir, we would ride all day long in the saddle, sometimes we got home by dark then other times it would be real late when we come in especially if we were marking and branding horses, yearlings and so on, cause Maser he did not ever farm. Maser he had several slaves there on the ranch something like 15 or 16, I don't remembers just how many. Son we worked from sun to sun if that is what you want to know. Maser he woke us up about 5 o'clock every morning to get in the saddle and we stayed there until dark drove us in, sometimes it would be long after dark when we got in from the pasture."

"Well yes sir, son I'se never did hardly know when Saturday came or Sunday either for that matter, cause Maser he made us ride right on after his stock. Well once and awhile on Saturday night Maser would let us have a dance where us negroes could be together for a while but not every Saturday night, and we could not stay out any later than midnight, cause Sunday we had to ride right on after his stock."

John Sneed, Texas

"Dere was 'bout four or five hundred acres an 'bout sixty slaves. Dey got up every mornin 'bout daylight an' come from de field in time to feed an do de chores 'fore dark. I didn't learn to read an write. I followed cattle from de time was 'bout eight years ole 'till I was twenty-six. I was a general cow-han went up de Chisholm Trail eight or nine times. I drove fer Marster Blocker, Judge Brackenridge an' odders."

"After work, at night, de ole folks would sit 'roun, fiddle, play de accordion, tell stories an' other things. But dat was after de crops was laid by or all gathered or on rainy days. On workin' time, dey was usually pretty tired an went to bed early. Dey didn't work as a usual thing on Marse Sneed's place on Saturday afternoon or on Sunday; jus on rush harvest time or w'en dey was gatnerin' de crop 'gin a rain or bad weather. Ole man Jim Piper was de fiddler on our plantation. He played de fiddle for dances fer black an white on nearby places. He mos' usuall got pay an' dat money was his'n to keep. Marster usually made all us niggers go to church every Sunday. Sometimes, us had dinner on de groun', an' all-day services."

Mariah Snyder, Texas

"The 'Driver' come round and woke us all up in the morning and had us in the fiel' by day-break. I'se seed a whole fiel' of Negroes abreast hoeing. The cotton rows was so long you could make only one round fore dinner. Master Sam had a gin on his place. I used to 'drive the gin.' It was run by two mules, and I driv' them. They baled the cotton pretty fast. It was wrapped in bagging and tied with ropes. It was long time after surrender fore I saw cotton tied with steel like they bale it now."

Ria Sorrell, North Carolina

"We worked from sunup till sunset wid a rest spell at 12 o'clock of two hours. He give us holidays to rest in. Dat wus Christmas, a week off den, den a day every month, an' all Sundays. He said he wus a Christian an' he believed in givin' us a chance. Marster died of consumption. He give us patches an' all dey made on it. He give slaves days off to work dere patches."

"A lot of de niggers in slavery time wurked so hard dey said dey hated to see de sun rise in de mornin'. Slavery wus a bad thing, 'cause some white folks didn't treat dare niggers right."

Leithean Spinks, Texas

"In de mornin' when de bell ring, everybody goes to work, but I is little and does de chores and am gap tender. De cattle am 'lowed to run where dey wants, here, there and all over. Fences am 'roun de fields and yards and there am gates to go through, but us calls dem gaps. It am my job to open and close dem, 'cause somebody allus wantin' to drive or walk through dem gaps."

"My sis am de fly chaser. She has de big fan make from de tail feathers of de peacock. 'Twas awful purty thing. She stands 'round de white folks and shoe off de flies."

"Massa Fay ain't hard on he cullud folks. He works dem steady but don't drive dem. Lots de slaves goes fishin' in de river on Saturday afternoon and Sunday, and dey cotches plenty fish."

Annie Stanton, Alabama

"De men did mos' ob de farm wurk, dey planted cotton, corn, potatoes, cane, and peas and pumpkins, an' dey ginned de cotton by hitching four horses tuh de gin, and dey run hit dat way."

Lydia Starks, Georgia

"In de winter, Massa Taggart tried to give 'em some kind of work which wouldn't make de slaves have ter go outside in de weather. Dey shucked corn and shelled it, dey cleaned de stable. And dere wuz plenty of weavin' goin' on. There wuz one great ole fat woman slave dat done de weavin' mos' o' de time. Den de elder people carded and spun too. I used to help my gran'ma put the thread into hanks. Yeah, I she learned how to spin."

Emeline Stepney, Georgia

No crops of any kind were sold and consequently the plantation had to be self-sustaining. Cotton was spun into clothing in the master's own spinning room and the garments were worn by the master and slaves alike. A small amount of flax was raised each year and from this the master's two sisters made household linens. Food crops consisted of corn, wheat (there was a mill on the plantation to grind these into flour and meal), sweet potatoes, and peas. In the smoke house there was always plenty of pork, beef, mutton, and kid. The wool from the sheep was made into blankets and woolen garments.

The Terry household was not like other menages of the time. There were only one or two house servants, the vast majority being employed in the fields. Work began each morning at eight o'clock and was over at sundown. No work was done on Saturday, the day being spent in preparation for Sunday or in fishing, visiting, or "jes frolickin'." The master frequently let them have dances in the yards on Saturday afternoon. To supply the music they beat on tin buckets with sticks.

Guy Stewart, Texas

"Ise starts work w'ens Ise seben yeahs ol' in de cotton an' con'n field. Ise j'st peddels 'round furst. In de field am whar de Marster works dis nigger alls de time. Marster Taylor he am sho good to weuns cullud fo'ks. He am so good dat de tudder w'ite fo'ks calls us de 'free niggers.' Marster ses, 'If youes wants to keep de nigger workin' good, treat him good,' and he sho do dat. He sho gets da work f'om weuns 'cause weuns am glad fo' to work hard fo' hims."

William Stone, Texas

"Dat sugar cane an' sorghum! We wuz happy ter do dis wukk fer us knowed dat hit mean dat us has it ter eat wid our bread an' butter in de winter. Lawdy, wish I knowed dat I cud hab all ob de 'lasses an' bread an' butter dat I wanted dis winter. Dem wuz good times, Lawd. Offen us'd sing dis song, seems like I kin hear hit now:

We'll stick ter de hoe, till de sun go down
We'll rise w'en de rooster crow,
An' go ter de fiel' whar de sun shine hot,
Ter de fiel' whar de sugar-cane grow,
Yes, chilluns, we'll all go!

"I kin shut my eyes an' dream 'bout de days w'en we wukkin in de fiels down in Louisian. I kin see de long, long rows of cotton an' de corn, see de niggers drivin' de oxen an' de mules ter de plow as dey ride, one in one row an' one in tother. I kin see dat oberseer as he come er ridin' on he horse, fust one place an den a'nuther."

"In de ole days dey had sartin hans to jes' plow an dey name plow hans. Yassum I kuld sing hit fer you effen yer wants me ter. I kin not sing no tune kase I ain't got no voice lef for de singin' now. Hit goes somethin' like dis:

Nigger mighty happy w'en he layin' by de corn,
Nigger mighty happy w'en he hear dat dinner horn;
But he's more happy w'en de night kum on.
Dat sun's a-slantin' sho's you born
De ole cow's er shakin' her bell,
En de frogs er tunin' up, fer de dew's done fell.

"Us'll nebber see dem happy days ergain. Dis wuz jes atter freedom w'en I wuz a boy. Dey hab de big plantations an' de oberseer's jes' like dey did in de days befo' freedom, but mos' of de oberseers by dis time wuz niggers. Dey didn't whup de fiel hands like dey did in slavery, but dey gib him he wukk an' w'en he does hit den he kin take de Saddy off effen he through he week's wukk."

Yach Stringfellow, Texas

"Ob course, I didn' carry no water till I wuz about fourteen years ole. 'Case we had to git it sometimes from a spring an sometimes from a deep well, an dere wuz danger dat a little chile would fall in an drown. Marster, he say dat niggers too valyble to risk dem dat way. It wuz hard work to be a water totter fer de niggers what wuz workin on de plantation. 'Cause dere wuz allus some body a hollerin' fer water. An you had to trot down a slippery bank through de thorns to de spring, or pull a heavy sweep to git it out ob a well. An when you trot all day wid a heavy bucket an mos' de time two heavy buckets, it shore makes you tired. Dey brought our dinner to de field or woods wherever we wuz workin' an' you only stopped long 'nuff to eat an den Marse Green Morgan, de over seer, he kracked dat ole black snake whip an nigger, you better git in dere an swing."

"Marster shore had a lot ob land an a lot ob slaves. Us got to de fields fore good light an wukked till 'bout dark. Den some went to de big house to git in de wood, to milk an do de chores an sech; de odders dey wuk on till plum dark. Marse had Mister John to oversee an he wuz shore a stepper. He could be every place you didn't think he gwine come. Ole man Jim he had a big boom voice an he allus singing; jes any kind song outen he haid. An he had one dat would wail kind-a an ef de oberseer wuz comin he'd wail out loud like an say; 'Look-a long black man, look-a long; dere's trouble comin shore.' Effen de black boy or wimmin be a-lyin in de corn row, dey's gwin git up quick an be mighty buzy right soon, case de black snake whip reach fer 'em an reach quick. Effen deres a boy a-nappin under a tree, he scramble he self togedder some fas', an he be de buziest in de bunch time Mister John git to see him. No'm twan't no jail ez you might say. Some ob de planters had a big strong crib dey put de troublesome niggers in an tie 'em up hard an fas'. De oberseer guine whup you effen you lazy er sassy er break something an effen you makin' somethin', you better watch close an not spoil it. My marster nebber whup me an he nebber let Mister John git me case I allus wurkked good an atter I not wurk in de field like on rainy days er in de winter, I made things wid my knife an Marse he like dat fine."

Emma Taylor, Texas

"De darkies had to get up at four in de morning and work and work till they couldn't see no more. Den dey had to work at night. De men had to chop wood, and haul up poles to help build fences and cut up for wood. De women folks had to spin four cuts of thread every night, and den make all de clothes for all de slaves on de place. Den some of dem had to card de cotton to make quilts, and to weave de cloth, and den knit stockings outtin big thread. Master gived each one a chore to do, and if it wasn't done before we went to bed, we were whipped. One time I fell plumb asleep befo I had finished shelling some corn, but I didn't git much of a whippin dat time. I never did run when I was fixin to git a whippin. I seen some of dem run, and den they tied dem up wid chains to a post, and dey got lots worse whippins dan iffin day had jist been still. Master never did whip any body lessin de needed it. Iffin dey done what he told dem to, and didn't talk back, dey didn't never git no whippins hardly ever."

"We worked all picking cotton, or choppin cotton, or howing corn; some nights then after all de work was done, de older darkies danced, and played de fiddle, while de chillerns played in de yard. We could stay up all night on nights like dat, but we had to work de next day, and we hardly ever stayed up all night. Dat was during de harvest, or at Christmas times."

Mollie Taylor, Texas

"De overse'er on de farm would ring a bell at 4:30 in de mornin' an' de slaves would git up an' wash an' go eat der breakfast, den dey would go to de fiel'.

Dey wokked from daylight til dark, ever day except Sunday. De marster waz purtty reasonably wid de wokke. Der wasn't much foolishness an' de marster very seldom had to whip any of de slaves. De most of de whippun's I's git waz from my mother an' I's needed 'em. I's hear tell dat on de other farms 'round dere dat dey sometimes kill de slaves cauze dey wouldn't wokke but I's never seen 'em do dat."

Jake Terriell, Texas

"Massa wake us 'bout four o'clock with de great iron and hammer and us work long as us could see."

"Us could rest when us git to de quarters or go by de big task and take de bath, and every Saturday night us git de holiday and have banjo and tin pan beatin' and dance. On Christmas massa kilt de big hawg and us fix it jus' like us wants and have big dinner."

J. W. Terrill, Texas

"Missy worked me on the farm and there was 'bout 100 acres and fifteen slaves to work 'em. The overseer waked us 'bout three in the mornin' and then he worked us jus' long as we could see. If we didn't git 'round fast 'nough, he chain us to a tree at night with nothin' to eat, and nex' day, if we didn't go on the run he hit us 39 licks with a belt what was 'bout three foot long and four inches wide."

Lucy Thomas, Texas

"All hands was up and in the field by daylight and Marse Baldwin allus kep's a fifty gallon barrel whiskey on the place and a demijohn on the front porch all the time for the niggers to git they drink on way to the field. But nobody ever got drunk."

Nancy Thomas, Texas

"Harvey Wheeler was de nigger overseer. He was a big nigger, not in looks, but 'cause he took orders only f'om Mawster Smith. So we looked up to him lak he was a big man. Harvey had a putty good education, and he was a preachah. He would always preach to us on Sunday afternoons. He was allowed to do dat, but we wasn't allowed to read no books."

Mary Thompson, Texas

"When we come home from de fields at night, de womon cooked de food and den dey was so tired dey jus' went to bed. We didn' have fun in de evenin's, but on Christmas mornin' de marster give us oggnog and sich. Den we'd sing but I don' 'member de songs now."

"De crops in Alabama would be cleared by July 4 and den we'd have sev'ral days off, all de slaves. Dey'd give us pits of barbecue and pies and cakes to eat."

Albert Todd, Texas

"But when we got to Lavernia, where we got a farm, I didn't do no work that was suff'ring. I used to scour the house and keep it clean."

"But they worked us plenty hard. Work was a religion we was taught. They said if we didn't work hard, God would come and put us in the fire. All they taught us was to work hard, obey your master, don't be sassy, and don't steal. That was the way we could get to heaven."

Alex Trimble, Texas

"My pa he uster wuk in de fiel' 'till freedom come. My ma she wuk in de kitchen. Dat how come I git so much outer de kitchen to eat. Sometime she hafter wuk in de fiel' too."

Neal Upson, Georgia

"Marster had one of dem old cotton gins what didn't have no engines. It was wuked by mules. Dem old mules was hitched to a long pole what dey pulled 'round and 'round to make de gin do its wuk. Dey had some gins in dem days what had treadmills for de mules to walk in. Dem old treadmills looked sorter lak stairs, but most of 'em was turned by long poles what de mules pulled. You had to feed de cotton by hand to dem old gins and you sho had to be keerful or you was gwine to lose a hand and maybe a arm. You had to jump in dem old cotton presses and treed de cotton down by hand. It tuk most all day long to gin two bales of cotton and if dere was three bales to be ginned as had to wuk most all night to finish up."

John Van Hook, Georgia

"Really, Miss, I couldn't say just how big that plantation was, but I am sure there must have been at least four or five hundred acres in it. One mighty peculiar thing about his slaves was that Marse George never had more than 99 slaves at one time; every time he bought one to try to make it an even hundred, a slave died. This happened so often, I was told, that he stopped trying to keep a hundred or more, and held on to his 99 slaves, and long as he did that, there warn't any more deaths than births among his slaves. His slaves. had to be in the fields when the sun rose, and there they had to work steady until the sun went down. Oh! yes, man, Marse Tommy Angel was mighty mean to his slaves, but Miss Jenny, his sister, was good as could be; that is the reason she gave my mother to her sister, Miss Ca'line Sellars; because she though Marse Tommy was too hard on her."

Addie Vinson, Georgia

"Pappy's Ma and Pa was Grandma Nancy and Grandpa Jacob. Day was field hands, and dey b'longed to Marse Obe Jackson. Grandma Lucy and Grandpa Toney Murrah was owned by Marse Billy Murrah. Marse Billy was a preacher what sho could come down wid de gospel at church. Grandma Lucy was his cook. Miss Sadie LeSeur got Grandma Lucy and tuk her to Columbus, Georgy, and us never seed our grandma no more. Miss Sadie had been one of de Vinson gals. She tuk our Aunt Haley 'long too to wait on her when she started out for Europe, and 'fore dey got crost de water, Aunt Haley, she died on de boat. Miss Sarah, she had a time keepin' dem boatsmens from th'owing Aunt Haley to de sharks. She is buried in de old country somewhar."

"Long 'fore day, dat overseer blowed a bugle to wake up de Niggers. You could hear it far as High Shoals, and us lived dis side of Watkinsville. Heaps of folkses all over dat part of de country got up by dat old bugle."

"I will never forgit one time when de overseer said to us chillun: 'You fellows go to de field and fetch some corn tops.' Mandy said: 'He ain't talkin' to us 'cause us ain't fellows and I ain't gwine.' Bless your sweet life, I runned and got dem corn tops, 'cause I didn't want no beatin'. Dem udder chillun got deir footses most cut off wid dem switches when dat overseer got to wuk to sho 'em dey had to obey him. Dat overseer sho did wuk de Niggers hard; he driv' 'em all de time. Dey had to go to de field long 'fore sunup, and it was way atter sundown 'fore day could stop dat field wuk. Den dey had to hustle to finish deir night wuk in time for supper, or go to bed widout it."

"When slave got in from de fields at night dey cooked and et deir supper and went to bed. Dey had done been wukin' since sunup. When dere warn't so much to do in de fields, sometimes old Marster let his Niggers lay off from wuk atter dinner on Saddays. If de chinches was most eatin' de Niggers up, now and den de 'omans was 'lowed to stay to de house to scald evvythirg and clear 'em out, but de manfolkses had to go on to de field. On Sadday nights de 'omans patched, washed, and cut off peaches and apples to dry in fruit season. In de daytime dey had to cut off and dry fruit for Old Miss. When slaves got smart wid deir white folkses, deir Marsters would have 'em beat, and dat was de end of de matter. Dat was a heap batter'n dey does now days, 'cause if a nigger gits out of place dey puts him on de chaingang."

Bean Walker, Texas

"Ebbery body worked ebbery day 'cep' Sunday. Us ware too tired to do anything but res' atter de day's work ware done. Sometime dere ware dances."

Edwin Walker, Mississippi

"My fust wuk wuz 'round de place at odd jobs lak pickin' up apples, a totin' in wood an' cleanin' yards; and later in de fields ob cotton, corn an' wheat. Hit took 'bout two or three weeks to thrust out de wheat."

Irella Battle Walker, Texas

"When I was about twelb years old I could pick about one hundred and fifty pounds ob cotton a day. It sure was hard work. Dere was one man, Israel Roberts, dat could pick his five hundred pounds a day. He sure was a good picker. But he never did git no pay fo' pickin' all ob dat cotton. He jes' got his food, clothes and a place to stay at night. None ob us got paid fo' our work. A lot ob folks would go along and pick de cotton and den make up songs to sing. I don't remembah none ob dem songs, but I sure know dat de folks sung 'em."

"De men was never allowed to go huntin' durin' de week 'xceptin' on Sunday. Durin' de week if it rained and we couldn't do no field work, we had to shuck and shell cawn. Dere was two laghe cawn shellers in de log crib and we had to do dat kind of work, or we had to go out and pull up all de weeds in de yard, and it was a big one too. A lot ob de wimmen would stay in de cabins and spin thread fo' de looms. Dere was two laghe looms on de place and every cabin had a spinnin' wheel."

John Walton, Texas

"I had to help break up de land, plant de cawn and cotton, chop de cawn and cotton and do a little of everything. Jes' whut ever had to be done at de time, I had to go out and do it."

"In clearin' land, we'd run across plenty of snakes. One day I was diggin' up sprouts and I was barefooted when a snake bit me right on top of my foot. Bein' virgin land dere was plenty of snakes. Dere was also plenty of varmints."

"Between three and four o'clock in de mawnin', de overseer rung de bell and we had to git up. We had a big fireplace about four foot across and dere'd be plenty of ashes in de mawnin' to make ash-cakes."

"Fo' breakfast we usually had meat, ash-cakes, bran-coffee and sassafras tea, which we made f'om de dried sassafras roots. Yo could keep dem dried sassafras roots de year 'round, and day'd be jes' as strong. Yo' could plow 'em up in de fields, cause dey growed wild. Sassafras tea was good fo' yo' blood, and also fo' de whole system."

"I done field work up dere and even us kids had to pick 150 pounds cotton a day, or git de whoppin'. Us puts de cotton in de white-oak baskets and some dem hold more'n 100 pounds. It 'cordin' to de way you stamps you cotton in. De wagon with de yoke of oxen standin' in de field for to pour de cotton in and when it full, de oxen pulls dat wagon to de hoss-power gin. Us gin'rally use 'bout 1,600 pounds cotton to make de bale."

Sol Walton, Texas

"The first work I done in slavery was totin' water and dinner to the field hands, in gourd buckets. We didn't have tin buckets then. The hands worked from sun to sun, and if the overseer seed 'em slackin' up he cussed 'em and sometimes whacked 'em with a bullwhip. I seed 'em whipped till their shirt stuck to their back. I seed my mammy whipped for shoutin' at white folks meetin'. Old massa stripped her to the waist and whipped her with a bullwhip. Heaps of 'em was whipped jus' 'cause they could be whipped. Some owners half fed their hands and then whipped them for beggin' for grub."

Annie Whitley Ware, Texas

"All de wimmin on de Whitley plantation but one er two had ter wukk in de fiel', in de house, de dairy, er whar dey wuz needed. Mammy hauled wood, ploughed, wukked 'roun' de house, spun thread an' wove clothe, cooked, dyed cloth an' whar ever Mis' arrange. Some ob de men slaves wuz good cattle hands an' could rope an' brand wid de bes' ob 'em."

Ella Washington, Texas

"De plan'ation was big, dey had 'bout a hundred an' fifty slaves jes' guessing on it. Most of 'em was field hands, but a couple of de women work in de house an' in de kitchen. When a woman jes' had a baby, dey wouldn't let 'er go to de fields for a while, dey put 'em in de loom, making 'em card an' spin. Dey make dere own cloth for de slaves to wear. I don' know much 'bout dat part of it, 'cause I never had nothing to do wit' it. Dey work 'em hard, too. Sometime dey work in de fields 'til nine 'clock at night when it got so dark dey couldn't see to work no more. I 'member sometimes in de summer time it was 'bout ten 'clock 'fore my mother an' father come in out of de fields."

Rosa Washington, Texas

"We had a good cabin on the plantation. Made out-a planks. Ole rip-rap plunder. Dey treat us good. I was a servant. Water garden, work in fields when ten years old. Hoed my row ev'ry day. Dey didn't whop me though. My mistress wouldn't let 'em. Marsa and missus good to me. I not tell no lie on 'em. Tell truf. Truf shines."

"My dad drive the carrage [carriage]. Carried 'em around all time. My mother worked in the field like I do."

Louis Watkins, Indiana

"All the slaves were well clothed, fed and housed. The master kept four grown slaves for the fields and the mistress kept two to do the work in the big house."

Foster Weathersby, Mississippi

"My first wuk in de fiel's was carryin' water, droppin' corn, and pickin' cotton. De slaves was kep' busy all through de farm season, which lasted 'bout nine months out of de year. Through de winter dey did all de repair wuk on de houses, fences and farm implements. At dis time new land was cleared and de log rollin' was done. De womens was kep' busy spinnin' and knittin'."

Robert Weathersby, Mississippi

"De fiel' wuk wuz done from sun to sun. De fiel' hands went out early in de mornings after de horn had blowed an' dey had all et breakfas' at Marse's house. When dey reached de fiels dey went to plowing, strowing fertlize, planting an' hoeing. At twelve o'clock a cowhorn wuz blowed an' dey would go in to dinner, den dey would go back an' wuk till nite. In gathering time fiels full ob 'em would cut rake, bind an' stack. Wagons would be coming an' gwine stacked high wid grain an' stuff dey had growed. Acres an' acres o' snowy white cotton would be dotted here an' deir wid bunches o' slaves a picking cotton wid deir long sacks dragging from deir sholdiers. De darkies had a big time a singing, shouting, an' hollering. Scary ghos' tales would be tole an' tales o hoo-doo an' all kinds o' superstion dat de darkies believed in. Dey believed in all kinds o' signs an' stuff lak dat. De Overseers wuz alwas' close by to see dat de wuk wuz kept a gwine. When nite come on dey took out, et supper an' den hit de hay [to bed, a negro saying as their beds were of hay] dead tired."

Steve Weathersby, Mississippi

"My fust wuk in de fields, I was a small slave boy ob about five years. I had to chop de grass from around de stumps. As I growed up I did uder things an' heaver wuk such as pickin' cotton, plowin' an' lookin' ader Mar's stock."

James West, Texas

"Sam, Buck, an' Rufus am de field wo'kahs. Deys 'ten' to de plantin' ob de cotton, co'n, an' sich. Dey looks aftah de stock too. Dey wo'ks hahd some times w'en de wo'k am rushed, udder times dey don'. All de Marster wants am dat de wo'k am done. He tells dat to de niggers often. W'en de wo'k am done, de cullud fo'ks am 'lowed to go afishin', to visit, or to res'. Jus' any thing dey wants to does."

"W'at wo'k Ise does? Well, befo' de wah, mos'ly, Ise keeps de bread an' buttah f'om gwine to waste. Den de Marster gives me de he goat. Buck, him was de shoemakah, makes me de harness an' a caht fo' de goat. W'en weuns gits dat goat trained to drive good, Ise have de job ob gittin' de chips fo' kindlin' de fiah, gits de fiah wood, an' totes de wuatah. Lawd, w'at didn't Ise do wid dat Billy. You see, Billy was his name."

William Wheeler, Mississippi

William Wheeler known as "Uncle Wheeler" says he was jes a "Shirt tail" boy at the time of the surrender. From other things he tells I judge him to be about 83 years old.

Wheeler was borned on de Walden place near Lexington Mississippi. His grandmother—old lady Tildy—wuz de prize pickin nigger on dat place. Pickin' or snappin' 650 to 700 pounds a day. She would have a cotton sack 9 to 12 feet long holding 50 to 100 pounds of cotton, slung over each shoulder crawling along a cotton row on her knees and snatching with both hands, sometimes bolls, small limbs and what ever came off as she snatched by, into these sacks. As one would be filled it was left on the ground to be picked up by some one. Tilda would be given another which she placed on her shoulder without much slacking."

Adeline White, Texas

"Us hab Sunday off but not Sadday. Us hafter wuk in de fiel' all day Sadday."

Mingo White, Alabama

"I warn't nothin' but a chile endurin' slavery, but I had to wuk de same as any man. I went to de fiel' and hosed cotton, pulled fodder and picked cotton wid to res' of de han's. I kep' up too, to keep from gittin' any lashes dat night when us got home. In de winter I went to de woods wid de men folks to hope git wood or to git sap from de trees to make turpentine an' tar. Iffen us didn't do dat us made charcoal to run de blacksmif shop wid."

Green Willbanks, Georgia

"The only one of my grandparents I can bring to memory now is Grandma Rose on my Pa's side. She was some worker, a regular man-woman; she could do any kind of work a man could do. She was a hot horse in her time and it took an extra good man to keep up with her when it came to work."

"That plantation covered a large space of land, but to tell you how many acres is something I can't do. There were not so many slaves. I've forgot how they managed that business of getting slaves up, but I do know we didn't get up before day on our place. Their rule was to work slaves from sunup to sundown. Before they had supper they had a little piddlin' around to do, but the time was their own to do as they pleased after they had supper."

Horatio W. Williams, Texas

"My w'ite folks move from Pine Bluff, Arkansaw, to Bastrop, Lou's'ana, an' den on to Texas, 'n' brung me wid 'em. W'en us wuk in d' fiel' us had a cook w'at put us food on big trays an' carry it to d' fiel', den we would stop 'n' eat under shade of a tree, if dey was any 'bout. Dey give us bread, meat 'n' sirup fo' dinner. Us had bacon 's long 's it last', den dey kill' d' beefs 'n' dat was our meat. Dey raise' cotton, 'n' co'n 'n' sweet 'taters 'n' peas."

Julia Williams, Texas

"Dey waited till de cotton pickin' was over to begin dere winter work de women would spin on de old spinnin' wheel or weave on de loom to make de close we wore de cold winters, while de men would clear de land, cut cord wood fer our fies, an' prepare de land fer de nex' year's crop."

Lewis Williams, Texas

"My Master was Captain Billie Sourlock, he married Miss Thompson. They was mighty good folks and was mighty good to us slaves. We lived like folks, had plenty to eat and wear and slaves on old Captain's plantation weren't whipped, he didn't allow it, and if any of the slaves got sick, Marster and Mistress tended on 'em and seed that they had plenty of medicine and 'tention. We got up at four o'clock ever' morning in the summer and winter alike, there weren't no horn blowed nor no bell rung, he told us to git up at that time and we knowed to do it."

Lizzie Williams, Mississippi

"My job back in dem days was to weave, spin thread, run de loom, an durin crop time I plowed an' hoed in de field. My mammy was a regular field hand."

"De overseer sent us to de field every mornin' by 4:00 o'clock an we stayed 'till after dark. By de time cotton was weighed up an supper cooked an et, it was midnight when we'd get to bed heep o' times. Dese overseers saw dat every nigger got his 'mount o' cotton. De grown ones had to pick 600, 700 an 800 pounds a day an' de 14 an 15 year old ones had to pick 400 an 500 pounds."

Mattie Williams, Texas

"Folks had to do whut yo' called a task each day, and yo' had to finish it befo' yo' was through fo' de day. Pappy was sich a poor picker, dat mammy had to drop cotton in his row, so he'd have enough to make up fo' his task each day."

Millie Williams, Texas

"Now 'bout de wokke, de overse'er would wake 'em up at four o'clock in de mornin'. Den dey would git ready to eat an' go to de fiel'."

Soul Williams, Texas

"I never did any work until I was freed. I'se always stayed around the house and drove my master where he wanted to go or saddled his horse for him. No sir, I never did have any money. Sometime the master would give me five or ten cents and I would spend that for candy."

"Our overseer, Master John Bates, would wake us every morning about 4 o'clock cause when he rung that old big bell, we came rolling out yessir. We would work all day and he would bring us in at sundown. He would make us fall in the creek ever night, clothes and all, and take a bath."

Wayman Williams, Texas

"When de cotton pickin' time cum den de nigger all are happy 'kaze dey gits a little money an den dey all has good times in de fiels a singin' an runnin' races to see who makes de rows first, dey had lots of songs dey sing, some long an some short. One goes like dis,

De top bolls aint open, de bottom bolls are rotton,
I caint git my numba here, I has to quit an go away,
Wen de sun goes down, an de moon goes up,
Efn I caint git my numba, I caint git my pay.

"When I was little, my father split de rails out of trees to make fences, and I have an aunt what was de big woman, and she help. She have a song what go like dis, and when she sing, she come down on a rail, 'biff.'"

Times are gittin' hard, (biff)
Money's gittin scarce, (biff)
Times don't git no better here, (biff)
I bound to leave dis place.

Frances Willingham, Georgia

"Our overseer got all de slaves up 'fore break of day and dey had to be done et deir breakfast and in de field when de sun riz up. Dat sun would be down good 'fore dey got to de house at night."

"When slaves come in from de fields at night de 'omans cleant up deir houses atter dey et, and den washed and got up early next mornin' to put de clothes out to dry. Mens would eat, set 'round talkin' to other mens and den go to bed. On our place evvybody wukked on Saddays 'til 'bout three or four o'clock and if de wuk was tight dey wukked right on 'till night lak any other day."

Adeline Willis, Georgia

"Her mother worked in the field: she drove stears and could do all kinds of farm work and was the best meat cutter on the plantation. She was a good spinner too, and was required to spin a broach of 'wool spinning' every night. All the negro women had to spin, but Aunt Adeline said her mother was specially good in spinning wool and 'that kind of spinning was powerful slow.' Thinking a moment, she added: 'And my mother was one of the best dyers anywhere 'round, and I was too. I did make the most colors by mixing up all kinds of bark and leaves. I recollect the prettiest sort of a lilac color I made with maple bark and pine bark, not the outside pine bark, but that little thin skin that grows right down next to the tree—it was pretty, that color was."

Sampson Willis, Texas

"We had good times when we was chillun growin up, played games, hollered and sang. Then when we got big enough to work in the field, Uncle Larry blew a horn just at day every morning to wake us. We had to get to work early. The cook blew the horn at 11:30 and we went back to work at one. We sang an hollered as we worked but mostly of a morning an late in the evening."

"When laying by time was over the hands went to clearing land some would be hauling the wood up to the house while others cut and split. Then there was rails to make fencin to do. There was plenty work for all the hands."

Claude Augusta Wilson, Florida

The Dexter plantation was quite a large place, covering 100 or more acres. There were about 100 slaves, including children. They had regular one room quarters built of logs which was quite insignificant in comparison with the palatial Dextor mansion. The slaves would arise early each morning, being awakened by a "driver" who was a white man, and by "sun-up" would be at their respective tasks in the fields. All day they worked, stopping at noon to get a bite to eat, which they carried on the fields from their cabins.

At "sun-down" they would quit work and return to their cabins, prepare their meals and gossip from cabin to cabin, finally retiring to await the dawn of a new day which signalled a return to their routine duties. At Sundays they would gather at a poorly constructed frame building which was known as the "Meeting House." In this building they would give praise and thanks to their

God. The rest of the day was spent in relaxation as this was the only day of the week in which they were not forced to work.

Claude Augusta worked in the fields, his mother and sister worked in the Dexter mansion. Their duties were general house work, cooking and sewing. His mother was very rebellious toward her duties and constantly harrassed the "Missus" about letting her work in the fields with her husband until finally she was permitted to make the change from the house to the fields to be near her man.

Lulu Wilson, Texas

"One day they truckled us all down in a covered wagon and started out with the family and my maw and step paw and five of us chilluns. I know I was past twelve year old. We come a long way and we passed through a free state. [Probably Missouri] Some places we drove for miles in the woods instead of the big road and when we come near to folks they hid us down in the bed of the wagon."

"We passed through a little place and my maw told me to look and I saw a man going up some steps toting a bucket of water. She said, 'Lulu, that man is your paw. He aint such a youngish man but he was good to me and good for me.' I ain't never think she was as considible of my step paw as she was of my paw and she gave me to think as much. My step paw never did like me but he was a fool for his own younguns. 'Cause at the end of the wars when they set the niggers free he tramped over half the world gathering up them younguns that they had sold away."

"He went to a place called Wadefield [Texas] and settled for some short passing of time and they was a Missionary Baptist church next to the house. When we was there Mrs. Hodges let me go twice and I was fancified with the singing and the preaching. They sang something 'bout the Glory Road. I set it in my mind that some day I'd jine with them and I spoke it over with my maw."

"We went on to Chatfield Point. [Navarro County, Texas] Wash Hodges built a log house and covered it with weather boarding and built my maw and paw quarters to live in. They turned to raising corn, taters and hogs. I had to work like a dog. I hoed and I milked ten cows twice a day."

President Wilson, Texas

"Dey worked us pretty hard, and dey'd whip us without no excuse lots of time. Make us lay down on a log and whip till de blood come."

Wash Wilson, Texas

"Back in Louisiana an' here in Texas, dar wuz a big bell in Marse's yard an' hit 'ud ring fer us ter go to wukk by an' ter stop by. Us had ter git ter wukk jes' ez soon as hit wuz light. De bell 'ud ring 'bout eleven thutty ob er mornin' an' us git back ter wukk in er little while an' wukk till dark. Mammy wukked in de fiel' in de day an' spun an' wove at night. On bad days an' in de winter, her

Wash Wilson. (Library of Congress)

did de mos' ob de spinnin' an' weavin'. Dar wuz a shoemaker on de plantation an' he made mos' ob de shoes. Dey wuz brogans wid one buckle, no shoe laces, an' dey had brass toes."

Willis Winn, Texas

"I still got the bugle he woke us with at four in the morning. When the bugle blowed you'd better go to hollering so the overseer could hear your. If he had to call you, it was too bad. The first thing in the morning we go to the lot and feed, then go to the wood pile till breakfast. They put our grub in the trough and giv' us so long to eat. Master hollered, if we was slow eating, 'Swallow that grub now and chaw it tonight. Better be in that fiel' by daybreak.' We worked from 'see to can't,' from the time you could see the furrow till you can't see it."

Rube Witt, Texas

"Master Witt had a big place, I don't recall how many acres, but he didn't have so many slaves. Slavery was a 'tight-fight.' We lived in small cabins, slep' on rough plank beds, and et bacon, peas, and parched co'n. We didn't hardly know what flour bread was. Master giv' us one outfit of clothes at a time, and sometimes we wore shoes. We wo'ked all day in the fiel', come in feed the stock and chores 'round the house, get what little grub [food] it took to do us and go to bed. You'd better not go anywhere without a pass 'cause the 'Pattyrollers' was rolling 'round every bush."

Rebecca Woods, Mississippi

"I wuz a fiel' han' an' toted water to de han' in de fiel'; dats what de chillun had to do befo' dey got big nuf to work in de fiel's; when hit cum time fer de chilluns to wuk, dey ole folks wu'd giv' dem a short handle how an' learn dem how to chop out cotton, an' den we wu'd have us short sacks in de fall when cotton pickin' time cum' we didn't hev' to wuk hard, but wid so many mouths to feed in de quarter us hed to do sumthin' to make our sumpthin' to eat."

Caroline Wright, Texas

"On de farm, us all lived in one an' two room log cabins, made out of cedar posts. My ma an' my pappy worked on de farm an' de boys. My sisters an' me worked in de house, doin' all de house work fo de Wortham fambly. Us didn't make any money, but us had plenty of hog meat, beef, butter, milk, corn bread an' vegetables to eat, lots mo den us hab dese days. Us did all de cookin' on de fireplaces. Yes mam, us sho did eat plenty of possum, an' rabbit, an' us cotched lots of fish out de Bosque ribber. Us eat all de food de white folks gabe us."

"De women slaves, eleven of us, had dere own gardens. Us eleben spun our own clothes. In de summer, us all wore cotton stripe an' in de winter linsey dresses. On Sunday us had lawn dresses, an' us sho did come out looking choicesome."

"Dr. Wortham had Si for a overseer. He worked and carried out the doctor's orders. It was a big farm an' had forty or fifty slaves to work it. Us had to get up about four o'clock in de mornin' an' did not have breakfas 'till 'bout nine. All de slaves had to work from sun to sun, an' when us was sick, Dr. Wortham treated us. He give us powder and pills."

Henry Wright, Georgia

As a youngster Mr. Wright had to pick up chips around the yard, make fires and keep the house supplied with water which he got from the well. When he was ten years of age he was sent to the field as a plow-boy. He remembers that his mother and father also worked in the fields. In relating his experience as a field hand Mr. Wright says that he and his fellow slaves were roused each morning about 3 o'clock by the blowing of a horn. This horn was usually blown by the white overseer or by the Negro foreman who was known among the slaves as the "Nigger Driver." At the sounding of the horn they had to get up and feed the stock. Shortly after the horn was blown a bell was rung and at this signal they all started for the fields to begin work for the day. They were in the field long before the sun was up. Their working hours were described as being from "sun to sun." When the time came to pick the cotton each slave was required to pick at least 200 lbs. of cotton per day. For this purpose each was given a bag and a large basket. The bag was hung around the neck and the basket was placed at the end of the row. At the close of the day the overseer met all hands at the scales with the lamp, the slate and the whip. If any slave failed to pick the required 200 lbs. he was soundly whipped by the overseer. Sometimes they were able to escape this whipping by giving illness as an excuse. Another form of strategy adopted by the slaves was to dampen the cotton or conceal stones in the baskets, either of which would make the cotton weigh more.

Sometimes after leaving the fields at dark they had to work at night—shucking corn, ginning cotton or weaving. Everyday except Sunday was considered a work day. The only form of work on Sunday was the feeding of the live stock, etc.

Fannie Yarbrough, Texas

"Ole Marster had a world of sheeps. Every day we take dem sheeps and watch 'em. The wolves was mean. We'd git to playin', all us little niggers, and forgit them sheeps and nex' thing you know an old wolf would have himse'f a sheep."

"Sometimes we'd keep playin' so late it was dark 'fore we knowed it and we'd start runnin' them sheeps home. Ol' Marster would be at de big gate to let us in. He says, 'Now, chillen, you didn' git back with all the sheep.' We'd say, 'Ol' wolf got 'em.' But he knowed ol' wolf didn't git all de ones missin' and he'd say, 'You're storyin'.' Then purty soon some of the little stray ones come home. Then he knowed we'd run the sneep home and he'd say, 'I 'spose I'll have to whip you,' but he never did. Those were sweet times! Ol' Marster was so good, and he give us more to eat than you ever saw. Hog meat every day and sweet 'tatoes so big we'd have to cut 'em with an ax."

"After we et our supper, we had to spin a broach of thread every night 'fore we went to bed. I larned all 'bout spinnin' and weavin' when I was little and by time I's 10 I'd make pretty striped cloth."

Litt Young, Texas

"When that big bell rung at four o'clock you'd better get up 'cause the overseer was standin' there with a whippin' strap if you was late. My daddy got a sleepin' most every morning for oversleeping. Them mules was standin' in the field at daylight, waitin' to see how to plow a straight furrow. If a nigger was a 500 pound cotton picker and didn't weigh up that much at night, that was not gitting his task and he got a whipping. The last weighin' was done by lightin' a candle to see the scales."

Louis Young, Texas

"'Twas de same wid de old fo'ks 'bout de wo'k. Wo'k, wo'k, wo'k, 'twas all dey do. De cullud fo'ks wo'ked f'om de time dey could see 'til dark comes, an'

Sunday am jus' de same as tudder days. Ise don't know what Sunday am s'posed to be 'til Ise come to Texas. Parties, dances, tudder good things, Ise don't know what dey am 'til Ise comes to Texas. No sar, not on Marster Atkinson's place, an' weuns am not 'lowed to go to tudder places. Him comes to de cabins ever night, an' looks to see if weuns am all thar."

Mary Young, Texas

"Master and his mistress they was young and fiery, but they was durn good to their black folks. Master he have about 30 acres in his farm. He growed tobacco. He have six grown slaves and I'se just about grown. Master he wake the slaves bout 4 o'clock every morning and they work just long as they could see how. Oh, yes, they whip the slave when they get unruly just like you do mule. He would hit him 39 lick that is just how the patter roller would get them."

Teshan Young, Texas

"How many houahs we uns wo'k? Dat depen's on de time ob de yeah it am. W'en its de time fo' de hoein' or de pickin' ob de cotton, dey wo'k late. 'Twarnt sich long houahs udder times."

DOMESTIC WORKERS

Household duties that slaveholders needed performed, such as cooking, serving, and caring for children, were often handled by the enslaved. Although not as physically arduous as field work, these tasks were physically and psychologically demanding. The household workers performed under the constant scrutiny of the slaveholder family and had to be available day and night. Some enslaved domestic workers received special favors and benefits as a result of their close relationship with the slaveholder family, but for others the proximity proved detrimental as they suffered constantly at the hands of slaveholders who were never satisified with their work.

The opportunity to work as an enslaved servant in the house certainly had its benefits. The living environment for enslaved house workers was generally better than that of field workers, and housing, food quality, and clothing were usually higher in quality. A wide range of tasks needed to be done, depending on the wealth of the slaveholder and his family. On the Georgia plantation where Alice Battle lived, "Her mother was the cook for the 'big house.' The mistress had a number of servants helping with the house work, the washing and ironing, the weaving and sewing. Alice's oldest sister was one of the maids." One of the benefits of serving as the cook was the access to better food for the cook and at times her family. Tom Mix of Texas reaped those benefits as a result of his mother's serving as the cook in "the big house": "My mother done the cookin' up at the house because she was workin' up there all the time, weavin' cloth, and of course we ate up there. The rest of 'em didn't like it much because we ate up there, but her work was there."

Other jobs as enslaved house workers also reaped benefits that made the worker's lives a little less onerous. Marshal Butler's Georgia mother had access to better clothing; she "was maid in de Collar's home and she had many fine dresses—some of them were give to her by her missus." In Georgia, Cornelia Whitfield's father received special privileges while working directly for his slaveholder: "My father and mother wuz house servants. My marster served my father's plate from his own table and sent it to him, every meal. He had charge of the work shop, and when marster was away he always stayed at the Big House, to take care of my Missis and the children." Also in Georgia, Mose Davis's "Father was the family coachman. 'All that he had to do was to drive the master and his family and to take care of the two big grey horses that he drove.' Compared to my mother and the other slaves he had an easy time." These were small benefits, but they could make working in the house advantageous.

However, there were negative aspects to working near the slaveholder family as well. The work could be physically draining:

> My mammy wus de cook an' she help in de house; she scrubbed de floors wid a big heavy mop dat had holes bored in it, an' shucks put in dat, an' she pulled dat crossed de rooms wid sand an' homemade soap, an' got de floors white. Den she poured clean water on de floors an' took a broom made uf broom sage straw an' swept dat off, an' den tuk a big sack an' laid it on to de floor an' put her feet on it an' kept walkin cross dat floor till she had wiped up all de water. Dat floor wus pritty an' white. (Henry Lewis McGaffey, Mississippi)

The work hours were long as one had to be constantly available to respond to the needs of others, no matter how tired one was. Stearlin Arnwine of Texas recalled: "As soon as dinner was over Massa John always took a nap, lie down for one hour each day an my job was to set by him an fan him, an lawsy me, I'd get so tired but I knowed I had to keep that fan a-gwine. I can hear him now, as he'd wake up he'd say, 'Colonel, go get me a drink outa the north east corner of the well.'" In addition, house workers were under constant scrutiny, so a misstep or displeasing action often resulted in punishment. Elizabeth Finley of Mississipi said: "Dey give us plenty to eat and wear but dey beat on us a plenty. 'Old Mis' would whup de house slaves wid a cowhide whup when dey didn't do to suit her. Dey sho' wuz scared of her and stepped wen she speak to dem."

For women there was the added problem of unwanted advances from the men of the household. Having to sleep and live on or near the main premises left them constantly vulnerable and defenseless. Sometimes these liaisons benefited the children that resulted, but more often they were treated the same as other enslaved children. Both Anne Clark of Texas and her mother suffered this fate on their plantation: "My mama did the washin' for the big house. . . . My mama had two white chillen by marster and they were sold as slaves. I had two chillen, too. I never married." The experiences of Anne and her mother illustrate the dangers associated with working in the "big house," which counterbalanced any benefits that might accrue.

Most enslaved children became field hands, but not all of them. The slaveholder needed many jobs filled that were separate from the planting cycle. Child care was one of those tasks. Not only did enslaved children care for their siblings, but they were also enlisted to watch the slaveholder's children. Often the mistress of the house selected an enslaved child to play with and care for her children to relieve herself of these duties. This is what happened in the case of

Julia Bunch of South Carolina: "I b'longed to Marse Jackie Dorn of Edgefield County, I was gived to him and his wife when dey was married for a weddin' gift. I nussed deir three chilluns for 'em and slep' on a couch in dier bedroom 'till I was 12 years old, den 'Mancipation come."

Child care was not the only task assigned enslaved children. They also served as housekeepers, cooks, yard cleaners, and weavers, and performed sundry other duties that needed doing. Both girls and boys were assigned these tasks, often without regard to gender. In Georgia, George Womble's "job was to wait tables, help with the house cleaning, and to act as nurse maid to three young children belonging to the master. At other times I drove the cows to and from the pasture and I often helped with the planting in the fields when the field hands were rushed."

Their work in the house did not always last, however, and as some enslaved children got older they were relegated to working in the fields. But for others, as they increased in skill or the family became attached to their working in the house, the work did become their full-time position. This selection process was carefully worked out in households like the one where Randall Lee of Florida grew up:

> Boys and girls under ten years of age were never sent into the field to work on the Miller plantation but were required to mind the smaller children of the family and do chores around the "big house" for the mistress and her children. Such work as mending was taught the domestic-minded children and tending food on the pots was alloted others with inborn ability to cook. They were treated well and taught "manners" and later was used as dining room girls and nurses.

NARRATIVES

Anthony Abercrombie, Alabama

"My mistis, Miss Lou, was raisin' me up to be a carriage driver, an' she was jes' as good to me as she could be. She useta dose me up wid castor oil, jimson root, and dogwood tea when I'd be feelin' po'ly, and she'd always take up for me when Marse Jim get in behind me 'bout somep'n. I reckon though I was a purty worrisome nigger in dem days; always gettin' in some kind of mischief."

James Calvin Alexander, Texas

"Fathaw did a lot ob fahmin' on de plantation. Mothaw done mos' ob de cookin' and mighty little fahm work. She was a good cook, too; and at times, she'd be in de loom-room, where day made de cloth. De loom-room, which had a loom, spinnin' wheel and cardin' rack, was up in de big house."

Barney Alford, Mississippi

"My mammy wus named Deliah, en she wus de best cook in de wurld, en ole Missus kno'ed it, en she kept her in dat kitchen all de time. When big meetin wud cum, my mammy wuld stack dem cakes up high on de shelf in er big room, en one time I slipped in dar en pinched offen a big piece uf cake, en dey sho whipped me dat time. En ernudder time I got my han' in er jar uf jam en culdnt git it out en my mammy hed to git it out fur me, en I wus whipped fur dat."

"My pappy wus named Jourdan, en he wurk in de field, en druv the team uf oxen ter Covin'ton, Louisiana, wid a big waggin loaded wid cotton, all dat four yoke uf oxen culd pull atter time. He wus allus gone er week en when he cum back de waggin wus filled wid flour, en salt, en sugar, en one time he brung a barrell of mackeral, en I stole sum uf dat en wus whipped er gin."

Jim Allen, Mississippi

"Did I work? Yes Mam, me and a girl worked in de field carrying one row, you know it took two chillerns to make one hand."

"As I done tole you, I was Mars Allens' pet nigger boy. I was called a 'stray.' I slep on de floor by ole Miss and Mars Bob. I could a slep on de trundle bed, but it was so easy jist to roll over and blow dem ashes and make dat fire burn."

"Ole Miss was so good, I'd do anything for her. She was so good and weighed around 200 pounds. She was Mars Bob's second wife. Nobody posed on me, No, Sir! I carried water to Mars Bob's store close by and he would allus give me candy by de double handsfull, and as many juice harps as I wanted. De best thing I ever did eat was dat candy. Marster was good to his only stray nigger boy."

Charity Anderson, Alabama

"Missy, peoples don't live now; and niggers ain't got no menners, and doan' know nothin' 'bout waitin' on folks. I kin remember de days when I was one of de house servants. Dere was six of us in de ole Massa's house—me, Sarai, Lou, Hester, Jerry and Joe. Us did'n' know nothin' but good times den. My job was lookin' atter de corner table what nothin' but de desserts set. Joe and Jerry, dey was de table boys. Dey neber tetched nothin' wid dere hen's, but used de waiter to pass things wid."

"My ole Massa was a good man. He treated all his sleves kind, and took good kere of 'em. But, honey, all de white folks wan't good to dere slaves. I's seen po' niggers 'mos' tore up by dogs and whupped 'tell dey bled w'en dey did'n' do lak de white folks say. But, thank de Lawd, I had good white folks and dey sho' did trus' me, too. I had charge of all de keys to de house, and I waited on de Missis' and de chillun. I laid out all de clo'se on Sat'dy night, and den Sunday mawnin's I'd pick up all de dirty things. Dey did'n' have a thing to do. Us house servants had a hard job keepin' de pickaninnies out er de dinin' room whar ole Massa at, cause w'en dey would slip in and stan' by his cheer, w'en he finished eatin' he would fix a plate for 'em end let 'em set on the hearth."

Charity Anderson. (Library of Congress)

"No mam, Missy, I ain't neber worked in de fields. Ole Messa he neber planted no cotton, and I ain't seen none planted 'tell after I was free. But, honey, I could sho 'nuff wash, iron and knit and weave. Sometimes I weaved six or seven yahds of cloth, and do my house work too. I lernt the chillun how to weave, and wash, and iron, and knit too, and I's waited on de fo'th generation of our fambly. I jes' wish I could tell dese young chillun how to do. Iffen dey would only suffer me to talk to dem, I'd tell dem to be more 'spectful to dere mammies and to dere white folks and say 'yes mam' and 'no mam,' instid of 'yes' and 'no' lak dey do now."

Cindy Anderson, Mississippi

"'Bout all I remembers 'bout slave time wuz Miss Betsy Ann an' my mother spinning wool or cotton an' makin' thread or cloth. Seems lak dats all dey ever done. Miss Betsy Ann would weave an' my mother would spin thread, reel it into hanks, then put it into shuttles; it took three shuttles full of thread goin' at once to weave a piece of cloth, an' you worked the loom pedal with yo' foot."

Manuel Armstrong, Texas

"Mother went to wuk in Cherokee county. She was give to de marster' daughter. Dey let father go to see her onct in a w'ile."

"Mother was de cook, an' father wuk on de farm."

Stearlin Arnwine, Texas

"I was the only one of my family to go to Mr. Moseleys but he took Aunt Winnie an her three chillun, Tom, Ed, an Viny. My mother worked in the government shoe-shop at Rusk during the war. She could make as good shoes as any body."

"I never did work in the field. When I was with Judge Jowell I jest run errands, toted water, watched the gaps and waited on Mr. Jowell. When Massa John took me to live with him he said I must be his house boy—an house boy I was. Massa was sho good to me, and I did love to be with him and follow him aroun'."

"The kitchen was out in the yard an I had to carry the victuals, when they was cooked, to the big dinin-room. As soon as dinner was over Massa John always took a nap, lie down for one hour each day an my job was to set by him an fan him, an lawsy me, I'd get so tired but I knowed I had to keep that fan a-gwine. I can hear him now, as he'd wake up he'd say, 'Colonel, go get me a drink outa the north east corner of the well.' One day while I was fannin Massa John I drapped off to sleep and he woke me up by slippin' a chaw of tobacco in my mouth, one he had already chawed."

Caroline Ates, Alabama

"We lived 'bout thirty-seven miles frum Macon; so all the crops wuz hauled there in great big wagons with six mules ter the wagon. We growed lots o' cotton, corn, peas, potatoes, rye an' wheat."

Tell me what kind of work your mother did, I suggested.

"She did some field work; but, most always, she cooked for all the slaves that lived near us. She had the nicest kitchen built 'speshully for that purpose. My brothers an' sisters worked in the field.'

Kose Banks, Arkansas

"The girls swept yards, cleaned the house, nursed, and washed and ironed, combed old miss' and the children's hair and cut their finger and toe nails and mended the clothes. The womens' job was to cook, attend to the cows, knit all the socks for the men and boys, spin thread, card bats, weave cloth, quilt, sew, scrub and things like that."

Amelia Dorsey Barragan-Redford, Georgia

"I jus' tuk care o' de babies," she said. "My mother was a real stout young plow-han'. She was some woman!"

Alice Battle, Georgia

Alice's father worked in the fields. There was no regular working hours, for he worked from "sun up to sun down." Her mother was the cook for the "big house." The mistress had a number of servants helping with the house work, the washing and ironing, the weaving and sewing. Alice's oldest sister was one of the maids. There were about fifty slaves on the plantation, and those who did not help at the house did field work. The first work that Alice remembers was "nursin' the chillun" though it was a pleasure for her as she enjoyed pulling the little wagon around and playing the games that they did.

Alice's mother wove the cloth for the clothes, which her mistress superintended the making of. Some of the other slave women did the sewing. Dresses were made very full, buttoned down the front, and with belts sewed in at the waist line.

Jasper Battle, Georgia

"Mammy's job was to make all de cloth. Dat was what she done all de time; jus' wove cloth. Some of de others ovardad de bats and spun thread, but Mammy, she jus' wove on so reg'lar dat she made enough cloth for clothes for all dem slaves on de plantation and, it's a fact, us did have plenty of clothes."

Frank Bell, Texas

"I worked 'round master's saloon, kep' everything cleaned up after they'd have all night drinkin' parties, men and woman. I earned nickels to tip off where to go, so's they could sow wild oats. I buried the nickels under rocks. If master done cotch me with money, he'd take it and beat me nearly to death. All I had to eat was old stuff those people left, all scraps what was left."

Oliver Bell, Alabama

"I reckerlecks my mammy was a plow han' an' she'd go to work soon an' put me under de shade of a big ol' post-oak tree. Dere I sat all day, an' dat tree was my nurse. It still standin' dere yit, an' I won't let nobody cut it down."

Virginia Bell, Texas

"When I got old enough I was housegirl and used to carry notes for Miss Mary to the neighbors and bring back answers. Miss Mary would say, 'How, Virginny, you take this note to sech and sech place and be sure and be back in sech and sech time,' and I allus was."

Hariette Benton, Alabama

"I wuz neber large 'nuff during dem days to work. But my maw, why she an' de res' o' dem po' slaves on dat plantation she did work. Mos' o' de women plowed in de cotton field or dey picked cotton. Jes' a few worked in de big house. De chillun whut wuz ol' enough fanned flies off de table and dey helped carry de food in de big house from de kitchen. You know dat de kitchen wuz way out from de big house, don't you? In rainy weather? Why dey done jes' lak dey always done. Dey had a kind o' cover to put over de trays an' dey jes' come on in de house. Cose, de slaves, dey always got drenched to de bone."

Ellen Betts, Texas

"I nussed de sick folk, too—white and black. Sometime I dose with 'Blue Mass' pills and den sometime Doc Fatchit [Fawcett] come along and leave rhubarb and epicac and calomel and castor oil and sech. Two year after de war, I git marry and git chillen of my own. Den I turn into a wet nuss. I wet nuss de white chillen and black chillen lak dey all de same color. Sometime I have a white un pullin' one de one side and a black one on t'other and dat de truth. I wish my sister was here to testify for me. I knowed as much 'bout mid-wifin' as some of dem touty ones but I git scare de law git on me do I go ahead and bring de chillen."

Charlotte Beverly, Texas

"My auntie she cook 'n' my mudder she was d' milker. Dey cook 'simmon [persimmon] bread 'n' 'tater pone 'n' d' like."

Nelson Birdsong, Alabama

Nelson says the first work he remembered doing was "nussing a baby boy of Mr. Bramwell Burden, a gran'son of old man Burden."

Francis Black, Texas

"Me and his two chil'ren played together. They was younger than me, and we used to fight mightly. When they fight me I fight them back, and scratch them up. Mistress Caroline use to say she was gwying [going] to thrash me if I didn't stop fighting her chil'ren. She never did—she was jist trying to scare me. We played, and fought every day till I had to go sot [set] the table. I was so small I had to get in a chair to get the dishes out of the safe. I had to pull a long fly brush over the table while the white fo'ks et."

Olivier Blanchard, Texas

"My mama he'p de ol' missus up in de big house. De ol' missus' name Josephine Allick. Dey mek country clo's but us go barefoot mos' of de time. Us hab plenty to eat—peaches and figs and pears and muscadines and grapes and hick'ry nuts and pecans. Dey mek lots of t'lings like wines and t'ings like dat. Dey was right smart woods and swamp 'roun' dere. Dere was redbirds, and mockin'birds and blackbirds. Dey was lots of robins in de summer time. Us uster mek robin gumbo and pie."

Manda Boggan, Mississippi

"My first wuk wuz 'round mar's house, totin' cule water a mile from a spring, an milkin' de cows. Hit took a heap ob us ter milk all dem cows. De milk den had to be strained in big stone crocks and put in de dairies dat wuz built out under de trees ter keep de milk cool. Deir wuz a heap o' churnnin' ter be done. Hit 'peared lak us had ter churn fer hours 'afore dat butter would be deir."

Georganna Bohannon, Mississippi

"I worked as Miss' maid and wus a house girl and I didn't see no fighting and I ate in de hous in Miss' kitchen. We had a big farm with over 100 slaves and we didn't never see no money."

"I helped make de clothes for de white folks and we spun and wove and picked cotton from de seeds. I never did learn to read nor write and I don't guess I needed to cause some of de educated folks I know aint got much common sense. We didn't have no church nor bible reading and de niggers gathered around de quarters to gab or have parties but mostly we worked and I didn't see no fighting but de yankees come to de house but dey jest wanted to be fed."

Ella Booth, Mississippi

"My mother worked in de fiel' and wash and iron fer de white folks. She had 18 chillun—five boys and twelve girls—most of dem now 'deceased.'"

Nancy Boudry, Georgia

"Mistis was sorta kin' to me, sometimes. But dey only give me meat and bread, didn' give me nothin' good—I ain' gwine tell no story. I had a heap to undergo wid. I had to scour at night at de Big House—two planks one night, two more de nex'. De women peoples spun at night and reeled, so many cuts a night. Us had to git up befo' daybreak be ready to go to de fiel's."

Harrison Boyd, Texas

"I never worked a day in the field for Master Trammel, but allus stayed round the house. I cleaned yards, odd-jobs and went places for Mistress. I never learned to read or write and only went to church once or twice a year fore surrender. I'se heard preachers read the Bible some fore they set us free."

Isabella Boyd, Texas

"My mistus kep' me right in d' house right by 'er sewin'. My wuk was sewin'. Dey teach me t' sew soon's I was big 'nuf t' hol' a needle. I could sew so fas' I git my task ovah fo' d' uders git start' good. Lots time' in d' evenin' w'en us gals want t' go t' dance' I help put in d' sleebe 'r' sew on d' pants so d' uders could go wid us. Dey say, 'Dat 'Bella, she done go way pas' all time.'"

Jacob Branch, Texas

"Mama, she work up in de big house, doin' cookin' and washin'."

"Old lady 'Liza, she have three women to spin when she git ready make de clothes for everybody. Dey spin and weave and make all us clothes. Us all wear shirt tail till us 'bout twelve or fourteen, boys and gals, too. You couldn't tell us apart."

William Branch, Texas

"How'd us slaves git de clothes? We carded de cotton, den de women spin it on a spinnin' wheel. After dat day sew de gahment togeddah on a sewin' machine. Yahsur, we's got sewin' machine, wid a big wheel and a handle. One woman tu'n de handle and de yuther woman do de sewin'."

William Branch. (Library of Congress)

"Dat's how we git de clothes for de 75 slaves. Marster's clothes? We makes dem for de whole fam'ly. De missis send de pattren and de slaves makes de clothes. Over nigh Richmond a fren' of Marster Woodson has 300 slaves. Dey makes all de clothes for dem."

Minerva Bratcher, Texas

"My Mistress learned me how to do all kinds of housework and I was busy all the time washing dishes, dusting, sweeping, combing chilluns hair, washing chilluns feet, knitting, hanking thread and weaving cloth. Laud Miss, you don't know how much folks had to do them days, and everybody worked, the old slave women who were too old to work in the field cooked, took care of the little niggars and helped spin and weave cloth. Ever morning over-seer blow a horn for the slaves to get up. When dinner time come the dinner for the slaves was put on big tables down in the quarters. I recon there was a 1000 acres in old Marsters plantation and about sixty slaves so it took a lot of cooking but everybody always had plenty."

"Yessum they worked on Saturday evening jest like any other day and when they went to the quarters at night they went to bed."

Alice Bratton, Arkansas

"The white folks ain't got no reason to mistreat the colored people. They need us all the time. They don't want no food unless a nigger cook it. They want niggers to do all their washing and ironing. They want niggers to do their sweeping and cleaning and everything around their houses. The niggers handle everything they wears and hands them everything they eat and drink. Ain't nobody can get closer to a white person than a colored person. If we'd a wanted to kill 'em, they'd a all done been dead. They ain't no reason for white people mistreating colored people."

Sam Broach, Mississippi

"My mother was name Vi'let, Vi'let Broach. She was old Miss's cook, cooked all time in de big house. Me, I cut wood an' play 'round wid de white chullun. Yes'm, ever'body work, dat is, work off an' on, you know. Some of de nigger women work in de fiel', an' some of 'em stay in de yard an' spin an' make soap an' drip candles."

Fred Brown, Texas

"Every one have deir certain wo'k an' duties fo' to do. My mammy am de fam'ly cook. Marster have no chillun, so 'twarnt much wo'k fo' her an' she he'p at de loom, makin' de cloth. My daddy am de black-smith, shoemakah an' de tanner. Ise 'splain how him do de tannin'. He puts de hides in de wauter wid black-oak bark, prutty soon de hair come off, den he rolls an' poun's de hides fo' to make dem soft."

"W'en Ise 'bout eight yeahs ol', or sich, deys stahts me to he'pin' do de yard wo'k an' he'pin' mammy in de house, totin' wauter, totin' fiah wood an' sich. As Ise grows ol'er deys give me othah wo'k to do. W'en de wah am ovah Ise den he'pin' in de field. Marster, him raises cane an' co'n mostly, no cotton."

"Marster have de overseer an' de overlooker. De overseer am in charge ob de wo'k an' de overlooker am in charge of de cullud women, him am a nigger. De overseer gives all de whuppin's."

Josie Brown, Texas

"I didn' do nuthin' but eat 'n' sleep 'n' foller d' ol' mistus 'bout. She gib me good clo's. My mudder was d' weaver. Dey jus' cut out slip', straight down, 'n' dyed wid all kin's 'r' bark. I hab t' keep my head comb, 'n' grease' wid lard. If us hab good hair dey wrip it in string but if it short dey jus' bresh it out."

Aunt Sally (Julia Brown), Georgia

"No, it's not there. Ah guess it's been put in the basement. Ah'll show it to you when you come back. It's a rock made of iron that the pot is set on befo' puttin' it on the fire coals. The victuals was good in then days; we got our vegetables out'n the garden in season and didn't have all the hot-house vegetables. Ah don't eat many vegetables now unless they come out'n the garden and I know it. Well, as I said, there wuz rocks fitted in the fireplace to put pots on. Once there wuz a big pot settin' on the fire, jest bilin' away with a big roast in it. As the water biled, the meat turned over and over, comin' up to the top and goin' down again. Ole Sandy, the dog, come in the kitchen. He sot there a while and watched that meat roll over and over in the pot, and all of a sudden-like he grabbed at that meat and pulls it out'n the pot. 'Course he couldn't eat it 'cause it wuz hot and they got the meat befo' he et it. The kitchen wuz away from the big house, so the victuals wuz cooked and carried up to the house. Ah'd carry it up mahse'f. We couldn't eat all the diffrent kind of victuals the white folks et and one mornin' when I wuz carryin' the breakfast to the big house we had waffles that wuz pretty golden brown and pipin' hot. They wuz a picture to look at and ah jest couldn't keep from takin' one, and that wuz the hardest waffle fur me to eat befo' I get to the big house I ever saw. Ah jest couldn't git rid of that waffle 'cause my owner once whipped me so."

"They tought me to de everything. Ah'd use battlin' blocks and battlin' sticks to wash the clothes; we all did. The clothes wuz taken out of the water an put on the block and beat with a battlin' stick, which wuz made like a paddle. On wash days you could hear them battlin' sticks poundin' every which-away. We made our own soap, used ole meat and grease, and poured water over used ashes which wuz kept in a rack-like thing and the water would drip through the ashes. This made strong lye. We used a lot o' sich lye, too, to bile with."

Lizzie Fant Brown, Mississippi

"I wus the little nigger always called on to roast the coffee and I wished then that Miss Liza would get somebody else sometime. I would tell the other chillun stories so they would stay with me while I worked. But I'm glad now 'cause she learnt me a lot."

"First I gathered bark, set it afire and put the big pot of green coffee on it, (we parched a half-bushel at a time) then I would stir it with a cedar paddle and when the coals burned out the coffee was roasted. When it began to cool off, Miss Liza would pour the whites of eggs in it while I rubbed and rubbed it, and that coffee would shine like glass."

Manus Brown, Mississippi

"Now my ma, she done general wuk round marse' house. She done de cooking, washing, scouring an' a helping wid de chilluns. Her and de gals had to make de soap, dry up de lard, make de candles, an' spin an' weave de cloth. Everything back in dem days had to be made by hand. What us colored folks called 'ho'made.' De washing wuz done in long wooden troughs, what had been hued out deep enough to hole de water an' de close. Dey would be two and three partitions in 'em. De troughs to water de stock in wuz made lak dat too."

Polly Turner Cancer, Mississippi

"I didn't never have to wurk hard den 'cause I wuz sickly; I had de rumatism, so ole Miss kep me in de house to wait on her; she tended to de garden an' when she wanted sumbody to wurk in de garden she's ask Marster fur sum han's an' she'd always say, 'I wants Poll.'"

Cato Carter, Texas

"I was trained for a houseboy and to tend the cows. The bears was so bad then, a 'sponsible pusson who could carry a gun had to look after them."

Allen Carthan, Texas

"Grandma Dicey used to do de cookin' on de place, and I used to go to de log-cabin kitchen, dat was set apart f'om de two-story frame house where de mawster lived, and put my hand through a crack in de wall and ask fo' a little bread."

Belle Caruthers, Mississippi

"I worked in the house, waited on my mistress, fanned her when she slept and nursed the baby."

Esther King Casey, Alabama

"There were eight or ten slaves in all," Esther continued. "We lived in a house in the backyard of Captain King's Big House. My mamma was the cook. Papa was a mechanic. He built houses and made tools and machinery. Captain King gave me to the 'white lady" that was Liss Susan, the Captain's wife. Captain King was a fine men. He treated all of us just like his own family. The 'white lady' taught us to be respectable and truthful."

Aunt Cicely Cawthon, Georgia

"My mother was Marster's house girl. People didn't do like they do now. She'd be called a chambermaid now. I just staid around the house with the Mistis. I was just, you might say, her little keeper. I stayed around, and waited on her, handed her water, fanned her, kept the flies off her, pulled up her pillow, and done anything she'd tell me to do. My mother combed her hair, and dressed her too. Her hair was long, down to here. [She measured below her waist]. She could sit on it. It was a light color, and it was so pretty! I'd call it silver."

Sally Banks Chambers, Texas

"Mama was de milker and washwoman and did de spinnin'. She mek all de clo's for de place and dey was good strong clo's too."

Clara Chappel, Texas

"I had a easy time myself, 'cause I was maid to missus, I had to keep her dress and wait on her jes' like dey do now. Some of de niggers sho' did have to work 'cause marster's place was big. I don't know how many acres he had, but he had a league of land, 'course it wasn't all plowed but he didn't have enough niggers so some of 'em sho' did have to work."

Anne Clark, Texas

"My mama did the washin' for the big house. She tuk a big tub on her head and a bucket of water in her hand. My mama had two white chillen by marster and they were sold as slaves. I had two chillen, too. I never married. They allus said we'd steal, but I didn' take a thing. Why, they'd put me on a hoss with money to take into town and I'd take it to the store in town, and when I'd git back, marster'd say, 'Anne, you didn' take a thing.'"

Betty Cofer, North Carolina

"I was lucky. Miss Ella (daughter of the first Beverly Jones) was a little girl when I was borned and she claimed me. We played together an' grew up together. I waited on her an' most times slept on the floor in her room. Kuh was cook an' when I done got big enough I holped to set the table in the big dinin' room. Then I'd put on a clean white apron an' carry in the victuals an' stand behind kiss Ella's chair. She'd fix me a piece of somethin' from her plate an' hand it back over her shoulder to me [eloquent hands illustrate Miss Ella's making of a sandwich]. I'd take it an' run outside to eat it. Then I'd wipe my mouth an' go back to stand behind Miss Ella again an' maybe get another snack."

"Yes'm, there was a crowd of hands on the plantation. I mind 'em all an' I can call most of their names. Mac, Curley, William, Sanford, Lewis, Henry, Ed, Sylvester, Hamp, an' Juke was the men folks. The women was Mellie, two Lucys, Martha, Nervie, Jane, Laura, Fannie, Lizzie, Cassie, Tensie, Lindy, an' MaryJane. The women mostly worked in the house. There was always two washwomen, a cook, some hands to help her, two sewin' women, a house girl, an' some who did all the weavin' an' spinnin'. The men worked in the fields an' yard. One was stable boss an' looked after all the horses an' mules."

John Coggin, North Carolina

"We wucked de fiel's, I totin' water fer de six or seben nan's what wucked dar. An' we jist wucked moderate like. We had plenty ter eat an' plenty ter w'ar, do' we did go barefooted most of de year. De marster shore wuz good ter us do'."

Fannie Coleman, Georgia

"I used to card and spin. Us used to spin and weave our clothes in them days. I worked in de fields too."

George Coleman, Mississippi

"I wuz trained to be a 'House servant' and kind of trusty about the 'big house.' I was sold to Mr. Dave Coleman, of West Point, Mississippi, his place is twenty-two miles from West Point, for $1490.00 when I was sixteen years old, I wuz way over six foot tall and weighed near two hundred pounds and could lift any thing, then."

"I milked the cows, 'tended the sheep and ran the loom in the weaving room. Lots of times I would weave at night. I could weave two and one half yards of cloth a day. We dyed the cloth with maple bark, Red Oak bark and copprice. The bark was boiled to make the dye. Red oak would make the cloth deep blue, so would maple bark, the copprice would make it yellow.

Then I carried special messages to Mr. Dave when he'd be out on the plantation. The thread we used to weave the cloth was 'soused' [meaning sized] and wound on a 'skittle' [meaning shuttle] and hit with a 'slay' [meaning sledge]. The 'skittle' was about sixteen inches long."

Tildy Collins, Alabama

"My Granmammy, her de head cook 'oman at de big house, an' us had to mine her lak us did Mammy. I hope Granmammy in de kitchen, atter I got big 'nough an' she sho' did keep me humpin'. Chilluns had to mine dey olders in dem days. Dey wan't lak dey is now, don't mine nobody, not eben dey Pa."

Martha Colquitt, Georgia

"Ma's house wuz right on de edge of Marse Billie's yard, 'cause she wuz de cook. Grandma lived in de same house wid ma and us chillun, and she worked in de loom house and wove cloth all de time. She wove de checkidy cloth for de slaves clo'es, and she made flannel cloth too, leaseways, it wuz part flannel. She made heaps of kinds of cloth."

Andrew Columbus, Texas

"Master John did all the bossin' hisself. None of his niggers ever run off 'cause he was too good for them to do that. I only got one whippin' from him and it was for stealin' eggs from a hen's nest. My pappy was carriage driver for Master. I didn't do much of the work when I was a boy, jes' stayed round the house."

Aunt Gertha Couric, Alabama

"I used to belong to Marse Rogers," she said. "After surrender, Marse Rogers moved to dis country, and bought a plantation 'twixt Merse Josiah Flourney's and General Toney's. He said his plentation j'ined theirs." She was a nurse-maid all of her life, even in Slave days, and never was a "field nigger." Asked if she saw any soldiers during the war she said she saw "thousands."

Julia Cox, Mississippi

"My master had a big family ob gals, an' he gib each one ob dem a maid. I wuz maid to Miss Vicky. I sho' did like her. She wuz purty and easy to please. I ust to love to iron and lay out her purty dresses, dey wuz all full ob laces, ruffles, and ribbons, and den her curls and big blue eyes would set dem off. One morning when I go up to her room she didn't git up lack she always did, tole me her head wuz a aching and that she won't a feeling well. I stayed wid her, toted her cool water and dainties and tried to git her to eat. Den de Doctor he come. De fust thing I knowed he would go down from her room and shake his head. I'd go off to our cabin and cry. One nite she died and I wuz a lonely little nigger after dey took her to de grave yard on de hill. I usto go up deir an' put red an' white roses, that she loved, in vases on her grave. After her died I wuz afraid I would be sont to de fields, but her sister she liked me and took me fer her maid."

Sara Crocker, Georgia

Her father worked in the fields for Mr. Hodge, while her mother was the cook for Mr. Fulton's family and also washed their clothes. Her brother and sisters worked in the fields. Sara's first recollection of any work was when she was quite a small girl, and this was field work. There were various kinds of work performed by other slaves on the plantation, such as plowing, chopping, hoeing, weaving cloth, spinning and washing. Most of them did their washing at night.

Adeline Cummins, Texas

"De women wuks in de fields until dey has chillun and when de chillun's ole enough to wuk in de fields den de mother goes to ole man Foley's house. Dere she's a house servant and wuks at spinnin' and weavin' de cotton. Dey makes all de clothes for ole man Foley and his fam'ly and for de slaves."

Julia Daniels, Texas

"Now, my mammy was cook in the Denman house and for our family and Uncle Joe's family. She didn't have much time for anythin' but cookin' all the time. But she's the bestes' cook. Us had fine greens and hawgs and beef. Us et collard greens and pork till us got skittish of it and then they quit the pork and kilt a beef. When they done that, they's jus' pourin' water on our wheels, 'cause us liked best of anythin' the beef, and I do to this day, only I can't never git it."

Carrie Davis, Alabama

"My grand-parents was from Virginny. When I was a slave I was used as a house-girl and to help keep de yards clean and bring in water. Us wore mostly slips, wove in homemade looms; an' dey was orsanburg an' homespun. We wore 'em Sunday and Monday de same. Us shoes was made at a tanyard and dey was brogans as hard as rocks."

Minnie Davis, Georgia

"My mother was the cook and looked after the house. Oh, yes indeed, we had good food to eat. Bread, milk, meat, collard greens, turnips, and potatoes. I would say we had just everything that was grown in the garden and on the plantations to eat at that time. The cooking was done in the kitchen in the yard. The fireplace was as wide as the end of this room, and a long iron bar extended from one end to the other. The great cooking pots were suspended over the coals from this bar by means of pot hooks. Heavy iron skillets with thick lids were much used for baking, and they had ovens of various sizes. I have seen my mother bake beautiful biscuits and cakes in those old skillets, and they were ideal for roasting meats. Mother's batter cakes would just melt in your mouth and she could bake and fry the most delicious fish. There was no certain thing that I liked to eat more than anything else in those days. I was young and had a keen appetite for all good things."

Mose Davis, Georgia

All slaves too old for field work remained at home where some took care of the young children, while others worked in the loom houses helping make the cloth and the clothing used on the plantation. Since no work was required at night, this time was utilized by doing personal work such as the washing and the repairing of clothing, etc.

Ella Dilliard, Alabama

Ella said that her mother was her madame's hairdresser, and that Mrs. Norris had her mother taught in Mobile. So Ella's life was very easy, as she stayed around the big house with her mother, although her grandmother, Penny Anne Norris, cared for her more than her mother did. One of the things she remembers quite distinctly was her grandmother's cooking on the fireplace, and how she would not allow any one to spit in the fireplace. She said her grandmother made corn-pone and wrapped it in shucks and baked it in ashes.

Ella said that there were three cooks at the big house, their names being Hannah, Judy, and Charlotte, and the gardener's name was Uncle John. Ella also said that one thing that she remembers so well about the kitchen in the big house was a large dishpan, that had a partition in the middle of it, one side you washed the dishes in, and the other side was used for scalding them.

Clara Dodge, Mississippi

Clara Dodge of Marcus Bottoms was born and reared in a family that took pride in their servants being thrifty. At an early age Clara took sole care of the two children of the family because of the early death of her young Mistress. She has all the love of a real mother for them, as they grow up to be a noble man and woman and from their own lips the writer heard them say that they "owe their rearing to their own Black Mammie, Clara."

Callie Donalson, Arkansas

"Ma mother was a field band and she washed and ironed. She was a good spinner. She carded and wove and spun all. She knitted too. She knitted mostly by nite. All the stockings and gloves had to be knit. She sewed and I learned from her. We had to sew with our fingers."

Simon Durr, Mississippi

"I wuked 'round de place when I wuz a little slave boy. I done fust one thing an' then another, but mostly 'round de lot an' horses. When I got big 'nuf to handle 'em Marse put me to drivin'. I sho did lak dat as I got to go to all de places de family went. It wuz plumb grand, me all dressed up a drivin' dem purty horses all hitched up to dat coach. Hit wuz one ob dem kind whar de driver rid on de outside. I wuz always ready to go too."

George Eason, Georgia

Those women who were too old for field work did the sewing in addition to other duties to be described later.

Indigo was cultivated for dyeing purposes and in some instances a dye was made by boiling walnut leaves and walnut hulls in water. In addition to her duties as cook, Mr. Eason's mother had to also weave part of the cloth. He told of how he had to sit up at night and help her and how she would "crack" him on the head for being too slow at times.

Mary Edwards, Texas

"I got give to Massa Felix Vaughn and he brung me to Texas. Dat long 'fore de war fer freedom, but I don't know de year. De most work I done for de Vaughns was wet nuss de baby son, what name Elijah. His mammy jes' didn't have 'nough milk for him."

"Den I knit de secks and wash de clothes and sometimes I work in de fields. I he'ped make de baskets for de cotton. De man git white-oak weed and we lets it stay in de water for de night and de nex' mornin' and it soft and us split it in strips for makin' of de baskets. Everybody try see who could make de bes' basket."

Callie Elder, Georgia

"Old Aunt Martha what nussed de chillun while deir Mammies wukked in de field was de quiltin' manager. It warn't nothin' for 'omans to quilt three quilts in one night. Dem quilts had to be finished 'fore dey stopped t'eat a bit of de quiltin' feast. Marse Billy 'vided dem quilts out 'mongst de Niggers what needed 'em most."

Gabe Emanuel, Mississippi

"I was de house boy on old Judge Stamps' plantation. He live 'bout nine miles east o' Port Gibson, an' he was a mighty well-to-do gent'man in dem days. He owned 'roun' 'bout 500–600 us Niggers. He made plenty o' money outto' his fiel's. Dem niggers wuk for dey keep, I 'clare dey did."

"I 'member I use to hate ever' Wednesday, 'cause dat was de day I had to polish de silver. Lawsy! It took me mos' all de day an' den when I'd think I was 'bout through de Missus was sho' to fin' some o' dat silver what had to be done over."

Jerry Eubanks, Mississippi

"You know I was dining room servant, and when de boss and Misses got up from de table den it was mine. Dey had so much, dat even what was left in de plate was nuff to feed me. Times wasn't like de is now. Other slaves eat out of de big garden."

"It was jes like dis. De had a big brown skin woman who set at de loom. She weaved for de whole plantation. Den what so and ever kind of garment was wanted, it was cut out and sent to the seamstress."

Martha Everette, Georgia

Prior to freedom, her first job was "toting in wood," from which she was soon "promoted" to waiting on the table, house cleaning, etc. She make no claims to have ever "graduated" as a cook, as so many old before-the-war Negresses do.

Sarah Felder, Mississippi

"Old Mistis wurk hard all de time. She hed a big room whar sum of de women wus busy wid de cards, an' spinnin' an' de looms. Miss Vickey niver lowed de women ter rest. She med 'em wurk at night an' when it wus rainin' she wus rite dar ter see dat dey wus wurkin'. She kep' de looms goin' an' made all kind uf pretty cloth, an' dey made 'coverlets' jes as pritty as dey make 'em now. She made sum uf de wimin git bark out uf de woods an' dye sum uf dat thread, an' it sho' made pritty coverlets. An' den she hed ter dye her thread ter make pants an' coats. She made de pants an' coats outern blue jeans. She kep' sum uf de wimin sewin an' dey made mity fine things fur old Mistis an' her chulluns, an' dey made sum things fur us, but whut we got wus made frum cloth spun dar at home, an' it niver out. De gurl chulluns jes wore long aprons, and de boys jes had long tail shirts, an' we niver hed anything under dem, an' when we wus bad Miss Vickey wuld lift our coat tails an' switch us on de naked hide. I wus allus gittin a switchin, an' de udder chaps wus too."

"Old Mistis made me larn ter spin, and made me larn ter sew but I niver got ter de loom, I jes seed de udders makin' de cloth."

"Old Mistis wud knit socks an' stockin' an' sum uf de wimen in de quarters wud knit at nite, but when old Mistis wuld go ter church, or hed fine com'ny she wud put on fine silks an' wear store bought stockin' an' she hed a lotta uf fine things."

Mary Ferguson, Georgia

Aunt' Mary said that the Littles trained her to be a nurse. Before the war ended, she was inherited by Mr. Gus (the late Hon. W. A.) Little. She remembers that all the "quality," young white men who went to the war from Talbotton took Negro men-servants (slaves) along with them. These were usually called body servants, and it was a body-servant's duty to cook, wash, and do general valet service for his master. In a pinch, he was also supposed to raid a hen roost, or otherwise rustle food for his "white fokes."

Reuben Fitzpatrick, Alabama

"My mother wuz de cook. She had rule over all the cookin'. She spinned thread an' reeled it off too."

William Flannagan, Mississippi

William's mother cooked for all the slaves, twenty or more in number, and if all did not have enough to eat at each meal, it was because she just miscalculated the amount needed. She used a big fireplace for cooking.

Cicero Gaulding, Mississippi

"I was born belongin' to Marsta William Gaulding, in what was then Panola County just a few miles east of Senatobia, but then Senatoby was no size atall. I never had to work in the fields or barns attall. 'Miss.' took me in the house soon as I can remember, I always helped in the house and garden and drove Miss wherever she went, my folks were always good to me, and I had plenty clothes and a good home and fine food to eat as long as Miss. lived. If she was here now I could go to her and she'd help me. I wouldn't be in this fix, why now I can't plow, I don't have nothin' it show is hard to live, I make a few little patches o' stuff and grow some turkeys and guineas, but not enough to have any clothes, my shoes are plumber worn out."

Frank Gill, Alabama

"As I said b'fore I was a boy between fourteen or fifteen years old b'fore de slaves was divided, an' when I was on de Ol' Missy's place, I stayed aroun' de house, an' wait on dem, an' 'tend de horses. Anudder thing I had to do, dey would send me for the mail. I had to go twelve miles atter hit an' I couldn't read or write, but I could bring everybody's mail to dem jes' right. I knowed I had better git hit right. You see I could kinder figure, so I could make out by de numbers."

Cora Gillam, Arkansas

"My work was to answer the door bell and wait on my mistress and go round with her wherever she went. I had to sleep in the house with her. Sometimes at night I would have to go down to the quarters for her, and I would run every step of the way."

Mattie Gilmore, Texas

"I worked in the fields till Rachel [his sister] was sold, den tooken her place, doin' kitchen work and fannin' files off de table with a great, long limb. I liked dat. I got plenty to eat and not so hot."

Esther Green, Alabama

"I never had no work to do myself, 'cause I always stayed in de big house wid Miss Mary Davis, ole Massa's wife. I was in de house one day and ole Massa asked me if I wanted to eat at de table wid dem, so I pulled up a chair and spite of de fact dere was all kinds of good stuff to eat in front of me, I called for lye hominy. I sho did love dat stuff better'n anything else I ever et. Ole Massa and de res' of dem jus' laugh fit to kill. I reckon dey thought I was crazy sho' nuff', but I et hominy jes' de same."

"De men and women worked in de field all day, but I never picked a bit of cotton all my life. At night de women would spin and weave cloth, but I never did learn to do dat. Den dey would dye de cloth different colors, mostly red and blue though, and make dem into clothes. Us chilluns had a one-piece dress or slip. Our shoes was all homemade too. Massa had one man who tanned de leather. He would take it and put it into a long trough for a long time and den whatever was done dat was supposed to be done to it, he would take it out and cut it and make shoes. Us chilluns' had shoes same as de grown folks."

Margaret Green, Georgia

[Margaret Green] said her mother was a seamstress and also a cook. Three other seamstresses worked on the plantation. There was a spinning wheel and a loom, and all the cotton cloth for clothing was woven and then made into clothes for all the slaves. There were three shoe makers on the place who made shoes for the slaves, and did all the saddle and harness repair.

Rosa Green, Texas

"My work was cleanin' up 'roun de house and nussin' de chillen. Only times I went to church when day tuk us long to min' de chillen."

Minerva Grubbs, Mississippi

"When I growed up a bit, I wuz made ter nurse de little slave chillun while deir mudders would in de fields a wukin'. I had ter nurse Mar's chillun too, an' he sho did hab a heap ob 'em."

Milton Hammond, Georgia

Although the Freemans owned a large plantation several miles from Criffin and had a large number of slaves, who lived on this plantation to do the work, they resided in town with only the Hammond family as their servants. Mr. Hammonds' grandmother acted as the cook for the household and his mother assisted her. His sister was the chamber-maid and kept the house spotlessly clean. Smiling, Mr. Hammond remarked, "Until I was older my job was that of playing, later I became my young mistress's carriage driver."

After the work in the fields was completed for the day, women were then required to work at night spinning thread into cloth. Each woman had a task which consisted of making som many cuts a night. As Mr. Hammond remarked, "You couldn't hear your ears at night on some plantations, for the old spinning wheels." At 9 o'clock the overseer would blow the horn for every one to go to bed. The cloth woven by women was used to make men clothing also, and was dyed different colors from dye which was made by boiling walnut hulls and berries of various kinds. Color varied according to the kind of berry used. One pair of shoes, made to order, was given each person once a year.

Julia E. Haney, Arkansas

"My mother was a cook and she knitted. She molded candles and milked the cows, and washed and ironed. She and her children were the only slaves they owned. They never whipped my mother at all. I stayed in the house. They kept me there. I never had to do anything but keep the flies off the table when they were eating."

Molly Harrell, Texas

"I was purty little den, but I done my share. I holp my mother dust and clean up de house and peel 'tatoes. Dere some old men dat too old to work so dey sot in de sun all day and holp with de light work. Dey carry grub and water to de field hands."

Anne Hawthorne, Texas

"My ma she was jis' a fiel' han' but my gramma and my aunt dey hab dem for wuk 'roun' de house. I didn' do nuthin' but chu'n [churn] and clean de yard, and sweep 'roun' and go to de spring and tote de water. I l'arn how to hoe, too."

Dinah Hayes, Mississippi

"I have worked for just two families since I was fourteen," says Dinah, "and I nursed for both of these and the children called me their black Mammie and I was. I loved those children like they be mine. I scolded and whipped them, too, when they needed it. I planned and cooked their meals, mended their clothes, took them to the park, bathed them and put them to bed, told them bedtime stories, and settled their disputes between themselves, and they would tell me all of their troubles. It was my white children that taught me how to read and write and how to speak. We taught each other things."

Emmaline Heard, Georgia

Every woman had a certain amount of weaving and spinning to do at home after coming in from the fields. Emmaline says her mother had to card bats at night so that the two older sisters could begin spinning the next morning. A loom was almost as large as a small kitchen and was operated by hands and feet. Until midnight, the spinning wheels could be heard humming in the slave cabins. At the hour of twelve, however, a bell was rung, which was the signal for the slaves to cease their spinning and go to bed.

Dye for coloring the cloth was provided by collecting sweet gum, dogwood bark, and red clay. Mixing these together produced different colors of dye. Sweet gum and clay produced a purple; dogwood, a blue.

Phoebe Henderson, Texas

"I worked in de house, too. I spinned seven curts a day and every night we run two looms, makin' large curts for plow lines. We made all our clothes. We didn't wear shoes in Georgia but in this place the land was rough and strong, so we couldn't go barefooted, A black man that worked in the shop measured our feet and made us two pairs a year."

Adeline Hodges, Alabama

"Lor!, yes'm, I libed in dose days, and I tells you I 'members all 'bout dem. Do come in and set down. De fust white people I b'longed to was a man named Jones, who was a colonel in de war, but I can't tell you much 'bout dem, 'caze I was jes' a li'l gal den. I was jes' big 'nuff to tote water to de fiel' to de folks wukking and to min' de gaps in de fence to keep de cattle out when dey was gatherin' de crops. I don't 'spec' you knows anything 'bout dose kind of fences. Dey was built of rails and when dey was gatherin' de crops dey jes' tuk down one section of de fence, so de wagons could git through."

After having been sold to Mr. Collins, of Shubuta, Mississippi, "Aunt" Adeline said that life was very hard, not so much for herself, but she saw how hard the other slaves worked. She was the house girl and helped clean house, wash dishes, and take care of the children. After finishing that work, she had to spin thread. Each day she would have to spin so many cuts, and if she did not finish the required number, she was punished.

Wayne Holliday, Mississippi

"My mammy did de cookin' for de white folks dere. Dey all thought a lot of her. I never knowed much what slavery was about, to tell de truf. De folks never treated us wrong and chillen in dem days diden get to run around lak dey do today and we diden get to hear no gossip bout de other niggers. Since we didn't live in no quarters we diden hear nothin'. Our folks never said nothin' cause dey was ver well satisfied lak dey was. We never hear of no whippin's or runaways either til after de war and when we got older."

Rebecca Hooks, Florida

She was born in Jones County, Georgia of Martha and Pleasant Lowe, who were slaves of William Lowe. The mother was the mulatto offspring of William Lowe and a slave woman who was half Cherokee. The father was also a mulatto, purchased from a nearby plantation.

Because of this blood mixture Rebecca's parents were known as "house niggers," and lived on quarters located in the rear of the "big house." A "house nigger" was a servant whose duties consisted of chores around the big house, such as butler, maid, cook, stableman, gardner and personal attendant to the man who owned him.

These slaves were often held in high esteem by their masters and of course fared much better than the other slaves on the plantation. Quite often they were mulattoes as in the case of Rebecca's parents. There seemed to be a general belief among slave owners that mulattoes could not stand as much laborious work as pure blooded Negro slaves. This accounts probably for the fact that the majority of ex-slaves now alive are mulattoes.

Emma L. Howard, Alabama

She explained her duties about the Big House as sweeping the rambling porches and yards. Sometimes she churned. Afterward she would join the white children and played most of the day.

Emma L. Howard. (Library of Congress)

"Edie was de laundress," she recalled, "an' Arrie, she was de weaver. Den dere was Becky, Melia, Aunt Mary, Ed, John, and Uncle George the house man, who married Aunt Evalina. Jake was de over-looker [overseer]. He was a great, big cullud man. Dar was more, but I can't 'member. I was jes' a little shaver den."

Talking further about work about the plantation, she said: "Louisa cleaned de parlor an' kept Mistis' room nice." She took up a recital of work on the plantation. "Atter dat she didn't do anything but sew, an' Sist' Liza hoped her wid dat. After de weavin', we done sewin', and it took a lot of sewin' for dat family. Eve'body had two Sunday dresses, summer and winter, as well as clothes for eve'day."

Annie Huff, Georgia

Among the "quarter" families were Annie Huff and her daughters, Mary being the elder. The mother cooked and the small children learned to sweep the yard and to do minor jobs in the field at a very early age. At the age of twelve, the girls were taught to card and spin as well as to knit and were required to do a certain task each day until they were large enough to assist with the heavier work. The adult females did this type of work after sunset, when their labor in the field was over. On rainy days they shucked and shelled corn or did some other kind of indoor labor.

Easter Huff, Georgia

"De big old cook house had a partition 'crost it, and on one side Aunt Peggy done all de cookin' for Old Marster's household and for de slaves too. On de udder side of de partition was de loom room whar Aunt Peggy weaved all de cloth and Mrs. Lacy Hines, what lived on another plantation not far f'um us, made all our clothes."

Lina Hunter, Georgia

"On wash days dat was a busy place, wid lots of 'omans bending over dem great big wash pots and de biggest old wooden tubs I ever seed. Dere was plenty racket 'round de battlin' block whar dey beat de dirt out of de clothes, and dey would sing long as dey was a-washin'."

Camilla Jackson, Georgia

Dr. Hoyle's family included his wife, three boys, and three girls. He owned a very large plantation, and a large number of slaves, probably 75 or more. All of them were required to work in the fields and tend the crops, which consisted mostly of sugar cane and cotton. Syrup was made from the sugar came. Mrs. Jackson remembers quite well that everyone was required to work in the fields, but not until Dr. Hoyle, who was a kind master, was sure that they were old enough. She was about 12 years old when she was given a job in the house, operating the fly-brush. The fly-brush was constructed so that a piece of cloth, fastened on a wooden frame with hinges, could be pulled back and forth with a cord. This constant fanning kept the room clear of flies. As she related this, she smiled to herself as if her job was particularly amusing.

Henrietta Jackson, Indiana

Just how old Mrs. Jackson is, she herself doesn't know, but she thinks she is about 105 years old. She looks much younger. Her youngest child is 73 and she had nine, two of whom were twins. Born a slave in Virginia, record of her birth was kept by the master. She cannot remember her father as he was soon sold after Mrs. Jackson's death. When still a child she was taken from her mother and sold. She remembers the auction block and that she brought a good price as she was strong and healthy. Her new master, Tom Robinson, treated her well and never beat her. At first she was a plough hand, working in the cotton fields, but then she was taken in to the house to a maid.

Adeline Johnson, South Carolina

"I never have to do no field work; just stayed 'round de house and wait on de mistress, and de chillun. I was whupped just one time. Det was for markin' de mentel-piece wid a dead coal of fire. They make mammy do de lashin'. Hadn't hit me three licks befo' Miss Dorcas, Miss Jemima, Miss Julia, and Marse Johnnie run dere, ketch de switch, and say: 'Dat enough Mauma Ann! Addie won't do it agin.' Dats all de beatin' I ever 'ceived in slavery time."

"Now does you wanna know what I do when I was a child, from de time I git up in de mornin' to de time I go to bed? I was 'bout raised up in de house. Well, in de evenin', I fill them boxes wid chips and fat splinters. When mornin' come, I go in dere and make a fire for my young mistresses to git up by. I help dress them and comb deir hair. Then I goes down stairs and put flowers on de breakfas' table and lay de Bible by Marse 'illiam's chair. Then I bring in de breakfas'. (Table have to be set de night befo') When everything was on de table, I ring de bell. White folks come down and I wait on de table."

"After de meal finish, Marse William read de Bible and pray. I clear de table and help wash de dishes. When dat finish, I cleans up de rooms. Then I acts as maid and waitress at dinner and supper. I warms up de girls' room, where they sleep, after supper. Then go home to poppy John and Mauma Anne. Dat was a happy time, wid happy days!"

Prince Johnson, Mississippi

"Master took me for the house boy, and I carried my head high. He would say to me, 'Prince, do you know who you were named for,' and I would say to him, 'Yes sir, Prince Albert.' And then he would say to me, 'Well, always carry yourself like he did.' To this good day I holds myself like Master said."

"On certain days of the week one of the old men on the place took us house servants to the field to learn us to work. We was brought up to know how to do anything that came to hand. Master would let us work at odd times for outsiders and we could use the money we made for anything we pleased. My grand-mother sold enough corn to buy her two feather beds. We always had plenty to eat. The old folks did the cooking for all the field hands, 'cept on Sunday when each family cooked for his self. Old Miss would come every Sunday morning with sugar and white flour. We would most generally have fish, rabbits, 'pos-sums or coons. Lord Child! those possums was good eating."

Emma Jones, Alabama

"I worked as a house gal an' when Miss Sarah ma'ied I went with her to nuss her chilluns. Besides Miss Sarah dere was Mista Billy, Mista Crick, Miss Lucy and Miss Emma. Dey had two uncles an' a Aunt of deres lived dere too."

Harriet Jones, Texas

"All us house women larned to knit de socks and head mufflers, and many is de time I has went to town and traded socks for groceries. I cooked, too, and helped 'fore old Marse died. For everyday cookin' we has corn pone and pot-licker and bacon meat and mustard and turnip greens, and good, old sorghun 'lasses. On Sunday we has chieken or turkey or roast pig and pies and cakes and hot, saltrisin' bread."

Lewis Jones, Texas

"Massa have de fine coach and de seat for de driver am up high in front and I's de coachman and he dresses me nice and de hosses am fine, white team. Dere I's sat up high, all dress good, holdin' a tight line 'cause de team am full of spirit and fast. We'uns goes lickity split and it am a purty sight. Man, 'twarnt any one bigger dan dis nigger."

Liza Jones, Texas

"'Bout all de work I did was 'tend to de rooms and sweep. Nobody ever 'low us to see nobody 'bused. I never seed or heared of nobody gittin' cut to pieces with a whip like some. Course, chillen wasn't 'lowed to go everywhere and see everything like dey does now. Dey jump in every corner now."

Lucy Kimball, Alabama

When a young girl, Mammy Lucy performed the duties of a children's nurse, and worked as a dining room servant. She had some education, and as she had worked in families of refinement and culture all her life, her manner was that of a well educated person. However, like the average educated Negro, she still displayed the characteristics of the Negro of the ante-bellum days. She said that she strictly adhered to old fashioned methods, such as: going to church twice a week, not believing in doctors, and always taking home-concocted remedies.

Charlie King, Georgia

"Niggers" on "ole Master's place had to work, even chillun over 7 or 8 years of age.

Charlie and all of his 10 brothers and sisters helped to card and spin the cotton for the loom. Sometimes they worked all night, Charlie often going to sleep while carding, when his mother would crack him on the head with the carder handle and wake him up. Each child had a night for carding and spinning, so they all would get a chance to sleep.

Silvia King, Texas

"Marse Jones and Old Miss finds out 'bout my cookin' and takes me to de big house to cook for dem. De dishes and things was awful queer to me, to what

I been brung up to use in France. I mostly cooks after dat, but I's de powerful big woman when I's young and when dey gits in a tight I holps out."

"On de cold winter night I's sot many a time spinnin' with two threads, one in each hand and one my feets on de wheel and de baby sleepin' on my lap. De boys and old men was allus whittlin' and it wasn't jes' foolishment. Dey whittles traps and wooden spoons and needles to make seine nets and checkers and sleds. We all sits workin' and singin' and smokin' pipes. I likes my pipe right now, and has two clay pipes and keeps dem under de pillow. I don't aim for dem pipes to git out my sight. I been smokin' clost to a hunerd years now and it takes two cans tobaccy de week to keep me goin'."

Annie Little, Texas

"In de cold days de women spin and weave de cloth on looms. I stands by and pick up de shuttle when dey fall. Us niggers all wore de clothes make on de spinnin' wheel, but de white folks wore dresses from de store. Dey have to pay fifty and seventy-five cents de yard for calico den."

Isaac Martin, Texas

"Dey had a ol' woman to look after de babies when dey mammies was out in de fiel'. Dey have a time sot for de mammies to come in and nuss de babies. De ol' woman she had helpers. Dey had a big house and cradle' for dem babies where de nuss tek care of 'em."

"Ol' mistus she had a reg'lar cook. Dat was my mudder's mudder. Eb'ryt'ing had to be jis' so, and eb'ryt'ing nice and clean."

Jim Martin, Mississippi

"My mammy wus named Annie, an' she wus whut yer wud call a 'handy woman'—she hed to milk an' churn, wash an' iron, card de bats, spin, weave an' sumtimes she hed ter help cook, an' sumtimes she hed to go to de fiel' an on rainy days old Mistis made all de wimen wurk in de loom room."

William Mathews, Texas

"When I got big 'nough I'd drive dere carriage. I was what dey calls de 'waitin' boy.' I sot in dat buggy and wait till dey come out of where dey was, and den driv 'em off. I wasn't 'lowed to git out and visit round with de other slaves. No, suh, I had to set dere and wait."

John Matthews, Mississippi

"I had to keep dat water bucket filled wid water all de time. Dey had a big well in de yard not fur frum de house and dat well had a windlass an' one bucket:

I let de bucket go down in de well an' turn dat windlass an' up come de bucket wid de best cold water. De water bucket wus made uf cedar wid brass band 'round it an' dat wus scrubbed ebery week to keep clean an' white."

Ann May, Mississippi

"No, I didn't work in the fields. I was raised with white folks right in the house, and ate in their kitchen. I was taught to keep the house clean and to sew. I learned to spin and help weave the cloth. All our clothes was home spun. Yes, sometimes they would whip me. Mr. Alford believe in making every body doing right, and when you would do right he was kind to you but when you would do wrong he would lay the lash on heavy. If folks would whip more today they would make this world a better world. We could not run wild like the young folks do these days."

Tom McAlpin, Alabama

"My job aroun' de place was to nuss de chilluns, white an' nigger. We all played 'roun' together. Sometimes we play coon an' rabbit, fox an' houn' and snatch, but what was de mostes' fun was a-ridin' ole Sut. Sut was a donkey an' us useta hitch him to a wagon, an' six of de chilluns would ride in de wagon an' I'd ride on his back. Sometimes us'd ride all de way into Talladega wid Sut."

Duncan McCastle, Mississippi

"I can recollect how dey had to spin, weave an' knit in dem days. I can see dem a cookin' on de big fire place an' a makin' soap, candles, cheese, an' molasses. I'se played under long scaffoles ob fruit a dryin fer winter use. I'se played around de fires whar dey wuz makin' lard and killin' hogs. De whole place wuz kept alive wid wuk, slave gwine dis way an' dat, each one wid his duties to carry out."

Amanda McCray, Florida

Children on the Pamell plantation led a carefree existence until they were about 12 years of age when they were put to light chores like carrying water and food, picking seed from cotton lint (there were no cotton gins), and minding the smaller children.

Amanda was trained to be a house servant, learning to cook and knit from the blind mother who refused to let this handicap affect her usefulness. She liked best to sew the fine muslins and silks of her mistress, making beautiful hooped dresses that required eight and ten yards of cloth and sometimes as many as seven petticoats to enhance their fullness.

Hoops for these dresses were made of grape-vines that were shaped while green and cured in the sun before using. Beautiful imported laces were used to trim the petticoats and pantaloons of the wealthy.

Amanda was an exceptionally good cook and so widespread was this knowledge that the Union soldiers employed her as a cook in their camp for a short while. She does not remember any of their officers and thinks they were no better nor worse than the others. These soldiers committed no depredations in her section except to confiscate whatever they wanted in the way of food and clothing. Some married southern girls.

Lucy McCullough, Georgia

"Mah mammy, she wuz cook at duh big house, en Ah wuz raised dah in de kitchen en de back yahd at de big house. Ah wuz tuh be uh maid fer de ladies in de big house. De house servants hold that dey is uh step better den de field niggers. House servants wuz niggah quality folks."

In all Mr. Hale had eleven children. "I had to nurse three of them before I was old enough to go to the field to work."

Henry Lewis McGaffey, Mississippi

"When I got big 'nuff I cud help her do dat. I brung in de wood fur de fires an' picked up de eggs, an' toted slop to de pig pin an' wus learnin to milk fore de surrender."

Matilda McKinney, Georgia

The adult female a who lived in the house did most of the weaving and sewing. All the summer, garments were made and put away for winter use. Two dresses of osnaburg were then given each person.

The field hands, always considered an inferior group by the house servants, worked from sunup to sun down.

William McWhorter, Georgia

"My Aunt Mary b'longed to Marse John Craddock and when his wife died and left a little baby—dat was little Miss Lucy—Aunt Mary was nussin' a new baby of her own, so Marse John made her let his baby suck too. If Aunt Mary was feedin' her own baby and Miss Lucy started cryin' Marse John would snatch her baby up by the legs and spank him, and tell Aunt Mary to go on and nuss his baby fust. Aunt Mary couldn't answer him a word, but my ma said she offen seed Aunt Mary cry 'til de tears met under her chin."

Annette Milledge, Georgia

Annette's mother did the family marketing for the Ransomes, on daily trips to the Augusta markets. The old woman recalled that in war times $70.00 in Confederate money was paid for a roast.

"We had anything we wanted to eat," she continued, "Marster had a store-room right next to my mother's room, and anything she wanted to get to cook, she would go dere and get it. When we got sick, Marster would send for de doctor. Mother was de mid-wife, she would tend to her Mistis, and if any of de women git dat way, she had to go to dem too."

Harriet Miller, Mississippi

"Marster Mike hed a big plantation en hed plenty slaves. Dar wus uncle Henry, his wife en six chilluns—uncle Washin'ton, his wife en seben chilluns—uncle Levi, his wife en four chilluns—aunt Aisley, who done de cookin—aunt Charity who hoped in de house en done de sewin en she hed two boys—aunt Liddy who done de milkin en her two small chilluns—aunt Terry en her chile—den dar wus my grand pappy en my grand mammy en me."

"My mammy died when her last chile wus born, en aunt Charity tuk me ter raise."

"Aunt Aisly wus de cook in de white folk's kitchen. She hed ter do de cookin en look atter de black chilluns whilst deir mammies wus in de field, en Missus Nancy hoped aunt Aisly ter tend ter de chilluns, en when we wus bad she wuld lift up our coat tails en switch us on de naked skin, en dat wuld hurt. We niver wore but one garment."

"Aunt Liddy done de milkin' en she wuld tek two big water buckets ter de pen ebery mornin en ebery nite en bring back de milk."

Tom Mills, Texas

"In Alabama we lived on Patterson's place. The grandmother of all these Pattersons was Betsy Patterson and we lived on her estate. My mother wove the cloth. It kep' her pretty busy, but she was stout and active. My uncle was blacksmith and made all the plows, too.

La San Mire, Texas

"Everyone raised cotton. In the evenings the slave women and girls seeded the cotton, corded it, made thread of it on the spinning wheel. They made it into cotton for dresses and suits. No shoes or socks. In winter the men might wear them in winter. Never the women or children."

"How many slaves? I do not recall. There were so many the yard was full. They worked from sun-up to sundown, with one hour for dinner. School? I hoed cotton and drove the oxen to plow the field."

Bob Mobley, Georgia

"My mother was the family cook, and also superintended the cooking for many of the slaves."

"I was raised in my master's house—slept in his room when I was a small boy, just to be handy to wait on him when he needed anything."

Laura Montgomery, Mississippi

"Marse would blow dat hour every mornin' an' we had to git out right now an' start dat wuk. My mammy had to cook, milk, wash, iron, spin, weave, and do de wuk in de fiel' lak de others."

"I had to he'p my mammy scrub dat house. We had shuck mops, an' we put san on de floor an' pore water on it and pull dat mop over it 'til dat floor was white an' clean an' iffen it didn' 'pear clean old Mistis would make us do it a-gin. Den we hed to scrub de water buckets an' mek dem clean. De buckets den was made of cedar an' had brass rings 'round 'em an' dey had long han'le gourds to drink out of an' de bucket sot on de shelf on de front of de house."

Isaam Morgan, Alabama

"Mr. James Morgan was my Massa, an' his wife, Miss Delia, was my Mistis. My mammy's name was Ann Morgan, an' as for my pappy, I done forgot his'n. I was raised raght dar in de white folks house, an' I had my own special place to sleep. I was de house boy, an' when I growed older I driv' Mistis aroun' in de Ca'iage."

Tom Morris, Mississippi

"My mammy wus de cook, an' she wus er good cook; dat wus to be her wurk. I wus raised in de kitchen, an' my mammy made me brung in de kindlin'; I had ter help her wash dishes an' she taught me how ter cook. She cooked on de fireplace. I roasted 'taters in de ashes, an' she wud rake de ashes to one side an' pore de bread dou'h down on de hot place, den civer it wid ashes an' let it cook, den we had fine hoe-cake. I roasted pinders in de ashes too an' sum times I put corn down an' let it brown an' eat dat."

"Yes Mam, mammy washed sumtimes; I allus had to brung up de wood to put 'round de pot to bile de water, an' den she hed er big end uf a stump, an' she washed de clo'se er while an' den put dem on dis stump an' give me a bo'rd wid a small end to it, an' made me beat dem clo'se, an' keep turnin' dem an' beat dem er gin till dey wus pritty an' white; She drawed water frum de well an' made me help tote it to de tibs."

George Morrison, Indiana

"There was two ladies in at the house, the Missus and her daughter, who was old enough to keep company when I was a little boy. They used to have me to drive 'em to church. I'd drive the horses. They'd say, 'George, you come in here to church. Byt I always slipped off with the other boys who was standing around outside waitin' for they folks, and played marbles."

Mandy Morrow, Texas

"Mammy and my crandma am cooks and powerful good and dey's larnt me end dat how I come to be a cook. Like everybody dem times, us raise everthing and makes preserves and cure de meats. De hams and bacons am smoked. Dere am no hickory wood 'round but we uses de corncobs and dey makes de fine flavor in de meat. Many's de day I watches de fire in dat smokehouse and keeps it low, to git de smoke flavor. I fellews de cookin' when I gits big and goes for myself and I never wants for de job."

Margrett Nillin, Texas

"De marster ain' de boss of dis nigger, 'cause I 'longs to Missy Corneallus and she don' 'low any other person boss me. My work was in de big house, sich as sewing, knitting and 'tending Missy. I keeps de flies off her with de fan and I does de fetching for her, sich as water and de snack for to eat, and de likes. When she goes to fix for sleep I combs her hair and rubs her feet. I can't 'member dat she speak any cross words to dis nigger."

Fanny Nix, Georgia

Rosetta Green, the mother of Fanny, "cooked and washed for Judge Green for yeahs and yeahs." Fanny "found her mammy a cookin' at the big house the fust thing she knowed."

As Fanny grew up, she was trained by "ole Miss" to be a house girl, and did "sech wuk" as churning, minding the flies "offen de table when de white folks et, gwine backards and forads to de smoke-house for my mammy."

She recalls that when she minded the flies offen the table she allus got plenty of biscuits and scraps o' fried chicken the white folks left on their plates. "But," Fanny added with a satisfied smile, "Marse Green's darkies never wanted for sumpin t'eat, case he give 'em a plenty, even molasses all dey wanted." Fanny and her mammy always ate in "de Missis kitchen."

Richard Orford, Georgia

"My Ma did'nt have many chillun—jes' ten boys an' nine girls. I went to work in marster's house when I wus five years old an' I stayed dere 'till I wus thirty-five. De fust work I had to do wus to pick up chips, feed chickens, an' keep de yard clean. By de time I wus eight years old I wus drivin' my missus in de carriage."

Annie Osborne, Texas

"Massa Bias refugees me and my mammy to Mansfield, in Louisiana when I's jus' a baby. They come in wagons and was two months on the way, and the big boys and men rode hossback, but all the niggers big 'nough had to walk. Massa Bias openes a farm twelve mile from Mansfield. My mammy plowed and hoed and chopped and picked cotton and jus' as good as the menfolks. I allus worked in the house, nussin the white chillen and spinnin' and house-work. Me and my brother, Frank, slep' in Missy Bias house on a pallet. No matter how cold it was we slep on that pallet without no cover, in front the fireplace."

"Old man Tom never give us no money and half 'nough clothes. I had one dress the year round, two lengths of cloth sewed together, and I didn't know nothin' 'bout playin' neither. If I made too much fuss they put me under the bed. My white folks didn't tench us nothin' 'cept how they could put the whip on us. I had to put on a knittin' of stockin's in the mornin' and and if I didn't git it out by night, Missy put the lash on me."

Mary Overton, Texas

"My marster had 'bout four slaves. He sold and bought slaves sev'ral times, but he couldn' sell me, 'cause I belonged to de mistis, and she wouldn' let him sell me. I cooked and washed and ironed and looked after de chillen, mostly. Dey had three chillen, but de mistis died when the least one was 'bout six months ole and I raised de two older ones. Dey was two boys, and dey was 'bout grown when I lef' after freedom."

Mary Patterson, Texas

"When I growed up it was my job to wet muss Rufe Burleson, 'cause he mammy didn't have 'nough milk for him. Beside dat, I helped in de loom room and have to spin five cuts de day, but I's fast 'nough to make eight cuts."

G. W. Pattillo, Georgia

Pattillo's mother was cook and general house servant, so well thought of by the Ingram family that she managed the house as she saw fit and planned the meals likewise. Young Pattillo was considered a pet by everyone and hung around the mistress, since she did not have any children of her own. His job was to hand her the scissors and thread her needles. "I was her special pet," said Pattillo, "and my youngest brother was the master's special pet."

Anna Peck, Georgia

How Baskets were Made in Slavery Time by Slaves: They took a number of wide splints, lapped the ends and tied them together strongly with a thong of wood about the size of a string, so that they looked like the spokes of a big wheel. Small pieces were woven in and out till the bottom was the right size and then they bent the splints upward, adding new ones as needed to make the sides solid enough. They wove the other wide splints round and round till the basket was deep enough, then around the top they put a stronger piece of wood, tied also with a thong of wood over this they bent the up and down splints, slipping the ends back under the splints which went around. This made a strong rim. They scraped the splints with a piece of broken glass till they were smooth, then colored some brown with walnut hulls, others a purple red with pokeberry juice.

Henderson Perkins, Texas

"Marster Garner runs a tavern, dey calls 'em hotels now. My mammy was cook for de tavern. De other nigger's named Gib, and I'se to do de work 'roun de place and take grist to de water mill for to grin'. Marster have de farm, too, and have seven niggers on dat place and sometimes I goes dere for to he'p."

Simon Phillips, Alabama

Simon Phillips was one of 300 Negroes belonging to Bryant Watkins, a planter of Greensboro, Alabama. He was a house man, which means that he mixed the drinks, opened the carriage doors, brought refreshments on the porch to guests, saw that the carriage was always in the best of condition and tented the front lawn. When asked about slave days, he gets a far-away expression in his eyes; an expression of tranquil joy.

Ellen Polk, Texas

"It was a fine, big plantation. De young women slaves wukked in de fields and de ole women slaves made de cloth on de spinnin' wheels and de looms. Den de women would go in de woods and take de bark frum de trees and pursley frum de groun' and mix dem wid copperas and put it all in a big iron pot and boil it. Den dey would strain de water off and dye de cloth. De color was brown and, O Lawd, all de slaves wore de same color clothes. Dey even made our socks on de plantation."

Alec Pope, Georgia

"I wuz de reg'lar water boy, and I plowed some too. 'Course dere wuz so many on dat plantation it tuk more'n one boy to tote de water. Money? dis Nigger couldn't git no money in dem days."

"De overseer got us up 'bout four o'clock in de mornin' to feed de stock. Den us et. Us allus stopped off by dark. Mist'ess dere's a old sayin' dat you had to brush a Nigger in dem days to make 'em do right. Dey brushed us if us lagged in de field or cut up de cotton. Dey could allus find some fault wid us. Marster brushed us sometime, but de overseer most gen'ally done it."

Mrs. Preston, Indiana

Mrs. Preston is an old lady, 83 years old, very charming and hospitable She lives on North Elm Street, Madison Indiana. Her first recollections of slavery were of sleeping on the foot of her mistress' bed, where she could get up during the night to "feed" the fire with chips she had gathered before dark or to get a drink or anything else her mistress might want in the night.

When Mrs. Preston was a little older, part of her work was to drive about a dozen cows to and from the stable. Many a time she warmed her bare feet in the cattle bedding. She said they did not always go barefooted but their shoes were old or their feet wrapped in rags.

Her next promotion was to work in the fields hauling shocks of corn on a balky mule which was subject to bucking and throwing its rider over its head. She was aided by a little boy on another mule. There were men to tie the shocks and place them on the mule.

Annie Price, Georgia

As Mr. Kennon owned only a few slaves it was necessary for these few persons to do all of the work. Says Mrs. Price: "My mother had to do everything from cultivating cotton to cooking." The same was true of her father and the other servant. Before the break of day each morning they were all called to prepare for the day's work. Mrs. Price then told how she has seen the men of her plantation and those of the adjoining one going to the fields at this unearthly hour eating their breakfast while sitting astride the back of a mule. After her mother had finished cooking and cleaning the house she was sent to the field to help the men. When it was too dark to see all field hands were permitted to return to their cabins. This same routine was followed each day except Sundays when they were permitted to do much as they pleased. When the weather was too bad for field work they shelled corn and did other types of work not requiring too much exposure. Holidays were unheard of on the Kennon plantation. As a little slave girl the only work that Mrs. Price ever had to do was to pick up chips and bark for her mother to cook with. The rest of the time was spent in playing with the "Marster's" little girls.

All cooking on Mrs. Price's plantation was done by her mother.

Aunt Nicey Pugh, Alabama

"When I was a little pickaninny I worked in Massa Jim's house, sweepin' an' a-cleanin'. Us slaves hed to be up at de house by sunup, build de fires an' git de cookin' started. Dey had big open fireplaces wid potracks to hang de pot on. Dats whar us boiled de vegetables. An' honey, us sho had plenty somp'n' t' eat: greens, taters, peas, rosenyurs an' plenty of home killed meat. Sometimes my oldest brother, Joe West, even' Friday Davis, anudder nigger, went huntin' at night an' kotched mo' possums dan we could eat. Dey'd ketch lots of fish; 'nuf to las' us three days."

Charlotte Raines, Georgia

[Charlotte Raines] seldom spoke unless spoken to and she would never tell very much about her early life. She had been trained as personal maid to one of her ex-master's daughters. This family, (that of Swepson H. Cox) was one of the most cultured and refined that Lexington, in Oglet Morpe County, could boast.

Fanny Randolph, Georgia

"When I wuz 'bout nine years ole, Marse Bob tuk me up ter de 'big house' ter wait on ole Mistis. I didn't hav' much ter do, Jes' had ter he'p 'er dress an' tie 'er shoes an' run eroun' doin' errands fur 'er. Yer know, in den times, de white ladies had niggers ter wait on 'em an' de big niggers done all de hard wuk 'bout de house an' yard."

Easter Reed, Georgia

There were from fifty to seventy-five slaves on the plantation, each with his separate job. Easter sat erect in her chair and began again, "My mother was the chief cook; she cooked for the marster right on down to the slaves. An', she could cook anything they gave her. She didn't just mess things up, she had 'em lookin' fresh an' nice on the dishes."

Easter's father worked the crops. Her sisters spun cloth and acted as house maids. Other slaves worked in the fields or helped with the house work. The first work that Easter remembers was helping her mistress. The mistress was a large stout woman who did not like to stoop. Easter was then a little girl about ten years old and would stay close to the mistress and pick up handkerchiefs and fans that she often dropped. A year or two later she began to spin.

Sallie Reynolds, Alabama

Sallie said Mrs. Albritton was kind to her, taught her to spin and sew, and she tried to learn herself to weave, but, somehow, could never master it.

Edd Roby, Mississippi

"Like I said befo', course I was born in 1863 an' don't have no recollection o' slavery days. All I know is what Pa an' Ma has told me 'bout de times dey had. Course Pa, bein' what dey called houseboy, coachman or driver, had a heep better time 'n most slaves did. From all 'counts tho' Ma went through de roughs tho'. See, Ma, she belonged to de Hammonds, an' Pa, he belonged to

Ki Roby, Ma was a regular field hand an' wasn't never treated so very good by her white folks."

Henry Rogers, Georgia

"In one corner of the kitchen set a loom my Mother use to weave on. She would weave way into the night lots of times."

"The fust thing I 'members is follerin' my Mother er 'round. She wuz the housegirl an' seamstress an' ev'rywhere she went I wuz at her heels. My father wuz the overseer on the Hunt place. We never had no hard work to do. My fust work wuz 'tendin' the calves an' shinin' my Master's shoes. How I did love to put a Sunday shine on his boots an' shoes. He called me his nigger an' wuz goin' ter make a barber out o' me if slavery had er helt on. As it wuz. I shaved him long as he lived."

"Ole Uncle Alex Hunt wuz the bugler an' ev'ry mornin' at 4:00 o'clock he blowed the bugle fer us ter git up, 'cept Sunday mornin's, us all slept later on Sundays."

John Rogers, Georgia

John could recall much about days before the war. He said that he was his old master's "house-boy" and that his duties were "jest to fetch and carry for old Mastah and Mistis." He also "minded off" flies with a pea-fowl-feather-fly-brush when either took a nap. What he liked to do most of all was to drive the big carriage and take Mr. and Mrs. Rogers to church on Sunday. "No man, I can't read and write. Mastah had most o' his darkies larned, but my head was too thick."

Mammie Rose, Mississippi

Mammie Rose lived in quality families and in her day she was the ruler of the nursery mammies. She says the white folks "don't raise dey chillon now. Dey jest let 'em come up."

Gill Ruffin, Texas

"De first marster I remember, marster Butler, lived in a big, two-story log house with a gallery. The slaves lived a short piece away in little log cabins. Marster Butler owned lots of land and niggers and he sho' believed in makin' 'em won. There wasn' no loafin' roun' dat white man. Missus name was Sarah and she made me a houseboy when I was small. I allus took de co'n to mill and went after things Missus would borrow from de neighbors. She allus made me ride a mule, 'cause de country was full of wild prairie cattle and varmints. Missus had a good saddle pony, and I allus rode behin' her when she went visitin'."

"We didn' have no gardene and all we et come from de white folks. They fed us turnips, greens, and meats and cornbread and plenty of milk. We worked every day 'cept Sunday and didn' know any more 'bout a holiday dan climbin' up a tree back'ard. They never give us money, and we hit de field by sunup and stayed dere till sundown. The niggers was whipped with a ridin' quirt."

Julia Rush, Georgia

For a while Mrs. Rush worked in the fields where she plowed and hoed the crops along with the other slaves. Later she worked in the master's house where she served as maid and where she helped with the cooking. She was often hired out to the other planters in the vicinity. She says that she liked this because she always received better treatment than she did at her own home. These persons who hired her often gave her clothes as she never received a sufficient amount from her own master.

Josephine Ryles, Texas

"My mother was de cook for de white folks and my li'l brother, Charlie Evans, was de water toter in de fields. He brung water in de bucket and give de hands a drink."

"My sis am de fly chaser. She has de big fan make from de tail feathers of de peacock. 'Twas awful purty thing. She stands 'round de white folks and shoe off de flies."

Clarissa Scales, Texas

"My job was tendin' fires and herdin' hawgs. I kep' fire goin' when de washin' bein' done. Dey had plenty wood, but used corn cobs for de fire. Dere a big hill corn cobs near de wash kettle. In de evenin' I had to bring in de hawgs. I had a li'l whoop I druv dem with, a eight-plaited rewhide whoop on de long stick. It a purty sight to see dem hawgs go under de slip-gap, what was a rail took down from de bottom de fence, so de hawgs could run under."

Janie Scott, Alabama

Her mother worked in the house, and when the field hands were working helped carry water out to them in buckets, each one getting a swallow or two a piece. Her father was Andy White, and was raised on the plantation of John Jewett at Stockton, Alabama.

Janie said her mother "was strong and could roll and cut logs like a man, and was much of a woman." Then they had a log rolling on a plantation the Negroes from the neighboring plantations came and worked together until all the jobs were completed.

Alice Shaw, Mississippi

"They struck a plow point to wake us up and git us to the field by daylight. We had planty to eat, milk, butter, bread and vegetables."

"My job wus to fan the flies off the table while the white folks eat and to tote the dishes to the kitchen, and if I dropped one Miss cracked me on the head. Miss—thats what we called her—wus good to me unless I broke a dish."

Lucindy Hall Shaw, Mississippi

"I used to nuss de chilluns, an' I wu'ud ride in de stage coach an' tote de baby; when dey wuz travellin'; dey didn't have no trains den, an' when dey went tradin' dey w'u'd sen' de wagons to Memphis, an' dey w'ud take a hole monf fer de trip; bymby Mister Jacob Thompson wanted a shorter way to go to Memphis an' he navigated dis railroad to cum by Oxford; hit look lak hit cost more to ride on dose ole stage co'ches dan de railroads."

Partheny Shaw, Georgia

"My grandmother was de cook woman and she cook all de meals, and my mother always carried hearn to her house to eat. She work in de fields. I would be playin' round, totin' chips, gittin' water at the well and at de spring. I could sweep yard and do things like that."

Robert Shepherd, Georgia

"De white ladies had nice silk dresses to wear to church. Slave 'omans had new calico dresses what dey wore wid hoopskirts dey made out of grapevines. Dey wore poke bonnets wid ruffles on 'em and, if de weather was sort of cool, dey wore shawls. Marster allus wore his linen duster. Dat was his white coat, made cutaway style wid long tails. De cloth for most all of de clothes was made at home. Marse Joe raised lots of sheep and de wool was used to make cloth for de winter clothes. Us had a great long loom house whar some of de slaves didn't do nothin' but weave cloth. Some cyarded bats, some done de spinnin', and dere was more of 'em to do de sewin'. Miss Ellen, she looked atter all dat, and she cut out most of de clothes. She seed dat us had plenty to wear. Sometimes Marster would go to de sewin' house, and Mist'ess would tell him to git on 'way from dar and look atter his own wuk, dat her and Aunt Julia could run dat loom house. Marster, he jus' laughed den and told us chillun what was hangin' round de door to jus' listen to dem 'omans cackle. Oh, but he was a good old boss man."

Tom Singleton, Georgia

"Marse Fred didn't have a very big plantation; jus' 'bout 70 or 80 acres I guess, an' he had 'bout 25 Niggers. He didn't have no overseer. My pa wuz de one in charge, an' he tuk his orders from Marse Fred, den he went out to de farm, whar he seed dat de Niggers carried 'em out. Pa wuz de carriage driver too. It wuz his delight to drive for Marster and Mist'ess."

Mr. and Mrs. Alex Smith, Alabama

Mrs. Smith was named after Elizabeth Stubblefield, a relative of Peter Stubbelfield. As a child of five years or less, Elizabeth had to spin "long reels five cuts a day," pick seed from cotton, and cockle burrs from wool, and perform the duties of a house girl.

Nancy Smith, Georgia

"De biggest, bestest fireplace up at de big house was in de kitchen whar Mammy done de cookin'. It had a great wide hearth wid four big swingin' racks and four big old pots. Two of de ovens was big and two was little. Dat was better cookin' 'rangements and fixin's den most of de other white folks in dis town had den. When dat fire got good and hot and dere was plenty of ashes, den Mammy started cookin' ash cakes and 'taters. One of Mammy's good ash-roasted 'taters would be awful good right now wid some of dat good old home-made butter to go wid it. Marster allus kept jus' barrels and barrels of good old home-made 'lasses sirup, 'cause he said dat was what made slave chilluns grow fast and be strong. Folks don't know how to have plenty of good things to eat lak us had den. Jus' think of Marse Joe's big old plantation down nigh de Georgia Railroad whar he raised our somepin' t'eat: *vegetables sich as green* corn, 'taters, cabbages, onions, collards, turnip greens, beans, peas—more dan I could think up all day—and dere was plenty of wheat, rye, and corn for our bread."

"Out dar de pastur's was full of cows, hogs and sheep, and dey raised lots of chickens and turkeys on dat farm. Dey clipped wool from dem sheep to weave wid de cotton when dey made cloth for our winter clothes."

"…Miss Julia used to make me sweep de yard wid a little brushbroom and I had to wear *a bonnet* den to keep dust out of my hair. Dat bonnet was ruffled 'round de front and had staves to hold de. brim stiff, but in de back it didn't have no ruffle; jus' de bottom of de crown what us called de bonnet tail. Dem bonnets looked good enough in front but mighty bob-tailed in de back."

Paul Smith, Georgia

"When us warn't out in de fields, us done little jobs 'round de big house, de cabins, barns, and yards. Us used to holp de older slaves git out whiteoak splits, and dey larnt us to make cheer bottoms and baskets out of dem splits. De best cheer bottoms what lasted de longest was dem what us made wid red ellum withes. Dem old shuck bottoms was fine too; dey plaited dem shucks and wound 'em 'round for cheer bottoms and footsmats. De 'omans made nice hats out of shucks and wheat straw. Dey plaited de shucks and put 'em together wid plaits of wheat straw. Dey warn't counted much for Sunday wear, but dey made fine sun hats."

Annie Stanton, Alabama

When asked by the writer about nursing these chidred, so as to be sure she [illegible text]id colored children, she replied, "dat de slaves libed on de plantation, and [illegible text]y had an oversear who libed on dis place, an' she neber seed de Marshall's place 'til after dey wuz freed. As I growed bigger into a big yearlin' gal I wuz tuk intuhe de overseer's home to 'tend tuh de dinin' room table sich as settin'nit an washin' de dishes an' cleanin' up, an' later on I wuz showed how to iron, spin thread, weave cloth, and make candles. Honey, folks talkin' bout depression now don't kno' nothin' 'bout hard times. In dem days folks din't hab nothin' 'ceptin' what dey made. Eben if yo' had a mint ob money, there wuz nothin' to buy. We made de candles to burn by tying stringd en the stick an' puttin' dem down in melted taller in moulds. In dem times we had no matches. Folks made fire by strikin' flint rocks together an' de fire droppin' on cotton. [illegible text] don't know whether dese rocks were ones dat de Indians lef' or me, but dey wuz dif'rent from other rocks. People usta carry dem an' de cotton roun' in boxes sumtin lak snuff boxes tuh keep de cotton dry. Sumtimes when dey could'nt get de fire no odder way, dey would put de cotton in de fireplace and shoot up in dere an' set hit on fire."

Liza Strickland, Mississippi

"I wuz waitin' maid in Mars' house. I jest done eber thing about a house in general, jest whut eber I wuz sont ter do. I help keep up de house an' wait on ole missus and and tended ter de chillun and waited on de table an' things lak dat. Deir wuz a heap o' us ter do de wuk but deir wuz a heap o' wuk ter be done."

Rachel Sullivan, Georgia

"I wus a nu's gal, 'bout 'leben years old. I nu'sed my Auntie's chillun, while she nu'sed de lady's baby whut come from Russia wid de Marster's wife—nu'sed dat baby fum de breas's I mean. All de white ladies had wet nusses in dem days. Her master had just returned from Russia, where he had been embassador. Her baby had the czarina for a godmother."

And so you used to look after you aunt's children?

"Yas'm. I used to play wid 'em in de big ground wid de monuments all around."

Salena Taswell, Florida

"I cleaned and dusted and waited on the table, made beds and put everything in order, ashed dishes, polished silverware and did the most trusty work."

Daniel Taylor, Alabama

"Mah grandfather's name was Mac Wilson an' mah grandmother's name was Ellan Wilson, an' de ol" Miss's name was Miss Mamie Herrin. All de colored folks' chillun called Mr. Herrin 'Ol' Marster,' an' he sho' was a good marster, too. I 'members dat atter I got to be a big boy dey put me in de fiel's choppin' cotton, but I neber could pick cotton. I knows dat mah paw said I was too crazy 'bout de girls, so he tuk me an' made me plow."

"Ol' marster had a big place, I don't jes' exactly knows how many acres dey was, but I knows us had plenty ob cotton, 'ca' se sometimes dey would pick four or five bales a day. An' den I knows durin' cotton time mah paw hauled cotton all day long to de gin whut was run by five or six mules."

"Durin' de busy season on de plantation ol' Marster had de older women cookin' an' sendin' de dinner to de fiel'. Dere was two big baskets, one to put de bread in, an 'de odder basket to put de meat in. Every mornin' at three o'clock de women begun cookin' an' each han' brought his own meat an' bread to this cabin to be cooked. Every person's plate had their names on 'em. Ever'body had to be up by daylight an' ready to begin work. De men had to get up before daylight an' begin to harness de mules, an' soon as light day was in de fiel's. Dere was two hundred and fifty head ob colored people, scusing chillun. Dey would raise four, five, and six hundred bales ob cotton, a year. Us worked den, dere warn't no walkin' 'bout den, not eben on Sat'day atternoons, but I believes I'd lack it betta dan I does now, 'cause de chillun was taught to be mannerable den, but now dey cuss if you say anything to dem."

Daniel Taylor. (Library of Congress)

Cordelia Thomas, Georgia

"Our Marster evermore did raise de cotton—lots, of it to sell, and plenty for clothes for all de folkses, white and black, what lived on his place. All de cloth was home-made 'cept de calico for de best Sunday dresses. Chillun had to spin de thread and deir mammies wove de cloth. 'Fore de end of de war, whilst I was still so little I had to stand on a box to reach de spinnin' wheel good, I could spin six reels a day."

Ellen Thomas, Alabama

In her childhood, Ellen had as her special mistress Miss Cornelia, one of the Kimball girls, who trained her in the arts of good housekeeping, including fine sewing, which was itself an art among the women of that period. Ellen relates with much pride, her ability to put in tucks and back-stitch them in the front of men's shirts, to equal the best machine work of the present day. Although hampered by failing eyesight in recent years, her work with the needle today is proof that her claims are not exaggerated.

Her training as a house servant was very broad and involved every feature of a well kept household of that period. She has especial pride in her ability to serve at table, particularly when there were guests present. A feature of the training given her and which Ellen says she never knew of anyone else receiving was, after being taught to set the dining table complete for guests, she would be blindfolded and then told to go through the motions of serving and so learn to do so without disturbing anything on the table. So proficient did she become in serving, that a few times when they had guests, Judge Kimball would for their amusement have Ellen blindfolded and direct her to serve the dinner. In passing dishes a small silver tray was used.

Maria Tilden Thompson, Texas

"At Engledow's ranch I had to do housework and nuss de chillun. I don't remember none ob de chillun's names. Durin' slavery time de folks whut owned us was putty mean to us. De Engledows was putty good folks, but dey would whoop us, too. Even when I was in my late twenties I still got a whoopin' fo' doin' somethin' dat I should of done better."

Mary Thompson, Texas

"I always felt mysef free even befo' freedom, 'cause I didn't have to do no field work. I cleaned house, nussed de chillun, and waited on table."

"We wusn't given no money. We wus given our room, food and clothes. I lived in de 'big house' wid de Marster and mistress, and slep' on a pallet on de floah. I had to git up durin' de night and wait on de chillun, … give 'em watah and so on."

"De chillun liked me and called me Mary, and de chillun's folks treated me all right, except once or twice. Some of dose chillun is still livin' in Alabama, and I could have a room wid 'em to dis day."

Margaret Thornton, Mississippi

"I wus brung up ter nurse an' I'se did my share of dat, too honey, let me tell you. I has nursed 'bout two thousand babies I reckins. I has nursed gran'maws an' den dere gran' chiles. I reckin dat I has closed as many eyes as de nex' one."

Phil Towns, Georgia

Phil Towns' father worked in the field and his mother did light work in the house, such as assisting in spinning. Mothers of three or more children were not compelled to work, as the master felt that their children needed care.

Young Phil was in his teens when be began his first job—coach driver for "Gov." Towns. This was just before they moved to Georgia. He traveled with him wherever he went, and as the Gov. purchased a plantation in Talbot County, (the house still stands), and a home in Mason, (the site of Mt. De Sales Academy), a great deal of his time was spent on the road. Phil never did any other work except to occasionally assist in sweeping the large yard. The other member of this group split rails, did field work, spinning, tailoring and any of the many things that had to be done. Each person might choose the type of work he liked best.

Neal Upson, Georgia

"Marse Frank said he wanted 'em to larn me how to wait on de white folkses' table up at de big 'ouse, and dey started me off wid de job of fannin' de flies away. Mist'ess Serena, Marse Frank's wife, made me a white coat to wear in de dinin' room. Missy, dat little old white coat made me git de onliest whuppin' Marse Frank ever did give me." Here old Neal paused for a hearty laugh. "Us had comp'ny for dinner dat day and I felt so big showin' off 'fore 'em in dat white coat dat I jus' couldn't make dat turkey wing fan do right. Dem turkey wings was fastened on long handles and atter Marster had done warned me a time or two to mind what I was 'bout, the old turkey wing went down in de gravy bowl and when I jerked it out it splattered all over de preacher's best Sunday suit. Marse Frank got up and tuk me right out to de kitchen and when he got through brushin' me off I never did have no more trouble wid dem turkey wings."

Charlie Van Dyke, Alabama

Uncle Charlie said his mother cooked for the white folks, and sometime she didn't get down to their cabin but on Sunday afternoon, that he being the oldest had to look after the younger children and that he was never required to do heavy work as he broke his leg when a boy, so the folks let him just work around the yard and look after his sisters and brothers and also the other slave children.

"Honey, I warn't no common eve'yday slave, I hoped de white folks in de big house. Mistus Lucy wouldn't let 'em take me to de fiel'. Dem was good days, chile; mighty good days. I wuz happy den, but since 'mancipation I has jes' had to scuffle an' work an' do de bes' I kin."

Addie Vinson, Georgia

"Pappy's Ma and Pa was Grandma Nancy and Grandpa Jacob. Day was field hands, and dey b'longed to Marse Obe Jackson. Grandma Lucy and Grandpa Toney Murrah was owned by Marse Billy Murrah. Marse Billy was a preacher what sho could come down wid de gospel at church. Grandma Lucy was his cook. Miss sadie LeSeur got Grandma Lucy and tuk her to Columbus, Georgy, and us never seed our grandma no more. Miss Badie had been one of de Vinson gals. She tuk our Aunt Haley 'long too to wait on her when she started out for Europe, and 'fore dey got crost de water, Aunt Haley, she died on de boat. Miss Sarah, she had a time keepin' dem boatsmens from th'owing Aunt Haley to de sharks. She is buried in de old country somewhar."

"De kitchen was sot'off a piece from de big house, and our white folkses wouldn't eat deir supper 'fore time to light de lamps to save your life; den I had to stan' 'hind Old Miss' cheer and fan her wid a turkey-feather fan to keep de flies off. No matter how rich folkses was dem days dere warn't no screens in de houses."

"I never will forgit pore old Aunt Mary; she was our cook, and she had to be tapped evvy now and den 'cause she had de drapsy so bad. Aunt Mary's old man was Uncle Harris, and I 'members how he used to go fishin' at night. De udder slaves went fishin' too. Many's de time I'se seed my Mammy come back from Barber's Crick wid a string of fish draggin' from her shoulders down to de ground. Me, I laked milk more'n anything else. You jus' oughta seed dat place at milkin' time. Dere was a heap of cows a fightin', chillun hollerin', and sich a bedlam as you can't think up. Dat old plantation was a grand place for chillun, in summertime 'specially, 'cause dere was so many branches and cricks close by what us chillun could hop in and cool off."

"Sunday was a day off for all de slaves on our plantation. Cause, de mens' had to look atter de stock in de lot right back of de cabins. De 'omans cooked all day for de next week. If dey tuk a notion to go to church, mules was hitched to wagons made lak dippers, and dey jigged off down de road. Us had four days holiday for Christmas, Old Miss give us lots of good things to eat dem four days; dere was cake, fresh meat, and all kinds of dried fruit what had been done stored away. All de Niggers tuk dat time to rest but my Mammy. She tuk me and went 'round to de white folkses' houses to wash and weave. Dey said I was a right smart, peart little gal, and white folkses used to try to hire me from Old Miss. When dey axed her for me, Old Miss allus told 'em: 'You don't want to hire dat gal; she ain't no 'count.' She wouldn't let nobody hire her Niggers, 'cept Mammy, 'cause she knowed Mammy warn't gwine to leave her nohow. On New Year's Day, if dere warn't too much snow on de ground, de Niggers burnt brush and cleared new ground."

Rhodus Walton, Georgia

As Rhodus' father did not come to this home with his family, he knows nothing of him. Except for brief intervals, his mother worked in the house. There cotton and wool were spun into thread and then woven into cloth from which the slaves' clothing was made. An elder sister nursed the master's smaller children—there were several in the family. Rhodus' first duties were to drive the cows to and from the pastures and to keep the calves from annoying the milkers.

Lula Washington, Georgia

"All de niggers on Marster Charlie's plantation had to work in de field 'cept Malindy Lu, a Mulatto nigger gal. Marster Charlie kept her in de house to take care of Missus Jane, dat wuz Marster Charlie wife."

Foster Weathersby, Mississippi

"My first wuk as a slave-child was when I was a little chap. Dey made me churn out in de back yard under de big trees. De churn was big an' tall, an' hel' gallons of milk. I had to churn, and churn, and den churn some mo'; dey just never would, look lack, let me stop; dey made me walk 'roun' and 'roun' dat churn. I jes natu'ally growed to lak dat job."

Jennie Webb, Mississippi

"When I got big 'nuf I wuz put to look after de other little slave chillun. I had to keep 'em quiet an' git de little babies to sleep; help to keep 'em a playin' an' to help feed de little uns, at meal times. Right here I wants to tell yo' how we wuz fed. We had big wooden bowls dat wuz alwas' left out deir. Our food wuz poured in dese bowls an we all et from 'em at de same time wid our hands. My aunt wuz de one dat cooked an' fixed hit up fer us. She never did have dese bowls took in an' washed. After we got through eatin' in 'em de flys swarmed over 'em an' de dogs licked 'um an' dey sho' did smell bad. When I got big 'nuf to know how nasty dis wuz I got to whar I couldn't half eat, but I'd take de little uns up an' feed 'em from my hands. Even dis got to whar hit sickened me. Mos' all de bigger chillun wuz lak me 'bout it. We began to git skinny from de lak of some'em to eat, an' one day I wuz a feedin' some ob de little uns at dinner time but couldn't eat nothin' my self. Marse come up an' stood lookin' up, den he called to me an' ast why I wasn't eatin'. I jes' up an' tole 'em it wuz nasty an' jes' ole sloppy stuff. He took a good look over an called de cook an' say, 'Adelene, how do you think I can raise de little niggers an' you feedin' 'em lak dis.' He got in behind 'em an' we wuz fed right from den on."

"When I wuz a little bigger I wuz put to spinnin' an' knittin'. All our clo'se wuz wove an' made by hand, our shoes wuz home made too an' we never wuz give no shoes 'till we wuz purty good size. Dey wuz heavy an' course, an' sho' did las' a long time."

Margaret White, Florida

"My father was a tailor and made the clothes for his master and his servants. I was never sold. My master just kept me. They liked me and wouldn't let me be sold. He never whipped me, for I was a slave, you know, and I had to do just as I was told."

"I worked around the house doing maid's work. I also helped to care for the children in the home."

Martha Whitfield, Mississippi

Fostine was recognized as one of the best cooks in the county, serving in the Gladney home for years. She taught her daughters to make servants. Martha, while never going to school very long has become a self educated woman, serving in the Bloominfield home for near forty years. She is an active member of the negro Methodist church and stands for good Christian citizenship.

Green Willbanks, Georgia

"Ma was a field hand and this time of the year when work was short in the field—laying-by time, we called it—and on rainy days she spun thread and wove cloth. As the thread left the spinning wheel it went on a reel where it was wound into hanks, and then it was carried to the loom to be woven into cloth. Pa had a little trade; he made shoes and baskets, and old Boss let him sell them. Pa didn't make shoes for the slaves on our plantation; old Boss bought them ready-made and had them shipped here from the West."

Callie Williams, Alabama

"My mammy say dat dey waked up in de mornin' when dey heard de sweep. Dat was a piece of iron hangin' by a string and it made a loud noise when it was banged wid another piece of iron. Dey had to get up at four o'clock and be at work by sunup. To do dis, dey mos' all de time cook breakfast de night befo'."

"Pappy was a driver under de overseer, but mammy say dat she stay at de little nursery cabin and look after all de little babies. Dey had a cabin fixed up with homemade cradles and things where dey put all de babies. Der mammies would come in from de field about ten o'clock to nurse 'em and den later in de day, my mammy would feed de youngest on pot-licker and de older ones on greens and pot-licker. Dey had skimmed milk and mush, too and all of 'em stayed as fat as a butter balls, me among 'em. Mammy saw dat I always got my share."

"While mammy was tendin' de babies she had to spin cotton and she was supposed to spin two 'cuts' a day. Four 'cuts' was a hard day's work. What was a cut? You oughta' know dat! Dey had a reel and when it had spun three hundred yards it popped. Dat was a 'cut.' When it had been spun, den another woman took it to do de loom to make cloth for de slaves. Dey always took Saturday afternoon to clean up de clothes and cabins, 'case dey always had to start work on Monday mornin' clean as a pin. If dey didn't dey got whupped for bein' dirty."

Daphne Williams, Texas

"My mudder was de cook. She like to die one time an' dey start breakin' me in to do de cookin'. Den w'en she die I tuk her cook' place an' I been cookin' two or t'ree year' w'en freedom come."

Lizzie Williams, Mississippi

"My job back in dem days was to weave, spin thread, run de loom, an durin crop time I plowed an' hoed in de field. My mammy was a regular field hand."

Millie Williams, Texas

"Now 'bout de wokke, de overse'er would wake 'em up at four o'clock in de mornin'. Den dey would git ready to eat an' go to de fiel'."

"I's wokke at de marster's house, I's help cook, clean house an' help tak care of de nigger chillen. In a pinch I's sent to de fiel' to wokke, but not often. All de slaves wokked from daylight till four o'clock in de evenin'. Dey would git off on Thursdays, Sat'day an' Sunday. De reason dat we'ns git Thursdays off is dat de marster's folks waz Germans an' dey didn't believe in wokkin' on Thursday. I's don' know if Thursday waz a German holiday or not, all I's know is dat de marster says we'ns didn't wokke on Thursday, so we'ns didn't wokke."

Olin Williams, Georgia

"I doan 'member what year I was borned, but Marster say, I was 'bout fo'teen when freedom comed. I doan' 'member 'bout my pappy, cyaze he died out an' my mammy mah'ied again."

"Us b'longed to Marster John Whitlow, and his plantation was 'bout th'ee miles b'low Watkinsville, whar Bishop is now. But dar won't nuffin' dar den."

"All de chillun my mammy had was me an' my twin brudder. My brudder wukked in de field, but I was de house boy, an' helped my mammy an' mist'ess in de house, cleaned yards, an' did a sight of churin' cyaze Marster sho' had a lots of cows."

"My job every Sadday was to scrub de wooden water buckets 'til dem brass hoops shine lak' gole. Mistess would look to see if dey was right an' if she fine jes' one little spot, hit was all to do ober."

"I had to come to Watkinsville th'ee times a week for to git de mail. Mail didn't go so fast den as it do now."

Stephen Williams, Texas

"Like I tell you, young Mr. Dan and me was 'bout the same age, and I liked him right from the start and I guess he liked me 'cause we use to eat together and sleep on the same pallet."

"Mamma is the cook and Jane helps her and papa help 'round the store keeping things clean. I don't do nothing much 'cept go 'round with young Mr. Dan. I guess old Mr. Dan sure likes me too, 'cause I know one day a man say to him, 'How much you want for that young nigger?' Mr. Dan tell him I ain't for sale, that I'm worth my weight in gold, and if he hadn't liked me pretty well I don't reckon he'd of said that."

Mary Wilson, Texas

"Ise never does much wo'k 'roun' de place 'cept runnin' errands. Ise 'membahs my aunt an' my mammy wo'kin' 'roun' de house, cleanin' up, makin' beds, an' runnin' de old spinnin' wheel. 'Sides runnin' de spinnin' wheel dem two done all de clothes sewin' fo' de whole place includin' de plantation. Tudder womens on de plantation he'ped spin de thread aftah dey's wo'kin' houahs. Deys have de spinnin' house in dey's qua'tahs. Ise don't 'membahs how many cabins am in dey's qua'tahs but 'twas lots."

Robert Wilson, Texas

"Ise tellin' 'bout de wo'k an' 'twas de Mistes dat done de house—wo'k mos'ly. Many's de time Ise stands an' fans her while she churns. Ise does dat fo' 'bout ha'f houah den falls over sleep. Ise he'ps her w'en she am weavin' cloth. She have to sat up on de high bench an' Ise gives her de shuttle w'en she draps it. She runs de spinnin' but Ise not needed den. My sistah knits de socks an' gloves dat am used. Ever'thing used on de place am made right dere 'cludin' de shoes de grown fo'ks weahs which Marster makes f'om de hides he gits w'en he kill fo' our meat."

Cornelia Winfield, Georgia

Cornelia Winfield, 1341 Ninth Street, was born in Crawford, Oglethorpe County, Georgia March 10, 1855. Her father, being the same age as her master, was given to him as a little boy. They grew up together, playing games, and becoming devoted to each other. When her master was married her father went to his home with him and became the overseer of all the slaves on the plantation. "My father and mother wuz house servants. My marster served my father's plate from his own table and sent it to him, every meal. He had charge of the work shop, and when marster was away he always stayed at the Big House, to take care of my Missis and the children. My mother was a seamstress and had three younger seamsters under her, that she taught to sew. We made the clothes for all the house servants and fiel' hans. My mother made some of the clothes for my marster and missis. My mother was a midwife too, and useter go to all the birthings on our place. She had a bag she always carried and when she went to other plantations she had a horse and buggy to go in."

Silvia Witherspoon, Alabama

"Yassmam," she continued, after I had asked a few questions, "I remembers some things 'bout de slavery days. 'Co'se I can't remember jus' 'zactly how old I is, but I mus' be mought nigh on to ninety, 'ca'se I was a raght sizable gal when de war ended. I was bawn on a plantation in Jackson, Mississi ppi, dat belonged to my Massa, Dr. Minto Witherspoon. My Pappy an' Mammy was name Lum an' Phyllis Witherspoon. De white folks lived in a big, white house made outten logs. Honey, Massa an' Mistis Witherspoon was quality: Yassmam, dey was quality. Us slaves was treated lak we was somp'n round dat place. Massa didn't 'low no oberseer to tote no strop 'hine his niggers. Besides dat we was fed good an' had good clothes. He useta done had brogans sont out in boxfuls folks' f'um Mobile. My job was to do little things aroun' de white/house, but befo' dat I stayed in de quarters an' nussed my mammy's chilluns, while she worked in de fiel's. She would tie de smalles' baby on my back so's I could play widout no inconvenience. I laked to stay at de big house, dough, an' fan de flies offen de white folks while dey et. Dat was de bes' job I eber had. Mistis gived me a dress dat de white chilluns done out-growed an' on Sunday I was de dressed-upest nigger in de quarter."

George Womble, Georgia

"I remember that he had one little boy whose job was to break these animals so that they could be easily sold. My job was to wait tables, help with the house cleaning, and to act as nurse maid to three young children belonging to the master. At other times I drove the cows to and from the pasture and I often helped with the planting in the fields when the field hands were rushed. Out of the forty-odd slaves that were held by the Ridleys all worked in the field with the exception of myself and the cook whose name was Harriet Ridley."

Mr. Womble was asked to tell what time he had to arise in the morning to begin his day's work and he replied that sometimes he did'nt even go to sleep as he had to keep one hand on the baby crib to keep it from crying. Most of the time he got up at four o'clock in the morning and went to the kitchen where he helped the cook prepare breakfast. After this was done and he had finished waiting on the master and his family he started to clean the house. When he had finished this he had to take care of the younger Womble children and do countless the other things to be done around a house.

Ruben Woods, Texas

"Beins I stayed in de house, Mistress allas gived me good cloths to wear, and shoes too. Some of de niggers didn't have no clothes."

"De most fun I guess I ever had was when Massa let me be footman for his carriage. He got me a uniform, mos like a soldier's uniform, ceptin mine was red, wid black stripes down de sides. I member it jist like it was yestidy, de first time I puts it on. Massa gave a big celebration at his house, and de regular doorman was sick. Massa handed me de suit, and tol me to hurry and put it on. Den he made me come to de front door, and let him in ova and ova, soas to git the hang of it. He told me to take his hat and cane and put it up, and to say 'thank you,' and 'this way please,' and not to say no mo to no body, and I didn't. After dat night, I opened de door lots of times, but I wore my red suit when I went to church wid de white folks, and held de horses, while dey listened to de serman."

"Well when we got settled in de new house, Massa's wife picked me out to be nurse to her childern, since she say dat I waz too little do much work in de field. No'm I never did work in de field till atter I waz freed. My maw didn't work in de field either. My maw wasn't strong in her back. She say she done been hurt when she got a whippin when she wasn't grown. Mistress say to her, 'Eva, you come in de kitchen, and make some chittlins, and iffin you can cook good, you can stay and work in my kitchen, iffen you can't, you will haft to work in de field wid de rest of de niggers.' Maw she make de chittlins, and Mistress say she let her stay in de house and do de cooking of de vittils. I didn't have nothin to do, ceptin look atter the childerns, and help bring in de wood."

Willis Woodson, Texas

"We gits to de new farm, long ways from where we lives befo', and starts clearin' land."

Henry Wright, Georgia

When Mr. Wright was asked about the treatment that was given the house slaves in comparison to that given the field slaves, he replied with a broad grin that "Old Marster" treated them much the same as he would a horse and a mule. That is, the horse was given the kind of treatment that would make him show off in appearance, while the mule was given only enough care to keep him well and fit for work. "You see," continued Mr. Wright, "in those days a plantation owner was partially judged by the appearance of his house servants." And so in addition to receiving the discarded clothes of "Old Marster" and his wife, better clothing was bought for the house slaves

The working hours of the house slave and the field slave were practically the same. In some cases the house slaves had to work at night due to the fact that the master was entertaining his friends or he was invited out and so someone had to remain up to attend to all the necessary details.

On the plantation of Mr. House the house slaves thought themselves better than the field slaves because of the fact that they received better treatment. On the other hand those slaves who worked in the fields said that they would rather work in the fields than work in the house because they had a chance to earn spending money in their spare or leisure time. House servants had no such opportunity.

Susannah Wyman, Georgia

"The house servants wuz trained to cook, clean up, de men wuz trained to make shoes. I don't think us had carpenters. I toted water in de fiel', hoed some, I was quite young. I spun but I didn't weave. Dere was a lady they had on the place done de weaving. I had a many a dress striped, woven on dat big loom and dey wuz pretty, too."

Mary Young, Texas

"I cooked, that was about all I did until after I was free. I have cooked hole calf at time and great big skillet plum full of corn bread. We did not have flour them days. Yessir, I have cooked rabbit and fish bos until I looked like rabbits. Oh, yessir, I like rabbit the best."

SKILLED WORKERS

Many of the needs of the plantation were fulfilled by enslaved artisans. They built furniture, sewed clothing, cobbled shoes, shoed horses, and performed numerous other skilled tasks. Their efforts gave greater self-sufficency to the slaveholders' operation and increased their profits. The enslaved's skills were a mixed blessing as they made that individual invaluable to the operation, but also more valuable when placed on the auction block.

When they could, slaveholders sought to have their operation be as economically independent as possible. The less they had to purchase at stores or from others the lower their costs of operation. Consequently, when they could have items they needed created by their enslaved labor they took advantage of it. If an enslaved person had special skills they could escape working in the fields. Blacksmiths, carpenters, weavers, seamstresses, hostlers (stable workers or groomsmen), shoemakers, or an especially skilled cook were among the workers who were considered of high value and had a special status. In Georgia, where Cicely Cawthon lived, "Uncle Jeff Names, the shoemaker, he made all of the shoes that all of 'em wore on the place. He was about the first slave Marster had. He come from Virginny. They paid big money for him cause he was a valuable darkey. He was 'bout as valuable as the blacksmith. I don't remember how much they paid for him, but it was big money."

On Tempie Herndon's plantation in South Carolina one of these valued skills belonged to Mama Rachel, who worked in the dyeing room:

> Dey wuzn' nothin' she didn' know 'bout dyein'. She knew every kind of root, bark, leaf an' berry dat made red, blue, green, or whatever color she wanted. Dey had a big shelter whare de dye pots set over de coals. Mammy Rachel would fill de pots wid water, den she put in de roots, bark an' stuff an' boil de juice out, den she strain it an' put in de salt an' vinegar to set de color.

Her knowledge, combined with the efforts of skilled enslaved weavers, enabled the slaveholder to produce all of the clothing needed by the people residing on his plantation. This translated into a major savings on larger operations with 20 or more slaves. Such skills also increased the value of workers if they were put up for sale. "The value of slaves varied from $500 to $10,000, depending on his or her special qualifications. Tradesmen such as blacksmiths, shoe makers, carpenters, etc., were seldom sold under $10,000," according to G. W. Pattillo of Georgia.

NARRATIVES

Aunt Adeline, Georgia

Adeline's mother worked in the field, drove steers, and was considered the best meat cutter on the plantation. The slave women were required to spin, and Adeline's mother was unusually good at spinning wool, "and that kind of spinning was powerful slow," added the old woman. "My mother was one of the best dyers anywhere around. I was too. I made colors by mixing up all kinds of bark and leaves. I made the prettiest sort of lilac color with maple bark and pine bark—not the outside pine bark, but that little thin skin that grows right down next to the tree."

James Calvin Alexander, Texas

"Uncle Elija Glasgow was the shoemaker on de place. Dat's all he had to do. He tanned de leather and made brass-toe brough-ans. A lot ob times we wo'e shoes wid tufts of hair still in de toe paht! Sometimes we blacked our shoes by goin' to de wash-pot and takin' a rag, we'd rub it against it and den put the blacknin' on our shoes. We'd also smear tallow on de shoes to make 'em shine."

George Anderson, Texas

"My work was to drive de surrey for de family and look atter de hosses and de harness and sich. I jis' have de bes' hosses on de place to see atter."

"Dey had plenty of hosses and mules and cows on de ol' plantation. I had to look atter some of de hosses, but dem what I hatter look atter was s'pose to be de bes' hosses in de bunch. Like I say, I drive de surrey and dey allus have de bes' hosses to pull dat surrey. Dey had a log stable. Dey kep' de harness in dere, too. Eb'ry-t'ing what de stock eat dey raise on de plantation, all de co'n and fodder and sich like."

Molly Arnond (Ammonds), Alabama

"My pappy made all de furniture dat went in our house an' it were might' good furniture too. Us useta cook on de fiareplace. Us would cook ash cakes. Dey wuz made outen meal, water and a little pinch of lard; on Sundays dey wuz made outen flour, buttermilk an' lard. Mammy would rake all de ashes out de fiareplace, den kivver de cake wid de hot ashes an' let it cool till it was done."

"De only work I done on de plantation was to nuss some little niggers when dere mammy an' pappy wuz in de fiel's. Twarn't hard."

Hanna Austin, Georgia

"Besides working as the cook for the Hall family my mother was also a fine seamstress and made clothing for the master's family and for our family. We were allowed an ample amount of good clothing which Mr. Hall selected from the stock in his store. My father worked as a porter in the store and did other jobs around the house. I did not have to work and spent most of my time playing with the Hall children. We were considered the better class of slaves and did not know the meaning of a hard time."

Bettie Massingale Bell, Alabama

"My gran'maw name Cely De Graffenreid, en my gran'paw name Peter en he wuz er shoe-maker fer de place en made a cudder stock plows en put er sweep on ter sweep cotton en er corey plow whut had er wooden wall board. Now dey has steel uns, but my Gran'pappy made all dem wooden ones on de place. He wuz er worker, en he larnt me how ter pull fodder en chop corn en cotton when I wa'r'nt so high, jes' er black nigger."

Charlie Bell, Mississippi

"My mother was bornd between Poplarville an' Picayune an' my father was bornd at Red Church forty mile below New Orleans. I have heard say my gran'father was bornd there too. My father was a carpenter an' a blacksmith, could make a whole wagon, go out an' cut him a gum tree an' make a whole wooden wagon, an' hubs an' ever'thing. That's how come they didn' take him to de War; leave him at home ter make mule shoes an' things. He was a powerful worker."

Oliver Bell, Alabama

"My gran'ma's name was Cely De Graffenreid an' my gran'pa's name was Peter. He was a shoemaker fur de place an' made plows, too. He was a worker an' he learnt me how to pull fodder an' chop corn an' cotton when I was jest a little scamp jes' a little black nigger."

Oliver Bell. (Library of Congress)

Carrie Bradley Logan Bennet, Arkansas

"My pa was the head blacksmith on Massa Tom's place, them other men helped him along."

Rias Body, Alabama

Many spinning wheels and looms were operated on the Body plantation by expert female spinners and weavers who made practically all the cloth for the slaves' clothes. This cloth was of four kinds—cotton, mixed cotton and flax, mixed cotton and wool, and all-wool. The women wore pantelettes that came to their shoe tops and usually had ruffles on their bottoms. All men wore "galluses" in lieu of belts, which were unknown among the Negroes.

Betty Bormer, Texas

"We'uns hab all de clothes we'uns needed. Dey was all made on de place. My mammy am de seamstress, my pappy de shoemaker. My wo'k 'twas nuss fo' de small chilluns ob de Marster, dey was Mart, Sally, and Veanna. Dat am my wo'k all de time till freedom."

Isabella Boyd, Texas

"My mistus kep' me right in de house, right by her, sewing. I could sew so fast I git my task over 'fore de others git started good."

"My mammy em de sewing woman and my pappy am de shoemaker. My work, for to nuss de small chillen of de marster."

Monroe Brackins, Texas

"I was then about six years old, but not big enough to do any work. I learned the stock business principally on the Adams' Ranch. They stayed there quite awhile. After I got large enough, I was a horse breaker. We thought it [horse-breaking] was all right. We had regular Spanish horses and some real broncos. We had shoes; I had to have some kind of shoes because they had me in the brush nearly all the time and I had to have something to keep the thorns out of my feet, and I wore rawhide leggin's too. I'll tell you, lady, we just had such clothes as we could get—old patched up clothes. They just had that jeans cloth, home made clothes, pants and jackets and such like. I was with George Reedes probably ten or twelve years. It was my first training—with George Reedes—learnin' the stock business and horse breakin'."

Fannie Brown, Texas

"My mistis learned me to spin an' weave an' dis chile got meny uh whuppen befo' I got to whar I could do it good, but it warn't long 'till she wuz makin' a show ob my work an' braggin' 'bout what a good job I could do; I knowed I had to do it or git whupped. I allus got whupped 'cause I couldn't handle de distaff. My mistis allus thought I wuz 'bout de bes' cook in de country. She allus had me start cookin' two or three days befo' she wuz goin' to hab big company an' dat is w'en we had de good ole poun' cake. De little chillun would stan' 'roun' w'en I wuz bakin' so as to git to lick de spoons an' pans. My, how dey would pop dere lips w'en dey wuz lickin' dat good dough."

Fred Brown, Texas

"Every one have deir certain wo'k an' duties fo' to do. My mammy am de fam'ly cook. Marster have no chillun, so 'twarnt much wo'k fo' her an' she he'p at de loom, makin' de cloth. My daddy am de black-smith, shoemakah an' de tanner. Ise 'splain how him do de tannin'. He puts de hides in de wauter wid black-oak bark, prutty soon de hair come off, den he rolls an' poun's de hides fo' to make dem soft."

Fred Brown. (Library of Congress)

James Brown, Texas

"Marster Blair did not hab a w'ite mans fo' da obs'ser, like most udder w'ite fo'ks. He hab one ob de niggers in charge ob de work."

"Da furst work da Ise does 'twas drivin' da marster to town. Has larned dis nigger to driv'n and to be thar co'chman, that am de work Ise does alls de time Ise wid de Marster."

"Ise sho liks de co'chman work. De Marster hab fine hooses, de co'ch hooses am greys, full ob life. Dey would stand wait, but soons youes picks up de lin' deys ready to go. Weuns dribe dat fouah miles to Waco in twenty minutes easy. No body could pass weuns. Lots ob times dey tries, den de Marster would say, 'Nigger show how youes can driv'.' Den Ise tight de lin', easy like and sez, 'gid dap,' den off de does. Ise talks to dem, Ise sez, 'come on dere boy, steady now steady, don'ts lets dem pass youes, Ise sez dat sort ob coaxin'. 'Narary a one could pass weuns. Dat when de Marster would laugh and sez to me, 'Thata boy, Jim.'"

Aunt Sally (Julia Brown), Georgia

"Ah help spin the cotton into thread fur our clothes. The thread wus made into big broaches—four broaches made four cuts, or one hank. After the thread wus made we used a loom to weave the cloth. We had no sewin' machine—had to sew by hand. My mistress had a big silver bird and she would always eatch the cloth in the bird's bill and this would hold it fur her to sew."

Queen Elizabeth Bunts, Georgia

"My father was a field hand and worked from sun up to sun down. My mother was considered a very fine seamstress and sewed for the Norris family. When she wasn't busy sewing she worked as house-woman for Mrs. Norris. My brothers and sisters did field work."

Augustus Burden, Georgia

The trades taught were carpentering and brick work. "Some men made shoes," Augustus remembered, "but how they learned it I never knew. They were funny shoes, all going over to one side. But there were some skilled workers on the place, and there was a woman named Mrs. Abe who had possession over other women at childbirth."

Aunt Phoebe Jane Burrell, Texas

"I had to work hard but they were good to me but never learned me to read nor write. None of Mr. Carter's slaves ever went to school any. Jest work, work."

"I never saw any slaves sold as I can remember but I know of course it was done. Some of Mr. Carter's slaves were Wyatt, he was the driver. Aunt

Fanny and Kathleen were the weavers. I could weave but not like they could, they wove jeans and could use three and four treadles, but I never learned to use but two treadles and I just wove plain cloth, about six yards a day was the best I could do. Elizabeth was the cook and twixt idle times she sewed."

Jeff Calhoun, Texas

"As soon as I got up big enuf to handle hosses, I wuz made carriage driver for mah marster eveh what he went or any of his family, I had to drive de hosses."

James Cape, Texas

"When I's old 'nough to set on de hoss, dey larned me to ride, tendin' hosses. 'Cause I's good hoss rider, dey uses me all de time gwine after hosses. I goes with dem to Mexico. We crosses de river lots of times. I 'members once when we was a drivin' 'bout 200 hosses north'ards. Dey was a bad hail storm comes into de face of de herd and dat herd turns and starts de other way. Dere was five of us riders and we had to keep dem hosses from scatterment. I was de leader and do you know what happens to dis nigger if my hoss stumbles? Right dere's whar I'd still be! Marster give me a new saddle for savin' de hosses."

Esther King Casey, Alabama

"There were eight or ten slaves in all," Esther continued. "We lived in a house in the backyard of Captain King's Big House. My mamma was the cook. Papa was a mechanic. He built houses and made tools and machinery. Captain King gave me to the 'white lady'; that was Liss Susan, the Captain's wife. Captain King was a fine men. He treated all of us just like his own family. The 'white lady' taught us to be respectable and truthful."

Aunt Cicely Cawthon, Georgia

"Darkey womens wore white and blue striped dresses, spun and wove; them that lived in the quarters had looms and reels. They spun their own cloth and made their own clothes. They made everything they wore 'cept shoes. Uncle Jeff Names, the shoemaker, he made all of the shoes that all of 'em wore on the place. He was about the first slave Marster had. He come from Virginny. They paid big money for him cause he was a valuable darkey. He was 'bout as valuable as the blacksmith. I don't remember how much they paid for him, but it was big money."

Willis Cofer, Georgia

"Dem bricklayers made all de bricks out of de red clay what dey had right dar on most all de plantations, and de blacksmith he had to make all de iron bars and cranes for de chimblies and fireplaces. He had to make de plow points too and keep de farm tools all fixed up. Somtimes at night dey slipped off de place to go out and wuk for money, a-fixin' chimblies and buildin' things, but dey better not let demselves git cotched."

"Mammy wove de cloth for our clothes and de white folkses had 'em made up. Quilts and all de bed-clothes wuz made out of homespun cloth."

Andrew "Smoky" Columbus, Texas

"My Pappy wuz carriage-driver fer Master Ellington. I didn't do much wo'k when I wuz a boy. Mos' of time I jes' stay 'round the house."

Hannah Costine, Mississippi

Hannah Costine, one of the mid-wives of the community, was born in New Orleans about 79 years ago but has lived in Mound Bayou for the past ten years. She remembers her people with the spinning wheel when she was between the ages of 9 and 10 years. She made herself useful by keeping the floor clear of threads or dust and by being ready to run errands. For this reason no objection was ever made to her watching the process. First, the seed were separated from the cotton and the cotton was then placed in the sun to be thoroughly dried. It was then fluffed so as to make it light and placed in baskets handy for use. After the cotton was carded and spun into thread it was wound on a shuttle, sometimes on two shuttles. The wheel of the spinning wheel had a diameter of about 5 feet.

In weaving wide breadths of cloth called cottonede, two widths were fastened together to make spreads. These were dyed yellow or brown by extracting the coloring from certain barks of trees. When striped the stripe was always crosswise the cloth.

Carey Davenport, Texas

"My father used to make them old Carey plows and was good at makin' the mould board out of hardwood. He make the best Carey plows in that part of the country and he make horseshoes and nails and everything out of iron. And he used to make spinning wheels and parts of looms. He was a very valuable man and he make wheels and the hub and put the spokes in."

Mose Davis, Georgia

Mose's Father was the family coachman. All that he had to do was to drive the master and his family and to take care of the two big grey horses that he drove. "Compared to my mother and the other slaves he had an easy time," said Uncle Mose, shaking his head and smiling. "My daddy was so crazy about the white folks and the horses he drove until I believe he thought more of them than he did of me. One day while I was in the stable with him one of the horses tried to kick me and when I started to hit him Daddy cussed me and threatned to beat me."

On this plantation there were quite a few skilled slaves mostly blacksmiths, carpenters, masons, plasterers, and a cobbler. One of Mose's brothers was a carpenter.

Ella Dilliard, Alabama

Ella said that her mother was her madame's hairdresser, and that Mrs. Norris had her mother taught in Mobile. So Ella's life was very easy, as she stayed around the big house with her mother, although her grandmother, Penny Anne Norris, cared for her more than her mother did. One of the things she remembers quite distinctly was her grandmother's cooking on the fireplace, and how she would not allow any one to spit in the fireplace. She said her grandmother made corn-pone and wrapped it in shucks and baked it in ashes.

Rufus Dirt, Alabama

"Boss, I don' rightly know jes' how old I is. I was a driver [Negro boss of other slaves] during slavery and I reckons I was about twenty sompin'. I don' remember nothin' in particular that caused me to get dat drivin' job, ceptin' hard work, but I knows dat I was proud of it 'cause I didn' have to work so hard no mo'. An' den it sorta' made de other niggers look up to me, an' you knows us niggers, boss. Nothin' makes us happier dan' to strut in front of other niggers. Dere ain't nothin' much to tell about. We jes' moved one crop atter de other till layin' by time come and den we'd start in on de winter work. We done jes' 'bout de same as all de other plantations."

Charles Green Dortch, Arkansas

"My father was not a field hand. He was what they called the first man 'round there. He was a regular leader on the plantation—boss of the tool room. He was next to the master of them, you might say. He was a kind of boss."

"I never heard of his working for other men besides his master. I believe he drove the stage for a time from Arkadelphia to Camden or Princeton."

Willis Easter, Texas

"Mammy de bes' cook in de county and & master hand at spinnin' and weavin'. She made her own dye. Walnut and elm makes red dye and walnut brown color, and shumake makes black color. When you wants yellow color, git cedar moss out de brake."

"All de lint was picked by hand on our place. It a slow job to git dat lint out de cotton and I's gone to sleep many a night, settin' by de fire, pickin' lint. In bad weather us sot by de fire and pick lint and patch harness and shoes, or whittle out something, dishes and bowls and troughs and traps and spoons."

Anderson Edwards, Texas

"Mammy was a weaver and made all the clothes and massa give us plenty to eat; fact, he treated us kind-a like he own boys. Course he whipped us when we had to have it, but not like I seed darkies whipped on other place. The other niggers called us Major Gaud's free niggers and we could hear 'em moanin' and cryin' round 'bout, when they was puttin' it on 'em."

Louis Fowler, Texas

"We makes de cloth and de wool and I could card and spin and weave 'fore I's big 'nough to work in de field. My mammy larned me to help her. We makes dye from de bark of walnut and de cherry and red oak trees, and some from berries but what dey is I forgit. Iffen we'uns wants clay red, we buries de cloth in red clay for a week and it takes on de color. Den we soaks de cloth in cold salt water and it stays colored."

Lizzie Gibbs, Mississippi

Lizzie became well known as a seamstress, and tells of making wedding dresses for the older generation, also pants for some of our prominent citizens. She often helped with wedding suppers, being an old time cook, especially making wedding cakes. Lizzie also relates many interesting stories about some of our prominent citizens.

Gabriel Gilbert, Texas

"My mammy weave cloth out cotton and wool. I 'member de loom. It go 'boom–boom–boom.' Dat de shuttle goin' cross. My daddy, he de smart man. I'll never be like him long as I live in dis world. He make shoes. He build house. He do anything. He and my mammy neither one ever been brutalize'."

Addy Gill, North Carolina

"My father wus David Gill and my mother wus Emily Gill. My father wus a black smith an he moved from place to place where dey hired his time. Dats why I wus born on Major Wilders place. Marster Gill who owned us hired father to Major Wilder and mother moved wid him. For a longtime atter de war, nine years, we stayed on wid Major Wilder, de place we wus at when dey set us free."

Andrew Goodman, Texas

"My paw was a shoemaker. He'd take a calfhide and make shoes with the hairy sides turned in, and they was warm and kept your feet dry. My maw spent a lot of time cardin' and spinnin' wool, and I allus had plenty things."

Isaiah Green, Georgia

Besides acting as midwife, Green's grandmother Betsy Willis, was also a skilled seamstress and able to show the other women different points in the art of sewing.

O. W. Green, Texas

"My old masta was a doctor and a surgeon. He trained my grandmother; she worked under him thirty-seven years as a nurse. When old masta wanted grandmother to go on a special case he would whip her so she wouldn't tell none of his secrets. Grandmother used herbs fo' medicine—black snake root, sasparilla, blackberry briar roots—and nearly all de young'uns she fooled with she save from diarrhea."

Dave Gullins, Georgia

"My father was carriage driver and foreman of the other niggers. My mother was cook for the family and the weaver. All of the clothing was made on the plantation from cotton and wool. The cotton was carded, spun and woven into cloth and died. Likewise, woolen garments was made from the wool clipped from the sheep raised for this purpose. All these garments were made right on the plantation."

Jane Harmon, Georgia

"My Ma wuz a 'spert spinner an' weaver, an' she spun an' wove things ter be sont ter de Soldiers in de War. I 'members dat, her ar spinnin' an' dey say hit wuz fer de soldiers."

Orris Harris, Mississippi

"My pappy, Warren Bonner, wus Marse Hughey kerrage driver, en w'en he wud start to church wid de Mistress en de giruls, Marse Hughey wud tell him not ter low de horses to run way wid de kerrage en not ter low enything to hap'en to dem. He allus rode horse back."

Charles Hayes, Alabama

"My mammy was a fiel' han' an' my pappy was a mechanic an' he use to be de handy man aroun' de big house, makin' eve'thing f'um churns an' buckets to wagon wheels. My pappy also useta play de fiddle for de white folks dances in de big house, an' he played it for de colored frolics too. He sho could make dat thing sing."

Wash Hayes, Mississippi

"My pappy done fiel' wuk in season but de mos' ob de time he wuz de shoe maker fer all de slaves on Marse's three plantations. Dat kept him busy mos' ob de time. De shoes wuz made from rough cow hide wid brass on put on de toes to keep 'em from wearin' out so soon. When de slaves wuz give a pair ob dem shoes he knowed dey sho' had to las' a long time."

Alonzo Haywood, North Carolina

"My father was Willis Haywood and in slavery days he belonged to Mr. William R. Pool. Mr. Pool liked father because he was quick and obedient so he determined to give him a trade."

Bill Heard, Georgia

"Dey had special mens on de plantation for all de special wuk. One carpenter man done all de fixin' of things lak wagons and plows, holped wid all de buildin' wuk, and made all de coffins."

Tempie Herndon, North Carolina

"My white fo'ks lived in Chatham County. Dey was Marse George an' Mis' Betsy Herndon. Mis Betsy was a Snipes befe' she married Marse George. Dey had a big plantation an' raised cawn, wheat, cotton an' 'bacca. I don't know how many field niggers Marse George had, but he had a mess of dem, an' he had hosses too, an' cows, hogs an' sheeps. He raised sheeps an' sold de wool, an' dey used de wool at de big house too. Dey was a big weavin' room whare de blankets was wove, an' dey wove de cloth for de winter clothes too. Linda Harnton an' Milla Edwards was de head weavers, dey looked after de weavin' of da fancy blankets. Mis' Betsy was a good weaver too. She weave de same as de niggers. She say she love de clackin' soun' of de loom an' de way de shuttles run in an' out carryin' a long tail of bright colored thread. Some days she set at de loom all de mawnin' peddlin' wid her feets an' her white han's flittin' over de bobbins."

"De cardin' an' spinnin' room was full of niggers. I can hear dem spinnin' wheels now turnin' roun' an' sayin' hum-m-m-m, hum-m-m-m, an' hear de slaves singin' while day spin. Mammy Rachel stayed in de dyein' room. Dey wuzn' nothin' she didn' know 'bout dyein'. She knew every kind of root, bark, leaf an' berry dat made red, blue, green, or whatever color she wanted. Dey had a big shelter whare de dye pots set over de coals. Mammy Rachel would fill de pots wid water, den she put in de roots, bark an' stuff an' boil de juice out, den she strain it an' put in de salt an' vinegar to set de color. After de wool an' cotton done been carded an' spun to thread, Mammy take de hanks an' drap dem in de pot of boilin' dye. She stir dem 'roun' an' lif' dem up an' down wid a stick, an' when she hang dem up on de line in de sun, dey was every color of de rainbow. When dey dripped dry dey was sent to de weavin' room whare dey was wove in blankets an' things."

"Wilson Morgan run the blacksmith shop at Falls of Neuse and it was him that taught my father the trade at Mr. Pool's insistence."

Ben Horry, North Carolina

"The grown-up slaves had to work in de field all day and then at night they spin cloth and make their clothes. We had one shoemaker what didn't do nothing else much 'cept make shoes for all of us. I was too young to do much work, so the missus mostly keep me in de house to nurse de chillun. When de chillun go to school, she make me go 'long wid them for to look after them and tote their books. I stayed wid them all day and brought their books home in de evening."

Fannie Hughes, Georgia

"My daddy was a blacksmith. He show was smart. Thar wasn't but two on the place an' my daddy'd take the young boys an' learn them the trade."

Everett Ingram, Alabama

"Master had us a two-room house, 'ca'se my mammy was de cook an' weaver. Dey made dey own silk den, too, an' raised de silk worms. Us useta get mulberry leaves to feed de silk worms wid. Us used indigo, which us cooked an' used for dye. Us would wear any kind of clothes on everyday an' Sunday; an' didn't have no shoes 'til us was big chilluns."

"Gran'mammy was a great doctor; useta give us turpentine an' castor oil an' Jerusalem oak fer worms. She'd give us all kinds of teas, too. I'members dat gran'mammy was also a *midwife*."

Squire Irvin, Mississippi

"There was a man on the place, I forgets his name that was taught the trade of shoemaker. He got the leather from the calves, that were killed. He tanned the leather and made us shoes that were much better than any shoes you can get now. I don't care what you pay for them."

Abraham Jones, Alabama

"Before de war my people took me up to Blount County, and when de war come dey left me to run de grist-mill. I was de fust man in Alabama to try to grind a bushel of oats. I ground 'em too. A lady brung de oats and ast me could I grind 'em, and I told her I would try. She say dey didn't had nothin' for de chillun to eat. I ground de oats, and told her, 'Ole Mistis, I knows jest how 'tis and I'll be glad to give you a peck of meal if you will use it.' She say, 'of course I will; jest put it in with the oat meal, and I sure will appreciate it.' Her husband was off to de war and she didn't had no way to feed de chillun."

Lucindy Jurdon, Alabama

"My mammy was a fine weaver and did de work for both white an' colored. Dis is her spinning wheel, an' it can still be used. I use it sometimes now. Us made our own cloth an' our stockings, too."

John Matthews, Mississippi

"My mammy wus one uf de boss weavers; she didnt spin de thread, she made de cloth an' dat wus fine cloth; she cud make any pattern. Den my mammy cud cut out any thing an' she cud do fine sewin' too. She cud cut out coats an' pants an' make dem to look like bought clothes. She cud hem dem pritty ruffles an' do it all by hand. She had to wurk in de fiel' some time but old Mistress kept her mi'ty busy at de house."

C. B. McRay, Texas

"The nigger women spinned and weaved cloth. I 'spec' dat's the onlies' place in Jasper whar you could go any time of day and see a parlor full of nigger women, sittin' up dere fat as dey could be and with lil' to do. Marster have no plantation for de men to wo'k but he rented lan' for them to cult'vate."

Josh Miles, Texas

"Pappy was de fam'ly coachman and druv de li'l surrey when Massa gwine see he plantations. On Sunday he druv de big coach to church. Den Old Massa wear de big stove-pipe hat and de long-skirt coat and he big boots. Pappy, he wear de tall hat with de blue uniform with brass buttons, and black, shiny boots. He have de long horsewhip to crack at des hosses—he drive four or six hosses, 'cause dat coach am big and heavy and de roads an often muddy."

Bob Mobley, Georgia

"My aunt's job was to weave the cloth. There was a house on the plantation built especially for spinnin' an' weavin'. Two or three of the other nigger women made the clothes and they had to make 'em to fit. The mist'ess would make them be careful so the clothes would look nice. Some of the slaves even learned to dye the wool so that we could have warm clothes in winter. We always had all the clothes we needed. Marster wouldn't have us dirty an' ragged. It took a lot o' cloth for the clothes, too, 'cause ever'thing was made full."

Joseph Mosley, Indiana

Joseph's father was the shoemaker for all the farm hands and all adults workers. He would start in Sepetember making shoes for the year. First the shoes for the folks in the house, then the workers.

Richard Orford, Georgia

"After I got big enough I learned to use a loom and used to weave six or seven yards of cloth a day. I wove and reeled some in Thomson, spun dere about nine or ten years."

"I was a shoemaker, too. Made many a pair of shoes. Old Uncle Jesse Shank taught me to shoemake."

"All of the clothing worn on this plantation was made there. Some of the women who were too old to work in the fields did the spinning and the weaving as well as the sewing of tie garments. Indigo was used to dye the cloth. The women wore callico dresses and the men wore ansenberg pants and shirts. The children wore a one piece garment not unlike a slightly lengthened dress. This was kept in place by a string tied around their waists. There were at least ten shoemakers on the plantation and they were always kept bust making shoes although no slave ever got but one pair of shoes a year. These shoes were made of very hard leather and were called brogans."

Martha Patton, Texas

"We made cotton and wool cloth both, yes'm, we made both. We raised cotton. The sheep were so po' they would die. We would go through de woods and find de dead sheep and pick de wool offen 'em. When we would wash de wool and spin it into thread and weave it into cloth to make wool clothes."

"My man, he worked in de tan ya'd. He fixed de hides to make us all de shoes we had, and dey made harness and saddles fo' de gov'nment—fo' de soldiers. To make de lime to take de hair off of de hides, dey would burn limestone rocks. Then dey would hew out troughs and soak de hides in lime water till all the hair come off. Den dey would take 'ooze' made from red oak bark and rub the hides till dey were soft and dry."

Betty Powers, Texas

"De field hands works early and late and often all night. Pappy makes de shoes and mammy weaves, and you could hear de bump, bump of dat loom at night, when she done work in de field all day."

Layfayette Price, Texas

"In de days I's a boy even de plows was made on de place. De blacksmith do de iron work and de wood work am done by pappy, and de plows am mostly wood. Jus' de point and de shear am iron. My grandpap made de mouldboards out of wood. No, sar, 'twarnt no steel mouldboards den. I's watch grendpap take de hard wood block and with de ax and de drawshave and de plane and saw and rule, him cut and fit de mouldboard to be turnin' plow. De mouldboard las' 'bout one year."

Beverly Pullin, Georgia

Mr. Peeples was considered by all his slaves as a kind master. He expected and received splendid work from all his 900 slaves. Each one was designated for some particular work, even the children. During the week all the slaves had plain but substantial food, but on Sunday there was always a feast for them.

There were a number of slaves belonging to this family who were taught to card, spin, and weave. This was their particular job, and they were kept busy making the coarser cloth to be made into garments for this large household. There was Sally Snow who, by her skilled workmanship, became better known than the others. She began her work as a helper to the pastry cook and seamstress in the Peeples family, but her natural talent for cooking and flying fingers with a needle, soon won her first place. She cut, fitted and made all the nicer things for the family from the beautiful bolts of materials her master, Mr. Hal Peeples, brought from Savannah for his wife and children. As the girls married she made up their trousseaus for them, and always it was she who "dressed the bride."

Bill Reese, Georgia

"My father was the personal property of Dr. B. J. Fritz, and soon as he was big enough to be trained for a trade his master arranged for him to learn how to be a barber. High-class white folks liked to have their own barbers then and they wanted 'em well trained, and professional men like pa's owner liked to have at least one slave that could do what they called valet service now. The man pa learnt his trade from was a Mexican who catered only to white people. When he took pa in hand he started him off blacking shoes, and before he finished with him he had trained him to do anything that come to hand in a first class barber shop. At the time of pa's death, him and his brother-in-law owned and run a barber shop together."

"Colored children learns to work mighty early. I wasn't but six years old when I started working. My first job was taking pa's meals to the barber shop, sweeping out the shop, washing spittoons, and shining shoes. By the time I was eleven or twelve years old I made from a dollar and a half to as high as three dollars a week."

Ferebe Rogers, Georgia

"All de slaves had diff'unt work to do. My auntie was one de weavers. Old Miss had two looms goin' all de time. She had a old loom and a new loom. My husband made de new loom for Old Miss. He was a carpenter and he worked on outside jobs after he'd finished tasks for his marster. He use to make all de boxes dey buried de white folks and de slaves in, on de Hart and Golden Plantations. Dey was pretty as you see, too."

Elvira Roies, Texas

"Marster Boles didn' have many slaves on de farm, but lots in brickyard. I toted brick back and put 'em down where dey had to be. Six bricks each load all day. That's de reason I ain't no 'count, I'se worked to death. I fired de furnace for three years. Stan'in' front wid hot fire on my face. Hard work, but God was wid me. We'd work 'till dark, quit awhile after sundown. Marster was good to slaves, didn' believe in jus' lashin' 'ex. He'd not be brutal but he'd kill 'em dead right on the spot. Overseers 'ud git after 'em and whop 'em down."

Annie Row, Texas

"De marster has two overseers what tends to de work and 'signs each nigger to do de certain work and keep de order. Shoes was made by a shoemaker what am also de tanner. Cloth for de clothes was made by de spinners and weavers and that what they larned me to do. My first work was teasin' de wool. I bets you don't know what teasin' de wool am. It am pickin' de burrs and trash and sich out of de wool for to git it ready for de cardin'."

Hamp Santee, Mississippi

"My Pa he knowed how to make shoes and when I wuz jes a little nigger he learned me bout leather—cutin' and shoe makin'—and when I growed up I used to make shoes fer de whole community and all of de settlement folks. We had a tanning vat near Mahned, and dare we tanned our leather. De settlers brung dey chulluns to our place and I measured dey feet and cut dey shoes out. Some day I made from two to three pairs of shoes, and I worked lack dat 'til I moved to dis place years ago."

Janie Scott, Alabama

Janie had heard her father say he was a coachman and drove the folks around, also came over in a boat with his master to Mobile to get supplies and groceries, and that they killed many a deer in neighborhoods just north of Bienville Square.

Millie Smith, Texas

"My grandpa made all the beds for the white folks and us niggers, too. Massa didn't want anything shoddy 'round him, he say, not even his nigger quarters."

"I's sot all day handin' thread to my mammy to put in the loom, 'cause they give us homespun clothes, and you'd better keep 'em if you didn't want to go naked."

Nancy Smith, Georgia

"Daddy, he was de car'iage driver. He driv Marse Joe 'round, 'cept when Mist'ess wanted to go somewhar. Den Daddy driv de coach for her, and Marse Joe let another boy go wid him."

Nellie Smith, Georgia

"All our clothes and shoes was home-made, and I mean by that they growed the cotton, wool, and cattle and made the cloth and leather on the plantation. Summer clothes was made of cotton homespun, and cotton and wool was wove together for winter clothin'. Marse Jack owned a man what he kept there to do nothin' but make shoes. He had another slave to do all the carpentarin' and to make all the coffins for the folks that died on the plantation. That same carpenter made 'most all the beds the white folks and us slaves slept on. Them old beds—they called 'em teesters—had cords for springs; nobody never heard of no metal springs them days. They jus' wove them cords criss-cross, from one side to the other and from head to foot. When they stretched and sagged they was tightened up with keys what was made for that purpose."

Tim Thornton, Georgia

"Dey made me ride from one court house to the other on marster's horse," he said, "I had to deliver 'portant papers in big carpet bags what hung down on each side of de horse. Den I had to work in de 'bacco factory. Dey come and tuk a passel of white men at the factory, we never did see de boss overseer no more."

Neal Upson, Georgia

"Daddy made de shoes for all de slaves on de plantation and Mammy was called de house 'oman. She done de cookin' up at de big 'ouse, and made de cloth for her own fambly's clothes, and she was so smart us allus had plenty t'eat and wear."

Rhodus Walton, Georgia

The slaves did most of the weaving on the plantation, but after the cloth was woven the problem of giving it color presented itself. As they had no commercial dye, certain plants were boiled to give color. A plant called Indigo, found in the cotton patch, was the chief type of dye, although there was another called copperas. The dresses made from this material were very plain.

Annie Whitley Ware, Texas

"All de wimmin on de Whitley plantation but one er two had ter wukk in de fiel', in de house, de dairy, er whar dey wuz needed. Mammy hauled wood, ploughed, wukked 'roun' de house, spun thread an' wove cloths, cooked, dyed cloth an' whar ever Mis' arrange. Some ob de men slaves wuz good cattle hands an' could rope an' brand wid de bes' ob 'em."

"Mammy wuz trained ter be a doctor. In dem days dey git deir medecine from de woods an' made deir salves, liniment an' sech. Mammy larned me what she knowed 'bout doctorin'. Ole Mis' wuz mighty good ter de sick an' she went far an' wide ter see ter de sick folks. Ebery night, come ebery boddy in bed an' she gwine slip outten de big house an' make de 'rouns ob de quarters ter see effen eny body be sick an' she think Mammy got ter go erlong too."

Sam Jones Washington, Texas

"Well, 'bout de wo'k. W'en I's a younguns, I's fust run errands, an' de Marster larnt me to ride, soon's I's able to sat on de hoss. Den, w'en I's 'bout 15 yeahs old, him puts me on de cattle ranch. I's stay dere mostest ob de time aftah dat, so f'om den on, I's don't know what am goin on 'roun' de fahm."

"I's tickled 'bout de wo'k on de ranch. I's sho lak to ride an' rope de cattle. De Marster always fix me up wid fine clothes, hoss an' saddle. I's stay on dat ranch, 'til 'way aftah surrendah."

Eliza White, Alabama

"Massa lived in a big, fine white house. He had two or three hundred slaves, and de quarters was in two long rows, runnin' up near'bout to de big house on de hill. Dey even raised deer on de place. De houses in de quarters was two-room log houses wid a shed room to cook in. My mammy was de cook at de big house was de weaver. Pappy was de bedmaker; he made most of de beds outen popular. I had a little chair in de corner where I sot and kept de flies offen Mistis wid a green twig brush."

Willie Williams, Texas

"Marster had a nigger dat was de shoemakah. De shoes was made f'om de hides dat was tanned dere an' de hides was off de cattle dat was killed fo' de meat weuns used. De tannah 'ten's to de tannin' ob de hides. Dere was a vat dat him puts de hides in. Him leaves dem soak in wautah dat had oak bahk an' udder stuff in it. Aftah a certain time, de hair comes off de hides. Den deys poun' dem fo' to git 'em limbah."

"Did yous ever see anybody cahd de wool or spin de yarn? Dere was certain women dat spin de yarn f'om de wool dat come off de sheep dat was raised on de place. Den dey makes de cloth, an' den de clothes, all dat was used dere."

Claude Augusta Wilson, Florida

The "missus" taught Claude's sister to sew and to the present day most of her female descendants have some ability in dress making.

Tanning and curing pig and cow hides was done, but Claude never saw the process performed during slavery. Claude had no special duties on the plantation on account of his youth. After cotton was picked from the fields the seeds were picked out by hand, the cotton was then carded for further use. The cotton seed was used as fertilizer. In baling cotton burlap bags were used on the bales. The soap used was made from taking hickory or oak wood and burning it to ashes. The ashes were placed in a tub and water poured oven them. This was left to set. After setting for a certain time the water from the ashes was poured into a pot containing grease. This was boiled for a certain time and then left to cool. The result was a pot full of soft substance varying in color from white to yellow, this was called lye soap. This was then cut into bars as desired for use.

For dyeing thread and cloth, red oak bark, sweet gum bark and shoe make roots were boiled in water. The wash tubs were large wooden tubs having one handle with holes in it for the fingers. Chicken and goose feathers were always carefully saved to make feather mattresses. Claude remembers when women wore hoop skirts. He was about 20 years of age when narrow skirts became fashionable for women. During slavery the family only used slats on the beds, it was after the war that he saw his first spring bed, and at that time the first buggy. This buggy was driven by ex-governor Reid of Florida who then lived in South Jacksonville. It was a four wheeled affair drawn by a horse and looked sensible and natural as a vehicle.

Henry Wright, Georgia

Mr. House wanted his slaves to learn a trade such as masonry or carpentry, etc., not because it would benefit the slave, says Mr. Wright, but because it would make the slave sell for more in case he had "to get shet [rid] of him."

The slaves who were allowed to work with these white mechanics, from whom they eventually learned the trade, were eager because they would be permitted to hire themselves out. The money they earned could be used to help buy their freedom, that is, what money remained after the master had taken his share. On the other hand the white mechanic had no particular objection to the slaves being there to help him, even though they were learning the trade, because he was able to place all the hard work on the slave which made his job easier. Mr. Wright remembers how his grandfather used to hire his time out doing carpentry work, making caskets and doing some masonry. He himself can plaster, although he never hired out during slavery.

HIRING OUT ENSLAVED WORKERS

The system of hiring out made the services of enslaved people more widely available to slaveholders and others who might not own slaves but needed access to workers. Hiring out also further emphasized how dependent the southern economy was upon the labor of enslaved people. There were very few occupations in the South in which enslaved people were not employed. They were often mistreated and forced to work long hours, but it was their efforts that made the institution of slavery so valuable to the success and economic well-being of the South.

At times the work produced by skilled and unskilled enslaved workers was leveraged to the benefit of the slaveholder. Other people who needed short-term help or specific skilled labor were willing to pay for the services rendered. The distribution of the wages varied depending on the circumstances. Sometimes the money went directly to the slaveholder and the enslaved worker saw no benefit. Other times the wages went to the enslaved worker, who paid a major portion of it to the slaveholder. This was an extra source of income for the slaveholder and an opportunity for enslaved workers to earn some money for themselves.

Sometimes when whites needed someone to provide a specific service they might hire an enslaved person to do the work. The length of the work varied from one special occasion to several months depending on the service needed and the contract. In Texas, Charley Mitchell's "mammy was willed to the Terrys and allus lived with them till freedom. She worked for them and they hired her out there in town for cook and house servant." In Georgia, Elsie Moreland's father was a carpenter whose "Marster hired him out ter other fokes. Sometimes he'd eben go 'way down ter Savannah, so I never saw him much."

Hiring out was most profitable when the worker had special skills, but unskilled workers could also produce income. For some slaveholders hiring out was a regular source of extra revenue. "Slaves not needed on the home plantation were 'hired out' to other land owners for from $200.00 to $300.00 a year. This was done the first of each year by an auction from a 'horse block,'" according to Mollie Malone of Georgia. In addition to contracting enslaved people to work the fields, a woman who needed household help might contract for an enslaved worker. George Womble of Georgia "was often hired out to the other white ladies of the community to take care of their children and to do their housework. Because of his ability to clean a house and to handle children he was in constant demand."

One benefit to the system of hiring out was that it allowed some enslaved people to have greater independence. Some slaveholders were willing to enter into an agreement with the enslaved which allowed the worker to pay a fixed fee for the opportunity to work independently. The slaveholder of Phil Towns of Georgia provided such an opportunity for enslaved people working for him: "A man or woman who paid Gov. Towns $150.00 might hire himself to the Gov. for a year. When this was done he was paid cash for all the work he did and many ware able to clear several hundred dollars in a year." Gov. Towns had a more liberal policy than most slaveholders, but this same system with slight variations was used by other slaveholders. Although it could be a challenge to earn the required money during the contract period, this system could work to the benefit of the enslaved, and some earned enough money to purchase freedom for themselves and their family members. The father of William Sherman of Florida bought his freedom this way:

> He hired himself out to some of the wealthy plantation owners and applied what he earned toward the payment for his freedom. He was a skilled blacksmith and cabinet maker and his services were always in demand. After procuring his freedom he bought a tract of land from his former master and built a home and black smith shop on it. He had hoped to buy the freedom of his wife and children, but died before he could accomplish that goal.

NARRATIVES

Lizzie Atkins, Texas

"We had terrible times here in Texas in them days for the Indians would kill our stock and steal everything we had. Maser made a trap one time and he caught an Indian stealing his corn. After that the Indians were more careful. After that they would come in the daytime when they thought Maser was gone. You asked me what kind of work I done in them days and here I is telling you about them Indians. Why, son, I'se cleared land, cut wood, chopped corn, not much cotton, cause the seed were too hard to pick out. I'se done that picking out of the cotton seed so we could spin that cotton. Then I'se cooked and washed dishes. Maser use to hire us out to work for other people and collect our wages, as he was an officer and did not have very good farm."

Bill Austin, Florida

Bill's father Jack was regarded as a fairly good carpenter, mason and bricklayer; at times his master would let him do small jobs of repairing of building for neighboring planters. These jobs sometimes netted his him hams, bits of cornmeal, bits of cornmeal, cloth for dresses for his wife and children, and other small gifts; these he either used for his small family or bartered with the other slaves. Sometimes he sold them to the slaves for money; cash was not altogether unknown among the slaves on the Smith place.

Julia Blanks, Texas

"My grandfather bought my grandmother's time and they run a laundry house. They hired my mother out, too."

George Taylor Burns, Indiana

The Burns brothers operated a wood yard at the Landing and the work of cutting and piling wood for the commerce was performed by slaves of the Burns plantation.

Nothing impressed the little boy with such unforgettable imagery as the cold which descended upon Greogery's Landing one winter. Motherless, hungry, desolate and unloved, he often cried himself to sleep at night while each day he was compelled to carry wood. One morning he failed to come when the horn was sounded to call the slaves to breakfast. "Old Missus went to the Negro quarters to see what was wrong" and "She was horrified when she found I was frozen to the bed."

She carried the small bundle of suffering humanity to the kitchen of her home and placed him near the big oven. When the warmth thawed the frozen child the toes fell from his feet. "Old Missus told me I would never be strong enough to do hard work, and she had the neighborhood shoemaker fashion shoes too short for any body's feet but mine," said Uncle George.

Uncle George doesn't remember why he left Missouri but the sister of Greene Taylor brought him to Troy, Indiana. Here she learned that she could not own a slave within the state of Indiana so she indentured the child to a flat boat captain to wash dishes and wait on the crew of workers.

George was so small of stature that the captain had a low table and stool made that he might work in comfort. George's mistress received $15.00 per month for the service of the boy for several years.

Killen Campbell, Georgia

"When I wus 'bout ten years old dey started me totin' water—you know ca'in water to de hands in de field. 'Bout two years later I got my first field job, 'tending sheep. When I wus fifteen my old Missus gib me to Miss Eva—you know she de one marry Colonel Jones. My young missus wus fixin' to git married, but she couldn't on account de war, so she brought me to town and rented me out to a lady runnin' a boarding house. De rent was paid to my missus. One day I wus takin' a tray from de out-door kitchen to de house when I stumbled and dropped it. De food spill all over de ground. De lady got so mad she picked up a butcher knife and chop me in de haid. I went runnin' till I come to de place where my white folks live. Miss Eva took me and wash de blood out mah head and put medicine on it, and she wrote a note to de lady and she say, 'Ellen is my slave, give to me by my mother. I wouldn't had dis happen to her no more dan to me. She won't come back dere no more.'"

Austin Grant, Texas

"After work at nights there wasn't much settin' 'round; you'd fall into bed and go to sleep. On Saturday night they didn' git together, they would jes' sing at their own houses. Oh, yes'm, I 'member 'em singin' 'Run, nigger, run,' but it's too far back for me to 'member those other songs. They would raise up a song when they was pickin' cotton, but I don' 'member much about those songs."

"We never got to play none. Our boss hired us out lots of times. I don' know what he got for us. We farmed, cut wood, grubbed, anything. I herded sheep and I picked cotton."

Sarah Grant, Nebraska

"In some ways they were pretty good as slave holders were considered those days, but as they were not well fixed they had to hire out some of their slaves to other plantation owners. My mother was one of these and the people she worked for treated her very badly. She was only allowed to come home on Christmas eve and had to go back New Years."

Jake Green, Alabama

"But dey wan't so mean. Sometimes us got whupped but Massa had fo' men he didn't 'low nobody to hit, white er black. Dey was Unker Arch, he was de main carriage driver; my father, he was de house sarvant; Unker Julius, de fo' man of de plow han's an' Unker Ed'erds, de fo' man of de hoe han's. Whenever anybody wanted to hire anybody to work for 'em, de Massa send dem fo' out an' hire 'em by de day to chop cotton or pick. An' dem fo' niggers could chop much cotton in a day as de mule could plow. Whenever dey'd stop de plow at twelve o'clock, dem niggers was right dere to lay de hoe handles on de plow, an' dat's choppin'. All four could pick a bale of cotton a day. Whenever anybody say, 'Mr. Whitehead, I want a bale of cotton picked today,' he'd send dem fo' men an' dey could pick five hundred pounds apiece an' leave de sun still runnin'. Dey was pickers in dem days!"

Martha Adeline Hinton, North Carolina

"Durin' slavery dey tried to sell daddy. De speculator wus dere an' daddy suspicion sumpin. His marster tole him to go an' shuck some corn. Dey aimed to git him in de corn crib an' den tie him an' sell him but when he got to the crib he kept on goin'. He went to Mr. Henry Buffaloe's an' stayed two weeks den he went back home. Dere wus nuthin' else said 'bout sellin him. Dey wanted to sell him an' buy a 'oman so dey could have a lot of slave chilluns cause de 'oman could multiply. Dey hired men out by the year to contractors to cut cord wood an' build railroads. Father wus hired out dat way. Ole man Rome Harp wus hired out day way. He belonged to John Harp."

Caroline Malloy, Georgia

After her master's death, Caroline's mistress hired her to a Mr. Mitchell. This man, according to Caroline, was in Hawkinsville looking after the "rations" for the Confederate soldiers. She was still working for him when peace was declared.

Mollie Malone, Georgia

Slaves not needed on the home plantation were "hired out" to other land owners for from $200.00 to $300.00 a year. This was done the first of each year by an auction from a "horse block". When Mollie was seven months old her mother, Clacy Brook, was "hired out" and she was taken care of by two old Negroes, too old to work, and who did nothing but care for the little "Niggers." Mollie grew up with these children between the "big house" and the kitchen. When she was old enough she was "put to mind" the smaller children and if they did'nt behave she pinched them, but "when the 'ole Miss found it out, she'd sure 'whup me,'" she said. These children were fed corn-bread and milk for breakfast and supper, and "pot licker" with cornbread for dinner. They slept in a large room on quilts or pallets. Each night the larger children were given so many "outs" to spin, and were punished if all weren't finished. The thread was woven into cloth on the loom and made into cloths by the slaves who did the sewing. There were no "store bought" clothes, and Mollie was free before she ever owned a pair of shoes. Clothes had to be furnished by the owner for the slaves he "hired out."

Charley Mitchell, Texas

"My mammy was willed to the Terrys and allus lived with them till freedom. She worked for them and they hired her out there in town for cook and house servant."

"They hired me out most times as nuss for white folks chillen, and I nussed Tom Thurman's chillen. He run the bakery there in Lunchburg and come

Charley Mitchell. (Library of Congress)

from the north, and when war broke they made him and 'nother northener take a iron clad oath they wouldn't help the north. Durin' the war I worked in Massa Thurman's bakery, helping make hard tack and doughnuts for the 'federate sojers. He give me plenty to eat end wear and treated me as well as I could hope for."

Elsie Moreland, Georgia

"My daddy wuz a carpenter," said Elsie. "Marster hired him out ter other fokes. Sometimes he'd eben go 'way down ter Savannah, so I never saw him much. I'd stay 'round at nights in other nigger cabins an' Granny'd look after me in the day time. Granny'd keep all the little nigger chillun ever' day while they fokes worked in the fields."

G. W. Pattillo, Georgia

The value of slaves varied from $500 to $10,000, depending on his or her special qualifications. Tradesmen such as blacksmiths, shoe makers, carpenters, etc., were seldom sold under $10,000. Rather than sell a tradesman slave, owners kept them in order to make money by hiring them out to other owners for a set sum per season. However, before the deal was closed the lessee would have to sign a contract which assured the slave's owner that the slave would receive the best of treatment while in possession.

Charlie Sandles, Texas

"I'se done most all kinds of farm work such as chop cotton, corn, plowed, cleared land and cut cordwood. Maser would hire us out most of the time and collect our wages. That is what he really wanted, for us to hire out to another man all the time as he never farmed much during slavery time or even before slavery time was over."

"No I never did earn any money during slavery time. My new Maser would give me a nickel or dime once and awhile, when I could I would spend it for candy or something like that."

Dorsey Scott, Texas

"W'en Ise seven yeahs old, de Marster hires me out fo' a nurse girl to his friend. De fam'ly's name am Murray. Dey used me real nice, an' Ise stays dere fo' two yeahs. 'Twas w'en de breakup come, dat Ise quits."

Tom Singleton, Georgia

When Tom was asked if he ever made any money, a mischievous smile illumined his face. "Yes ma'am, you see I plowed durin' de day on old Marster's farm. Some of de white folks what didn't have many Niggers would ax old Marster to let us help on dey places. Us had to do dat wuk at night. On birght moonshiny nights, I would cut wood, fix fences, and sich lak for 'em. Wid de money dey paid me I bought Sunday shoes and a Sunday coat and sich lak, cause I wuz a Nigger what always did lak to look good on Sunday."

Neal Upson, Georgia

"Dem days it was de custom for marsters to hire out what slaves dey had dat warn't needed to wuk on deir own land, so our marster hired out two of my sisters. Sis' Anna was hired to a fambly 'bout 16 miles from our place. She didn't lak it dar so she run away and I found her hid out in our 'tater'ouse. One day when us was playin' she called to me right low and soft lak and told me she was hongry and for me to git her somepin t'eat but not to tell nobody she was der. She said she had been der widout nothin' t'eat for several days. She was skeered Marster might whup her. She looked so thin and bad I thought she was gwine to die, so I told Mammy. Her and Marster went and brung Anna to de 'ouse and fed her. Dat pore chile was starved most to death. Marster kept her at home for 3 weeks and fed her up good, den he carried her back and told dem folkses what had hired her dat dey had better treat Anna good and see dat she had plenty t'eat. Marster was drivin' a fast hoss dat day, but bless your heart, Anna beat him back home dat day. She cried and tuk on so, beggin' him not to take her back dar no more dat he told her she could stay home. My other sister stayed on whar she was hired out 'til de war was over and dey give us our freedom."

Mattie Williams, Texas

"Mawster Richardson never had no plantation here, but he hired us out to other fahmers. De men folks was hired out to plow, plant, gather crops, split rails, cut wood, and do a little of everything; de wimmen was hired out fo' cooks, nusses, and sich."

Frank Ziegler, Alabama

Frank went to Billy Ziegler. Billy was too young to handle his property so his slaves were rented out to the smaller plantations whose owners did not have enough slaves but were unable to buy more. Frank stayed with his family until he was old enough to work himself. When he worked for different people at the usual jobs on a farm, plowing, hoeing and the duties around the home. The mistress cooked for the slaves at the same time that she cooked for her own family. There were no overseers on the plantations where Frank worked. The owner was his own overseer. When the slaves were punished the master did it himself.

6

Physical Abuse and Intimidation

As the institution of slavery took root in British North America, first in Virginia and then in other colonies, rules of engagement were established. These regulations or slave codes spelled out the roles and responsibilities of the enslaved and their enslavers. Virginia began this process in the mid-17th century with the passage of a series of laws that restricted the rights of "Negroes" and strengthened the prerogatives of slaveholders. These statutes made Africans servants for life, defined them as property not people, forbade them from striking a Christian, and allowed the slaying of a slave who resisted his master.

Other colonies desiring to regulate slavery soon followed suit. The strictest slave codes were crafted in South Carolina, which passed major legislation in 1712 and 1740. The latter was referred to as the "Negro Act." These pieces of legislation removed any protection for the enslaved from violent actions taken against them by their slaveholder. These laws paralleled those enacted in Virginia but added more restrictions. Runaway slaves were subject to losing an ear, being branded with an "R" for runaway, or death. In addition, they were not allowed to learn to read or write, to dress above their station, or gather in small groups. The laws reflected residents' concerns about the growing numbers of enslaved people living in their midst. Before the American Revolution, the enslaved population in South Carolina outnumbered their white counterparts. Throughout the South the slave population generally represented 33 percent of the total population. By the end of the Civil War this percent had risen to approximately 38 percent of the southern population.

Southerners' concerns with this growing population increased with the discovery of several plans by enslaved people to rise up against their enslavers and take their freedom by force. Plots were uncovered in 1800 near Richmond, Virginia, lead by Gabriel Prosser and in Charleston, South Carolina, under the leadership of Demark Vesey in 1822. Actual uprisings took place near New Orleans, Louisiana, in 1811 and Southampton County, Virginia, in 1831. The Louisiana rebellion included 200 rebels under the leadership of Charles Deslondes, while Nat Turner's rebellion in Virginia left 51 whites dead. Although none of these actions attained their intended goals, their existence was a source of great concern for southerners.

Southern slaveholders recognized how vulnerable their situation was. Enslaved workers were an integral part of their environment and affected nearly every aspect of their lives. The enslaved cooked for them, cared for their children, made their clothes, drove their vehicles, and toiled in their fields. On larger plantations the

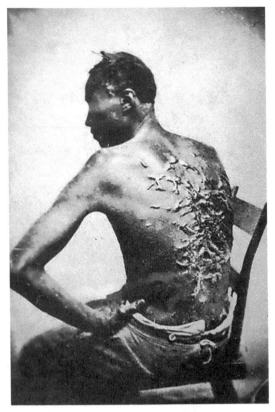

Beaten enslaved man. (National Archives)

number of enslaved people easily outnumbered the enslavers and their families. Larger plantations might have 100 or more enslaved workers. Even on smaller operations with 20 or fewer workers, which were most of the farms with slaves, the enslaved were often in the majority. Under these circumstances maintaining control over the situation was essential for the slaveholders. Slavery was not a condition enslaved workers enjoyed or preferred. They lived under these circumstances against their will and as a result of the power the slaveholder exercised over them. Slaveholders knew very well that they had to maintain the upper hand if they were to control their enslaved work force and keep their operation smoothly functioning.

One of the strategies some slaveholders used was to cultivate a strong personal connection between themselves and their workforce. By doing so they hoped to gain the loyalty of the enslaved and undercut their desire to remove themselves from their circumstances. The more benevolent slaveholders could take a variety of actions to encourage this loyalty, such as ensuring that the enslaved were well clothed and had plenty of food to eat so they did not feel deprived. Taking care of these basic needs provided a sense of well-being and made a strong impression on the enslaved. It certainly affected Zeb Crowder of North Carolina, who felt very kindly toward his slaveholder: "I belonged ter ole man William Crowder durin' slavery, Tom Crowder's daddy. Ralph is Tom's son. My missus wus named Miss Melvina an' if I lives ter be a hundred years old I will never forget dem white folks. Yes sir, dey shore wus good ter us. We had good food, good clothes and a good place ter sleep."

This positive feeling was even stronger if they were aware of conditions on neighboring places where the enslaved lived under much more severe circumstances. In her testimony, Annie Price of Georgia noted, "Food on the elder Mr. Kennon plantation was just as scarce as it was plentiful on his son's." When asked how she knew this Price said she had seen her father take meat from his master's smoke house and hide it so that he could give it to those slaves who invariably slipped over at night in search of food. "The elder Mr. Kennon had enough food but he was too mean to see his slaves enjoy themselves by having full stomachs." While Price and her family did not enjoy enslavement, they did appreciate the manner in which they were treated by their slaveholder.

The other strategy was to use things other than physical violence to get the enslaved to perform the tasks necessary for the operation of the farm. Some slaveholders did not abuse their enslaved workers but sought to use rewards and kind treatment as an incentive. Mary Williams of South Carolina appreciated her enslaver's decision to follow that course. In her remembrance, she refers to "paterollers" (patrollers), who were groups of armed white men who could legally whip, beat, or shoot (if they resisted) any enslaved people caught off their farm or plantation without a pass:

> She said her master was a kind man, didn't allow any "paterollers" on his place, yet she had seen other slaves on other plantations with bloody backs and arms from the whippings they got. When asked why they were whipped, she replied, "Just because their masters could whip them; they owned them and could do what they wanted to them". Her master didn't allow any whipping on his place. One time he kept a slave from another plantation who was fleeing the "paterollers" on his place and in his own house until he was set free.

Unfortunately, Mary Williams's slaveholder was the exception rather than the rule. To maintain a balance of power in their favor most slaveholders thought the use of intimidation and physical violence was the best course to follow. In their minds, a heavy dose of fear was the most effective method of control. In his groundbreaking book *The Peculiar Institution* (Vantage, 1956), Kenneth Stampp wrote about the attitude of many slaveholders with regard to the treatment of their workers. In the chapter "To Make Them Stand in Fear," he used the testimony of plantation owners to illustrate their belief in the necessity of using force to extract obedience from enslaved workers and to affirm their control over them. Testimonies in the slave narratives support this assertion. For example, Tucker Smith of Texas asserts, "we were whipped if we were sassy or stubborn or if we did not exactly work like Maser thought we should."

Corporal punishment was a powerful lesson on two levels: it punished the individual who experienced it and served as an object lesson to those who witnessed it, looking on in helpless horror as a family member or neighbor suffered. The screams of pain and the carnage wrought left a powerful impression. As David Byrd of Texas explained, "Maser he never had to whip very many negroes. They knew what that whipping meant. There was not very many negroes that liked that whipping." Slaveholders clearly understood the power of this lesson and made sure their enslaved workers were reminded of who held the balance of power. And if a whipping did not reinforce the lesson enough they found other forms of punishment that served a similar purpose. Slaveholders could deprive the enslaved of food, string them up by their thumbs and leave them for hours, or put them in isolation for an extended period of time. In Texas, Gus Johnson's mistress used the following as chastisement: "She punish de slaves iffen day bad, but not whip 'em. She have de jail builded undergroun' like de stormcave and it have a drop door with de weight on it, so dey couldn't git up from de bottom. It sho' was dark in dat place."

PUNISHING FIELD WORKERS

The productivity of enslaved field workers was critical to the plantation's economic success, so slaveholders, overseers, and slave drivers used physical punishment and abuse as incentives to make the enslaved work steadily. Nearly every enslaved worker felt the sting of the lash at least once in their work lives if not more frequently. The less fortunate suffered even harsher punishments—and sometimes death—for perceived transgressions. The mistreatment of enslaved workers served as an object lesson that was intended to encourage the others to work hard and at least outwardly seem compliant.

Where the enslaved most often suffered from the sting of the lash or other forms of physical punishment was in the fields. With the cultivation of the crops there were expectations of a certain level of productivity each workday, and if field hands fell short punishment almost always followed. Most slaveholders or overseers carried a whip, which they used liberally to provide incentives to workers they believed were dawdling. On the Texas plantation where Sol Worth lived, "The hands worked from sun to sun, and if the overseer see them slacking up on their work he stormed out at them, cussed [cursed] them and sometimes whacked them with a bull whip. I'se seed Niggers whipped till their shirt stuck to their back till it took salt water to get it loose." No one was spared from this kind of treatment. Men, pregnant women, aged workers, and children could expect to suffer if they lagged in their duties. Getting the work done was all important.

The objective of the work was to make the farm as profitable as possible, and to accomplish this the labor force had to meet the expectations of the slaveholder. This was especially true at harvest time when the crop must be gathered as quickly as possible to ensure that it did not go bad before reaching market. Failing to accomplish this task was money lost, which was not acceptable. For enslaved field hands like Ellen Vaughn in Georgia, the expectations were clearly defined, as was the punishment: "Ellen, with the other women, had to be in the fields so early in the day that they couldn't see to plow. Certain tasks were set, such as a certain number of pounds of cotton to be picked by each negro. If they fell short of the amount, Merritt's overseers whipped them."

The weighing in at the end of the day was a moment every worker likely dreaded because of the consequences of falling short. But this trepidation was not only associated with picking cotton. Any chore assigned to the enslaved had to be accomplished according to the preference of the person in authority or they suffered the consequences. Feeding the animals, building fences, plowing, or any task assigned was watched carefully. And if the person in charge was not happy or was just in a bad mood punishment would follow. Mrs. John Barclay of Texas recalled, "He would whip us 'til we was raw and then put pepper and salt in de sores. If he thought we was too slow in doin' anything he would kick us off de groun' and churn us up and down. Our punishment depended on de mood of de overseer." As a result it was almost impossible for enslaved workers to avoid punishment no matter how hard they tried. Heard Griffin of Georgia had a slaveholder he described as "the meanest man I've ever known. . . . He would sit down with nothing else to do, think of some man, send for him and for no reason at all, give him a good beating." Consequently, the enslaved people on the Griffin farm, as was the case on many other places, stood in constant fear of the temper and mean spirit of the person supervising them, and they could do nothing to protect themselves.

NARRATIVES

Frank Adamson, South Carolina

"First one name Mr. Cary, he a good man. Another one Mr. Tim Gladden, burn you up whenever he just take a notion to pop his whip. Us boys run 'round in our shirt tails. He lak to see if he could lift de shirt tail widout techin' de skin. Just as often as not, though, he tech de skin. Little boy holler and Marster Tim laugh. They done move de whippin' post dat was in de backyard. Yes sah, it was a 'cessity wid them niggers. It stood up and out to 'mind them dat if they didn't please de master and de overseer, they'd hug dat post, and de lend of dat whip lash gwine to flip to de hide of dat back of their's. I ain't a complainin'. He was a good master, bestest in de land, but he just have to have a whippin' post, 'cause you'll find a whole passle of bad niggers when you gits a thousand of them in one flock."

John Aldrich, Texas

"De marster's name was Michelle Thibedoux. Dat was de same as Mitchell Thibedoux, and some of de people called him dat. He was my Gran'pa too, my mother's father. You know in dem times de women had to do what dere masters told 'em to do. If dey didn't dey pick on 'em and whip 'em. If she do what he want he stop picking on 'em and whipping 'em. Old Marster was bad 'bout dat, and his sons was bad too."

"Marster would come 'round to de cabins in de quarters. Sometime he go in one and tell de man to go outside and wait 'til he do what he want to do.

Her husband had to do it and he couldn't do nothing 'bout it. Marster was tough 'bout dat. He had chillen by his own chillen. Some of de marsters sell dere own chillen."

"Marster was mean. He hardly ever whip 'em over dere clothes. He whip 'em on de bare skin. He make de women throw dere dress up over dere head, and make de men undress."

"Dey didn't 'low you to go 'way from your plantation. If you go off, any 'peck' what find you catch you and whip you and carry you back."

"Sometime Marster punish his slaves like dis. He had two heavy plank with a hole for your neck and two little holes for your wrists. Dey had a iron strap at de end to lock it down. Dey have another for your feet. Dey give you twenty-five licks and clamp you in it. Next morning dey give you twenty-five more and tell you to git your breakfast and git to work. Dey whip you with a half-inch bull whip. When dey git through with you, you need a doctor. How you 'spect anybody to rest in dat thing? Dey too sore to work. I seen dat thing since free time. Sometime dey put salt and pepper on your back after dey whip you."

"He say dare was one nigger on Mr. William Bearsland place done something and Mr. William go to whip him. Nigger had a hoe and he say if anybody try to whip him he gwinter kill 'em. Mr. William tell him to put dat hoe down, but he wouldn't. Den he git he shotgun. When de nigger still won't put de hoe down, he shoot him in de legs. Still he say he ain't gwine to be beat, dey might as well give him de other load. I think dey kill him."

Rev. W. B. Allen, Alabama

"Whipping, of course, was a part of the system employed by owners to control their serfs. One popular method of whipping a Negro was called the 'Buck' and another was the 'Rolling Jim.' Throwing a Nigger into the 'Buck' consisted in first stripping him (all Nigger whipping was applied to the bare body), making him squat and tying his hands between his knees to a stout stick run behind the bends of his knees. Then, the Nigger was pushed over and the performance begun. In the 'Rolling Jim' system, a Nigger was stretched on his stomach at full length on a large log, about eight feet long. Into holes bored in each end of this log, wooden pegs were driven. The feet were securely tied to one set of these pegs—at one end of the log, and the hands to the pegs at the other end. The victim was then ready to be worked on."

"Sometimes the 'Buck' and the 'Rolling Jim' candidates were flogged with a rawhide strap, and sometimes they were 'persuaded' with a paddle. The rawhide cut the flesh and brought streams of blood. The paddle had holes in it which raised blisters. The muscular contortions of the Negro on the log caused it to sway—hence the name, 'Rolling Jim.'"

"Cruel masters and overseers, after 'Bucking' and 'Rolling Jimming' a Negro, would then rub salt and red pepper into his wounds, causing him to go into convulsions, developing fever, resulting frequently in a state of coma lasting for several days. Serious and lasting illnesses also resulted, in many instances, from these ordeals."

Sarah Ashley, Texas

"I uster hafter pick cotton. Sometime' I pick t'ree hunnerd poun' 'r' cotton 'n' tote it a mile t' d' cotton house. Some pick t'ree hunnerd t' eight hunnerd poun's 'r' cotton 'n' hafter tote d' bag fo' a whole mile' t' d' gin. Iffen dey didn' do dey wuk dey git whip 'til dey hab blister on 'em. Den iffen dey didn' do it a man on a hoss went down d' rows 'n' whip wid a paddle mek wid holes in it 'n' bus' d' blisters. I neber git whip cause I alays git my t'ree hunnerd poun'. Us hab t' go in d' fiel' so early, dey blow d' ho'n [horn] so early sometime dey don' hab time to' cook fo' [before] daylight. Us hafter tek us wittles [victuals] t' d' fiel' in a bucket iffen we didn' hab time t' cook 'em."

"W'en I was wid d' w'ite lady one time I seed a man in d' fiel' run 'way. D' w'ite men git d' dogs out t' hunt d' nigger. Dey kotch him 'n' put him in d' front room. He so scare' he jump t'roo d' big winder 'n' break d' glass all up. He jump out w'lle us was eatin' breakfus'. Dey sho' did whip him w'en dey kotch him ag'in."

"D' way dey whip d' niggers was t' strip dem off neckid, 'n' whip dem 'til dey mek blisters 'n' bus' d' blisters. Den dey tek salt 'n' red pepper 'n' put in d' Woun's. Atterward dey wash 'n' grease dem 'n' put sumpthin' on de, t' keep dem from bleed t' def' [death]. I hear some folks tell 'r' whippin' dem t' def' [death], but I neber see dem do it. I hear dat sometime' dey put d' nigger dawgs atter dem 'n' d' dawgs kotch dem 'n' eat dem up but I neber see nuthin' 'r' dat."

Josephine Bacchus, South Carolina

"Just like as I been hear talk, some of de people fare good in slavery time en some of dem fare rough. Dat been accordin to de kind of task boss dey come up under. Now de poor colored people in slavery time, dey give dem very little rest en would whip some of dem most to death. Wouldn' none of dem daresen to go from one plantation to another widout dey had a furlough from dey boss. Yes, mam, if dey been catch you comin back widout dat walkin paper de boss had give you, great Jeruseleum, you would sho catch de devil next mornin. My blessed a mercy, hear talk dey spill de poor nigger's blood awful much in slavery time. Hear heap of dem was free long time fore dey been know it cause de white folks, dey wanted to keep dem in bondage. Oh, my Lord, dey would out dem so hard till dey just slash de flesh right off dem. Yes, mam, dey call dat thing dey been whip dem wid de cat o' nine tail. No, darlin, I hear talk it been made out of pretty leather plaited most all de way en den all dat part down to de bottom, dey just left it loose to do de cuttin wid. Yes, honey, dem kind of whips was made out of pretty leather like one of dese horse whips. Yes, mam, dat been how it was in slavery time."

Joe Barnes, Texas

"I kin kinder rec'leck 'em whippin' slaves. Marster was mean to 'em. Dey tie 'em down 'cross a bar'l or log and whip' 'em. Mos' de time dey whip 'em 'bout wuk. Dey wuk 'em by task and if a nigger ain't git he task done dey whip 'em. Some of 'em run away. Dey had w'at dey call de nigger dog to ketch 'em. One nigger run away one time. He could run fas'er dan de dog and de dog ain't kin ketch 'im. He stay in de woods a long time, but atter dat he tek a notion to come back and let 'em whip 'im."

Alice Battles, Alabama

The slaves on the plantation were whipped for idleness and disobedience, but Alice was never whipped. Her mother and father were punished in this manner; however, this was the only form of punishment ever administered.

Harrison Beckett, Texas

"Old massa was kind and good, though. He have partiality 'bout him, and wouldn't whip nobody without de cause. He whip with de long, keen switch and it didn't bruise de back, but sho' did sting. When he git real mad, he pull up you shirt and whip on de bare hide. One time he whippin' me and I busts de button off my shirt what he holdin' on to, and runs away. I tries to outrun, him, and dat tickle him. I sho' give de ground fits with my feets. But dem whippin's done me good. Dey break me up from thievin' and make de man of me."

Sarah Benjamin, Texas

"I don't know how many slaves there was, but it was a lot, maybe 60 or 70. Dey worked hard every day 'cept Sunday. Iffen they was bad they night git whuppin's, but not too hard, not to de bloom. Iffen dey was still bad, dey puts chains on dem and puts dem in de stocks, 'cause there wasn't no jail there."

Harriet Benton, Alabama

"Occasionally, a Negro was whipped for stealing, jes' as Niggers ought to be whooped now for takin' things that don't belong to 'em."

"My Massa wuz a nice white man. He wuz good as he could be to his slaves. But ol' Missus, Lor! She wuz a devil in her own way. She uster have her slaves beat jes' to hear 'em holler. Dey didn't have to do somethin' wrong; she jes' had 'em beat fer nothin'."

Ellen Betts, Texas

"When a whuppin' got to be done, old Marse do it hisself. He don't 'low no overseer to throw his gals down and pull up dere dress and whup on dere bottom lak I hear tell dat some of 'em do. When dat have to be done, he do it hisself. Was he still livin' I s'pec' one part of his hands would be with him to dis day. I know I would."

Francis Black, Texas

"Master lived there in Jefferson, but had a farm 'bout four miles from town. He had a overseer that rode a horse over the farm. I'se seed him buckle the Niggers cross a log and whip them."

Gordon Bluford, South Carolina

"Master had a big plantation of several farms, near about 1,000 acres or more. It was said he had once 250 slaves on his places, counting children and all. His overseers had to whip the slaves, master told them to, and told them to whip them hard. Master Calms was most always mean to us. He got mad spells and whip like the mischief. He all the time whipping me 'cause I wouldn't work like he wanted."

Nancy Boudry, Georgia

"I had to work hard, plow and go and split wood jus' like a man. Sometimes dey whup me. Dey whup me bad, pull de close off down to de wais'—my master did it, our folks didn' have overseer."

Samuel Boulware, South Carolina

"Marster was good, in a way, to his slaves but dat overseer of his name John Parker, was mean to us sometimes. He was good to some and bad to others. He strung us up when he done de whippin'. My mammy got many whippin's on 'count of her short temper. When she got mad, she would talk back to de overseer, and dat would make him madder than anything else she could do."

Wes Brady, Texas

"Some white folks might want to put me back in slavery if I tells how we was used in slavery time, but you asks me for the truth. The overseer was 'straddle his big horse at three o'clock in the mornin', roustin' the hands off to the field. He got them all lined up and then come back to the house for breakfas'. The rows was a mile long and no matter how much grass was in them, if you leaves one sprig on your row they beats you nearly to death. Lots of times they weighed cotton by candlelight. All the hands took dinner to the field in buckets and the overseer give then fifteen minutes to git dinner. He'd start cuffin' some of them over the head when it was time to stop eat in' and go back to work. He'd go to the house and eat his dinner and then he'd come back and look in all the buckets and if a piece of anything that was there when he left was et, he'd say you was losin' time and had to be whipped. He'd drive four stakes in the ground and tie a nigger down and beat him till he's raw. Then he'd take a brick and grind it up in a powder and mix it with lard and put it all over him and roll him in a sheet. It'd be two days or more 'fore that nigger could work 'gain. I seed one nigger done that way for stealin' a meat bone from the meathouse. That nigger got fifteen hundred lashes. The li'l chaps would pick up egg shells and play with them and if the overseer seed them he'd say you was stealin' eggs and give you a beatin'. I seed long lines of slaves chained together driv by a white man on a hoss, down the Jefferson road."

"One time the stock got in the field and the overseer 'cuses a old man and jumps on him and breaks his neck. When he seed the old man dead, he run off to the woods, but massa sent some nigger after him and say for him to come back, the old man jus' got overhet and died."

Della Briscoe, Georgia

Punishment was administered, though not as often as on some plantations. The little girl, Della, was whipped only once—for breaking up a turkey's nest she had found. Several were accused of this, and because the master could not find the guilty party, he whipped each of the children.

Men were sometimes placed in "bucks," which meant they were laid across blocks with their hand and feet securely tied. An iron bar was run between the blocks to prevent any movement; then, after being stripped, they were whipped. Della said that she knew of but one case of this type of punishment being administered a Ross slave.

The "old man" kept account of the increase or decrease in live stock and poultry and reported anything missing each day. When suspicion fell on a visitor of the previous night, this information was given to his master, who then searched the accused's dinner pail and cabin. If meat was found in either the culprit was turned over to his accuser for punishment. After being whipped, he was forbidden for three months to visit the plantation where he had committed the theft.

Sally Brown, Georgia

"I wuz give to the Mitchell Fambly and they done everything mean to me they could. I wuz put to work in the fields when I wuz five year ole, pickin' cotton and hoein'. And I slep on the flo' nine years, winter and summer, sick or well. I never wore nothin' but a cotton dress and my shimmy and draw's. I had sich hard time. That Mistress Mitchell didn't care what happened to us. Sometimes she would walk us to church but we never went nowhere else. That 'oman took delight in sellin' slaves. She used to lash me with a cowhide whip. Then she died and I went frum one fambly to another. All the owners wuz pretty much the same, but this is still the Mitchell 'oman I'm telling you about now."

"We wuzn't 'lowed to go around and have pleasure as the folks does today. We had to have passes to go wherever we wanted."

Wesley Burrell, Texas

"De people was mighty cruel on us in slavery time. Some would take us an' stake us to four stakes an' whip us until de blood run down; some times dey hit five-hundred or more licks. Some of de women, when pregnant would be beaten with dere stomach down in a hole an' dey was tied to a stake. Dey was not allowed to sing or pray; if caught doing so we would git a whippen. We was not allowed to go from one place to another without consent of de boss. De pat-roller would whip dem if dey should be caught without a pass from de boss. Many days when snow was knee deep an' my old marster had his boots an' over coat on, I would have to go with him an be bare foot an' with nothing on my head."

Richard Bush, Mississippi

"Marse Easterlin wuz sho' a stern master. He believed in whippin' his slaves. I'se seed him put my ma 'cross a barrel an' whip her. She wuz a fiel' hand an' wuked powerfully hard. One ob de cruelest things I ever seen done to a slave wuz done by my Master. He wanted to punish one ob de slaves what had done some 'em dat he didn't lak, a kinda subborn one. He took dat darkie an' hitched him to a plow an' plowed him jes' lak a hors. He beat him an' jerked him 'bout 'till he got all bloody an' sore, but ole Marse he kept right on day after day. Finally de buzzards went to flyin' over 'em [a superstitious idea] dem buzzards kept a flyin' an' ole Marse kept on a plowin him 'till one day he died."

Dave Byrd, Texas

"Yes, Maser would whip the slaves if he got contrary or stubborn. I saw him whip several negroes, although he never spoke a cross word to this here negro. He would tie rope to them negroes hand, tie both hands together and pull their hands high above the head and back of them and take that cat-o-nine tails and hit that negro 25 licks for the first licks, then 50 the next time and so on. Every time he had to whip one he just increased the licks every time. No sir, Maser he never had to whip very many negroes. They knew what that whipping meant. There was not very many negroes that liked that whipping. Sometimes he would send the negroes to their quarters after working all day without anything to eat, and when they got up in the morning he would send them to the field still without anything to eat. That would hurt him worse than whipping, because all negroes like to eat plenty good things, but of course the poor negroes they don't get it just like the poor white folks."

"No sir, he did not exactly have a jail for the slaves, but Maser had a place built that he could lock negro in it if he wanted to."

Louis Cain, Texas

"Yes, we very often got whipped or had to do without anything to eat. I'se seen Maser tie them slaves hands to their feet and tie them to a tree and hit them about 25 or 50 licks with a raw-hide belt. Everytime he hit that negro, hide and blood both would just fly. Then I'se seen him tie their feet to their hands and tie them to a tree and leave them all night cause they would be stubborn. Next morning he would turn them loose and make them work without anything to eat all that day. They would be so tired and hungry when he turned them loose. He had what he called jail for the negro women and girl slaves. Of course he would whip them too, but he would have better luck by chaining and locking them in jail with nothing to eat but cornbread and one glass of water 3 times a day. Maser was pretty rough with some of his slaves. Once he had a slave that tried to run away from him and go to the woods. He was going to be a jungle negro, but Maser found him with some dogs he had. When he brought that negro home he took a hot iron and branded that negro; after he branded him he made a bell and put on him. It was made in a wooden frame so it would slip down over his shoulders and under his arm so it would not come off. The bell was high enough above his head so he could not reach it, and keep it from clapping when he moved. You know Mister, Maser made that negro wear that bell almost a year, finally he took it off one Christmas Day as a present to him. It sure did make a good negro out of him. He never did give Maser anymore trouble, no sir, as long as he was a slave."

Solomon Caldwell, South Carolina

"Marse Gillam sho was rapid. I saw him whip my mammy till you couldn't put a hand on her shoulder and back widout touching a whelp."

Fanny Cannady, North Carolina

"Dey took Buitus to de whippin' post. Dey strip off his shirt, den dey put his head an' hands through de holes in de top, an' tied his feets to de bottom, den Ole Marse took de whip. Dat lash hiss like col' water on er red hot iron when it come through de air, an' every time it hit Burrus it lef' er streak of blood.

Time Ole Marse finish, Burrus' back look like er piece of raw beef. Dey laid Burrus face down on er plank den dey poured turpentine in all dem cut places. It burned like fire but dat niggah didn' know nothin' 'bout it kaze he done passed out from pain. But, all his life dat black man toted dem scares on his back."

Richard Carruthers, Texas

"His name was Tom Hill, but us niggers call him 'Devil Hill.' At first when my missy find out the overseers mean, she fire them out and turn them off, but when she git a new one, he jus' as mean."

"Old Devil use to whup me and the other niggers if we don't jump quick enough when he holler and if we run away and if we don't work fast as he have a mind to it. He stake us out like you stake out a hide and whup till we bleed and that the truth. Many the time I set down and make a eight-plait whup so he could whup from the heel to the back of the head until he figger he get the proper ret'ibution. He never make me plait my own whup, but many's the whupping I persecuted with. I hear tell and see some-time when a overseer take salt and rub on the nigger, so he smart and burn proper and suffer misery according to how the overseer think he ought. They was a caliboose right on the plantation. It look like a ice-house, 'bout that size, and it were sure bad to git locked up. He soon as leave you there until you die."

Aunt Cicely Cawthon, Georgia

"Overseers didn't do no more than what Marster told him to," Aunt Cicely said. "He'd come to the field and if he saw a slave sitting under a tree he'd ask him if he was sick, and it was all right if he was sick, but if he was well and laying out under a tree, he got a whipping. The overseer would go back and tell Marster, and that night he'd give 'em just as many licks as Marster said, but, he was keerful with the darkies. I never seed the overseer have a billie in his hand. His whip was wropped around the horn of his saddle. He'd unwrop it, and put you on the clock and give you whatever Marster said. Overseers didn't have no rules, but if you resisted him, he'd double your whipping. For killing time or being lazy, you got 25 licks; for stealing, 50 licks; and for running away, that was the worst, if they got you back, you got a hundred licks. I had a cousin to run away, and they got her back from Charleston. The overseer give her a hundred licks. One lick out the blood, and my Mistis got so mad she threwed that long hair back, I can see that long hair now, and quarreled at Marster. He said he had to make a zample for the other slaves. Mistis said it injured the woman to whip her that way, so then Marster made 'em be more careful. Even that warn't as bad as going to the chaingang now. Young darkies now gets mad with me for saying that, but they pertected you, and nobody didn't need to bother you. They pertected you wherever you went."

Jeptha Choice, Texas

"Course, sometimes the niggers in the field would get o'nry and not work good, but the overseer on our place wasn' 'lowed to whup. At night, when they came in he would tell the old Massa what the trouble was about, and then the Massa would whup the nigger what he thought he deserved. Our Massa had a tree he tied a bad nigger to to whup him, but some white folks had ring posts, and tied a nigger around the neck with a rope—and run the rope through the ring—and tied him up like a mule to whup him."

Anthony Christopher, Texas

"But de overseer sho' use to whip dem niggers what work in de field. I seed dem hold bacon over a fire and let de hot grease drop on de bare hide of a nigger what was tie down on de ground and den lash him from de head down to de feet. Yes, suh, I sho' has seed it, jes' like I's tellin' you."

Peter Clifton, South Carolina

"How long was they whipped? Well, they put de foots in a stock and clamp them together, then they have a cross-piece go right across de breast high as de shoulder. Dat cross-piece long enough to bind de hands of a slave to it at each end. They always strip them naked and some time they lay on de lashes wid a whip, a switch or a strap. Does I believe dat was a great sin? No sir. Our race was just lak school chillun is now. De marster had to put de fear of God in them sometime, somehow, and de Bible don't object to it."

Charles Coates, Florida

On the Hall plantation there was a contraption, similar to a gallows, where the slaves were suspended and whipped. At the top of this device were blocks of wood with chains run through holes and high enough that a slave when tied to the chains by his fingers would barely touch the ground with his toes. This was done so that the slave could not shout or twist his body while being whipped. The whipping was prolonged until the body of the slave was covered with wects and blood trickled down his naked body. Women were treated in the same manner, and a pregnant woman received no more leniency than did a man. Very often after a severe flogging a slave's body was treated to a bath of water containing salt and pepper so that the pain would be more lasting and aggravated. The whipping was done with sticks and a whip called the "cat o' nine tails," meaning every lick meant nine. The "cat o' nine tails" was a whip of nine straps attached to a stick; the straps were perforated so that everywhere the hole in the strap fell on the flesh a blister was left.

The treatment given by the overseer was very terrifying. He relates how a slave was put in a room and locked up for two and three days at a time without water or food, because the overseer thought he hadn't done enough work in a given time.

Another offense which brought forth severe punishment was that of crossing the road to another plantation. A whipping was given and very often a slave was put on starvation for a few days.

Hattie Cole, Texas

"Whuppin's am not so often, an' w'en 'tis given, dey don't tie de cullud fo'ks down to a post, or put dem over de barrel. Dey jus' puts dey face down on de ground, den dey am lashed wid a rawhide. De Marster don't 'lows fo' to draw blood. Co'se thar am wales on thar body. De whuppin's am given mos'ly 'cause young fo'ks goes off de place an' gits catched at it."

William Coleman, Texas

"Maser woke us up every morning about 4:30 o'clock with a great large bell that hung just outside of his bed. Son I'se dressed several times out behind my quarters cause if we did not get right up when Maser rung that bell, here he come with a rawhide whip and gun buckled on him, and he would whip us all the time we were trying to dress. Maser he would work us from sun to sun or we would be in the field in the morning waiting for daylight to come, then we stayed in th' field and worked just as long as we could see how. When we went to the house we had all our night work to do after dark before we got our supper, and went to bed. Well son, I'se seen the slaves whipped for nothing, but then if they did do something to be whipped for they were almost killed before Maser would quit working on them. Yes sir, if one was the least bit stubborn or even acted like he would sass Maser, he was whipped. I'se seen Maser ride up close to a slave when he was working and whip him good, cause he would be 3 or 4 feet behind the rest of the slaves. One time one of the slaves was helping Mistress there in the yard and he passed too close to her as he was hurrying fast as he could, and sort of bumped into her. She never paid him no attention, but Maser saw him and he let him go on ahead and finish what he was doing then he called that poor negro to him and took him out in the pasture, tied his hands together, throwed the other end of the rope over a limb on a tree and pulled that negro's hands up in the air to where that negro had to stand on his tiptoes, and Maser he took all that negro's clothes off and whipped him with that rawhide whip until that negro was plum bloody all over. Then he left that poor negro tied there all the rest of the day and night."

"When Maser did let that negro down he could not stand up or get his hands down from over his head, but that did not keep Maser from giving him another whipping as he thought the negro was putting on, but he found out he was not. Then Maser called old negro mama that he had there on the plantation to rub and work with that poor negro until she finally got him

824 PHYSICAL ABUSE AND INTIMIDATION

limbered up so he could move around some. Son, that was one of the sickest negroes you ever saw after that. Maser thought for more than a week he was going to die, but the old negro mama just kept working with him until she pulled him through. Maser did have to kill him after that as it made an outlaw out of him. He got to where he would not work and Maser whipping him all the time, and he would sass Maser right out. Then Maser sold him to another man and his new Maser carried him to the field and thought he would work, but no sir, he just lay his hoe down and walked right off from his new Maser and right back to his old Maser; said if he ever got a chance he was going to kill his Maser. Maser had to give that man money back, then he sold him to another man that lived in another state and just as soon as he turned him loose and thought he would be satisfied, why he just walked off from that new Maser and come right back home. Maser had to give that mans money back as he could not keep him cause he come and got him 3 or 4 times. His old Maser done got scared of him and put him in chains, but of course, he would have to unfasten his hands in the daytime so he could work, but he never took the chains off his legs. At night he was locked in his quarters. We was all locked in at night for that matter. Then one day Maser had this negro working and he was not watching him and went to show some of the other slaves something about what he was doing and turned his back on this negro and that negro thought that was his chance, so he jumped right on Maser's back and pinned him to the ground and was trying to choke Maser and keep him from getting his gun all at the same time, but with his feet chained he could not do it. Some of us run in and started to pull him off Maser and he made us get away cause he did not want to shoot some of us when he did get his gun, which he finally did, and shot that negro off of him. He sure hated to kill one of his slaves cause they were a valuable piece of property in them days, but he had to kill that one. He just drug that negro off and throwed him in a brush pile, never even buried him. No sir, said he was not worth burying."

"Well no sir, they was not exactly a jail there on the plantation for the slaves, but Maser he had our quarters fixed so he could lock us in there every night and if he wanted to punish us that way, all he had to do was lock us in our quarters and let us stay there just as long as he wanted to and we were afraid to try to get out if we could cause we knew just what Maser would do to us if we did. I have stayed in my quarters locked up 3 days at a time without a bit to eat or drink. Son I sure would get dry and hungry but all the good it would do me cause I knew Maser would'nt let me out until he got good and ready anyway."

Jane Cotton, Texas

"They have great big house built out logs, the over seer he mean man. He whipped negro when he didnt go in run cause he didnt like negro. Master he have about 100 acres in the plantation. They was about eight grown slave and seven little negro slaves. The over seer he gets us up about four o'clock every week day and Sunday he lets us sleep until the sun is real high. I'se seen a few slaves whipped just like you would a mule cause they would get stubbering and contrary. I'se seen them lay slave over log or barrel and take their clothes down sos they could whip on the naked hide, then they would hit them thrity-nine licks, with cat-o-nine tails."

Elijah Cox, Texas

"Life for the slaves was pretty hard. On the plantation where my parents were slaves, there was an overseer who was cruel to the slaves. Besides having to do the regular farm work they had to split rails and make boards to shingle the houses. The overseer was to see that they worked and to whip them if they didn't work. If they picked up a newspaper they were whipped for that too. The owners didn't want the slaves to learn to read because they were afraid they would get too smart. And if they picked up a gun they were whipped for that."

Green Cumby, Texas

"Durin' slavery I had purty rough times. My grandfather, Tater Cumby, was cullud overseer for forty slaves and he called us at four in de mornin' and we worked from sun to sun. Most of de time we worked on Sunday, too."

"De best times was when de corn shuckin' was at hand. Den you didn't have to bother with no pass to leave de plantation, and de patter rolls didn't bother you. If de patter rolls cotch you without de pass any other time, you better wish you dead, 'cause you would have yourself some trouble."

"De white overseers whipped us with straps when we didn't do right. I seed niggers in chains lots of times, 'cause there wasn't no jails and they jus' chained 'em to trees."

Campbell Davis, Texas

"I seed one my sisters whip 'cause she didn't spin 'nough. Dey pull de clothes down to her waist and laid her down on de stomach and lash her with de rawhide quirt. I's in de field when dey whips my Uncle Lewis for not pickin' 'nough cotton. De driver pull he clothes down and make him lay on de groun'. He wasn't tied down, but he say he scart to move."

Mama Duck, Florida

"I never got no beatins fum my master when I was a slave. But I seen collored men on de Bradley plantation git frammed but plenty. De whippin boss was Joe Sylvester. He had pets amongst de women folks, an let some of em off light when they desarved good beatins."

How did he punish his "pet"?

"Sometimes he jus bop em crosst de ear wid a battlin stick."

A what?

"Buttlin stick, like dis. You doan knew what a battlin stick is? Well, dis here is one. Use it for washin clothes. You lift em outa de wash pot wid de battlin stick; den you lay em on de battlin block, dis here stump. Den you beat de dirt but wid de battlin stick."

A stick like that would knock a horse down!

"Wan't nigh as bad as what some of do others got. Some of his pets amongst de mens got it wusser dan de womens. He strap em croast de sharp side of a barrel an give em a few right smart licks wid a bull whip."

And what did he do to the bad ones?

"He make em cross dere hands, den he tie a rope roun dey wrists an throw it over a tree limb. Den he pull em up so dey toes jus touch de ground am smack em on de back an rump wid a heavy woden paddle, fixed full o'holes. Den he make em lie down en de ground while he bust all den blisters wid a raw-hide whip."

Didn't that kill them?

"Some couldn't work for a day or two. Sometimes dey threw salt brine on dey backs, or smear on turpmtine to make it git well quicker."

Lewis Evans, South Carolina

"Whippin's? Yes sir, I got 'most skinned alive once, when I didn't bring up de cows one Sunday. Got in a fight wid one of Miss Betsie Aiken's hands and let de cows git away, was de cause of de whippin'. I was 'shamed to tell him 'bout de fight. Maj. Bell, dis time, whipped me hisself. "Who-ee! Don't talk to dis nigger 'bout patrollers. They run me many a time. You had to have a pass wid your name on it, who you b'long to where gwine to, and de date you expected back. If they find your pass was to Mr. James' and they ketch you at Mr. Rabb's, then you got a floggin', sure and plenty."

Charlotte Foster, South Carolina

She said her master never whipped any of the slaves, but she had heard cries and groans coming from other plantations at five o'clock in the morning where the slaves were being beaten and whipped. Asked why the slaves were being beaten, she replied rather vehemently, "Just because they wanted to beat 'em; they could do it, and they did." She said she had seen the blood running down the backs of some slaves after they had been beaten. One day a girl about 16 years of age came to her house and said she'd just as leave be dead as to take the beatings her master gave her, so one day she did go into the woods and eat some poison oak. "She died, too." On one plantation she saw an old woman who used to get so many beatings that they put a frame work around her body and ran it up into a kind of steeple and placed a bell in the steeple. "Dat woman had to go around with that bell ringing all the time."

John Glover, South Carolina

"Dey have a driver dat tote whip on see dat you do what you know to do. Didn' have no jail in dat day, but if you ain' do your task on dey catch you, dey punish you by de whip. Some of de time, dey put em in de screw box what dey press bales of cotton wid. Put em in dere en run press right down whe' can' crush en dey couldn' move till dey take em out in de mornin en whip em en put em to work. See plenty whipped on de place. Dey make one fellow go over a barrel en de other peoples hold he head down en de driver whip him. Give em 50 en 75 licke fore dey stop sometimes. Use chains to hold em when dey break ropes so dey couldn' get away."

Thomas Goodwater, South Carolina

"Lisa Winning wusn' a mean man. He couldn' lick pa cus dey grow up togedder or at least he didn' try. But he liked his woman slave. One day ma aus in de field workin' alone an' he went there an' try to rape 'er. Ma pull his ears almos' off so he let 'er off an' gone an' tell pa he better talk to ma. Pa wus workin' in the salt pen an' w'en Mr. Winning tell him he jus' laugh cus e know why ma did it. . . . "

"I wus by the 'nigger quarters' one day w'en Blake, the overseer stars' to lick a slave. She take the whip frum him an' close de door an' give him a snake beatin'."

Austin Grant, Texas

"My grandfather, he would tell us things, to keep the whip off our backs. He would say, 'Chillen, work, work and work hard. You know how you hate to be whipped, so work hard!' And of course we chillen tried, but of course we would git careless sometimes."

"The master had a 'black snake'—some called it a 'bull whip,' and he knew how to use it. He whipped, but I don' 'member now whether he brought any blood on me, but he cut the blood outta the grown ones. He didn' tie 'em, he always had a whippin' block or log to make 'em lay down on. They called 500 licks a 'light breshin,' and right on your naked back, too. They said your clothes wouldn' grow but your hide would. From what I heered say, if you run away, then was when they give you a whippin, prob'ly 1500 or 2000 licks. They'd shore tie you down then, 'cause you couldn' stan' it. Then you'd have to work on top of all that, with your shirt stickin' to your back."

Charlie Grant, South Carolina

"I tellin you dat was a good place to live in slavery time. I didn' have to do nothin but mind de sheep en de cows en de goats in dat day en time. All de slaves dat was field hands, dey had to work mighty hard. De overseer, he pretty rough sometimes. He tell dem what time to get up en sound de horn for dat time. Had to go to work fore daybreak en if dey didn' be dere on time en work like dey ought to, de overseer sho whip dem. Tie de slaves clear de ground by dey thumbs wid nigger cord en make dem tiptoe en draw it tight as could be. Pull clothes off dem fore dey tie dem up. Dey didn' care nothin bout it. Let everybody look on at it. I know when dey whip my mamma. Great God, in de mornin! Dey sho had whippin posts en whippin houses too in dem days, but didn' have no jail. I remember dey whipped dem by de gin house. De men folks was put to de post what had holes bored in it whe' dey pull strings through to fasten dem up in dere. Dey catch nigger wid book, day ax you what dat you got dere en whe' you get it from. Tell you bring it here en den dey carry you to de whippin post for dat. No men folks whip me. Women folks whip me wid four plaitted raw cowhide whip."

Dosia Harris, Georgia

"I couldn't rightly say how big dat plantation of hers was. Oo-o! But it sho' was one more big place, and Niggers was scattered all 'round dar lak black-birds. Dat old overseer, he sho' was mean to de slaves. He whupped 'em and he kept on whuppin' 'em, 'til sometimes it seemed lak he jus' beat on 'em to hear 'em holler. It warn't long atter midnight when he got 'em up to go to wuk and he kept 'em at hard labor 'til way atter sundown. De biggest things he whupped Niggers for was for runnin' 'way and for not doin' deir wuk. right."

"Jails! Did you say jails? Yessum, dey had jails. You know slaves warn't civilized folks den—all dey knowed was to fuss and fight and kill one 'nother. Dey put de Niggers in dem jails 'til dey hung 'em."

Mrs. Lancy Harris, Arkansas

"Old man Henry Downing [nigger-driver] he wud eat you alive—L-o-r-d he wus so mean. Yo' ud better not let him see you wid a book let alone learning to read."

Benjamin Henderson, Georgia

Benjamin heard from his elders that some masters constructed stocks like those of old, and sometimes slaves were whipped while fastened in the stocks. One slave owner named Gay kept wristbands of iron, and also a gag made to fit into the mouth and fasten around the neck, which prevented rolling while being whipped. Besides being punished for disobedience, a slave was often punished because he failed to complete the required amount of work. There were certain amounts of work specified for each slave: 150 rails had to be split a day by the rail splitters; cotton pickers were supposed to pick 150 pounds of cotton a day. Should anyone fail to complete his daily task, a sound whipping was given.

Jeff Henry, Georgia

"Marse Robert done his own whippin' of his slaves and, let me tell you, they didn't have to do much for him to whip 'em; he whipped 'em for most anything. They was tied, hand and foots, to a certain tree, and he beat 'em with a heavy leather strop. I'se seed him whip 'em heaps of times, and it was 'most allus in the mornin's 'fore they went to wuk. Thar warn't no jailhouse nigh whar us lived and Marse Robert never had no place to lock slaves up when they got too bad, so he just beat the meanness out of 'em. Thar was one slave he never tetched; that was his foreman and his name was Robert too, lak I done told you."

Jerry Hill, South Carolina

He said, that when a slave had to have a whipping, he was taken to a whipping post in Jonesville. A bull-whip was used for the punsihment and it brought the blood from the bare back of the man or woman being whipped. One day a grown slave was given 150 lashes with the bull-whip, for teaching the young boys to gamble. He saw this punishment administered. He had climbed a tree where he could get a better view. He said that several slaves were being whipped that day for various things, and there were several men standing around watching the whipping. He said that he was laughing at the victim, when some by-stander looked up and saw him; "that boy needs 150 lashes, too," he said. "He is laughing at the punishment being given." So his master told the by-stander to get the boy and give him the lashing if he thought he needed it. When he was led up to the whipping post, some man there shook his head at the by-stander; so the boy did not get whipped. Jerry says that the sister of Jim Fernandes used to carry a bull-whip around her neck when she walked out on the farm, and would apply it herself to any slave she thought needed it.

Uncle Ben Horry, South Carolina

"The worst thing I members was the colored oberseer. He was the one straight from Africa. He the boss over all the mens ad womens and if omans don't do all he say, he lay task on 'em they ain't able to do. My mother won't do all he say. When he say, 'You go barn and stay till I come,' she ain't do em. So he

Ben Horry. (Library of Congress)

have it in for my mother and lay task on 'em she ain't able for do. Then for punishment my mother is take to the barn and strapped down on thing called the Pony. Hands spread like this and strapped to the floor and all two both she feet been tie like this. And she been give twenty five to fifty lashes till the blood flow. And my father and me stand right there and look and ain't able to lift a hand! Blood on floor in that rice barn when barn tear down by Hontingdon [A. M. Huntingdon]. If Marse Josh been know 'bout that obersheer, the oberseer can't do 'em; but just the house servant get Marse Josh' and Miss Boss' ear. Them things different when my father been make the head man. What I tell you happen fore Freedom, when I just can remember."

Charles Hudson, Georgia

"Dat overseer, he was a clever man, but I can't ricollect his name. He never paid no heed to what sort of clothes slaves wore, but he used to raise merry cain if dey didn't have good shoes to ditch in. Marse David was de cussin' boss, but de overseer called hisself de whuppin' boss. He had whuppin's all time saved up special for de 'omans. He made 'em take off deir waistes and den he whupped 'em on deir bar backs 'til he was satisfied. He done all de whuppin' atter supper by candle light. I don't 'member dat he ever whupped a man. He jus' whupped 'omans."

"Dey didn't have no jail house or nothin' lak dat 'round dat plantation, 'cause if slaves didn't please Marster dey was jus' made to come up to de yard at de big house and take deir beatin's."

Margaret Hughes, South Carolina

"My massa never whip de slaves very much, but he do sometime. Once I saw my poor old daddy in chains. They chained his feet together, and his hands too, and carry him off to whip him, 'cause he wouldn't tell who stole a trunk that was missing. He couldn't tell though, 'canse he didn't know though, but they thought he did."

Auntie Johns, Texas

"Colonel Sims had a farm 'oinin' Major Odom's farm, and his niggers was treated mean. He had a overseer, J. B. Mullinax, I 'member him, and he was big and tough. He whipped a nigger man to death. He would come out of a mornin' and give a long, keen yell, and say, 'I'm J. B. Mullinax, just back from a week in Hell, where I got two new eyes, one named Snap and Jack, and t'other Take Hold. I'm goin' to whip two or three niggers to death today.' He lived a long time, but long 'fore he died his eyes turned backward in his head. I seen 'em thataway. He wouldn' give his niggers much to eat and he'd make 'em work all day, and just give 'em boiled peas with just water and no salt and cornbread. They'd eat their lunch right out in the hot sun and then go right back to work. Mama said she could hear them niggers bein' whipped at night and yellin', 'Pray, marster, pray,' beggin' him not to beat 'em."

"My husban's tol' me about slavery times in Alabama. He said they would make the niggers work hard all day pickin' cotton and then take it to the gin and gin away into the night, maybe all night. They'd give a nigger on Sunday a peck of meal and three pounds of meat and no salt nor nothin' else, and if you et that up 'fore the week was out, you jus' done without anything to eat till the end of the week."

Thomas Johns, Texas

"We done a good day's work, but didn' have to work after night 'less it was necessary. We was allowed to stop at 12 o'clock and have time for rest 'fore goin' back to work. Other slave owners roun' our place wasn't as good to dere slaves, would work 'em hard and half starve 'em. And some marsters or overseers would whip dere niggers pretty hard, sometimes whip 'em to death. Marster Johns didn' have no overseer. He seed to the work and my father was foreman. For awhile after old Marster died, in 1862 or 1863, I forget which now, we had a overseer, John Sewell. He was mean. He whipped the chillen and my mother told Miss Lucy, old marster's oldest girl."

Ella Johnson, Georgia

"Dr. Lyles was a fine man. He was very rich and had a good education. He wouldn't beat a slave for anything. A rich man wouldn't ever whip a slave. They always hired someone to do this. Whipping was the only form of discipline used on our plantation, as far as I can remember."

"Getting back to the whipping of slaves. . . I had an Aunt named Annice Henry. She was given to one of Dr. Lyles sons when he married. Young Lyles' new wife said she was going to whip Annice. Annice said she wouldn't let her 'missus' whip her. So she was told that she would be sold if she didn't submit to being whipped. Annice didn't and so she was sold to the 'Nigger Traders,' a group of white men who bought and sold slaves. Annice was forced to leave her husband and mother but was allowed to take her little girl, Mariah with her. The 'Nigger Traders' took her from Greenville, South Carolina, to New Orleans, and on the way one of the traders saw Annice crying, and whipped her terribly. So when they got to New Orleans and Annice was put on the slave block at auction, nobody wanted to buy her because she had been whipped. You see her back was just raw, and the white folks said a slave was bad if they had to be whipped. Finally a French woman saw Annice and thought she was pretty and that she didn't look to be a bad slave. So this woman bought Annice. She gave her a good home and got her well. Annice's duties were to just wait on her missus. When she was through with her duties, she could hire herself to other people, and in this way make extra money. Little Mariah learned how to speak French as well as she could English, and she also learned to play piano as well as anybody. After the war, Annice and Mariah came back to South Carolina to see their relatives and Mariah just tickled us all to death speaking French. And the Lyles had her to play piano for them all the time. And believe it or not Annice had saved more than five-hundred dollars [$500.00]."

Gus Johnson, Texas

"Old massa, he name Aden and he brother name John, and dey was way up yonder tall people. Old massa die soon and us have missy to say what we do. All her overseers have to be good. She punish de slaves iffen day bad, but not whip 'em. She have de jail builded undergroun' like de stormcave and it have a drop door with de weight on it, so dey couldn't git up from de bottom. It sho' was dark in dat place."

"In slavery time us better be in by eight o'clock, better be in dat house, better stick to dat rule."

Mary Johnson, Texas

"Old massa he never clean himself up or dress up. He look like a vagrant thing and he and missy mean, too. My pore daddy he back allus done cut up from the whip and bit by the dogs. Sometime when a woman big they make a hollow out place for her stomach and make her lay down 'cross that hole and whip her behind. They sho' tear thatthing up."

Easter Jones, Georgia

"Dey whip you so hard your back bleed, den dey pour salt and water on it. And your shirt stick to your back, so you hadder get somebody to grease it fore you kin take it off."

Sam Kilgore, Texas

"Dat place am so well manage dat whippin's am not nec'sary. Massa have he own way of keepin' de niggers in line. If dey bad he say. 'I 'spect dat nigger driver comin' round tomorrow and I's gwine sell you.' Now, when a nigger git in de hands of de nigger driver it am de big chance he'll git sold to de cruel massa, and dat make de niggers powerful skeert, so dey 'haves. On de next plantation we'd hear de niggers pleadin' when dey's whipped, 'Massa, have mercy,' and sich. Our massa allus say, 'Boys, you hears dat mis'ry and we don't want no sich on dis place and it an up to you.' So us all 'haves ourselves."

Mollie Kinsey, Georgia

"My father uster b'long to Mr. Sam Ellington. He sold him to Dick Petite, a spec'later, from Mississippi. I don't 'member it but ma tole us chilluns 'bout it when we grow'd up."

"Dey had slaves in pens, brung in droves and put in dem pens jes' lak dey wus cows. Dey sold dem by auctionin' off to the highest bidder. I wus only a chile and nevah went 'round much. Dey put girls on the block and auctioned dem off. 'What will you give fer dis nigger wench?' Lot of the girls wus being sold by their master who wus their father, taken rat out uv the yards with their white chilluns and sold lak herds uv cattle."

"My sister was given away when she wus a girl. She tole me and ma that they'd make her go out and lay on a table and two or three white men would have in'ercourse with her befo' they'd let her git up. She wus jes' a small girl hone. She died when she wus still in her young days, still a girl. Oh! You is blessed to live in this day and don't know the tortures the slaves went through. Honey, slavery wus bad, but I wus so young I missed all the evil but chile I know'd 'bout it."

"My master whipped me once and he nevah jes' whipped me fer nothin'. It wus somethin' I'd done. I wus scared uv him too. I see chilluns doin' things they shouldn't do, but I can't say nuthin' fer I 'member I wus a chile and did the same thing once. I got a lot uv whippings from my ma fer I wus a bad chile. My master would tell me to do a job and I would do it, willingly, but I went 'bout it slow lack and he'd holler, 'Concarn it, get a move on yer.' I'd say, 'I make hase terreckly, Marse George, I make hase.'"

Hagar Lewis, Texas

"My father was a slave from another farm. My mother was the cook. She cooked it all in the same place for white folks and us. We ate the same, when the white folks was finished. They's a big light bread oven in the yard of the big house and in front of the quarters, under a big tree. That one baked the pies. The cabins had a big fire-place der than that piano there. They'd hang meat and sausage and dry them in the fireplace. Cut holes in has and hang them there. Had big hogsheads filled up with flour, corn and wheat."

"Some pore niggers were half starved. They belonged to other people. Missus Mary would call them in to feed 'em, see 'em outside the fence pickin' up scraps. They'd call out at night, 'Marse John, Marse John.' They's afraid to come in daytime. Marse John'd say, 'What's the matter now! They'd say, 'I'se hongry.' He'd say, 'Come in and git it.' He'd cure lots of meat, for we'd hear 'em hollerin' at night when they'd beat the pore niggers for beggin' or stealin', or some crime."

"Marse John would saddle up Old Charlie and go'see. He had a big shot gun across his lap. We'd hear that ole bull whip just a poppin'. They'd turn 'em loose when Marse John got after 'em. He prosecuted some marsters for beatin' the slaves. He knew they was half feedin' 'em. One time he let us go see where they'd drug two niggers to death with oxen. For stealin' or some-thin'. I can't say we were treated bad, 'cause I'd tell a story. I've always been treated good by whites, but many of the niggers was killed. They'd say bad words to the bosses and they'd shoot 'em. We'd ask Miss Mary why did they kill old Uncle so end so, and Miss Mary would say, 'I don't know. It's not right to say when you don't know.' I'm glad to see slavery over."

"Some whites had a dark hole in the ground, a'dungeon,' they called it, to put their slaves in. They'd carry 'em bread and water once a day. I'se afraid of the hole, they'd tell me the devile was in that hole."

"Dey used to have old slavery-day jedge and jury of white folks and dey hear de case and 'cide how many lashes to give de darky. Dey put de lash on dem, but dey never put no jail on dem. I seed some slaves in chains and I heared of one massa what had de place in de fence with de hole cut out for de nigger's neck. Dey hist up de board and de nigger put he head through de hole and den dey beat him with a lash with holes bored in it and every hole raise de blister. Den he bus' dem blisters with de handsaw and dey put salt and pepper in de bucket water and 'noint dem blisters with de mop dip in de water. Dey do dat when dey in 'ticular bad humor, iffen de nigger ain't chop 'nough cotton or corn. Sometime a overseer kilt a nigger, and dey don't do nothin' to him 'cept make him pay for de nigger. But our massa good."

Louis Love, Texas

"I git ship one time. Dat time de overseer give me de breshin'. Dey have stocks dey put a man in. Dey put de man leg through de holes and shut it down. De man jus' lay dere and bawl."

Adeline Marshall, Texas

"Cap'n he a bad man, and he drivers hard, too, all de time whippin' and stroppin' de niggers to make dem work harder. Didn't make no difference to Cap'n how little you is, you goes out to de field mos' soon's you can walk. De drivers don't use de bullwhip on de little niggers, but dey plays de switch on us what sting de hide plenty. Sometimes dey puts a nigger in de stocks and leaves dem two or three days, don't give dem nothin' to eat or a drink of water, jes' leaves dem till dey mos' dead. Does dey die, jes' put dem in a box and dig a hole out back of de hoss lot and dump dem in and cover up. Ain't no preachin' service or nothin', but de poor nigger out he mis'ry, dat's all."

"Old Cap'n jes' hard on he niggers and I 'member one time dey strops old Beans what's so old he can't work good no more, and in de mornin' dey finds him hangin' from a tree back of de quarters. He done hang himself to 'scape he mis'ry!"

Susan Merritt, Texas

"Massa Watt didn't have no overseer, but he have a nigger driver what am jus' as bad. He carry a long whip 'round the neck and I's seed him tie niggers to a tree and cowhide 'em till the blood run down onto the ground. Sometimes the women gits slothful and not able to de their part but they makes 'em de it anyway. They digs a hole, 'bout body deep, and makes them women lie face down in it and beats 'em nearly to death. That nigger driver beat the chillen for not keepin' their cotton row up with the lead man. Sometimes he made niggers drag long chains while they works in the field and some of 'em run off, but they oughtn't to have done it, 'cause they chase 'em with hounds and nearly kilt 'em."

La San Mire, Texas

"The old master was mean—made slaves lie on the ground and whipped them. I never saw him whip my father. He often whipped my mother."

"I'd hide to keep from seeing this. I was afraid."

Why did he whip them?

"I do not remember. He did not have a prison, just 'coups de fault' [beatings]. But not one slave from our plantation tried to escape to the north that I can remember."

John Moore, Texas

"Dey have miggers in de fields in different squads, a hoe squad and a plow squad, and de overseer was pretty rapid. Iffen dey don' do de work dey buck dem down and whip dem. Dey tie dey hands and feet togedder and make 'em put de hands 'tween de kneew, and put a long stick 'tween de hands so dey can't pull 'em out, and den dey whip dem in good fashion."

Van Moore, Texas

"Iffen old Missy Cunningham ain't in heaven right now, den dere ain't none, 'cause she so good to us we all loved her. She never took de whip to us, but I heered my mammy say she knowed a slave woman what owned by Massa Ricksts, and she workin' in de field, and she heavy with de chile what not born yet, and she has to set down in de row to rest. She was havin' de misery and couldn't work good, and de boss man had a nigger dig a pit where her stomach fit in, and lay her down and tie her, so she can't squira 'round none, and flog her till she lose her mind. Yes, suh, dat de ruf, my mammy say she knowed dat woman a long time after dat, and she never right in de head 'gain."

Annie Osborne, Texas

"Old man Tom never give us no money and half 'nough clothes. I had one dress the year round, two lengths of cloth sewed together, and I didn't know nothin' 'bout playin' neither. If I made too much fuss they put me under the bed. My white folks didn't teach us nothin' 'cept how they could put the whip on us. I had to put on a knittin' of stockin's in the mornin' and and if I didn't git it out by night, Missy put the lash on me."

"My mammy was sceered of old Tom Bias as if he was a bear. She worked in the field all day and come in at night and help with the stock. After supper they made her spin cloth. Massa fed well 'nough, but made us wear our old lowel clothes till they most fell off us. We was treated jus' like animals, but some owners treated they stock better'n old Tom Bias handled my folks. I still got a scar over my right eye where he put me in the dark two months. We had a young cow and when she had her first calf they sent me to milk her, and she kicked me and run me round a li'l pine tree, fightin' and tryin' to hook me. Massa and missy standin' in the gate all the time, hollerin' to me to make the cow stand still. I got clost to her and she kicked me off the stool and I run to the gate, and massa grab me and hit me 'cross the eye with a leather strap and I couldn't see out my right eye for two months. He am dead now, but I's gwine tell the truth 'bout the way we was treated."

Horace Overstreet, Texas

"Dat old plantation must have been 'bout 200 acres or even mo', and 'bout 500 head of slaves to work it. Massa Hall, he big lawyer and bought more niggers every year. He kap' a everseer what was white and a nigger driver. Sometime dey whip de slaves for what dey call disbedjonce. Dey tie 'em down and whip 'em. But I was raise' 'round de house, 'cause I a fav'rite nigger."

Lee Pierce, Texas

"Marse Fowler worked 'bout a hundred and fifty acres of land and had sev'ral cullud families. He done overseeing hisself, but had a black man for foreman. I seed plenty niggers whopped for not doin' dey tasks. He'd whop 'em for not pickin' so many hundreds of cotton a day, buckle 'em down hawg fashion and whop 'em with a strap. Us never stopped work no day, lessen Sunday, and not then iffen grass in de field or crops sufferin'."

Betty Powers, Texas

"Mammy and pappy and us twelve chillen lives in one cabin, so mammy has to cook for fourteen people, 'sides her field work. She am up way befo' daylight fixin' breakfast and supper after dark, with de pine knot torch to make de light. She cook on de fireplace in winter and in de yard in summer. All de rations measure out Sunday mornin' and it have to do for de week. It am not 'nough for heavy eaters and we has to be real careful or we goes hongry. We has meat and cornmeal and 'leases and 'taters and peas and beans and milk. Dem short rations causes plenty trouble, 'cause de niggers has to steal food and it am de whippin' if dey gits cotched. Dey am in a fix if dey can't work for bein' hongry, 'cause it am de whippin' den, sho', so dey has to steal, and most of 'em did and takes de whippin'. Dey has de full stomach, anyway."

"De massa and he wife am fine, but de overseer am tough, and he wife, too. Dat woman have no mercy. You see dem long ears I has? Dat's from de pullin' dey gits from her. De field hands works early and late and often all night. Pappy makes de shoes and mammy weaves, and you could hear de bump, bump of dat loom at night, when she done work in de field all day."

"Misay know everything what go on, 'cause she have de spies 'mongst de slaves. She purty good, though. Sometimes de overseer tie de nigger to a log and lash him with de whip. If de lash cut de skin, dey puts salt on it. We ain't 'low to go to church and has 'bout two parties a year, so dere ain't much fun. Lawd, Lawd, most dem slaves too tired to have fun noway. When all dat work am finish, dey's glad to git in de bed and sleep."

"Did we'uns have weddin's? White man, you knows better'n dat. Dem times, cullud folks am jus' put together. De massa say, 'Jim and Nancy, you go live together,' and when dat order give, it better be done. Dey thinks nothin' on de plantation 'bout de feelin's of de women and dere ain't no 'spect for dem. De overseer and white mens took 'vantage of de women like dey wants to. De woman better not make no fuss 'bout sich. If she do, it am de whippin' for her. I sho' thanks de Lawd surrender done come befo' I's old 'nough to have to stand for sich. Yes, sar, surrender saves dis nigger from sich."

Mary Reynolds, Texas

"Slavery was the worst days was ever seed in the world. They was things past tellin', but I got the scars on my old body to show to this day. I seed worse than what happened to me. I seed them put the men and women in the stock with they hands screwed down through holes in the board and they feets tied together and they naked behinds to the world. Solomon the overseer beat them with a big whip and massa look on. The niggers better not stop in the fields when they hear them yellin'. They cut the flesh most to the bones and some they was when they taken them out of stock and put them on the beds, they never got up again."

"We was scart of Solomon and his whip, though, and he didn't like frolickin'. He didn't like for us niggers to pray, either. We never heared of no church, but us have prayin' in the cabins. We'd set on the floor and pray with our heads down low and sing low, but if Solomon heared he'd come and beat on the wall with the stock of his whip. He'd say, 'I'll come in there and tear the hide off you backs.' But some the old niggers tell us we got to pray to Gawd that he don't think different of the blacks and the whites. I know that Solomon is burnin' in hell today, and it pleasures me to know it."

"Seems like after I got bigger. I member' more'n more niggers run away. They's most allus cotched. Massa used to hire out his niggers for wage hands. One time he hired me and a nigger boy, Turner, to work for some ornery white trash name of Kidd. One day Turner goes off and don't come back. Old man Kidd say I knowed 'bout it, and he tied my wrists together and stripped me. He hanged me by the wrists from a limb on a tree and spraddled my legs round the trunk and tied my feet together. Then he beat me. He heat me worser than I ever been beat before and I faints dead away. When I come to I'm in bed. I didn't dere so much iffen I died."

"I didn't know 'bout the passin' of time, but Miss Sara come to me. Some mite folks done it word to her. Mr. Kidd tries to talk hisself out of it, but Miss Sara fotches me home when I'm well 'nough to move. She took me in a cart and my maw takes care of me. Massa looks me over good and says I'll git well, but I'm ruin for breedin' chillun."

Martin Ruffin, Texas

"The overseer was named Charley and there was one driver to see everyone done his task. If he didn't, they fixed him up. Them what fed the stock got up at three and the overseer would tap a bell so many times to make 'em git up. The rest got up at four and worked till good dark. They'd give us a hundred lashes for not doing our task. The overseer put five men on you; one on each hand, one on each foot, and one to hold your head down to the ground. You couldn't do anything but wiggle. The blood would fly 'fore they was through with you."

"When I's a li'l fellow, I seed niggers whipped in the field. Sometimes they'd take 'em behind the big corn crib and fix 'em up."

Martin Ruffin. (Library of Congress)

Aaron Russel, Texas

"Massa have special place in woods where he have meanes' niggers whip. He never whip much, but wartime comin' on. Some de growed ones runs away to dem Yankees. He have to whip some den. He have stocks to put dey neck in when he whip dem. Massa never chain he slaves. I seed talkin' parrots. Massa didn't have one, but other massas did. Dat parrot talk. He tell when de nigger run away or when he not work."

Hannah Scott, Texas

"When I gits bigger, de overseer puts me in de field with de rest. Marse Bat grow mostly cotton and it don't make no dif'ence is you big or li'l, you better keep up or de drivers burn you up with de whip, sho' 'nough. Old Marse Bat never put a lick on me all de years I 'longs to him, but de drivers sho' burnt me plenty times. Sometime I gits so tired come night, I draps right in de row and gone to sleep. Den de driver come 'long and, wham, dey cuts you 'cross de back with de whip and you wakes up when it lights on you, yes, suh! 'Bout nine o'clock dey hollers 'cotton up' and dat de quittin' signal. We goes to de quarters and jes' drap on de bunk and go to sleep without nothin' to eat."

Abram Sells, Texas

"The li'l folks slep' mos' as long as they want to in daylight, but the big niggers have to come out'n that bed 'bout fo' o'clock when the big horn blow. The overseer have one nigger, he wake up early for to blow the horn and when he blow this horn he make sich a holler then all the res' of the niggers better git out'a that bed and 'pear at the barn 'bout daylight. He might not whip him for being late the fus' time, but that nigger better not forgit the secon' time and be late!"

"Massa Rimes didn't whip them much, but iffen they was bad niggers he jes' sold them offen the place and let somebody else do the whippin'."

George Selman, Texas

"I never seen runaway slaves, but Marster Tom had a neighbor mean to slaves and sometimes when they was whipped we could hear 'em holler. The neighbor had one slave called Sallie, and she was a weaver and was so mean she had to wear a chain."

Ben Simpson, Texas

"But what I'se fixin to tell you was when [Massa Earl Stielszen] gets in to trouble there in Georgia. He got him two good stopping horses, and has him covered wagon then he chaines all the slaves he have around the necks and fastens to the horses and makes all the slaves walk same way and that was sister Emma and she had to walk some time all she get to ride was the couplin pole that come out behind the wagen bed about three feet. Somewhere on the road it went to snowing, and master would not let us have shoes or anything to wrap around our feet, and then we had to sleep on the ground in all that snow. Boss, he had great long whip platted out of raw hide, and when one of the negro begins to fall behind or give out, he would hit him with that whip. And he would take all the hide every time master hit a negro. Mother, she give out on the way some where about the line of Texas. Her feet got raw and bleeding and her legs swell plum out of shape. Then master he just take out his gun and shot her and while she was dying he kick her two or three times and say dam a negro that couldnt stand anything. He didnt need them anyway, cause he could get plenty more when he gets us boss, you know that man. Wouldnt bury mother just left her laying where he shot her at. He come plum to Austin Texas through that snow. Boss you know that time they wasnt any law against killing negro slaves. After he got to Austin he take up farm and changes his name to Alex Simpson."

Millie Ann Smith, Texas

"Master had an overseer and a 'Nigger-driver' named Jacob Green, but he 'lowed no one to whip one of his Niggers but his-self. If one was hard to control he was tied to a tree. Some of the bosses tied them down 'cross a barrell and beat them might nigh to death. I give justice to Master Trammell, he didn't do nothing like that, but allus call us up and talk to us and then whip us right. Master didn't have no chil'ren of his own. It was the white fo'ks that had a pacel of chil'ren that was so hard on them, and worked them nearly to death. Them what had a bunch of chil'ren would cuse the 'Niggers' of doing something to them so they could whip them."

Millie Ann Smith. (Library of Congress)

Tucker Smith, Texas

"Yes sir, we were whipped if we were sassy or stubborn or if we did not exactly work like Maser thought we should. Maser he was pretty rough on the slaves if he did not think they were doing like he thought they ought to do. The overseer he sure enough was hard on us slaves when Maser was gone. I'se seen him get pretty rough on one slave that Maser had there on the plantation, I'se believes he really had it in for that slave, it seemed that way sure enough. He tied that slave's hands around a tree and whipped him one time unmerciful, then again he tied his hands together up over a limb and whipped him again another time until that poor negro could not hardly walk, and all that slave done was slow about his work, as he would be scared of the overseer and he would try to get in a hurry and not do his job right and the overseer would be right on him with that cat-o-nine tails. Yes sir, all us slaves were afraid of that overseer as he would just soon kill a negro as not, cause they did not cost him one cent and he did not care what he done to us negroes or how he treated us cause he did not think that we would ever be free and that we might cause him plenty of trouble some day. They were some of the slaves that would have done him a lot of damage if they could have. Well no sir, we did not exactly have a jail there on the ranch for the slaves but Maser he always had a place where he could take care of the unruly negroes. He could just stake them out somewhere till they would behave themselves."

"Yes sir, I'se seen Maser chain slaves to a tree and left them there a week at a time cause they would get unruly. You asked me while ago about jail there fore us, that was his jail, a good heavy chain and lock, that was a pretty severe punishment to some of us slaves. He chained me one time and left me one whole week cause I just let a horse that he was trying to break get a loose and it took us several days before we could capture him again. Boss that was the longest week that I ever spent in my whole life and all he would give me to eat was just cornbread and water twice a day."

Leithean Spinks, Texas

"Ise see de whuppin's. 'Twarnt given in private but am public so allus niggers could see it, an' dat makes de 'pression on our minds. 'Twas a cullud fellow gits catched w'en he run off. W'en dey ties him down to de log, dey gives him 20 lashes. W'en dey let him up, he starts runnin' 'way 'gain. De overseer pulls his pistol, an' lets him have it. Down goes de nigger. W'en dey gits to him, blood am runnin' in a stream. Dey looks him over, an' 'twas de bottom of his right ear shot off. Dat nigger never tries to run off 'gain."

Bert Strong, Texas

"They was a overseer a while, but massa fires him for cuttin' and slashin' he niggers. He made my uncle Freeman overlooker. We is heared slaves on

Bert Strong. (Library of Congress)

farms close by hollerin' when they git beat. Some the neighbors works they hands till ten at night and weighed the last weighin' by candles. If the day's pickin' wasn't good 'nough, they beat them till it a pity."

Mariah Snyder, Texas

"Missy was name Patsy and she was purty good, and Massa Sam was purty good, too. He'd whip us if we needed it. He'd pull of our clothes and whip in the field. But he wouldn't 'low the driver to whip us if we didn't need it. No, sar. And he wouldn't have no patterrollers on the place."

"I seed plenty niggers whipped while I driv that gin. They tied the feets and hands and rawhided 'em good. They tied a bell on one woman what run away all the time. They locks it round her head."

Allen Thomas, Texas

"I walk in blood up to my ankle w'ere it come up to here on my foot. I's walk over many a dead pusson. De reason dey beat 'em 'cause dey wouldn' wuk."

Allen Thomas. (Library of Congress)

William Thomas, Texas

"He whipped me with a dogwood switch, but he never did bring no blood. He thought a heap of us, but I guess I thought I was a man and my mother said, 'He needed to whip you, you talk so sassy.' But it taken seven men to whip my father. When one couldn't whip you they would go and get two or three to whip you, but he never did do that to me. He was pretty good to me after all. One time when he whipped me I told him if I ever lived to be a man he never could whip me again. He said, 'You mustn't talk to your master like that.' He was pretty good to me, after all. But some of them was awful good."

Penny Thompson, Texas

"As for de whappin,' dere wasn't any on massa's place. Him have only one nigger what am unruly and dat am Bill McClure, and a bigger thief never lived."

"On de nex' plantation dey gives de whuppin' and we hears dem niggers beller. On dat plantation dey trades and sells de niggers all de time and de speculation wagon comes by often. Sometime it am awful to see de babies sold from de mothers and de wife from de husban'. Sich bemoanin' at some of dem sales, yous jus' can't 'magine."

Albert Todd, Texas

"There was one white man near us who would get a new set of niggers every year. He said, if they didn't die, there wasn't any good work left in them anyhow. He would cut off a ear so he would know them if they runs off."

Joe Vaughn, Georgia

Joe Vaughn, ex-slave, is 76 years old. His father belonged to Joe Vaughn of Monroe County, who lived near Forsyth. "Mr. Vaughn was a farmer and a good master." Joe said he was a small boy at the close of the war, but he could recall many things his parents told him. Ellen Vaughn, his mother, belonged to Mickleberry Merritt. She died four years ago at the age of 97.

She told Joe that her master was very mean to them. He whipped them with a long leather whip, such as they drive mules and oxen with. The whip had a cracker on the end of it, which Mr. Merritt liked to hear snap. If it broke or came off, he hitched up his horse and went to town to get another so that he might hear it crack when he whipped the negroes. He had overseers, and they were allowed to whip the negroes. Ellen, with the other women, had to be in the fields so early in the day that they couldn't see to plow. Certain tasks were set, such as a certain number of pounds of cotton to be picked by each negro. If they fell short of the amount, Merritt's overseers whipped them."

John Walton, Texas

"I had to do field work. Us slaves had to do a certain amount of tasks a day. Even us kids had to pick 150 pounds of cotton a day… or we got a whoopin'. We picked cotton and put it into laghe and small white-oak baskets. Some of dem baskets would hold more'n a hunnert pounds of cotton. It was accordin' to de way yo' stamped de cotton in. A wagon wid a yoke of oxen hitched to it was standin' in de field ready fo' us to pour our cotton in. When de wagon was full de oxen pulled de wagon to de hoss-power gin. We ginerally used about 1,600 pounds of cotton to make a bale. Soon after Mawster Walton opened his fahm he died. Mistress Walton den married a captain or Dr. Richardson. Mawster Walton didn't never allow no overseer on his place but Dr. Richardson did. Dis overseer got putty rough wid us. Durin' de cotton hoein' time, de overseer wanted all of us—dat is de biggest ones—to stay right in line and chop along. We had to keep up wid one another. And if we didn't we jes' got de bull-whoop. De overseer would ride up and hit us over de back if we didn't do our job right. At times de overseer would git off'n his hoss, have two other slaves hold another one down and give him de bull-whoop. They'd give it to him, too."

Rhodus Walton, Georgia

His master was a very cruel man whose favorite form of punishment was to take a man (or woman) to the edge of the plantation where a rail fence was located. His head was then placed between the two rails so that escape was impossible and he was whipped until the overseer was exhausted. This heartless form of punishment was an almost daily occurrence, which was administered on the slightest provocation.

Sol Walton, Texas

"Master allus blowed a horn at four o'clock and you'd better be ready to gwye [go]. The hands worked from sun to sun, and if the overseer see them slacking up on their work he stormed out at them, cussed [cursed] them and sometimes whacked them with a bull whip. I'se seed Niggers whipped till their shirt stuck to their back till it took salt water to get it loose. I seed my mother whipped for shouting at the white fo'ks meeting. Old Master stripped her clothes down to her waist and whipped her with a bull whip. Heaps of them was whipped just cause they could be whipped. Some of the owners half fed their hands and then whipped them for begging for grub."

"My Master never had but one white overseer. He got kilt [killed] fighting. The hands was burning logs and trash and the overseer knocked an old man down and made some of the other Niggers hold him while he bull-whipped him. The old man got up and picked up a stick and knocked him in the head and then took a ax and cut off his hands and feet. Master said he didn't ever want another white overseer, and made my cousin 'overlooker' after that."

Rosa Washington, Texas

"I seed niggers put in stocks, put 'em in stocks hand in fust. Tear their clothes off backs, whop till sores come, den dey pour coal oil and turpentine in sores. I see det with my own eyes."

Dianah Watson, Texas

"But the oldes' boy, William, got the debbil in him and hires a overseer, and he rid in the fields with a quirt and rope and chair on his saddle. When he done take a notion to whip a nigger, he'd make some the men tie that nigger to the chair and beat him somethin' scand'lous. He got mad at my mother's sister, Aunt Susie Ann, and beat her till the blood run off her on the ground. She fall at his feets like she passed out and he put up the whip and she trips him and gits the whip and whips him till he couldn't stand up. Then some the niggers throwed him off a cliff and broke his neck. His folks gits the sheriff but master's boys orders him off the place with a gun. There warn't no more overseers on the place after that."

"If the Niggers of now days had seed what I seed in slavery time, they would pray and thank their God every day. My Master's place sot right cross a big road from a place where they cut and slashed their Niggers. You could hear that man's black folks bellowing like cows. I didn't go over there. I'se stood many times on our front porch and seed them cut and slash the blood out of them till it run off on the ground. I'se seed ole wimmen, half bent from beatings, gwyning to the field. The overseer rode a horse and carried a chair behind his saddle. On the saddle horn he kept a tie rope, a raw-hide quirt, and a wooden paddle with nails in it. I'se seed them take them ole half bent wimmen and beat them till they couldn't walk for three days. I used to say to my Mistress, 'Why are they cutting and slashing them black folks that-a-way?' She say, 'Dianah, that white man has got the devil in him.'"

Adeline White, Texas

"I was 'bout eight year' ol' w'en freedom come. I was bo'n at Op'lousas. My marster and mistus was Doctor and Missus Bridget. Dey was mean. Dey beat us and put houn's atter us. Dey done dat for meanness I guess. Dey beat de li'l ones and de big ones. W'en marster ain't beat 'em he mek his wife beat 'em. I don' see nuttin' else. He had a plantation, it was a pritty big plantation wid lots of slaves. It was 'bout nine mile' from Op'lousas and I guess it was nor'f."

"Yessir, ol' marster sho' whip' us. He mean—awful mean. W'en he whip' 'em he put 'em 'cross a barrel. Sometime' he chain' 'em and stake 'em out to grass wid a rope. Dey didn' give de cullud folks anyt'ing to eat. He sho' treat' de cullud folks mean in slav'ry."

Jack White, Texas

"Though Marster was a Mef'dis' preacher, he whip' his slaves, an' den drap pitch an' tuppentine on dem from a bu'nin' to'ch."

Mingo White, Alabama

"De white folks was hard on us. Dey would whup us 'bout de leas' li'l thang. Hit wouldn't a been so bad iffen us had a had comforts, but to live lack us did was 'nouf to make anybody soon as be dead. De white folks tol' us born to work for 'am an' dat us was doin' fine at dat."

"Hit was hard back in dem days. Ever' mornin' fo' day break you had to be up an' ready to git to de fiel'. Hit was de same ever' day in de year 'cep' on Sunday, an' den we was gitten' up earlier dan the folks do now on Monday. De drivers was hard too. Dey could say what ever dey wanted to an' you couldn't say nothin' for yourse'f. Somehow or yuther us had a instinct dat we was goin' to be free. In de event when de day's wuk was done de slaves would be foun' lock in dere cabin prayin' for de Lawd to free dem lack he did de chillun of Is'ael. Iffen dey didn't lock up, de Marsa or de driver would of heard 'em an' whupped 'em. De slaves had a way of puttin' a wash pot in de do' of de cabin to keep de soun' in de house. I 'member once ol' Ned White was caught prayin'. De drivers took him de nex' day' an' carried him to de pegs, what was fo' stakes drove in de groun'. Ned was made to pull off ever'thang but his pants an' lay on his stomach 'tween de pegs whilst some-body stropped his legs an' arms to de pegs. Den dey whupped him 'twell de blood run from him lack he was a hog. Dey made all of de han's come an' see it, an' dey said us'd git de same thang if us was cotched. Dey don't 'low a man to whup a horse lack dey whupped us in dem days."

Lou (Granny) Williams, Texas

"All de slaves wasn't so lucky as we was though. We lived close to de meanest owner in de country. Our Massa wouldn't keep no over-seers 'cause he say his niggers wasn't dogs, but dis other man, he keeps over-seers to beat de niggers and he had a big leather bull whip with lead in de end and he beats some of de slaves to death. We could hear dem holler and holler 'til dey couldn't holler no mo' den dey jes' sorta grunt every lick 'til dey die. We could find big streams of blood where he had whooped dem and when it rained de whole top of de groun' jes' looked like a river of blood dere. Sometimes he bury his niggers and sometime de law comes out and makes him bury dem. He put dem in chains and stockades and sometimes he would buck and gag dem. We could see his niggers goin' by our plantation with der oven on der heads around 3 o'clock in de mornin' on der way to de fields. Dose ovens was made of wood and tin over a tin cap dat fits de slaves' head. Each nigger would have his bread and some old hairy bone meat a cookin' with fire coals in dese ovens as he went to work. Dey was made so as not to burn der heads and when dey got to de fields dey would set dem down to finish cookin' while dey worked 'til breakfast time. De mothers what was expectin' babies was whooped to make 'em work faster and when any babies was sick de mothers would have to put dem in a basket on top of der heads and take dem to de cotton patch and put dem under de cotton stalks and try to 'tend to dem. Lawd, Lawd, honey! dem was awful times, but I sho' is glad I had good white folks."

Rose Williams, Texas

"And dey was in de field fore sun up and works til after sun down, and if you wants a licken jest fool roun likes dey do now, er gets sacy when you is tole ter do a little more. But marster George didnt have but two whipped while I was with him, and one of dem got a little cross with de drivah, de other lied bout feeden de pigs; he feeds dem bout half what he sposed to one night cause he didn't want ter shell so much co'n. Dey jest ties der hands ter gether and above der heads ter a pole and de drivah hits dem with a cat o'nine tails but he didn't whip dem as hard as some de others round there, but jest a few licks wid dis cat-o-nine tails was hurtin bad nuff when you was turned lose."

Stephen Williams, Texas

"But all the colored folks wasn't treated like us, no suh. The slaves what worked the plantations were driven jes' like mules, and when a colored girl get 'bout 12 years old, she mighty liable to get mistreated by some low-down overseer. If her folks make a fuss 'bout it, the owner don't pay no 'tention to 'em, and they jes' bring on trouble for themselves and get whipped or mebbe worse."

"I mind the time I see six slaves hung by the sheriff there in Alexandria, 'cause they had killed a overseer what had mistreated their families."

"Do I rec'lec' right, these folks what was hung belong to Mr. Thomas what had a plantation. The overseer on the place had been taking the young colored girls of these folks and mistreating 'em. So one night they slip out and catch de overseer and kill him and tie a plowshare to the body to weigh it down and throw him in the river. But somebody see 'em and they is caught and hung, jes' for trying to pertect their own children. The law was jes' for white folks, and colored folks didn't have no rights at all, jes' do what they were told or get whipped or sold off away from their folks or mebbe killed even."

Sampson Willis, Texas

"I've seed a good many slave whipped the unruly ones. Most generally take off their shirts, sometimes Marster would make them stretch out with a man on each side of them with a piece of raw hide. I've seed the dogs running the slaves too, but Mr. Philco Guinn, a white man, had one nigger that the dogs wouldn't run. His name was Calvin Philco. Don't know why the dogs just naturally wouldn't run that nigger."

President Wilson, Texas

"My master never whipped the slaves, but he had a overseer named Bill Ditto who whip them. When he would whip a slave he would say, 'Don't thank me for this. Thank your master.' So I reckon by that de master had him whip us. When my father wuz whipped he would run away and hide in the river bottom. I seen them bring him several times. If dey whipped when dey brought him in, he would run away ag'in, but if dey didn' whip him, he would stay awhile, maby a year."

Willis Winn, Texas

"I'se seed many Niggers whipped on a 'buck and gag' bench. You don't know what that is, do you? They buckle you down hard and fast on a long bench, gag your mouth with cotton, and when Master got through laying on that cowhide the blood was running off on the ground. Next morning after he whip you, he come around to the quarters when you get up and say, 'Boy, how is you feeling?' No matter how sore you is, you'd better jump and kick your heels and show how lively you is. Master hated me to his dying day cause I told Mistress 'bout him whipping a girl scandously in the fiel' cause she wanted to go to the house to her sick baby. Mistress Callie didn't whip us, but she twist our nose and ears nearly off. Them fingers felt like a pair of pinchers [plyers]. She stropped on her guns and rode a big bay horse to the fiel'. She wouldn't let Master whip us."

Rube Witt, Texas

"My Mistress was name Kate, and had two chil'ren, Edward and Lucy. The Witts had a good set of Niggers. Sometime he giv' us a light brushing for piddling 'round at work. I's seed plenty of Niggers whipped on ole man Ruff Perry and Pratt Hughes places. They was death on them. Lawyer Marshall used to whip his Niggers goin' and comin' every day that come round."

Willis Woodson, Texas

"I never did see no niggers whipped, but I done see dat whip hangin' in de barn. It a big, long thing, lots bigger'n a horsewhip, and I know it must have been used, 'cause it all wore out at one end."

Litt Young, Texas

"When that big bell rang at four o'clock in the mo'ning, you'd better rise, cause the overseer was standing there with a whipping strap if you was late. My daddy got a whipping most every mo'ning for oversleeping. Them mules was standing in the fiel' at daylight waiting to see how to plow a straight furrow. The overseer whipped us for not getting our task. Every Nigger had so much cotton to pick a day, 'cording to what he picked the first week of picking. If a Nigger was a 500 pound picker and didn't weigh up that much at night, that was not getting his task. The last weighing was done by lighting a candle to see the scales. Some of them was whipped scandously for running off."

Mary Young, Texas

"Master and his mistress they was young and fiery, but they was durn good to their black folks. Master he have about 30 acres in his farm. He growed tobacco. He have six grown slaves and I'se just about grown. Master he wake the slaves bout 4 o'clock every morning and they work just long as they could see how. Oh, yes, they whip the slave when they get unruly just like you do mule. He would hit him 39 lick that is just how the patter roller would get them."

"Yes sir, master he have jail on his farm for slave, when whipping wouldnt do good. It was about high enough for him to stand good but he couldnt lay down he could sit down. He put him in there the first three days without anything to eat, but little piece of bread and water that would make good negro out most slaves."

Teshan Young, Texas

"But de Marster makes de cullud fo'ks wo'k an' whups dem w'en dey don' an' w'en dey gits bad an' don' mine de o'dahs. Ise membah one slave dat gits whupped so bad hims neber gits up, hims died. We uns chilluns would go roun' whar hims was an' look at 'im. De Marster lets we uns do dat. Ise guess, fo' to larn we uns dat 'tis bes' fo' to mine. Yes sar, dey whupped pow'ful hahd sometimes. My mammy gits whupped one time 'cause she come f'om de field fo' to nuss her baby, an' once fo' de 'cause she don' keep up her row. My pappy gits shoot in de shoulder by de obersee', 'cause hims runs f'om de whuppin'. 'Twas dis way, de obersee' sez: 'Come hyar, Ise gwine whup you fo' not doin' de wo'k lak Ise sez.' Dere was a fence dere an' my pappy runs fo' dat an' am crawlin' ober it w'en de obersee' shoots. Some ob de shots hit 'im in da shoulda but 'twant bad; him get ober dat in a s'ort w'ile."

Teshan Young. (Library of Congress)

PUNISHING DOMESTIC WORKERS

Working regularly for the slaveholder family in and near their home did not necessarily provide better working conditions for the enslaved. Family members both young and old were often temperamental and difficult bosses. They could be as cruel and mean spirited as an overseer in the fields. Like their male counterparts, women enslavers demanded compliance and productivity of their enslaved workers and punished workers when they thought it necessary. Domestic servants suffered whippings and other abuse as frequently as did field workers. Working inside did not protect them from mistreatment or physical abuse. It was the lot of all enslaved workers.

Because working in or near the home of the slaveholder family forced close physical interaction between the enslaved and their enslavers, it could have positive or negative consequences for the servant. In some instances the personal bond served to mitigate the severity of the punishment one might suffer. The slaveholder needed to reaffirm his or her authority, but not in a devastating way. The punishment given would be more perfunctory than damaging. This was the case for Georgian Amanda McDaniel, for whom corporal punishment was a rarity: "Whippings were very uncommon on the Hale plantation. Sometimes Mr. Hale had to resort to this form of punishment for disobedience on the part of some of the servants. Mrs. McDaniel says that she was whipped many times but only once with the cowhide. Nearly every time that she was whipped a switch was used. She has seen her mother as well as some of the others punished but they were never beaten unmercifully." McDaniel did not avoid punishments altogether, but her situation was better than the challenges faced by other enslaved servants.

More often proximity made the enslaved more vulnerable to the moodiness of the person for whom they worked. Repercussions might result if they did not perform a task in the manner in which it was expected, did not show appropriate deference, or just found themselves in the wrong place at the wrong time. The punishment might vary greatly depending on what the slaveholder had available at the time. In Georgia, William McWhorter's mother was beaten over the head with a stick when she fell asleep while holding her enslaver's baby late one night. In Texas, Willis Winn's Mistress Callie did not beat him but violently twisted his nose or ears with pincher-like fingers when she was not pleased.

Although painful, such impulsive actions were over quickly. More often, however, the abuse suffered by servants rivaled the painful punishment given to field workers. Extended sessions of 50 or more lashes were not unusual. As Fannie Griffin of South Carolina recalls, her mistress, Missy Grace, "was mean to us. She whip us a heap of times when we ain't done nothing bad to be whip for. When she go to whip me, she tie my wrists together wid a rope and put that rope thru a big staple in de ceiling and draw me up off de floor and give me a hundred lashes. I think 'bout my old mammy heap of times now and how I's seen her whipped, wid de blood dripping off of her."

Mistreatment by Female Enslavers

As was evident from the experiences of Fannie Griffin, working for the woman of the house did not shield enslaved workers from abuse. Female slaveholders also sought to assert control and were not hesitant to mete out punishment as they saw fit. This impulse was not necessarily confined to the matriarch of the family. Agatha Babino of Texas discovered this when the daughter of the household attacked her: "Young miss come home from college. She slap my face. She want to beat me. Mama say to beat her, so dey did. She took de beatin' for me." What prompted this aggressiveness is not clear, but the college student believed she had the right to strike and abuse Babino if she so pleased.

Sometimes there was a deeper reason for the mistreatment on the part of the wife of the family. In Georgia, the abuse of Julia Rush sprang from her mistress's inability to control her own husband:

> When Colonel De Binion's wife died he divided his slaves among the children.
> Mrs. Rush was given to her former playmate to who was at the time married and

Woman whips an enslaved woman. (Corbis)

living in Carrollton, Georgia. She was very mean and often punished her by beating her on her forearm for the slightest offense. At other times she made her husband whip her [Mrs. Rush] on her bare back with a cowhide whip. Mrs. Rush says that her young mistress thought that her husband was being intimate with her and so she constantly beat and mistrusted her. On one occasion all of the hair on her head (which was long and straight) was cut from her head by the young mistress.

Even though Julia was either not guilty of the wife's suspicions or an innocent victim of the husband, there was nothing she could do to protect herself. She became the outlet for the frustrations of an unhappy spouse. Gender was no predictor of the treatment an enslaved person might receive. Authority and power were important for enslavers to maintain under slavery and both men and women exerted their control when they thought it necessary.

NARRATIVES

Victoria Adams, South Carolina

"De massa and missus was good to me but sometime I was so bad they had to whip me. I 'members she used to whip me every time she tell me to do something and I take too long to move 'long and do it. One time my missus went off on a visit and left me at home. When she come back, Sally told her that I put on a pair of Bubber's pants and scrub de floor wid them on. Missus told me it was a sin for me to put on a man's pants, and she whip me pretty bad. She say it's in de Bible dat: 'A man shall not put on a woman's clothes, nor a woman put on a man's clothes.' I ain't never see that in de Bible though, but from then 'til now, I ain't put on no more pants."

"De grown-up slaves was punished sometime too. When they didn't feel like taking a whippin' they went off in de woods and stay 'til massa's hounds track them down; then they'd bring them out and whip them. They might as well not run away. Some of them never come back a-tall, don't know what become of them."

Andy Anderson, Texas

"I's git one whuppin' while on de W.T. House place. De scahs am on my ahms, see thar, an' on my back too. Dem I's will carry to my grave. De whuppin' I's git am fo' de cause as I's will 'splain. 'Twas dis away; De overseer sent me fo' de dry fiah wood. W'en I's gits de wood loaded an' stahts to drive, de wheel hits a sho't stump, de team jerks an' dat breaks de whippletree. I's tries to fix dat so dat de load could be hauled in. I's delayed quite a spell while de cook am waitin' fo' de wood. Aftah I's tries an' tries, it am necessary fo' me to walk to de bahn fo' anudder whippletree. De overseer am at de bahn w'en I's gits dere. He am gittin' ready to staht aftah me. I's tell w'at am de delay. He am powe'ful mad 'cause I's hit de stump an' sich."

"De overseer ties me to de stake an' ever' ha'f hour, fo' fouah hours, deys lay 10 lashes on my back. Fo' de fust couple ob hours, de pain am awful. I's never fo'git it. Aftah I's stood dat fo' a couple ob hours, I's could not feel de pain so much an' w'en dey took me loose, I's jus' ha'f dead. I's could not feel de lash 'cause my body am numb, an' my mind am numb. De last thing I's 'membahs am dat I's wishin' fo' death. I's laid in de bunk fo' two days gittin' over dat whuppin'. Dat is, gittin' over it in de body but not in de heart. No Sar! I's have dat in my heart 'til dis day."

"Aftah dat whuppin', I's don't have my heart in de wo'k fo' de Marster. If I's see some cattle in de co'n field, I's tu'n my back 'stead ob chasin' dem out. I's guess de Marster sees dat I's not to be d'pended on an' dat's m'ybe de reason he sol' me to his brothah, John."

Mary Anderson, North Carolina

"Marster had three children, one boy named Dallas, and two girls, Bettie and Carrie. He would not allow slave children to call his children marster and missus unless the slave said little marster or little missus. He had four white overseers but they were not allowed to whip a slave. If there was any whipping to be done he always said he would do it. He didn't believe in whipping so when a slave got so bad he could not manage him he sold him."

"Marster didn't quarrel with anybody, missus would not speak short to a slave, but both missus and marster taught slaves to be obedient in a nice quiet way."

Mary Armstrong, Texas

"You see when I was born, my mamma belong to old Wm. Cleveland an' old Polly Cleveland, an' they was the meanest two white folks what ever lived, 'cause they was always beatin' on their slaves. I know 'cause mamma told me, an' I hear about it other places, an' besides, old Polly—she was a Polly devil if there ever was one—whipped my little sister what was only 9 months old an' jes' a little baby, to death. She came an' took the diaper off my little sister an' whipped 'til the blood jes' ran jes' cause she cry like all babies do an' it killed my sister. I never forgot that, but I got some even with that old Polly devil, 'cause when I was about 10 years old I belonged to Mis' Olivia, what was their daughter, an' one day old Polly devil come to where Mis' Olivia lived after she got married, an' tried to give me a lick out in the yard, an' I picked up a rock 'bout as big as half your fist an' hit her right in the eye an' busted the eyeball an' told her that was for whippin' my baby sister to death. You could hear her holler for five miles, but Mis' Olivia when I told her, say,

Mary Armstrong. (Library of Congress)

'Well, I guess mamma has learnt her lesson at last'.' But she was mean like old Cleveland 'til she die, an' I hopes they is burnin' in torment now."

Smith Austin, Texas

"Old Marster was bad. He beat his slaves till dey bleed. Sometime he rub salt and pepper and grease where dey been beat. Sometime he tie dey feet and dey hands. One time I was sweeping de yard and young mistus jist come back from college. I had one aunt what run 'way 'cause dey whip her so much. Dey found her and brung her back and beat her. We didn't have no dogs but dere was some in de neighborhood what had 'em and dey lend 'em to other men what didn't have none."

Agatha Babino, Texas

"Old Marse bad. He beat us till we bleed. He rub salt and pepper in."

"My aunt run off 'cause dey beat her so much. Dey brung her back and beat her some more."

Charlie Barbour, North Carolina

"I can 'member, do' I wuz small, dat de slaves wuz whupped fer disobeyin' an' I can think of seberal dat I got. I wuz doin' housewuck at de time an' one of de silber knives got misplaced. Dey' cused me of misplacin' it on purpose, so I got de wust beatin' dat I eber had. I wuz beat den till de hide wuz busted hyar an' dar."

Lucy Barnes, Texas

"I knows all about how hard dey were on de niggers. I'se seen 'em staked out in the boiling sun an' whipped with cows' hides. My white fo'ks were hard on me! No'm, dey didn't treat me good. Didn't gib me nothin' to eat but co'n pone an' so'ghum 'lasses. I wuz nevah 'lowed to be with other niggers 'ceptin' my grandma."

"I 'members how my ole grandma had to git up in de dead hours ob de night an' put on de skillet an' cooks up food fo' de patter-olers when dey wuz out searchin' fo' run-'way niggers an' come to our house an' make her fix 'em sumpin' to eat. I'se seen patter-olers whup niggers 'til dey'd fall on de groun' an' beg fo' dey life."

John Belcher, Mississippi

"Effen you wuz caught off yo place at night without dat pass you wuz whipped. Dat wuz cause dey 'specked the niggars to be runnin away. My Boss had a cast iron cook stove he paid a hundred dollars fer and it was a show to all us case we cooked on our fireplaces and dat stove wuz something fine, too. I 'members hearin my Boss whippin and cussin dem womens that worked 'roun de house, case dey didn' keep dat stove clean."

Virginia Bell, Texas

"There was might little whippin' goin' on at our place 'cause Massa Lewis an' Mis' Mary treated us good. They wasn't no overseer goin' to whip 'cause Massa wouldn' low him to. Les' see, I don't rec'lec' more than two whippins' I see anyone get from Massa, an' that has been so long ago I don't rec'lec' what they was for."

Sallie Blakely, Alabama

Although Mr. and Mrs. Cobb were exceptionally kind to their own slaves, there were other masters who punished them unmercifully. Besides the whip there was another form of punishment known as branding. This practice is still known even today. If a man broke some rule he was branded on the jaw with a hot iron. Sometimes women visiting Mrs. Cobb would make remarks in order to get the slaves punished. Mrs. Blakely always worked in the house and often overheard visitors trying to influence her mistress. For instance, if a slave servant appeared wearing earrings or some other piece of cheap Jewelry, some one of them would make remarks about allowing the slaves to wear such things, etc. Mrs. Cobb very seldom paid them attention since the trinkets were always given to them by Mr. Cobb, who would bring them back as gifts after a business trip. It was not often that a master would punish a slave for killing another; but if a crime was committed against a white person they were punished severely. Mrs. Blakely remembers an occasion when two slave cousins quarrelled over a girl; one became so infuriated he picked up a rack and hit the other in the head killing him. He was not punished in spite of this fact, there was very little killing among the slaves.

Jacob Branch, Texas

"My po' mama. Eb'ry washday de ol' mistus give her a beatin'. She couldn' keep de flies from speckin' de clo's overnight. Ol' mistus git up soon in de mawnin', befo' mama have time git de specks off. Den she snort and say, 'Renee, soon's you git breakfas' and wash dem dishes I's gwineter teach you how to wash.' Den she beat her wid a cowhide. Look like she gwineter cut my po' mama in two. Many's de time I edge up and try to tek some dem licks off my mama."

Hattie Brown, Texas

"I was born near Woodville, Mississippi, March 8, 1822, er somewheres 'bout dat year. I don' 'member de name of my mahster. I'se so ol' I can't 'member things like I used to could. Use to I could tell you lots things 'bout de ol' slavery times, but it's jes' hard for me to 'member back that fur now. I 'member ol' mahster's wife wanted him to hang me 'cause she wanted my boy, and he tuk me out in de woods to hang me, but he conscience hurt him, and he said he wouldn' hang me 'cause he already nearly blind and he 'fraid de Lawd make him more blinder. I don' like to talk much of slavery times 'cause I wasn' treated ve'y well den."

Lewis Brown, Arkansas

"I was born in 1854 and 'co'se I wasn't big enough to work much in slavery times, but one thing I did do and that was tote watermelons for the overseer and pile 'em on the porch."

"I 'member he said if we dropped one and broke it, we'd have to stop right there and eat the whole thing. I know I broke one on purpose so I could eat it and I 'member he made me scrape the rind and drink the juice. I know I eat till I was tired of that watermelon."

"And then there was a lake old master told us to stay out of. If he caught you in it, he'd take you by the shirt collar and your heels and throw you back in."

"I know he nearly drowned me once."

Sarah Woods Burke, Ohio

"I remembers quite clearly are scene that happened jus' afore I left that there part of the country. At the slaveholders home on the plantation I was at it was customary for the white folks to go the church on Sunday morning and to leave the cook in charge. This cook had a habit of making cookies and handing them out to the slaves before the folks returned. Now it happened that on one Sunday for some reason or tother the white folks returned before the regular time and the poor cook did not have time to get the cookies to the slaves so she just hid them in a drawer that was in a swing chair."

"The white folks had a parrot that always sat on top of a door in this room and when the mistress came in the room the mean old bird hollered out at the top of his voice, 'Its in the rocker. It's in the rocker.' Well the Missus found the cookies and told her husband where upon the husband called his man that done the whipping and they tied the poor cook to the stake and whipped her till she fainted. Next morning the parrot was found dead and a slave was accused because he liked the woman that had been whipped the day before. They whipped him then until the blood ran down his lags."

Tempie Cummins, Texas

"Marster was rough. He take two beech switches and twist them together and whip 'em to a stub. Many's the time I's bled from them whippin's. Our old mistus, she try to be good to us, I reckon, but she was turrible lazy. She had two of us to wait on her and then she didn' treat us good."

Douglas Dorsey, Florida

Mrs. Matair being a very cruel woman, would whip the slaves herself for any misdemeanor. Dorsey recalls an incident that is hard to obliterate from his mind, it is as follows: Dorsey's mother was called by Mrs. Matair, not hearing her, she continued with her duties, suddenly Mrs. Matair burst out in a frenzy of anger over the woman not answering. Anna explained that she did not hear her call, thereupon Mrs. Matair seized a large butcher knife and struck at Anna, attempting to ward off the blow, Anna received a long gash on the arm that laid her up for some time. Young Douglas was a witness to this brutal treatment of his mother and he at that moment made up his mind to kill his mistress. He intended to put strychnine that was used to kill rats into her coffee that he usually served her. Fortunately freedom came and saved him of this act which would have resulted in his death.

Young Douglas had the task each morning of carrying the Matair children's books to school. Willie, a boy of eight would teach Douglas what he learned in school, finally Douglas learned the alphabet and numbers. In some way Mrs. Matair learned that Douglas was learning to read and write. One morning after breakfast she called her son Willie to the dining room where she was seated and then sent for Douglas to come there too. She then took a quill pen the kind used at that time, and began writing the alphabet and numerals as far as ten. Holding the paper up to Douglas, she asked him if he knew what they were; he proudly answered in the affirmative, not suspecting anything. She then asked him to name the letters and numerals, which he did, she then asked him to write them, which he did. When he reached the number ten, very proud of his learning, she struck him a heavy blow across the face, saying to him "If I ever catch you making another figure anywhere I'll cut off your right arm." Naturally Douglas and also her son Willie were much surprised as each thought what had been done was quite an achievement. She then called Mariah, the cook to bring a rope and tying the two of them to the old colonial post on the front porch, she took a chair and sat between the two, whipping them on their naked backs for such a time that for two weeks their clothes stuck to their backs on the lacerated flesh.

Ryer Emmanuel, South Carolina

"My mammy; she was de housewoman to de big house en she say dat she would always try to mind her business en she never didn' get no whippin much. Yes, mum, dey was mighty good to my mother, but dem other what never do right, dey would carry dem to de cow pen en make dem strip off dey frock, bodies clean to de waist. Den dey would tie dem down to a log en paddle dem wid a board. When dey would whip de men, de boards would often times have nails in dem. Hear talk dey would wash dem wid dey blood. Dat first hide dey had, white folks would whip it off dem en den turn round en grease dem wid tallow en make dem work right on. Always would inflict de punishment at sunrise in de mornin fore dey would go to work. Den de women, dey would force dem to drop dey body frock cross de shoulders so dey could get to de naked skin en would have a strap to whip dem wid. Wouldn' never use no board on de women. Oh, dey would have de lot scatter bout full of dem what was to get whip on a mornin."

Leah Garrett, Georgia

"I know so many things 'bout slaver time 'til I never will be able to tell 'em all," she declared. "In dem days, preachers wuz just as bad and mean as anybody else. Dere wuz a man who folks called a good preacher, but he wuz one of de meanest mens I ever seed. When I wuz in slavery under him he done so many bad things 'til God soon kilt him. His wife or chillun could git mad wid you, and if dey told him anything he always beat you. Most times he beat his slaves when dey hadn't done nothin' a t'all. One Sunday mornin' his wife told him deir cook wouldn't never fix nothin' she told her to fix. Time she said it he jumped up from de table, went in de kitchen, and made de cook go under de porch whar he always whupped his slaves. She begged and prayed but he didn't pay no 'tention to dat. He put her up in what us called de swing, and beat her 'til she couldn't holler. De pore thing already had heart trouble; dat's why he put her in de kitchen, but he left her swingin' dar and went to church, preached, and called hisself servin' God. When he got back home she wuz dead. Whenever your marster had you swingin' up, nobody wouldn't take you down. Sometimes a man would help his wife, but most times he wuz beat afterwards."

"Another marster I had kept a hogshead to whup you on. Dis hogshead had two or three hoops 'round it. He buckled you face down on de hogshead and whupped you 'til you bled. Everybody always stripped you in dem days to whup you, 'cause dey didn't keer who seed you naked. Some folks' chillun took sticks and jobbed [jabbed] you all while you wuz bein' beat. Sometimes dose chillun would beat you all 'cross your head, and dey Mas and Pas didn't know what stop wuz."

"Another way marster had to whup us wuz in a stock dat he had in de stables. Dis wuz whar he whupped you when he wuz real mad. He had logs fixed together wid holes for your feet, hands, and head. He had a way to open dese logs and fasten you in. Den he had his coachman give you so many lashes, and he would let you stay in de stock for so many days and nights. Dat's why he had it in de stable so it wouldn't rain on you. Everyday you got dat same number of lashes. You never come out able to sit down."

"I had a cousin wid two chillun. De oldest one had to nuss one of marster's grandchildren. De front steps wuz real high, and one day dis pore chile fell down dese steps wid de baby. His wife and daughter hollered and went on turrible, and when our marster come home dey wuz still hollerin' just lak de baby wuz dead or dyin'. When dey told him 'bout it, he picked up a board and hit dis pore little chile 'cross de head and kilt her right dar. Den he told his slaves to take her and throw her in de river. Her ma begged and prayed, but he didn't pay her no 'tention; he made 'em throw de chile in."

Fannie Griffin, South Carolina

"I was de youngest slave, so Missy Grace, dats Massa Joe's wife, keep me in de house most of de time, to cook and keep de house cleaned up. I milked de cow and worked in de garden too. My massa was good to all he slaves, but Missy Grace was mean to us. She whip us a heap of times when we ain't done nothing bad to be whip for. When she go to whip me, she tie my wrists together wid a rope and put that rope thru a big staple in de ceiling and draw me up off de floor and give me a hundred lashes. I think 'bout my old mammy heap of times now and how I's seen her whipped, wid de blood dripping off of her."

David Goodman Gullins, Georgia

"There were strict rules governing slaves, but our master was never brutal. I being a child, never received any punishment from any one except my mother and my Mistress. Punishment was inflicted with a raw cow hide, which was cut in a strip about three inches wide, one end being twisted. This made a very powerful and painful weapon. There were unruly slaves, what we called desperadoes. There were 'speculators,' too, who would get possession of these, and if a slave come into possession of one of these speculators, he either had to come under or else he was sure to die. The Lynch law was used extensively. Those slaves committing crimes against the state were more often considered unworthy of trial, though some were brought to trial, punishment being so many licks each day for so many days or weeks, or capital punishment. It is true that many crimes put upon the slaves when the white man was guilty."

"In 1863, Miss Elizabeth was going to have big company at her house, she was saving her strawberries for the occasion. I spied all these nice, ripe strawberries through the paling fence, and the whole crowd of us little niggers thought they needed picking. We found an opening on the lower side of the fence and made our way in, destroying all of those luscious ripe strawberries. When we had about finished the job, Mistress saw us, and hollered at us. Did we scatter! In the jam for the fence hole I was the last one to get through and Mistress had gotten there by that time and had me by the collar. She took me back to the house, got the cow hide down, and commenced rubbing it over me. Before she got through, she cut me all to pieces. I still have signs of those whelps on me today. In the fight I managed to bite her on the wrist, causing her to almost bleed to death. I finally got away and ran to a hiding place of safety."

"They used soot and other things trying to stop the bleeding. When Marstor come home he saw Miss Elizabeth with her hand all bandaged up, and wanted to know what the trouble was. He was told the story, so he came out to look for me. He called me out from my hiding place, and when he saw me with those awful whelps on me, and how pitiful looking I was, he said, 'Elizabeth, you done ruint my little nigger, David.' 'I wouldn't have him in this fix for all the strawberries.'"

Susan Hamlin (Hamilton), South Carolina

"I'll always 'member Clory, de washer. She wus very high-tempered. She wus a mulatra with beautiful hair she could sit on; Clory didn't take foolishness frum anybody. One day our missus gone in de laundry an' find fault with de clothes. Clory didn't do a t'ing but pick her up bodily an' throw 'er out de door. Dey had to sen' fur a doctor 'cause she pregnant an' less than two hours de baby wus bo'n. Afta dat she begged to be sold fur she didn't want to kill missus, but our master ain't nebber want to sell his slaves. But dat didn't keep Clory frum gittim' a brutal whippin'. Dey whip' 'er until dere wusn't a white spot on her body. Dat wus de worst I ebber see a human bein' got such a beatin'. I t'ought she wus goin' to die, but she got well an' didn't get any better but meaner until our master decide it wus bes' to rent ner out. She willingly agree' since she wusn't 'round missus. She hated an' detest' both of them an' all de fembly."

"W'en any slave wus whipped all de other slaves wus made to watch. I see women hung frum de ceilin' or buildin's an' whipped with only supin tied 'round her lowen part of de body, until w'en dey wus taken down, dere wusn't breath in de body. I had some terribly bad experiences."

Molly Harrell, Texas

"Dey use to have de little whip dey use on de women. Course de field hands got it worse, but den, dey was men."

Emmaline Heard, Georgia

Besides working as a plow hand, Emmaline's mother assisted Aunt Celia Travis in preparing the meals for the Harper family. Four or five pots each containing a different kind of food hung over the fire along the long fireplace. Just before dinner, the mistress would come in to inspect the cooking. If the food in any of the pots was not cooked to her satisfaction, she would sometimes lose her temper, remove her slipper and strike the cook.

Auntie Johns, Texas

"My husban' said a family named Gullendin was mighty hard on their niggers. He said ole Missus Gullendin, she'd take a needle and stick it throgh one of the nigger women's lower lips and pin it to the boson of her dress, and the woman would go 'round all day with her head drew down thataway and slobberin'. There was knots on the nigger's lip where the needle had been stuck in it."

Susan Merritt, Texas

"I stay mos' the time in the big house and massa good but missy am the devil. I couldn't tell you how I treated. Lots of times she tie me to a stob in the yard and cowhide me till she give out, then she go and rest and come back and beat me some more. You see, I's massa nigger and she have her own niggers what come on her side and she never did like me. She stomp and beat me nearly to death and they have to grease my back where she cowhide me and I's sick with fever for a week. If i have a dollar for ev'ry cowhidin' I git, I'd never have to work no more."

"Young missy Betty like me and try larn me readin' and writin' and she slip to my room and have me doin' right good. I lern the alphabet. But one day Missy Jane cotch her schoolin' me and she say, 'Niggers don't need to know anything,' and the lams me over the head with the butt of a cowhide whip. That white mans so rough, one day us makin' soap and some little chickens gits in the fire 'round the pot and she say I let 'em do it and make me walk barefoot through that bed of coals sev'ral times."

Anna Miller, Texas

"Dey sho whups us. I'se gits whupped lots a times. Marster whups de men and missus whups de women. Sometimes she whups wid de nettleweed. When she uses dat, de licke ain't so bed, but de stingin' and de burnin' after am sho' misery. Dat jus' plum runs me crazy. De mens use de rope when dey whups."

Bob Mobley, Georgia

"Well, you see," he replied. "I reckon they was some better to me 'cause I lived right there in the house with them. But he was mighty good to all of us. Sometimes he had to whip some of the boys but he never did touch the grown niggers. Whenever they'd disobey, he'd cut off their hair an' that was a bad punishment to them 'cause they'd try to make their hair grow long. He never did whip me but I needed it plenty of times."

William Moore, Texas

"Marse Tom was a fitty man for meanness. He jus' 'bout had to beat somebody every day to satisfy his cravin'. He had a big bullwhip and he stake a nigger on the ground and make 'nother nigger hold his head down with his mouth in the dirt and whip the nigger till the blood run out and red up the ground. We li'l niggers stand round and see it done. Then he tell us, 'Run to the kitchen and git some salt from Jane.' That my mammy, she was cook. He'd sprinkle salt in the cut, open places and the skin jerk and quiver and the man slobber and puke. Then his shirt stick to his back for a week or more."

"My mammy had a terrible bad back once. I seen her tryin' to git the clothes off her back and a woman say, 'What's the matter with you back?' It was raw and bloody and she say Marse Tom done beat her with a handsaw with the teeth to her back, She died with the marks on her, the teeth holes goin' crosswise her back. When I's growed I asks her 'bout it and she say Marse Tom got mad at the cookin' and grabs her by the hair and drug her out the house and grabs the saw off the tool bench and whips her."

"One day I'm down in the hawg pen and hears a loud agony screamin' up to the house, when I git up close I see Marse Tom got mammy tied to a tree with her clothes pulled down and he's layin' it on her with the bullwhip, and the blood am runnin' down her eyes and off her back. I goes crazy. I say, 'Stop, Marse Tom,' and he swings the whip and don't reach me good, but it cuts jus' the same. I sees Miss Mary standin' in the cookhouse door. I runs round-crazy like and sees a big rock, and I takes it and throws it and it cotches Marse Tom in the skull and he goes down like a poled ox, Miss Mary comes out and lifts her paw and helps him in the house and then comes and helps me undo mammy. Mammy and me takes to the woods for two, three months, I guess. My sisters meets us and grense mammy's back and brings us victuals. Purty soon they say it am safe for us to come in the cabin to eat at night and they watch for Marse Tom."

"One day Marse Tom's wife am in the yard and she calls me and say she got somethin' for me. She keeps her hand under her apron. She keeps beggin' me to come up to her. She say, 'Gimme you hand.' I reaches out my hand and she grabs it and slips a slip knot rope over it. I sees then that's what she had under her apron and the other end tied to a li'l bush. I tries to get loose and runs round and I trips her up and she falls and breaks her arm. I gits the rope off my arm and runs."

Jenny Proctor, Texas

"I'tended to de chillun when I was a little gal and tried to clean de house jes' like ole miss tells me to. Den soon as I was 10 years ole, ole marster, he say, 'Git dis yere nigger to dat cotton patch.' I recollects once when I was tryin' to clean de house like ole miss tell me, I finds a bisouit and I's so hungry I et it, 'cause we nev'r see sich a thing as a bisouit only some times on Sunday mornin'. We jes' have co'n braid and syrup and some times fat baeon, but when I et dat bisouit and she comes in and say, 'Whar dat biscuit?'"

"I say, 'Miss, I et it 'cause I's so hungry.' Den she grab dat broom and start to beatin' me over de head wid it and callin' me low down nigger and I guess I jes' clean lost my head 'cause I know'd better den to fight her if I knowed anything 'tall, but I start to fight her and de driver, he comes in and he grabs me and starts beatin' me wid dat cat-o'-nine-tails, and he beats me 'til I fall to de floor nearly dead. He cut my back all to pieces, den dey rubs salt in de cuts for mo' punishment. Lawd, Lawd, honey! Dem was awful days. When ole marster come to de house he say, 'What you beat dat nigger like dat for?' And de driver tells him why, and he say, 'She can't work now for a week, she pay for several biscuits in dat time.' He sho' was mad and he tell ole miss she start de whole mess. I still got dem scars on my ole back right now, jes' like my grandmother have when she die and I's acarryin' mine right on to de grave jes' like she did."

"We might a done very well if de ole driver hadn' been so mean, but de least little thing we do he beat us for it, and put big chains 'round our ankles and make us work wid dem on 'til de blood be cut out all around our ankles. Some of de marsters have what dey call stockades and puts dere heads and feet and arms through holes in a big board out in de hot sun, but our old driver he had a bull pen, dats only thing like a jail he had. When a slave do anything he didn' like he takes 'em in dat bull pen and chains 'em down, face up to de sun and leaves 'em dere 'till dey nearly dies."

Susan Ross, Texas

"Massa have li'l houses all over de plantation for he slaves. Massa and he folks punich dey slaves awful hard, and he used to tie 'em up and whip 'em, too. Once he told my mammy do somethin' and she didn't and he tie and whip her, and I skeert and cry. Mammy cook and work in de field."

"I jes' 'member I used to see sojers dress in blue uniforms walkin' all over de country watchin' how things goin'. Massa want one my brothers go to war, but he wouldn't, so I seed him buckle my brother down on a log and whip him with whips, den with hand saws, till when he turn him loose you couldn't tell what he look like. My brother lef' but I don't know whether he went to war or not."

Annie Row, Texas

"Now for ne treatment, does yous want to know 'bout that? Well, 'twarnt good. When dis nigger am five year old, de marster give me to him's son, Marster Billy. That am luck for me, 'cause Marster Billy am real good to me, but Marster Charley am powerful cruel to hims slaves. At de work, him have de overseers drive 'em from daylight 'til dark, and whups 'em for every little thing what goes wrong. When dey whups dey ties de nigger over de barrel and gives so many licks with de rawhide whup. I seed slaves what couldn't git up after de whuppin's. Some near died 'cause of de punishment."

"Dey never give de cullud folks de pass for to go a-visitin', nor 'lons parties on de place. As for to go to church, shunt that from yous head. Why, we'uns wasn' even 'lowed to pray. Once my mammy slips off to de woods near de house to pray and she prays powerful loud and she am heard, and when she come back, she whupped."

"My mammy and me not have it so hard, 'cause she de cook and I 'longs to Marster Billy. Him won't let 'em whup me iffen he knows 'bout it. But one time, when I's 'bout six year, I stumbles and breaks a plate and de missy whups me for that. Here am de scar on my arm from that whuppin'."

Mary Thompson, Texas

"My mistress' niece had a big plantation, and she had a place whah she had de slaves whooped. She had a reg'lah whoopin'-post whah de slaves was whooped."

"My Marster jes' had a large cowhide whoop. Yes, I got a whoopin' more'n once. Well, I was jes' a slave, and I have never forgotten it. If dey treated me right, I tried to do right. Several times de Marster took hold of my eahs and bumped my haid against de wall ... otherwise dey was good to me. I'm jes' tellin' you de truf."

Horatio W. Williams, Texas

"My boss man was mean to his niggers. I 'member crawlin' down thr'oo d' weeds 'n' lis'inin' one time w'en dey beat one 'r' dem. Eb'ry time he hit him he pray. Boss hab fi'teen slaves. I recollec' one time dey was gwinter beat my mudder. She run t' d' kitchen 'n' jump behin' d' kitchen do' 'n' kiver herse'f up in d' big pile 'r' dirty clo's dat was dere. Dey neber t'ink t' look dere fo' her 'n' she stay dere all day. But d' nex' day dey kotch her 'n' whip her."

"I rec'lect once our w'ite folks had comp'ny. A white gemman 'n' his wife dey come 'n' stay all night. D' gemman was some kin' 'r' trablin' man 'n' he hab some big suit case. Dat night one 'r' our nigger men slep' on d' po'ch jes' outside d' room w'er d' comp'ny slep'. In d' night he slip in d' room 'n' t'iefed a fine w'ite shu't [shirt] outn' d' gemman's suit case 'n' was wearin' it 'roun' d' nex' mornin'. Co'se he couidn' read 'n' he ain' know d' w'ite man have he name on d' shu't. W'en d' boss fin' it out dey tuk dat nigger down in d' bottom. I crawl thr'oo d' bresh 'n' watch. Dey tie he foots togedder ober a lim' 'r' a tree, 'n' let he haid hang down 'n' beat him 'til d' blood run down on d' roots 'r' dat tree. W'en dey tuk him down his back look like raw meat. He nearly die."

"If our oberseer hab a darky w'at he couldn' make min' him he put a chain to one foot 'n' a ball on it 'bout 's big's dat nigger's head 'n' dat darky hab t' wuk 'n' drag dat t'ing 'roun' wid him all day."

Lulu Wilson, Texas

"Now Mrs. Hodges studied 'bout meanness more than Wash done. She was mean to anybody she could lay her hands to, but special mean to me. She

Lulu Wilson. (Library of Congress)

beat me and she used to tie my hands and make me lie flat on the floor and she put snuff in my eyes. I ain't lyin' before God when I say that I knows why I went blind. I did see white folks sometimes that spoke right friendly and kindly to me."

Sallie Wroe, Texas

"Mike Burdette was our mawster and he had a laghe cotton plantation. Mawster Burdette had an overseer, and he sure was rough. I think dat his name was Bebil. My sister, Mollie, was a weaver at de loom, and at one time she didn't git de amount she had to git for de day, and she was tied up in a sittin'-lak form and she was whopped putty hard. She had stripes all over her shoulders."

CRUSHING SIGNS OF REBELLIOUSNESS

Enslaved persons who refused to follow instructions, ran away, or secretly traveled to visit family and friends on other farms risked severe punishment. If they were not punished slaveholders feared their authority might be undermined. Slave patrols, leg chains, branding, severe lashings, and other actions were implemented as deterrents. These acts discouraged the enslaved but did not stop them, and instances of running away and defying slave patrols continued to regularly occur. When caught, they were physically beaten, but their spirits were not broken.

Maintaining authority was so crucial for slaveholders that they especially sought to exert physical control over those taking actions they regarded as absolute defiance. Among the worst actions in the eyes of slaveholders was running away to escape punishment or to gain freedom. Quite often the penalties for those who did this were quite severe. What Matilda Mumford saw happen to runaways from her farm in Georgia made a lasting impression:

> All five overseer so mean, de slaves run away. Dey dug cave in de wood, down in de ground, and dey hide dere. Dey gits de blood-houn's to fin' 'em—den they whips 'em in de wood, dey buckle 'em down to a log and beat de breaf' outter dem till de blood run all over everywhere. When night come, dey drug 'em to dey house and greases 'em down wid turpentine, and rub salt in dey woun's to mek 'em hurt wuss.

The slaveholder's intention was to make an example of these people so others would not try to imitate their actions. It certainly worked in the case of Matilda who remained enslaved until the end of the Civil War despite the severe mistreatment she suffered.

Slave patrols were another control device put in place to reinforce the slaveholders' authority and to stop unauthorized travel, including running away. These bands of about six armed men were given legal authority to guard the countryside at night and question any enslaved person they encountered. If that person did not have a pass the patrol could detain and whip him. An enslaved person who resisted or tried to escape could be shot or killed as a last resort. The patrols were especially on the lookout for gatherings of enslaved people they suspected might be up to no good or fugitives seeking freedom or hiding in the countryside. Traveling without a pass meant a person did not have permission to be away from his or her farm and therefore was operating against the wishes of their enslaver. For the family of Isom Blackshear of Arkansas, the threat of the patrol had the intended effect:

> My father said that the patrollers would run you and ketch you and whip you if you didn't have a pass, when you was away from the place. But they didn't bother you if you had a pass. The patrollers were mean white people who called themselves making the niggers stay home. I think they were hired. They called their selves making the niggers stay home. They went all through the community looking for people, and whipping them when they'd leave home without a pass. They said you wasn't submissive when you left home without a pass.

This was one more reminder for the enslaved of the absolute power white society had over their lives. They could not visit family or friends on another farm without written permission from their enslaver. Some people risked punishment to see someone special, but they risked paying dearly for their decision, as was the father of Miller Barber of South Carolina who was stripped and beaten in front of his wife, whom he had gone to visit.

Strong actions also resulted when an enslaved worker openly defied the rules or a direct order from the slaveholder. Most slaveholders saw their relationship with the enslaved much in the same way as a Virginia planter who argued in an 1846 essay in the *Southern Cultivator* that "a slave should know that his master is to govern absolutely, and he is to obey implicitly" (Stampp, *Peculiar Institution,* p.145). If this sacred bond was undermined or broken by the enslaved quick retribution often followed. A less volatile slaveholder might respond as Tempie Herndon Durham of North Carolina recalled, "If a nigger cut up an' got sassy in slavery times, his Ole Marse give him a good whippin' an' he went way back an' set down an' 'haved hese'f."

Durham describes a more tempered response, but the response to defiance could be devastating for the enslaved, and death was a real possibility. That was the fate suffered by Anne Clark's father when he defied his Texas enslaver:

> My poppa was strong. My father never had a lick in his life. He helped the marster, but one day the marster says: "Si, you got to have a 'whoppin' [whipping], and my father says: "I never had a whoppin and you caint whop me," and the marster he says: "But I can kill you." And he shot my father down. My momma tuk him in the cabin and put him on a pallet. He died.

This was a loss of valuable property and a good worker, but Clark's enslaver believed quashing any manifestation of defiance was more important than the money lost with her father's death.

Other slaveholders were less impulsive and more calculating in how they responded to defiance or stubbornness. Rather than suffer a monetary loss with the death of the enslaved malcontent, they chose to sell them and recoup their investment. The important thing was to hide the defiant nature of the worker being sold. Slave traders and slave buyers did not want troublemakers, who might be a bad influence on other enslaved people. Getting rid of malcontents quickly was the best way to ensure that their stubborn tendencies did not affect their value. Selling the malcontent was also a lesson to others who might consider defiance. They, too, might be sold and separated from friends and family, possibly never to see them again. Plus, there was no way of knowing what fate awaited them in their new location under another slaveholder. The possibility of being sold made the disadvantages of defiance very real, and it made Sarah Debro's North Carolina grandfather decide that defiance was not in his best interest:

> Marse Cain was good to his niggers. He didn' whip dem like some owners did but if dey done mean he sold dem. Dey knew dis so dey minded him. One day gran'pappy sassed Mis' Polly White an' she told him dat if he didn' 'have hese'f dat she would put him in her pocket. Gran'pappy wuz er big man an' I ax him how Mis' Polly could do dat. He said she meant dat she would sell him den put de money in her pocket. He never did sass Mis' Polly no more.

The decision made by Debro's grandfather not to openly resist the power and authority of his slaveholder was one made by many enslaved people. The possible repercussions for defiance made that choice a very risky one. Slaveholders wanted a workforce that would obey their commands and operate in the ways they thought best. If it took violence and physical abuse to make this happen the slaveholders were more than ready to use it. They recognized that their resolve would be tested periodically by the enslaved, and they were determined to win any battle of the wills. Even the kindlier enslavers, though they used less harsh methods, expected their enslaved workers to follow their directives. Violence was integral to the day-to-day operation of most farm operations. It made for a difficult life that left many of the enslaved bruised and scarred. Louisa Gause of North Carolina summed it up best:

> Colored people had to live under a whip massa en couldn' do nothin, but what he say do. Yes, mam, dey had dese head men, what dey call overseers, on all de plantations dat been set out to whip de niggers. I tell you, it was rough en tough in dem days. Dey would beat you bout to death. My grandfather en my grandmother, dey die wid scars on dem dat de white folks put dere.

The scars were both physical and emotional and made enslavement a daunting endeavor. Enslaved workers would remember those painful experiences decades after having gained their freedom.

NARRATIVES

Frank Adams, Texas

"Some marsters was'n' good to dere slaves like ours. One time, w'en I was ober in Tyler county, a cullard woman run 'way from her marster. Well, dey tie' a rope to her, put it ober de ho'n er de saddle an' drag her home, tie' her to de bed, den nex' mawnin' dey cut off bofe her breastes, den ram' a hot i'on down her throat an' kilt her. Dat was de wustest treatment I eber knowed a marster to git a slave. But sometime' our near neighbors was mean to dere slaves. You could hear de whip a-poppin'."

S. B. Adams, Texas

"Ef you tried to go wid out a pass an' de patroller caught you, he would give you a whippen' an' a good'un too. Some de slaves run 'way, most of dem was caught an' brought back an' dey got a good whippen. My marster was pretty good didn' whip us lessen we done somethin' we knowed not to do."

William M. Adams, Texas

"Lots of overseers was mean. Sometimes dey'd whip a nigger wid a leather strap 'bout a foot wide and long as your arm and wid a wooden handle at de and."

"We didn' have to have a pass but on other plantations dey did, or de paddlerollers would git you and whip you. Dey was de poor white folks dat didn' have no slaves. We didn' call 'em white folks dem days. No, suh, we called dem 'Buskrys.'"

Rev. W. B. Allen, Alabama

"Runaway slaves were hunted with packs of 'Nigger dogs,' bred and trained to trail Negroes. And when rounded up and brought in, the runaway was whipped differently from ordinary offenders. He was swung by his thumbs from some convenient rafter or overhead beam and whipped and let hang, with just his toes touching the floor for hours. Then, while still agonizing from the effects of the beating he had received and the torture of his suspension by his thumbs, he was further tormented by having his wounds 'doctored' with salt and red pepper. Often, strong men would tear their thumbs out at the roots and drop to the floor unconscious. Sir, you can never know what some slaves endured; but they could take it in those days and times."

"I never heard or knew of a slave being tried in court for anything. I never knew of a slave being guilty of any crime more serious than taking something or violating plantation rules. And the only punishment that I ever heard or knew of for slaves was a whipping of some sort."

"I have personally known of a few slaves who were beaten to death for one or more of the following offenses: leaving home without a pass, talking back to a white person, hitting another Negro, fussing, fighting, 'ruckusing' in the quarters, lying, loitering on the job, taking things (the Whites called it 'stealing'). Plantation rules forbade a slave to: own a firearm, leave home without a pass, sell or buy anything without his master's consent, have a light in his cabin after a certain hour of night, attend any secret meeting, harbor or in any manner assist a runaway slave, abuse a farm animal, mistreat a member of his family, and do a great many other things."

I asked the Reverend if he ever heard slaves plot an insurrection, and he answered in the negative. When I asked if he had personal knowledge of a slave offering resistence to corporal punishment, the Reverend shook his head, but said: "Sometimes a stripped Negro would say hard things to the white man with the strap in his hand, though he [the Negro] knew that he would pay dearly for it; for when a slave showed spirit that way, the master or overseer laid the lash on all the harder."

I asked him how the women took their beatings, and he said, "They usually screamed and prayed, though a few never made a sound."

Smith Austin, Texas

"Slaves from Marsters' place have to get a slip if dey go. If dey don't have a slip dey get beat. De patter rollers go to de place where de dance was and make de folks show dere slips. If dey ain't had no slip—oo-oo-ooh, dat was too bad. Dey git beat. Dey didn't have nothing to eat at dem dances and dey had to be back to de quarters by sundown."

Celestia Avery, Georgia

Mr. Heard was a very mean master and was not liked by any one of his slaves. Secretly each one hated him. He whipped unmercifully and in most cases unnecessarily. However, he sometimes found it hard to subdue some slaves who happened to have very high tempers. In the event this was the case he would set a pack of hounds on him. Mrs. Avery related to the writer the story told to her of Mr. Heard's cruelty by her grandmother. The facts were as follows: "Every morning my grandmother would pray, and old man Heard despised to hear any one pray saying they were only doing so that they might become free niggers. Just as sure as the sun would rise, she would get a whipping; but this did not stop her prayers every morning before day. This particular time grandmother Sylvia was in 'family way' and that morning she began to pray as usual. The master heard her and became so angry he came to her cabin siezed and pulled her clothes from her body and tied her to a young sapling. He whipped her so brutally that her body was raw all over. When darkness fell her husband cut her down from the tree, during the day he was afraid to go near her. Rather than go back to the cabin she crawled on her knees to the woods and her husband brought grease for her to grease her raw body. For two weeks the master hunted but could not find her; however, when he finally did, she had given birth to twins. The only thing that saved her was the fact that she was a mid-wife and always carried a small pin knife which she used to cut the navel cord of the babies. After doing this she tore her petticoat into two pieces and wrapped each baby." Grandmother Sylvia lived to get 115 years old.

Not only was Mr. Henderson cruel but it seemed that every one he hired in the capacity of overseer was just as cruel. For instance, Mrs. Henderson's grandmother Sylvia, was told to take her clothes off when she reached the end of a row. She was to be whipped because she had not completed the required amount of hoeing for the day. Grandmother continued hoeing until she came to a fence; as the overseer reached out to grab her she snatched a fence railing and broke it across his arms. On another occasion grandmother Sylvia ran all the way to town to tell the master that an overseer was beating her husband to death. The master immediately jumped on his horse and started for home; and reaching the plantation he ordered the overseer to stop whipping the old man. Mrs. Avery received one whipping, with a hair brush, for disobedience; this was given to her by the mistress.

Josephine Bacchus, South Carolina

"Just like as I been hear talk, some of de people fare good in slavery time en some of dem fare rough. Dat been accordin to de kind of task boss dey come up under. Now de poor colored people in slavery time, dey give dem very little rest en would whip some of dem most to death. Wouldn' none of dem daresen to go from one plantation to another widout dey had a furlough from dey boss. Yes, mam, if dey been catch you comin back widout dat walkin paper de boss had give you, great Jeruseleum, you would sho catch de devil next mornin. My blessed a mercy, hear talk dey spill de poor nigger's blood awful much in slavery time. Hear heap of dem was free long time fore dey been know it cause de white folks, dey wanted to keep dem in bondage. Oh, my Lord, dey would cut dem so hard till dey just slash de flesh right off dem. Yes, mam, dey call dat thing dey been whip dem wid de cat o' nine tail. No, darlin, I hear talk it been made out of pretty leather plaited most all de way en den all dat part down to de bottom, dey just left it loose to do de cuttin wid. Yes, honey, dem kind of whips was made out of pretty leather like one of dese horse whips. Yes, mam, dat been how it was in slavery time."

Henry Baker, Texas

"I's 'member de time my mother gits a whippin', dat waz becuze her an' a nigger dat dey called Uncle Dick, had a fight. De marster, he cum up while dey waz fightin' an' whipped my mother wib a cowhide whip. He whipped her till de blood jus' streamed from her. Dat lak to kill me, I's cried a long time, it jus' broke my heart. Uncle Dick, he run away while de marster waz whippin' my mother an' de marster had to run hem down wib de hounds."

Millie Barber, South Carolina

"My pa have to git a pass to come to see my mammy. He come sometimes widout de pass. Patrollers catch him way up de chimney hidin' one night; they stripped him right befo' mammy and give him thirty-nine lashes, wid her cryin' and a hollerin' louder than he did. Did I ever git a whippin? Dat I did. How many times? More than I can count on fingers and toes. What I git a whippin' for? Oh, just one thing, then another. One time I break a plate while washin' dishes and another time I spilt de milk on de dinin' room floor. It was always for somethin', sir. I needed de whippin'."

Mrs. John Barclay (nee Sarah Sanders), Texas

"My marster and mistress was good to all de slaves dat worked for dem. But our over-seer, Jimmy Shearer, was sho' mean. One day he done git mad at me for some little somethin' and when I take de ashes to de garden he catches me and churns me up and down on de groun'. One day he got mad at my brother and kicked him end over end, jes' like a stick of wood. He would whip us 'til we was raw and then put pepper and salt in de sores. If he thought we was too slow in doin' anything he would kick us off de groun' and churn us up and down. Our punishment depended on de mood of de overseer."

John Barker, Texas

"Talk about times! De blood houn's on deir trail! Dey had what you call de common houn's and when you couldn' get 'em by de common houn's, you put de blood houn's dat don't make no racket atall on deir trail. Dey run my gran'fadder ovah one hun'erd miles and never caught 'im till about t'ree or fo' days an' nights an' dey found 'im under a bridge. What dey put on him was e-nuf. I have seen 'em whip 'em till de blood run down deir backs and den dey would put common salt in de places where dey whipped 'em an' dey would have to go right on nex' mawnin' and do deir tasks dey puts on 'em. I've seen 'nuf o' dat! Yes, mam, dat was up in Ohio I seen all dat. Oh, yes'm, dey had slaves up dere too. Maybe dey puts you on a task dis mawnin' and dat dare task got to be finished by seben o'clock dis evenin' an' if it ain't, dey whip you. I have seen many a nig—person go out in de mawnin' and deir backs cut jus' like it was cut wid a knife. De overseer was a white man an' he rode hossback and wo' [wore] dese big, tall beaver hats an' had a wide strap hangin' down from de saddle, wide as yo' han'. Jus' like a belt 'round yo' waist, only wider, you know. No, it didn' have no holes in it, but it raised a blister, jes' de same, an' cut yo' back like a knife."

Frank Bell, Texas

"When I'se about 17 years old I'se married girl while master was on drunk spell. We have home wedding bless my sole and master he run her off and I'se slipping off late at night to see her and master he finds it out some how and he take great long knife and cuts her head plum off, ties great heavy weight to her and makes me throw her in the river. Then he puts me in chains and every night he come give me whipping for long time. I dont remember the exact time."

Sallie Blakely, Alabama

After work hours slaves were allowed to amuse themselves by attending "frolics" however before anyone could leave the plantation it was necessary to obtain a pass. If a slave was caught off with out a pass, there were men known as "Patter Rollers" who appointed themselves to punish the slaves. Often they were carried to the calaboose and whipped almost to death. Mr. Cobb did not allow the "Patter Rollers" on his premises.

Julia Blanks, Texas

"They had what they called patros, and if you didn't have a pass they would whip you and put you in jail. Old man Burns was hired at the courthouse, and if the marsters had slaves that they didn't want to whip, they would send them to the courthouse to be whipped. Some of the marsters was good and some wasn't. There was a woman, oh, she was the meanest thing. I don't know if she had a husband—I never did hear anything about him. When she would get mad at one of her slave women, she would make the men tie her down, and she had what they called cat-o'-nine-tails, and after she got the blood to come, she would dip it in salt and pepper and whip her again. Oh, she was mean! My mother's marster was good; he wouldn't whip any of his slaves. But his wife wasn't good. If she got mad at the women, when he would come home she would say: 'John, I want you to whip Liza. Or Martha.' And he would say, 'Them are your slaves, You whip them.' He was good and she was mean."

Clay Bobbit, North Carolina

"Massa Dick ain't good ter us, an' on my arm hyar, jist above de elbow am a big scar dis day whar he whupped me wid a cowhide. He ain't whupped me fer nothin' 'cept dat I is a nigger. I had a whole heap of dem whuppin's, mostly case I won't obey his orders an' I'se seed slaves beat 'most ter deff."

Rias Body, Alabama

During the course of the interview we discussed the disciplining of slaves at some length, and he told me that during antebellum days the "patrollers" were quite active. According to Uncle Rias, the patrol consisted of six men who rode nearly every night and was composed of planters and overseers who took turns about policing each militia district in the county. All slaves were required to procure passes from their masters or overseers before they could go visiting or leave their homes at all. If the patrollers caught a Negro out without a pass, they gave him a "brushing" and sent him home. Sometimes, however, if a man did not run—and told a straight story—he was let off with a lecture and a warning.

In speaking of punishment, Uncle Rias said that when a mean Negro or one guilty of some serious offense was whipped, the white folks usually "put him in the buck." This consisted in making the Negro squat, running a stout stick under his bended knee, and then tying his hands firmly to the stick—between the knees. Then, the lash was laid on his back parts. An offense that was punished by such a whipping during slavery times would probably draw a jail or chain gang sentence today.

Uncle Rias said that he never heard of a slave being killed; and, since slaves were valuable property, none was ever whipped to the point that he or she was incapacitated for work. The majority of slave holders were humane, God-fearing men; though Uncle Rias admitted that a few were "a little fractious" and wielded a "stingin' lash." He never heard of a Negro being underfed or insufficiently clothed in the days of slavery; and, as a rule, the slaves ate about the same food as the Whites, excepting the dainties and hot waffles "an' sich." Uncle Rias summed up by saying that they "got plenty o' hog an' hominy; an' when a man has dat, his belly is satisfied."

"Mah employer, Ah mean, mah marster, never 'lowed no overseer to whup none er his niggers. Marster done all the whuppin' on our plantation hisself. He never did make no big bruises an' he never drawed no blodd, but he sho' could bunn 'em up with that lash. Niggers on our plantation was whupped for laziness mos'ly. Next to that, whuppin's was fer stealin' eggs an' chickens. They fed us good an' plenny, but a nigger is jes' boun' to pick up chickens an' eggs effen he kin, no matter how much he done eat. He jes' cyan' help it. Effen a nigger ain' busy, he gwine to git into mischief."

W. L. Bost, North Carolina

"Then the paddyrollers they keep close watch on the pore niggers so they have no chance to do anything or go anywheres. They jes' like policeman, only worser. 'Cause they never let the niggers go anywhere without a pass from his master. If you wasn't in your proper place when the paddyrellers come they lash you till' you was black and blue. The women got 15 lashes and the men 30. That is for jes bein' out without a pass. If the nigger done anything worse he was taken to the jail and put in the whippin' post. They was two holes cut for the arms stretch up in the air and a block to put your feet in, then they whip you with cowhide whip. An' the clothes shores never get any of them licks."

"I remember how they kill one nigger whippin' him with the bull whip. Many the pore nigger nearly killed with the bull whip. But this one die. He was a stubborn Negro and didn't do as much work as his Massa thought he ought to. He been lashed lot before. So they take him to the whippin' post, and then they strip his clothes off and then the man stan' off and cut him with the whip. His back was cut all to pieces. The cuts about half inch apart. Then after they whip him they tie him down and put salt on him. Then after he lie in the sun awhile they whip him agin. But when they finish with him he was dead."

"I remember how the driver, he was the man who did most of the whippin', use to whip some of the niggers. He would tie their hands together and then put their hands down over their knees, then take a stick and stick it 'tween they hands and knees. Then when he take hold of them and beat 'em first on one side then on the other."

John Boyd, South Carolina

Aunt Polly Meador had no patrollers on her place. She would not allow one there, for she did her own patrolling with her own whip and two bull dogs. She never had an overseer on her place, either. Neither did she let Uncle Johnny do the whipping. Those two dogs held them and she did her own whipping. One night she went to the quarter and found old "Bill Pea Legs" there after one of her negro women. He crawled under the bed when he heard Aunt Polly coming. Those dogs pulled old "Pea Legs" out and she gave him a whipping that he never forgot. She whipped the woman, also.

Monroe Brackins, Texas

"I was with George Reedes 10 or 12 years. It was my first trainin' learnin' the stock business and horse breakin.' He was tol'able good to us, to be slaves as we was. His brother had a hired man that whipped me once, with a quirt. I've heard my father and mother tell how they whipped 'em. They'd tie 'em down on a log or up to a post and whip 'em till the blisters rose, then take a paddle and open 'em up and pour salt in 'em. Yes'm, they whipped the women. The most I remember about that, my father and sister was in the barn shuckin' co'n and the master come in there and whipped my sister with a cowhide whip. My father caught a lick in the face and he told the master to keep his whip offen him. So the master started on my father and he run away. When he finally come in he was so wild his master had to call him to get orders for work, and finally the boss shot at him, but they didn't whip him any more. Of course, some of 'em whipped with more mercy. They had a whippin' post and when they strapped 'em down on a log they called it a 'stroppin' log.' I remember they tasked the cotton pickers in Mississippi. They had to bring in so many pounds in the evenin' and if they didn't they got a whippin' for it. My sister there, she had to bring in 900 pounds a day. Well, cotton was heavier there. Most any of 'em could pick 900 pounds. It was heavier and fluffier. We left the cotton country in Mississippi, but nobody knew anything about cotton out here that I knew of."

"I heard my mother and father say they would go 15 or 20 miles to a dance, walkin', and get back before daylight, before the 'padderollers' got 'em. The slaves would go off when they had no permission and them that would ketch 'em and whip 'em was the 'padderollers.'"

Clara Brim, Texas

"When us slaves go to some of de other brudders' places us hafter git passes. Iffen us didn' have pass de patterrollers ketch us and whip us. Sometimes some of de niggers git out and go 'thout a pass, but dey hafter tek de chance."

"Dem patterrollers was 'bout six men on hossback ridin' de roads to ketch niggers what out 'thout passes. Dey jis' ride de roads and iffen dey ketch a nigger what ain't got no pass dey whip him."

Sylvester Brooks, Texas

"De nex' thing dat I members mighty well is de patty rollers, kase dey whipped me ebery time dat dey ketch me away wid-out a pass, an' many is de times dat I have seen dem ridin' aroun' at night lookin' to see efn dey any niggers out dat ought to be at home, dat is de way dey made us stay home at night, hit made good niggers out of us fer we did'nt have a chance to chase aroun' an' git into meanness, when we did go off de plantashun we had to have a pass from de overseer er de old Marster, dat's why dey sung, 'Run Nigger Run,' about de Patty Rollers."

Easter Brown, Georgia

"Marster wuz real cruel. He'd beat his hoss down on his knees and he kilt one of 'em. He whupped de Niggers when dey didn't do right. Niggers is lak dis; dey wuz brought to dis here land wild as bucks, and dey is lak chicken roosters in a pen. You just have to make 'em 'have deyselves. Its lak dat now; if dey'd 'have dey-selves, white folkses would let 'em be."

"Dere warn't no jails in dem days. Dey had a gyuard house what dey whupped 'em in, and Mondays and Tuesdays wuz set aside for de whuppin's, when de Niggers what had done wrong got so many lashes, 'cordin' to what devilment dey had been doin'. De overseer didn't do de whuppin', Marster done dat. Dem patterrollers wuz sompin else. mankind! If dey ketched a Nigger out atter dark widout no pass dey'd most nigh tear de hide offen his back."

Fred Brown, Texas

"Dem fool niggers what sneak off without de pass, have two things for to watch, one is not to be ketched by de overseer and de other am de patterrollers. De nigger sho' am skeert of de patters. One time my pappy and my mammy goes out without de pass and de patters takes after dem. I'se home, 'cause I's too young to be pesterin' roun'. I sees dem comin,' and you couldn' catched dem with a jackrabbit. One time anoudder nigger am runnin' from de patters and hides under de house. Dey fin' him and make him come out. You's seen de dawg quaver when him's col'? Well, dat nigger have de quaverment jus' like dat. De patters hits him five or six licks and lets him go. Dat nigger have lots of power—him gits to de quarters ahead of his shadow."

Sally Brown, Georgia

"I wuz give to the Mitchell Fambly and they done everything mean to me they could. I wuz put to work in the fields when I wuz five year ole, pickin' cotton and hoein'. And I slep on the flo' nine years, winter and summer, sick or well. I never wore nothin' but a cotton dress and my shimmy and draw's. I had sich hard time. That Mistress Mitchell didn't care what happened to us. Sometimes she would walk us to church but we never went nowhere else. That 'oman took delight in sellin' slaves. She used to lash me with a cowhide whip. Then she died and I went frum one fambly to another. All the owners wuz pretty much the same, but this is still the Mitchell 'oman I'm telling you about now."

"We wuzn't 'lowed to go around and have pleasure as the folks does today. We had to have passes to go wherever we wanted."

"When we'd git out there wuz a bunch of white men called the 'patty rollers.' They'd come in and see if all us had passes and if they found any who didn't have a pass he wuz whipped; give fifty or mo' lashes—and they'd count them lashes. If they said a hundred, you got a hundred. They wuz somethin' lak the Klu Klux. We wuz 'fraid to tell our mastahs 'bout the patty rollers 'cause we wuz skeared they'd whip us again, fur we wuz tol' not to tell. They'd sing a little ditty. I wish I could remember the words, but it went somethin' lak this:

Run, nigger, run, de patty rollers'll git you,
Run, nigger, run, you'd bettah git away.

"We wuz 'fraid to go any place."

Augustus Burden, Georgia

"We could not leave the plantation without a ticket," he said, "if the Patterolers caught us away from home and we didn't have the ticket, they could whip us and send us back home."

Marshal Butler, Georgia

"Yes sah! I got paddled. Et happened dis way. I'se left home one Thursday to see a gal on the Palmer plantation—five miles away. Come gal! No, I didn't get a pass—de boss was so busy! Everythings was fine until my return trip. I wuz two miles out an' three miles to go. There come de 'Paddle–Rollers' I wuz not scared—only I couldn't move. They give me thirty licks—I ran the rest of the way home. There was belt buckles all over me. I ate my victuals off de porch railing. Some gal! Um-m-h. Was worth that paddlin' to see that gal— would do it over again to see ary de next night."

O Jane! love me lak you useter,
O Jane! chew me lak you useter,
Ev'y time I figger, my heart gits bigger,
Sorry, sorry, can't be yo' piper any mo'.
Um-m-mh-Some gal!

Henry H. Buttler, Texas

"On the Sullivan place there existed consideration for human feelings but on the Rector place neither the master nor the overseer seemed to understand that slaves were human beings. One old slave called Jim, on the Rector place, disobeyed some rule and early one morning they ordered him to strip. They tied him to the whipping post and from morning until noon, at intervals, the lash was applied to his back. I, myself, saw and heard many of the lashes and his cries for mercy."

"One morning a number of slaves were ordered to lay a fence row on the Rector place. The overseer said, 'This row must be laid to the Branch and left in time to roll those logs out in the back woods.' It was sundown when we laid the last rail but the overseer put us to rolling logs without any supper and it was eleven when we completed the task. Old Pete, the ox driver, became so exhausted that he fell asleep without unyoking the oven. For that, he was given 100 lashes."

Dave Byrd, Texas

"We were not allowed to go from one plantation to another without a pass. If we did the Patter Roller would get Mr. Negro, and what they did to him was plenty. The first time they would get hold of the negro it would be 39 licks. Of course, lots of the negroes would slip off and prowl around and they would never catch them. I was one of them, and like to have been caught one time, but just out run them Patter Rollers."

William Byrd, Texas

"If a nigger was mean Marse Sam give him fifty licks over a log the first time and seventy-five licks the second time and 'bout that time he most gen'rally had a good nigger. If they was real mean and he couldn't do nothin' with 'em, he put them in the jail with a chain on the feets for three days, and fed 'em through a crack in the wall."

Louis Cain, Texas

"We had to have a pass if we went from one plantation to another. Our Maser would give it to us if he wanted us to have it. If we did not have a pass them Patter Rollers would get that negro, and Lord! what they would do was plenty. They would give them 39 licks with a rawhide and believe me we was tore up good. I'se slipped off and them Patter Rollers failed to catch me, but they would catch lots of negroes slipping off."

Jeff Calhoun, Texas

"Mah ole marster wuz shore good to us but mah last marster de first marster son-in-law, he not so good but dey both feed us good and did not whip us only when one got sulky er onery den dey would punish dem other ways and ifen dis did not work dey would whip, dis de drivah done, didn make no difference if hit wuz his wife er chile, er yer pappa er yer mamma you'se had to do hit, er git licked yer self, and dem you'se couldnt be drivah no more, de boss would make anouthur drivah."

"Der wuz several reasons fer whippens, but der wuz little done, fer mah marster fer gittin smart wid de drivah wuz de thing de most of dem wuz punished fer, er gittin sulky er not doin der work right and several things."

"I hab seed de slaves hands tied to a pole above der heads and de blood whipped outen dem, dey hab to be carried away. Den I seed dem tied hand and foot and a stick run under der nees and oveh der arms at de elbows and kicked oveh and whipped worsen a dog. Dey too had to be carried away. I helped to carry two eb dem away, dey wuz whipped fer runnin away. No der wuznt no jail on our plantation."

Richard Carruthers, Texas

"My pappy had to have a pass to visit my mamma. When he come to see us, or we goes to see him, the watchman say, 'Fetch yo' pass, nigger.' And if we don't have one, the paddle roller conk you on the head."

Cato Carter, Texas

"They whupped the women and they whupped the mens. I used to work some in the tan'ry and we made the whups. They'd tie them down to a stob, and give 'em the whuppin'. Some niggers, it taken four men to whup 'em, but they got it. The nigger driver was meaner than the white folks. They'd better not leave a blade of grass in the rows. I seed 'em beat a nigger half a day to make him 'fess up to stealin' a sheep or a shoat. Or they'd whup 'em for runnin' away, but not so hard if they come back of their own 'cordance when they got hungry and sick in the swamps. But when they had to run 'em down with the nigger dogs, they'd git in bad trouble."

"The Carters never did have any real 'corrigible niggers, but I heard of 'em plenty onother places. When they was real 'corrigible, the white folks said they was like mad dogs and didn't mind to kill them so such as killin' a sheep. They'd take 'em to the graveyard and shoot 'em down and bury 'em face downward, with their shoes on. I never seed it done, but they made some the niggers go for a lesson to them that they could git the same."

George Caulton, Georgia

He was never whipped by his master, but the overseer would often "clean him up." He would not stop his work to administer the punishment but would promise George a whipping that night. With this promise in mind, George would hie to the woods and there hide in safety. The overseer, for fear of losing one of the master's slaves and thereby losing his own job, would send slaves with torches to find him. By the time he was found, the overseer would be so thankful that he would forget his promise and George would escape the punishment. All of the slaves were whipped by the overseer, not by the master.

A pass was absolutely necessary for a slave to have if he wanted to leave the plantation. George seemed to think it was a great sport to leave his home without the pass and try to outrun the "patterroll." If he once reached the gate of the plantation he could not be whipped. George said that, by the time he was fifteen, no "patterroll" could catch him. If ever caught "you wuz tore up," he said.

Aunt Cicely Cawthon, Georgia

"Our Marsters kept patrollers to keep us straight. There was some hard-headed darkies like they is now who wanted to go without a pass, and if they didn't have a pass, the patrollers got 'em and brought 'em back home. There's a song about the patrollers." Here Aunt Cicely sang in her musical voice, patting one foot all the while: "Run, nigger, run, the paddy-role will catch you, run, nigger, run, the paddy-role will catch you, run, nigger, run, the paddy-role will catch you, you better get away, you better get away."

Mary Childs, Georgia

Were you whipped because you didn't pay attention to your work and didn't do it right?

"Yes'm. I had to whip them seams perfectly straight. They treat me good mos' of de time, dat was de only thing I got whip for. But Thomas, de red-headed young marster was mean about slaves stayin' out over pass time. If dey went off and stay too long, when they come back, he'd strip 'em stark mother nekked, tie 'um to a tree and whip 'um good. But old master he didn't believe in whipping. It was different when the boys taken possession after he died."

Was Thomas mean all the time, Mary?

"Yes'm. You know us had plenty to eat, a smokehouse full o' meat, syrup and things like dat, but sometimes when Mister Thomas got mad and he saw you eatin', he would take everything in de pans and tho' it in de slop pail, and you had to wait till de nex' meal to git somethin'. Dere was three families of Roofs, Thomas, Franklin and de old man, but de lan' was work by all of 'em togedder. I was belongs to de ole man."

Mary was asked about what other slaves had called "the gameron stick" method of tying up a disobedient slave.

"Waren' so on our plantation," she said. "But I yeared people say that niggers was sometimes punished wid de 'gamlin' stick on other plantations."

Anne Clark, Texas

"When women were with child they'd dig a hole in the ground and put their stomach in the hole and then beat em. They'd allus whop us." She remembers Abe Lincoln as a name. "He done set us free."

Willis Cofer, Georgia

"Our Marster done de overseein' at his place hisself, and he never had no hired overseer. Nobody never got a lickin' on our plantation lessen day needed it bad, but when Marster did whup 'em dey knowed dey had been whupped. Dere warn't no fussin' and fightin' on our place and us all knowed better'n to take what didn't b'long to us, 'cause Old Marster sho' did git atter Niggers what stole. If one Nigger did kill another Nigger, dey tuk him and locked him in de jailhouse for 30 days to mak his peace wid God. Evvy day de preacher would come read de Bible to him, and when de 30 days wuz up, den dey would hang him by de neck 'til he died. De man what done de hangin' read de Bible to de folkses what wuz gathered 'round dar while de murderer wuz a-dyin'."

Thomas Cole, Texas

"But us lucky, 'cause Massa Cole don't whip us. De man what have a place next ours, he sho' whip he slaves. He have de cat-o-nine tails of rawhide leather platted round a piece of wood for a handle. De wood 'bout ten inches long and de leather braided on past de stock quite a piece, and 'bout a foot from dat all de strips tied in a knot and sprangle out, and makes de tassle. Dis am call de cracker and it am what split de hide. Some folks call dem bullwhips, 'stead of cat-o-nine tails. De first thing dat man do when he buy a slave, am give him de whippin'. He call it puttin' de fear of Gawd in him."

Eli Coleman, Texas

"Yes, Maser would whip a slave if he got stubborn or lazy and did not want to work. He whipped one slave so hard one day that slave said he would kill Maser before long, he was so mad at him. But, Mister, Maser got hold of what that slave done said and believes me when Maser got through with him he was a Christian. Maser took him to his quarters and put a chain around that negroes legs so he just could hardly walk and brings him back to the field and puts that negro to work. At night when he got to his quarters Maser put another chain around his neck, and didn't give him half enough to eat for 3 solid weeks. When he would snap this chain around his neck he fastened the other end to a tree and let that negro sleep on the ground, then he would beg Maser to let him loose as on Saturday he could not go to see his wife or go to the negro dances we would have. Just have to stay chained up to that tree."

"After the 3 weeks was up Maser turned him loose and I's believes that was the proudest negro in the world. That night Maser give him pass so he could see his wife who lived on the next plantation from ours. That negro was the hardest working negro Maser had after that."

Arthur Colson, Georgia

If a slave wished to leave the plantation, he first had to secure a pass from the master or else he would be soundly thrashed. This whipping was not administered by the master, but by the white men of the community.

Sara Crocker, Georgia

Sara told us that she, as well as her brothers and sisters, were whipped by their master. "But he didn't whup much," she answered. There was no other punishment for a slave, so if he were idle or disobedient he knew what to expect.

Adeline Cunningham, Texas

"One of de slaves runs away and dey ketches him and puts his eyes out. Dey catches anudder slave dat run away and dey hanged him up by de arm. Yassuh, I see dat wid my own eyes; dey holds de slave up by one arm, dey puts a iron on his knee and a iron on his feet and drag 'im down but his feet cain't reach de groun'."

Minnie Davis, Georgia

"I heared 'em talkin' 'bout paterollers, but I never did see one. Folkses said dey would git you and beat you if dey cotch you off de plantation whar you b'longed 'thout no pass. If any of Marse Billie's slaves got cotched by de paterollers, I never knowed nothin' 'bout it."

Elige Davison, Texas

"I seed some few run away to the north and massa sometime cotch 'em and put 'em in jail. Us couldn't go to nowhere without a pass. The patterrollers would git us and they do plenty for nigger slave. I's went to my quarters and be so tired I jus' fall in the door, on the ground, and a patterroller come by and hit me several licks with a cat-o-nine-tails, to see if I's tired 'nough to not run 'way. Sometimes them patterrdlers hit us jus' to hear us holler."

Douglas Dorsey, Florida

Sometimes the young men on the plantation would slip away to visit a girl on another plantation. If they were caught by the "Patrols" while on these visits they would be lashed on the bare backs as a penalty for this offense.

A whipping post was used for this purpose. As soon as one slave was whipped, he was given the whip to whip his brother slave. Very often the lashes would bring blood very soon from the already lacerated skin, but this did not stop the lashing until one had received their due number of lashes. .

Hattie Douglas, Arkansas

"He [her father] used to say his owner tried to whip him but he wouldn't stand for that. He was mean as the devil, but he was good in some ways. He provided for his family—I give him credit for that. We had plenty to eat and plenty to wear. Why, when you'd go in the smoke house it would look like a young store."

"I heard my mother say one time her owner was gone and the overseer ordered her to wash some socks and she wouldn't do it cause she was not under his supervision and he struck her and knocked her out."

Victor Duhon, Texas

"I was always in good hands. Some slaves were treated bad. Mr. Natale Vallean beat up a slave for stealing. He beat him so hard he lay in front of the gate a whole day and the night."

George Eason, Georgia

Although the master or the overseer were not as cruel as some he had heard of they tolerated no looseness of work and in case a person was suspected of loafing the whip was applied freely. Although he was never whipped, he has heard the whip being applied to his mother any number of times. It hurt him, he says, because he had to stand back unable to render any assistance whatever. (This happened before he was sent to the plantation.)

When his mother got these whippings she always ran off afterwards and hid in the woods which were nearby. At night she would slip to the cabin to get food and while there would caution him and the other children not to tell the master that they had seen her. The master's wife who was very mean was always the cause of her receiving these lashings.

Mr. Ormond permitted few if any celebrations or frolics to take place on his farm. When he did grant this privilege his slaves were permitted to invite their friends who of course had to get a "pass" from their respective masters. They, too, were required to secure a pass from Mr. Ormond if they wanted to visit off the premises. If caught by the "Paddle Rollers" [Patrollers] without this pass they were soundly whipped and than taken to their master.

Callie Elder, Georgia

"If one slave kilt another, Marse Billy made de overseer tie dat dead Nigger to de one what kilt him, and de killer had to drag de corpse 'round 'til he died too. De murderers never lived long a-draggin' dem daid ones 'round. Dat jus' pyorely skeered 'em to death. Dere was a guard house on de farm, whar de wust Niggers was kept, and while dey was in dat guard house, dey warn't fed but once a day. It warn't nothin' unusual for Marse Billy to sell slaves, but he never sold his best Niggers. De ones he sold was allus dem he couldn't git no wuk out of."

Phillip Evans, South Carolina

"Who was de overseers? Mr. Wade Rawls was one and Mr. Osborne was another. There was another one but 'spect I won't name him, 'cause him had some troube wid my Uncle Dennis. 'Pears like he insult my aunt and beat her. Uncle Dennis took it up, beat de overseer, and run off to de woods. Then when he git hungry, him come home at night for to eat sumpin'. Dis kept up 'til one day my pappy drive a wagon to town and Dennis jined him. Him was a settin' on de back of de wagon in de town and somebody point him out to a officer. They clamp him and put him in jail. After de 'vestigation they take him to de whippin' post of de town, tie his foots, make him put his hands in de stocks, pulled off his shirt, pull down his britches and whip him terrible."

Lewis Favor, Georgia

Sometimes there were slaves who were punished by the overseer because they had broken some rule. Mr. Favors says that at such times a cowhide whip was used and the number of lashes that the overseer gave depended on the slave owner's instructions. He has seen others whipped and at such times he began praying. The only punishment that he ever received was as a little boy and then a switch was used instead of the whip. If the "Patter-Roller" caught a slave out in the streets without a pass from his master they proceeded to give the luckless fellow five lashes with a whip called the cat-o-nine-tails. They gave six lashes if the slave was caught out at night regardless of whether he had a pass or not.

John Finnely, Texas

"De worst whuppin' I seed was give to Clarinda. She hits massa with de hoe 'cause he try 'fere with her and she try stop him. She am put on de log and give 500 lashes. She am over dat Iog all day and when dey takes her off, she am limp and act deadlike. For a week she am in de bunk. Dat whuppin' cause plenty trouble and dere lots of arg'ments 'mong de white folks 'round dere."

Sarah Ford, Texas

"Massa Charles run dat plantation jus' like a factory. Uncle Cip was sugar man, my papa tanner and Uncle John Austin, what have a wooden leg, am shoemaker and make de shoes with de brass toes. Law me, dey heaps of things go on in slave time what won't go on no more, 'cause de bright light come and it ain't dark no more for us black folks. Iffen a nigger run away and dey cotch him, or does he come back 'cause he hongry, I seed Uncle Jake stretch him out on de ground and tie he hands and feet to posts so he can't move none. Den he git de piece of iron what he call de 'slut' and what is like a block of wood with little holes in it, and fill de holes up with tallow and put dat iron in de fire till de grease sizzlin' hot and hold it over de pore nigger's back and let dat hot grease drap on he hide. Den he take de bullwhip and whip up and down, and after all dat throw de pore nigger in de stockhouse and chain him up a couple days with nothin' to eat. My papa carry de grease scars on he back till he die."

Louis Fowler, Texas

"Dere am only one time dat a nigger gits whupped on dat plantation and dat am not given by massa but by dem patterrollers. Massa don't gin'rally 'low dem patterrollers whup on his place, and all de niggers from round dere allus run from de patterrollers onto massa's land and den dey safe. But in dis 'ticlar case, massa make de 'ception."

"'Twas nigger Jack what dey chases home and he gits under de cabin and 'fused to come out. Massa say, 'In dis case I gwine make 'ception, 'cause dat Jack he am too unreas'able. He allus chasin' after some nigger wench and not satisfied with de pass I give. Give him 25 lashes but don't draw de blood or leave de marks.'"

"Well, sar, it am de great sight to see Jack git dat whippin'. Him am skeert, but dey ain't hurtin' him bad. Massa make him come out and dey tie him to a post and he starts to bawl and beller befo' a lick am struck. Say! Him beg like a good fellow. It am, 'Oh, massa, massa, Oh, massa, have mercy, don't let 'em whup me. Massa, I won't go off any more.' De patterrollers gives him a lick and Jack lets out a yell dat sounds like a mule bray and twice as loud."

"Dere used to be a patterroller song what sent like dis:

Up de hill and down de holler
White man cotch nigger by de collar
Dat nigger run and dat nigger flew,
Dat nigger tore he shirt in two.

"Well, while dey's whuppin' dat nigger, Jack, he couldn't run and he couldn't tear he shirt in two, but he holler till he tear he mouth in two. Jack say he never go off without de pass 'gain and he kept he word, too."

Fannie Fulcher, Georgia

"At night dey couldn't leave de place 'less marster give 'um a pass to go whenever dey said dey wanted to go. If the Patterolers got 'em anywhere else, and dey couldn't out-run 'em dey got a whipping."

Fannie said that the whipping was done by the master himself, he seldom allowed the overseer to whip his slaves. Some were bad and did many things displeasing to the owner, but as a whole there was not much whipping done by Dr. Miller.

Mary Gladdy, Georgia

"My father was a very large, powerful man. During his master's absence in '63 or '64, a colored foreman on the Mines Holt place once undertook to whip him; but my father wouldn't allow him to do it. This foreman then went off and got five big buck Negroes to help him whip father, but all six of them couldn't out-man my daddy! Then this foreman shot my daddy with a shotgun, inflicting wounds from which he never fully recovered."

Andrew Goodman, Texas

"Old man Briscoll, who had a place next to ours, was vicious cruel. He was mean to his own blood, beatin' his chillen. His slaves was afeared all the time and hated him. Old Charlie, a good, old man who 'longed to him, run away and stayed six months in the woods 'fore Briscoll cotched him. The niggers used to help feed him, but one day a nigger 'trayed him, and Briscoe put the dogs on him and cotched him. He made to Charlie like he wasn't goin' to hurt him none, and got him to come peaceful. When he took him home, he tied him and beat him for a turrible long time. Then he took a big, pine torch and let burnin' pitch drop in spots all over him. Old Charlie was sick 'bout four months and then he died.

George Govan, Arkansas

"Both my parents was slaves on de plantation of a Mr. Govan near Charleston, South Carolina. Dat's where we got our name. Folks come to Arkansas after dey was freed. No sir, I ain't edicated—never had de chance. Parents been dead a good many years."

"Yes suh, my folks used to talk a heap and tell me lots of tales of slavery days, and how de patrollers used to whip em when dey wanted to go some place and didn't have de demit to go. Yes suh, dey had to have a demit to go any place outside work hours. Dey whipped my mother and father both sometimes, and dey sure was afraid of dem patrollers. Used to say, 'If you don't watch out de patrollers'll git you.' Dey'd catch de slaves and tie em up to a tree or a pos' and whip em wid buggy whips and rawhides."

Charlie Grant, South Carolina

"I was sittin up in de corner en look up en patrol was standin in de door en call patrol. When dey hear dat, dey know something gwine to do. Dey took Uncle Mac Gibson en whip him en den dey take one by one out en whip dem. When dey got house pretty thin en was bout to get old man Gibson, he take hoe like you work wid en put it in de hot ashes. People had to cut wood en keep fire burnin all de year cause didn' have no matches den. Old man Gibson went to de door en throwed de hot ashes in de patrol face. Dey try to whip us, but de old man Gibson tell dem dey got no right to whip his niggers. We run from whe' we at to our home. Dey tried four years to catch my daddy, but dey couln' never catch him. He was a slick nigger."

Alice Green, Georgia

"Now my daddy, he was a plum sight sho' 'nough. He said dat when evvythin' got still and quiet at night he would slip off and hunt him up some 'omans. Patterollers used to git atter him wid nigger hounds and once when dey cotch him he said dey beat him so bad you couldn't lay your hand on him nowhar dat it warn't sore. Dey beat so many holes in him he couldn't even wear his shirt. Most of de time he was lucky enough to outrun 'em and if he could jus' git to his marster's place fust dey couldn't lay hands on him. Yes Mam, he was plenty bad 'bout runnin' away and gittin' into devilment."

O. W. Green, Texas

"My old masta was good, but when he found you shoutin' he burnt your hand. My grandmother said he burnt her hand several times. Masta wouldn't

O. W. Green. (Library of Congress)

let de cullud folks have meetin', but dey would go out in de woods in secret to pray and preach and shout."

Sarah Anne Green, North Carolina

"Marse Billy an' Mis' Roby teached de Sunday School, but day didn' teach us to read an' write, no suh, dey sho didn'. If dey'd see us wid er book dey'd whip us. Dey said niggers didn' need no knowledge; dat dey mus' do what dey was tole to do."

Heard Griffin, Georgia

"Mike Griffin was the meanest man I've ever known," he continued. "He would sit down with nothing else to do, think of some man, send for him and for no reason at all, give him a good beating. He kept a long cow-hide, which was almost an inch thick and with this he would almost beat folks to death. First you had to remove your clothing so that whipping would not wear them out. One day he beat a woman named Hannah so badly that she died the same night. . . . We never knew the burial place. Overseers too, were very mean, particularly those on the Griffin plantation. They followed the example of the man who hired them and as a result this plantation was known far and wide for its cruelty, fear, and terror. Many slaves would have attempted to run away but for fear of the pack of blood hounds kept for the purpose of tracking run away slaves."

"'Petter-rollers' were busy, too, looking up slaves and whipping them for the flimsiest of excuses. Slaves often outran them to the woods and managed to return to their plantations unobserved. If a pass had a certain hour marked in it, for the slaves return and he failed to return at the designated houses, this was an offense for which they were punished by the 'patter-rollers.'" "Yes," remarked Mr. Griffin, "We were not even allowed to quarrel among ourselves. Our master would quickly tell us, 'I am the one to fight, not you.'" When a slave visited his relatives on another plantation the master would send along one or two of his children to make sure they did not attempt to run away.

Milton Hammond, Georgia

Slaves on the Freeman plantation never knew anything but kind treatment. Their mistress was a religious woman and never punished unless it was absolutely necessary. On other plantations however, some slaves were treated cruelly. When a slave resented this treatment he was quickly gotten rid of. Many were sent to Mississippi and Texas. White offenders were sent to chain gangs, but there were no gangs for slaves. "Patter rollers" were known more for their cruelty than many of the slave owners and would often beat slaves unmercifully. "I remember one," remarked Mr. Hammond. "The Patter rollers fot after a man on our place. Booker went to see his wife and took along an old out of date pass. The Patter-rollers asked to see the pass which he quickly handed to them and kept walking. After inspecting the pass closely they called Booker and told him the pass was no good. 'Well this is,' he replied and started running just as fast as he could until he safely reached the plantation. I never needed a pass."

Pierce Harper, Texas

"The masters couldn't whip the slaves there. The law said in black and white no master couldn't whip no slave, no matter what he done. When a slave got bad they took him to the county seat and had him whipped. One day I seen my old daddy get whipped by the county and state 'cause he wouldn't work. They had a post in the public square what they tied 'em to and a man what worked for the county whipped 'em."

Tom Hawkins, Georgia

"Miss Annie was her own whuppin' boss. She beat on 'em for most anything. She had a barrel wid a pole run thoo' it, and she would have a slave stretched out on dat barrel wid his clothes off and his hands and foots tied to de pole. Den Miss Annie would fire up her pipe and set down and whup a Nigger for a hour at a time. Miss Annie would pull my ears and hair when I didn't do to suit her, but she never whupped me. Miss Annie didn't need no jail for her slaves. She could manage 'em widout nothin' lak dat, and I never did hear of no jails in de country 'roun' whar us lived."

"Dere warn't no schools whar slaves could git book larnin' in dem days. Dey warn't even 'lowed to larn to read and write. When Dr. Cannon found out dat his carriage driver had larned to read and write whilst he was takin' de doctor's chillun to and f'um school, he had dat Niggers thumbs cut off and put another boy to doin' de drivin' in his place."

Emmaline Heard, Georgia

Slaves who chanced to be visiting away from his plantation without a pass from his owner would be severely handled if caught by the Ku Klux Klan or "patterrollers" as they were more commonly called. Fear of the "patterrollers" was involved to frighten children into good behaviour.

Benjamin Henderson, Georgia

Slaves were punished by "Patter Rollers" or the government patrol, if caught off of their plantations without a pass. Often slaves outran the "Patter Rollers" and escaped the 75 lashes which were in store for them if they were caught. "Patter Rollers" carried a crooked-handle stick which they would try to fasten around the slaves' necks or arms. Morever, the slaves soon learned that the "patter-rollers" stick would slide off their bare arms and backs, so they left their shirts if planning to make a visit without a pass.

Julia Henderson, Georgia

"My grandmother said my grandfather uster slip off widout askin' for no pass. Sometimes de young bucks would bus' in de smoke-'ouse and steal roasin' potatoes and broilin' meat. De overseer come lookin' and grandfather tore out to git home, but dey whip de res' whatever dey caught. Yes, dey whip 'em bad—dey raise a fence and put dey head under de fence and whip 'em. Onc't dey whip my grandmother. She were plyin' [ploughing] and mule go all right, but when it come back to dis end, he would make a dart, and dat would jerk de fer [furrow] crooked, and den she went around to see what make dat dart, and a great big coach-whip snake big as she, jus' rear up and look at her! She taken de whip and cut 'im around de neck, des de easies' way to kill 'em. Boss-man come down dere to see what de matter, 'cause she quit workin'. She give him stiff talk, and he whip her from one end of de road to de udder, and de blood run down in her shoes, and she plyin'!" Julia shuddered. "O am so glad I ain't slave! But I reckon I'd git along all right, be jus' like I is now, nice and good and dey wouldn' whip me none."

Essex Henry, North Carolina

"Der wus a few spirited slaves what won't be whupped an' my uncle wus one. Es wus finally sold fer dis."

Tom Holland, Texas

"If we went off without a pass we allus went two at a time. We slipped off when we got a chance to see young folks on some other place. The patter-rollers cotched me one night and, Lawd have mercy me, they stretches me over a log and hits thirty-nine licks with a rawhide loaded with rock, and every time they hit me the blood and hide done fly. They drove me home to massa and told him and he called a old mammy to doctor my back, and I couldn't work for four days. That never kep' me from slippin' off 'gain, but I's more careful the next time."

Bill Homer, Texas

"Some work was hard and some easy, but massa don' 'lieve in overworkin' his slaves. Sat'day afternoon and Sunday, dere was no work. Some whippin' done, but mos' reasonable. If de nigger stubborn, deys whips 'nough for to change his mind. If de nigger runs off, dat calls de good whippin's. If any of de cullud folks has de misery, dey lets him res' in bed and if de misery bad de massa call de doctor."

Bill Homer. (Library of Congress)

Bryant Huff, Georgia

Bryant's early life was not one to inspire pleasant memories for his master, a highly educated man; ardent church workers, had a cruel nature and a temper that knew no bounds. Owning 800 acres of land in a fairly level section, he ruled his small kingdom with an iron hand. Bryant's father, Daniel, was the only man who did not fear "Marse" Rigerson.

While most of the punishment was given by the "patty-roller" and the Master, in some instances overseers were allowed to administer it. Some of these overseers were Negroes and occasionally there was trouble when they attempted to punish another slave. Huff recalls having seen one of these "bosses" approach his mother as she toiled in the field and questioned her regarding her whereabouts on the previous evening. She refused to answer and as he approached her in a threatening manner, she threw piles of twigs upon him. (She was loading a wagon with small limbs cut from trees on "new ground.") He fled in terror. That night, as the mother and her children were seated in their cabin, the same man accompanied by their Master entered, tied her hands and led her from the home. She was carried quite a distance down the road and severely beaten.

Easter Huff, Georgia

"I seed dem patterollers on hosses jus' goin' it down de big road. I seed 'em axin' Niggers dey met if dey had passes. Atter dey looked at de passes, dey would let 'em go on. But if a slave was cotched widout no pass dey would beat him mos' nigh to death. If us had patterollers to keep Niggers f'um gallivantin' 'round so much now days, dar wouldn't be so much devilment done."

"Some of de slaves jus' had to be whupped 'cause dey wouldn't behave. On our plantation, de overseer done de whuppin'; Marse Jabe never totched 'em. Mammy told us 'bout seein' slaves put on de block in Virginny and sold off in droves lak hosses."

Amanda Jackson, Georgia

"Dere wuz'nt much whuppin on our plantation—not by de marster. Dey usually got whupped fer not workin'. Others got whupped by de Paddie-Rollers when dey wuz cot off'n de plantation widout a pass. Dey would come to de plantation an' whup you if dey knowed you had been off wid out a pass. Des man whose plantation we wuz on did pretty well by us—he did'nt like fer de Paddie-Rollers to come on his place to do no whuppin."

James Jackson, Texas

"Marster Duvall would whip de niggers who was disobedience and he jus' call dem up and ask dem what was de trouble, den he would whip dem wid a cowhide or a rope whip. We could go anywhere iffen we had a pass, but if we didn' de paddlerollers would ketch us. They was kinda like policemen we got today."

James Jackson. (Library of Congress)

Richard Jackson, Texas

"They was a white overseer on the place, and mammy's stepdaddy, Kit, was nigger driver and done all the whippin', 'cept of mammy. She was bad 'bout fightin' and the overseer allus tended to her. One day he come to the wuarters to whip her and she up and throwed a shovel full of live coals from the fireplace in his bosom and run out the door. He run her all over the place 'fore he cotched her. I seed the overseer tie her down and whip her. The niggers wasn't whipped much 'cept for fightin' 'mongst themselves."

Thomas Johns, Texas

"We was allus well treated by old marster. We was called, 'John's free niggers,' not dat we was free, but 'cause we was well treated. Jesse Todd, his place joined ours, had 500 slaves, and he treated 'em mighty bad. He whipped some of 'em to death. A man sold him two big niggers which was brothers and they was so near white you couldn' hardly tell 'em from a white man. Some people thought the man what sold 'em was their daddy. The two niggers worked good and dey hadn' never been whipped and dey wouldn' stand for bein' whipped. One mornin' Todd come up to 'em and told de oldest to take his shirt off. He say, 'Marster, what you wan' me to take my shirt off for?' Todd say, 'I told you to take your shirt off.' De nigger say, 'Marster, I ain' never took my shirt off for no man.' Todd run in de house and got his gun and come back and shot de nigger dead. His brother fell down by him where he lay on de groun'. Todd run back to load his gun again, it bein' a single shot. Todd's wife and son grabbed him and dey had all dey coul' do to keep him from comin' out and killin' de other nigger."

Benjamin Johnson, Georgia

"You go off to see somebody at night—jes' like you an' me want to laff an' talk—an' if dey ketch an' you ain't got no pass den dey gwine to whup you. You be glad to git away too 'cause when dey hit you, you wus hit. I wus down to ol' John Brady's place one night talkin' to a lady an' ol' man Brady slipped up behin' me an' caught me in de collar an' he say: 'Whut you doin' over here? —I'm goin' to give you twenty-five lashes' an' den he say to me: 'come here.' He wus jes' bout as tall as I am an' when I got to 'im he say turn 'roun' and' I say to 'im dat I ain't doin' nuthin' an' den he say: 'dats whut I'm goin to whup you fer 'cause you ought to be home doin' sumpin'. 'Bout dat time when I stooped over to take off my coat I caught 'im in his pants an' throwed 'im in a puddle o' water an' den I lit out fer home. If you git home den dey couldn't do nuthin' to you. He tried to chase me but he did'nt know de way through de woods like I did an' he fell in a gulley an' hurt his arm. De next mornin' when I wus hitchin' up de boss man's horse I seed 'im comin' an' I tol de boss dat he tried to whup me de night befo' an' den de boss man say 'did he have you?' 'I tol' 'im dat he did but dat I got away. An' den de boss say: 'He had you an 'he did'nt have you—is dat right?' Den he say 'don't worry 'bout dat I can git you out of dat. If he had you he shoulda whupped you an' dat woulda been his game but he let you git away an' so dat wus yo' game.' 'Bout dat time ol' man Brady had done got dere an' he tol' de marster dat I wus on his place de night befo' an' dat I got away an' when he tried to whup me an' de marster say to him: 'dat wus his game—if you had him you shoulda whupped 'im. Dats de law. If you had whupped 'im dat woulda been yo' game, but you let 'im git away an' so dat wus his game.' Ol' man Brady's face turned so red dat it looked like he wus gonna bus'."

"Sometimes ol' missus would come 'long an' she would be mad wid some of de women an' she would want to go to whuppin' on 'em."

"Sometimes de women would'nt take it an' would run away an' hide in de woods. Sometimes dey would come back after a short stay an' den again dey would have to put de hounds on dere trail to bring dem back home. As a general rule dere wus'nt much whuppin' on our plantation. 'Course if you did'nt do what dey tol' you to do dey would take you out an' put yo' hands round a pole an' tie you so yo' feet would jes' touch de groun' an' den dey would go to work on you wid a cowhide. Everytime dey hit you de blood would fly wid de whip."

Ella Johnson, Georgia

"Oh, before I forget it, I must tell you about the 'paddlerollers.' These were a bunch of white men who banded together to beat slaves when they were caught off their plantation without a pass. They beat them unmercifully with huge wooden paddles. After the war they were called the Ku Klux Klan. The beatings that some of those poor slaves got was horrible."

Harry Johnson, Texas

"It don't look reas'able to say it, but it's a fac'—durin' slavery iffen you lived one place and your mammy lived 'cross de street you couldn't go to see her without a pass. De paddlerollers would whip you if you did. Dere was one woman owns some slaves and one of 'em asks her for a pass and she give him de piece of paper sposed to be de pass, but she writes on it:

His shirt am rough and his back am tough,
Do pray, Mr. Paddleroller, give 'im 'nough

"De paddlerollers beat him nearly to death, 'cause that's what's wrote on de paper he give 'em."

"I 'member a whippin' one slave got. It were 100 lashes. Dey's a big over-seer right here on de San Marcos river. Clem Polk, him and he massa kilt 16 niggers in one day. Dat massa couldn't keep a overseer, 'cause de niggers wouldn't let 'em whip 'em, and dis Clem, he say, 'I'll stay dere,' and he finds he couldn't whip dem niggers either, so he jus' kilt 'em. One nigger nearly got him and would havd kilt him. Dat nigger raise de ax to come down on Polk's head and de massa stopped him jus' in time, and den Polk shoots dat nigger in de breast with a shotgun."

Toby Jones, Texas

"Our owner was Massa Felix Jones and he had lots of tobacco planted. He was real hard on us slaves and whipped us, but Missie Janie, she was a real good woman to her black folks."

"The overseer was a mean white man and one day he starts to whip a nigger what am hoein' tobacco, and he whipped him so hard that nigger grabs him and made him holler. Missie come out and made them turn loose and massa whipped that nigger and put him in chains for a whole year. Every night he had to be in jail and couldn't see his folks for that whole year."

Lucindy Jurdon, Alabama

"Ef us tried to learn to read or write, dey would cut your forefingers off."

Jennie Kendricks, Georgia

The whipping on most plantation were administerd by the overseers and in some cases punishment was rather severe. There was no overseer on this plantation. Only one of Mr. Moore's sons told the field hands what to do. When this son went to war it became necessary to hire an overseer. Once he attempted to whip one of the women but when she refused to allow him to whip her he never tried to whip any of the others. Jennie Kendricks' husband, who was also a slave, once told her his master was so mean that he often whipped his slaves until blood ran in their shoes.

There was a group of men, known as the "Patter-Rollers," whose duty it was to see that slaves were not allowed to leave their individual plantations without passes which they were supposed to receive from their masters. "A heap of them got whippings for being caught off without these passes." She stated adding that sometimes a few of them were fortunate enough to escape from the "Patter-Rollers." She knew of one boy who, after having out-run the "Patter-Rollers," proceeded to make fun of them after he was safe behind his master's fence. Another man whom the Patter-Rollers had pursued any number of times but who had always managed to escape, was finally caught one day and told to pray before he was given his whipping. As he obeyed he noticed that he was not being closely observed, whereupon he made a break that resulted in his escape from them again.

Charlie King, Georgia

[Charlie King] said though "ole Marster" "whupped" when it was necessary, but he was not "onmerciful" like some of the other "ole Marsters" were, but the "paterolers would sho lay it on if they caught a Nigger off his home plantation without a pass." The passes were written statements or permits signed by the darkies' owner, or the plantation overseer.

Julia Larken, Georgia

"'Fore Grandma Mary got too old to do all de cookin, Mammy wuked in de field. Mammy said she allus woke up early, and she could hear Marster when he started gittin' up. She would hurry and git out 'fore he had time to call 'em. Sometimes she cotch her hoss and rid to the field ahead of de others, 'cause Marster never laked for nobody to be late in de mornin'. One time he got atter one of his young slaves out in de field and told him he was a good mind to have him whupped. Dat night de young Nigger was tellin' a old slave 'bout it, and de old man jus' laughed and said: 'When Marster pesters me dat way I jus' rise up and cuss him out.' Dat young fellow 'cided he would try it out and de next time Marster got atter him dey had a rukus what I ain't never gwine to forgit. Us was all out in de yard et de big house, skeered to git a good breath when us heared Marster tell him to do somepin, 'cause us knowed what he was meanin' to do. He didn't go right ahead and mind Marster lak he had allus been used to doin'. Marster called to him again, and den dat fool Nigger cut loose and he evermore did cuss Marster out. Lordy, Chile, Marster jus' fairly tuk de hide off dat Nigger's back. When he tried to talk to dat old slave 'bout it de old man laughed and said: 'Shucks, I allus waits 'til I gits to de field to cuss Marster so he won't hear me.'"

Amos Lincoln, Texas

"Elisha Guidry he my master in slavery. He had lots of slaves. He whip my pa lots of times. He was unwillin' to work. He whip my ma, too. One time he cut her with the whip and cut one her big toes right off. Ma come up on the gallery and wrap it up in a piece of rag."

Caroline Malloy, Georgia

To leave the plantation all slaves had to have passes from the master. If they were caught outside the boundaries of the plantation without this pass or ticket, the "patteroll" or white men in the community punished them. The master had no authority over them then.

Charlotte Mitchell Martin, North Carolina

Charlotte was a slave of Judge Wilkerson on a large plantation near Sixteen, Florida, a little town near Madison. Shepherd Mitchell was a wagoner who hauled whiskey from Newport News, Virginia for his owner. Wilkerson was very cruel and held them in constant fear of him. He would not permit them to hold religious meetings or any other kinds of meetings, but they frequently met in secret to conduct religious services. When they were caught, the "instigators"—known or suspected—were severely flogged. Charlotte recalls how her oldest brother was whipped to death for taking part in one of the religious ceremonies. This cruel act halted the secret religious services.

James Martin, Texas

"Did they whip the slaves? Well, they jus' about half killed 'en. When it was too rough, they slipped into Canada."

Carrie Mason, Georgia

"Effen my mammy or pappy ever runned away from Marster, I ain't heered tell uv it, but Mammy said dat when slaves did run away, dey wuz cotched an' whupped by de overseer. Effen a man or a 'oman kilt another one den dey wuz branded wid er hot i'on. Er big S wuz put on dey face somewhars. S stood fer 'slave,' an' evvybody knowed dey wuz er mudderer. Marster din't have no overseer; he overseed hisself."

William Mathews, Texas

"Sometimes dey run 'way. It ain't done dem no good, for de dawgs am put on dey trail. If you clumb de tree, dem dogs hold you dere till de white folks comes, and den dey let de dogs git you. Sometimes de dogs tore all dey clothes off, and dey ain't got nary a rag on 'em when dey git home. If dey run in de stream of water, de dogs gits after 'em and drowns 'em. Den Nick, de overseer, he whop 'em. He drive down four stakes for de feets and hands and tie 'em up. Den he whop 'em from head to feets. De whip make out a hide, cut in strips, with holes punch in 'em. When dey hits de akin it make blisters."

John McCoy, Texas

"Old Marse John have a big place round Houston and raises cotton and corn and hawgs and cows. Dere was lots of wilderness den, full of varmints and wildcats and bears. Old Marse done larn me 'bedience and not to lie or steal, and he larn me with de whip. Dat all de larnin' we gits. Does he cotch you with de book or paper, he whip you hand down. He don't whip de old folks none, jes' de young bucks, 'cause dey wild and mean and dat de onlies' way dey larns right from wrong."

Ed McCree, Georgia

"Don't talk 'bout dat overseer whuppin' Niggers. He beat on 'em for most anything. What would dey need no jail for wid dat old overseer a-comin' down on 'em wid dat rawhide bull-whup?"

"'Bout dem patterollers! Well, you knowed if dey cotched you out widout no pass, dey was gwine to beat your back most off and send you on home. One night my Pa 'lowed he would go to see his gal. All right, he went. When he got back, his cabin door was fastened hard and fast. He was a-climbin' in de window when de patterollers got to him. Dey 'lowed: 'Nigger, is you got a pass?' Pa said: 'No Sir.' Den dey said: 'Us can't beat you 'cause you done got home on your marster's place, but us is sho' gwine to tell your Marster to whup your hide off.' But Old Marster never tetched him for dat."

Bill McRay, Texas

"Us have good marster, but some of de neighbors treat dere slaves rough. Ole Dr. Neyland of Jasper, he have 75 or 80 slaves and he was rich and hard on de slaves. One day two run away. Tom and Ike, and Dr. Neyland takes de bloodhoun's and ketch dose two niggers and brung 'em in. One of de niggers takes a club and knock one of de houn's in de head and kilt him. Dey cook dat dog and make dem niggers eat part of him. Den dey give both of 'em a beatin'."

"De ole log jail in Jasper, it useter stan' whar de Fish Store is now. Dey have a place t'other side de jail whar dey whip niggers. De whippin' pos' was a big log. Dey make de niggers lie down on it and strap 'em to it. I was a lil' boy den and me and two white boys, Doley McRay end Henry Munn, we useter slip 'round and watch 'em. Coley and Henry both grow up and go to war but neither one come back."

"Sam Swan, he was sheriff and he ketch two runaway niggers one day. Dey was brudders and dey was name Rufe and John Grant. Well, he takes 'em and puts dem in jail and some of de men gits 'em out and takes 'em down to de whippin' pos' and den strap 'em down and give 'em one terrible lashin' and den throw salt in dere wounds and you could hear dem niggers holler for a mile. Den dey took 'em back to de farm to wo'k."

"Dey hanged good many niggers 'round Jasper. In slavery times dey hangs a nigger name Jim Henderson, at Maynew Pond. Us boys wen' dere and mark de tree. Two cullud men, Tom Jefferson and Sam Powell, dey kill anudder nigger and dey hang dem to de ole white oak tree what is south of Jasper Court House."

C. B. McRay, Texas

"Us have a foreman, name Charlie. It was his duty to keep de place stock' with wood. He take slaves and wo'k de wood patches when it needed, but onct marster come home from New Orleans and roux' dem all suferin' for want of fire. He call ole Charlie and ask him why he not git up plenty wood. 'Well,' old Charlie say, 'wood was short and 'fore I could git more did col' spell come and it too awful col' to git wood.' Marster say, 'You keep plenty wood or I gwinter sell you to a mean marster.' Charlie git better for a while, then he let wood git low again. So he was sol' to Ballard Adams, who had the name of bein' hard on his slaves. Charlie couldn' do enough wo'k to suit Marster Adams, so he put him in what's knowed as the 'Louisiana shirt.' Dat was a barrel with a hole cut in the bottom jus' big enough for Charlie to slip he head through. Dey pull dis on to him every mornin' and then he couldn' sit down or use he arms, coul' jus' walk 'rous' all day, de brunt of other slaves jokes. At night dey took it off and chain him to he bed. After he have wo'n dis Louisiana shirt a month de marster task he again. He fail and run off to the woods. So Marster Adams, he come to Marster McRay and want to sell Charlie back again, but he couldn' 'cause freedom jus' come and they couldn' sell slaves no more, but Marster McRay say Charlie coul' come back and stay on he place if he wanted to."

Annette Milledge, Georgia

There were no whippings on the Ransome place, but Annette had dreadful recollections of slaves being punished on adjoining plantations.

"Sometimes dey would w'hoop dem terrible. Dey tied dem acros't a barrel and w'hooped dem until de blood run out. De leas' little thing dey w'hoop de hide off 'em. Better not let 'em ketch you with a book, neider."

"You had to go to yo' marster for a piece of paper, a pass. If dey did ketch you widout dat paper, dey would w'hoop you. Marster never 'low Patterolers to w'hoop his servants. We had a Patteroler in de cullud people's church, too. You know we had our own church wid a cullud preacher. It was Providence Baptis' Church."

Charlie Mitchell, Texas

"Course, I didn't git no schoolin'. The white folks allus said niggers don't need no larnin'. Some niggers larnt to write their initials on the barn door with charcoal, then they try to find out who done that, the white folks, I mean, and say they cut his fingers off iffen they jus' find out who done it."

"Lynchburg was good sized when war come on and Woodruff's nigger tradin' yard was 'bout the bigges' thing there. It was all fenced in and had a big stand in middle of where they sold the slaves. They got a big price for 'em and handcuffed and chained 'em together and led 'em off like convicts. That yard was full of Louisiana and Texas slave buyers mos' all the time. None of the niggers wanted to be sold to Louisiana, 'cause that's where they beat 'em till the hide was raw, and salted 'em and beat 'em some more."

"Course us slaves of white folks what lived in town wasn't treated like they was on most plantations. Massa Nat and Missy Julia was good to us and most the folks we was hired out to was good to us. Lynchburg was full of patty-rollers jus' like the country, though, and they had a fenced in whippin' post there in town and the pattyrollers sho' put it on a nigger iffen they cotch him without a pass."

Matilda Mumford, Georgia

"Yes, she here, visitin'," she said, inviting the visitors to the back porch. Matilda was sitting there, rocking and mumbling, senile, patiently waiting for death to release her from "dis yere hard worl' when I has so much trouble, honey, I kain't 'member nuthin' 'bout dem days but whupping, whup, whup—all de overseers what come from de Norf, jus' whuppin' my mother and me, all de time, when I working, plowing."

"All five overseer so mean, de slaves run away. Dey dug cave in de wood, down in de ground, and dey hide dere. Dey gits de blood-houn's to fin' 'em—den dey whips 'em in de wood, dey buckle 'em down to a log and beat de breaf' outter dem till de blood run all over everywhere. When night come, dey drug 'em to dey house and greases 'em down wid turpentine, and rub salt in dey woun's to mek 'em hurt wuss. I see de man, drinkin' whiskey to mek him mean, while de overseer look on and tell him what to do."

"Dey whup me—cut de breaf outter me—dey tie my mother to a tree and whip her—I crawl under de house and cry."

Matilda moaned. The listening women sighed in sympathy, and her friend said: "When Matilda's mind was clearer she told us terrible stories. It made us thankful we weren't born in those times."

Matilda raised her head. She was "rekellecting" again: "De las' overseer come down befo' de war start, he like to kilt us. He'd strip us down to de wais'—tie men to trees and drink and beat 'em jus' to be whipping."

Matilda's voice was filled with past horror as she went on breathlessly: "I 'member dere wuz two old women, dey couldn't work much. De overseer so mean, he tie 'em to a buggy, stark mother nekked, put a belly band on 'em, and driv' 'em down de road like dey wuz mules, whippin' 'em till dey drap down in de road. Dere wuz some white ladies what see it, and dey reported him and prosecuted him, and he got run out of de county."

Hannah Murphy, Georgia

"I seen many mens runnin' away fum de bloodhoun's. Sometimes we chilluns be in de quarter playin', and a man would come runnin' along fast, breathin' hard, so skeared! De houn's be behind him. Den I kin 'member how they'd whip 'em when dey ketch him. Dey would make de men drop down dey pants and lay down across big logs and dey'd whip 'um. De womans dey'd drop dey bodies and dey'd whip 'em across de back and 'round de waises till de blood come."

George Owens, Texas

"De patterrellers neber git me. I see 'em chase slaves. When dey ketch 'em dey whip 'em, and tell 'em nex' time be sho' to have a pass from ol' marster."

Harre Quarls, Texas

"Sir, us got one day a week and Christmas Day, was all de holiday us ever heered of, and us couldn't go anywhere 'cept us have pass from our massa to 'nother. If us slips off dem patterrollers gits us. Patterroller hits 39 licks with de rawhide with de nine tails. Patterroller gits 50 cents for hittin' us 39 licks. Captain, hera am de words to de patterroller song:

Run, nigger, run, patterroller cotch you,
How kin I run, he got me in de woods
And all through de pasture?
White man run, but nigger run faster.

Easter Reed, Georgia

"No mam, my marster never did whip me," said Easter. "But the mistress would if she caught us tellin' a lie. She'd whip her chillun as well as us. My sisters were whipped for leavin' the cows out in the pasture when they were s'posed to be shut up."

If a slave ever left the plantation he was required to have a pass. Without this written permission, if caught, he would be whipped by the white men of the community. As Easter had a kind master, she had no trouble in securing a pass.

Walter Rimm, Texas

"Massa and missus took dey goodness by spells like. Sometimes dey was hard to git 'long with and sometimes dey was easy to git 'long with. I don't know de cause, but it am so. De mostest trouble am 'bout de work. Dey wants you to work if you can or can't. My pappy have de back mis'ry and many de time I seed him crawl to de grist mill. Him am buyed 'cause him am de good mill-hand. He tells us his pappy am white, and dat one reason he am de run-awayer. I's scairt all de time, 'cause he run away. I seed him git one whippin' and nothin' I can do 'cept stand dere and cry. Dey gits whippin's every time massa feels cross. One slave name Bob Love, when massa start to whip him he cuts his throat and dives into de river. He am dat scairt of a whippin' dat he kilt himself."

Elvira Roies (Boles), Texas

"Marster Boles didn' have many slaves on de farm, but lots in brickyard. I toted brick back and put 'em down where dey had to be. Six bricks each load all day. That's de reason I ain't no 'count, I'se worked to death. I fired de furnace for three years. Stan'in' front wid hot fire on my face. Hard work, but God was wid me. We'd work 'till dark, quit awhile after sundown. Marster was good to slaves, didn' believe in jus' lashin' 'ex. He'd not be brutal but he'd kill 'em dead right on the spot. Overseers 'ud git after 'em and whop 'em down."

"Iffen dey had a pretty girl dey would take 'em, and I'se one of 'em, and my oldest child, he boy by Boles, almost white."

"We had to steal away at night to have church on de ditch bank, and crawl home on de belly. Once overseers heered us pravin', give us one day each 100 lashes."

Tom Rosboro, South Carolina

"I hear mammy say dat daddy's mistress was name Miss Emma but her mistress and my mistress was name Miss Margaret. My daddy have to have a pass every time he come to see mammy. Sometime they give him a general pass for de year. Sometime him lose de pass and then such a gwine on you never did see de lak. Make more miration [hullabaloo] over it than if they had lost one of de chillun. They was scared de patarollers [patrollers] would come ketch him, and lay de leather whip on his naked back. He wouldn't dare stay long. Him would go back soon, not on de big road but through de woods and fields, so as not to meet de patarollers."

Matilda Shepard, Arkansas

Tell about singing and praying around the black kettle. How did you fix it so your voices could not be heard? Did you ever get caught praying this way?

"My mother and other negroes turned the Black Kettle bottom side up left a hole so voices could be heard out of the room. Then after all my old Master and Mistress could hear us. Yes I got caught and they stripped all of our close off—ant put us on the whipping block. Beat us so we could not half walk."

Callie Shepherd, Texas

"Miss Fannie and de Doctor had five field laborers. Some of de white folks dey got more. Some of de Niggers dey don' like de way of their treatment and dey run away to de woods to get away. I used to hear de Nigger dogs a runnin' and when dey ketch de Niggers dey bites 'em all over and tears dey clothes and gets de skin too. And de Niggers dey would holler. I seed' dem when dey whupped de Niggers. Dey used to tell us little childers to look. Dey buckled 'em down on de groun' and laid it on dey backs. Sometimes dey laid on with a mighty heavy han'."

Marshall Showers, Texas

"In de slavery days de boss man buy you den he come an' beat you up. Dey say you can't see your family. It don't make no diffrance. You runs off den you gits a whippin'. Iffen you wants to see your mammy you better git a pass. Dere's a paytroll wid a long bull whip. An' he walk up an' down de road, up an' down, up an' down. He run up on you an he say, 'What you doin' out dis time er night?' You better talk nice. Iffen you don't he open you back wid de bullwhip."

"De paytroll listen while you's talkin' to you wife an' you gotter talk, 'ch, ch, ch,' An' he walk up an' down wid de ole bullwhip, tryin' to hear what you say, 'ch, ch, ch.'"

"You sass de boss man an' dey whips you. You sass his wife an' dey stakes you face down on de ground. Den dey takes down you britches an' cuts your ass all to pieces wid a bullwhip. An' dat aint all. Times de boss's wife she make up stories 'bout you, say you lazy, say you hides out, say you sass 'er when you aint done it. Den dey stakes you out again an' de ole bullwhip make de blood fly. An' you lay dere on de ground bellerin', 'Oh marster, oh, marster.'"

Betty Simmons, Texas

"Dey was one nigger name' John Harper. He was 's mean 's a nigger could git to be. He's truly mean. Dey whip him near' to de'f [death], but he's so no 'count dey atter w'ile jes' t'rowed him 'way."

"W'en us come down Minard's Riber to Gran' Cane to locate, dey was sump'n' funny happen'. Dey's w'ite fambly w'at hab a carriage criber, a big nigger boy 'bout 15 year' ol' dat dey thought a lot of. Dat boy git stuck on one us house gals. De crazy t'ing tuk up a min' [mind] to foller us. It w'er a woodly country an' de boy slip off an' foller. Marse drove he niggers at night. De w'ite folks was so 'sturb' dat dey sont down to hab him brung back. De boy outrun dem a mile, 'long down to Boggy Tu'n road. He's runnin' like de dickens. I year [hear] de dogs runnin' clear 'cross de fiel'. De po' boy he so to'

[torn] an' bleedin' wid bresh scratch' dat he ain' able to move hardly. He run in de yard an' upstair' 'n de gin house. De dogs sot down 'roun' de do' [door] like dey done tree' a 'possum. De dog-man, dat de man w'at own' de dog, he drug de boy down by he foot an' pull' he jacket off. Ol' man Hanlon, us oberseer, he tol' dem it no use to punish dat boy no mo'. He been punish' 'nuf. Dat don' he'p though. Dey t'row de boy in de Horse Hol' an' de two dogs w'at train' to swim dey go in atter him. De boy so scare' he yell an' holler. But de dogs train' an' dey nip an' pinch him good wid dey claw' an' teef. Atter dey 'low him out ol' man Hanlon put med'cine on de bite'. De boy so scare' he cryin'. W'en he marster fin' how mean de dog-man been to de boy he so mad he 'fuse to pay de fee. De dog-man 'cess a fee for all de niggers w'at he kotch wid he dogs."

James W. Smith, Texas

"Our Marster gives weuns reasonable priviledge to go off de place. 'Twas de rule dat de cullud fo'ks must have de pass fo' to go off de plantation. Dat am fo' de reason to keep o'dah, an' to hold de cullud fo'ks on de place. If dey tries to run away, de Patrollers would catch dem. De Patrollers, deys ride over de country, an' demand de pass be shown by de niggers dat am on de road, or whar deys finds dem off dere plantation. If dey finds de cullud person widout de pass, dey whups him, an' tooks him home. 'Cause ob de Patrollers, de sensible nigger stays home 'less him have de pass."

James W. Smith. (Library of Congress)

Jordon Smith, Texas

"Missus didn't 'low her niggers to work till they's 21, and the chillen played marbles and run round and kick their heels. The first work I done was hoeing and us worked long as we could see a stalk of cotton or hill of corn. Missus used to call us at Christmas and give the old folks a dollar and the rest a dinner. When she died me and my mother went to Ab Smith at the dividement of the property. Master Ab put us to work on a big farm he bought and it was Hell 'mong the yearlin's if you crost him or missus either. It was double trouble and a cowhidin' whatever you do. She had a place in the kitchen where she tied their hands up to the wall and cowhided them and sometimes cut they back 'most to pieces. She made all go to church and let the women wear some her old, fine dresses to hide the stripes where she'd beat them, Mammy say that to keep the folks at church from knowin' how mean she was to her niggers."

"Master Ab had a driver and if you didn't do what that driver say, master say to him, 'Boy, come here and take this nigger down, a hunerd licks this time.' Sometimes us run off and go to a dance without a pass and 'bout time they's kickin' they heels and getting sot for the big time. in come a patterroller and say, 'Havin' a big time, ain't you? Got a pass?' If you didn't, they'd git four or five men to take you and when they got through you'd sho' go home."

"If a nigger ever run off the place and come back, master'd say, 'If you'll be a good nigger, I'll not whip you this time.' But you couldn't 'lieve that. A nigger run off and stayed in the woods six month. When he come back he's hairy as a cow, 'cause he lived in a cave and come out at night and pilfer round. They put the dogs on him but couldn't cotch him. Fin'ly he come home and master say he won't whip him and Tom was crazy 'nough to 'lieve it. Master say to the cook, 'Fix Tom a big dinner,' and while Tom's eatin', master stand in the door with a whip and say, 'Tom, I's change my mind; you have no business runnin' off and I's gwine take you out jus' like you come into the world.'"

"Master gits a bottle whiskey and a box cigars and have Tom tied up out in the yard. He takes a chair and say to the driver, 'Boy, take him down, 250 licks this time.' Then he'd count the licks. When they's 150 licks it didn't look like they is any place left to hit, but master say, 'Finish him up.' Then he and the driver sot down, smoke cigars and drink whiskey, and master tell Tom how he must mind he master. Then he lock Tom up in a log house and master tell all the niggers if they give him anything to eat he'll skin 'em alive. The old folks slips Tom bread and meat. When he gits out, he's gone to the woods 'gain. They's plenty niggers what stayed in the woods till surrender."

Tucker Smith, Texas

"Well son, we had to have a pass before we could go from one ranch to another and maser he would send a note by us to other men and he would give us a pass so we would not get in trouble with the white people or the patterrollers either, cause them patterrollers they would sure get the negro if they caught him off his ranch without a pass. The negroes they would carry their passes in their hand and if they met someone on their way he would show his pass whoever he met would let him continue on his way to where his Maser had sent him and the patterroller would not bother the poor negro. But if he should be caught off his ranch without a pass and the patterroller did get hold of that poor negro it was just too bad, cause they would stretch him over a log and hit him 39 licks with a red-heifer on the naked hide, that meant he would sure be tore up to where he could not hardly sit down for more than a week. All us negroes that wanted to do right sure did have to be very careful if we stayed out of trouble. Son, then sometimes we accidently got into trouble before we knew what we had done, but that was the way of the poor slave he had to be very careful. Course some did'nt care of being in trouble as that was all they were looking for anyway, but that did'nt help them any either with their Maser."

Mariah Snyder, Texas

"I'se seed lots of Negroes whipped while I was 'driving the gin.' They tied their feet and hands and raw-hided them good. I seed them tie a bell on one woman that was bad about running away. They locked it round her head someway. I'se seed lots of Negroes put on the block and bid off and carried away in chains like cattle. I 'members one woman, Venus, who raised her hands and hollered 'Weigh 'em cattle'; 'Weigh 'em cattle' while she was on the block being big off."

Patsy Southwell, Texas

"Marster' plantation had fifteen hunnerd acre' in it. At fus' he had only six ol' slaves and a lot of chillen. Sometime' dey punish' awful hard. I see 'em hit my mother five hunnerd licks, and my father six hunnerd. Father had run 'way and been gone a long time. Dey ketch' him in the water in the Neches River. He hab meat and staff, and dey say Mother was feedin' him, but I t'ink it the other way. I t'ink he was gittin' and sen'in' her stuff."

Lydia Starks, Georgia

Mrs. Starks informed the interviewer that "paddle rollers" didn't necessarily wait for slaves to be caught after dark off their plantations without a pass. They oft time just came on various plantations and whipped slaves. Some slave holders permitted such, others didn't, as was the case of her particular owner. She continued: "I can remember seeing the ole over-seer on the plantation joinning ours, jes' whippin' dem po' ole slaves till de couldn't even stan' up."

"When a slave did some crime which couldn't be purnished by whippin' him dey jes' hung him lak dey always have done folks, 'til these new-fangled ideal 'bout 'lectrocution came about."

Billy Taylor, Texas

"The massa whipped me with a dogwood switch, but he never did bring no blood. But it taken 7 men to whip my father."

Ellen Thomas, Texas

"I never did hear much about hard times. I was treated good but I got switched many a time. Oh, yes'm, I've been whipped, but not like some of 'em was. They used to tie some of 'em down. I've heered tell, they shore whopped 'em. They used to be a runaway that got away and went to Mexico now and then, and if they caught him they shore whopped him awful."

William M. Thomas, Texas

"'Bout de whuppin's, 'twarnt any. Dere am once dat a nigger gits de whuppin'. Dat am 'cause him stole Marster's favorite pun'kin. 'Twas dis away, de Marster am savin' de pun'kin fo' to git de seed. It am big as de ten gallon keg. De co'n field am full ob pun'kins an' dat nigger can tooks what him wants fo' to make sauce, but him tooks de Marster's choice pun'kin. Well, dat cullud gent'man must be awful hongry dat time, 'cause he tooks dat big pun'kin so to make lots ob sauce. Dat pun'kin am so big, de nigger have to tussle wid it befo' he gits it to his cabin. 'Twas lak stealin' de elephant, yous can't hide it in de watch pocket. Co'se, lots ob de cullud fo'ks see dat cullud gent'mans wid de pun'kin, an' 'twarnt long 'til de Marster knows it."

"Well Sar, 'twas funny sight to see de Marster punish dat fellow. Fust, de Marster sats him down on de groun' in f'ont on de cullud quatahs, whar allus can see him. Den de Marster gives him de big bowl ob pun'kin sauce wid a spoon, an' says to him, 'Eat dat sauce.' De cullud gent'mans eats, an' eats, an' eats. Him gits so full dat it am hahd fo' him to swallow, an' him stahts to gag. Den de Marster says, 'Eat some mo', 'tis awful good'. Dat nigger tries 'gain, but him gags, an' can't tooks any mo'. De Marster hits him a lick, an' says, 'It am good. Eat some mo'" an' den hits sev'ral light licks. Sho was funny to see. Dere sat de cullud gent'mans wid pun'kin sauce smeared on his face, an' tears runnin' down his cheeks."

Reeves Tucker, Texas

"He had a big place and lived in a good house, but didn't have so powerful many slaves. He never 'lowed no overseer on his place. Master Tucker didn't believe in having his 'Niggers' beat up, they cost too much. I'se saw slaves on other places whipped till the blood run off them onto the ground. When they cut them loose from the tree they fell over like they was dead. I' se saw lots of slaves bid off like stock, and babies sold from their mothers breast. Some of them brought $1,500, owing to how strong they was. Speculators rode all over the country buying up

'Niggers.' I'se seed as many as fifty in a gang being driven like convicts. The bosses 'round where we lived made the old wimmen what was too old to work, tend to the chil'ren while the slaves worked. They built them a house to themself and first thing in the mo'ning everybody had to take the chil'ren to them."

"Master Tucker was good to his darkies, and give us plenty to eat and wear. We et po'k and flour bread jest like the white fo'ks. Every woman had to spin so many yards of cloth 'fore she go to bed after we come in from the field. None of Master Tuckers 'Niggers' ever run off 'cept my father. One night he started to go 'cross a 'shirt' of woods to one of the neighbors. Young Master was a Pattyroller and told him to wait and go with him, but Pappy was hard headed as a mule and went on by his-self. The Pattyrollers cotched him might nigh beat him to death. Young Master was sho' mad as fire, cause he didn't want his 'Niggers' skinned up. I think them Pattyrollers kinda beat some sense in his head, for after that he allus went with young Master or got a pass."

Henry Turner, Arkansas

No Negro slave was allowed to go beyond the confines of his owner's plantation without written permission. This was described by "Uncle" Henry Turner as a "pass"; and on this "pass" was written the name of the Negro, the place he was permitted to visit, and the time beyond which he must not fail to return. It seems that numbers of men were employed by the County or perhaps by the slaveowners themselves whose duty it was to patrol the community and be on constant watch for such Negroes who attempted to escape their bondage or overstayed the time limit noted on their "pass." Such men were known then as "Paddy Rolls" by the Negroes and in the Southern states are still referred to by this name. Punishment was often administered by them, and the very mention of the name was sufficient to cause stark terror and fear in the hearts of fugitive slaves.

At some time during that period when slavery was a legal institution in this country, the following verse was composed by some unknown author and set to a tune that some of the older darkies can yet sing:

Run nigger run, the Paddy Roll will get you
Run nigger run, it's almost day.
That nigger run, that nigger flew
That nigger tore his shirt into.
Run nigger run, the Paddy Roll will get you
Run nigger run, it's almost day.

Manda Walker, South Carolina

"My pappy name Jeff and b'long to Marse Joe Woodward. He live on a plantation 'cross de other side of Wateree Crick. My mammy name Phoebe. Pappy have to git a pass to come to see mammy, befo' de war. Sometime dat crick git up over de bank and I, to dis day, 'members one time pappy come in all wet and drenched wid water. Him had made de mule swim de crick. Him stayed over his leave dat was writ on de pass. Patarollers [patrollers] come ask for de pass. They say: 'De time done out, nigger.' Pappy try to explain but they pay no 'tention to him. Tied him up, pulled down his breeches, and whupped him right befo' mammy and us chillun. I shudder, to dis day, to think of it. Marse Tom and Miss Jane heard de hollerin' of us all and come to de place they was whuppin' him and beg them, in de name of God, to stop, dat de crick was still up and dangerous to cross, and dat they would make it all right wid pappy's marster. They say of pappy: 'Jeff swim 'cross, let him git de mule and swim back.' They make pappy git on de mule and follow him down to de crick and watch him swim dat swif' muddly crick to de other side. I often think dat de system of patarollers and bloodhounds did more to bring on de war and de wrath of de Lord than anything else. Why de good white folks put up wid them poor white trash patarollers I never can see or understand. You never see classy white buckra men a patarollin'. It was always some low-down white men, dat never owned a nigger in deir life, doin' de patarollin' and a strippin' de clothes off men, lak pappy, right befo' de wives and chillun and beatin' de blood out of him. No, sir, good white men never dirty deir hands and souls in sich work of de devil as dat."

John Walton, Texas

"When we'd go a courtin' we'd have to have a pass or de patrol would git yo'. Day'd sho whoop yo' too, if yo' didn't have yo' pass. Befo' day got through wid yo', yo'd wished yo' had four passes."

Ella Washington, Texas

"A lot of 'em run 'way from dere, but dey sic de nigger dogs on dere trail an' most of de time dey catched 'em. My cousin run 'way all de time. He use to run through de cow pen an' shinny over de fence an' run in de woods. De dogs use to go to de cow pen an' stay dere an' look under de cow shed an' wait for him to come out. Den time de marster found out he wasn't under dere, dey'd take de dogs out in de woods an' hunt him dere. Dey always, found him 'til he run 'way during de War. When dey catched him dey use to whup him, but it shore never done no good 'cause he was gone 'gain in no time."

"Dey use to put sticks down in de ground an' tie dere hands an' feet to de sticks an' whup 'em like dat. Some places dey say dey strip 'em naked an' whup 'em. I know dat overseer we use to have was mean as Jim Ross. He use to pull de women's dress down an' whup 'em. I get mad every time I think 'bout him. I like to git my hands on him, I'd pull all dat hay-colored hair off'n his head."

Allen Williams, Texas

"There warn't much to Marshall when I first seed it. It was growed up in bushes all where the stores is now. When I was just a boy I'se slipped 'round and peeped at the Pattyrollers whipping Niggers for stealing chickens and other things. The whipping block was right there where the Marshall National Bank is now. The block was built like a bed and filled with sawdust, and had a plank fence round it. Us kids peeped through the cracks. They buckled the Niggers down by the feet and whipped them with a cat-of-nine-tails. A Pattyroller warn't 'lowed to hit a darky more than thirty-nine licks. The law could give him as many as they wanted to. If a Nigger was cotched [caught] out at night without a pass from his owner, the Pattyrollers give him thirty-nine licks at the whipping block."

Millie Williams, Texas

"We'ns go any whur we'ns wanted to go on Sat'day an' Sunday, dat is if we'ns had a pass from de marster. Cauze if you didn't have no pass an' de padder-rollers caught you it waz to bad. Ever'time de padder-rollers caught a nigger wid out a pass dey would give de nigger thirty nine licks wid a bullwhip. De padder-rollers waz men dat parole de country side watchin' de niggers."

Willie Williams, Texas

"As fo' de whuppin' deys give dat punishment. W'en de niggers gits stubbo'n an' 'fuses to obey de rules or de o'dahs. W'en deys give de whuppin', deys strap de nigger over de barrel. De Marster have one nigger dat does de

Willie Williams. (Library of Congress)

whuppin', but de Marster stan's dere an' counts de licks, an' hims won't 'low fo' to draw de blood."

George Young, Alabama

"Dey didn't l'rn us nothin' an' didn't 'low us to l'arn nothin'. Iffen dey ketch us l'arnin' to read an' write, dey cut us han' off. Dey didn't 'low us to go to church, neither. Sometimes us slip off an' have a little prayer meetin' by usse'ves in a ole house wid a dirt flo'. Dey'd git happy an' shout an' could't nobody hyar 'em, 'caze dey didn't make no fuss on de dirt flo', an' one stan' in de do' an' watch. Some folks put dey head in de wash pot to pray, an' pray easy, an' somebody be watchin' for de overseer. Us git whupped fer ev'ything iffen hit was public knowed."

"Us wasn't 'lowed visit nobody from place to place, an' I seed Jim Dawson, dis here same Iverson Dawson' daddy; I seed him stobbed out wid fo' stobs. Dey laid him down on his belly an' stretch his han's out on bofe sides an' tie one to one stob, an' one to de yuther. Bofe his feet was stretch out an' tied to dem stobs. Dem dey whupped him wid a whole board whut you kiver a house wid. De darkies had to go dere in de night an' take him up in a sheet an' carry him home, but he didn't die. He was 'cused of gwine over to de neighbor's plantation at night. Nine o'clock was de las' hour us had to be closed in. Head man come out an' holler, 'Oh, yes! Oh yes! Ev'ybody in an' do's looked.' An' iffen you wan't, you got whupped."

7

Runaways and the Quest for Freedom

The desire for freedom was the one constant in the lives of the enslaved. Regardless of whether they lived on a large plantation or in an urban setting, freedom or escape from the challenges endemic to slavery was often on the minds of the enslaved. They prayed, discussed, and sang about freedom when they were away from their enslavers. They found ways to act on it, in ways large and small, when the opportunity arose or when circumstances became unbearable. They did this despite the steps taken by enslavers to discourage or prevent them from running away. the enslaved were valuable property, so the enslavers crafted a variety of ways—both dramatic and severe—to protect their investment and avoid loss of labor and capital. The penalties for seeking freedom ranged from flogging to wearing balls and chains, separation from family, or even death. Like so many aspects of slavery, the punishments and penalties varied based on the idiosyncrasies and preferences of the slaveholder. In Texas, Charley Bowen observed, "One owner what lived on an jinning farm kept a bell on one of his Niggers ca'se he was allus running away. It was fixed on a steel band and locked round his head."

Even with these deterrents, the enslaved's quest for freedom posed a problem for slaveholders throughout the entire period of slavery. The disappearance of an enslaved worker was a frequent occurrence from the time slavery was established in the New World. In 1640, after the escape and capture of an African servant in Virginia, the court decided that his punishment would be to serve his master for the remainder of his life; it was the first documented case of someone being legally enslaved. In addition, fugitive slave advertisements appeared regularly in newspapers and on posters throughout the nation as early as the 18th century. Worry about runaways prompted the creation of article 2, section 3, in the United States Constitution, which addressed the return of fugitive slaves. This article, in turn, became the basis for the fugitive slave laws Congress passed in 1793 and 1850 to ensure the rights of slaveholders to recapture runaways, even when they had reached territory in which slavery was banned. The goal of these laws, created primarily for southern slaveholders, was to protect the slaveholder's investment in those whom they saw as valuable property.

Ironically, the fugitive slave legislation helped create vivid and sympathetic images of escaping fugitives in the minds of residents in northern states where slavery had ended or was gradually disappearing. In many ways, the image of a man or a women fleeing from bondage is one of the most enduring images in

RUNNING AWAY. (*See page 345.*)

Runaway enslaved family. (Library of Congress)

American cultural history. Harriet Beecher Stowe capitalized on this imagery in *Uncle Tom's Cabin* (1852) in the famous scene of Eliza desperately attempting to cross the thin ice of the Ohio River to gain her freedom and that of her baby. Harriet Tubman also gained great fame in the North for her efforts to return to the South to help others gain their freedom via the Underground Railroad.

REASONS FOR DECIDING TO RUN

The fictional Eliza and the real life Tubman were motivated by similar concerns: protecting their family. Eliza sought to prevent the sale of her infant child, and Tubman often returned to help guide family members to freedom. Family also caused other enslaved persons to flee, sometimes to follow a family member who had been sold and taken to a new location, and sometimes to try to protect a loved one from mistreatment at the hands of the enslaver. This was the case with Adah Isabelle Suggs of Kentucky, whose mother worried so much about her owner's unwelcome attentions toward her young daughter that the need to escape outweighed all the risks and dangers of escape.

The desire to reunite with family was an important motivation for running away. Husband and wives frequently lived on different plantations and in order to see one another more regularly one of them would leave their place of residence and hide near the other. In Mississippi, when July Ann Halfen's father was left behind after she and her mother were sold, her mother "tuck me an' we run 'way an' tried to go back whar my pappy wus."

There were innumerable additional reasons why the enslaved resolved to take the risk to run away. Anger after receiving punishment prompted many to take off. This was particularly true after an enslaved person had suffered a severe beating and refused to allow that to happen again. At that point they determined they would prefer to risk being caught rather than suffer any longer at the hands of their enslavers. How far they ran depended on their resourcefulness and knowledge of their environment. Some were quickly caught and returned, some remained free for a long period before capture, and others were never caught. Mississipian Heywood Ford recalled how his friend Jake Williams told him: "I is gonna run away to a free State. I ain't a-gonna put up wid dis treatment no longer. I can't stand much mo'." For Williams the mistreatment had brought him to a breaking point where it was worthwhile to risk running. He was lucky that his escape was successful.

Sometimes just the desire to be free from the control of their enslavers, regardless of how they were physically treated, motivated escape efforts. In William Still's book, *The Underground Railroad* (1872), many of the fugitives he interviewed said they ran because they were tired of working for someone else and not receiving any of the benefits from their efforts. In short, they wanted to be paid for their work and have greater control over their lives.

Similar sentiments were expressed in the interviews in the slave narratives in this chapter. These people also wanted the benefits of independence. They did not want to be told when to rise, when to head out to work, how much work they had to do each day, what tasks they had to perform, how to worship, or to hold their tongue when they thought they were being mistreated. Leah Garrett of Georgia remembered a newlywed who disputed an order from her mistress and, with the aid of her husband, ran off and lived for several years in the nearby mountains. She did this rather than accept the punishment threatened for her impudence. But even enslaved workers who were not mistreated contemplated taking off. Martin Jackson of Texas declared, "Even with my good treatment, I spent most of my time planning and thinking of running away."

Although Jackson thought carefully about what he would do if he ran away, for many fugitives their escape was an impulsive response to an immediate situation. If they realized they were about to get punished for not working hard enough or failing to perform at the expected level, they might take off rather than face a whipping or worse. The enslaved person might also run away after physical abuse, deciding he or she could not bear the mistreatment any longer. Someone might also run fearing repercussions after talking back to or disputing the orders of their enslaver. Monroe Brackins of Texas remembers that "my father and sister was in the barn shuckin' co'n and the master come in there and whipped my sister with a cowhide whip. My father caught a lick in the face and he told the master to keep his whip offen him. So the master started on my father and he run away."

Thus, the motivations of the enslaved varied greatly. Although freedom was the overarching goal for many of those held in bondage, the impetus to flee was often based on more practical considerations. How can one escape the violence that was so central to the institution of slavery? How can one find ways to be reunited with loved ones? And how can one exercise greater control over one's existence? So although freedom motivated some to flee, other factors may have forced the enslaved person to make such a life-altering decision.

NARRATIVES

Samuel Simeon Andrews, Florida

"Parson" describes himself as being very frisky as a boy and states that he did but very little work and got but very few whippings. Twice he ran away to escape being whipped and hid in asparagus beds in Sparta, Georgia until nightfall; when he returned the master would not whip him because he was apprehensive that he might run away again and be stolen by poorer whites and thus cause trouble.

Bill Austin, Florida

Bill learned much about the operation of the store, with the result that when Mr. Smith left with the Southern Army he left his wife and Bill to continue its operation. By this time there used to be frequent stories whispered among the slaves in the neighborhood—and who came with their masters into the country store—of how this or that slave ran away, and with the white man-power of the section engaged in war, remained at large for long periods or escaped altogether.

These stories always interested Austin, with the result that one morning he was absent when Mrs. Smith opened the store. He remained away "eight or nine days, I guess," before a friend of the Smiths found him near Macon and threatened that he would "half kill him" if he didn't return immediately.

Either the threat—or the fact that in Macon there were no readily available foodstuffs to be eaten all day as in the store—caused Austin to return. He was roundly berated by his mistress, but finally forgiven by the worried woman who needed his help around the store more than she needed the contrite promises and effusive declarations that he would "behave alright for the rest of his life."

And he did behave; for several whole months. But by this time he was "a great big boy," and he had caught sight of a young woman who took his fancy on his trip to Macon. She was free herself; her father had bought her freedom with that of her mother a few years before, and did odd jobs for the white people in the city for a livelihood. Bill had thoughts of going back to Macon, marrying her, and bringing her back "to work for Missus with me." He asked permission to go, and was refused on the grounds that his help was too badly needed at the store. Shortly afterward he had again disappeared.

"Missus," however, knew too much of his plans by this time, and it was no difficult task to have him apprehended in Macon. Bill may not have had such great objections to the apprehension, either, he says, because by this time he had learned that the young woman in Macon had no slightest intention to give up her freedom to join him at Greensboro.

A relative of Mrs. Smith gave Austin a sound beating on his return; for a time it had the desired effect, and he stayed at the store and gave no further trouble. Mrs. Smith, however, thought of a surer plan of keeping him in Greensboro; she called him and told him he might have his freedom. Bill never attempted to again leave the place—although he did not receive a cent for his work—until his master had died, the store passed into the hands of one of Mr. Smith's sons, and the emancipation of all the slaves was a matter of eight or ten years' history!

Smith Austin, Texas

"I had one aunt what run 'way 'cause dey whip her so much. Dey found her and brung her back and beat her. We didn't have no dogs but dere was some in de neighborhood what had 'em and dey lend 'em to other men what didn't have none."

Anna Baker, Mississippi

"I doan remembers much 'bout my ma 'fore she runned off, case I guess I was most nigh too little but she tole me after she come after us. When de war was over, all 'bout why she had to run away. It was case de nigger overseers, dey had niggers over de hoers and white mens over de plow han's, dey kept a tryin' to mess 'round wid her and she wouldn't have nothing to do wid dem. One time while she was in de field de overseer asked her to go over to de woods wid him and she said, all right, she'd go find a nice place and wait for him and she just kept a goin' and swam de river and runned away. She slip back once or twice at night to see us but dat was all. She hired out to some folks who woan rich enough to have no slaves of dey own. Dey was good to her too, and she never lacked work to do."

Sarah Benjamin, Texas

"Dey would whip dem cause dey wouldnt do right, little whippen was done on dis plantation. I seed my daddy put in stocks fer runnin off. De niggah dogs brought him back. Dey had dogs ter go git you when you run away."

"Yes a few did run away to de north, one ole man run away, he traveled all night den de next mornin he hollered and he was home. Dey put him in stocks, he had been travelin in a circle all night and kem back ter whar he started from."

Frank Berry, Florida

It was during the war between the Indians and settlers that Berry's grandmother, serving as a nurse at Tampa Bay was captured by the Indians and carried away to become the squaw of their chief; she was later re-captured by her owners. This was a common procedure, according to Berry's statements. Indians often captured slaves, particularly the women, or aided in their escape and almost always intermarried with them. The red men were credited with inciting many uprisings and wholesale escapes among the slaves.

Harry Bridges, Mississippi

Bridges tells of his father running away after receiving a severe whipping at the hands of Major Sartin's overseer just before the negroes were freed. He hid in the Pearl river Swamp and escaped capture until negroes were finally set free.

George Brooks, Georgia

One of "Uncle" George's stories is to the effect that he once left a chore he was doing for his second "Marster's" wife, "stepped" to a nearby well to get a drink of water and, impelled by same strange, irresistible "power," "jes kep on walkin 'til he run slap-dab inter de Yankees," who corraled him and kept him for three months.

F. H. Brown, Arkansas

"When an overseer got rough, she would fire him. Slaves would run away sometimes and stay in the woods if they thought that they would get a whipping for it."

Fred Brown, Texas

"Marster have de overseer an' de overlooker. De overseer am in charge ob de wo'k an' de overlooker am in charge of de cullud women, him am a nigger. De overseer gives all de whuppin's. Mos' of dat am fo' leavin' wid out de pass an' runnin' away. Some times w'en a nigger leaves wid out de pass, he gets overlayed an' am not dere fo' wo'k in de mo'nin', den de overseer knows dat de nigger violates de rule 'bout leavin'. Dat calls fo' de whuppin', sho. Sometimes w'ens de nigger gets overlayed, 'stead of comin' home an' takin' de whuppin', deys goes to de caves ob de river an' stays, an' jus' come in de night fo' eats. W'ens deys do dat, de dawgs am put aftah dem. Den it am de fight 'tween de nigger an' de dawg. Jus' once a nigger kills a dawg wid de knife. Only once deys fail to git de nigger, dat was close to freedom. Freedom come befo' deys catch him. W'ens deys whups fo' runnin' off, de nigger am tied down over a barrel an' whupped hard, till deys draws blood sometimes. Fo' failure to do de wo'k right de whuppin' 'twarnt so hard an' not so often."

Killen Campbell, Georgia

What happened, Auntie, if a slave from one plantation wanted to marry a slave from another?

She laughed significantly. "Planty. Old Mr. Miller had a man name Jolly and he wanner marry a woman off annoder plantachun, but Jolly's Marster wanna buy de woman to come to de plantachun. He say, 'Whut's fair fer de goose is fair fer de gander.' When dey couldn't come to no 'greament de man he run away to de woods. Den dey sot de bloodhounds on 'im. Dey let down de rail fence so de hounds could git fru. Dey sarch de woods and de swamps fer Jolly but dey neber find him."

"De slaves dey know whar he is, and de woman she visit him. He had a den down dare and plenty o' grub dey take 'im, but de white folks neber find him. Five hundred dollars wus what Miller put out for whomsover git him."

And you say the woman went to visit him?

"Yes, ma'm. De woman would go dere in de woods wid him. Finally one night when he was outer de swamp he had to lie hidin' in de ditch all night, cross from de nigger hospital. Den somebody crep' up and shot him, but he didn't die den. Dey ca'yed his crost to de hospital and he die three days later."

Fanny Cannady, North Carolina

"Marse Jordan's two sons want to de war; dey went all dressed up in dey fightin' clothes. Young Marse Jordan wuz jus' like Mis' Sally but Marse Gregory wuz like Marse Jordan, even to de bully way he walk. Young Marse Jordan never come back from de war, but 'twould take more den er bullet to kill Marse Gregory, he too mean to die anyhow kaze de debil didn' want him an' de Lawd wouldn' have him."

"One day Marse Gregory come home on er furlo'. He think he look pretty wid his sword clankin' an' his boots shinin'. He wuz er colonel, lootenent er somethin'. He wuz struttin' 'roun' de yard showin' off, when Leonard Allen say under his breath, 'Look at dat God damn sojer. He fightin' to keep us niggahs from bein' free.'"

"'Bout dat time Marse Jordan come up. He look at Leonard an' say: 'What yo' mumblin' 'bout?'"

"Dat big Leonard wuzn' skeered. He say, 'I say, Look at dat God dann sojer. He fightin' to keep us nigghas from bein' free.'"

"Marse Jordan's face begun to swell. It turned so red dat de blood near 'bout bust out. He turned to Pappy an' tole him to go an' bring him dis shot gun. When Pappy come back Mis' Sally come wid him. De tears wuz streamin' down her face. She run up to Marse Jordan an' caught his arm. Ole Marse flung her off an' took de gun from Pappy. He leveled it on Leonard an' tole him to pull his shirt open. Leonard opened his shirt an stood dare big as er black giant sneerin' at Ole Marse."

"Den Mis' Sally run up again an' stood 'tween dat gun an' Leonard."

"Ole Marse yell to pappy an' tole him to take dat woman out of de way, but nobody ain't moved to touch Mis' Sally, an' she didn' move neither, she jus' stood dare facin' Ole Marse. Den Ole Marse let down de gun. He reached over an' slapped Mis' Sally down, den picked up de gun an shot er hole in Leonard's ches' big as yo' fis'. Den he took up Mis' Sally an' toted her in den house. But I wuz so skeered dat I run an' hid in de stable loft, an' even wid my eyes shut I could see Leonard layin' on de groun' wid dat bloody hole in his ches' an' dat sneer on his black mouf."

"After dat Leonard's brother Burrus hated Ole Marse wus'n er snake, den one night he run away. Mammy say he run away to keep from killin' Ole Marse. Anyhow, when Ole Marse foun' he wuz gone, he took er bunch of niggahs an' set out to find him. All day long dey tromped de wods, den when night come dey lit fat pine to'ches an' kept lookin', but dey couldn' find Burrus. De nex' day Ole Marse went down to de county jail an' got de blood houn's. He brung home er great passal of dem yelpin' an' pullin' at de ropes, but when he turned dem loose dey didn' find Burrus, kaze he done grease de bottom of his feets wid snuff an' hog lard so de dogs couldn' smell de trail. Ole Marse denn tole all de nigiahs dat if anybody housed an' fed Burrus on de sly, dat he goin' to shoot dem like he done shot Leonard. Den he went every day an' searched de cabins; he even looked under'de houses."

"One day in 'bout er week Mis' Sally wuz feedin' de chickens when she heard somethin' in de polk berry bushes behin' de hen house. She didn's go 'roun' de house but she went inside house an' looked through de crack. Dare wuz Burrus layin' down in de bushes. He wuz near 'bout starved kaze he hadn' had nothin' to eat since he done run away."

"Mis' Sally whisper an' tole him to lay still, dat she goin' to slip him somethin' to eat. She went back to de house an' made up some more cawn meal dough for de chickens, an' under de dough she put some bread an' meat. When she went 'cross de yard she met Marse Jordan. He took de pan of dough an' say he goin' to feed de chickens. My mammy say dat Mis' Sally ain't showed no skeer, she jus' smile at Ole Marse an' pat his arm, den while she talk she take de pan an' go on to de chicken house, but Ole Marse he go too. When dey got to de hen house Ole Marse puppy begun sniffin' 'roun' Soon he sta'ted to bark; he cut up such er fuss dat Ole Marse went to see what wuz wrong. Den he foun' Burrus layin' in de polk berry bushes."

"Ole Marse drag Burrus out an' drove him to de house. When Mis' Sally seed him take out his plaited whip, she run up stairs an' jump in de bed an' stuff er pillow over her head."

"Dey took Buitus to de whippin' post. Dey strip off his shirt, den dey put his head an' hands through de holes in de top, an' tied his feets to de bottom, den Ole Marse took de whip. Dat lash hiss like col' water on er red hot iron when it come through de air, an' every time it hit Burrus it lef' er streak of blood. Time Ole Marse finish, Burrus' back look like er piece of raw beef. Dey laid Burrus face down on er plank den dey poured turpentine in all dem cut places. It burned like fire but dat niggah didn' know nothin' 'bout it kaze he done passed out from pain. But, all his life dat black man toted dem scares on his back."

Aunt Cicely Cawthon, Georgia

"We had one man to run away to the North," said Aunt Cicely. "He run away because the overseer whipped him because he went to the adjoining planta- tion to see a woman. You had to have a pass to go off the place, and he went without a pass. They never did hear nothing of him. They put the hounds on his trail but they never did ketch him. Mistis said there was a trick in it somewhere."

Hannah Chapman, Mississippi

"After being whipped some o' de slaves would hide fer days an' weeks in de woods. Some ob 'em stay hid out mos' all de times. My father and mother wuz strict on us. How dey would whip!"

Bill Collins, Texas

"Never did see a jail for the darkies but remember one night when a slave from a close plantation came and stayed in our woods. He was trying to run away but got cought. These slaves would run away from their masters be- cause they did not treat them right. Some times when they were caught and carried back to their plantations they were put in chains for safe keeping."

Laura Cornish, Texas

"I rec'lec's one time we chillen is playin' out near some woods whar dey is a big briar patch, an' we see two old men what look like wild men sure 'nuff. Dey had long hair all over dere faces an' dere shirts was all bloody, an' when dey see us lookin' dey hides down in de brush. Lord have mercy, we sure was scairt an' we run as fas' as we could to de house an' tell papa Day what we has seen. He tells us to take him to whar we has seen de men an' we goes to de place an' sure 'nuff dey is still dere. Papa Day goes in de briar patch an' me an' Lucy, one of de chillen I'se playin' with, go 'long, too, but de rest stays out, an' de old men takes papa Day 'round de knees an' begs him do he not tell dere master whar dey is at 'cause dey get whipped some more an' mebbe kilt. Papa Day ask 'em who dey belong to, an' dey say dey is old Lodge an old Baldo an' dey has run 'way 'caused dey is old an' dere master whips 'em 'cause dey can't work so good no more. I don't rec'lec' now who dey say dey belong to, but I 'member papa Day has tears comin' in his eyes an' he says 'dat is de sin of sins, to bloody flesh dat way.'"

"I don't know how long dey has hid in de briar patch, but dey can't hardly walk, an' papa Day sends me to de house an' tells me to have Aunt Mandy, de cook, to fix up some food an' to hurry an' bring it back. Lord have mercy, I never see sech eatin', dere wasn't 'nough left for a ant to feed hisself, dey was so hungry."

Elijah Cox, Texas

"My parents were treated so cruelly they ran away from their master. They escaped with their children through the woods about twenty miles below Memphis, Tennessee. They crossed over to Quebec, in Canada, just across from Detroit. Then they went into the free state of Michigan where they could live in peace. They lived in that state until their death, which was in 1876, about the time of General Custer's Massacre."

Green Cumby, Texas

"To see de runaway slaves in de woods scared me to death. They'd try to snatch you and hold you, so you couldn't go tell. Sometimes dey cotched dem runaway niggers and dey be like wild animals and have to be tamed over 'gain. Dere was a white man call Henderson had 60 bloodhounds and rents 'em out to run slaves. I well rec'lect de hounds run through our place one night, chasin' de slave what kilt his wife by runnin' de harness needle through her heart. Dey cotch him and de patter rolls took him to Henderson and hangs him."

Alice Dixon, Arkansas

"Ah had a good ole pa too. He died a long time ago. Ah member one night he started to whoop mah brudder and mah pa and mah brudder had hit. So mah brudder runned off, an de marster called ole Dinah, Dinah wuz a dog yo know but Dinah was a big dog ovah the other dogs yo know and dem dogs went and got me brudder and dem Newtons sho did beat him."

Ambrose Douglass, Florida

"I was a young man," he continues, "and didn't see why I should be anybody's slave. I'd run away every chance I got. Sometimes they near killed me, but mostly they just sold me. I guess I was pretty husky, at that."

"They never did get their money's worth out of me though I worked as long as they stood over me, then I ran around with the gals or sneaked off to the woods. Sometimes they used to put dogs on me to get me back."

George Eason, Georgia

When his mother got these whippings she always ran off afterwards and hid in the woods which were nearby. At night she would slip to the cabin to get food and while there would caution him and the other children not to tell the master that they had seen her. The master's wife who was very mean was always the cause of her receiving these lashings.

Callie Elder, Georgia

"Yes Ma'am, dey whupped de Niggers. My Pappy and grandpa was de wust ones 'bout gittin' licked. Evvy time Pappy runned away Marse Billy sicked dem hounds on his heels and dey was sho' to ketch him and fetch him back. Dey had to keep knives from Pappy or when dem dogs cotch him he would jus' cut 'em up so dey would die. When dey got him back to de house, dey would buckle him down over a barrel and larrup him wid a plaited whup. 'Omans warn't whupped much. My grandpa York was so bad 'bout runnin' 'way Marse Billy made him wear long old horns. One Sunday Marse Billy went by our church to see if all his Niggers was dar what was sposen to be dar. And dere grandpa was a-sottin' wid dem horns on his head. Marse Billy told him he could take de horns off his head whilst he was in de meetin' house. At dat grandpa dropped dem horns, and lit a rag to de woods and it tuk de dogs days to find him."

Ryer Emmanuel, South Carolina

"Oh, dey would beat de colored people so worser till dey would run away en stay in de swamp to save dey hide. But Lord a mercy, it never do no good to run cause time dey been find you was gone, dey been set de nigger dog on you."

Mattie Fannen, Arkansas

"I seen mama whooped. They tied some of them to trees and some they just whooped across their backs. It was 'cordin' to what they had done. Some of them would run off to the woods and stay a week or a month. The other niggers would feed them at night to keep them from starving."

Ida May Fluker, Arkansas

"I heered papa talk about how he was sold. He say the overseer so mean he run off in the woods and eat blackberries for a week."

Ruben Fox, Mississippi

"The only person that ever ran off was my mother. She said, she was going to try to make it to the free country. She didn't have no cause for leaving, sept she wanted to be free. She didn't get far before them patrollers catched her and brought her back. That was the patrollers business to catch the folks wahat ran off and bring them back."

Leah Garrett, Georgia

"One of de slaves married a young gal, and dey put her in de 'Big House' to wuk. One day Mistess jumped on her 'bout something and de gal hit her back. Mistess said she wuz goin' to have Marster put her in de stock and beat her when he come home. When de gal went to de field and told her husband 'bout it, he told her whar to go and stay 'til he got dar. Dat night he took his supper to her. He carried her to a cave and hauled pine straw and put in dar for her to sleep on. He fixed dat cave up just lak a house for her, put a stove in dar and run de pipe out through de ground into a swamp. Everybody always wondered how he fixed dat pipe, course dey didn't cook on it 'til night when nobody could see de smoke. He ceiled de house wid pine logs, made beds and tables out of pine poles, and dey lived in dis cave seven years. Durin' dis time, dey had three chillun. Nobody wuz wid her when dese chillun wuz born but her husband. He waited on her wid each chile. De chillun didn't wear no clothes 'cept a piece tied 'round deir waists. Dey wuz just as hairy as wild people, and dey wuz wild. When dey come out of dat cave dey would run everytime dey seed a pusson."

"De seven years she lived in de cave, diffunt folks helped keep 'em food. Her husband would take it to a certain place and she would go and git it. People had passed over dis cave ever so many times, but nobody knowed dese folks wuz livin' dar. Our Marster didn't know whar she wuz, and it wuz freedom 'fore she come out of dat cave for good."

Cora Gillam, Arkansas

"There was one man down there so mean to the people that they were scared all the time. None of the slaves ever tried any uprising. Only sometimes they would take up for themselves when they were being beaten. Then they would run away, too. If the overseer ran a man away, some of the masters would take it out of the overseer's wages."

Hector Godbold, South Carolina

"Another thing I had to do was to carry de baby cross de swamp every four hour on let my mamma come dere en suckle dat child. One day I go dere en another fellow come dere what dey call John. He en my mamma get in a argument like en he let out en cut my mamma a big lick right cross de leg en de blood just pour out dat thing like a done a what. My mamma took me en come on to de house en when Miss Jane see dat leg, she say, 'Cindy, what de matter?' My mamma say, 'John call me a liar en I never take it.' Miss Jane tell em to send after Sam Watson right den. Sam Watson was a rough old overseer en he been so bowlegged dat if he stand straddle a barrel, he be settin down on it just as good as you settin dere. Sam Watson come dere en make dat fellow lay down on a plank in de fence jam en he take dat cat o' nine tail he have tie round his waist en strike John 75 times. De blood run down off him just like you see a stream run in dat woods. Dat sho been so cause all we chillun stand bout dere en look on it. I suppose I was bout big enough to plough den. When dey let John loose from dere, he go in de woods en never come back no more till freedom come here. I tellin you when he come back, he come back wid de Yankees."

Arnold Gragston, Florida

"I almost ran the business in the ground after I had been carrying the slaves across for nearly four years. It was in 1863, and one night I carried across about twelve on the same night. Somebody must have seen us, because they set out after me as soon as I stepped out of the boat back on the Kentucky side; from that time on they were after me. Sometimes they would almost catch me; I had to run away from Mr. Tabb's plantation and live in the fields and in the woods. I didn't know what a bed was from one week to another. I would sleep in a cornfield tonight, up in the branches of a tree tomorrow night, and buried in a haypile the next night; the River, where I had carried so many across myself, was no good to me; it was watched too close."

"Finally, I saw that I could never do any more good in Mason County, so I decided to take my freedom, too. I had a wife by this time, and one night we quietly slipped across and headed for Mr. Rankin's bell and light. It looked like we had to go almost to China to get across that river; I could hear the bell and see the light on Mr. Rankin's place, but the harder I rowed, the ferther away it got, and I knew if I didn't make it I'd get killed. But finally, I pulled up by the light house, and went on to my freedom—Just a few months before all of the slaves got their's. I didn't stay in Ripley, though; I wasn't taking no chances. I went on to Detroit and still live there with most of 10 children and 31 grandchildren."

Mary Ella Grandberry, Alabama

"De slaves would git tired of de way dey was treated an' try to run away to de No'th. I had a cousin to run away one time. Him an' anudder fellow had got 'way up in Virginny 'fo' Massa Jim foun' out whar dey was. Soon as Massa Jim foun' de whar' bouts of George he went atter him. When Massa Jim gits to George an' 'em, George pertended lack he didn' know Massa Jim. Massa Jim as' him, 'George don't you know me?' George he say, 'I neber seed you 'fo' in my life.' Den dey as' George an' 'em whar did dey come from. George an' dis yuther fellow look up in de sky an' say, 'I come from above, whar all is love.' Iffen dey had owned dey knowed Massa Jim he could have brung 'em back home. My pappy tried to git away de same time as George an' dem did, but he couldn' see how to take all us chillun wid him, so he had to stay wid us. De blacks an' de whites would have de terr'bles' battles sometimes. Dat would be when de blacks would slip off to de No'th an' was caught an' brung back. De paterollers'd ketch de colored folks an' lock 'em up twell de owner come atter 'em."

Evie Herrin, Mississippi

"My mother wasn't born in slavery. I is never understood just how that came about. She came from North Carolina, and she told me many times that she was free before she came to Mississippi. My mother was smart and apt, and old Miss took her for a houseservant. One day she got mad about something what happened at the big house, so she runned off. When she couldn't be found, they hunted her with dogs. Them dogs went right straight to the ditch where my mother was hid, and before the men could get to them, they had torn most of her clothes off her, and had bitten her all over. When they brought her in, she was a sight to see, all covered with blood and dirt. Old Miss flew into a rage, and she told those men not to never again hunt nobody on her place with dogs. I just can't tell you how many slaves were on that place, there were so many, but there warn't none of them ever hunted again with dogs."

William George Hinton, North Carolina

"A slave by the name of Gallie Temples run away 'cause her missus, Mary Temples, wus so mean to her. She stuck hot froms to her. Made 'em drink milk an' things for punishment is what my mother an' father said. Gallie never did come back. Nobo'y never did know what become of her."

Eliza Holman, Texas

"After we been in Texas 'bout a year, missy Mary gits married to John Olham. Missy Mary am massa's daughter. After dat I lives with her and Massa John and den hell start poppin' for dis nigger. Missy Mary am good but Massa John

Eliza Holman. (Library of Congress)

am de devil. Dat man sho' am cruel, he works me to death and whups me for de leas' thing. My pappy say to me, 'You should 'come a runaway nigger.' He runs 'way hisself and dat de las' time we hears of him."

Martha Jackson, Alabama

"When de War fus' started," said Martha Jackson who was born in 1850, "dey wouldn't let none of de cullud people go to chu'ch 'thout dey had a pass, and mighty few white folkses would give 'em a pass. Dare was a heap of men (hit mou't have been six or twelve, my recollection is short, but anyhow 'twuz jus' a big crowd) whut went back'erds en ferwerds jes' lack sher'fs and de calls de'se'fs de 'Patterrollers.' Ef de white folks give de niggers a pass, den dey could go, and ef dey was to go'thout one, dem Patterrollers would have 'em a-runnin thoo de woods jes' lack dey was a lot of deer, and ef dey ever cotch 'em, dey'd take 'em to dey Marster and he'd jes' natchelly wear 'em out!"

"Den dey didn't 'low 'em for to go nowhurs much, eben when de plantation j'ined one ernudder, did, dey'd ketch 'em over dere and fetch 'em back and dey'd git whooped ag'in, and dat's 'zackly how come a heap uv 'em run'd away. I knowed a nigger onc't whut was gone nigh 'bout a year, and he wa'n't gone nowhur but right up de big road a piece, livin' in a cave whut he dug outer de side uv a clay bank. And Miss Betty say, 'Marthy, whur you reckon Dan at?' And I never said nothin'. De Patterrollers couldn't fine him or nobody, and he ain't never showed hisse'f in daylight 'tel he peered up atter de S'render."

"And I knowed a woman name Tishie, Miss Mollie's house sarvant. She run away 'case dey so mean to her, I reckon, and de cullud folks harbored her and

Martha Jackson. (Library of Congress)

hid her up in de grain house wid de peas and sech lac', stedder down in de corn crib. And who ever 'twuz 'trayed her I ain't sayin' but a crowd uv dem Patterrollers come and got 'er one night, and tuck her away, and l ain't nebber seed Tishie no mo'."

Benjamin Johnson, Georgia

"Sometimes ol' missus would come 'long an' she would be mad wid some of de women an' she would want to go to whuppin' on 'em."

"Sometimes de women would'nt take it an' would run away an' hide in de woods. Sometimes dey would come back after a short stay an' den again dey would have to put de hounds on dere trail to bring dem back home. As a general rule dere wus'nt much whuppin' on our plantation."

Abe Kelley, Mississippi

"Overseers was pretty tight, so tight that Old Master would tell them to stop, that they was being too tight. Some of the niggers would run away off in the woods. Old Master had a woman, Nancy, that stayed in the woods three years."

"I don't know why they didn't catch her because there was certain men that raised 'nigger dogs', they could follow a nigger's tracks. But they used them on white folks too."

Jennie Kendricks, Georgia

The treatment on some of the other plantations was so severe that slaves often ran away. Jennie Kendricks told of one man who was lashed and who ran away but was finally caught. When his master brought him back he was locked in a room until he could be punished. When the master finally came to administer the whipping, Lash had cut his own throat in a last effort to secure his freedom. He was not successful; his life was saved by quick action on the part of his master. Sometime later after rough handling Lash finally killed his master and was burned at the stake for this crime.

William McWhorter, Georgia

"Dey told me, atter I was old enough to take it in, dat de overseer sho did drive dem slaves; dey had to be up and in de field 'fore sunup and he wuked 'em 'til slap, black dark. When dey got back to de big house, 'fore dey et supper, de overseer got out his big bull whip and beat de ones dat hand't done to suit him durin' de day. He made 'em strip off deir clothes down to de waist, and evvywhar dat old bull whip struck it split de skin. Dat was awful, awful! Sometimes slaves dat had been beat and butchered up so bad by dat overseer man would run away, and next day Aunt Suke would be sho to go down to de spring to wash so she could leave some old clothes dar for 'em to git at night. I'se tellin' you, slaves sho did fare common in dem days."

"None of our Niggers never knowed enough 'bout de North to run off up dar. Lak I done told you, some of 'em did run off atter a bad beatin', but dey jus' went to de woods. Some of 'em come right on back, but some didn't; Us never knowed whar dem what didn't come back went. Show me a slavery-time Nigger dat ain't heared 'bout paterollers! Mistess, I 'clar to goodness, *paterollers was de devil's own hosses.* If dey cotched a Nigger out and his Marster hand't fixed him up wid a pass, it was jus' too bad; *dey most kilt him.* You couldn't even go to de Lord's house on Sunday 'less you had a ticket sayin': 'Dis Nigger is de propity of Marse Joe McWhorter. Let him go.'"

Charity Moore, South Carolina

"What do I t'ink ob slavery? I t'ink slavery is jest a murdering of de people. I t'ink Freedom been a great gift. I lak my Maussa and I guess he was as good to his slave as he could be, but I ruther [rather] bee free."

Charlie Pye, Georgia

"The whipping was done by a 'Nigger Driver,' who followed the overseer around with a bull whip; especially for this purpose. The largest man on the plantation was chosen to be the 'Nigger Driver.'"

Mary Reynolds, Texas

"Aunt Cheyney was jus' out of bed with a sucklin' baby one time, and she run away. Some say that was 'nother baby of massa's breedin'. She don't come to the house to nurse her baby, so they misses her and old Solomon gits the nigger hounds and takes her trail. They gits near her and she grabs a limb and tries to hist herself in a tree, but them dogs grab her and pull her down. The men hollers them onto her, and the dogs tore her naker and et the breasts plumb off her body. She got well and lived to be a old woman, but 'nother woman has to suck her baby and she ain't got no sign of breasts no more."

Josephine Riles, Texas

"Plenty times de niggers run 'way, 'cause dey have to work awful hard and de sun awful hot. Dey hides in de woods and Mr. Snow keep nigger dogs to hunt 'em with. Dem dogs have big ears and dey so bad I never fools 'round dem. Mr. Snow take of dere chains to git de scent of de nigger and dey kep' on till dey finds him, and sometimes dey hurt him. I knows dey tore de meat off one dem field hands."

Irene Robinson, Arkansas

"I was sold. Yes mam I sho was. Jes put up on a platform and auctioned off. Sold rite here in Des Are. Non taint right. My old mistress [Mrs. Snibley] whoop me till I run off and they took me back when they found out where I lef from. I stayed way bout two weeks."

"Mama said her owners wasn't good. Her riding boss put a scar on her back she took to her grave. It was deep and a foot long. He wanted to whoop her naked. He had the colored men hold her and he whooped her. She run off and when her owner come home she come to him at his house and told him all about it. She had been in the woods about a week she reckon. She had a baby she had left. The old mistress done had it brought to her. She was nursing it. She had a sucking baby of her own. She kept that baby. Mama said her breast was way out and the doctor had to come wait on her; it nearly ruined."

Henry Ryan, South Carolina

"None of Major Pickens Butler's slaves ever went away from him, but some in de neighborhood did run away, and dey never heard of dem again."

Callie Shepherd, Texas

"Miss Fannie and de Doctor had five field laborers. Some of de white folks dey got more. Some of de Niggers dey don' like de way of their treatment and

Callie Shepherd. (Library of Congress)

dey run away to de woods to get away. I used to hear de Nigger dogs a runnin' and when dey ketch de Niggers dey bites 'em all over and tears dey clothes and gets de skin too. And de Niggers dey would holler. I seed' dem when dey whupped de Niggers. Dey used to tell us little childers to look. Dey buckled 'em down on de groun' and laid it on dey backs. Sometimes dey laid on with a mighty heavy han'."

Amos Sims, Texas

"De overseer dere use to whip de colored lots, too. Dey wouldn' let me work, I was too little, but I can 'member lots of whippin's. One time my father run 'way an' hid in de woods. Dey hunt him with dogs dey kep' for huntin' colored folks. Me an' my mother could hear 'em hollerin' an' we cried. Oh, I was jus' a li'l boy den."

"It took 'em a long time to find 'im, but when dey got 'im dey tied 'im to a post an' whipped 'im. Yes, Ma'm, I 'member dat. He never run 'way no more."

Millie Ann Smith, Texas

"When Master George Washington Trammell (my Master) come to Texas with his wife and three chil'ren, he brought my mother and her three chil'ren. Pappy belonged to a George Moore there in Mississippi and Master Trammell hadn't bought him when we left to come to Texas. Pappy run off and come to Texas and begged Master into buying him so he could be with his wife and chil'ren."

Laura Sorrell, North Carolina

"My mammy, Virginia Burns, wus borned in Fayetteville, Cumberland County. She never knowed her parents an' frum . . . de fust she could 'member she wus bound out ter a Mis' Frizelle what beat her, give her scraps lak a dog, an' make her wuck lak a man. Dey eben makes her git on de well sweep an' go down in de well an' clean hit out. She said dat she wus skeerd nigh ter death."

"She wus a grown woman when she 'cided dat she can't stand de treatment no mo'. She has cut wood since she wus big enough ter pick up de axe an' she makes up her min' ter quit."

"Dey wus a-fixin' ter chain her up an' beat her lak dey usually done when she 'cides ter go away. She has ter go den or take de whuppin' an' she ain't got time ter make no plans."

"Fust she runs ter de Marster's bedroom an' slips on a pair of his ole shoes, den she goes out ter de big chicken house back of de barn. She hyars de Marster a-cailin' fer her 'fore she gits ter de woods so she runs back an' hides in de chicken house."

"Dey calls an' dey calls, an' de chickens comes ter de roost but she lays low an' doan make no fuss, so dey goes on ter sleep. She hyars de folkses a-callin' her but she lays still, den she sees de torches what dey am usein' ter find her an' she thanks God dat she ain't in de woods. Atter awhile she thinks dat she can sneak out, but she hyars de bayin' of de bloodhoun's in de swamp so she lays still."

"Hit am four o'clock 'fore all gits quiet. She knows dat hit am safe ter go now, case she has done hyard Mister Frizelle an' one of de patterollers a-talkin' as dey goes back ter de house. Dey 'cides ter go home an' start out ag'in de nex' mornin' bright an' early."

"Mammy am skeerd pink but she knows dat unless she am keerful dey am gwine ter ketch her. She lays still till daybreak den she flies fer de woods.

"I'se hyard mammy say dat dem nights she slept in de woods wus awful. She'd find a cave sometimes an' den ag'in she'd sleep in a holler log, but she said dat ever'time de hoot owls holler or de shiverin' owls shiver dat she'd cower down an' bite her tongue ter keep frum screamin'."

"She said dat de woods wus full of snakes an' hit wus near 'bout two weeks 'fore she got ter Guilford County. She had stold what she et on de way der, an' dat hadn't been much so she wus weak."

"One day she crept outen de woods an' look roun' her an' hit bein' in July, she spies a watermillion patch. She looks roun' an' den flies out dar an' picks up a big million, den she shakes a leg back ter de woods."

"While she wus settin' dar eatin' de watermillion a young white man comes up an' axes her her business an' she, seein' dat he am kind-lookin', tells him her story."

"She fully 'specks him ter turn her ober ter de sheriff but 'stid of dat he tells her dat his name am Daniel Green, an' dat he am a Union sympathizer, an' den he takes her ter some colored folkses house."

"Dese colored folkses am named Berry an' my mammy am stayin' dar when she falls in love wid paw, Jake Sorrell, an' marries him."

"She ain't never been ter dances an' sich before but now she goes some, an' hit wus at one of dese dances whar she met my paw. When she gits engaged ter him she won't let him kiss her till she axes Marster Daniel iffen she can marry him. Yo' see she wus wuckin' fer Marse Dan."

"Well he give his consent an' dey wus married. Dey had me soon, case I wus eight months old when de Yankees come, an' we wus freed by de law."

Patsy Southwell, Texas

"Marster' plantation had fifteen hunnerd acre' in it. At fus' he had only six ol' slaves and a lot of chillen. Sometime' dey punish' awful hard. I see 'em hit my mother five hunnerd licks, and my father six hunnerd. Father had run 'way and been gone a long time. Dey ketch' him in the water in the Neches River.

He hab meat and staff, and dey say Mother was feedin' him, but I t'ink it the other way. I t'ink he was gittin' and sen'in' her stuff."

Adah Isabelle Suggs, Indiana

Among the interesting stories connected with former slaves one of the most outstanding ones is the life story of Adah Isabelle Suggs, indeed her escape from slavery planned and executed by her anxious mother, Harriott McClain, bears the earmarks of fiction, but the truth of all related occurences has been established by the aged negro woman and her daughter Mrs. Harriott Holloway, both citizens of Evansville, Indiana.

Born in slavery before January the twenty-second, 1852 the child Adah McClain was the property of Colonel Jackson McClain and Louise, his wife.

· According to the customary practice of raising slave children, Adah was left at the negro quarters of the McClain plantation, a large estate located in Henderson county, three and one half miles from the village of Henderson, Kentucky. There she was cared for by her mother. She retains many impressions gained in early childhood of the slave quarters; she remembers the slaves singing and dancing together after the day of toil. Their voices were strong and their songs were sweet. "Master was good to his slaves and never beat them," were her words concerning her master.

When Adah was not yet five years of age the mistress, Louisa McClain, made a trip to the slave quarters to review conditions of the negroes. It was there she discovered that one little girl there had been developing ideas and ideals; the mother had taught the little one to knit tiny stockings, using wheat straws for knitting needles.

Mrs. McClain at once took charge of the child, taking her from her mother's care and establishing her room at the residence of the McClain family.

Today the aged negro woman recalls the words of praise and encouragement accorded her accomplishments, for the child was apt, active, responsive to influence and soon learned to fetch any needed volume from the library shelves of the McClain home.

She was contented and happy but the mother knew that much unhappiness was in store for her young daughter if she remained as she was situated.

A custom prevailed throughout the southern states that the first born of each slave maiden should be the son or daughter of her master and the girls were forced into maternity at puberty. The mother naturally resisted this terrible practice and Harriott was determined to prevent her child being victimized.

One planned escape was thwarted; when the girl was about twelve years of age the mother tried to take her to a place of safety but they were overtaken on their road to the ferry where they hoped to be put across the Ohio river. They were carried back to the plantation and the mother was mildly punished and imprisoned in an upstair room.

The little girl knew her mother was imprisoned and often climbed up to a window where the two could talk together.

One night the mother received directions through a dream in which her escape was planned. She told the child about the dream and instructed her to carry out orders that they might escape together.

The girl brought a large knife from Mrs. McClain's pantry and by the aid of that tool the lock was pried from the prison door and the mother made her way into the open world about midnight.

A large tobacco barn became her refuge where she waited for her child. The girl had some trouble making her escape; she had become a useful and necessary member of her mistress' household and her services were hourly in demand. The Daughter "young missus" Annie McClain was afflicted from birth having a cleft palate and later developing heart dropsy which made regular surgery imperative. The negro girl had learned to care for the young white woman and could draw the bandages for the surgeon whey "Young Missus" underwent surgical treatment.

The memory of one trip to Louisville is vivid in the mind of the old regress today for she was taken to the city and the party stopped at the Gault House and "It was a grand place," she declares, as she describes the surroundings; the handsome dreperies and the winding stairway and other artistic objects seen at the grand hotel.

The child loved her young mistress and the young mistress desired the good slave should be always near her; so, patient waiting was required by the negro mother before her daughter finally reached their rendezvous.

Under cover of night the two fugitives traveled the three miles to Henderson, there they secreted themselves under the house of Mrs. Margaret Bentley until darkness fell over the world to cover their retreat. Imagine the frightened negroes stealthily creeping through the woods in constant fear of being recaptured. Federal soldiers put them across the river at Henderson and from that point they cautiously advanced toward Evansville. The husband of Harriott, Milton McClain and her son Jerome were volunteers in a negro regiment. The operation of the Federal Statute providing for the enlistment of slaves made enlisted negroes free as well as their wives and children, so, by that statute Harriott McClain and her daughter should have been given their freedom.

When the refugees arrived in Evansville they were befriended by free negroes of the area. Harriott obtained a position as maid with the Parvine family, "Miss Hallie and Miss Genevieve Parvine were real good folks," declares the aged negro Adah when repeating her story. After working for the Misses Parvine for about two years, the negro mother had saved enough money to place her child in "pay school" there she learned rapidly.

Penny Thompson, Texas

"Once Jus' befoah de wah stahts, 'twas some men come to de nigger qua'ters. Ise don' know w'at dey am called, but dey come at night. Marster am sick abed den. De mens says to my mammy an' some udder niggers, dat dey would be back sich an' sich a night, an' those dat wants freedom, deys am gwine to take wid dem an' warns dem not to says a word."

"De next day, Ise am a thinkin' 'bout dat. Ise love my Marster an' Ise 'fraid dat dey am gwine to takes me away. Ise begin to cry. Ise den goes to de Marster's bed a cryin' an' says to him, 'Ise don' want to go away.' He ask w'at Ise mean 'bout go away. So Ise tol' him w'at de mans says. He says to me, 'Stop cryin', yous aint goin' away wid any mens.' He send me over to John Barrow's house wid a note to him. Marster Barrow den come to de Marster's house an' de Marster tells him w'at Ise tol'. Now, de night w'en de mens am 'spose to come, Marster have all de niggers hade out an' de w'ite men am in de qua'ters

Penny Thompson. (Library of Congress)

wid de long pistols. Ise don' know w'at am said w'en de fellahs come, but weuns heahs couple shots, 'twarnt any killed. Dat am de last weuns heahs ob sich."

Mother Tid, Mississippi

"Mother Tid" as she is called by her neighbors lives on Lanes Hill and is a very spry old person of ninety or more years. She says that her Master, whose name she would not give, was mean to her and to all of his slaves. Said she ran away once because her Master slapped her in the face because of something she did not do. She said she ran and hid in some bushes and would have gone away or tried to but she could hear her Master's little son calling her, "Tid, Tid, come back to me. I won't let you get hurt any more." And she says her love for the little lad of four caused her to go back.

William Henry Towns, Alabama

"Ever once er while slave would run away ter de North. Most times dey was caught and bou't back. Sometimes dey would git desperate aand would commit suicide 'fore dey would stand ter be bou't back. One time I heard of a slave that had 'scaped and when dey tried ter ketch him he jumped in er creek and drown hisse'f. He was 'bout frum ter Geo'gia. He hadn't been in Alabama long 'fore him and two more tried ter 'scape; two

William Henry Towns. (Library of Congress)

uv 'em was cau't and bou't back but dis odder one went ter der lan uv' sweet dreams."

Callie Washington, Mississippi

"Lots of slaves ran off. I don't know if they went to the North. They said they was going to make it to the free country. Most of them did make it there, 'cause they never did get them back. By the time the freedom came, most every one had gone. My mammy and Daddy ran off. I didn't see them no more till after peace was declared. She came after me and brought two colored Yankee soldiers with her. I seed them coming and ran in the house and told old Miss, 'Yonder comes some of them blue jackets.' She says, 'They is coming to set you free, but you is going to stay with me, ain't you?' Before I could answer, my mammy decided that question. She said she come to get me, and she was going to carry me back. Old Miss knowed wan't no use trying to keep me, so she says, 'If Callie wants to go, carry her on.' I loved Old Miss, and I hated to leave her but you know how children is. They is always ready, when they hears the word go. There wasn't never no trouble between the colored folks and the whites. They didn't run off for no reason of that kind, nor because they was mistreated. They just heared about that freedom, from one person and another, who would picture it to be something grand, and they all wanted to be free. The only way news was carried was from one to the other. Whenever you see them gang together telling that 'They say' so and so, you know right then, they don't know who 'They' is."

Ella Washington, Texas

"A lot of 'em run 'way from dere, but dey sic de nigger dogs on dere trail an' most of de time dey catched 'em. My cousin run 'way all de time. He use to run through de cow pen an' shinny over de fence an' run in de woods. De dogs use to go to de cow pen an' stay dere an' look under de cow shed an' wait for him to come out. Den time de marster found out he wasn't under dere, dey'd take de dogs out in de woods an' hunt him dere. Dey always found him 'til he run 'way during de War. When dey catched him dey use to whup him, but it shore never done no good 'cause he was gone 'gain in no time."

Eugenia Weatherall, Mississippi

"Did I tell you 'bout my grandma runnin' away from the blood hounds? Well, twas three times she done it. She was living in Tuscaloosa then and it was fore she was sold to the Bramletts. I is forgotten who twas she belong to then but I is heared her call de marster, Marse Fred. He was a regular slave trader and my grandma was born on his place. He sold niggers just like I do chickens and eggs. My grandma was right peart and had a head of her own even when she was a young gal. She tried to run off from Marse Fred and he sont the blood hounds after her. They called them nigger hounds in those days and the first time she run off it twaren't long fore they cotch her. They didn't do much to her that time but just put her back to work and tell her she better not try that stunt again. She was set on running away tho' and it wasn't very long fore she tried it again. This time she got away from the blood hounds and hid out til she got hungry and then come creeping back beggin' fore mercy from de marster. He didn't give her much mercy tho' but just sent her to his whippers and they put stripes on her back with the big lashes they had. That made her so mad that she was more 'termined than ever and this time she runned off over on the ferry across the black water and hid out. Some of the patrollers found her tho and carried her back and that time cured her cause when Marse Fred saw her he took her out to the fodder block, that was where they crushed feed for the stock, and showed her where they put men who disobeyed they marsters. They would let the block down on them til it most nigh crushed them to death. He told her he was gwineter put her down there and try her out but she was so scared and cried and begged so hard he told her if she would promise never to try to run off again he would let her go. She did and he let her off and after that she was one of the best niggers on the place."

Lou (Granny) Williams, Texas

"Some niggers was always runnin' away and dey would set de nigger dogs on dem and ketch dem mos' times and put dem in jail, den dey would treat dem so bad dey wouldn' never want to run away no mo'. Most of de white folks wouldn' teach de niggers nothin' 'cause dey say dey learn too much and know more den de white folks."

President Wilson, Texas

"My master never whipped the slaves, but he had a overseer named Bill Ditto who whip them. When he would whip a slave he would say, 'Don't thank me for this. Thank your master.' So I reckon by that de master had him whip us. When my father wuz whipped he would run away and hide in the river bottom. I seen them bring him several times. If dey whipped when dey brought him in, he would run away ag'in, but if dey didn' whip him, he would stay awhile, maby a year."

"Lots of slaves run away, but dey'd most always ketch 'em and bring 'em back."

Willis Winn, Texas

"No slaves ever run off to the North. They couldn't get away, I'se seed too many try it. If the Pattyrollers didn't cotch you, some of the white fo'ks put you up and send for your Master. They had a 'greement to be on the watch for run-a-way Niggers. The young boys run off cause Master was so hard on them. They'd go to a neighbors house and ask for something to eat. The Master of the house would say, 'Boy, who you belong to?' You tell him why you leave, and he say, 'That's a shame; he ought to be whipped his-self; you is going to stay right here with us; and if you be good and work we'll take care of you and treat you right.' Then he feed you and send you off to do some task. That evening you see the Master leave and 'bout night when he come back your Master was with him. When he got you back home and got through with you, you'd sho' stay home."

George Womble, Georgia

On one occasion Mr. Womble says that he has seen his master and a group of other white men beat an unruly slave until his back was raw and then a red hot iron bar was applied to his back. Even this did not make the slave submissive because he ran away immediately afterwards. After this inhuman treatment any number of the slaves ran away, especially on the Ridley plantation. Some were caught and some were not. One of the slaves on the Womble plantation took his wife and ran away. He and his wife lived in a cave that they found in the woods and there they raised a family. When freedom was declared and these children saw the light of day for the first time they almost went blind stated Mr. Womble.

CRAFTING A PLAN OF ESCAPE

The ability to flee from the peculiar institution took equal amounts of daring, resilience, planning, and luck. Although some of the enslaved had sophisticated and well-developed escape plans, others, spurred by the need for immediate action, fled with more excitement than planning. For example, on rare occasions an enslaved person might physically confront his or her enslaver and flee, realizing the magnitude of what had been done. But sometimes the attack on the slaveholder and the escape that followed were well thought out in advance. In South Carolina, Susan Hamlin's (also known as Hamilton) father resented the whipping he received and carefully plotted revenge on his enslaver:

> De next day which wus Monday, pa carry him 'bout four miles frum home in de woods an' give him de same 'mount or lickin' he wus given on Sunday. He tied him to a tree an' unhitched de horse so it couldn't git tie-up an' kill e self. Pa den gone to de landin' an' cotch a boat dat wus comin' to Charleston wood fa'm products. He was permitted by his master to go to town on errands, which helped him to go on de boat without bein' question'. W'en he got here he gone on de water-front an' ax for a job on a ship so he could git to de North.

The steps Hamilton took were extraordinary in how well they were planned, but less well planned escapes were also successful. A sense of improvisation often allowed the enslaved to take advantage of the moment. These narratives suggest that almost all the enslaved had experienced or heard stories about the use of bloodhounds, also known as slave hounds, which were a key tool used by the patrollers, the men hired to enforce the racial strictures of the day and to capture those brazen enough to flee. The slaves developed tricks to deter or fool the dogs, including putting pepper in their socks to make the dogs sneeze. John Barker's Texas grandfather sprinkled dried horned toads where he walked to throw pursuing dogs off the scent. Turpentine was another successful deterrent.

Avoiding the hounds was one of the escape strategies the fugitives used. Some came up with ingenious transport plans, like the father of Sallie Wroe of Texas who drove a wagon full of cotton to market for his slaveholder and then "pappy and de other men left de wagons along de river bank, rolled a bale ob cotton into de river, and all four ob 'em got on dat bale and rowed across de Rio Grande over into Mexico." Mexico, like Canada, had abolished slavery years earlier.

Traveling near the border of Mexico or a northern state made the possibility of escape more tempting. Ben Kinchlow of Texas described how Mexican citizens along the border tried to persuade enslaved workers to cross to freedom. Each time an enslaved wagon driver brought a load of cotton to those locations the temptation to flee must have gotten stronger.

Similar temptations were provided by other persons, black and white, who offered help to those seeking freedom. Sometimes these people were part of the Underground Railroad, a loosely defined network of people who, for religious, moral, or cultural reasons, risked much to assist those seeking freedom. Sometimes they were just folks opposed to slavery and willing to help. Whatever their motivation, their encouragement and support were critical for freedom seekers ready to leave behind their lives of slavery. This source of help was not frequently available but was invaluable when it was offered. Help sometimes came from surprising sources, too, including the Texas slaveholder of Lorenza Ezell, who regularly helped enslaved workers fleeing from those he considered cruel masters:

> Old massa didn't hold with de way some mean massa treat dey niggers. Dere a place on our plantation what us call "De old meadow." It was common for runaway niggers to have place 'long de way to hide and res' when dey run off from mean massa. Massa used to give 'em somethin' to eat when dey hide dere. I saw dat place operated, though it wasn't knowed by dat den, but long time after I finds out dey call it part of de "Underground railroad." Dey was stops like dat all de way up to de north.

In running away, enslaved people might collaborate with others or trust only in their own devices. They knew failure would have painful consequences, so they did whatever was necessary to get to safety. No plan was foolproof, and both courage and luck were important parts of the equation.

NARRATIVES

Frank Adams, Texas

"My marster he would tell run-a-way slaves dat come to him, 'Gwan an' lay down in dat big cotton shed. Nobudy gwinter hu't [hurt] you.' He would keep slaves, an' as many as he want' to, an' wouldn' 'low no patter-roles to git an' whip any dat come to him, an' iffen eber dere was a Christian among de w'ite folks, Uncle Abel was one."

John Aldrich, Texas

"My pa run off one time when Marster first move to Houma. He send pa to git some hogs what got out. He tell him he better not come back 'thout dem hogs. Dat was in February. He didn't git catch 'til September. He went to Algiers or some of dem places 'round New Orleans. De way he git catch was dis—one Sunday dere was a crowd of 'em gambling. Dey raise a fuss and git put in jail. De owners of de other niggers come and git dere niggers out but dere warn't nobody to git pa out. After while a man come 'round what knowed pa. He went back and told Marster. Marster say he didn't want him, he sell him. De man ax how much he want for pa, and Marster say $1500.00. De man say dat too much so pa have to come back. Marster beat him and put him to work. He say pa owed him sixty cords of wood for de time he was off and made him work every Sunday 'til he got dat sixty cords cut."

"Mother tell 'bout a gal what run off. She say de gal stay with her. She never know she run off. Two men come with dogs and ask her if she knew where de gal was. She say, 'In de field 'cross de fence.' Dey sic de dogs on her and dey tear every rag of cloth off her."

John Barker, Texas

"Talk about times! De blood houn's on deir trail! Dey had what you call de common houn's and when you couldn' get 'em by de common houn's, you put de blood houn's dat don't make no racket atall on deir trail. Dey run my gran'fadder ovah one hun'erd miles and never caught 'im till about t'ree or fo' days an' nights an' dey found 'im under a bridge. What dey put on him was e-nuf. I have seen 'em whip 'em till de blood run down deir backs and den dey would put common salt in de places where dey whipped 'em an' dey would have to go right on nex' mawnin' and do deir tasks dey puts on 'em. I've seen 'nuf o' dat! Yes, mam, dat was up in Ohio I seen all dat."

"In dese days an' times you see dese hawned toads dat runs ovah de worl'. My gran'father would gather dese toads and lay 'em up in de fireplace till dey dried an' den roll 'em wid bottles till dey get jes' like ashes an' den dey take it an' rub it on de bottom of de shoes. Dey take dat powder and t'row it as fuh [far] as dey could jump an' den jump ovah it, an' do dis again till dey use all de powder, den when dey make de last jump, dey is gone. Dat would t'row de common houn's off de trail all togedder. But when dey put de 'hell houn's' on de trail, dey would come right up to de do' [door] an' take de trail an' you nevah heah 'em say a word, dey was quiet, an' dey could pick up dat trail. I ust to ask my gran'father, 'What you gonna do wid dat powder?' an' he say, 'You will know some day when you is old enough. I'm gwine put it on my shoes!' You see, dat stuff don't stick all togedder on de shoes, it stick to dat track. When you make dat jump, you gonna threw dat stuff right in front o' you."

Ank Bishop, Alabama

"Dey was good to us 'caze Lady Liza's son, Mr. Willie Larkin, was de overseer for his ma, but cose sometime dey git among 'em an' thrashed 'em out. One time one de niggers runned away, old Caesar Fownsy, an' dey sarnt for Dick Peters to come an' bring his 'nigger dogs.' Dem dogs was trained to ketch a nigger same as rabbit dogs is trained to ketch a rabbit. So Mr. Willie Larkin told Stuart for to say to old man Dick Peters when he come, 'I'm gone,' but for him to come on. 'I'm gwineter keep de road,' he say, 'an' cross 'Bigbee at Moscow landin'.' So ol' Dick Peters, he kept de road lack he tole him to, an' he cross 'Bigbee at Moscow landin' over in de canebrake. But dem nigger dogs didn't never ketch ol' man Caesar. He stayed right wharever he was at 'twell after S'render, an' de War done ceasted. Den he come out, but iffen he had a been caught, dey'd a used him up pretty rough, but he stayed hid twell de time done passed."

Rias Body, Alabama

Uncle Rias said that some of the slaves frequently became restless and ran away; and when on these excursions they did not hesitate, when hunger overtook them, "to knock anybody's pig in the head." Furthermore, runaway slaves learned that fresh pork, though killed during the hottest months of the year, will cure nicely if packed down in shucked corn-on-the-cob. And, as a bag of corn was easy for a slave to steal, all runaways began taking along corn with which to cure meat while they were hiding in the woods.

"Now an' then slaves 'ud run away an' go in the woods an' dig dens an' live in 'em. Sometimes they runned away on 'count o' crool treatment, but mos' uv the time they runned away kyazen they jes' diden' wanner wuk, an' wanner to laze aroun' fer er spell. The marsters allus put de dawgs atter 'em an git 'em back. They had black and brown dawgs called 'nigger houn's,' whut woan' used fer nuthin' but to track down niggers."

Sally Brown, Georgia

"My grandmother run away from her mastah. She used sand fur soap. Yes, chile, I reckon they got 'long all right in the caves. They had babies in there and raised 'em, too."

Midge Burnett, North Carolina

"De patterollers 'ud watch all de paths leadin' frum de plantation an' when dey ketched a nigger leavin' dey whupped him an' run him home. As I said de patterollers watched all paths, but dar wus a number of little paths what run through de woods dat nobody ain't watched case dey ain't knowed dat de paths wus dar."

Thomas Cole, Texas

"I thoughts yessum, Mr. Anderson will takes good care of me, he'll give me dat cat-o-nine tails de first chance he gits, but I makes up mah mind right dar he wasn't goin ter gits no chance, cause I'se goin ter stay wid de rest of de slaves, and runs off de first chance I gits. I didnt know much about how ter gits outten dar, but I'se goin ter try it de first chance I gits I was goin north whar dar wasnt no slave owners."

"Purty soon mah mother comes out and tells me ter be a good and do all dat Mr. Anderson tells me ter do and ter stay up wid de rest of de slaves and dat she would comes ter see me de first chance she gits and fer me ter do de same thing. Bout dat time de boss hollers fer all of us ter goes ter work so I tole mah mother good bye, dat was de last time I ever seed her, she never did gits ter come back ter see me and I never could goes in ter see her, and I never seed mah brother and sister any more, dey never did brings dem back ter de plantation. I dont knows whether dey was sold er not after dey gits bigger, and I dont know whether mah mother marries any more er not."

"I got mah dinner and goes on ter de fiel and de first thing Mr. Anderson says ter me, 'Now Thomas, you got ter do as much work as de rest of dese niggers.' I says, 'Yassah,' and flies in ter it and I kept up all de time, but from dat day on I didnt has no use fer dat overseah. He wants ter whips me and I knows it but I never did gives him a chance."

"Missus Coles kept some of de slaves at de house ter help packs and loads things and when we comes in from work dat evenin dey was all gone. Dis movin was done wid ox wagons and was loaded heavy. I stayed on de planta-tion and worked fer two, three, four maybe five years and works every day cept Sundays and holidays till I got de chance dat I wanted ter run off. I done every thing de overseah toles me ter do and zactly laks he toles me ter do it."

"Mr. Anderson got him a better job in a year or so and missus Coles hires another man his name was Mr. Sandson. He was purty good ter us, he was more lak marser Coles fer bout two years, den he shore gits hard on us."

"De overseah gives me a log house and furnished me a girl ter do mah cookin and make mah clothes and other things dat had ter be done. He gives us a garden and we raised our own garden and roasting ears. I worked on day after day wantin a good chance ter run off and finally dar was talk bout de north and south seperatin and iffen dey did it would cause a war, dat de north wants de south ter turn de slaves loose and de south wouldnt do it. I dont know how it all happened but I thinks de north declares de slaves free and de south declares their selves free from de north and den things begins happening. Missus Coles begans comin ter de plantation quite a lot after de war started. John de oldes boy comes wid her quite a bit at first den finally John quits all of a sudden like. Isaac begins comin wid her. I heard dat John went ter war. I dont know fer shore, but John was bout eighteen er nineteen years ole bout dat time and was jest lak his papa. Sho was a nice lookin man. John was serious bout ever thing, but Isaac he was a happy go lucky kind of a feller and knows ever thing til de time comes and den he backs up. I ast Isaac iffen John jined de war, he said no, John jest gone off and dats all I could gits out of him."

"We begin goin ter de fiel earlier and stayin a little later each day den we did de year befo, corn was hauled off, cotton was hauled off, hogs and cattle was rounded up and hauled off, and things begins lookin bad. Instead eatin corn bread made outen corn meal, we eats corn bread made outten kaffir corn and maize jest stuff lak dat."

"We raised lots of okra dat year. Dey said dat okra was goin ter be parched and ground or beat up ter make coffee out off fer a person to drink, white folks was goin ter drink dat. Now dat didnt look good ter us either. Dat wintah instead killin from three hundred to four hundred hogs laks we had allus done befo, we only done one killin and kilt one hundred and seventy five and dey was not all big ones either. When de meat supply begins ter runs low in de wintah time er early spring, de overseah Mr. Sandson would sends some of de slaves ter kill a deer, wild hogs wid out any marks er brand on em er jest any kind of game dey could gits. He had sent out some of dem several times, but never had sent me out in any of de bunches. I hoped dat he would send me out but he didnt til he had sent out some of dem de second time, den one day he calls me up wid some of dem dat had gone befo and tole us not ter go off de plantation too far, but ter be shore and bring home some meat. All dat bunch of slaves was purty good ter do what dey was tole ter do amd master Sandson wasnt scared dey would run off either, but he didnt knows me too well. Dis was de chance I had been wantin, so when we all gits ter de hunting groun, de leader says now lets us all scatters out. I tole him me and another man would go north and makes a circle roun ter de rivah and I would cross ovah and come down on de east side and mah partner would comes down on de west side and we would meet back what we started bout sun down. So we started and when we got roun ter de rivah, I crossed de rivah to de east side but I didnt go very far east of de rivah til I turns back north steadda goin south. I was goin ter a free country, de north whar dar wasnt no slaves. I traveled all dat day and night up de rivah in de day and followed de north star dat night. Several times dat night I thought I could hear de blood houn trailin me and I would gits in a big hurry. I was already so tired dat I couldnt hardly move cause I had traveled as fast as I could all day, but when I would thinks sho hears dem blood houns, I would gits in a trot."

"I was hopin and prayin all de time dat I could meets up wid dat Harriet Tubman woman. She a colored woman dey say dat she comes down dar next ter us and gits a man and his wife and takes dem out and dey didnt gits ketched either. I heard after de war dat she was takin all dem slaves ter Canada and dat she had a regular town up dar jest slaves, negroes in it a good sized little town too. She allus travels de undergroun rail road dey calls it, travels at night and hides out in de day at different places and den travels all night again til she gits what dey was all safe. She sho sneaked lots of dem out of de south but she knowed what she was doin and who would help her. I never did see dis woman but I thinks she was a brave woman any way."

"I traveled dis way fer several nights and hidin in de day time in de thickets. I would eats all de nuts I could as there was lots of dem in de bottoms. I killed a few swamp rabbits and ketched a few fish I built one fire, puts lots of chunks and lots together and goes off bout half mile and hides in a thicket dis thicket lead right up to mah fire, but I goes back bout half mile in it and waits fer de fire ter burns down der coals, and I goes back and bakes me some fish and a rabbit. I was shakin all de time, fraid I would gits caught, but I was nearly starved to death and I did not much care iffen I did gits ketched. Maybe I would gits sumpin ter eat. But I didnt and I eats mah rabbit and three er four big fish and I puts de rest of de fish in mah ole cap and starts out again feelin purty good. I traveled on dat night follerin de north star and hides out de next day and eats de rest of mah fish and some more nuts and travels all de night again and hides in a big thicket de next day and along dat evenin I hears de guns begin shootin. I sho was skaired dis time sho nuff. I'se skeared ter come out and skeared ter stay in dar and while I was standin dar thinkin and shakin I heard two man say, 'Stick yo hands up boy, what you goin?' I puts mah hands up as high as I could reach and says, 'ah, ah, ah, dunno what I'se goin, you'se aint goin ter take me back ter de plantation is you.' Dey said, 'No, you want ter fight fer de north?' I toles dem I did cause I could tell by de way dey talked dat dey was northern men and dey turns me with them, and dey are spies fer de north."

Bill Collins, Texas

"The bell called and said, get up I'm coming after you, and said if they did not answer the call the over-seer would whip them. The slaves had to have passes to go and come from one plantation to another. I just can remember the 'Nigger Dogs,' that were used to catch the slaves. The darkies from the old states were lots smarter than the Texas negroes, they hoo-hoed the dogs, by putting red pepper in their shoes. After they had put pepper in their shoes the dogs wouldn't chase them any further. I was mis-treated lots of times, I went to sleep and old Master come in and hit me over the head. Some times we were tied to stakes and beat when we did not do what the master or over-seer said do."

"One man was beat from nine in the morning until sun-down."

Henry Davis, South Carolina

"Does I 'members anything 'bout patrollers? 'Deed, I do! Marster didn't 'ject to his slaves gwine to see women off de place. I hear him say so, and I hear him tell more than once dat if he over hear de patrollers a comin' wid blood hounds, to run to de lot and stick his foots in de mud and de dogs wouldn't follow him. Lots of run'ways tried it, I heard, and it proved a success and I don't blame them dogs neither."

Sarah Ford, Texas

"Massa Charles run dat plantation jus' like a factory. Uncle Cip was sugar man, my papa tanner and Uncle John Austin, what have a wooden leg, am

Sarah Ford. (Library of Congress)

shoemaker and make de shoes with de brass toes. Law me, dey heaps of things go on in slave time what won't go on no more, 'cause de bright light come and it ain't dark no more for us black folks. Iffen a nigger run away and dey cotch him, or does he come back 'cause he hongry, I seed Uncle Jake stretch him out on de ground and tie he hands and feet to posts so he can't move none. Den he git de piece of iron what he call de 'slut' and what is like a block of wood with little holes in it, and fill de holes up with tallow and put dat iron in de fire till de grease sizzlin' hot and hold it over de pore nigger's back and let dat hot grease drap on he hide. Den he take de bullwhip and whip up and down, and after all dat throw de pore nigger in de stockhouse and chain him up a couple days with nothin' to eat. My papa carry de grease scars on he back till he die."

"Massa Charles and Uncle Jake don't like papa, 'cause he ain't so black, and he had spirit, 'cause he part Indian. Do somethin' go wrong and Uncle Big Jake say he gwine to give papa de whippin', he runs off. One time he gone a whole year and he sho' look like a monkey when he gits back, with de hair standin' straight on he head and he face. Papa was mighty good to mama and me and dat de only reason he ever come back from runnin' 'way, to see us. He knowed he'd git a whippin' but he come anyway. Dey never could cotch papa when he run 'way, 'cause he part Indian. Massa Charles even gits old Nigger Kelly what lives over to Sandy Point to track papa with he dogs, but papa wade in water and dey can't track him."

Arnold Gragston, Florida

"I didn't have no idea of ever gettin' mixed up in any sort of business like that until one special night. I hadn't even thought of rowing across the river myself."

"But one night I had gone on another plantation 'courtin,' and the old woman whose house I went to told me she had a real pretty girl there who wanted to go across the river and would I take her? I was scared and backed out in a hurry. But then I saw the girl, and she was such a pretty little thing, brown-skinned and kinda rosy, and looking as scared as I was feelin', so it wasn't long before I was listenin' to the old woman tell me when to take her and where to leave her on the other side."

"I didn't have nerve enough to do it that night, though, and I told them to wait for me until tomorrow night. All the next day I kept seeing Mister Tabb laying a rawhide across my back, or shootin' me, and kept seeing that scared little brown girl back at the house, looking at me with her big eyes and askin' me if I wouldn't just row her across to Ripley. Me and Mr. Tabb lost, and soon as dust settled that night, I was at the old lady's house."

"I don't now how I ever rowed the boat across the river the current was strong and I was trembling. I couldn't see a thing there in the dark, but I felt that girl's eyes. We didn't dare to whisper, so I couldn't tell her how sure I was that Mr. Tabb or some of the others owners would 'tear me up' when they found out what I had done. I just knew they would find out."

"I was worried, too, about where to put her out of the boat. I couldn't ride her across the river all night, and I didn't know a thing about the other side. I had heard a lot about it from other slaves but I thought it was just about like Mason County, with slaves and masters, overseers and rawhides; and so, I just knew that if I pulled the boat up and went to asking people where to take her I would get a beating or get killed."

"I don't know whether it seemed like a long time or a short time, now—it's so long ago; I know it was a long time rowing there in the cold and worryin'. But it was short, too, 'cause as soon as I did get on the other side the big-eyed, brown-skin girl would be gone. Well, pretty soon I saw a tall light and I remembered what the old lady had told me about looking for that light and rowing to it. I did; and when I got up to it, two men reached down and grabbed her; I started tremblin' all over again, and prayin'. Then, one of the men took my arm and I just felt down inside of me that the Lord had got ready for me. 'You hungry, Boy?' is what he asked me, and if he hadn't been holdin' me I think I would have fell backward into the river."

"That was my first trip; it took me a long time to get over my scared feelin', but I finally did, and I soon found myself goin' back across the river, with two and three people, and sometimes a whole boatload. I got so I used to make three and four trips a month."

"What did my passengers look like? I can't tell you any more about it than you can, and you wasn't there. After that first girl—no, I never did see her again—I never saw my passengers. It would have to be the 'black nights' of the moon when I would carry them, and I would meet 'em out in the open or in a house without a single light. The only way I know who they were was to ask them, 'What you say?' and they would answer, 'Menare.' I don't know what that word meant—it came from the Bible. I only know that that was the password I used, and all of them that I took over told it to me before I took them."

Susan Hamlin (Hamilton), South Carolina

"My pa b'long to a man on Edisto Island. Frum what he said, his master was very mean. Pa real name wus Adam Collins but he took his master' name; he wus de coachman. Pa did supin one day en his master whipped him. De next day which wus Monday, pa carry him 'bout four miles frum home in de woods an' give him de same 'mount or lickin' he wus given on Sunday. He tied him to a tree an' unhitched de horse so it couldn't git tie-up an' kill e'self. Pa den gone to de landin' an' cotch a boat dat wus comin' to Charleston wood fa'm products. He was permitted by his master to go to town on errands, which helped him to go on de boat without bein' question'. W'en he got here he gone on de water-front an' ax for a job on a ship so he could git to de North. He got de job an' sail' wood de ship. Dey search de island up an' down for him wood houndogs en w'en it wus t'ought he wus drowned, 'cause dey track him to de river, did dey give up. One of his master' friend gone to New York en went in a store w'ere pas wus employed as a clerk. he reconise' pa is essy is pa reconise' him. He gone back home an' tell pa master who know den dat pa wusn't comin' back an' before he died he sign' papers dat pa wus free. Pa's ma wus dead an' he come down to bury her by de permission of his master' son who had promised no ha'm would come to him, but dey wus fixin' plans to keep him, so he went to de Work House an' ax to be sold 'cause any slave could sell a self if a could git to de Work House. But it wus on record down dere so dey coulan't sell 'im an' told him his master' people couldn't hold him a slave."

Pierce Harper, Texas

"The masters couldn't whip the slaves there. The law said in black and white no master couldn't whip no slave, no matter what he done. When a slave got bad they took him to the county seat and had him whipped. One day I seen my old daddy get whipped by the county and state 'cause he wouldn't work. They had a post in the public square what they tied 'em to and a man what worked for the county whipped 'em."

"After he was whipped my daddy run away to the north. Daddy come by when I was cleanin' the yard and said, 'Pierce, go 'round side the house, where nobody can't see us.' I went and he told me goodbye, 'cause he was goin' to run away in a few days. He had to stay in the woods and travel at night and eat what he could find, berries and roots and things. They never caught him and after he crossed the Mason-Dixon line he was safe."

Josh Horn, Alabama

"De fust thing I 'members 'bout slave'y time, I wan't nothing but a boy, 'bout fifteen I reckon, dat's what Marse Johnnie Horn say. Us belong to Marse Ike Horn, Marse Johnni's pa, right here on did place whar us is now, but dis here didn't belong to me den, dis here was all Marse Ike's place. Marse Ike's gin got outer fix and we couldn't git it fixed. Colonel Lee had two gins and one of 'em was jes' below old Turner house. Recolleck a big old hickory tree? Well dar's whar it was."

"I was plenty big 'nough to drive de mules to de gin. Set on de lever and drive 'em, jes lak a 'lasses mill, so dat night Marse Ike told us he want everybody go wid him to Colonel Lee's gin nex' morning, and didn't want nobody to git out and go ahead of him. Dat held up de ginning; made us not to go to de ginhouse tell sunup."

"Us got de mules and jes' waited. 'Twixt daylight and sunup, us all standing dar at de gate and we heared a little fine horn up de road. Us didn't know what it meant coming to de house. And bimeby Mr. Beesley, what live not fur from Marse Ike, he rode up and had five dogs, five nigger dogs, what dey call 'em, and soon as he come, Marse Ike's hoss was saddled up and Marse Ike and him rode off down de road and de dogs wid 'em, 'head of us. Us followed 'long behind 'em, stay close as dey' low us, to see what dey was up to. When dey got close to de ginhouse, ginhouse right 'side de road, dey stop us and Mr. Beesley told old Brown to go ahead. Old Brown was de lead dog and had a bell on him and dey was fasten togedder wid a rod, jes' lak steers, He turn 'em loose, and den he popped de whip and hollered at old Brown and told him 'nigger.' Old Brown hollered lak he hit. He want to go. And dey was a fence on bofe sides made it a lane, so he put old Brown over de fence on de ginhouse side, and told Brown to 'go ahead.' He went ahead and run all aroun' de ginhouse and dey let him in de gin-room and he grabbled in de cottonseed in a hole."

"Den somebody holler 'Guinea Jim.'"

"I looks and I didn't see him. Didn't nobody see him, but dey know dat's whar he been hiding. Mr. Beesley told old Brown he jes' fooling him, and Old Brown holler ag'in, lak he killing him, and Mr. Beesley say: 'Go git dat nigger' and old Brown started 'way from dar lak he hadn't been hunting nothing, but he went aroun' and aroun' dat gin and Mr. Beesley told him he hatter do better dan dat or he'd kill him, 'cause he hadn't come dar for nothing."

"Brown made a circle aroun' dat gin 'way down to de fence dat time, and he was so fat he couldn't git through de fence. You know what sort of fence, a rail fence it was. Den he stop and bark for help. Now I seed dis wid my own eyes. Dey put Brown on top de fence and he jump way out in de road, didn't stay on de fence. He jump and run up and down in de road, and couldn't find no scent of Jim. You knows how dey used to make dem rail fences?"

"Well, Brown come back dar, and dis is de trufe, so help me Gawd. He bark, look lak, for dem to lift him back up on de fence, and bless God, if dat dog didn't walk dat rail fence lak he walking a log, as fur as from here to dat gate yonder, and track Jim jes' lak he was on de groun'. He fell off once, and dey had to put him back, and he run his track right on to whar Jim jumped off de fence way out in de road. Old Brown run right cross de road to de other fence and treed ag'in on t'other side de road toward Konkabia. Old Brown walk de fence on dat side de road a good piece, jes' lak he done on de other side, and dem other dogs, he hadn't never turned dem loose."

"When Brown he jump off dat fence, he jump jes' as fur as he kin on de fiel' side, lak he gwine ketch Jim lak a gnat or somepin' and he never stop barking no more, jes' lak he jumping a rabbit. Den, Mr. Beesley turn dem other dogs loose dat he hadn't never turned loose, 'ca'se he say old Brown done got de thing straight. And he had it straight. Dem dogs run dat track right on down to Konkabia and crossed it to de Blacksher side. Dey was a big old straw field dar den and dey cross it and come on through dat field, all dem dogs barkin' jes' lak dey looking at Jim. 'Beckley, dey come up on Jim running wid a pine bresh tied behind him to drag his scent away, but it didn't bother old Brown."

"When dem dogs 'gin to push him, Jim drap de bresh and runned back toward Konkabia. Now on Konkabia dere used to be beavers worse den on Sucarnatchee now. Dey was a big beaver dam 'twixt de bridge and de Hale place, and Jim run to dat beaver dam. You know when beavers build dey dam, dey cut down trees and let 'em fall in de creek, and pull in trash en bresh same as folks, to dam de water up dar tell its knee-deep. De dogs seen him, old Brown looking at him, jes' 'fore he jump in 'bove de dam right 'mongst de trash and things dey'd drug in dar. Brown seed him and he jump in right behind him. Jim jes' dive down under de raff, en let he nose stick outer de water. Every once in a while Jim he put he head down under, he holding to a pole down dar, and once Mr. Beesley seed him, he jes' let him stay dar."

"Brown would swim 'bout 'mongst de bresh, backerds and for'erds, and terreckly Mr. Beesley tole old Brown, 'Go git him.' Den all de men got poles and dug 'bout in de raff hunting him. Dey knowed he was dar, en Marse Ike had a pole giggen aroun' trying to find him too. Den he told Mr. Beesley to give him de hatchet and let him fix he pole. He sharpen de pole right sharp, den Marse Ike start to jug aroun' wid de pole, and he kinder laugh to hisse'f, 'ca'se he knowed he done found Jim. 'Bout dat time Jim poke he head up and say: 'Dis here me,' and everybody holler. Den he ax 'em please, for God's sake, don't let dem dogs git him. Dey told him come on out."

"You see, Jim belonged to Miss Mary Lee, Mr. John Lee's Ma, and his Pa was kilt in de war, so Mr. Beesley was looking out for her. Well, dey took Jim outer dar, and Mr. Beesley whipped him a little and told him: 'Jim, you put up a pretty good fight and I's gwine to give you a start for a run wid de dogs.'"

"Jim took out towards Miss Mary's, and Mr. Beesley helt old Brown as long as he could. Dey caught Jim and bit him right smart. You see dey had to let em bite him a little to satisfy de dogs. Jim could have made it, 'cept he was all hot and wore out."

Annie Huff, Georgia

Those seeking to escape from a cruel Master used to rub turpentine on the soles of their feet to prevent capture. Others collected quantities of soil from a graveyard and sprinkled it in their tracks for a certain distance. Both of these precautions were used to throw the dogs off scent. Refugee slaves often found shelter on Mr. Huff' estate, where they were assisted in further flight by the Huff Negroes. Those who remained in the woods were fed regularly.

Ben Kinchlow, Texas

"While I was yet on the border, the plantation owners had to send their cotton to the border to be shipped to other parts, so it was transferred by Negro slaves as drivers. Lots of times, when these Negroes got there and took the cotton from their wagon, they would then be persuaded to go across the border by Meskins, and then they would nevee return to their master. That is how lots of Negroes got to be free. The way they used to transfer the cotton—these big cotton plantations east of here—they'd take it to Brownsville and put it on the wharf and ship it from there. I can remember seeing, during the cotton season,

Ben Kinchlow. (Library of Congress)

fifteen or twenty teams hauling cotton, sometimes five or six, maybe eight bales on a wagon. You see, them steamboats used to run all up and down that river. I think this cotton went out to market at New Orleans and went right out into the Gulf."

Amie Lumpkin, South Carolina

"There was pretty good order on de plantation, generally at de time in 1856, when I was 'bout seven years old. Most of de slaves go right along doin' their chores, as expected of them, but a few was restless, and they break de rules, by runnin' 'bout without askin', and always there was one or two who tried to escape slavery by goin' far away to the North."

"I 'member seein' one big black man, who tried to steal a boat ride from Charleston. He stole away one night from Master Mobley's place and got to Charleston, befo' he was caught up with. He tell the overseer who questioned him after he was brought back: 'Sho', I try to git away from this sort of thing. I was goin' to Massachusetts, and hire out 'til I git 'nough to carry me to my home in Africa.'"

"It was de rule when a trial was bein' held lak this, for all de bosses and sometimes de missus to be there to listen and to ask the run'way slave some questions. After this one talked, it was Missus Mobley herself who said: 'Put yourself in this slave's shoes, and what would you do? Just such as he has. The best way to treat such a slave is to be so kind and patient with him, that he will forget his old home.'"

"He was led away and I never did hear if he was whipped. He lak a Cherokee Indian, he never whimper if he should be whipped 'til de blood stream from him; but I do know he never got away again. He was de first one to pick up his hat and laugh loud, when President Lincoln set all slaves free in January, 1863; He say: 'Now I go, thank de Lord, and he strike right out, but he not git much beyond de barn, when he turn and come back. He walked in de yard of de big house, and he see Missus Mobley lookin' out at him. He take off his hat and bow low and say: Missus, I so happy to be free, that I forgits myself but I not go 'til you say so. I not leave you when you needs a hand, 'less de master and all de white folks gits home to look after you.'"

"De missus look down at her feet and she see de black man, so big and strong, sheddin' tears. She say to him: 'You is a good nigger and you has suffered much; make yourself at home, just as you have been doin' and when you want to go far away, come to me and I'll see that you git 'nough money to pay your way to Boston and may be to Africa.' And that is what happen' a year or two later."

Walter Rimm, Texas

"My pappy wasn't 'fraid of nothin'. He am light cullud from de white blood, and he runs away sev'ral times. Dere am big woods all round and we sees lots

Walter Rimm. (Library of Congress)

of run-awayers. One old fellow name John been a run-awayer for four years and de patterrollers tries all dey tricks, but dey can't cotch him. Dey wants him bad, 'cause it 'spire other slaves to run away if he stays a-loose. Dey sots de trap for him. Dey knows he like good eats, so dey 'ranges for a quiltin' and gives chitlin's and lye hominey. John comes and am inside when de patterrollers rides up to de door. Everybody gits quiet and John stands near de door, and when dey starts to come in he grabs de shovel full of hot ashes and throws dem into de patterrollers faces. He gits through and runs off, hollerin', 'Bird in de air!'"

"One women name Rhodie runs off for long spell. De hounds won't hunt her. She steals hot light bread when dey puts it in de window to cool, and lives on dat. She told my mammy how to keep de hounds from followin' you is to take black pepper and put it in you socks and run without you shoes. It make de hounds sneeze."

"One day I's in de woods and meets de nigger runawayer. He comes to de cabin and mammy makes him a bacon and egg sandwich and we never seed him again. Maybe he done got clear to Mexico, where a lot of de slaves runs to."

Gill Ruffin, Texas

"The woods was full of runaways and I heered them houn's a runnin' 'em like deer many a time, and heered dat whip when they's caught."

"I never knew but one nigger to run away from Marster Hargrave. He slip off and goes to Shreveport. That was Peter Going. Marster missed him and he goes to fin' him. When he fin's him in Shrevaport, he say, 'Come on, Peter, you knowed what you was doin' and you's goin' to pay for it.' Marster tied him behin' de buggy and trots de hosses all way back home. Then he ties Peter to a tree and makes him stay dere all night with nothin' to eat. Peter, nor none of the res' of the niggers didn' ever try to run off after that."

William Sherman, Florida

On another occasion one of the Stokes' slaves ran away and he sent Steven Kittles, known as the "dog man," to catch the escape. (The dogs that went in pursuit of the runaway slaves were called "Nigger dogs"; they were used specifically for catching runaway slaves.) This particular slave had quite a "head start" on the dogs that were trailing him and he hid among some floating logs in a large pond; the dogs trailed him to the pond and began howling, indicating that they were approaching their prey. They entered the pond to get their victim who was securely hidden from sight; they dissapeared and the next seen of them was their dead bodies floating upon the water of the pond; they had been killed by the escapee. They were full-blooded hounds, such as were used in hunting escaped slaves and were about fifty in number. The slave made his escape and was never seen again. Will relates that it was very cold and that he does'nt understand how the slave could stand the icy waters of the pond, but evidently he did survive it.

John Morgan Smith, Alabama

"I remembers a slave on our plantation dat was always arunnin' away. De Massa try beatin' him but dat didn't do no good. Dat nigger would run away in spite of nothin' they could do. One day de massa decided he was goin' to take de nigger to Mobile an' swap him for anudder one. De Misstis tol' him to leave de ole fool alone, said it warn't warth the trouble. Well, de massa started out to Mobile wid de nigger, an' when de got dere an' de train stop, de nigger, he lit out an' de massa runned right behine him. Dey musta runned a mile or mo' till finaly de massa he gib out an' let de nigger go. Two days later de massa he died f'm a-chasin' dat low down burr head."

Mary Smith, South Carolina

"Befo' ma died and I was a little gal, a terrible thing happened to us. Across de Enoree on another place, de Miller place, Fannie Miller run away. Dey couldn't find her fer a long time. Dey told my marster to git her. One Sunday my ma got ready to dress me fer Sunday school. She bathed me and when she looked in de drawer she couldn't find my clothes. All of her clothes was gone, too. I cried 'cause I couldn't go to Sunday school. Maude, de woman what lived next to us, went to church. She saw Fannie dar wid all ma's clothes on. She told Marse about it and he sont out and had Fannie caught. She had come to our house and got de clothes on Saturday evening. She had dem hid in a old house on our place. Dey put her in jail, and den her marster come and whupped her and sont de clothes back to ma. She never tried to run off agin."

Tucker Smith, Texas

"Well no sir, boss, I'se never heard of any negroes that ever tried to run off to the north but we had one negro that run off and joined up with Jesse James, that there bad man that the people talked about, but he was one of the best men that I'se ever seen. Son I'se wants to tell you I'se cooked lots of meals for him out there on the prairie and on the mountains when he was hiding out from the law. Course the law could have captured him lots of times but they did not want him, no sir, cause they knew it meant death to contrary him and so they let him alone. He went just about where he pleased."

Maria Tilden Thompson, Texas

"Durin' slavery time dere was lots ob times when de scared slaves would git together and talk about gittin' dere freedom. Dey would git together, polish up dere huntin' guns, and be ready to staht somethin'. Dis was jes' befo' freedom. De main thing dat de slaves wanted was to git dere freedom, but de mawsters had better not hear about it."

Sallie Wroe, Texas

"Pappy was a putty good man, considerin' dat he was a slaveman. One day pappy, Uncle Paul, Uncle Andy, and Uncle Joe—dey wasn't our uncles, but we always called de older folks uncle and auntie—was takin' bales of cotton on ox wagons down to de Rio Grande River. Each man was drivin' a ox wagon down to Brownsville, where dey was to wait and meet Mawster Burdette. But, pappy and de other men left de wagons along de river bank, rolled a bale ob cotton into de river, and all four ob 'em got on dat bale and rowed across de Rio Grande over into Mexico. Dis was durin' de Civil War, I believe. Pappy told us later dat he done got along fine wid dem Mexicans over in Mexico. He learned to talk jes' lak a Mexican. Pappy and Uncle Andy could talk lak two Mexican brothaws. I don't remembah whut type ob work dey done ovah in Mexico. I know dat pappy never married no Mexican woman."

"Me and mammy stayed on at Mawster Burdette's place durin' de whole time dat pappy was gone. He didn't come back till aftah slavery time, and we was livin' at Chappel Hill, Washington County. Aftah slavery, and when we was free, my Cousin Mitchell—we always called him Mitch—come and

Sallie Wroe. (Library of Congress)

got us f'om de Burdette place and brought us to Chappel Hill, and looked out fo' us till pappy come."

FLEEING NOT TOO FAR DISTANT

Escapes by the enslaved were often short in distance and of varying duration. Ties to family could cause the runaway to return after a period of absence, as could the inability to find enough food. In addition, the distance to free territory might be forbidding and the alternative of hiding in nearby areas more feasible. Such practical considerations influenced where and how long the enslaved went missing.

Enslaved workers who lived far from northern communities and Mexican borders often chose to find safe havens nearby. They found a variety of places to hide, including caves, cliff dwellings, and places concealed in the woods. The key was to create a space that was difficult for the whites searching for them to discover. Some places were so well hidden that the inhabitants occupied them for years without discovery.

After receiving a whipping for leaving a Georgia plantation without a pass, Celestia Avery's uncle ran off into the nearby woods and found a cave large enough to live in comfortably. After he prepared it, "he came back to the plantation unobserved and carried his wife and two children back to this cave where they lived until after freedom. When found years later, his wife had given birth to two children. No one was ever able to find his hiding place." The hideaway created by Celestia's uncle was extraordinarily successful and illustrates the ingenuity some fugitives put into their escape and concealment. It also was a reminder that runaways did not always leave the region.

The narratives in this section illuminate a part of history that, although well documented in such places as Cuba or Brazil, shows how small runaway or maroon communities were created in the United States. These communities were a source of comfort to those who fled bondage and an area of concern and worry for those who profited by the labor of the enslaved.

Running away did not always result in permanent disappearance. Many people only left for short periods, and after a few days or weeks they voluntarily returned. This decision was prompted by a variety of circumstances. Some runaways found it difficult to survive on their own in the wild. Obtaining food could be especially challenging, and many returned extremely hungry and tired, willing to receive whatever punishment was to come. Loneliness at being separated from loved ones brought others back. Not seeing their children, spouse, or other loved ones was too heavy a burden to bear and so they returned despite the consequences. This was the case for the Georgia mother of Charlie Pye: "My mother resented being whipped and would run away to the woods and often remained as long as twelve months at a time. When the strain of staying away from her family became too great, she would return home. No sooner would she arrive than the old overseer would tie her to a peach tree and whip her again."

NARRATIVES

Samuel Simeon Andrews, Florida

"My mother's brother, 'Uncle Dick,' and 'Uncle July' swore they would not work longer for masters; so they ran away lived in the woods. In winter they would put cotton seed in the fields to rot for fertilizer and lay in it for warmth. They would kill hogs and slip the meat to some slave to cook for food. When their owners looked for them, 'Bob Amos' who raised 'nigger hounds' [hounds raised solely to track Negro slaves] was summoned and the dogs located them and surrounded them in their hide-out; one went one way and one the other and escaped in the swamps; they would run until they came to a fence—each kept some 'graveyard dust and a few light-wood splinters' with which they smoked their feet and jumped the fence and the dogs turned back and could track no further. Thus, they stayed in the woods until freedom, when they came out and worked for pay. Now, you know 'Uncle Dick' just died a few years ago in Sparta, Georgia."

Celestia Avery, Georgia

Mrs. Avery related the occasion when her Uncle William was caught off the Heard plantation without a pass, and was whipped almost to death by the "Pader Rollers." "He stole off to the depths of the woods where he built a cave large enough to live in. A few nights later he came back to the plantation unobserved and carried his wife and two children back to this cave where they lived until after freedom. When found years later his wife had given birth to two children. No one was ever able to find his hiding place and if he saw any one in the woods he would run like a lion."

James Barber, Texas

"I see slaves from other plantations run off in de woods. After freedom come one woman that had been in de woods come up to our w'ite folks. De briers an' thorns had cut sores on her an' in some er de sores dere was screwworms. They was one man Mike Mitchell allus in de woods."

Joe Barnes, Texas

"I kin kinder rec'leck 'em whippin' slaves. Marster was mean to 'em. Dey tie 'em down 'cross a bar'l or log and whip' 'em. Mos' de time dey whip 'em 'bout wuk. Dey wuk 'em by task and if a nigger ain't git he task done dey whip 'em. Some of 'em run away. Dey had w'at dey call de nigger dog to ketch 'em. One nigger run away one time. He could run fas'er dan de dog and de dog ain't kin ketch 'im. He stay in de woods a long time, but atter dat he tek a notion to come back and let 'em whip 'im."

Nathan Best, Mississippi

"I run away once, [he laughed] I didn' start to go nowhere jes' laid out in de wood, hidin from de overseer. He come down the street in de Quarters dat mawnin' jes' a beatin' an' whuppin' an' de niggahs all a cryin' an' a screamin' an' befoe he got to where I was, I done lef'an hid in de woods. My ole mistis, thought dat de overseer had kilt me, an' she tole him not to bother me ef I was foun'. Ole mistis was mean too, she would tell de overseer to whup de niggah, but she didn' low him to kill none of us, 'kase dat would lose her money. Well, dey foun' me an' took me to de Great House, but dey didn' whup me. Dey ship me off from dat place ober to her son's plantation. He was mah'ied off an his place was about 3 miles from ole mistis."

Julia Blanks, Texas

"No'm, I don't know if they run off to the North, but some of them runned off and stayed in the swamps, and they was mean. They called them runaways. If they saw you, they would tell you to bring them something to eat. And if you didn't do it, if they ever got you they sure would fix you."

James Bolton, Georgia

"Now and then slaves 'ud run away and go in the woods and dig dens and live in 'em. Sometimes they runned away on 'count of cruel treatment, but most of the time they runned away kazen they jus' didn't want to wuk, and wanted to laze around for a spell. The marsters allus put the dogs atter 'em and git 'em back. They had black and brown dogs cailed 'nigger hounds' what waren't used for nothin' but to track down niggers."

James Boyd, Texas

"De slaves did run off an' try to go north, but nigger stealers mos' offen got dem an den dey would be sold again an maybe git worse hans holt of 'em. Mos' en general 'round our part of de country, effen a nigger want to run away, he'd light out fer ole Mexico. Dat was nigger heaven dem days, dey thought, but soon as de Freedom come, I thought I'd try it an git me a rich Mex wife an live like a big bug, but all I got shore worked hard to get it."

Sally Brown, Georgia

"Sometimes the slaves would run away. Their mastahs wuz mean to 'em and that caused 'em to run away. Sometimes they'd live in caves. How'd they git along? Well, chile, they got along all right—what with other people slippin' things in to 'em. And then they'd steal hogs, chickens, and anything else they could git their hands on. Some white people would help, too, fur their wuz some white people who didn't believe in slavery. Yes, they'd try to find them slaves that run away and if they wuz found they'd be beat or sold to somebody else."

Solbert Butler, South Carolina

"My uncle was so whip he went into de woods, an' live dere for months, Had to learn de independent life."

Jeff Calhoun, Texas

"Only two slaves tried to run away to de north dat I know of but dey didnt git far, dey didnt know the Kentucky and didnt know what to go er how to go."

Hannah Chapman, Mississippi

"After being whipped some o' de slaves would hide fer days an' weeks in de woods. Some ob 'em stay hid out mos' all de times. My father and mother wuz strict on us. How dey would whip!"

Pierce Cody, Georgia

Connected with nearly every home were those persons who lived "in the woods" in preference to doing the labor necessary to remain at their home. Each usually had a scythe and a bulldog for protection. As food became scarce, they sneaked to the quarters in the still of the night and coaxed some friend to get food for them from the smokehouse. Their supply obtained, they would leave again. This was not considered stealing.

Neil Coker, Florida

Negro slaves from the region around St. Augustine and what is now Hastings used to escape and use Bellamy's Road on their way to the area about Micanopy. It was considered equivalent to freedom to reach that section, with its friendly Indians and impenetrable forests and swamps.

Preely Coleman, Texas

"Jack Little was almost a wild man. I think he came from Africa, caused a world of trouble, wouldn't work, finally ran off and lived in the woods two years. Somebody slipped a frying pan to him and he had his gun. Just lived on wild turkeys and rabbits. He was staying in woods when freedom came."

Silva Durant, South Carolina

"I hear Tom Bostick tell 'bout when he run 'way one time. Say he use'er run 'way en hide in de woods aw de time. Den de o'erseer ketch him one time when he been come back en wuz grabblin' 'bout de tatoe patch. Say he gwinna make Tom Bostick stay outer de woods ur kill him 'fore sun up dat day. Tom say dey take him down 'side de woods en strip he clothes offen him. (I hear em say dere plenty people bury down 'side dem woods dat dere ain' nobody know 'bout). Den he say dey tie him to uh tree en take uh fat light'ud torch en le' de juice drap outer it right on he naked body. He say he holler en he beg en he ax em hab mercy but dat ne'er didn't do no good. He meck how de tar make uh racket when it drap on he skin. Yuh know it gwinna make uh racke't. Dat t'ing gwinna make uh racket when it drap on anyt'ing wha' fresh. Ain' yuh ne'er hear no hot grease sizzle lak? Yas'um, hear Tom Bostick tell dat more times den I got fingers en toe."

John Elliott, Arkansas

"Yes, ma'am, I was a slave. I was about 8 years old when they mustered 'em out the last time."

"My daddy went along to take care of his young master. He died, and my daddy brought his horse and all his belongings home."

"You see it was this way. My mother was a run-away slave. She was from, what's that big state off there—Virginia—yes, ma'am, that's it. There was a pretty good flock of them. They came into North Carolina—Wayne County was where John Elliott found them. They was in a pretty bad way. They didn't have no place to go and they didn't have nothing to eat. They didn't have nobody to own 'em. They didn't know what to do. My mother was about 13."

"By some means or other they met up with a man named John Elliott. He was a teacher. He struck a bargain with them. He pitched in and he bought 200 acres of land. He built a big house for Miss Polly and Bunk and Margaret. Miss Polly was his sister. And he built cabins for the black folks."

"And he says 'You stay here, and you take care of Miss Polly and the children. Now mind, you raise lots to eat. You take care of the place too. And if anybody bothers you you tell Miss Polly.' My Uncle Mose, he was the oldest. He was a blacksmith. Jacob was the carpenter. 'Now look here, Mose,' says Mister John, 'you raise plenty of hogs. Mind you give all the folks plenty of meat. Then you take the rest to Miss Polly and let her lock it in the smoke-house.' Miss Polly carried the key, but Mose was head man and had dominion over the smokehouse."

Isaiah Green, Georgia

Mr. John Branch was considered one of the meanest slave owners in Green County, and the Negroes on his plantation were always running away. Another slave owner known for his cruelty was Colonel Calloway, who had a slave named Jesse who ran away and stayed 7 years. He dug a cave in the ground and made fairly comfortable living quarters. Other slaves who no longer could stand Col. Calloway's cruelty, would join him. Jesse visited his wife, Lettie, two and three times a week at night. Col. Calloway could never verify this, but became suspicious when Jesse's wife gave birth to two children who were the exact duplicate of Jesse. When he openly accused her of knowing Jesse's whereabouts, she denied the charges, pretending she had not seen him since the day he left.

Molly Harrell, Texas

"Somebody run 'way all de time and hide in de woods till dere gut pinch dem and den dey have to come back and git somethin' to eat. Course, dey got beat, but dat didn't worry dem none, and it not long till dey gone 'gain."

Shang Harris, Georgia

"But law chile, eve'ybody didn't have dat. Some de marsters tied dey niggers to posts and whupped 'em till dey nigh killed 'em. Lots of 'em run away and hid in de woods. De marsters would put de dogs after you jes' like a coon. Dey'd run you and tree you—imitating the sound of baying dogs—oh, glory, hallelujah—dat's de way dey done 'em! I'se seed bare feets all cracked up wid de cold. We don't have no cold weather now. Why, I'se seed big pine trees bust wide open—done froze, and de niggers would be out in dat kind o' weather. But dey'd ruther do dat dan stay and git beat to death. Many a night jes' 'bout dark, I'd be a-settin' in my cabin wid my ole lady (dat was after I got older) and see somebody prowlin' roun' in de bushes, and I'd know hit was some po' nigger was hidin' and didn't had nuttin' to eat. My marster nuse to say, Harris, when you see somebody hongry, gi' 'im sumpin' to eat'. We didn't ever turn 'em down even when dey look so bad dey was right scarey."

Tom Hawkins, Georgia

"Niggers didn't run to no North. Dey run to de South, 'cause dem white folks up North was so mean to 'em. One Nigger, named Willis Earle, run off to de woods and made hisself a den in a cave. He lived hid out in dat cave 'bout 15 years."

Felix Haywood, Texas

"Sometimes someone would come 'long and try to get us to run up North and be free. We used to laugh at that. There wasn't no reason to run up

Felix Haywood. (Library of Congress)

North. All we had to do was to walk, but walk South. and we'd be free as soon as we crossed the Rio Grande. In Mexico you could be free. They didn't care what color you was, black, white, yellow or blue. Hundreds of slaves did go to Mexico and got on all right. We would hear about 'em and how they was goin' to be Mexicans. They brought up their children to speak only Mexican."

Jeff Henry, Georgia

"Slaves on our plantation never thought about runnin' off to no North. Marse Robert allus treated 'em fair and square, and thar warn't no need for 'em to run nowhar. That foreman of his, Robert Scott, did go off and stay a few days once. Marse Robert had started to whip his wife and he had jumped 'twixt 'em; that Marse Robert so made he run to the house to git his gun, so the foreman he got out of the way a day or two to keep from gittin' shot. When he come back, Marse Robert was so glad to git him back he never said a word to him 'bout leavin'.'"

Fred James, South Carolina

"Some slaves dat lived on places close to us would run off sometimes and hide in de woods, and live dar in a den which dey dug. At night dey would go out and hunt food, like hogs; den kill 'em at night and dress 'em. Most of de day dey would stay in de den."

Cinto Lewis, Texas

"Marse Dave wasn't mean like some. Sometimes de slaves run away to do woods and iffen they don't cotch em fust they finally gits hongry and comes home, and then they gits a hidin'. Some niggers jus' come from Africa and old Marse has to watch 'em close, 'cause they is de ones what mostly runs away to de woods."

Aunt Harriet Mason, Kentucky

A slave owner, in West Virginia, bought a thirteen year old black girl at an auction. When this girl was taken to his home she escaped, and after searching every where, without finding her, he decided that she had been helped to escape and gave her up as lost. About two years after that a neighbor, on a close-by farm, was in the woods feeding his cattle, he saw what he first thought was a bear, running into the thicket from among his cows. Getting help, he rounded up the cattle and searching the thick woodland, finally found that what he had supposed was a wild animal, was the long lost fugitive black girl. She had lived all this time in caves, feeding on nuts, berries, wild apples and milk from cows, that she could catch and milk. Returned to her master she was sold to a Mr. Morgan Whittaker who lived near where Prestonsburg, Kentucky now is.

Jake McLeod, South Carolina

"I hear tell bout one man runnin away from Black Creek en gwine to Free State. Catch ride wid people dat used to travel to Charleston haulin cotton en things. He come back bout 15 years after de war en lived in dat place join to me. Come back wid barrels en boxes of old second hand clothes en accumulated right smart here. Talk good deal bout how he associated wid de whites. Don' know how-come he run away, but dey didn' catch up wid him till it was too late. De community have man den call pataroller en dey business was to catch dem dat run away. Say like you be authorized to look after my place, you catch dem dat slipped off to another man place. Couldn' leave off plantation to go to another place widout you ask for a pass en have it on you."

Anna Miller, Texas

"Jus' 'bout a month befo' freedom, my sis and nigger Horace runs off. Dey don' go far, and stays in de dugout. Ev'ry night de'd sneak in and git 'lasses and milk and what food dey could. My sis had a baby and she nuss it ev'ry night when she comes. Dey runs off to keep from gettin' a whuppin'. De marster was mad 'cause dey lets a mule cut hisself wid de plow. Sis says de bee stung de mule and he gits unruly and tangle in de plow. Marster says, 'Dey can' go far and will come back when dey gits hongry.'"

Josephine Ryles, Texas

"Plenty of times people run 'way out of de fields. Dey use to work awful hard an' de sun was awful hot, so dey jus' run 'way. De only place dey could go to was de woods an' dey use to hide dere."

Harriet Sanders, Mississippi

"I used to hear my daddy say he was sold to a man who wanted to whip him, and he run away to de woods and stayed dar fo' ah year. Dars whar he was when de niggers was freed. He cum out de woods den. You know dey tell nobody until May."

Janie Satterwhite, Georgia

"My brudder he wusn't happy den and he run away—he run away fer five year."

Where was he all that time, Aunt Janie?

"Lawd knows, honey. Hidin', I reckon, hidin' in de swamp."

Hannah Scott, Texas

"Sometimes one of de darkies runs off and hides out in de woods, but dey ain't gone long, 'cause dey gits hungry and comes back, or de paddy-rollers fotch 'em back. Den dey gets a burning with de bullwhip. Does one run away de second time, Marster Bat say he's got too much 'rabbit' in him, and when he gits caught, 'sides getting a burning, old Marster chains him up 'til he has time to go to Little Rock, den he takes de 'rabbit' darky with him and sells him off."

Will Shelby, Texas

"Some of us neighbors' slaves run 'way and go down in ol' man Smith' fiel' and mek a camp in a under-groun' tunnel. Dey hab cans, skillets, and all sich to cook wid. Me and another fin' dere camp w'ile us was fishin' one day, but co'se, us wouldn' tell on 'em."

Tom Singleton, Georgia

"Yes Ma'am! dar always wuz a little trouble twixt de white folkses an' Niggers; always a little. Heaps of de Niggers went Nawth. I wuz told some white men's livin' in town hyar helped 'em git away. My wife had six of 'er kinfolkses what got clean back to Africa, an' dey wrote back here from dar."

Jordon Smith, Texas

"If you ever run off the place and come back and Master say to you, 'If you be a good Nigger, I'll not whip you this time,' don't you believe that. We had a man run off that stayed on our place and stayed in the woods six months. When he come back he was as hairy as a cow. He lived in a cave and come out at night and pilfer 'round and steal sugar, meat and stuff to eat. They put the dogs on him several times but didn't catch him. Finally he decide to come home. Master say to him, 'Tom, how you been gettin' along.' Tom say, 'I'se been living rich in that cave.' Master say then, 'If you be a good Nigger, I'll not whip you this time.' Tom was crazy nuff to believe it. Master then say to the cook, 'Go fix Tom a big dinner.' While Tom was eating, he look up and Master was standing in the door with a whip, and say, 'Tom, I'se changed my mind; you must learn to mind your Master, you had no business running off, and I'se going to take you out just like you come into the world.' He then gets him a bottle of whiskey and a box of cigars and has Tom tied up out in the yard. He takes a chair and say to the 'Driver,' 'Boy, take him down. 250 licks this time.' Then he'd count the licks as 'Puh-wow' that cowhide would say. Mind you, when the 'Driver' had put on 150 licks it didn't look like there is any place left to hit, but Master say, 'Finish him up.' Then he and the 'Driver' would set down, smoke cigars and drink whiskey and Master would talk to the run-away 'bout how he must learn to mind his Master. Then they took him and locked him up in a log house and Master tell the other Niggers if they give him anything to eat that he will skin them alive. The old fo'ks would slip him bread and meat. He stayed there 'bout a week, and as soon as he was loose, he was gone again. There was plenty of Niggers that stayed in the woods till surrender."

Mary Smith, South Carolina

"Jack Gist, a slave of Gov. Gist, run away once and lived in a cave fer five months befo' de white folks found him. He went down on 'de forest' and dug a cave near de road in sight of de Harris Bridge which still spans de Fairforest Creek at dat p'int. De cave wasn't dug on Governor Gist's land, but on a place know'd den as de old Jackson place. In de mid hours of night Jack come to see his friends and dey give him things to eat. When dey got him he had a hog, two geese, some chickens and two middles of meat. Cose de hog and de middles was stole."

"One night he was crossing de Fairfcrest Creek on a foot-log and he met Anderson Gist, one of de Governor's slaves. Dey talked fer awhile. Next morning, Anderson come wid his marster to de cave whar Jack was. Dey took all his things on to de big house, and he was whupped and put back to work. Governor Gist and our marster was good to deir slaves and dey didn't punish 'em hard like some of 'em did. We had lots more den dan we has had ever since."

Paul Smith, Georgia

"Granddaddy told us 'bout how some slaves used to run off from deir marsters and live in caves and dugouts. He said a man and a 'oman run away and lived for years in one of dem places not no great ways from de slave quarters on his marster's place. Atter a long, long time, some little white chillun was playin' in de woods one day and clumb up in some trees. Lookin' out from high up in a tree one of 'em seed two little pickaninnies but he couldn't find whar dey went. When he went back home and told 'bout it, evvybody went to huntin' 'em, s'posin' dey was lost chillun. Dey traced 'em to a dugout, and dere dey found dem two grown slaves what had done run away years ago, and dey had done had two little chillun born in dat dugout. Deir marster come and got 'em and tuk 'em home, but de chillun went plumb blind when dey tried to live out in de sunlight. Dey had done lived under ground too long, and it warn't long 'fore bofe of dem chillun was daid."

John Sneed, Texas

"Some of de slaves would run away an' go to my ole Marster, but Marster would allus send 'em back home an' he would go talk to de white owners an' tell 'em to be merciful to de niggers."

Leithean Spinks, Texas

"'Twas consid'able trouble wid runawayers. Yous see, 'twarnt far f'om de plantation to de river, an' 'long de river am lots of caves an' cliffs whar de fo'ks could hide. De Marster used de blood hounds to track de runawayers an' mostly, dey am catched. Dem dey don't catch, always comes back after a spell. 'Twas w'en dey gits hongry an' comes a-sneakin' back. 'Twas only once a nigger never comes back, an' 'twas one come back after freedom."

Jake Terriell, Texas

"I'se seen slaves run to the south. Boss, we sure did catch hell too, when we run to the south. They would whip us and then they wouldnt let us have certain food that we like and wouldnt let us stay with our wives."

Nancy Thomas, Texas

"Lots of slaves on other plantations would git a pass, and go to de Colorado River nearby, and start swimmin' to de other side, and nobody would hear f'om 'em agin. A lot of 'em would hide out in de woods and bottom lands fo' awhile, and den go back to dere mawsters. If dey run away f'om dere mawsters, dey didn't have no place to go."

Phil Towns, Georgia

On nearly all plantations there were some slaves who, trying to escape work, hid themselves in the woods. They smuggled food to their hiding place by night, and remained lost in some instances, many months. Their belief in witchcraft caused tham to resort to most ridiculous means of avoiding discovery. Phil told the story of a man who visited a conjurer to obtain a "hand" for which he paid fifty dollars in gold. The symbol was a hickory stick which he used whenever he was being chased, and in this manner warded off his pursuers. The one difficulty in this procedure was having to "set up" the stick at a fork or cross roads. Often the fugitive had to run quite a distance to reach such a spot, but when the stick was so placed human beings and even bloodhounds lost his trail. With this assistance, he was able to remain in the woods as long as he liked.

Mingo White, Alabama

"Lots of times when de patterollers would git after de slaves dey would have de worse fight an' sometimes de patterollers would git killed. After de war I saw Ned, an' he tol' me de night he lef' the patterollers runned him for fo' days. He say de way he did to keep dem frum ketchin' him was he went by de woods. De patterollers come in de woods lookin' for him, so he jes' got a tree on 'em an' den followed. Dey figured dat he was headin' for de free states, so dey headed dat way too, and Ned jes followed dem far as dey could go. Den he clumb a tree and hid whilst dey turned 'roun' an come back. Ned went on wid out any trouble much. De patterollers use ter be bad. Dey would run de folks iffen dey was caught out after eight o'clock in de night, iffen dey didn't have no pass from de marsa."

Olin Williams, Georgia

"Some white folkses had overseers what was awful mean, but Marster's overseer was good to us. We diden' git whippin's an' none of us ever wanned to run away. Sometimes slaves runned away f'um de yudder places an' would hide out in woods an' caves to keep dey overseers f'um ketchin' 'em, cyaze dat meant a whippin'. Us had to have a pass to leave de place on Sunday, so de paddyrollers wouldn't git us."

DISCOURAGING FREEDOM

Slaveholders sought to make their enslaved workers so fearful of the consequences of failed escapes that the workers would not make the attempt. Psychological and physical coercion were employed to this end. Through beatings and assaults by bloodhounds, captured fugitives were displayed as examples to intimidate others. Their injuries or deaths reminded family and friends who might be contemplating similar acts what fate awaited those who failed.

The threat of punishment upon return was not the only way in which slaveholders sought to deter runaways. They also used bloodhounds to track down escapees. These fierce animals were tireless in their pursuit of their victims and vicious in their attacks once they caught them. Anyone who was caught by bloodhounds or observed the dogs' ferocity had to think carefully about the pros and cons of fleeing. Ryer Emmanuel described the frightening hounds used in South Carolina:

> Oh, dem hounds would sho get you. Don' care whe' you was hidin, dem dogs would smell you. If you been climb up a tree, de dog would trail you right to de foot of dat tree en just stand up en howl at you. Dey would stand right dere en hold you up de tree till some of de white folks been get dere en tell you to come down out de tree. Den if you never do like dey say, dey would chop de tree down en let you fall right in de dog's mouth. Would let de dog bite you en taste your blood, so dey could find de one dey was lookin for better de next time.

Along with the dogs, packs of white patrollers were also used to capture and return fugitives. Any enslaved person found traveling alone, especially at night, was considered a runaway unless he or she had a pass from the slaveholder. Slave patrols were authorized to stop any enslaved persons and demand proof that they had permission to travel beyond the confines of their farm. If their answer was not satisfactory, the patrollers had the authority to punish the transgressors and return them to their plantation. Enslaved persons who considered running had to account for the patrollers and problems they posed to a successful escape. In Mississippi, according to Gabe Butler, "All de patrollers wus mean men; dey wud run yo' down wid dogs an' den whup yo'." Although they did not catch everyone, those they caught suffered painful consequences.

Yet, despite the many obstacles to a successful escape, the enslaved continued to flee. It was not unusual for an enslaved worker to escape several times, marking his or her determination to gain freedom despite the possible consequences. Enslavement was not a natural or preferred condition for the enslaved. They tolerated and survived it in the face of the power welded by slaveholder, but they did not embrace a destiny of enslavement. Their ultimate hope was to escape the bonds of slavery and control their lives. As Barney Alford of Mississippi expressed this aspiration, "all uf 'em wanted to be sot free. Dey jes' didnt want to wurk under a whup; dey all wanted to be free to cum an' go when dey wanted."

NARRATIVES

Victoria Adams, South Carolina

"White folks never teach us to read nor write much. They learned us our A, B, C's, and teach us to read some in de testament. De reason they wouldn't teach us to read and white, was 'cause they was afraid de slaves would write their own pass and go over to a free county. One old nigger did learn enough to write his pass and got' way wid it and went up North."

Rev. W. B. Allen, Alabama

"Runaway slaves were hunted with packs of 'Nigger dogs,' bred and trained to trail Negroes. And when rounded up and brought in, the runaway was whipped differently from ordinary offenders. He was swung by his thumbs from some convenient rafter or overhead beam and whipped and let hang, with just his toes touching the floor for hours. Then, while still agonizing from the effects of the beating he had received and the torture of his suspension by his thumbs, he was further tormented by having his wounds 'doctored' with salt and red pepper. Often, strong men would tear their thumbs out at the roots and drop to the floor unconscious. Sir, you can never know what some slaves endured; but they could take it in those days and times."

Samuel Simeon Andrews, Florida

With changed expression he told of an incident during the Civil War: Slaves, he explained had to have passes to go from one plantation to another and if one were found without a pass the "patrollers" would pick him up, return him to his master and receive pay for their service. The "patrollers" were guards for runaway slaves.

Harriet Barnett, Texas

"Yessir, I'se members when some slave run off. Dey was going to the north. Master he catch them and he give them 39 licks a piece with rawhide, then he kept them locked up at night. In the day time he kept chain on them. We didn't go from one plantation to another unless Master he give us pass."

Robert Barr, Arkansas

"According to my old father and mother, the Patteroles went and got the niggers when they did something wrong. They lived during slave time. They had a rule and government over the colored and there you are. When they caught niggers out, they would beat them. If you'd run away, they'd go and get you and beat you and put you back. When they'd get on a nigger and beat him, the colored folks would holler, 'I pray, Massa.' They had to have a great war over it, before they freed the nigger. The Bible says there is a time for all things."

W. L. Bost, North Carolina

"Then the paddyrollers they keep close watch on the pore niggers so they have no chance to do anything or go anywheres. They jes' like policeman, only worser. 'Cause they never let the niggers go anywhere without a pass from his master. If you wasn't in your proper place when the paddyrellers come they lash you till' you was black and blue. The women got 15 lashes and the men 30. That is for jes bein' out without a pass. If the nigger done anything worse he was taken to the jail and put in the whippin' post. They was two holes cut for the arms stretch up in the air and a block to put your feet in, then they whip you with cowhide whip. An' the clothes shores never get any of them licks."

"I remember how they kill one nigger whippin' him with the bull whip. Many the pore nigger nearly killed with the bull whip. But this one die. He was a stubborn Negro and didn't do as much work as his Massa thought he ought to. He been lashed lot before. So they take him to the whippin' post, and then they strip his clothes off and then the man stan' off and cut him with the whip. His back was cut all to pieces. The cuts about half inch apart. Then after they whip him they tie him down and put salt on him. Then after he lie in the sun awhile they whip him agin. But when they finish with him he was dead."

Charley Bowen, Texas

"I ain't got a scar on me put there in slavery time. I allus had my bread and milk twixt meals when I was coming up. My white folks treated us as people and not as beasts. Old Master never was wroth. There was some reporbate folks in the country and we could hear the whips whining on their place long fore day. One owner what lived on an jinning farm kept a bell on one of his Niggers ca'se he was allus running away. It was fixed on a steel band and locked round his head."

Dave Byrd, Texas

"Yes sir, I'se seen few negroes what tried to run away and go to the North, but they never got very far, When some white man would stop and ask for something to eat, he would capture him and fasten him up until his Maser could come after that negro. If Maser had to go get that negro he would whip him nearly all the way back, or everytime he would get tired or holler for his Maser to stop and camp so he could rest, why that Maser would tap him up good with that cat-o-nine tails. Them negroes they were glad when they would get back home."

Louis Cain, Texas

"One nigger run to the woods to be a jungle nigger, but massa cotched him with the dogs and took a hot iron and brands him. Then he puts a bell on him, in a wooden frame what slip over the shoulders and under the arms. He made that nigger wear the bell a year and took it off on Christmas for a present to him. It sho' did make a good nigger out of him."

Jeff Calhoun, Texas

"An I hab a uncle what runned off too, his marster wuz barbarous, he sho wuz mean, Mah uncle runned off, dey took a pack of hounds—a pack is twelve—well dey got on his trail. I herred dem runnin him. Dey run him fer three days and nights. Dey took a gun loaded wid buck shot dey wuz not sposed to shoot above de legs, dey come back and said mah uncle got away, but a few days later some boys wuz out huntin and found him. He had been shot fo times wid dis buck shot."

Richard Carruthers, Texas

"We uster go huntin' lots on off-days. Yes, they allow us to go huntin' and they had lots of game in them days: bear, panther, couger, pole cat, 'coon, and all sorts of game. We have bear dawg, fox dawg and rabbit dawg that mos'ly go by the name of jus' hound dawg. Then they had the dawg to run niggers. When a nigger try to run away, he sure have to up and fly to keep away from them dawgs. Do one of them dawg git on the track of a nigger, he run him for a 1000 miles jus' as long as long as stay on this earth. You could hear them hounds in the woods jus' a-bayin' mos' any night a-chasin' some nigger."

Alice Cole, Texas

"Well son, I'se don't believes I'se ever heard of any slaves running off and trying to go to the north because they were afraid to try as they knew them there patterrollers would get them and all the negroes were afraid of the patterrollers."

William Coleman, Texas

"No sir, I'se never heard of a slave trying to run away to the north cause they were all afraid to go there, and if a negro was caught off his plantation without a pass it was just 39 licks from a cat-o-nine tails given to us by them padder-rollers. I am telling you son all the negroes were afraid of them padderrollers cause they were sure rough on the negroes."

Martha Colquitt, Georgia

"No slave never runned away from Marse Billie's plantation. Dey never even wanted to try. Dey wuz always 'fraid dey might not be able to take as good keer of deyselves as Marse Billie did for 'em, and dey didn't know what would happen to 'em off de plantation."

"I heared 'em talkin' 'bout paterollers, but I never did see one. Folkses said dey would git you and beat you if dey cotch you off de plantation whar you b'longed 'thout no pass. If any of Marse Billie's slaves got cotched by de pater-ollers, I never knowed nothin' 'bout it."

Jane Cotton, Texas

"I'se seen one or two slaves run off to the north, when the war started, and the soldiers they kill every one of them they could. We carry news with pass if we got off the plantation without pass the patter roller would get negro. Yessir, when he get negro, it was too bad."

Sallie Crane, Arkansas

"Have I seen slaves sold! Good God, man! I have seed them sold in droves. I have worn a buck and gag in my mouth for three days for trying to run away. I couldn't eat nor drink—couldn't even catch the slobber that fell from my mouth and run down my chest till the flies settled on it and blowed it. Scuse me but jus' look at these places." [She pulled open her waist and showed scars where the maggots had eaten in—ed.]

Hannah Crasson, North Carolina

"Yes, we seed the paterollers, we called 'em pore white trash, we also called patterollers pore white pecks. They had ropes around their necks. They came

Hannah Crasson. (Library of Congress)

to our house one night when we were singin' and prayin'. It wuz jist before the surrender. Dey were hired by de slave owner. My daddy told us to show 'em de brandy our marster gib us, den dey went on a way, kase dey knowed John Waitor wuz a funny man about his slaves."

Carey Davenport, Texas

"Old man Jim, he run away lots and sometimes they git the dogs after him. He run away one time and it was so cold his legs git frozen and they have to cut his legs off. Sometimes they put chains on runaway slaves and chained 'em to the house. I never knowed of 'em puttin' bells on the slaves on our place, but over next to us they did. They had a piece what go round they shoulders and round they necks with pieces up over they heads and hung up the bell on the piece over they head."

John N. Davenport, South Carolina

"De patrollers was sometimes mean. If dey catch'd a nigger away from home widout a pass dey sho whipped him, but dey never got any of us. Dey come to our house once, but didn't git anybody."

Moses Davis, Georgia

"The fame of the 'Paddle-Rollers' was widespread among the slaves, but none of Colonel Davis' servants attempted to run away or leave the plantation often without the required pass (if they did they were never caught)."

Callie Elder, Georgia

"None of our Niggers ever runned away to de North. Dey was too busy runnin' off to de woods. Jus' to tell de truth dem Niggers on our place was so dumb dey didn't even take in 'bout no North. Dey didn't even know what de war was 'bout 'til it was all over. I don't know whar to start 'bout dem patterollers. Dey was de devil turned a-loose. Dere was a song 'bout 'Run Nigger run, de patteroller git you' and dey sho' would too, I want to tell you."

Ryer Emmanuel, South Carolina

"Yes, mam, white people would let de dog gnaw you up en den dey would grease you en carry you home to de horse lot whe' dey would have a lash en a paddle to whip you wid. Oh, dey would have a swarm of black people up to de lot at sunrise on a mornin to get whip. Would make dem drop dey body frock en would band dem down to a log en would put de licks to dem. Ma was whip twice en she say dat she stay to her place after dat. I hear talk dey give some of dem 50 lashes to a whippin. Dat how it was in slavery time. Poor colored people couldn' never go bout en talk wid dey neighbors no time widout dey Massa say so."

Lewis Evans, South Carolina

"Who-ee! Don't talk to dis nigger 'bout patrollers. They run me many a time. You had to have a pass wid your name on it, who you b'long to, where gwine to, and de date you expected back. If they find your pass was to Mr. James' and they ketch you at Mr. Rabb's, then you got a floggin', sure and plenty."

Sam and Louisa Everett, Florida

"Sam and Norfolk spent part of their childhood on the plantation of 'Big Jim' who was very cruel; often he would whip his slaves into insensibility for minor offences. He sometimes hung them up by their thumbs whenever they were caught attempting to escape—'er fer no reason atall."

Aaron Ford, South Carolina

"Dey had jails in slavery time at Marion for de slaves. If dey caught slaves dat had run away, dey would put dem in jail till dey Massa sent after dem. Sometimes dey would hold dem en sell dem for debt. Dey tell me some put on stand en sold dere at Marion, but I never saw any sold. Just hear bout dat, but I remembers I saw dis. Saw six men tied together wid a chain one Saturday evenin dat was comin from Virginia en gwine to Texas."

Anderson Furr, Georgia

"If slaves did run off to de North, I never heared nothin' 'bout it. Oh, Lord ! I jus' can't talk 'bout dem patterollers, for it looked lak all de white folks tried to jine up wid 'em. How dey did beat up us pore Niggers! Us had to git a pass for dis and a pass for dat, and dere jus' warn't nothin' us could do widout dem patterollers a-beatin' us up. Dey beat you wid a cowhide lash what cut a gash in your back evvy time it struck you. Yessum, white folks and Niggers was all time quar'ellin' and fightin'."

Charlie Grant, South Carolina

"I hear tell bout de slaves would run away en go to Canada. Put nigger dogs after dem, but some of dem would get dere some-how or another. If I was livin on your place, I wouldn' dare to go to another house widout I had a permit from my Massa or de overseer. We slip off en de patroller catch on whip us."

Elijah Green, South Carolina

"W'en slaves run away an' their masters catch them, to the stockade they go w'ere they'd be whipp' every other week for a number of months. An' de [illegible text]er: [illegible text]ade sake don' let a slave be catch with pencil an' paper. That was a major crime. You might as well had kill your master or missus."

James Augustus Holmes, Mississippi

"I wus 22 year old when freedom come. I remembers seeing my grandfather and my great-grandfather. His name wus Henry Holmes. He come from Bedford, Mass. Dats whar old Marsta bought him. He bought 300 slaves at one time and brought them all to Georgie. He kept most of these slaves til' freedom. He sold some and den some run away. When dey run away he puts the 'nigger hounds' on dem. Sometimes dey ketch 'em and bring 'em back; some of dem come back on der own 'cord, and den some nevver did come back. Ef dey didn't promise not to run off any more, an' wuz stubborn about it, he had 'em whupped, or if dey wus onusually rebellious, he put 'em in stocks. He usually sold dat kind first chance, 'ef dey didn't repent of der stubborness."

Hester Hunter, South Carolina

"I hear talk bout how some of de white folks would bout torture dey niggers to death sometimes, but never didn' see my white folks allow nothin like dat. Dey would whip dey niggers dat runaway en stay in de woods, but not so worser. No, mam, my Missus wouldn' allow no slashin round bout whe' she was."

Solomon Jackson, Alabama

"My granma wuz de cook den, an' one day us heard her holler out, 'Dem little devils in here done et up all my cheese an' crackers, an' slung sugar all over my clean flo! Jes' let me git my hands on 'em one mo' time!' An' wid dat she tuck de broom an' run us outen de house an' daseened us ter darken de door. We stayed up under de house tell hit looked lack we seed a runaway nigger, squattin' berhind a post under dere, an' den is when we took out! 'Cause runaway niggers wuz worse'n ha'nts or anything."

"Right across't de road frum usses house, on the very spot where dat ole Methodist church stood so long, wuz where de stake wuz. Dat wuz whar de patterrollers brung de runner-way niggers an' tied'm to de stake an' whupped'm. Yes lawd! Us little niggers shore wuz scairt er dat place! Everybody tole us dat runner-way niggers couldn' git nuthin' ter eat, so dey et little nigger boys, when dey got hungry fer meat."

"Dem patterollers kep' a passel er niggers' dawgs dat didn' do nothin' but hunt down runaway niggers. One dawg wuz de leader, an' he went ahead ter scent de nigger, while de res' wuz coupled together an' when dey closed in on de nigger dey wuz ketchin', the patteroller turnt loose one dawg at a time till they wuz all er runnin' after the nigger. No little niggers better not git in de way neither!"

Andrew Jackson Jarnagin, Mississippi

"During the war the slaves wasn't 'lowed to leave the plantation without a written permit from the marster or mistiss. If we wuz caught off'n de place widout a permit, the patrolman (we called him 'patterole') would take us and whip us with a huge bull whip. Some could outrun the 'patterole,' and if they got back home, they wusn't bothered. Sometimes the 'niggers' would run away to the woods, and then marster would set 'nigger-dogs' on his trail. These dogs wuz trained fur dat purpose."

Hattie Jefferson, Mississippi

"My grandpappy run way frum Marse Hillery and dey put de patterollers dogs after him an' he jes' run an' jumped in de river an' most drown; when dey fotched him out dey had to put him on a barrel an' roll him an' roll him to git de water out uf him. No, he wus not whupped fur dat but he wus tied up ebery night fur a long time, so as to keep him frum runnin' way ergin."

Uncle Gable Locklier, South Carolina

"I ain' never see any slaves punished but I hear tell bout it. Some of dem run away cause dey get tired of workin en if dey catch em, dey sho whip em. Used to have to get ticket from boss or Missus to go any place off de plantation widout you get punish for it. I hear tell bout de overseer en de driver whip plenty of de slaves en some of de time, dey would put em in de screw box over night. Sell em if dey didn' do like dey tell em to do. Speculator come dere to buy slaves en dey sell em to de highest bidder. I hear 'em say a certain one bring $1400 or $1500. I know a man offered my boss $1000 for my brother, Joe, but he wouldn' sell him."

Edward Lycurgas, Florida

Edward often heard his mother tell of the "patter-rollers," a group of white men who caught and administered severe whippings to these unfortunate slaves. Thye also corraled slaves back to their masters if they were caught out after nine o'clock at night without a pass from their masters.

William Mathews, Texas

"Sometimes dey run 'way. It ain't done dem no good, for de dawgs amput on dey trail. If you clumb de tree, dem dogs hold you dere till de white folks comes, and den dey let de dogs git you. Sometimes de dogs tore all dey clothes off, and dey ain't got nary a rag on 'em when dey git home. If dey run in de stream of water, de dogs gits after 'em and drowns 'em. Den Nick, de overseer, he whop 'em. He drive down four stakes for de feets and hands and tie 'em up. Den he whop 'em from head to feets. De whop make out a hide, cut in strips, with holes punch in 'em. When dey hits de akin it make blisters."

Henry Maxwell, Florida

Just a tot when the Civil War gave him and his people freedom, Maxwell's memories of bondage-days are vivid through the experiences related by older Negroes. He relates the story of the plantation owner who trained his dogs to hunt escaped slaves. He had a Negro youth hide in a tree some distance away, and then he turned the pack loose to follow him. One day he released the bloodhounds too soon, and they soon overtook the boy and tore him to pieces. When the youth's mother heard of the atrocity, she burst into tears which were only silenced by the threats of her owner to set the dogs on her. Maxwell also relates tales of the terrible beatings that the slaves received for being caught with a book or for trying to run away.

Watt McKinney, Arkansas

"Mr. Harvey Brown, the overseer, he mean sure 'nough I tell you, and de onliest thing that keep him from beatin' de niggers up all de time would be old mars er Mr. Mark Sillers. Bofe of dem was good and kind most all de time. One time dat I remembers, ole mars, he gone back to Panola County for somepin', en Mr. Mark Sillers, he attendin' de camp meeting. That was de day dat Mr. Harvey Brown come mighty nigh killin' Henry. I'll tell you how dat was, boss. It was on Monday morning that it happened. De Friday before dat Monday morning, all of de hands had been pickin' cotton and Mr. Harvey Brown didn't think dat Henry had picked enough cotton dat day en so he give Henry er lashin' out in de field. Dat night Henry, he git mad and burn up his sack and runned off and hid in de canebrake 'long de bayou all of de nex' day. Mr. Harvey, he missed Henry from de field en sent Jeff an' Randall to find him and bring him in. Dey found Henry real soon en tell him iffen he don't come on back to de field dat Mr. Harvey gwine to set de hounds on him. So Henry, he comed on back den 'cause de niggers was skeered of dem wild bloodhounds what they would set on 'em when dey try to run off."

"When Henry git back Mr. Harvey say, 'Henry, where your sack? And how come you ain't pickin' cotton stid runnin' off like dat?' Henry say he done burnt he sack up. Wid dat Mr. Harvey lit in to him like a bear, lashin' him right and left. Henry broke en run den to de cook house where he mammy, 'Aunt Mary,' was, en Mr. Harvey right after him wid a heavy stick of wood dat he picked up offen de yard. Mr. Harvey got Henry cornered in de house and near 'bout beat dat nigger to death. In fact, Mr. Harvey, he really think too dat he done kilt Henry 'cause he called 'Uncle Nat' en said, 'Nat, go git some boards en make er coffin for dis nigger what I done kilt.'"

"But Henry wasn't daid though he was beat up terrible en they put him in de sick house. For days en days 'Uncle Warner' had to 'tend to him, en wash he wounds, en pick de maggots outen his sores. Dat was jus' de way dat Mr. Harvey Brown treated de niggers every time he git a chanct. He would even lash en beat de wimmens."

Bill McRay, Texas

"Us have good marster, but some of de neighbors treat dere slaves rough. Ole Dr. Neyland of Jasper, he have 75 or 80 slaves and he was rich and hard on de slaves. One day two run away. Tom and Ike, and Dr. Neyland takes de bloodhoun's and ketch dose two niggers and brung 'em in. One of de niggers takes a club and knock one of de houn's in de head and kilt him. Dey cook dat dog and make dem niggers eat part of him. Den dey give both of 'em a beatin'."

Bill McRay. (Library of Congress)

"Sam Swan, he was sheriff and he ketch two runaway niggers one day. Dey was brudders and dey was name Rufe and John Grant. Well, he takes 'em and puts dem in jail and some of de men gits 'em out and takes 'em down to de whippin' pos' and den strap 'em down and give 'em one terrible lashin' and den throw salt in dere wounds and you could hear dem niggers holler for a mile. Den dey took 'em back to de farm to wo'k."

Hannah Murphy, Georgia

"I seen many mens runnin' away fum de bloodhoun's. Sometimes we chilluns be in de quarter playin', and a man would come runnin' along fast, breathin' hard, so skeared! De houn's be behind him. Den I kin 'member how they'd whip 'em when dey ketch him. Dey would make de men drop down dey pants and lay down across big logs and dey'd whip 'um. De womans dey'd drop dey bodies and dey'd whip 'em across de back and 'round de waises till de blood come."

Louis Napoleon, Florida

The various plantations had white men employed as "patrols" whose duties were to see that the slaves remained on their own plantations, and if they were caught going off without a permit from the master, they were whipped with a "raw hide" by the "driver." There was an exception to this rule, however, on Sundays the religious slaves were allowed to visit other plantations where religious services were being held without having to go through the matter of having a permit.

Richard Orford, Georgia

"Our ol' marster wus'nt like some of de other marsters in de community—he never did do much whuppin of his slaves. One time I hit a white man an' ol' marster said he wus goin' to cut my arm off an' dat wus de las' I heard of it. Some of de other slaves uster git whuppins fer not workin' an' fer fightin'. My mother get a whuppin once der fer not workin'. When dey got so bad ol' marster did'nt bother 'bout whuppin' 'em—he jes' put 'em on de block an' n' sold 'em like he would a chicken or somthin', slaves also get whuppins when dey wus caught off the plantation wid out a pass—de Paddie-Rollers whupped you den. I have knowed slaves to run away an hide in de woods—some of 'em even raised families dere."

George Patterson, South Carolina

Going back to slavery times, he said that on most plantations were kept squirrel dogs, 'possum dogs, snake dogs, rabbit dogs and "nigger" dogs. Each dog was trained for a certain kind of tracking. He used to train the "nigger" dogs which were used to track slaves who had run away from the plantation. He said he had two dogs that were sure never to lose the scent when they had taken it up. "If I put them on your track here and you went to Greenville, they would track you right to Greenville."

He said his master did not allow his slaves to be whipped but he had seen slaves on other pantations wearing chains to keep them from running away.

Sam Polite, South Carolina

"If slabe don't do tas', de git licking wid lash on naked back. Driver nigger gib licking, but Maussa 'most always been dere. Sometime maybe nigger steal hawg or run 'way to de wood, den he git licking too. Can't be no trouble 'tween white folks and nigger in slabery time for dey do as dey choose wid you. But Maussa good to slabe if dey done dey's tas' and don't be up to no meanness. Missis don't hab nutting to do wid nigger."

Alec Pope, Georgia

"Some of de Niggers run away to de Nawth—some dey got back, some dey didn't. Dem patterollers had lots of fun if dey cotch a Nigger, so dey could brush 'im to hear 'im holler. De onlies' trouble I ever heard 'bout twixt de whites and blacks wuz when a Nigger sassed a white man and de white man shot 'im. H'it served dat Nigger right, 'cause he oughta knowed better dan to sass a white man. De trouble ended wid dat shot."

Mary Reynolds, Texas

"Seems like after I got bigger I member' more'n more niggers run away. They's most allus cotched. Massa used to hire out his niggers for wage hands. One time he hired me and a nigger boy, Turner, to work for some ornery white trash name of Kidd. One day Turner goes off and don't come back. Old man Kidd say I knowed 'bout it, and he tied my wrists together and stripped me. He hanged me by the wrists from a limb on a tree and spraddled my legs round the drunk and tied my feet together. Then he beat me. He beat me worser than I ever been beat before and I faints dead away. When I come to I'm in bed. I didn't dere so much iffen I died."

Ferebe Rogers, Georgia

"When slaves run away, dey always put de blood-hounds on de tracks. Marster always kep' one hound name' Rock. I can hear 'im now when dey was on de track, callin', 'Hurrah, Rock, hurrah, Rock! Ketch 'im!'"

"Dey always send Rock to fetch 'im down when dey foun' 'im. Dey had de dogs trained to keep dey teef out you till dey tole 'em to bring you down. Den de dogs 'ud go at yo' th'oat, and dey'd tear you to pieces, too. After a slave was caught, he was brung home and put in chains."

Gill Ruffin, Texas

"The woods was full of runaways and I heered them houn's a runnin' 'em like deer many a time, and heered dat whip when they's caught."

"I never knew but one nigger to run away from Marster Hargrave. He slip off and goes to Shreveport. That was Peter Going. Marster missed him and he goes to fin' him. When he fin's him in Shrevaport, he say, 'Come on, Peter, you knowed what you was doin' and you's goin' to pay for it.' Marster tied him behin' de buggy and trots de hosses all way back home. Then he ties Peter to a tree and makes him stay dere all night with nothin' to eat. Peter, nor none of the res' of the niggers didn' ever try to run off after that."

Josephine Ryles, Texas

"Mr. Snow use to keep 'Nigger dogs' to hunt 'em with. Dey was de kind of dogs dat has de big ears. I don' know 'bout 'em. Dey was so bad I never fool 'round 'em. Mr. Snow use to keep 'em chained up 'til one of de field hands run 'way. Den he turn 'em loose to git de scent. Dey kep' on 'til dey found him, an' sometimes dey hurt him. I 'member hearin' dem talk 'bout how dey tore de meat off one of de field hands when dey found him. I was 'fraid of 'em. I never went 'round 'em even when dey was chain."

"Mr. Snow use to whip de fields hands when dey caught 'em from runnin' 'way. I never seen no whippin's an' I don' want to. But mostly dey was 'fraid of de dogs."

Will Sheets, Georgia

"Didn't none of Marse Jeff's Niggers run off to no North, but I heared of a Nigger what did on de place whar my Pa was at. De only thing I knowed what might a made him run to de North was dat Niggers thought if dey got dar dey would be in Heb'en. Dem patte- rollers was somepin' else. I heared folkses say dey would beat de daylights mos' out of you if dey cotched you widout no pass. Us lived on de big road, and I seed 'em passin' mos' anytime. I mos' know dere was plenty trouble twixt de Niggers and de white folkses. Course I never heared tell of none, but I'm sho' dere was trouble jus' de same," he slyly remarked.

Betty Simmons, Texas

"When us come to Gram' Come a nigger boy git stuck on one us house girls and he run away from he massa and feller us. It were a woodly country and

Betty Simmons. (Library of Congress)

de boy outrun he chasers. I heared de dogs after him and he tern and bleedin' with de bresh and he run upstair in de gin house. De dogs not down by de door and de dog-man, what hired to chase him, he drug him down and throw him in de Horse Hole and tells de two dogs to swim in and git him. De boy so scairt he yell and holler but de dogs nip and pinch him good with de claws and teeth. When dey lots de boy out de water hole he all bit up and when he massa larn how mean de dog-man been to de boy he 'fuses to pay de fee."

George Simmons, Texas

"Some of dere slaves would run away and hide in de woods and mos' of 'em was kotched with dogs. Fin'ly dey took to puttin' bells on de slaves so ifren dey run away, dey could hear 'em in de woods. Dey put 'em on with a chain, so dey couldn' get 'em off."

Smith Simmons, Mississippi

"It was very seldom a slave ever ran off. My oldest brother tried that once. He was caught by the patrollers and brought back so quick he never tried that no more."

Burke Simpson, Texas

"During de war dey wuz a man by de name of Jerry Steward, he wuz a w'ite man an' lived 'bout six miles from de Stroud place. He kept blood hounds to track de run-a-way slaves. I kin 'member dey names as well as if hit wuz today, dey wuz named Milo, Jenny Lane, Rock an' Red. I kin hear in my memory how dey would go thro' de country a yelpin' as dey chase de niggers thro' de bottom an' den w'en dey had him up a tree yer could tell by de way dey would bark."

"W'en dey ketch de nigger dey bring him back an' turn him over to de overseer, an' sometimes dey would lock him up or give him a whippin' an' send him to de field. Dey jes had to whip de lazy ones an' de ones dat would not work. De Massa Stroud an' Oliver, all dey had mostly wuz good niggers dat stayed wid dem. Maybe because dey wuz good to de slaves."

Amos Sims, Texas

"De overseer dere use to whip de colored lots, too. Dey wouldn' let me work, I was too little, but I can 'member lots of whippin's. One time my father run 'way an' hid in de woods. Dey hunt him with dogs dey kep' for huntin' colored folks. Me an' my mother could hear 'em hollerin' an' we cried. Oh, I was jus' a li'l boy den."

"It took 'em a long time to find 'em, but when dey got 'im dey tied 'im to a post an' whipped 'im. Yes, Ma'm, I 'member dat. He never run 'way no more."

James Singleton, Mississippi

"I seen 'pattyrollers' ridin' 'bout to keep de darkies frum runnin' 'roun' widout passes. I never seen 'em whup none but dey tol' us we'd git twen'y-nine licks iffen we got caught by 'em. I seen darkies git whuppin's on other plantations— whup 'em half a day sometimes, gen'ly when dey tried to run away."

Jordon Smith, Texas

"If you ever run off the place and come back and Master say to you, 'If you be a good Nigger, I'll not whip you this time,' don't you believe that. We had a man run off that stayed on our place and stayed in the woods six months. When he come back he was as hairy as a cow. He lived in a cave and come out at night and pilfer 'round and steal sugar, meat and stuff to eat. They put the dogs on him several times but didn't catch him. Finally he decide to come home. Master say to him, 'Tom, how you been gettin' along.' Tom say, 'I'se been living rich in that cave.' Master say then, 'If you be a good Nigger, I'll not whip you this time.' Tom was crazy nuff to believe it. Master then say to the cook, 'Go fix Tom a big dinner.' While Tom was eating, he look up and Master was standing in the door with a whip, and say, 'Tom, I'se changed my mind; you must learn to mind your Master, you had no business running off, and

I'se going to take you out just like you come into the world.' He then gets him a bottle of whiskey and a box of cigars and has Tom tied up out in the yard. He takes a chair and say to the 'Driver,' 'Boy, take him down. 250 licks this time.' Then he'd count the licks as 'Puh-wow' that cowhide would say. Mind you, when the 'Driver' had put on 150 licks it didn't look like there is any place left to hit, but Master say, 'Finish him up.' Then he and the 'Driver' would set down, smoke cigars and drink whiskey and Master would talk to the run-away 'bout how he must learn to mind his Master. Then they took him and locked him up in a log house and Master tell the other Niggers if they give him anything to eat that he will skin them alive. The old fo'ks would slip him bread and meat. He stayed there 'bout a week, and as soon as he was loose, he was gone again. There was plenty of Niggers that stayed in the woods till surrender."

Melvin Smith, Georgia

"Did you ever hear how the niggers was sold? They was put on a stage on the courthouse square an' sold kinder like they was stock. The prettiest one got the biggest bid. They said that they was a market in North Ca'lina but I never see'd it. The ones I saw was jest sold like I told you. Then they went home with they marsters. If they tried to run away they sont the hounds after them. Them dogs would sniff around an' first news you knowed they caught them niggers. Marster's niggers run away some but they always come back. They'd hear that they could have a better time up north so they think they try it. But they found out that they wasn't no easy way to live away from Marster."

Mariah Snyder, Texas

"I'se seed lots of Negroes whipped while I was 'driving the gin.' They tied their feet and hands and raw-hided them good. I seed them tie a bell on one woman that was bad about running away. They locked it round her head someway. I'se seed lots of Negroes put on the block and bid off and carried away in chains like cattle. I 'members one woman, Venus, who raised her hands and hollered 'Weigh 'em cattle'; 'Weigh 'em cattle' while she was on the block being bid off."

Leithean Spinks, Texas

"Thar am some whuppin's on de place, but 'twas mostly fo' runnin' off. Ise 'splain how de whuppin's am given by de Marster. Fo' runnin' off, 'twas hard whuppin' de Marster gives. De party am tied to a log, an' de Marster lays de whuppin' on de party's back. Fo' tudder dis'bedience, dey jus' stand thar an' lash few times wid de cullud fellow standin' up."

"Ise see de whuppin's. 'Twarnt given in private but am public so allus niggers could see it, an' dat makes de 'pression on our minds. 'Twas a cullud fellow gits catched w'en he run off. W'en dey ties him down to de log, dey gives him 20 lashes. W'en dey let him up, he starts runnin' 'way 'gain. De overseer pulls his pistol, an' lets him have it. Down goes de nigger. W'en dey gits to him, blood am runnin' in a stream. Dey looks him over, an' 'twas de bottom of his right ear shot off. Dat nigger never tries to run off 'gain."

Mary Thompson, Texas

"Heap of de slaves would run away and go up Nawth. De Marsters would try to find 'em by sendin' 'nigger houns' aftah 'em. Once de houns caught a slave and he kep' sayin', 'Oh, Lawd ... oh, Lawd!'"

Mary Thompson. (Library of Congress)

Stephen Varner, Alabama

The only thing that Stephen can remember about the patroller was a little chant that his mother use to frighten the children: "run nigger run, run nigger run, the 'pat-er-rollers' will get you if you don't look out."

George Ward, Mississippi

"Jesse Harris had sixteen hounds; he used these to catch Negroes when they ran away from their 'marster,' and for every Negro he caught he was paid ten dollars."

"The owners had about fifteen 'patterrolls' [patrols], for to catch the Negroes when they went off on Sundays without a pass. When this happened, the Negroes got thirty lashes."

William Ward, Georgia

"Few slaves ever attempted to escape from Mr. Brown, partially because of his kindliness and particlly because of the fear inspired by the pack of blood hounds which he kept. When an escaped slave was caught he was returned to his master and a sound beating was administered."

Anderson Williams, Mississippi

"When slaves run away, dey would catch 'em wid dogs an' den beat 'em nearly to death wid de 'Bull Whup.' I 'member once when I tol' 'bout seein' a nigger runnin' away, boss got his hymn book, set down, put me 'cross his knees an' as he'd sing de hymns, he'd whup me to de tune o' 'em. Believe me when he got through I didn' set down for a week an' I ain't never seed no more niggers runnin' away neither!"

Callie Williams, Alabama

Relative to runaway slaves, Callie said that some got away entirely, but if caught by the "patrollers" they were whipped and returned to their masters who would then put shackles on the slaves loose enough so they could work but the shackels prevented their running away again.

Horatio W. Williams, Texas

"Dem w'at run 'way, dey git bloodhoun's 'n' hunt 'em wid. W'en dey hear d' houn's comin' dey clum' a tree but dey couldn' stay dere long cause dey marsters mek 'em git down 'r' dey shoot dem. 'N' w'en dey did git down d' dawgs all jump on dem 'n' tear dem t' pieces if'n d' marster warn't dere t' beat dem off. I nebber done nuthin' t' git d' houn's after me but lots 'r' niggers did."

Henry Wright, Georgia

For the most part punishment consisted of severe whipping sometimes administered by the slaves' master and sometimes by the white men of the community known as the Patrol. To the slaves this Patrol was known as the "Paddle" or "Paddle-Rollers." Mr. Wright says that he has been whipped numerous times by his master for running away. When he was caught after an attempted escape he was placed on the ground where he was "spread-eagled," that is, his arms and feet were stretched out and tied to stakes driven in the ground. After a severe beating, brine water or turpentine was poured over the wounds. This kept the flies away, he says. Mr. House did not like to whip his slaves as a scarred slave brought very little money when placed on the auction block. A slave who had a scarred back was considered as being unruly. Whenever a slave attempted to escape the hounds were put on his trail. Mr. Wright was caught and treed by hounds several times. He later found a way to elude then. This was done by rubbing his feet in the refuse material of the barnyard or the pasture, then he covered his legs with pine tar. On one occasion he managed to stay away from the plantation for 6 months before he returned of his own accord. He ran away after striking his master who had attempted to whip him. When he returned of his own accord his master did nothing to him because he was glad that he was not forever lost in which case a large sum of money would have been lost. Mr. Wright says that slave owners advertised in the newspapers for lost slaves, giving their description, etc. If a slave was found after his master had stopped his advertisements he was placed on the block and sold as a "stray." While a fugitive he slept in the woods, eating wild berries, etc. Sometimes he slipped to the plantation of his mother or that of his father where he was able to secure food.

He took a deep puff on his pipe and a look of satisfaction crossed his face as he told how he had escaped from the "Paddle Rollers." It was the "Paddle-Rollers" duty to patrol the roads and the streets and to see that no slave was out unless he had a "pass" from his master. Further, he was not supposed to be any great distance away from the place he had been permitted to go. If a slave was caught visiting without a "pass" or if at any time he was off his plantation without said "pass" and had the misfortune to be caught by the "Paddle-Rollers" he was given a sound whipping and returned to his master.

George Young, Alabama

"I seed slaves plenty times wid iron ban's 'roun' dey ankles an' a hole in de ban' an' a iron rod fasten to hit what went up de outside of dey leg to de wais' an' fasten to another iron ban' 'roun' de waist. Dis yere was to keep 'em from bendin' dey legs an' runnin' away. Dey call hit puttin' de stiff knee on you, an' hit sho' made 'em stiff! Sometimes hit made 'em sick, too, caze dey had dem iron ban's so tight 'roun' de ankles, dat when dey tuck 'em off live things was under 'em, an' dat's whut give 'em fever, dey say. Us had to go out in de wood an' git May-apple root an' mullen weed an' all sich, to bile for to cyore de fever. Miss whar was de Lord in dem days? Whut was he doin'?"

"But some of 'em runned away, anyhow. My brother, Harrison, was one, an' dey sot de 'nigger dogs' on him lack fox houn's run a fox today. Dey didn't run him down till 'bout night but finely dey cotched him, an' de hunters feched him to de do' an' say: 'Mary Ann, here Harrison.' Den dey turned de dogs loose on him ag'in, an' sich a screamin' you never hyared. He was all bloody an' Mammy was a-hollerin', 'save him, Lord, save my chile, an' don' let dem

George Young. (Library of Congress)

dogs eat him up!' Mr. Lawler said, 'De Lord ain't got nothin' do wid dis here, an' hit sho' look lack He didn't', caze dem dogs nigh 'bout chewed Harrison up. Dem was hard times, sho'."

THE IMPACT OF THE CIVIL WAR

The beginning of the Civil War dramatically altered the likelihood of success for runaways. Rolling Union troop lines meant freedom might be only miles from the point of departure of a fugitive. By the first year of the war Union policy, in an effort to undermine the Confederate war endeavors, stated that fugitives reaching their lines were not to be returned. As word of this decision spread among the enslaved more were emboldened to leave. Even the murder of intercepted fugitives by southern soldiers was not enough to stop them.

Consequently, as the Civil War unfolded and Union troops came into proximity to southern plantations, more and more enslaved workers considered fleeing. If they could reach the Union lines they would be free, but this was not always easy to accomplish. It was not unusual for Confederate soldiers and slaveholders to shoot runaways caught trying to escape. They needed enslaved workers to take care of their farms while they were fighting and made examples of captured fugitives to discourage others from escaping. In many instances their actions had the hoped-for effect, as it discouraged some individuals from leaving because they, like Dave Byrd of Texas, feared it was futile. "After the war started between the States all that tried to run over to the North the white soldiers would shoot them like

The start of the Civil War made freedom available to formerly enslaved workers like these who escaped to Union army camps. (Library of Congress)

shooting rattle snakes. There was never a negro got away by trying to go over to the North."

But the lure of freedom was too tempting for others who decided the reward was worth the risk. When they had the opportunity they took off. Reaching Union lines was a much more realistic goal than previous escape strategies that involved traveling to a northern state hundreds of miles away. Northern army encampments might be only a day or two's travel away. And as with Mack Henderson of Mississippi a new life quickly followed.

Mack allways liked music. So when he ran away and got with the "Yankees" he was taught to blow the bugle this he played thruout the time he spent with the Union Army. He never carried a gun. Today Mack still looks like a man around seventy five altho he is much older (does not know his age) but for years he has played his horn and taken an active part in the May 30th Memorial Services at the National Cemetary Celebration. The reason I ran away to the Yankees says Mack is because I wanted to be free.

By the later stages of the war, thousands of the enslaved self-liberated. Some found work near the Union camps, and some enlisted in the northern army, an action that helped to guarantee their freedom and the freedom of the nearly four million in bondage. In the end, to be free is what most enslaved people wanted, but especially those who ran away. They fled because they wanted the opportunity to make their own decisions and have greater control over their lives and their relationship with family members. Under slavery those decisions were in the hands of their slaveholders, which left the enslaved vulnerable to their whims and disposition. Punishment came arbitrarily, families were broken apart, and the enslaved were treated as property not people. Escape held the possibility of a better life as a free person, and for those who chose to run, the chance for a better life, if even for a short period, was preferable to accepting things as they were. Charity Moore of South Carolina captured the sentiment best when she talked about life under slavery: "What do I t'ink ob slavery? I t'ink slavery is jest a murdering of de people. I t'ink Freedom been a great gift. I lak my Maussa and I guess he was as good to his slave as he could be, but I ruther [rather] bee free."

NARRATIVES

Barney Alford, Mississippi

"Dey sed de big war wus cumin' an' sed de south culdnt be beat, an' men wud cum to de big house an' stan' round under de trees an' prop deir foot up on de roots uf de trees an' dey wud stan' dar an' talk bout how quick de war wud be ober."

"Sum uf de slaves wud git to gedder at night time, an' go down by de crick an' pray for to be sot free. Sumtimes udder slaves frum udder plantations wud cum an' jine in de prayin'. I never went down dar, fur I wus 'sleep at dat time."

"One day Marse Edwin rode way on one uf his fine hosses, an' Mistiss, she cried an' cried an' sed he wus gone an' maybe git kilt. Sum uf de slaves wanted ole man Abe to whip de south an' sum uf dem wus for de south beatin', but all uf 'em wanted to be sot free. Dey jes' didnt want to wurk under a whup; dey all wanted to be free to cum an' go when dey wanted."

Mary Barbour, North Carolina

"We had our little log cabin off ter one side, an' my mammy had sixteen chilluns. Fas' as dey got three years old de marster sol' 'em till we las' four dat she had wid her durin' de war. I wuz de oldes' o' dese four; den dar wuz Henry an' den de twins, Liza an' Charlie."

"One of de fust things dat I 'members wuz my pappy wakin' me up in de middle o' de night, dressin' me in de dark, all de time tellin' me ter keep quiet. One o' de twins hollered some an' pappy put his hand ober its mouth ter keep it quiet."

"Atter we wuz dressed he went outside an' peeped roun' fer a minute den he comed back an' got us. We snook out o' de house an' long de woods path, pappy totin' one of de twins an' holdin' me by de han' an' mammy carryin' de udder two."

"I reckons dat I will always 'member dat walk, wid de bushes slappin' my laigs, de win' sighin' in de trees, an' de hoot owls an' whippoorwhills hollerin' at each other from de big trees. I wuz half asleep an' skeered stiff, but in a little while we pass de plum' thicket an' dar am de mules an' wagin."

"Dar am er quilt in de bottom o' de wagin, an' on dis dey lays we youngins. An' pappy an' mammy gits on de board cross de front an' drives off down de road."

"I wuz sleepy but I wuz skeered too, so as we rides 'long I lis'ens ter pappy an' mammy talk. Pappy wuz tellin' marry 'bout de Yankees comin' ter dere plantation, burnin' de co'n cribs, de smokehouses an' 'stroyin' eber'thing. He says right low dat dey done took marster Jordan ter de Rip Raps down nigh Norfolk, an' dat he stol' de mules an' wagin an' 'scaped."

"We wuz skeerd of de Yankees ter start wid, but de more we thinks 'bout us runnin' way from our marsters de skeerder we gits o' de Rebs. Anyhow pappy says dat we is goin' ter jine de Yankees."

"We trabels all night an' hid in de woods all day fer a long time, but atter awhile we gits ter Doctor Dillard's place, in Chowan County. I reckons dat we stays dar seberal days."

"De Yankees has tooked dis place so we stops ober, an' has a heap o' fun dancin' an' sich while we am dar. De Yankees tells pappy ter head fer New Bern an' dat he will be took keer of dar, so ter New Bern we goes."

"When we gits ter New Bern de Yankees takes de mules un' wagin, dey tells pappy something, an' he puts us on a long white boat named Ocean Waves an' ter Roanoke we goes."

"Later I larns dat most o' de reffes [refugees] is put in James City, nigh New Bern, but dar am a pretty good crowd on Roanoke. Dar wuz also a ole Indian Witch 'oman dat I 'members."

"Atter a few days dar de Ocean Waves comes back an' akes all ober ter New Bern. My pappy wuz a shoemaker, so e makes Yankee boots, an' we gits 'long pretty good."

John Bates, Texas

"When de war comes on and sometimes before de war de slaves would try ter run away ter de north, some never would be heard of again, sometimes dey would be caught and be whipped to death and maybe other things would happen. Dey always knew dey had sumpin comin iffen dey was caught. Well durin dem times jest like today nearly every body knew what was goin on, news traveled purty fast, iffen de slaves couldnt gits it ter each other by gitten a pass, dey would slip out after dark and go in ter another plantation from de back way ter gits it scattered and sometimes dey was caught and would gits a good whippen fer it."

Boston Blackwell, Arkansas

"Do you want to hear how I runned away and jined the Yankees? You know Abraham Lincoln 'claired freedom in '63, first day of January. In October '63, I runned away and went to Pine Bluff to get to the Yankees. I was on the Blackwell plantation south of Pine Bluff in '63. They was building a new house; I wanted to feel some putty in my hand. One early morning I clim a ladder to get a little chunk and the overseer man, he seed me. Here he come, yelling me to get down; he gwine whip me 'cause I'se a thief, he say. He call a slave boy and tell him cut ten willer whips; he gwine wear every one out on me. When he's gone to eat breakfas', I runs to my cabin and tells my sister, 'I'se leaving this here place for good.' She cry and say, 'Overseer man, he kill you.' I says, 'He kill me anyhow.' The young boy what cut the whips—he named Jerry—he come along wif me, and we wade the stream for long piece. Heerd the hounds a-howling, getting ready for to chase after us. Then we hide in dark woods. It was cold, frosty weather. Two days and two nights we traveled. That boy, he so cold and hongry, he want to fall out by the way, but I drug him on. When we gets to the Yankee camp all our troubles was over. We gets all the contraband we could eat. Was they more run-aways there? Oh, Lordy, yessum. Hundreds, I reckon. Yessum, the Yankees feeds all them refugees on contraband. They made me a driver of a team in the quatemasters department. I was always keerful to do everything they telled me. They telled me I was free when I gets to the Yankee camp, but I couldn't go outside much. Yessum, iffen you could get to the Yankee's camp you was free right now."

Gus Bradshaw, Texas

"The first work I done was picking cotton. Every fellow was in the fiel' at day light picking cotton, hoeing, or plowing. There was one overseer and two 'Nigger-Drivers.' The overseer whipped them in the fiel' for not doing like he say. I had a Uncle Joe to run off just when the war got gwying [going] good; he never did come back."

Jacob Branch, Texas

"Atter de war start lots of de slaves runned off to try to git to de Yankees. All de slaves in dis part de country when dey runned off dey headed for de Rio Grande Riber. Iffen dey could reach de riber and swim ha'f way 'cross dey was free. De Mexicans rig up flatboats out in de middle of de riber tied to stakes wid rope. When de cullud peoples git to de rope dey kin pull deyse'fs 'cross de res' of de way on de boats. De w'ite folks ride de 'Merican side of de riber all de time but lots of de slaves git through anyway. Some de niggers runned and hide out in de woods. Atter freedom dey have lots of trouble wid de wil' niggers what been hidin' in de woods and ain' knowed dey was free yit."

Easter Brown, Georgia

"Some of de Niggers runned away. Webster, Nagar, Atney, an' Jane runned away a little while 'fore freedom. Old Marster didn't try to git 'em back, 'cause 'bout dat time de war wuz over."

Lyttleton Dandridge, Arkansas

"We had two or three men run off and joined the Yankees. One got drowned fore he got there and the other two come back after freedom."

James Davis, Arkansas

"When I was twenty-one I was sold to the speculator and sent to Texas. They started me at a thousand and run me up to a thousand nine hunnerd and fifty and knocked me off. He paid for me in old Jeff Davis' shin plasters."

"I runned away and I was in Mississippi makin' my way back home to North Carolina. I was hidin' in a hollow log when twenty-five of Sherman's Rough Riders come along. When they got close to me the horses jumped sudden and they said, 'Come out of there, we know you're in there!' And when I come out, all twenty-five of them guns was pointin' at that hole. They said they thought I was a Rebel and 'serted the army. That was on New Years day of the year the war ended. The Yankees said, 'We's freed you all this mornin', do you want to go with us?' I said, 'If you goin' North, I'll go.' So I stayed with em till I got back to North Carolina."

Sebert Douglas, Arkansas

"I 'member Billy Chandler and Lewis Rodman run off and j'ined the Yankee a but they come back after the War was over."

Willis Dukes, Florida

Willis remembers the time when a slave on the plamtation escaped and went north to live. This man managed to communicate with his family somehow, and it was whispered about that he was "living very high" and actually saving money with which to buy his family. He was even going to school. This fired all the slaves with an ambition to go north and this made them more than usually interested in the outcome of the war between the states. He was too young to fully understand the meaning of freedom but wanted very much to go away to some place where he could earn enough money to buy his moter a real silk dress. He confided this information to her and she was very proud of him but gave him a good spanking for fear he expressed this desire for freedom to his young master or mistress.

John Finnely, Texas

"I becomes a runaway nigger short time after dat fight. De war am started den for 'bout a year, or somethin' like dat, and de Fed'rals am north of us. I hears de niggers talk 'bout it, and 'bout runnin' 'way to freedom. I thinks and thinks 'bout gittin' freedom, and I's gwine run off. Den I thinks of de patter rollers and what happen if dey cotches me off de place without de pass. Den I thinks of some joyment sich as de corn huskin' and de fights and de singin' and I don't know what to do. I tells you one singin' but I can't sing it:

De moonlight, a shinin' star,
De big owl hootin' in de tree;
O, bye, my baby, ain't you gwineter sleep,
A-rockin' on my knee?

Bye, my honey baby,
A-rockin' on my knee,
Baby done gone to sleep,
Owl hush hootin' in de tree.

She gone to sleep, honey baby sleep,
A-rockin' on my, a-rockin' on my knee.

"Now, back to de freedom. One night 'bout ten niggers run away. De next day we'uns hears nothin', so I says to myself, 'De patters don't cotch dem.' Den I makes up my mind to go and I leaves with de chunk of meat and cornbread and am on my way, half skeert to death. I sho' has de eyes open and de ears forward, watchin' for de patters. I steps off de road in de night, at sight of anything, and in de day I takes to de woods. It takes me two days to make dat trip and jus' once de-patters pass me by. I am in de thicket watchin' dem and I's sho' dey gwine search dat thicket, 'cause dey stops and am a-talkin' and lookin' my way. Dey stands dere for a li'l bit and den one comes my way. Lowd A-mighty! Dat sho' look like de end, but dat man stop and den look and look. Den he pick up somethin' and goes back. It am a bottle and dey all takes de drink and rides on. I's sho' in de sweat and I don't tarry dere long."

"De Yanks am camped nere Bellfound and dere's where I gits to. 'Magine my 'sprise when I finds all de ten runaway niggers am dere, too. Dat am on a Sunday and on de Monday, de Yanks puts us on de freight train and we goes to Stevenson, in Alabama. Dere, us put to work buildin' breastworks. But after de few days, I gits sent to de headquarters at Nashville, in Tennessee."

"I's water toter dere for de army and dere am no fightin' at first but 'fore long dey starts de battle. Dat battle am a 'sperience for me. De noise am awful, jus' one steady roar of de guns and de cannons. De window glass in Nashville am all shoke out from de shakement of de cannons. Dere am dead mens all over de ground and lots of wounded and some cussin' and some prayin'. Some am moanin' and dis and dat one cry for de water and, God A-mighty, I don't want any sich 'gain. Dere am men carryin' de dead off de field, but dey can't keep up with de cannons. I helps bury de deed and den I gits sent to Murphyrsboro and dere it am jus' de same."

Henry Gibbs, Mississippi

"Yes I knowed of slaves to run away to the north—er somewhures. Sometimes dey would go whur de come from. Dey followed de yankees away from West Point when dey was here. I seed one after de surrender."

Cora Gillam, Arkansas

"I never knew of any that run away and never come back. I have heard people say that some ran away and went to the free states. But I never knew of their doing that until the war started. Some of my people on the Johnson place were the first Negroes to settle in Minneapolis. They were the Youngs—Jack Young and Lovey, my Uncle Tom's brother and my mother's sister. Bill Gales was the first Negro to go up to Cincinnati after the war. Gales took his regular father's name while Johnson took his master's name."

Pierce Harper, Texas

"I seed a lot of Southern soldiers and they'd go to the big house for something to eat. Late in '63 they had a fight at a place called Kingston, only 12 miles from our place, takin' how the jacks go. We could hear the guns go off when they was fightin'. The Yankees beat and settled down there and the cullud folks flocked down on them and when they got to the Yankee lines they was safe. They went in droves of 25 or 50 to the Yankees and they put 'em to work fightin' for freedom. They fit till the war was over and a lot of 'em got kilt. My mother and sister run away to the Yankees and they paid 'em big money to wash for 'em."

Virginia Harris, North Carolina

"None of the slaves ran off to the North till after the Yankees came. They carried my father away one night when we was all asleep. None of us knowed nothing about it 'till the next day. After that my sister ran off to the Refugee Camp. She couldn't be got back out of there."

Mack Henderson, Mississippi

Mack Henderson was born in Copiah County and came to Vicksburg to live just before the Civil War "broke out." He was a slave and came here with his "marster" who came here to go in business.

"The reason I ran away to the Yankees," says Mack, "is because I wanted to be free, I wont talk of slavery it is too long past."

"When the war was over we colored men were all called together and told 'not to ever talk of the past,' we were told this by our Union officers they said 'this is a new day forget the past you are free men, but you are black men and you have still a hard way to go.' Since the war I settled in Vicksburg worked hard for my living and now that I get my Soldiers pension I still work my garden and flowers, and I expect to go to the Parade on the 30th, I am not going to ride either unless they make me, why ride? I walk everywhere else over town."

Bryant Huff, Georgia

The attitude of the slaves toward freedom varied and as they were not allowed to discuss it, their hope was veiled in such expressions as the "Lord will provide." Some were even afraid to settle any statement and silently prayed that their release would come soon. Some feared that something might prevent their emancipation so they ran away and joined the Yankee Army, hoping to be able to destroy their former master.

Alex Huggins, North Carolina

"I was born in New Bern on July 9, 1850. My father and mother belonged to Mr. L. B. Huggins. My father was a carpenter and ship builder an' the first things I remember was down on Myrtle Grove Sound, where Mr. Huggins had a place. I was a sort of bad boy an' liked to roam 'round. When I was about twelve years old I ran away. It was in 1863 when the war was goin' on."

"Nobody was bein' mean to me. No, I was'nt bein' whipped. Don't you know all that story 'bout slaves bein' whipped is all Bunk [with scornful emphasis]. What pusson with any sense is goin' to take his horse or his cow an' beat it up. Its prope'ty. We was prope'ty. Val'able prope'ty. No, indeed, Mr. Luke give the bes' of attention to his colored people, an' Mis' Huggins was like a mother to my mother. Twa'nt anythin' wrong about home that made me run away. I'd heard so much talk 'bout freedom I reckon I jus' wanted to try it, an' I thought I had to get away from home to have it."

"Well, I coaxed two other boys to go with me, an' a grown man he got the boat an' we slipped off to the beach an put out to sea. Yes'm, we sho' was after adventure. But, we did'n get very far out from she', an' I saw the lan' get dimmer an' dimmer, when I got skeered, an' then I got seasick an' we was havin' more kinds of adventure than we wanted, an' then we saw some ships. There was two of 'em, an' they took us on board."

Squire Irvin, Mississippi

"Plenty of the slaves ran off to the North. They didn't get them back cause when they got out of reach the Yankee soldiers was near enough to protect them. Course they had Patrollers to go after them with the dogs, but that didn't do no good against them Yankee soldiers. Them soldiers is been known to come right on the white folks places and take all the slaves that wanted to go with them."

Martin Jackson, Texas

"Even with my good treatment, I spent most of my time plaming and thinking of running away. I could nave done it easy, but my old father used to say, 'No use running from bad to worse, hunting better.' Lots of colored boys did escape and jeined the Union army, and there are plenty of them drawing a pension today. My father was always counseling me. He said, 'Every man has to serve God under his own vine and fig tree.' He kept pointing out that the War wasn't going to last forever, but that our forever was going to be spent living among the Southeners, after they got licked. He'd cite examples of how the whites would stand flatfooted and fight for the blacks the same as for members of their own family. I know that all was true, but still I rebelled, from inside of me. I think I really was afraid to run away, because I thought my conscience would haunt me. My father knew I felt this way and he'd rub my fears in deeper. One of his remarks still rings in my ears: 'A clear conscience opens bowels, and when you have a guilty soul it ties you up and death will not for long desert you.'"

Rev. Squires Jackson, Florida

He remembers the start of the Civil war with the laying of the Atlantic Cable by the "Great Eastern" being nineteen years of age at the time. Hearing threats of the War which was about to begin, he ran away with his brother to Lake City, many times hiding in trees and groves from the posse that was looking for him. At night he would cover up his face and body with spanish moss to sleep. One night he hid in a tree near a crook, over-slept himself, in the morning a group of white women fishing near the creek saw him and ran to tell the men, fortunately however he escaped."

After four days of wearied travelling being guided by the north star and the Indian instinct inherited from his Indian grandmother, he finally reached Lake City. Later reporting to General Scott, he was informed that he was to act as orderly until further ordered. On Saturday morning, February 20, 1861, General Scott called him to his tent and said "Squire; "I have just had you appraised for $1000 and you are to report to Col. Guist in Alachua County for service immediately." That very night he ran away to Wellborn where the Federals were camping. There in a horse stable were wounded colored soldiers stretched out on the filthy ground. The sight of these wounded men and the feeble medical attention given then by the Federals was so repulsive to him, that he decided that he didn't want to join the Federal Army. In the silent hours of the evening he stole away to Tallahassee, throughly convinced that War wasn't the place for him. While in the horse shed make-shift hospital, a white soldier asked one of the wounded colored soldiers to what regiment he belonged, the negro replied "54th Regiment, Massachusetts."

At that time, the only railroad was between Lake City and Tallahassee which he had worked on for awhile. At the close of the war he returned to Jacksonville to begin work as a bricklayer. During this period, Negro skilled help was very much in demand.

Gabe Lance, South Carolina

"Some my people run away from Sandy Islant. Go Oaks sea-shore and Magnolia Beach and take row-boat and gone out and join with the Yankee. Dem crowd never didn't come back."

"Any slave run way or didn't done task, put 'em in barn and least out they give 'em (with lash) been twenty-five to fifty. Simply cause them weak and couldn't done task—couldn't done task! 'Give 'em less rations to boot."

July Miles, Nebraska

He and five others "ran away." They fled in a boat and had rowed about 20 miles pursued by rebels, when they came upon some Union soldiers who took them into Camp, where they enlisted as Union soldiers. Miles fought as a Blue soldier for two and one-half years until the end of the war at the Battle of Mobile Bay. He was, however, never wounded, but he says he was so badly frightened in his first battle, that he remembers nothing of what happened. After that, he had no fear. As the war continued and the South became more and more depleted, rails were sawed into pieces like stove wood and shot from cannon like grape shot.

Louis Napoleon, Florida

He proudly tells you that his master was good to his "niggers" and cannot recall but one time that he saw him whip one of them and that when one tried to run away to the Yankees. Only memories of a kind master in his days of servitude remain with him as he recalls the dark days of slavery.

John Ogee, Texas

"I haven't got 'lection like I used to, but I 'members when I's in the army. Long 'bout '63 I go to the army and there was four of us who run away from home, me and my father and 'nother man named Emanuel Young and 'nother man, but I disremember his name now. The Yankees comed 'bout a mile from us and they took every ear of corn, kilt every head of stock and thirteen hawgs and 'bout fifteen beeves, and feed their teams and themselves. They pay the old lady in Confed'rate money, but it weren't long 'fore that was no money at

John Ogee. (Library of Congress)

all. When we think of all that good food the Yankees done got, we jus' up and jine up with them. We figger we git lots to eat and the res' we jus' didn't figger. When they lef' we lef'. My father got kilt from an ambush, in Miss'ippi—I think it was Jackson."

Aaron Russel, Texas

"Massa have special place in woods where he have meanes' niggers whip. He never whip much, but wartime comin' on. Some de growed ones runs away to dem Yankees. He have to whip some den. He have stocks to put dey neck in when he whip dem. Massa never chain he slaves. I seed talkin' parrots. Massa didn't have one, but other massas did. Dat parrot talk. He tell when de nigger run away or when he not work."

Charlie Sandles, Texas

"I'se heard that some negroes tried to get away and go to the north when the war started, but I'se always heard that they were killed. I don't think they ever got very far trying that. We had to have a pass before we could go from one plantation to another or the Patter Rollers would get you. The negroes were all scared of them cause they could hit him 39 licks with that cat-o-nine tails

Aaron Russel. (Library of Congress)

and believe me son, they would take the hair and hide both everytime they hit you."

William Sherman, Florida

Civil War: It was rumored that Abraham Lincoln said to Jefferson Davis, "work the slaves until they are about twenty-five or thirty years of age, then liberate them." Davis replied: "I'll never do it, before I will, I'll wade knee deep in blood." The result was that in 1861, the Civil War, that struggle which was to mark the final emancipation of the slaves began. Jefferson Davis' brothers, Sam and Tom, joined the Confederate forces, together with their sons who were old enough to go, except James, Tom's son, who could not go on account of ill health and was left behind as overseer on Jack Davis' plantation. Jack Davis joined the artillery regiment of Captain Razors Company. The war progressed, Sherman was on his famous march. The "Yankees" had made such sweeping advances until they were in Robertsville, South Carolina, about five miles from Black Swamp. The report of gun fire and cannon could be heard from the plantation. "Truly the Yanks are here" everybody thought. The only happy folk were the slaves, the whites were in distress. Jack Davis returned from the field of battle to his plantation. He was on a short furlough. His wife, "Missus" Davis asked him excitedly, if he thought the "Yankees" were going to win. He replied: "No if I did I'd kill every damned nigger on the place." Will who was then a lad of nineteen was standing nearby and on hearing his master's remarks, said: "The Yankees aint gonna kill me cause um goin to Laurel Bay" (a swamp located on the plantation.) Will says that what he really meant was that his master was not going to kill him because he intended to run off and go to the "Yankees." That afternoon Jack Davis returned to the "front" and that night Will told his mother, Anna Georgia, that he was going to Robertsville and join the "Yankees." He and his cousin who lived on the Davis' plantation slipped off and wended their way to all of the surrounding plantations spreading the news that the "Yankees" were in Robertaville and exhorting them to follow and join them. Soon the two had a following of about five hundred slaves who abandoned their masters' plantations "to meet the Yankees." En masse they marched breaking down fences that obstructed their passage, carefully avoiding "Confederate pickets" who were stationed throughout the countryside. After marching about five miles they reached a bridge that spanned the Savannah River, a point that the "Yankees" held. There was a Union soldier standing guard and before he realized it, this group of five hundred slaves were upon him. Becoming cognizant that someone was upon him, he wheeled around in the darkness, with gun leveled at the approaching slaves and cried "Halt." Will's cousin then spoke up, "Doan shoot boss we's jes friends." After recognizing who they were, they were admitted into the camp that was established around the bridge. There were about seven thousand of General Sherman's soldiers camped there, having crossed the Savannah River on a pontoon bridge that they had constructed while enroute from Green Springs Georgia, which they had taken. The guard who had let these people approach so near to him without realizing their approach was court martialed that night for being dilatory in his duties. The Federal officers told the slaves that they could go along with them or go to Savannah, a place that they had already captured. Will decided that it was best for him to go to Savannah. He left, but the majority of the slaves remained with the troops. They were enroute to Barawell, South Carolina, to seize Blis Creek Fort that was held by the Confederates. As the Federal troops marched ahead, they were followed by the volunteer slaves. Most of these unfortunate slaves were slain by "bush whackers" (Confederate snipers who fired upon them from ambush). After being killed they were decapitated and their heads placed upon posts that lined the fields so that they could be seen by other slaves to warn them of what would befall them if they attempted to escape. The battle at "Blis Creek Fort" was one in which both armies displayed great heroism; most of the Federal troops that made the first attack, were killed as the Confederates seemed to be irresistible. After rushing up reinforcements, the Federals were successful in capturing it and a large number of "Rebels."

Polly Shine, Texas

"Well no I never saw or heard of a slave trying to leave his southern Maser until after the war started between the states, then they were a few that tried to run off and get under the protection of the northern army but they did not get very far, as they had to have a pass before they could travel or someone would be sure and ask them for their pass and if they could not show a pass from their Mistress it would be just too bad for that negro. The one that ask him for a pass would be more than likely to give that negro a beating of his life and bring him home or send him back to her, and when they got there with that slave he would not be able to run off again for some time, as he would be whipped in an inch of his life. One or two that did try to get under protection of the northern soldiers were shot by the southern armies, as they could not take time to carry these slaves back to their Masers and that put fear in the ones that were at their homes and they would not try to run off as they would be afraid that they would be killed or beat nearly to death."

Barney Stone, Mississippi

"At the out-break of the Civil War and when the Northern army was marching into the Southland, hundreds of male slaves were shot down by the Rebels, rather than see them join with the Yankees. One day when I learned that the Northern troops were very close to our plantation, I ran away and hid in a culvert, but was found and I would have been shot had the yankee troops not scattered them and that saved me. I joined that Union army and served one year, eight months and twenty-two days, and fought with them in the battle of Fort Wagnor, and also in the battle of Milikin's Bend. When I went into the army, I could not read or write. The white soldiers took an interest in me and taught me to write and read, and when the war was over I could write a very good letter. I taught what little I knew to colored children after the war."

Charlie Trotty, Texas

"Yes'm lots of slaves tried to run away, but mostly dey allus got caught. All de marsters had blood hounds and when a slave runned away, dey set de blood hounds on em and dey nearly allus caught em. Lots of times dey nearly tore em up fo any body could git to em when dey caught de run-a-way. Jist member one nigger what got away. Dat was durin de war. He jumped in de creek and swam down de stream, and de dogs lost de scent, and we never did see him anymo. Don't know whether he got to some Yankee camp, or drowned in de creek. I heard tell dey was fixin to burn him, de reason he run away, guess I would of too iffin my Marster was mean to me."

Ella Washington, Texas

"A lot of 'em run 'way from dere, but dey sic de nigger dogs on dere trail an' most of de time dey catched 'em. My cousin run 'way all de time. He use to run through de cow pen an' shinny over de fence an' run in de woods. De dogs use to go to de cow pen an' stay dere an' look under de cow shed an' wait for him to come out. Den time de marster found out he wasn't under dere, dey'd take de dogs out in de woods an' hunt him dere. Dey always, found him 'til he run 'way during de War. When dey catched him dey use to whup him, but it shore never done no good 'cause he was gone 'gain in no time."

Mollie Williams, Mississippi

"Some of de darkies went off wid de Yankees. My brudder Howard did, an' we aint' heerd tell of him since. I'll tell you 'bout it. You see, Mr. Davenpo't owned him an' when he heard 'bout de Yankees comin' dis way, he sont his white driver an' Howard in de carrige wid all his valuables to de swamp to hide, an' while dey was thar de white driver, he went off to sleep an' Howard was prowlin' 'roun' an' we all jes reckin he went on off wid de Yankees."

Mollie Williams. (Library of Congress)

Dilly Yellady, North Carolina

"My father an' his brothers run away an' went to de Yankees. I heard daddy tell 'bout it. He got sick an' dey shipped him back home to North Carolina. Dey shifted niggers from place to place to keep de Yankees frum takin' 'em. When dere got to be too many Yankees in a place de slaves wus sent out to keep 'em from bein' set free."

EMANCIPATION

Abraham Lincoln's signing of the Emancipation Proclamation legally made freedom a reality for the enslaved. The Civil War became a war to end slavery. The moment they became free was not the same for every enslaved person, however. What freedom meant in reality in the short term and in the long term had to be worked out geographic location by geographic location. The process was not always a smooth one, but for most of the enslaved it was a dream come true and a positive change in their lives.

When the arrival of Union troops carried freedom across the South it was a momentous moment for the enslaved. How they received the news and their reactions to their change in status varied. Most were overjoyed and celebrated enthusiastically. Others were saddened because of their emotional bond to their slaveholder, and they were not sure they wished to leave. Others were pleased but unsure about the future. Although they had dreamed of freedom in the abstract, actually obtaining it presented new challenges. In the end most of the enslaved shared the sentiments of Kiziah Love of Oklahoma about slavery versus freedom: "I was glad to be free. What did I do and say? Well, I jest clapped my hands together and said, 'Thank God Almighty. I'se free at last!'"

No matter what challenges it brought, freedom was far superior to enslavement. Hamp Santee of Mississippi captured both the joy and the importance of freedom:

> After surrender, I can remember that the negroes were so happy. They just rang bells, blowed horns and shouted like they were crazy. Then they brought a brand new rope, and cut it into little pieces and they gave everyone a little piece. And whenever they look at the rope they should remember that they were free from bondage.

NARRATIVES

Nora Armstrong, Texas

"Everett Armstrong was my ol' man's marster. My ol' man, he jes' fa'm and wuk at the mills eber since us is free, but now us jes' fa'min'. W'en I's bo'n in Geo'gie, the war was purty heaby dar den. Mudder say she'd sot me on the flo' and w'en I hear the cannon roar, and the big shells bust, I'd try to peep out the door' and winder' to see w'at it was all 'bout. Mudder say dey didn' let dem know w'en dey is free, dey jes' kep' dem and mek' 'bout t'ree mo' crop', den my fadder and mudder hear dey's free, and dey 'cided to run 'way."

"I 'member fadder and mudder each tuk one of the younger chillen and tote 'em and as I's the ol'es' chile, dey lead me by the han'. Dey slip' out in the night and w'en us go down into the deep woods, I's awful 'fraid and I 'gin to cry. The moon was shinin' and us hab to cross a big creek. W'en I seed the 'flection of the moon and the stars and clouds in the water, I lit into screamin' for I's sho' I's goin' to drown. Den fadder and mudder tol' me to shut up or the Boss-man sho' come and git me."

"In the mawnin' us come to anudder w'ite man's house and he tol' fadder and mudder it true dat dey's free. Den befo' long, us come on Wes' and fadder wuk at the saw mills, and fa'm the res' of his life."

Lucy Barnes, Texas

"When de war wuz ovah—I wuz 'bout fo'teen—all de white fo'ks went to a gatherin' in de church. Den w'en dey comed back, a white man came with a paper, he read it out to us, call us in de yard—we didn't know—even know what he wuz readin' an' grandma say, 'Marster, what he say?' Den ol' Marster sez, 'You free, ever one, as I am.' I wuz standin' thar with my milk pail an' I jest drap it on the groun' an' begin gettin' 'way. Missie hollar, 'Lucy come back he'ah, and milk de cows.' I kept runnin' an' hollar back, 'Milk de cows yo'self!' I didn't like it dere an' now I could go an' I did! Yes, ma'm, I went to Columbus an' begin cookin' in white fo'ks' homes an' cooks 'til I gits too ol'."

Sarah Benjamin, Texas

"De day we was freed, slaves jest scattered every whar, dey was all free ceptin me. Mrs. Gilbert tole me I wasnt no slave but I had ter stay there and help her fer my board until I was grown, my daddy didnt try to git me back. I worked fer Mrs. Gilbert til I was sixteen years old jes doin house work, helpin do chores roun de house. When I was sixteen, I runs away and jest works any whar fer bout two years, den I marrys Cal Benjamin and we comes ter Texas, right here ter Corsicana and we goes ter work."

James Boyd, Texas

"When dey said we was free all us niggers throwed our hats in de air an hollered. Ole Marse say, 'How you gwine eat an git clothes an sech?' An' den we shore was scairt an mos ob us stayed near our white folks long as dey lived."

Matilda Brooks, Florida

The coming of the Yankee soldiers created much excitement among the slaves on the Pickens plantation. The slaves were in ignorance of activities going on, and of their approach, but when the first one was sighted the news spread "just like dry grass burning up a hill." Despite the kindness of Governor Pickens the slaves were happy to claim their new-found freedom. Some of them even ran away to join the Northern armies before they were officially freed. Some attempted to show their loyalty to their old owners by joining the Southern armies, but in this section they were not permitted to do so.

Mary Colbert, Georgia

"When news came that Negroes had been freed there was a happy jubilee time. Marse John explained the new freedom to his slaves and we were glad and sorry too. My mother stayed with Marse John until he died. I was still a child and had never had to do anything more than play dolls, and keep the children in the yard. Lord, Honey! I had a fine time those days."

Hattie Cole, Texas

"W'en surrendah comes, den life changed some. Weuns den stahted to have parties an' sich. No sar, 'twarnt any time dat de Marster called allus together an' told weuns dat weuns am free. De Bluecoats come an' does it. One ob de sojers reads a papah to weuns. Gosh, Ise don't know what it am in de papah, but w'en de sojer am through readin', him says, 'Yous am free, an' citizens ob de United States. Dat means yous can go whar yous lak.' But de sojers am mistaken, 'cause 'twarnt so. Weuns am not 'lowed to do as weuns please. Weuns am in'fered wid by de Ku Klux Klan, white caps weuns calls dem. Dat am o'gnation dat come aftah de wah."

Sara Crocker, Georgia

After the War the master was much poorer than before. Many of his slaves had left him and the Confederate money could not be used. You could see the money everywhere, Sara told us. The slaves were glad to be freed and many of the women began to sing songs of praise. Sara's daughter, who was just a child at the close of the War, said she remembered hearing them sing and thought they "wuz having meetin'." She began to sing one of the songs she remembered, "I am glad salvation is free for us all, I am glad salvation is free."

Many of the slaves saw very little change in the conditions after the War. Those who remained with the master had their duties to perform just as they did before the War began. Sara went to live with her husband. He had remained with his master, Mr. Bill Kelly, but they lived near her old master's plantation so she saw him often.

Charlie Davenport, Mississippi

"Lak all de fool Niggers o' dat time I was right smart bit by de freedom bug for awhile. It sounded pow'ful nice to be tol': 'You don't have to chop cotton no more. You can th'ow dat hoe down an' go fishin' whensoever de notion strikes you. An' you can roam 'roun' at night an' court gals jus' as late as you please. Aint no marster gwine a-say to you, "Charlie, you's got to be back when de clock strikes nine."'"

"I was fool 'nough to b'lieve all dat kin' o' stuff. But to tell de hones' truf, mos' o' us didn' know ourse'fs no better off. Freedom meant us could leave where us'd been born an' bred, but it meant, too, dat us had to scratch for us ownse'fs. Dem what lef' de old plantation seemed so all fired glad to git back dat I made up my min' to stay put. I stayed right wid my white folks as long as I could."

Minnie Davis, Georgia

"Mother was glad and sorry too that she was free. Marse John had been so good to all his slaves that none of them really wanted to leave him. We stayed on a while, then mother left and rented a room. She worked hard and bought a house as soon as she could; others did the same. There were very few slaves that had any money at all to begin on."

Moses Davis, Georgia

Uncle Mose says that when freedom was declared, his father came rushing to their cabin waving his arms like a wind mill, shouting: "Boy we is free—you can go and git yourself a job 'cause I ain't goin' to hitch up no more horses." Some of the slaves remained on the plantation where they worked for wages until their deaths. His father was one of them and after his death, his mother moved to another plantation to live with another son. Meanwhile Mose started traveling from place to place as soon as he was told that he was free to go as he pleased. He paid one visit to the plantation where he learned of his father's death. He then asked Manning, who was operating the plantation, for the ox that had belonged to his father and when Manning refused to part with this animal, he made a secret visit back, that night, and took the animal away. He has not been back since.

Ambrose Hilliard Douglass, Florida

"I guess we musta celebrated 'Mancipation about twelve times in Hornett County. Every time a bunch of No'thern sojers would come through they would tell us we was free and we'd begin celebratin'. Before we would get through somebody else would tell us to go back to work, and we would go. Some of us wanted to jine up with the army, but didn't know who was goin' to win and didn't take no chances."

"I was 21 when freedom finally came, and that time I didn't take no chances on 'em taking it back again. I lit out for Florida and wound up in Madison County. I had a nice time there; I got married, got a plenty of work, and made me a little money. I fixed houses, built 'em, worked around the yards, and did everything. My first child was already born; I didn't know there was goin' to be 37 more, though. I guess I would have stopped right there."

Lewis Favor, Georgia

Further he says that it was a happy day for him when he was told that he could do as he pleased because he realized then that he could do some of the things that he had always wanted to do.

Dora Franks, Mississippi

"When de war was over, my brother Frank slipped in de house where I was still a-stayin'. He tol' me us was free an' for me to come out wid de res'. 'Fore sundown dere warnt one Nigger lef' on de place. I hear tell later dat de Mistis an' de gals had to git out an' work in de fiel's to he'p gather in de crop."

Mary Gaines, Arkansas

"In Alabama at this new master's home mother was nursing. Grandma and another old woman was the cooks. Mother want to their little house and told them real low she had the baby and a strange man in the house said, 'Is that the one you goiner let me have?' The man said, 'Yes, he's goiner leave in the morning b'fore times.'"

"The new master come stand around to see when they went to sleep. That night he stood in the chimney corner. There was a little window; the moon throwed his shadow in the room. They said, 'I sure do like my new master.' Another said, 'I sure do.' The other one said, 'This is the best place I ever been they so good to us.' Then they sung a verse and prayed and got quiet. They heard him leave, seen his shadow go way. Heard his house door squeak when he shut his door. Then they got up easy and dressed, took all the clothes they had and slipped out. They walked nearly in a run all night and two more days. They couldn't carry much but they had some meat and meal they took along. Their grub nearly give out when they come to some camps. Somebody told them, 'This is Yankee camps.' They give them something to eat. They worked there a while. One day they took a notion to look about and they hadn't gone far 'fore Grandpa Harris grabbed grandma, then mama. They got to stay a while but the Yankees took them to town and Master Harris come got them and took them back. Their new master come too but he said his wife said bring the girl back but let that old woman go. Master Harris took them both back till freedom."

Annie Hawkins, Oklahoma

"We was the happiest folks in the world when we knowed we was free. We couldn't realize it at first but how we did shout and cry for joy when we did realize it. We was afraid to leave the place at first for fear old Mistress would bring us back or the pateroller would git us. Old Mistress died soon after the War and we didn't care either. She didn't ever do nothing to make us love her.

We was jest as glad as when old Master died. I don't know what become of the three gals. They was about grown."

"We moved away jest as far away as we could and I married soon after."

John Henry Kemp, Florida

The possible loss of his slaves upon the declaration of freedom on January 1, 1866 caused Gay considerable concern. His liquor-ridden mind was not long in finding a solution, however, he barred all visitors from his plantation and insisted that his overssers see to the carrying out of this detail. They did, with such efficiency that it was not until May 8, when the government finally learned of the condition and sent a marshall to the plantation, that freedom came to Gay's slaves. May 8, is still celebrated in this section of Mississippi as the official emancipation day.

Relief for the hundreds of slaves of Gay came at last with the declaration of freedom for them. The government officials divided the grown and growing crops; and some land was parcelled out to the former slaves.

George Kye, Oklahoma

"I never had a hard time as a slave, but I'm glad we was set free. Sometimes we can't figger out the best thing to do, but anyways we can lead our own life now, and I'm glad the young ones can learn and get some where these days."

George Lewis, Georgia

All of the slaves on the plantation were glad when they were told that they were free but there was no big demonstration as they were somewhat afraid of what the master night do. Some of them remained on the plantation while others of them left as soon as they were told that they were free.

Several months after freedom was declared Mr. Lewis' father was able to join his family which had not seen since they had moved to Georgia.

Kiziah Love, Oklahoma

"One of Master Sam Love's women was stole and sold down in Texas. After freedom she made her way back to her fambly. Master Frank sent one of my brothers to Sherman on an errand. After several days the mule come back but we never did see my brother again. We didn't know whether he run off or was stole and sold."

James Lucas, Mississippi

"Slaves didn' know what to 'spec from freedom, but a lot of 'em hoped dey would be fed an' kep' by de gov'ment. Dey all had diffe'nt ways o' thinkin' 'bout it. Mos'ly though dey was jus' lak me, dey didn' know jus' zackly what it meant. It was jus' samp'n dat de white folks an' slaves all de time talk 'bout. Dat's all. Folks dat ain' never been free don' rightly know de feel of bein' free. Dey don' know de meanin' of it. Slaves like us, what was owned by quality-folks, was sati'fied an' didn' sing none of dem freedom songs."

Ed McCree, Georgia

"It was a happy day for us slaves when news come dat de war was over and de white folks had to turn us loose. Marster called his Niggers to come up to de big house yard, but I never stayed 'round to see what he had to say. I runned 'round dat place a-shoutin' to de top of my voice. My folks stayed on wid Old Marster for 'bout a year or more. If us had left, it would have been jus' lak swappin' places from de fryin' pan to de fire, 'cause Niggers didn't have no money to buy no land wid for a long time atter de war."

Willie McCullough, North Carolina

"Mother said she loved my father before the surrender and just as soon as they were free they married."

Maggie Mials, North Carolina

"I think slavery wus a bad thing but when freedom come dere wus nuthin' else we could do but stay on wid some of de white folks 'cause we had nuthin to farm with an nuthin to eat an wear."

Fannie Moore, Florida

"After de war pappy go back to work on de plantation. He make his own crop, on de plantation. But de money was no good den. I played wif many a Confed'rate dollar. He sho was happy dat he was free. Mammy she shout fo' joy an' say her prayers war answered. Pappy git pretty feeble, but he work til jest fore he die. He made patch of cotton wif a hoe. Dey was enough cotton in de patch to make a bale. Pappy die when he 104 years old. Mammy she live to be 105."

Van Moore, Texas

"When freedom come, old missy tell my mammy, 'You is free now, and you all jus' have to do de best you kin.' But mammy she never been 'way from old

Van Moore. (Library of Congress)

missy is her life, and she didn't want no more freedom dan what she had, so we jus' stays with old missy till she moved back to Crosby."

Charlie Moses, Mississippi

"Slavery days was bitter an' I can't forgit the sufferin'. Oh, God! I hates 'em, hates 'em. God Almighty never meant for human beings to be like animals. Us Niggers has a soul an' a heart an' a min'. We aint like a dog or a horse. If all marsters had been good like some, the slaves would all a-been happy. But marsters like mine ought never been allowed to own Niggers."

"I didn' spec nothin' out o' freedom 'ceptin' peace an' happiness an' the right to go my way as I pleased. I prays to the Lord for us to be free, always."

"That's the way God Almighty wants it."

Mack Mullen, Florida

Mullen vividly recalls the day that they heard of their emancipation; loud reports from guns were heard echoing through the woods and plantations;

after awhile "Yankee" soldiers came and informed them that they were free. Mr. Snellings showed no resistance and he was not harmed. The slaves on hearing this good news of freedom burst out in song and praises to God; it was a gala day. No work was done for a week; the time was spent in celebrating. The master told his slaves that they were free and could go wherever they wanted to, or they could remain with him if they wished. Most of his 200 slaves refused to leave him because he was considered a good master."

Mary Overton, Texas

"I don' 'member much 'bout de war. Dere wasn' no fightin' whar we was, on de farm on Nolan river. On de day we was made free, de marster come and called us out one at a time and tol' us we was free. He said to me, 'Mary, you is free by de law. You don' belong to me no more. You can go wherever you wan' to. I ain't got no more to say 'bout you.' He tol' us if we'd stay awhile he'd treat us good and maybe we'd better stay, as de people was pretty much worked up. De rest of 'em stayed 'bout a week, den dey went off, and never come back, 'cept Isaac. I didn' go, but I stayed a long time after we was made free. I didn' care nothin' 'bout bein' free. I didn' have no place to go and didn' know nothin' to do. Dere I had plenty to eat and a place to stay and dat was all I knowed 'bout."

Lilly Perry, North Carolina

"I wus 'bout twelve years old when de Yankees come. I wus pickin' up chips in de yard when dey comes by wid dere hosses steppin' high an' dere music playin' a happy chune. I wus skeered, but I don't dasent run case marster will sho have me whupped, so I keeps on wid my wuck."

"Dey pass fast on down de road an' dey doan bother nothin' in our community but de white folkses hates 'em jist de same."

"Marster Jerry tells us 'bout a week later dat we am free an' all of de two hundret 'cept 'bout five er six goes right off. He tells all of us dat he will pay us effen we will stay an' wuck, so me an' my family we stays on."

Hannah Plummer, North Carolina

"When the war ended mother went to old marster and told him she was goin' to leave. He told her she could not feed all her children, pay house rent, and buy wood, to stay on with him. Marster told father and mother they could have the house free and wood free, an' he would help them feed the children, but mother said, 'No, I am goin' to leave. I have never been free and I am goin' to try it. I am goin' away and by my work and the help of the Lord I will live somehow.'"

Annie Price, Georgia

When Mrs. Kennon informed them that they were free to go or to stay as they pleased, her father, who had just come out of hiding, told Mrs. Kennon that he did not want to remain on the plantation any longer than it was necessary to get his family together. He said that he wanted to get out to himself so that he could see how it felt to be free. Mrs. Price says that as young as she was she felt very happy because the yoke of bondage was gone and she knew that she could have a privelege like everybody else. And so she and her family moved away and her father began farming for himself. His was prosperous until his death. After she left the plantation of her birth she lived with her father until she became a grown woman and then she married a Mr. Price who was also a farmer.

Lafayette Price, Texas

"When news of de surrender come lots of cullud folks seem to be rejoicin' and sing, 'I's free, I's free as a frog' 'cause a frog had freedom to git on a log and jump off when he please. Some jus' stayed on wid dere w'ite folks. One time dey say day sen' all de niggers back to Africa. I say dey never git me. I bin yere, and my w'its folks bin yere, and yere I goin' to stay. My young marster say he want me for a nigger driver, so he teach me how to read and spell so I could ten' to business."

Sarah Ross, Florida

Sarah remembers the coming of the Yankees and the destruction wrought by their appearance. The soldiers stripped the plantation owners of their meats, vegetables, poultry and the like. Many plantation owners took their own lives in desperation. Donaldson kept his slaves several months after liberation and defied them to mention freedom to him. When he did give them freedom, they lost no time in leaving his plantation which held for them only unpleasant memories.

Susan Ross, Texas

"We go to school after us free. When my oldes' brother hear us is free he give a whoop, run and jump a high fence, and told mammy goodbye. Den he grab me up and hug and kiss me and say, 'Brother gone, don't 'spect you ever see me no more.' I don't know where he go, but I never did see him 'gain."

Robert Shepherd, Georgia

"When dem yankees had done gone off Marster come out to our place. He blowed de bugle to call us all up to de house. He couldn't hardly talk, 'cause somebody had done told him dat dem yankees couldn't talk his Niggers into stealin' nothin'. Marster said he never knowed 'fore how good us loved him. He told us he had done tried to be good to us and had done de best he could for us and dat he was mighty proud of de way evvy one of us had done 'haved ourselfs. He said dat de war was over now, and us was free and could go anywhar us wanted to, but dat us didn't have to go if us wanted to stay dar. He said he would pay us for our wuk and take keer of us if us stayed or, if us wanted to wuk on shares, he would 'low us to wuk some land dat way. A few of dem Niggers drifted off, but most of 'em stayed right dar 'til dey died."

Rev. James Singleton, Mississippi

"No'm, didn' none of de slaves run off wid dem dat I knows of, an' de Yankees didn' try to bother us none. Well, afte' de War, Marse Elbert tol' us dat we was free now, an' pappy come an' got us an' taken us to live wid de cook on Mr. Elisha Bishop's place, an' he paid Mr. Barren Bishop to teach us. He taught us out of Webster's Blue Back Spellin' Book."

Melvin Smith, Georgia

"In a sense the niggers is better off since freedom come. Ol' Marster was good an' kind but I like to be free to go whar I please. Back then we couldn't go nowhar 'less we had a pass. We don't have no overseer to bother us now. It ain't that I didn't love my Marster but I jest likes to be free. Jest as soon as Marster said I didn't b'long to nobody no more I left an' went to Tallahassee. Mr. Charlie Pearce come an' wanted some hands to work in orange groves an' fish for him so that's what I done. He took a whole crew. While we was down thar Miss Carrie Standard, a white lady, had a school for the colored folks. 'Course, my ol' Miss had done taught me to read an' write out of the old blue back Webster but I had done forgot how. Miss Carrie had 'bout fifteen in her class."

Nancy Smith, Georgia

"When dem yankee sojers come, us warn't much skeered 'cause Marse Joe had done told us all 'bout 'em and said to spect 'em 'fore long. Sho' 'nough, one day dey come a-lopin' up in Marse Joe's yard. Dey had dem old blue uniforms on and evvy one of 'em had a tin can and a sack tied to his saddle. Marster told us dey kept drinkin' water in dem cans and dey called 'em canteens. De sacks was to carry deir victuals in. Dem fellows went all through our big house and stole whatever dey wanted. Dey got all of Mist'ess' best silver cause us didn't have no time to hide it atter us knowed dey was nigh 'round de place. Dey tuk all de somepin' t'eat dere was in de big house. When dey had done et all dey wanted and tuk evvything else dey could carry off, dey called us Negroes up 'fore deir captain, and he said all of us was free and could go any time and anywhar us wanted to go. Dey left, and us never seed 'em in dat yard no more. Marse Joe said all of us dat wanted to could stay on wid him. None of us had nowhar else to go and 'sides nobody wanted to go nowhar else, so evvy one of Marse Joe's Negroes stayed right on wid him dat next year. Us warn't skeered of dem Kluxers [Ku Klux Klan] here in town, but dey was right bad out on de plantations."

Rachel Sullivan, Georgia

"Lawdy yas'm. Mr. DeLoach come riding up to de plantachun in one o' dem low-bellied ca'yages. He call to Jo and James—dem boys what stay round de house to bring wood and rake de grass and sich—he sont Jo and Jin down to all de fields to tell all de hands to come up. Dey unhitch de mules fum de plows and come wid de chains rattlin', and de cotton hoers put dey hoes on dey shoulders—wid de blades shinin' in de sun, and all come hurrying to hear what Mr. DeLoach want wid'em. Den he read de freedom warrant to 'em. One man so upset he start runnin' and run clear down to de riber and jump in."

Jane Sutton, Mississippi

"After freedom I went back to 'Old Mis'. I walked all de way back from Rankin County. It was a long way, but I wanted to see Old Mis' an' my Mammy an' my brothers an' sisters."

"When de surrender come by pappy come to git me. I didn' wan'-a go. I tol' 'im I's gwine stay wid Old Mis'. So he goes an' gits de sheriff an' takes me anyway. I runned away twict an'come back to Old Mis'. He whupped me de firs' time, but de nex' time I hid from him an' he couldn' catch me. He went back home an' 'lemme 'lone. Den I went wid my mammy to live wid Marse Tally Berry. He was one of Old Marster's sons. Dey used to come an' tell me dat dat old Nigger was gwine kill me if I didn' come wid him. But I jus' stayed hid out till he went away."

J. W. Terrill, Texas

"When we heered war was over and we's free, we all jus' jumped up and hollers and dances. Missy, she cries and cries, and tells us we is free and she hopes we starve to death and she'd be glad, 'cause it ruin her to lose us. They was a big bunch of us niggers in town and we stirrin' 'round—like bees workin' in and out a hive. We was jus' that way. I went wild and the first year I went north, but I come back 'gain to Texas."

Ellen Thomas, Texas

"I was born in Mississippi. We come to Texas and my mother died, so grandma raised me. I was jes' a baby when we come to Texas. Mr. Harper owned us. I remember the war, but it's so long ago I don't remember much. I remember when John Harper read the free paper to us. He had a big lot of slaves, but when he read the free papers they jes' flew out like birds. But I didn't. I was

Ellen Thomas. (Library of Congress)

stickin' to my grandmother. She was on crutches and she stayed on at the Harper place."

Jane Mickens Toombs, Georgia

"I recollects when dey say Freedom had cum. Dare wuz a speakin' fer de slaves up here in town in Barnett's Grove. Dat mornin' Ole Miss sont all de oldes' niggers to de speakin' an' kep' us little 'uns dat day. She kep' us busy sweepin' de yards an' sich as dat. An' she cooked our dinner an' give hit to us herself."

"I 'members de grown folks leavin' early dat mornin' in a great big waggin."

Phil Towns, Georgia

Phil says his fellow slaves laughed when told they were free, but Gov. Towns was almost indifferent. His slaves, he said, were always practically free, so a little legal form did not count much. Nearly every one remained there and worked for wages.

Jane Anne Privette Upperman, North Carolina

"When de war ended father come an' got ma an' took her on to his marsters plantation. My father wus named Carroll Privette an' my mother wus Cherry Brantly, but after she wus free she begun to call herself by my fathers name, Privette."

Millie Williams. (Library of Congress)

Millie Williams, Texas

"I stays with Massa Ellis after we's freed. Dere sho' was a mighty purty sight when de slaves knows dey's free. Dey hug one 'nother and almos' tear dere clothes off. Some cryin' for de husban', and some cryin' for de chillen."

Rose Williams, Texas

"Cose every body knew de war was comin on and dey all knew when de war was on cause de white marsters sent some one er went dem selves and sent some hosses, co'n and meat of all kinds, dey sent wheat and dey sent lots of it too, dey also sent money too, cose we didnt know how much but we knows dey sends it. De day we was freed, Marster George call us all up and says yoah is all free ter do as yoah please wid yoah selves go what yoah please, now iffen yoah all wants ter stay yoah is welcome. But dare didnt none of us stayed, we all left, why de niggahs day jest scatter like quails dey goes in every dereck-shun, and none of dem knows what dey is goin, dey was jest goin dats all."

Stephen Williams, Texas

"When freedom comes to us colored folks, Mr. Dan tell us we is free to do what we want and he ask papa and mamma what they want to do. They tell him they don't want to do nothing 'cept stay with him and do jes' like they's been doing, and Mr. Dan tells 'em they won't never want for nothing long as they live, and they stay with Mr. Dan 'til mamma died in July 1870 and papa followed her 'bout three years after."

Wayman Williams, Texas

"When de slaves were set free den dey had big times an felt like dey did not has to work at all, but when de ole Marster give dem little crop of dar own an tell dem ef'n dey don' work dey wont have anything to eat dey stays wid him an works de crops on de halves mostly, dat is de nigger do de work an de Marster feed him an furnish de team an tools an give him half what he make. Dey like dis an mos all de niggers whar I live stayed on wid de ole Marster."

"De slaves dat went up Nawth an' cum back after freedom would tell how dey wuz called Contrabands up dar. Dey did not know wat hit meant but dey did not like to stay dar so dey cum back."

"At first a few white teachers from up Nawth would cum to teach de chillun an have a school, but dey did not talk like de folks here an dey did not know how to talk to us, dey could not understan our language, dey did not know what we meant wen we said 'titty' fer sister an 'budder' fer frother an 'nanny' fer mammy, dey had to learn how we talk."

Adeline Willis, Georgia

"When they all come home from the war and Marster called us up and told us we was free, some rejoiced so they shouted, but some didn't, they was sorry. Lewis come a runnin' over there an' wanted me and the chillun to go on over to his white folks' place with him, an' I wouldn't go—No man. I wouldn't leave my white folks. I told Lewis to go on and let me 'lone, I knowed my white folks and they was good to me, but I didn't know his white folks. So we kept living like we did in slavery, but he come to see me every day. After a few years he finally 'suaded me to go on over to the Willis place and live with him, and his white folks was powerful good to me. After a while, tho' we all went back and lived with my white folks and I worked on for them as long as I was able to work and always felt like I belonged to 'em, and you know, after all this long time, I feel like I am their's."

Sarah Wilson, Texas

"One day, I hears Marse Eden a tellin' he wife dat he guess he 'ud hab to read dem 'free papers' to de niggers in de mo'nin'. I slipped out jes' lak a mouse, an' hunt my Mammy an' whisper an' tell what I done heard. But I knowed better dan ter tell eny one 'cept her. W'en Marse come down to our cabin, he wuz er cryin'. Atter he read dat paper my Mammy clapped her hands an' shouted fer a long time. Me an' de odder young nigger jes' went wild. I jumped de fences lak a wild buck, me an' George Herod. Den w'en us ca'am down, de next' day er so, ole Mars' tole Mammy dat he wanted us to help him gather de crops an' he would gib her a load ob corn, two meat hogs, one wagon ob potatoes an' a keg ob 'lasses. So, us stayed an' wukked fer Marse seberal years."

Rube Witt, Texas

"I 'members the white fo'ks say the War started concerning keeping the slaves. Then I seed them mending harness and fixing wagons to go fight. I was a house-boy for the Witts during the war. 'Bout the time it was over I was enlisted at Alexandria, La. as a soldier and sent to Mansfield. The Yankees had done won the victory when our reg'ment got there. They turned us loose to get home the best way we could. I come back to the Witts and stayed 'bout a year after the war. Master calls all the slaves up and say we was free. He promised we would have plenty to eat and wear if we stayed on and worked for him, and if we left it was 'root hog or die.' Most of them left. You ought to seed them pulling off them 'croaker-sack' [home-spun] clothes when Master say we was free."

Henry Wright, Georgia

When freedom was declared he says that he was a vary happy man. Freedom to him did not mean that he could quit work but that he could work for himself as he saw fit to. After he was freed he continued working for his master who was considerably poorer than he had ever been before.

Clara C. Young, Mississippi

"De Yankees come 'roun' afte' de War an' tol' us we's free an' we shouted an' sang, an' had a big celebration fer a few days. Den we got to wonderin' 'bout what good it did us. It didn' feel no diffrunt; we all loved our marster an' missus an' stayed on wid 'em jes' lak nothin' had happened."

Litt Young, Texas

"After surrender the Yanks arrested my old missy and brought her out to the farm and locked her up in the black folks church. She had a guard day and night. They fed her hard-tack and water for three days 'fore they turned her a-loose. Then she freed all her niggers. 'Bout that time Massa Gibbs run out of corn to feed he stock and he took my daddy and a bunch of niggers and left to buy a boatload of corn. Missy seized a bunch us niggers and starts to Texas. She had Irishmen guards, with rifles, to keep us from runnin' 'way. She left with ten six-mule teams and one ox cook wagon. Them what was able walked all the way from Vicksburg to Texas. We camped at night and they tied the men to trees. We couldn't git away with them Irishmen havin' rifles. Black folks nat'rally scart of guns, anyway. Missy finally locates 'bout three miles from Marshall and we made her first crop and on June 19th, the next year after 'mancipation, she sot us free."

Appendix: The Long Road to the Cabin Door: Historians on American Slavery

On August 28, 1963, at the March on Washington, the Reverend Martin Luther King Jr. used the nation's most powerful metaphor, slavery, to draw attention not directly to slavery, but to the incompleteness of the Great Emancipation for the progeny of the nation's beleaguered 19th-century laborers on the South's plantations, farms, docks, and households. He did so 100 years after the Great Emancipation began and was given immediate worldwide significance by President Lincoln's Emancipation Proclamation. In his "I Have a Dream" speech, King said:

> Five score years ago a great American, in whose symbolic shadow we stand today signed the Emancipation Proclamation. This momentous decree is a great beacon light of hope to millions of Negro slaves who had been seared in the flames of withering injustice. It came as a joyous daybreak to end the long night of their captivity. But 100 years later the Negro still is not free.

An astute observer of American history, Dr. King surely knew Negroes were no longer chattel. And yet his words, now memorialized as one of the great speeches of the past century, revealed once again that over most of the nation's history slavery was both a reality and a metaphor. It took root early in the colonial era and evolved along with the nation. It created paradoxes in a colonial society that increasingly professed the importance of liberty and freedom while placing nearly all of its inhabitants within slavery's grip. When the colonies revolted against the British Crown, extolling the virtues of liberty in the Declaration of Independence, slavery survived the lofty rhetoric, the War of Independence, and creation of the American Republic.

Historian Eric Foner has argued that slavery was linguistically deployed by American revolutionaries, many of whom were slaveholders, to claim rights denied them by the British Crown. "Even though rarely mentioned explicitly," Foner observed, "black slavery was intimately related to the meaning of freedom for men who made the American Revolution" (Foner 1994, 435–60). No less than Thomas Jefferson, the author of the Declaration of Independence and a slaveholder, wrote of freedom as if it did not share the American experience with slavery, as if the clamoring for freedom by men such as he was not a crude hoax.

The history and memory of American slavery, as undertaken by those once enslaved, by those who in various ways bore witness to the lives of the enslaved, and by three generations of scholars who have given us an increasingly compli-cated picture of the institution, have intersected in recent years. There is now a comprehensive view of a tragic experience that was, in fact, among the nation's most important. Indeed, what has been written about slavery is now at the center of American historical scholarship on the making of two important parts of the story of America—its early life and times under slavery and as a modern society in search of a more perfect Union while still recovering from the long shadow cast by slavery.

At the time when the crafting of America's historical narrative was taken over by professionally trained historians, during the late 19th and early 20th centuries, research on American slavery placed it at or near the center of a decades-long con-troversy about the true nature of the Republic, its ideals and its ultimate purpose. Was America essentially a slave society? Was slavery a horrendously brutal experi-ence, or was it, essentially, a benign, civilizing institution for its victims? Indeed, were blacks victims at all? Were they so inferior that their enslavement was a "civi-lizing experience," one that converted many to Christianity and to standards of civilization that actually served them well when emancipation finally came? Much of the early scholarship, dominated in the history profession by Southern-born white mem, reflected, as historical scholarship often does, contemporary social mores. Indeed, early 20th-century America, when the study of slavery first came into high relief, was marked by the collapsing fortunes of African Americans in the life of the Republic. The disenfranchisement of black male voters in the southern states, the establishment of a rigid custom of racial separation in public life, and widespread violence against blacks had become a formidable part of modern American life. by the early years of the 20th century

It is also true that the first generation of historians on the making of the United States tended to be silent on those issues that future historians would find so riveting. To a great extent, pioneering historians crafted historical narratives they thought were deserving of a nation born out of an anticolonial revolution and seemingly destined, indeed divinely ordained, to sweep across the continent and to fulfill the promise of liberty and opportunity. From George Bancroft (1800–1891) to Woodrow Wilson (1856–1924), early American historians acknowledged the presence of slavery while largely ignoring the disturbing experience of the slaves. As an example, Bancroft's *History of the United States from the Discovery of the American Continent,* which covers the years 1854 to 1878, embraced and proselytized American romantic nationalism, but that was hardly a context in which the nation's racial customs and slavery could be studied in any meaningful way. The silence or indifference over slavery that marked the volumi-nous writings by Bancroft and successive historians as the 19th century was ending reveals how the lives of enslaved African Americans were seemingly incompatible with the nation's story and self-image.

All but imperceptible to the emerging historical profession at that time, the first generation of Negro historians mounted a considerable challenge to the founda-tional assumptions about slavery and African American slaves. George Washington Williams (1848–1891), among the most persuasive of those historians, wrote wrenchingly about slavery in his monumental 1883 text, *History of the Negro Race in America*:

> I have tracked my bleeding countrymen through the widely scattered documents of American history; I have listened to their groans, their clanking chains, and melting prayers, until the woes of a race and the agonies of centuries seem to crowd upon my soul as a bitter reality. Many pages of this history have been blistered with my tears; and, although having lived but a little more than a generation, my mind feels as if it were cycles old. (Williams 1883, iii)

Over the following years, professionally trained black historians, of whom Williams was not one, viewed slavery through the lens of the black experience within an institution controlled by powerful whites. W. E. B. Du Bois, for example, examined the cultural expression of the slave in his magisterial 1903 opus, *The Souls of Black Folk,* making him arguably the first scholar to shed light on ways in which blacks held on to their dignity within a system determined to demean them. He wrote the following:

> They that walked in darkness sang song in the olden days—Sorrow Songs—for they were weary at heart. . . . Little of beauty has America given the world save the rude grandeur God himself stamped on her bosom; the human spirit in this new world has expressed itself in vigor and ingenuity rather than in beauty. And so by fateful chance the Negro folk-song—the rhythmic cry of the slave—stands today not simply as the sole American music, but as the most beautiful expression of human experience born this side of the seas. It has been neglected, it has been, and is, half despised, and above all it has been persistently mistaken and misunderstood; but notwithstanding, it still remains as the singular spiritual heritage of the nation and the greatest gift of the Negro people. (Du Bois 1999, 154, 155)

Du Bois's ode to the folk culture of the enslaved would influence scholarship more than a generation later as historians and other scholars examined sacred and secular music, folktales, and dance, among other legacies of Africa that were woven in an African American cultural ethos.

By comparison, slavery was placed under a harsh light by Carter G. Woodson in his pioneering study, *The Negro in Our History,* first published in 1922. Woodson examined the essential cruelty of the slave system, its policing of black bodies, its injurious influence on slave families, and the prevalence of punishment in the lives of many enslaved people. Again, it is important to keep in mind that the study of slavery, through a part of the early Negro History Movement, largely steered far away from narratives informed by black cultural agency and the troubling presence of violence and other forms of cruelty at the heart of the institution. It would take more than a generation before the foundational work of Du Bois, Woodson, and other early 20th-century Negro scholars would be accepted as credible by a cross section of white Americans within and beyond the academy. The most important feature of scholarship on slavery during the early years of the negro history movement was its acknowledgment of the fundamental humanity and racial equality of the enslaved. That these scholars did so at a time when most black Americans, the progeny of slaves, were still on the margins of American society, was arguably the most enduring contribution to African American historiography and the larger narrative of the American Republic.

Despite efforts by the first generation of black historians to tell the story of slavery from the experience of the slaves, the prevailing interpretation on the institution of slavery, and by extension those within its grip, was Ulrich B. Phillips's *American Negro Slavery,* published in 1918, and his *Life and Labor in the Old South,* published in 1929. Both books had an enormous influence on nearly two generations of American historians. Convinced that Africans were inferior, Phillips concluded that slavery, though morally indefensible, brought Christian civilization to the enslaved. In his view, moreover, slavery was essentially a paternalistic institution that had at its core white supremacy over an inferior, uncivilized race of Africans. As he put it, "On the whole, the plantations were the best schools yet invented for the mass training of that sort of inert and backward people which the bulk of the American negroes represented" (Phillips 1918). In retrospect, Phillips, despite his extensive research of extant plantation records, wrote a study of slavery that was quintessentially American at a time when black scholarship by blacks was all but ignored by white scholars and when the academy was as racially segregated as was the Christian church on a Sunday morning in the United States.

That Phillips and those who followed his path long held sway over the historiographical trajectory on American slavery speaks to at least two important themes in the relationship of scholarship to contemporary American life: As long as blacks could be constructed as inferior beings without a credible past, their position in the present would be subjected to an array of injustices. Also, from the vantage point of Phillips and other contributors to early studies of slavery, blacks were not real historical actors but, rather, objects in the past. They were largely without voices, without stories, and without substantive roles in the making of American life in slavery and freedom.

Over the years that marked the maturation of the historical profession profound changes in American scholarship, especially in the social sciences and humanities, and the activism of African Americans on multiple fronts set the stage for a reconsideration of the foundational premises of the early historiography on slavery. Perhaps the most important revisionist interpretation was Kenneth Stampp's 1956 book, *The Peculiar Institution: Slavery in the Ante-Bellum South,* which signaled a reshuffling of perspectives not only of slavery as an institution and a way of life but also, and equally important, of its primary actors, the slaves themselves. In words that strike us now as reflecting post–World War II liberal assumptions about race, Stampp wrote, "I have assumed that slaves were merely ordinary human beings, that innately Negroes are, after all, only white men with black skins, nothing more, nothing less" (1956, vii–viii). His assertion of human and racial equality, though seemingly oblivious to the formidable presence of women, opened up a nearly revolutionary reconsideration of the enslaved as active participants in the life and times of an institution that Stampp found harsh, demeaning, racist, and profitable.

Arguably, with the publication of *The Peculiar Institution* during the early years of the modern civil rights movement, historians, including Stampp, were influenced by the rising cadence of black protest against long-standing injustices in the nation's public and private spheres. The daily rhythm of historians, not unlike that of other Americans, includes taking in the morning news, which during the 1950s increasingly carried stories about black resistance against racial discrimination and violence.

Historians at the time *The Peculiar Institution* was published easily recognized its game-changing influence on slavery studies. Hampton Institute's Charles H. Nichols viewed it as "the first really comprehensive study of slavery which is not an apology, a cherished dream, or an indictment" (Nichols 1956, 395), while the University of North Carolina's Frank W. Klingberg acknowledged that important conclusions drawn by Stampp "merely took away from the African his native culture and gave him, in exchange, little more than vocational training" (Klingberg 1957, 139). In the years to follow, the legacy of *The Peculiar Institution* was hard to ignore. "The interpretative advances of *The Peculiar Institution* and the ongoing struggle for black equality," southern historian Fitzhugh Brundage observed in 1997, "inspired a generation of talented historians to study African American history, especially slavery" (Brundage 1997, 119).

But if Stampp's rigorous revisionist sensibility during the civil rights era brought into question the foundational assumptions about race laid bare by Phillips, it also sparked an outpouring of scholarship exploring how enslavement affected slaves, how the slaves coped with their predicament, and the extent to which historians from Phillips to Stampp rarely drew from what the enslaved left for future generations to reveal and discern. Among the most influential of the then young historians was Sterling Stuckey, who, in his seminal 1968 article "Through the Prism of Folklore: The Black Ethos in Slavery," urged historians to explore folk culture, that is, the African antecedents that enslaved blacks kept alive over time. In 2008, historian George Frederickson referred to Stuckey's article as arguably "the most historiographically important journal article on slavery ever published. More than any other work of the 1960s it signaled [and] heralded the paradigm shift in the representation of the slave experience that came to fruition in the 1970s and 80s" (Hill 2006, 368).

Indeed, should one be in search for a nearly final declaratory blow against old paradigms that placed the memory, culture, and vigilance of blacks beyond the pale of historical scholarship on slavery it would be Stuckey's 20-page opus. "My thesis," he wrote in 1968, "which rests on an examination of folk songs and tales, is that slaves were able to fashion a life style and set of values—an ethos—which prevented them from being imprisoned altogether by the definitions which the larger society sought to impose" (Stuckey 1994, 4). This view showed the influence of earlier black scholars and artists, notably Sterling Brown, W. E. B. Du Bois, and Paul Robeson, on a generation of scholars that is often times referred to as the Nationalist School. Such scholars, most especially Stuckey, acknowledged the centrality of African cultures to the experience, adjustment, and influence of Africans in New World societies, including North America.

It may be true, too, that as the Nationalist School took form American scholarship reflected a racial chasm of long standing, where many white scholars, with the exception of Stampp, Herbert Aptheker, and a few others, seemed to be on the wrong side of historical scholarship because of their racial assumptions about Africans. Stuckey made such an observation in 1971 (263):

> When one realizes that the field of slavery has been more effectively dominated by white historians than any other in which black people were crucially involved, it is easier to understand the responses of black and white intellectuals to the [William] Styron novel on the slave prophet [*The Confessions of Nat Turner*]. It should also be borne in mind that there is a larger number of intact stereotypes about Afro-Americans during this period (despite the monumental work of Stampp) than other forms because in addition to providing the base for most of the other cherished American assumptions about African American personality, whole dimensions of the black experience, in this case music and religion, are all but unknown to historians. Historians continue to assert, with real certitude, that the slave experience went unrecorded by the slaves. And so they confidently march onward—in lockstep with their mentors of previous generations. (Stuckey 1971, 263)

The Nationalist School of African American history forged an evolving scholarly consensus over race, racism, and the formidable presence of Africans in Western societies, ennobling the power of memory, culture, and African survival in the United States and across the African diaspora. The making of such a consensus was, in fact, an early 20th-century phenomenon that began with Du Bois, the Harlem Renaissance, Franz Boas, Gunnar Myrdal, and indeed the Negro History Movement. It was strengthened by the gathering momentum of post–World War II black liberation struggles in Africa, the various elements of a heightened black consciousness advocacy in the arts, especially in literature and painting, as well as politics, religion and community life. Those years are best known through the lens of the modern civil rights movement, but a much broader geographical territory and cross section of the African diaspora nurtured an unprecedented expression of modern Africanity.

To a significant degree, the Nationalist School provided a substantive criticism of an earlier work by Professor Stanley Elkins to which it brought sustained attention within academic and nonacademic circles. His iconic study *Slavery: A Problem in American Institutional & Intellectual Life* (1959) was presented as a proposal for new questions about slavery within the context of the Americas, the effects of enslavement on the slaves, and the role of social psychology in slavery studies. It was arguably the most controversial study of slavery to emerge after World War II, at a time when the civil rights movement was soon to be transformed into a black liberation struggle. Elkins explicitly sought to till new ground in slavery historiography, which he boldly claimed had hit a dead end as virtually no other important questions were being raised or answered. Moreover, he claimed that the constellation of treatises ranging from James Ford Rhodes to Ulrich Bonnell Phillips, and encompassing Phillips's belief in the paternalistic as well as the famous rebuttal by Stampp, had settled a litany of scholarly and morally intense questions about the peculiar institution's importance in the nation's history. In a fascinating, if problematic, overview of the historiography on slavery and the resonance of racism in American society from the late 19th century to the waning of Phillips's influence over slavery's narrative, Elkins raised questions about antebellum slavery within and beyond the southern realm of the United States. Indeed, his comparative framework in which the slave systems of the United States and in Latin America were examined was all but path breaking, exploring topics not considered since Frank Tannebaum's *Slave and Citizen* appeared in 1947. The historiographical questions raised by Elkins, especially his provocative arguments on the personality traits of the enslaved, influenced the next generation of scholarship on the institution, the effect of enslavement on blacks, and the methodologies that, in effect, brought a flourish of new thinking about everyone involved in the enterprise of slavery and the lives affected by it over time, and well after emancipation. In short, Elkins's most controversial argument, in a book profuse in its controversies, focused on the powerful and disturbing southern stereotype of the enslaved black as Sambo. In academic circles Sambo, until Elkins's magnum opus, was rarely directly confronted, though as caricature the personality type found its way into American popular culture in movies, literature, television, and theater. Such a person within the ordeal of enslavement, Elkins argued (1959, 82),

> was docile but irresponsible, loyal but lazy, humble but chronically given to lying and stealing; his behavior was full of infantile silliness and his talk inflated with childish exaggeration. His relationship with his master was one of utter dependence and childlike attachment: it was indeed this childlike quality that was the very key to his being. Although the merest hint of Sambo's "manhood" might fill the Southern breast with scorn, the child, "in his place," could be both exasperating and lovable.

According to Elkins, no such personality trait emerged in the Latin American slave system, including the largest part of the system, Brazil. Moreover, Sambo, or a type cast of similar psychological characteristics, was not evident in the West African societies from which most American slaves were taken (Elkins 1959, 81–139).

Sambo, then, according to Elkins was not a crude, racialized invention of the white South. He was real, the result of a "closed society" that was uniquely harsh and unmediated by religious institutions and traditions found in Latin America, where no such image of blacks existed because, Elkins posited, such people did not exist. Fluidity, institutional mediation by the Catholic Church, and a modicum of rights accessible to slaves in Latin America marked profound differences in the lives and times of slaves there and slaves in the United States. "Neither in Brazil nor in Spanish America," Elkins observed, "did slavery carry with it such precise and irrevocable categories of perpetual servitude, 'durante vita' and 'for all generations,' as in the United States." Moreover,

> in extending its moral authority over men of every condition, the church naturally insisted on bringing slave unions under the holy sacrament. Slaves were married in church and the banns published; marriage was a sacred rite and its sanctity protected in law. In the otherwise circumspect United States, the only category which the law could apply in conjugal relations between slaves—or to unions between master and slave—was concubinage. (Elkins 1959, 72, 73).

In an extraordinary and controversial leap from antebellum slavery into another oppressive and even more horrific system—the Nazi concentration camps created during the Holocaust—Elkins compared the infantilization of survivors of the camps with the American South's Sambo. "The most immediate aspect of the old inmates' behavior which struck these [those who saw the survivors when the camps were liberated] was its childlike quality. The prisoners developed types of behavior which are characteristic of infancy or early youth" (Elkins 1959, 111). Depending on the length of time which inmates survived or ultimately perished during the Holocaust they, as kidnapped prisoners, had already endured a series of shocks that brought into retrospective focus a comparison with the way enslaved Africans were treated on their way across the Atlantic Ocean to the slave systems of the Americas. "If transported in cattle cars instead of passenger cars," Elkins wrote, "the prisoners were sealed in, under conditions not dissimilar to those of the Middle Passage" (Elkins 1959, 106, 159). Comparatively, then, Elkins argued that slavery in the United States and the Nazi concentration camps were closed systems that obliterated their victims' prior connections, essentially the parts of their memories and histories that fundamentally mattered to what they were, or used to be, as human beings.

Elkins's *Slavery* was received with ambivalence, and scholars saw it as an important if seriously flawed contribution to new ways of looking at the old debate over slavery. Some, most notably the aforementioned Frank Tannenbaum, commended Elkins for challenging old assumptions while calling for new ways of looking at slaves and the societies in which they labored. As Tannenbaum put it, Elkins explored "new ways of looking at the place of slavery in American history, as a part of the social, economic, political, and cultural history of the United States and not just of the Negro" (1960, 93–94).

Many more scholars questioned Elkins's controversial assumptions about slave personality in the South and his dubious deployment of social psychology to explain the similarities of the behaviors of 19th-century slaves and 20th-century concentration camp survivors. "One looks in vain for some effort to link these speculations with material from the substantial body of slave and Negro literature," observed Oscar Handlin. Indeed, Handlin bluntly claimed that "The disaster of this book is not due to the use of either concepts drawn from the social sciences or of imaginative analogies, but to a much simpler and older deficiency—the misuse of evidence" (Handlin 1961, 254, 255).

Disaster or not, and conceptual errors notwithstanding, Elkins's proposal for new research agendas on slavery drew multiple scholarly responses, though not necessarily what he anticipated, as the field significantly expanded in the 1960s and beyond. As historian Peter Parish put it in his book *Slavery: History and Historians*, "The incisiveness and daring—perhaps the outrageousness—of [Elkins's] argument stimulated a wealth of new insights and ideas, most of them sharply critical" (Parish 1989, 68). (For an insightful discussion of the enduring significance of and challenges to Elkins over the years after the publication of *Slavery*, see: Fredrickson, George M. 1988. *The Arrogance of Race: Historical Perspectives on Slavery, Racism, and Social Inequality*, 112–124. Hanover, NH: Wesleyan University Press.)

And so Stuckey's exploration of a black ethos in slavery was more than a rebuke of Elkins. It marked a broadening reexamination of slavery through sources theretofore ignored by historians, though many had been taken up by artists, activists, and others who found significant value in what slaves bequeathed to the future. In exploring folk culture, artifacts, texts, and memory—including the Works Progress Administration Slave Narratives—scholars fundamentally altered the trajectory of American historiography. Greater attention than ever was focused on the slave as an individual whose predicament was confronted in varying ways that enabled men and women to navigate slavery's harsh realities. As the contemporary climate of race relations and social activism likely shaped the scholarship of Stampp and Elkins, much of the work in the 1960s and 1970s was influenced by a new generation of scholars, many of whom were African American. The diversification of the history profession coincided with and was likely a major reason for the profound changes then underway in slavery studies and the larger narrative of the nation. Moreover, by the 1960s, the long-standing aversion to telling the story of Americans on the margins or at the bottom of the society—easily the position of the nation's slaves—all but ended. "For our purposes," the cultural historian Lawrence W. Levine observed,

> the advent of a stream of modern American historiography beginning in the late 1960s and blossoming in the mid-1970s that was—and is—convinced that there can be no real sense of the whole without exploring the parts, without understanding—often for the first time—the consciousness and actions of workers, women, ethnic, religious, racial, and national minorities, immigrants and their progeny, who participated in a myriad of separate geographical, occupational, fraternal, and religious communities that together constituted the larger society. (Levine 1993, 6)

Over the decades that followed the 1960s, the study of slavery was complicated by a deepening interest in the African antecedents and survivals of colonial, 19th century, and particularly antebellum slaves. John Blassingame, in his well-received *The Slave Community: Plantation Life in the Ante-Bellum South,* dismissed the one-dimensionality of Sambo, suggesting that slave behavior was hardly monolithic and hardly compliant and submissive. Equally important, Blassingame was one of a long line of equally talented scholars who found a communal ethos on many plantations, which encouraged comradery, secrecy, familial bonds, the sharing of news, recreation, and a form of order that was not simply imposed upon enslaved blacks by whites. Chaos within the slave quarter was not in the best interests of the quarter, and many adhered to realistic standards of behavior. This might explain why there were so few slave insurrections during the antebellum period, and it might also explain why when freedom came blacks were remarkably disciplined in facing the challenges placed before them. Complicating the lives of slaves, including contextualizing slave personality types in ways that further distanced historians from Elkins's rigid focus on Sambo, Blassingame's *The Slave Community* relies on slave narratives and other sources left by enslaved and free blacks. It created a stage from which the voices, actions, and complexity of black life fully emerged. Its publication in 1972 marked the maturity of scholarship on the world the slaves made and what that world made of blacks and whites within slavery and freedom.

Once the historiography on slavery was freed from the burden of racism that once ensured deeply adverse perceptions of Africans on American soil, the story of the slaves and those who exploited them forever changed, opening vistas onto the culture, behavior, and complexity of black life in slavery and freedom that is still unfolding. Following Blassingame's grand acknowledgment of the communal lives and forbearance of the enslaved, Robert Fogel and Stanley Engerman's 1974 opus, *Time on the Cross: The Economics of American Slavery,* further complicated the world of the slaves. Their controversial study portrayed slavery as a profitable capitalist system in which the slaves collaborated with those who exploited them. Moreover, they argued, it was a system in which slaves profited in limited but important ways, not the least in their sustenance as workers, in their ability to keep their families intact while receiving a modicum of privileges that amounted to a kind of compensation. This view struck some scholars as an apology for slavery that cast a blind eye toward the oppressiveness and cruelty to which slaves were vulnerable. It made *Time on the Cross* at once problematic and deserving of challenges on multiple fronts. Appearing at a time when most historians acknowledged black agency, an ethos of solidarity on the plantation, and a willingness by slaves to challenge the worse aspects of their enslavement, *Time on the Cross*, similar to Elkins's *Slavery,* largely mattered as a study to confront as being way off the mark of the increasingly known world of slaves and slavery. Indeed, the controversy surrounding *Time on the Cross* further demonstrated the complicated intersection where the study of slavery has historically existed. Did the slaves carve out ways to minimize their predicament? If so, were their efforts marked by resigned complicity or determined defiance, irresponsible feigns or forthrightness of purpose? Or were the daily rhythms of the slaves an array of actions and reactions, some of them quite contradictory, that historians must sift through in search of complicated human beings under pressure. Fogel and Engerman's claim that the South's peculiar institution was profitable, efficient, and largely benign was obviously questionable, if not completely irrelevant, at a time when the nation's moral compass had changed with the ascent of black people in the nation's historical narrative

Overshadowing much of the scholarship that surfaced in the years that followed the work of Stampp, Elkins, Stuckey, Blassingame, and other writers interested in placing the slaves at the center of the story of slavery, two works, Eugene D. Genovese's *Roll, Jordan, Roll: The World the Slaves Made* (1972) and Herbert Gutman's *The Black Family in Slavery and Freedom, 1750–1925* (1976) brought added distinction to what George Fredrickson once called "the historiographic weight" (Frederickson 1988) of slavery studies from the mid-1950s to the mid-1970s. Genovese's *Roll, Jordan, Roll* was preceded by a litany of important publications that explored the political economy of slavery, life on the plantation, slave rebellion within a diasporic context, and comparative analysis of slavery in the Americas. Genovese was admired as one of the nation's preeminent historians, as well as the most consistently provocative and challenging of scholars, and his interrogations of slavery covered vast areas of historical and economic determinism. His writings placed slavery at the crosshairs of a withering criticism of powerful interests within the capitalist system. Equally important, he explored how oppression, particularly oppression marked by racism and the exploitation of labor, was negotiated by both masters and slaves. Such was arguably the most daring and controversial part of *Roll, Jordan, Roll,* a tome in excess of 800 pages. The book is important for its persuasive, though controversial, argument that the lives of the enslaved and those who held slaves was a reciprocal relationship found in pre-capitalistic "seigneurial" societies. Slaveholders and slaves engaged each other within a social context characterized by paternalism, an agreement that wedded the slaves to the labor required of them, and an acceptance of their subservience, in exchange for acceptable treatment by their owners. Genovese argued that

> paternalism defined the involuntary labor of the slaves as a legitimate return to their masters for protection and direction. But, the masters' need to see their slaves as acquiescent human beings constituted a moral victor for the slaves themselves. Paternalism's insistence upon mutual obligations—duties, responsibilities, and ultimately even rights—implicitly recognized the slaves humanity. (Genovese 1972, 5)

Genovese's ambitious exploration of slave acquiescence, rebelliousness, religion, social status, and the importance the enslaved gave to spaces within and beyond the scrutiny of whites was consistent with a historiographic trajectory begun many years earlier. He depicted blacks as active participants in their own welfare. They were hardly hapless, marginal figures in the making of a slave society that in important ways acknowledged their humanity even as it kept them enslaved. However, for some scholars, given the antecedents of Genovese's argument that slavery involved an organic relationship between those seemingly with absolute power— the slave owners—and those seemingly without power—the slaves—was unconvincing (see Anderson 1974). Indeed, to some extent such a relationship had been put forth years earlier by Phillips. Genovese's views, some observers thought, were far too closely aligned with old-school thinking about paternalism, which he claimed "grew out of the necessity to discipline and morally justify a system of exploitation. It did encourage kindness and affection, but it simultaneously encouraged cruelty and hatred. The racial distinction between master and slave heightened the tension inherent in an unjust social order." Elaborating on paternalism as the glue that kept the system intact and problematic, in Genovese's mind, the slaves seemed complicit, defiant, shrewd, potentially dangerous, resistant, and, alas, accommodating to their enslavement. Obviously, such a view of slavery during the post–civil rights movement years would be for some problematic. Writing in the *Journal of Negro History,* James D. Anderson wrote:

> *Roll, Jordan, Roll* is presented as a book about slaves and the world they made. In actuality it is an attempt to capture the slave experience through an analysis of white paternalistic hegemony. Genovese confronts the slaves with a world in which resistance could be quickly and severely punished, whereas obedience or accommodation placed slaves in a position to benefit from the favor of a master who, according to the author, generally held a genuine interest in the welfare of the slaves. (Anderson 1974, 105)

For those far more persuaded by the scope of Genovese's vision of a world that slaves survived because of their adaptability to whatever few opportunities they had to be treated humanly, *Roll, Jordan, Roll* was a triumphant contribution to

American scholarship on slavery. Writing in *Political Science Quarterly* in 1976, Norman R. Yetman (90:774) called it "a monumental achievement, the most penetrating and profound analysis of slavery in the United States yet written, a work unlikely to be surpassed for years to come." Almost wistfully, Bertram Wyatt-Brown notes:

> In an age of doubt that desperately seeks utopian solutions to problems of order and freedom through violence, political fantasy, and leaden bureaucracies it is comforting to find a work that confronts hard questions in a spirit of splendid individuality and affirms the humanity of forgotten people, whose workaday heroism and self-recognition far transcend both the cant and merits of sloganeers of whatever partisan or racial coloration. Genovese's poetic memorial to the black American spirit, like that spirit itself, will endure. (Wyatt-Brown 1975, 41:242)

Herbert Gutman's contributions to the field are no less significant than those made by the historians covered thus far. And yet, his *The Black Family in Slavery and Freedom* stands as a unique study of black autonomy and social development over a vast number of years under various historical circumstances. When his book appeared in 1976, the conventional view of African Americans in slavery and freedom had changed in substantive ways. As George Fredrickson put it, "Whatever else the civil rights movement of the 1960s may have accomplished or failed to accomplish, it at least liberated Afro-Americans from historical invisibility" (Frederickson 1988, 112). And so as they made their way to or near the center of American slavery's history, slaves increasingly appeared as individuals capable of navigating their predicament while living in cohesive though vulnerable families and communities hardly cleaving to the ways of "their" white folks.

Accordingly, Gutman's exhaustive study sheds light on the durability of many slave marital unions and the resulting "inner strength" such unions fostered in the slave community. Although slave marriages were notoriously vulnerable to the exigencies of an institution and a legal system that did not recognize them, Gutman found that large numbers of slave families were headed by two parents. He also found fealty was given customarily to kinfolk when children were named after grandparents, aunts, and uncles. He argued that slave life, especially family life, is best examined over long historical periods. This approach enables researchers to take into account the creativity, adaptability, and cohesion of black families in slavery and freedom. Black families were pivotally important, indeed essential, to communal identity and purpose; they also harbored the folk heritage that sustained black people through the ordeal of slavery into the uncertain transition to freedom. And those families, we are told, carried unique customs, including taboos against blood cousin marriage and permissiveness of premarital sexual activity and child-bearing by women. That black families were often intact and quite different from the white family in their midst underscores, once again, the importance of examining the life and culture of enslaved and free blacks on terms informed by their experience, not the experience of whites (Gutman 1976). What Gutman revealed about the black family not only challenged long-held views of its history and weakness in contemporary American society but also encouraged succeeding scholars to examine black family life and culture through various lenses, including gender, children, work, and folk traditions, setting the stage for further study on the foundational institution of African American life.

In many ways what followed the enormously rich and often provocative scholarship over the four decades after World War II has been nothing short of a groundswell of research that broadly conceptualizes black life under slavery in the New World African diaspora. Building upon earlier, contemporary explorations on black slavery, scholars brought shapely, focused attention to the multiple ways Africans across the vast terrain of the Americas sustained ancestral folk traditions, defied and resisted the most egregious aspects of enslavement, used their ancestral religions and Christianity as bulwarks on behalf of their humanity and the presence of spiritual powers in their lives, forged familial networks and traditions that nurtured and protected children and adults, escaped from their owners' premises in goodly numbers and ways that manifest courage and fortitude over time, and sought to give meaning to their freedom when emancipation came or when they seized freedom on their own. The men, women, and children, we come to know of in the early years of the making of a black Atlantic world, as well as their progeny living on the cusp of revolutionary changes destined to sweep away slavery, are far more prescient in the past than at any previous time in the history of slavery in the Americas. As the view of slavery benefited from a longer view of its historical development and its presence throughout New World societies and nations, the institution's influence on all within its reach marked a substantial change in thinking about modern history. Indeed, it can be said, and has been said, that we all still live in the era of the slave trade.

More than any other recently published work, Ira Berlin's *Many Thousands Gone: The First Two Centuries of Slavery in North America* (1998) places slavery within a dauntingly broad context of African life, "the seedtime and the flowering of American slavery," as Nell Painter observed in her 2000 review (34:515–16). Berlin's book is a sophisticated rendering of slavery's evolution as modern way of life for Africans caught up in the making and remaking of British North America. Berlin substantiates the importance of slavery in different regions on the continent and delineates how African cultures, though removed from the continent where they were forged, survived and changed over time and how the institution changed, often not in ways favorable to the enslaved. In tracing the evolution of slavery from what he calls the "charter generations" of African immigrants forced out of native lands and ultimately onto North America—those who lived in "societies with slaves"—to their descendants whose existences were far more racialized and riddled with setbacks Berlin has powerfully influenced what is known about the making of an Afro-American foundation in the places destined to become the United States. It is likely that future scholarship on African American slavery in the Republic will continue to disproportionately focus on the last generation of black life in the South—the antebellum years—and yet considerations of the prior condition of early American blacks will figure more prominently in the narrative of slavery's apex and its long, embittered ending than ever before. That is one of many contributions and legacies of *Many Thousands Gone*.

As scholarship on slavery matured, becoming more diverse in the 1980s and 1990s forward, so has understanding that the slave experience was predicated on the hierarchy of labor, locale, and gender. Among the most important local studies on slavery from this period are Charles Joyner's *Down by the Riverside: A South Carolina Slave Community* (1984) and William Dusinberre's *Them Dark Days: Slavery in the American Rice Swamps* (1996). In these two books, especially Dusinberre's, the interpretative focus on white paternalism and black cultural agency that is customarily found in large, synthetic works (such as those discussed earlier) is modified, if not outrightly refuted, by evidence of intensely harsh labor, high mortality rates, and the degradation of slaves. (See also Peter A. Coclanis's review.)

Among the most important transformations came in the mounting attention given to women as slaves, mothers, bearers of culture, and change agents. Deborah Gray White in, her path-breaking study, *Ar'nt I a Woman? Female Slaves in the Plantation South* (1987) shows that gender mattered in ways that made women at once uniquely vulnerable and burdened. Sexual exploitation was forever present from white and black men. The bond women forged with their children was emotionally strong, yet susceptible to the vagaries of the slave marketplace and the indifference of slave owners to black families. Relying heavily on the WPA Slave Narratives, White nonetheless conceded the enduring challenge posed by a paucity of sources on the lives and times of black women on southern plantations. "The source problem," she wrote, "is directly related to what was and still is the black women's condition. Few scholars who study black women fail to note that black women suffer a double oppression: that shared by all African Americans and that shared by most women" (White 1987, 23). And yet over the years, scholars have found considerable evidence of ingenuity, courage, and folk wisdom among women, qualities that helped them, and their children and men, to navigate slavery and freedom. (For comprehensive information with interpretative insights on enslaved black women in America see Berry [2012]. For a compilation of essays that examine enslaved women within a diasporic context, focusing mainly on the United States, the Caribbean, and South America, see Gasper and Hine [1996].)

Recent scholarship on children has also brought attention to a dimension long ignored despite the large percentage of young slaves throughout the South. Children grew up in conditions that interrupted their youth, often placing them in harm's way, including harsh treatment from white overseers and owners. They could be separated from their kinfolk, which was often the most searing part of their young lives and, too, a poignant chapter in the early season of emancipation. The leading authority on the subject of black slave children, Wilma King, argues in *Stolen Childhood: Slave Youth in Nineteenth-Century America* (1995) that they learned early from kinfolk about the peculiar predicament of being young, black, and enslaved, which resulted in what she calls a stolen childhood marked by traumas and tragedies and a situation "akin to living in a war zone." Such harsh conditions faced by the most vulnerable of enslaved are preserved in the testimony given by the more than 2,000 former slave participants, narrators, in the WPA Slave Narratives. Obviously, that effort arguably gave children a formidable role, through their oral testimony, in shedding light on the waning years, months and days of the South's peculiar institution (King 1995).

Gender and generation played a role in one of slavery's most persistent features: runaway slaves, the vast majority of whom were young men ranging from the teenagers to men in their early twenties. In 1999, John Hope Franklin and Loren Schweniger's *Runaway Slaves: Rebels on the Plantation* drew attention to what was arguably one of the first indelible steps that led to a much larger and grander defiance of the slave system, that being the massive flight of slaves during the early months of the Civil War until the war's end in 1865. Indeed, it is clear that the Great Emancipation began quiet modestly when three young male slaves, Shepard Mallory, Frank Baker, and James Townsend, made their way, on May 23, 1861, to Fort Monroe, Virginia. There fort commander General Benjamin Butler declared them contraband, essentially property intended by the Confederacy to render harm against the Union. Of course, the hundreds of escaping slaves who preceded Mallory, Baker, and Townsend before the war could not have known that they were a part of a growing tide of resistance manifested in dangerously uncertain journeys away from places of enslavement. But their motivations, not unlike those of the three men seeking refuge at Fort Monroe, were similar: the risk of flight from slavery was, by comparison to continued enslavement, worthy of the effort. In that sense, *Runaway Slaves* contributes to what historian Douglas R. Egerton calls a national portrait of African American resistance (1999, 997).

Localized and regional studies of slavery yield important insights into the essence of an institution that was, in fact, a way of life for blacks and whites, though obviously race and status fundamentally shaped one's experience within the system. *In Soul by Soul: Life Inside the Antebellum Slave Market* (1999), Walter Johnson's focus on the New Orleans slave market takes us, shockingly for uninitiated readers of new scholarship on American slavery, into the essential meaning, purpose, and horror of slavery. In short, the slave market was the place and an experience where all that truly mattered in antebellum slavery came together—the commodification of black bodies, the wariness and camaraderie of slaves toward each other, the fantasy world inhabited by slave owners whose imagination of slaves and themselves was at once twisted and horrifically self-serving, and, most sadly, "the soul-destroying wretchedness" of the plight faced by the slaves (Wyatt-Brown 2001, 1359).

The serious study of American slavery is far more than an evolving historiographical debate among historians and other scholars. For more than two generations, the examination of a terrible way of life that was countenanced in colonial laws, the U.S. Constitution, state laws, and the attitudes of most white Americans brought into question foundational assumptions about the nature of American society. Slavery's longevity, over 200 years, and its sweeping influence on the nation's economy, politics, and social values, demanded of historians, indeed a cross section of Americans, a deepening interest in how enslaved black Americans survived their seemingly interminable ordeal and in remarkable ways influenced a nation that hustled them to its bottom early on. What blacks thought of themselves; the content of their character; their heroism and attempts to sustain elements of their African past; and their interactions with each other across gender, generational, and color lines are the stuff of extraordinary narratives now coming under a brilliant light. All the more, as the humanity, mental prowess, and cultural integrity of the slaves has become a normative point of departure for scholars, research agendas are now far bolder and the conclusions drawn by scholars are breathtakingly transformative.

As an example, historian Steven Hahn has opened relatively new vistas in the study of slavery and slaves, including a persuasive argument that slaves were consciously political actors during slavery and after slavery ended, that their resistance to slavery was a part of a sweeping diasporic phenomenon that turned the New World, including the United States, into a veritable and enduring slave revolt. The constellation of revolts, the largest being the Haitian Revolution, were in fact manifestations of a persistent quest for freedom and liberty that hastened the ending of slavery throughout the Americas over the course of the 19th century (Hahn 2003). And so as much as the slave and the former slave in the United States have been exceptionalized in scholarship, that increasingly heroic figure is now a part of a much larger, more complicated and contemporary story. In retrospect, George Washington Williams's acknowledgment of his brethren and sisters, his "bleeding countrymen," whose "clanking chains and melting prayers" crowded upon his soul "as a bitter reality" has resonated over time, as did the work of scholars who saw within the slavery experience a peculiar and intensely human drama that defined what America used to be and, too, what it would have to become if African Americans and others on the margins were ever to be truly free.

References

Anderson, James D. 1974. "Aunt Jemima in Dialectics: Genovese On Slave Culture." *Journal of Negro History* 61 (1): 99–114.

Bancroft, George. 1854. *History of the United States from the Discovery of the American Continent.* Boston: Little, Brown, and Company.

Berlin, Ira. 1998. *Many Thousands Gone: The First Two Generations of Slavery in North America.* Cambridge, MA: Harvard University Press.

Berry, Daina, with Deleso Alford. 2012. *Enslaved Women in America: An Encyclopedia.* Santa Barbara, CA: Greenwood.

Blassingame, John W. 1972. *The Slave Community: Plantation Life in the Ante-Bellum South.* New York: Oxford University Press.

Brundage, Fitzhugh. 1997. "American Slavery: A Look Back at the Peculiar Institution." *The Journal of Blacks in Higher Education* 15 (Spring): 118–20.

Coclanis, Peter A. 1996. Review, "Them Dark Days." *Journal of American History* 83 (4): 1375–76

Du Bois, W. E. B. 1999. *The Souls of Black Folk.* New York: W.W. Norton. First published 1903.

Dusinberre, William. 1996. *Them Dark Days: Slavery in the American Rice Swamps.* New York: Oxford University Press.

Egerton, Douglas R. 1999. Review, "Runaway Slaves: Rebels on the Plantation." *The Journal of American History* 87 (3): 997–98.

Elkins, Stanley M. 1959. *Slavery: A Problem in American Institutional and Intellectual Life.* Chicago: University of Chicago Press.

Fogel, Robert, and Stanley Engerman.1974. *Time on the Cross*. 2 vols. New York: Norton.

Foner. Eric. 1994. "The Meaning of Freedom in the Age of Emancipation." *The Journal of American History* 81 (2): 435–451.

Franklin, John Hope, and Loren Schweninger. 1999. *Runaway Slaves: Rebels on the Planatation*. Oxford: Oxford University Press.

Fredrickson, George M. 1988. *The Arrogance of Race*. Hanover, NH: Wesleyan University Press.

Gasper, David Barry, and Darlene Clark Hine, eds. 1996. *More Than Chattel: Black Women and Slavery in the Americas*. Bloomington: Indiana University Press.

Genovese, Eugene D. 1972. *Roll, Jordan, Roll: The World the Slaves Made*. New York: Vintage Books.

Gutman, Herbert G. 1976. *The Black Family in Slavery & Freedom, 1750–1925*. New York: Pantheon.

Hahn, Steven. 2003. *A Nation Under Our Feet: Black Political Struggles in the Rural South From Slavery to the Great Migration*. Cambridge, MA: Belknap Press.

Hahn, Steven. 2009. *The Political Worlds of Slavery and Freedom*. Cambridge, MA: Harvard University Press.

Handlin, Oscar. 1961. Review, "Slavery: A Problem in American Institutional and Intellectual Life." *The New England Quarterly* 34 (2): 253–55.

Hill, Robert A. 2006. "Introduction: P. Sterling Stuckey: In Praise of an Intellectual Legacy." *The Journal of African American History* 91 (4): 367–71.

Johnson, Walter. 1999. *Soul By Soul: Life Inside the Antebellum Slave Market*. Cambridge, MA: Harvard University Press.

Joyner, Charles. 1984. *Down by the Riverside: A South Carolina Slave Community*. Urbana: University of Illnois Press.

King, Wilma. 1995. *Stolen Childhood: Slave Youth in Nineteenth-Century America*. Bloomington: Indiana University Press.

Klingberg, Frank W. 1957. "The Peculiar Institution: Slavery in the Ante-Bellum South by Kenneth M. Stampp." *The American Historical Review* 63 (1): 139–40.

Lane, Ann J., ed. 1972. *The Debate Over "Slavery": Stanley Elkins and His Critics*. Urbana: University of Illinois Press.

Levine, Lawrence W. 1993. "Reflections on Recent American Historiography." In *The Unpredictable Past: Explorations in American Cultural History*, 3–13. New York: Oxford University Press.

Lewis, Jan Ellen. 2000. "Slavery and the Market." *Reviews in American History* 28 (4): 539–46.

Nichols, Charles H. 1956. "Realities of the Plantation Economy." *Phylon* 17 (4): 395.

Painter, Nell Irvin. 2000. Review, "African American Review." 34: 515–16.

Parish, Peter J. 1989. *Slavery: History and Historians*. New York: Harper & Row.

Phillips, Ulrich B. 1918. *American Negro Slavery: A Survey of the Supply, Employment and Control of Negro Labor as Determined by the Plantation Regime*. New York: D. Appleton.

Phillips, Ulrich B. 1929. *Life and Labor in the Old South*. Boston: Little, Brown & Company.

Stampp, Kenneth M. 1956. *The Peculiar Institution: Slavery in the Ante-Bellum South*. New York: Vintage Books.

Stuckey, Sterling. 1971. "Twilight of Our Past: Reflections on the Origins of Black History." In *Amistad 2: Writings on Black History and Culture*, edited by John A. Williams and Charles F. Harris, 261–95. New York: Vintage Press.

Stuckey, Sterling. 1994. "Through the Prism of Folklore: The Black Ethos in Slavery." In *Going Through the Storm: The Influence of African American Art in History*, 3–18. New York: Oxford University Press.

Stuckey, Sterling. 1987. *Slave Culture: Nationalist Theory and the Foundations of Black America*. New York: Oxford University Press.

Tannenbaum, Frank. 1947. *Slave and Citizen*. New York: Alfred A. Knopf.

Tannenbaum, Frank. 1960. Review, "Slavery: A Problem in American Institutional and Intellectual Life." *Journal of Southern History* 26 (1): 92–94.

White, Deborah Gray. 1987. *Ar'n't I a Woman?: Female Slaves in the Plantation South*. New York: W.W. Norton.

Williams, George Washington. 1883. *History of the Negro Race in America, From 1619 to 1880: Negroes as Slaves, as Soldiers, and as Citizens*. Vol. II. New York: G.P. Putnam's Sons.

Woodson, Carter G. 1922. *The Negro in Our History*. Washington, DC: Association for the Study of Negro Life and History.

Wyatt-Brown, Bertram. 1975. "*Roll, Jordan, Roll: The World the Slaves Made* by Eugene D. Genovese. Review by: Bertram Wyatt-Brown." *The Journal of Southern History* 41 (2): 240–242.

Wyatt-Brown, Bertram. 2001. Review, Walter Johnson, *Soul By Soul: Life Inside the Antebellum Slave Market. The American Historical Review* 106 (4): 1359–60.

Yetman, Norman R. 1975–76. Review, Eugene D. Genovese, *Roll, Jordon, Roll: The World the Slaves Made. Political Science Quarterly* 90: 774–76,

Recommended Resources

BOOKS

Aptheker, Herbert. 1983. *American Negro Slave Revolts*. New York: International Publishers Company.

Ball, Charles. 2003. *Fifty Years in Chains*. Mineola, NY: Dover.

Bancroft, George. 1854. *History of the United States from the Discovery of the American Continent*. Boston: Little, Brown, and Company.

Baptist, Edward, and Stephanie Camp. 2006. *New Studies in the History of Slavery*. Athens: University of Georgia Press.

Berlin, Ira. 1998. *Many Thousand Gone: The First Two Centuries of Slavery in North America*. Cambridge, MA: Belknap Press.

Blackburn, Robin. 2011. *The American Crucible: Slavery, Emancipation and Human Rights*. London: Verso.

Blassingame, John. 1974. *The Slave Community: Plantation Life in the Antebellum South*. New York: Oxford University Press.

Camp, Stephanie. 2004. *Closer to Freedom: Enslaved Women and Everyday Resistance in the Plantation South*. Chapel Hill: University of North Carolina Press.

Catterall, Helen, ed. 1926–37. *Judicial Cases Concerning American Slavery and the Negro*. 5 vols. Washington, DC: Carnegie Institution of Washington.

Crew, Spencer, and Goodman, Cynthia. 2002. *Unchained Memories Readings from the Slave Narratives*. Boston: Bulfinch Press.

Davis, David Brion. 1988. *The Problem of Slavery in Western Culture*. New York: Oxford University Press.

Du Bois, W. E .B. 1903. *The Souls of Black Folk*. Chicago: A. C. McClurg.

Elkins, Stanley. 1959. *Slavery: A Problem in American Institutional and Intellectual Life*. Chicago: University of Chicago Press.

Escott, Paul D. 1979. *Slavery Remembered: A Record of Twentieth-Century Slave Narratives*. Chapel Hill: University of North Carolina Press.

Fogel, Robert, and Stanley Engerman. 1974. *Time on the Cross*. 2 vols. New York: Norton.

Fox-Genovese, Elizabeth. 1989. *Within the Plantation Household: Black and White Women of the Old South*. Chapel Hill: University of North Carolina Press.

Franklin, John Hope, and Loren Schweninger. 1999. *Runaway Slaves: Rebels on the Plantation*. New York: Oxford University Press.

Genovese, Eugene. 1988. *The Political Economy of Slavery: Studies in the Economy and Society of the Slave South*. 2nd ed. Middletown, CT: Wesleyan University Press.

Genovese, Eugene. 1974. *Roll, Jordan, Roll: The World the Slaves Made*. New York: Pantheon.

Gutman, Herbert. 1977. *The Black Family in Slavery and Freedom, 1750–1925*. New York: Vintage Books.

Hahn, Steven. *The Political Worlds of Slavery and Freedom*. Cambridge, MA: Harvard University Press, 2009.

Halasz, Nicholas. 1966. *Rattling Chains: Slave Unrest and Revolt in the Antebellum South.* New York: D. McKay Company.

Horton, James, and Lois Horton. 2005. *Slavery and the Making of America.* New York: Oxford University Press.

Jacobs, Harriet A. 1987. *Incidents in the Life of a Slave Girl.* Edited by Jean Fagan Yellin. Cambridge, MA: Harvard University Press.

Johnson, Walter. 1999. *Soul by Soul: Life Inside the Antebellum Slave Market.* Cambridge, MA: Harvard University Press.

Joyner, Charles. 1984. *Down by the Riverside: A South Carolina Community.* Urbana: University of Illinois Press.

King, Wilma. 2011. *Stolen Childhood: Slave Youth in Nineteenth-Century America.* Bloomington: University of Indiana Press.

Levine, Lawrence. 1978. *Black Culture and Black Consciousness: Afro-American Folk Thought from Slavery to Freedom.* New York: Oxford University Press.

McDonogh, Gary W., ed. 1993. *The Florida Negro: A Federal Writers' Project Legacy.* Jackson: University Press of Mississippi.

Mullin, Gerald. 1972. *Flight and Rebellion: Slave Resistance in Eighteenth-Century Virginia.* New York: Oxford University Press.

Northrup, Solomon. 1968. *Twelve Years a Slave.* Edited by Sue Eakin and Joseph Logsdon. Baton Rouge: Louisiana State University Press.

Oakes, James. 2013. *Freedom National: The Destruction of Slavery in the United States, 1861–1865.* New York: W.W. Norton and Company.

Osofsky, Gilbert. 1969. *Puttin' On Ole Massa.* New York: Harper and Row.

Owens, Leslie H. 1976. *This Species of Property: Slave Life and Culture in the Old South.* New York: Oxford University Press.

Parish, Peter J. 1989. *Slavery: History and Historians.* New York: HarperCollins.

Phillips, Ulrich B. 1918. *American Negro Slavery.* New York: D. Appleton and Company.

Phillips, Ulrich B. 1929. *Life and Labor in the Old South.* Boston: Little, Brown & Company.

Raboteau, Albert. 1978. *Slave Religion: The Invisible Institution in the Antebellum South.* New York: Oxford University Press.

Rhodes, James Ford. 1893. *History of the United States.* New York: Harper and Brothers.

Rogers, Molly. 2010. *Delia's Tears: Race, Science and Photography.* New Haven, CT: Yale University Press.

Rose, Willie Lee. 1964. *Rehearsal for Reconstruction: The Port Royal Experiment.* Athens: University of Georgia Press.

Schwartz, Marie Jenkins. 2000. *Born in Bondage: Growing Up Enslaved in the Antebellum South.* Cambridge, MA: Harvard University Press.

Stampp, Kenneth. 1956. *The Peculiar Institution: Slavery in the Antebellum South.* New York: Vintage.

Stevenson, Brenda. 1996. *Life in Black and White: Family and Community in the Slave South.* New York: Oxford University Press.

Still, William. 1872. *The Underground Railroad.* Philadelphia: B&R Samizdat Express.

Stowe, Harriet Beecher. 1852. *Uncle Tom's Cabin.* Boston: John P. Jewett and Company.

Stuckey, Sterling. 1987. *Slave Culture: Nationalist Theory and the Foundations of Black America.* New York: Oxford University Press.

Tannenbaum, Frank. 1946. *Slave and Citizen.* Boston: Beacon Press.

Wade, Richard. 1972. *Slavery in the Cities: The South 1820–1860.* Westport, CT: Greenwood Press.

White, Deborah Gray. 1999. *Ar'nt I a Woman? Female Slaves in the Antebellum South.* New York: Norton.

Williams, George Washington. 1883. *History of the Negro Race in America*. New York: G. P. Putnam's Sons.

Willis, Deborah, and Barbara Krauthamer. 2013. *Envisioning Emancipation: Black Americans and the End of Slavery*. Philadelphia: Temple University Press.

Woodson, Carter G. 1926. *The Mind of the Negro as Reflected in Letters Written During the Crisis, 1800–1860*. Washington, DC: Association for the Study of Negro Life and History.

Woodson, Carter G. 1922. *The Negro in Our History*. Washington, DC: Association for the Study of Negro Life and History.

WEBSITES

The African American: A Journey from Slavery to Freedom. Web Resources on Slavery. B. Davis Schwartz Memorial Library. Long Island University. Lhttp://www2.liu.edu/cwis/cwp/library/aaslvwww.htm.

Freedmen's Bureau Online: Records of the Bureau of Refugees, Freedmen, and Abandoned Lands. http://www.freedmensbureau.com.

Gilder Lehrman Center for the Study of Slavery, Resistance and Abolition. Yale University. http://www.yale.edu/glc.

Handler, Jerome S., and Michael L. Tuite Jr. 2011. The Atlantic Slave Trade and Slave Life in Americas: A Visual Record. Virginia Foundation for the Humanities and University of Virginia. http://hitchcock.itc.virginia.edu/slavery.

H-Slavery. 2013. The History of Slavery. H-Net Humanities and Social Sciences Online. http://www.h-net.org/~slavery/.

Library of Congress. 2001. Born in Slavery: Slave Narratives from the Federal Writers' Project, 1936–1938. http://memory.loc.gov/ammem/snhtml/.

Schomburg Center for Research in Black Culture. New York Public Library. http://nypl.org/research/sc/sc.html.

VIDEOS/ FILMS

The African Americans: Many Rivers to Cross. 2013. PBS.

Africans in America: America's Journey through Slavery. 1998. 360 mins. PBS/WGBH. Boston 1998. http://www.pbs.org/wgbh/aia/home.html.

Amistad. 1997.

Beloved. 1998.

Digging for Slaves: The Excavation of Slave Sites. 1993. BBC Television.

Roots: The Saga of an American Family. 1976. ABC Television. 10 episodes.

Slavery and the Making of America. 2004. PBS; a production of Thirteen/WNET New York. Educational Broadcasting Corporation.

Twelve Years A Slave: The Narrative of Solomon Northrup. 2013.

Unchained Memories: Readings from the Slave Narratives. 2002. HBO. 75 minutes.

A Woman Called Moses. 1978. National Broadcasting Company. Original television airing. 1998. Xenon Pictures. DVD.

Name Index

Subject Index

About the Editors

Spencer Crew, PhD, is the Clarence J. Robinson Professor of History at George Mason University, Fairfax, Virginia. His published works include *Field to Factory: Afro-American Migration 1915–1940* and *Black Life in Secondary Cities: A Comparative Analysis of the Black Communities of Camden and Elizabeth, N.J., 1860–1920.* He is also coauthor of *The American Presidency: A Glorious Burden* and *Unchained Memories: Readings from the Slave Narratives.* Crew holds a doctorate in history from Rutgers University.

Lonnie Bunch is the founding director of the National Museum of African American History and Culture at the Smithsonian Institution, Washington, D.C. His published works include *Call the Lost Dream Back: Essays on History, Race and Museums* and *Picturing the Promise: The Scurlock Studio and Black Washington.* He is coauthor of *The American Presidency: A Glorious Burden* and *The Smithsonian's America: An Exhibition on American History and Culture.*

Clement Price, PhD, is the Board of Governors Distinguished Service Professor of History and director of the Institute on Ethnicity, Culture, and the Modern Experience at Rutgers University–Newark College of Arts and Science. His publications include *Freedom Not Far Distant: A Documentary History of Afro-Americans in New Jersey* and *Many Voices, Many Opportunities: Cultural Pluralism and American Arts Policy.* Price holds a doctorate in history from Rutgers University.